AMERICAN EXPERIENCE

Crime and Punishment in America

David B. Wolcott and Tom Head

☑Checkmark Books®
An imprint of Infobase Publishing

Crime and Punishment in America

Copyright © 2010 by David B. Wolcott and Tom Head
Maps and graphs copyright © 2010 by Infobase Publishing, Inc.

Checkmark Books
An imprint of Infobase Publishing
132 West 31st Street
New York NY 10001

Library of Congress Cataloging-in-Publication Data

Wolcott, David B.
Crime and punishment in America / David Wolcott and Tom Head.
p. cm.
Includes bibliographical references and index.
ISBN 978-0-8160-6247-8 (hardcover : alk. paper)
ISBN 978-0-8160-7897-4 (pbk. : alk. paper)
1. Crime—United States—History. 2. Criminal justice, Administration of—United States—History. 3. Punishment—United States—History. I. Head, Tom. II. Title.
HV6799.W65 2008
364.973—dc22   2008013372

Checkmark Books are available at special discounts when purchased in bulk quantities for businesses, associations, institutions, or sales promotions. Please call our Special Sales Department in New York at (212) 967-8800 or (800) 322-8755.

You can find Facts On File on the World Wide Web at http://www.factsonfile.com

Text design by Joan M. McEvoy
Maps and graphs by Dale Williams
Composition by Mary Susan Ryan-Flynn
Cover printed by Art Print, Taylor, PA
Book printed and bound by Maple Press, York, PA
Date printed: February 2010
Printed in the United States of America

10 9 8 7 6 5 4 3 2 1

This book is printed on acid-free paper and contains 30 percent postconsumer recycled content.

Note on Photos

Many of the illustrations and photographs used in this book are old, historical images. The quality of the prints is not always up to modern standards, as in many cases the originals are damaged. The content of the illustrations, however, made their inclusion important despite problems in reproduction.

To my wife, Elizabeth. Thanks for your loving support.
—D. W.

In loving memory of my nephew, James David Head (2003–2005).
—T. H.

Contents

Authors' Preface   vi

Introduction   vii

Chapter One	Old Crimes in the New World: 1500–1699	1
Chapter Two	A New System of Justice: 1700–1789	21
Chapter Three	The American Experiment: 1790–1829	41
Chapter Four	The American City: 1830–1854	58
Chapter Five	A Nation Dissolved: 1855–1869	81
Chapter Six	East and West: 1870–1889	100
Chapter Seven	The Gilded Age and Progressive Era: 1890–1913	121
Chapter Eight	Bootleggers and G-Men: 1914–1933	145
Chapter Nine	World War II and the Cold War: 1934–1957	170
Chapter Ten	Civil Disobedience and Civic Reform: 1958–1970	193
Chapter Eleven	A Crisis of Confidence: 1971–1981	220
Chapter Twelve	Responding to Urban Crime: 1982–1992	238
Chapter Thirteen	Crime and Justice as Public Issues: 1993 to Present	260

Appendix A: Documents   294

Appendix B: Biographies of Major Personalities   322

Appendix C: Maps   356

Appendix D: Graphs and Tables   361

Glossary   370

Notes   376

Bibliography   385

Index   405

Authors' Preface

This book is intended to offer readers an introduction to the multiple and overlapping stories of crime and justice in American history. In particular, through its structure it offers readers many different points of entry into the history of crime and punishment. The chapters are organized chronologically, and each chapter begins with a narrative introduction that discusses key themes, issues, people, and events in that period. Chronologies follow, explaining major events factually and precisely.

Most central to this volume, however, are the original primary sources. Each chapter features an extensive selection of primary source materials from the period under consideration. These sources articulate the visions of their time, how contemporaries understood issues surrounding crime and justice. They include newspaper accounts, eyewitness testimonies, laws, trial transcripts, and judicial decisions; they include the perspectives of leaders, of ordinary people, of criminals, and of practitioners of criminal justice. Some of these sources contain views that modern readers might consider admirable and prescient, while others express ideas that today would be regarded as reprehensible. All, however, express or imply a perspective, and understanding those perspectives is crucial to understanding the sources. To begin this process it is necessary to try to understand the context in which each document was created. When reading original sources, it is useful to consider how the document connects to the larger story. Who expressed what ideas when? Under what circumstances were these ideas expressed? For what purpose?

The appendices to the book also offer a number of useful tools. A biographical encyclopedia highlights key individuals, explaining who they were and what they contributed to the history of crime and punishment. Figures and maps represent visually crucial trends and patterns in this history. And a detailed bibliography directs readers to the sources used for this book and to the most important scholarly literature in the field.

An alert reading of the materials presented here—both the primary sources and the information illuminating the larger context—can reveal how people throughout American history have come to terms with issues of crime and punishment. These materials demonstrate the ways in which the history of crime and punishment is tied inextricably to the history of the United States.

Introduction

In the years immediately following the American Revolution, the young United States lacked most of the criminal justice institutions that are familiar to Americans today. In the 1780s, courts met only occasionally, jails held inmates only temporarily, prisons for long-term incarceration had not yet been invented, and full-time professional police did not exist.

Today, the United States maintains an array of institutions devoted to criminal justice at the local, county, state, and federal levels. In 2005, federal and state prisons and local jails incarcerated more than 2.2 million people, roughly one out of every 142 Americans. State governments alone spent almost $37 billion on corrections. Likewise, full-time policing and courts had become ubiquitous. Almost 18,000 state and local law enforcement agencies employed more than 1 million people in 2004 and more than 30 federal agencies employed a total of roughly 90,000 officers. Prosecutors' offices employed another 78,000.[1]

In less than two and a half centuries, the justice system in the United States has experienced a massive expansion and transformation. Did these changes take place because crime became more pervasive in modern America? Probably not, although the limitations of long-term statistics on crime make it difficult to answer this question with any certainty. Instead, the expansion and transformation of the criminal justice system reflect the transformation of the United States itself during this period. One premise of this book is that the history of crime and punishment is the history of America. Concerns about crime and justice emerge from the concerns of their day, and they change as the more general issues important to the public change. Crime and justice also provide a window into historical divisions between Americans; inequalities of class, of ethnicity and race, and of gender have all shaped patterns of crime and the operations of justice. Finally, the expansion, reform, and transformation of criminal justice exemplify changes in the American state as a whole and reflect the debates and conflicts that surrounded changes in American government. In short, criminal justice history is American history.

Crime and Punishment in the Popular Imagination

Crime and justice have long fascinated Americans, a fascination reflected in popular entertainment. Films have shaped many Americans' perceptions of crime. Movies have made icons of fictional criminals ranging from gangster Tom Powers in *The Public Enemy* (1931) to drug lord Tony Montana in *Scarface* (1983) to serial killer Hannibal Lector in *The Silence of the Lambs* (1991). Television has concentrated less on criminals and more on police, but it too has informed popular perceptions of law enforcement. Shows such as *Dragnet* (which aired between 1951 and 1959 and was revived between 1967 and 1970), *Hill Street Blues* (broadcast between 1981 and

1987), *Law and Order* (which debuted in 1990), and the long-running reality series *Cops* (which debuted in 1989) help fashion ideas about crime fighting for multiple generations of Americans.[2] In a similar way, mystery fiction focusing on the work of detectives has been a staple of popular literature at least since Sir Arthur Conan Doyle published his stories about Sherlock Holmes in the 1890s. Likewise, much of the gothic literature of the 19th century—such as the detective stories by Edgar Allan Poe published in the 1840s—focused on crime and justice. And finally, what are Westerns if not stories of crime and justice transposed to the American frontier?

Widely publicized crimes and criminals have often become prominent because they touched a nerve in some part of the American public mind, because they resonated in the culture of the times. For example, the trial of former football star O. J. Simpson, accused of killing his former wife, Nicole Brown Simpson, and her male friend, Ronald Goldman, in 1993, initially came to prominence because it overlapped with the late 20th-century news media's increasing focus on celebrities. By the time a jury acquitted Simpson—a black man—in 1995, the case had evolved into a forum for considering American divisions over race. Likewise, the bootlegger and organized crime figure Al Capone came to prominence in the 1920s because he embodied, in an odd way, the American Dream. Capone had risen from obscurity to wealth, power, and fame through personal competitiveness and aggressive business practices. Although a criminal, he embodied the masculine values most highly celebrated in the 1920s. In a similar way, bandits such as Charles Arthur "Pretty Boy" Floyd in the 1930s and Jesse James in the 1870s achieved prominence because, in times of economic and social change, they presented themselves as champions of the little people, robbing from the same interests that oppressed the poor and disenfranchised.

Public understandings of crime and justice have also been linked inextricably to the intellectual and cultural currents of their day. In fact, crime and punishment can constitute a forum where these trends are most evident. To a large degree, crimes become crimes because they violate the norms of a community. Thus, criminal law reflects community values by identifying what *not* to do, what actions lie outside of the realm of acceptable behavior. This pattern is perhaps most evident in 17th-century Massachusetts, when criminal law reflected the Puritan faith of that colony. Congregational churches regulated individual comportment and behavior, regarding violations of community norms as punishable crimes. Courts of law also became forums for debates over how to apply the evidence of faith to temporal life. The 1692 witch trials in Salem, Massachusetts, for example, turned on the question of whether spectral evidence, visible only to those confronted by evil spirits, could be admitted in court. By the late 19th century, few Americans connected crime to sin, but many connected it to a different pseudoscientific obsession of that era, heredity. Scholars such as the American investigator Richard Dugdale and the Italian criminologist Cesare Lombroso sought to demonstrate that criminal behavior resulted from biological failings and could be transmitted to future generations. In the public mind, purported criminal traits became the best example of the biological science of the time. Finally, in the late 20th century, criminal justice focused heavily on fighting a war against illegal drugs. This focus perhaps reflects a public concern with psychoactive substances and a loss of self-control more powerful than at any previous time.

In short, for much of American history, crime and justice have provided a window through which many people have viewed their worlds. Narratives involving crime—both fictional and real—become focal points for understanding the issues of the day. Stories of cops and robbers, cowboys and Indians, killers and detectives, all help reveal what mattered to Americans at the time.

Routine Crime and Social History

The reality of crime in U.S. history is far less dramatic than movies, television, and stories suggest. For that reason, ordinary crimes represent a useful window into the ways in which people actually lived in the past, their social history.

Despite the attention that serial killers and celebrity defendants receive, spectacular crimes are quite rare. Most homicides are motivated by jealousy, alcohol, or a momentary burst of anger. Furthermore, murder is far less common than casual opportunistic theft, which is far less common than disorderly conduct. In 2003, homicide represented far less than 1 percent of the eight serious offenses that constitute the Federal Bureau of Investigation's key nationwide measure of "index crimes." By contrast, larceny and theft accounted for approximately 60 percent of index crimes that year.[3] This same pattern is even more striking in earlier periods. For example, in Alameda County (includes Oakland and Berkeley), California, between 1872 and 1910, only 6 percent of arrests involved felony offenses, and only 27 percent involved any other sort of offense against persons or property. By contrast, 64 percent of arrests resulted from efforts to maintain public order—apprehending the drunken and the disruptive, shooing vagrants off the streets.[4] For these very reasons, crime and justice become a good measure of what people really did and how they really lived.

Much of ordinary crime and justice has been driven by inequalities of race and class, power and wealth. American history virtually begins with the inequitable treatment of Native Americans in criminal justice systems established by European colonists in the 17th and 18th centuries. When colonists and American Indians disagreed over whether accused offenders should be tried under Native or European systems of justice, American Indians almost invariably found themselves at a disadvantage. In addition, the poor, the powerless, and the economically marginal have always represented the majority of people accused of crimes and brought before the courts. This pattern has persisted even as the particular ethnic groups that tended to be poor and disadvantaged changed. As a result, immigrants and their children—particularly the new immigrants from eastern and southern Europe—constituted the vast majority of people in trouble with the law during the 19th and early 20th centuries. In modern times, this pattern has meant that African Americans have been overrepresented in the criminal justice system.

This concentration of blacks involved in both crime and justice builds on the long-term connections between race and power in the United States. Slavery—which persisted in North America for more than two and a half centuries until finally abolished in 1865—was built on the subjugation of African Americans. Masters used both violence and the threat of violence to exercise authority over their unwilling workers. For slaves themselves, crime and insurrection represented avenues of resistance. Their actions could range from simple and subtle, such as appropriating food from a master's garden, to spectacular, such as an 1831 insurrection in Southampton County, Virginia, led by Nat Turner that resulted in the deaths of 57 whites. Maintaining slavery required an elaborate system of informal controls and formal mechanisms, such as slave patrols. In the 19th-century South, these patrols evolved into the earliest systems of policing. Following the end of slavery, vigilante actions such as lynching continued to maintain a degree of control over the black population.

A similar pattern of efforts to reassert control over African Americans in the 1950s and 1960s helps explain violent resistance to the Civil Rights movement. At the same time, exclusion from equal opportunities in life and from equitable treatment before the law has led many African Americans to embrace crime and violence. The legacy of racial subjugation has been the disproportionate representation of African Americans as both the victims and the perpetrators of crime throughout the 20th century.

The gender dimensions of the history of crime are less often noted, not because they do not exist, but because they are so enormous that they seem natural. Men constitute the overwhelming majority of people accused of crimes (and the more serious a crime is, the more often the perpetrator is male). Until the late 20th century, men also constituted the overwhelming percentage of people working in all aspects of the criminal justice system, from policing to courts to corrections. As a result, the nature of crime and justice have been shaped by masculine notions of honor, whether it be in disputes such as the 1804 duel in which Vice President Aaron Burr killed former Treasury secretary Alexander Hamilton or in rumbles between street gangs in New York City in the 1950s. That said, women have also played substantial roles in the history of crime and justice. Like men, women have also been subject to criminal laws and also engaged in criminal enterprises. As women's roles in society developed in the 20th century, they too became increasingly likely to commit crimes against persons and property. In addition, women such as Dorothea Dix and Alice Stebbins Wells stand out for exercising disproportionate influence in the reform of criminal justice. By the late 20th century, women increasingly assumed professional roles in the justice system alongside men as police officers, attorneys, and corrections officers.

In short, the story of race and gender in the history of crime and justice reflects and parallels the story of race and gender in American society. Thus, the routine crimes that constitute the vast bulk of the justice system's work are just as significant as the spectacular crimes that earn most of the attention. These ordinary offenses help illuminate the contours of life for ordinary Americans.

Law and Order and the American State

In a comparable fashion, the growth of the apparatus of justice parallels the transformation of government. For much of U.S. history, criminal justice has been overwhelmingly local. States have largely determined which behaviors are to be treated as crimes, local officials have been in charge of enforcement, and county courts have decided most criminal cases. Prior to the 20th century, the federal government played almost no part in the criminal justice system. As a result of this very loose federal system, the United States maintains an incredibly diverse array of policies and institutions. Rather than discussing a single criminal justice system, it is more accurate to think about hundreds, if not thousands, of frequently overlapping criminal justice *systems.*

This pattern of dividing power between local, state, and national governments reflects general trends in American history more closely than early 21st-century observers can easily appreciate. Today, the federal government has assumed the paramount role in U.S. governance, but that development is fairly recent in historical terms and still does not fully characterize criminal justice. For most of the history of the United States, the federal government has played an extraordinarily limited role in people's day-to-day lives. In criminal justice in particular, the federal government has traditionally had no jurisdiction unless offenses crossed state lines, and it counted few agencies to take action. The U.S. Marshals Service was the first federal law enforcement agency, proudly dating its origins to 1789, but for most of its history it existed mainly to transport prisoners. The Treasury Department established the Secret Service in 1865 to protect the new national currency against counterfeiting and other threats; the Secret Service only assumed its more famous modern function of protecting political leaders following the 1901 assassination of President William McKinley. President Theodore Roosevelt established a Bureau of Investigation—the predecessor of today's Federal Bureau of Investigation (FBI)—in 1908 as a sort of national police force, but, like its sister agencies, it had very little to do. Only with the passage of federal laws against offenses involving interstate transport did the Bureau of Investigation assume clear (albeit limited) functions.

The expansion of federal law enforcement capabilities in the 20th century paralleled American political development. Under the New Deal of the 1930s, the FBI assumed a much larger role, leading a "war on crime" directed against depression-era bandits, bank robbers, and kidnappers. The FBI also positioned itself at the apex of a nationwide pyramid of law-enforcement agencies, becoming a national clearinghouse for information and expertise. The federal government expanded this clearinghouse role in the 1960s in the context of Lyndon Johnson's Great Society programs with the creation of the Law Enforcement Assistance Administration in 1968 to funnel federal money to local police. A growing "war on drugs" in the 1980s and 1990s and a new "war on terror" in the 2000s led to legislation extending federal jurisdiction over crime, a sharp expansion of federal criminal justice administrative capacity and a dramatic increase in the number of inmates housed in federal, rather than state, prisons. The extension of federal authority in criminal justice matters was really a phenomenon of the latter two-thirds of the 20th century, and even then it did not supersede the on-the-ground work of state and local agencies.

Police also represent a comparatively new innovation in American history. Boston established what is generally accepted as the first full-time professional police force in the United States in 1838; New York City followed suit in 1845. Prior to this, American cities had been guarded by casual, part-time, ill-organized "watches" (often composed of men moonlighting from their day jobs) or constables who served court orders in exchange for payment. Even with the creation of police forces, police functioned mainly as all-purpose guardians of public order rather than law enforcers. As they walked their beats, 19th-century police officers might be seen checking locks or street lamps, arresting drunks, herding stray cows off the street, forcefully reprimanding suspected offenders, or slipping into a saloon for a drink. Only in the late 19th century did police administrators even begin to consider law enforcement their primary function, and police reform became a project that dominated the 20th century.

For the most part, courts represent the primary components of the local justice systems. In the 19th century, they served as neutral arbiters when citizens filed complaints against one another. With the arrival of police, courts supported their work of maintaining order, issuing quick and summary judgments of the many minor offenses that came before them. But like the police, courts changed gradu-ally in the late 19th and 20th centuries. Public prosecutors and trained defense attorneys increasingly used courts as forums to make cases against and for alleged offenders. These more professional court officials and lawyers helped make court operations more routine by encouraging plea bargaining—trading admissions of guilt for reduced sentences. On the one hand, courts represented the entry point for most offenders to penalties and incarceration. On the other hand, courts also represented the best protectors of the rights of the accused, a function increasingly apparent in the 20th century.

Prisons and jails also exemplify the expansion of criminal justice in American history. In the 17th and 18th centuries, jails were small and little used. Offend-ers might be held there while they awaited trial or until they paid debts, but they would not be sentenced to a term in jail as their primary punishment. This pattern changed, however, when 18th-century Enlightenment ideas that punishment should be proportionate to crimes swept the United States; the length of a sentence could be fixed to the perceived severity of an offense. Larger prisons became America's primary mode of punishing criminals in the early 19th century; not only did pris-ons offer a mechanism for proportionate punishment, they also offered a means of removing offenders from society and potentially rehabilitating them. Despite their high ideals and lofty rhetoric, prison administrators more often reverted to using various forms of brutality to control inmates than working to achieve the goal of reforming inmates. Nonetheless, the ongoing tension between the opposite goals of punishment and rehabilitation has become the driving force in the history of prisons even as prisons themselves have become the most visible emblems of the criminal justice system.

The history of the death penalty reflects even more sharply ongoing questions about the purposes of punishment. Should punishment incapacitate offenders, pre-venting them from committing future crimes by locking them away (or doing away with them)? Or should punishment rehabilitate them, teach them the error of their ways, and make them into better people? Should punishment act as a deterrent to others? Or is punishment's purpose to enact society's retribution, taking an eye for an eye or a life for a life? Controversies over the death penalty have helped to crystallize these debates and forced advocates on all sides to make their assumptions explicit. Executions for crimes have been fairly common in American history. That said, the 19th-century emergence of the prison as a viable alternative to execution was accompanied by a more general humanitarian criticism of the death penalty. Over the course of the 19th century, most jurisdictions gradually replaced public, "outdoor" executions in town squares with private, "indoor" executions behind prison walls so as not to offend popular sensibilities. By the middle of the 20th century, the death penalty fell into disrepute due to obvious inequities of race and class, and in 1972 the U.S. Supreme Court found it unconstitutional in the form in which it then existed. The Supreme Court reversed this decision when confronted with new, less arbitrary death penalty laws in 1976, and executions have increased sharply but not nearly so sharply as sentences of death; in California, for instance, only 13 prisoners have been executed since 1976 despite the 669 prisoners under sentence of death in 2008.[5] In this modern climate, proper respect for due process and civil rights demands that cases be examined closely and at length before the ultimate penalty can be applied.

All of these transformations—in police, in courts, in prisons, and in the death penalty—have been shaped by reform movements, efforts to foster a more orderly society while improving the effectiveness of justice. In many cases, these reform movements have reflected the noblest aspirations of Americans. Juvenile courts, for example, were first established in Chicago in 1899 in order to separate young offenders from criminal courts and jails, to protect them from the harsh consequences of incarceration, and to offer rehabilitation to the most malleable of offenders. Juvenile courts also reflect the ways in which the perceptions and aspirations of reformers were shaped by and confined to their times. These institutions, which in the 1900s understood informal procedure and judicial discretion to be the keys to saving young offenders, were widely criticized in the 1960s for this same inattention to due process. The protective juvenile court had itself become a massive correctional bureaucracy, capable of incarcerating juveniles for years without the protections that would be afforded to adults. And in the 1990s, juvenile courts faced a new wave of criticism for their purported ineffectiveness as a bulwark against youthful crime. As in the case of juvenile courts, reform movements and an ongoing quest to improve society have been key dynamics in American history. Yet as was also the case with the juvenile court, the outcome has often been an expansion of the power of the state, the growth of bureaucracy, and criticism on all sides by subsequent generations.

CHAPTER ONE

Old Crimes in the New World
1500-1699

During the 16th and 17th centuries, there was no United States and no U.S. system of crime and punishment. American Indian peoples, who had inhabited the North American continent for at least 25,000 years, were confronted by colonists from Spain, France, Great Britain, and the Netherlands, each with its own distinct legal systems. In the colonies, the crime rate—like the population—was fairly low. Laws generally focused on establishing colonial power, maintaining social order, and preventing smuggling. Imprisonment was not a viable option in a frontier setting, so punishment at the hands of the state consisted of fines, humiliation, physical torment, banishment, or (for some offenses) death.

Crime and Punishment in Native America

In a 1787 letter to James Madison, Thomas Jefferson described the most free society as being "[w]ithout government, as among our Indians."[1] The belief that American Indian societies had no government at all was popular among framers of the American democracy, who found the example inspiring and cited it as evidence that strong governmental control is not necessary and should be abolished. This dovetailed with the concept of the Noble Savage popularized by French philosopher Jean-Jacques Rousseau, who held that human beings are inherently good when living in a natural state but become evil through excessive civilization, particularly through its political and economic trappings. The conventional view that precolonial American Indian societies had no form of government is partly true, relative to European governments of the time (as American Indian societies were not governed by complex written legal codes), but it does not accurately reflect the breadth of precolonial American Indian government.

This is particularly evident in the case of the Aztec. The Aztec kingdom, in what is now Mexico and Central America, was ruled by 20 clans of nobles (pipiltin), each of which elected a representative to serve as part of the kingdom's legislature. Of these 20, one was selected to serve as king for life and three others were appointed to a special executive committee answerable only to the king. Those who had not been born into the noble caste were classified either as commoners (macehualtin) or as serfs (mayeques) living under the jurisdiction of a clan; they could not

1

The Aztec, pictured here in 1910, arguably the most powerful American nation at the time of European contact, had an intricate judicial system enforcing an informal code of law. *(Library of Congress, Prints and Photographs Division [LC-USZ62-99677])*

fully participate in the political system and were usually prohibited from owning land (though exceptions were made for war heroes). Many members of the noble caste also functioned as judges and were expected to enforce the judgment of the kingdom and to resolve disputes.

At the opposite end of the spectrum were the Comanche, who lived in what is now the American Great Plains and in Texas and Mexico. Their leadership was based on informal democracy. Individual bands of hunters simply elected their leaders and, for the most part, let it go at that. Comanche leaders were always male; women had an important role in Comanche society but were excluded from the political process. At times different groups of Comanche met in common councils, but they did not follow a common hierarchy. Each leader was responsible for judging disputes that arose within his band, and he frequently relied on trusted advisers to help render fair verdicts and on swift hunters to help capture fugitives, but there is no evidence of a formal legal code.

American Indian nations were most often made up of small, semiautonomous governments held together by a common leader or group of leaders. Most systems were neither as complex and entrenched as that of the Aztec nor as simple and informal as that of the Comanche. Nations that relied most heavily on agriculture were more likely to settle into cities and establish complex systems of government, while nations that relied on hunting were more likely to be seminomadic and use a simpler, less formal approach to governance. There is no evidence whatsoever that any American Indian tribe operated without relying on some form of governance, but the formality of Native governments varied considerably.

The nations' specific approaches to crime and punishment also varied considerably. For the Cherokee nation, in what is now the southeastern United States, the operative value was harmony. The Cherokee harmony ethic called on all members of the tribe to deal with conflicts indirectly, using mediators, and never express an-

This photograph is a portrait of Chief Quanah Parker (1845–1911), last chief of the Kwahadie (Quahadi) Comanche. Comanche Indian chiefs, who were most often democratically elected, served both executive and judicial functions. *(National Archives and Records Administration [ARC 530911])*

This late 19th-century American Indian police unit included both American Indian and non-Indian members. This reflects a degree of cooperation that is not often found in policing. Jurisdictional conflicts between European-American and American Indian governments, common in the colonial era, continue to this day. *(National Archives and Records Administration [523707])*

ger directly at another person. In situations involving personal conflict, the better Cherokee was expected to perform an act of generosity—regardless of who was to blame. Those who consistently violated the harmony ethic were shunned or subject to dark magic. The emphasis in Cherokee culture was on the preservation of the tribe as a loving, familial unit; in all but the most severe cases, it was not as important to provide retribution as it was to preserve a safe environment. Direct retribution, even in cases of murder, was frowned upon. Retribution was to occur, as quietly as possible, at the hands of objective third parties.

In other cultures, such as the Choctaw nation in what is now the southern United States, justice and retribution went hand in hand. If one Choctaw murdered another, the offender was expected to surrender immediately to the victim's family and face direct retribution. If the murderer refused to surrender, a member of his or her family was offered up instead. The most important consideration was that the victim's family be allowed to seek justice.

One common theme among American Indian systems of crime and punishment is that in disputed cases, tribal elders were expected to render a verdict. This is why the trait of wisdom was so highly valued among tribal leaders. An ideal judge would be prepared to place the needs of the tribe above his or her own prejudices and deliver a verdict that affirmed the tribe's values as effectively as possible.

As European empires established colonies in the Americas, these colonies interacted with American Indian governments on issues of criminal justice. Initially, crime between American Indians and colonists was sometimes regarded as an act of war committed by one culture against another rather than the actions of specific individuals. In other instances, crime and punishment were addressed in a particularly commonsense way: The offenders were punished by whichever nation or tribe happened to capture them, without extradition. Over time, due in part to a series of treaties between British colonists and American Indians in the late 18th century, extradition to the colonies or states became an almost universal practice, while extradition to tribal authorities became increasingly rare.

Spanish Conquest and the French Trade

On October 19, 1469, a wedding decided the future of Spain. Crown Prince Ferdinand II, heir to the Aragon kingdom in northeastern Spain, married Princess Isabella I, heir to the Castile kingdom of northwest and central Spain. The two regions were united after Ferdinand inherited the throne of Aragón in 1479 (Isabella had already become queen in 1474), placing them in control of the bulk of Spain—and they wanted the rest. Devout Roman Catholics, Ferdinand and Isabella soon turned their attention to conquest of the Islamic kingdom of Granada in southern Spain, which fell to their soldiers in 1492. They had successfully made a single nation of most of the Iberian Peninsula, and it was one of the most powerful nations on Earth.

Seeking additional trade revenue to fund their military conquests, the Spanish monarchy sent Italian explorer Christopher Columbus to find a faster trade route to India. He landed on the island of San Salvador (today called Watling Island) on October 12, 1492, and discovered the Americas without initially realizing it. By December 6, however, he became aware that he had discovered a new world—and he established a base on the island of Quisqueya, which he renamed Hispaniola. Hispaniola would serve as the de facto capital of the Spanish conquistadores until their conquest of Mexico City in 1521. Initially, there was some disagreement over which nations would be allowed to settle the Americas. These concerns were addressed by Pope Alexander VI in 1493, when he declared in his papal bull titled *Inter Caetera* that Spain owned the bulk of the Americas and was responsible for converting its inhabitants to Christianity.

Spain did this by conquering land by force and making American Indians into serfs under the *encomienda* system, whereby a group of American Indians would be assigned to a Spanish administrator and forced to labor on the administrator's behalf—sometimes as farmers, sometimes to mine silver and gold. Many *encomiendas*—or groups of serfs under the control of an administrator—lived under very harsh conditions in a sort of walking prison. More than 90 percent of American Indians living in Mexico, South and Central America, and the Caribbean died during the Spanish occupation, due primarily to the introduction of European diseases for which they had no natural immunity. The death toll was exacerbated by casualties from combat, executions, starvation, and overwork. Reformers—such as the outspoken priest and human rights activist Bartolomé de Las Casas, who condemned Spanish abuses of American Indians in his *Short Account of the Destruction of the West Indies* (1552)—attempted to improve the living conditions of American Indians laboring under the *encomienda* system. These attempts went largely ignored, however. The Spanish government's gradual and halfhearted attempts at regulation, along with the introduction of African slaves (which began in 1538 in Brazil), rendered the *encomienda* system unprofitable and relatively uncommon by the end of the 16th century—but the damage had already been done.

During its peak in the mid-16th century, New Spain was made up of the southwestern United States, Florida, Mexico, Central America, most of the Caribbean, and the Philippines and included the modern cities of Santa Fe, New Mexico, and St. Augustine, Florida. For the first few decades of its existence, New Spain was essentially a military dictatorship overseen by conquistadores who ruled their *encomiendas* with little or no oversight. This changed in 1524, when the Spanish government established the Consejo de Indias (Council of the Indies) to oversee New Spain, and even more so in 1527, when the *audiencia* (court) system came into effect.

Each *audiencia* was made up of local *oidores* (justices), who ruled on a wide range of criminal, civil, and legislative matters. Unlike in Spain, where the *audiencias* were responsible only for interpreting and enforcing the law, *audiencias* in New Spain had almost unlimited power to create new laws, strike down old laws, and enforce existing laws. New Spain's status as a frontier colony gave immense power to those charged with ruling over it.

For New Spain, crime was less of an issue than war and treason. When Mexico City fell in 1521, Cuauhtémoc—king of the Aztec—was captured by the conquistadores, held as a prisoner for some time, and then abruptly executed for "treason" based on the whims of the military commander who had captured him. Frequently, other American Indians were imprisoned or executed by the Spanish military. The *audiencia* provided some oversight to this process, but only to a point; until the mid-16th century, Spain's conquistadores held almost unlimited power over their subjects. The power of New Spain in North America faded with time, and the Viceroyalty of New Spain was finally dissolved after the Mexican revolution of 1821.

The French attempt at colonizing the Americas was far less violent but also far less successful. In part, this was due to a series of wars with the Spanish; the first French colony, Fort Caroline in Florida, was destroyed by Spanish conquistadores. France's empire was also limited by its approach to colonization. Rather than establish military control as Spain had done, France sought to establish viable ports for international trade. At its peak, French territory extended throughout Canada, the Mississippi Valley, and the Gulf Coast and included what would later become the cities of Montreal, Quebec; New Orleans, Louisiana; and Detroit, Michigan, but it included few French people other than fur traders and colonial administrators. As a result, the French colonies remained geographically large but sparsely settled and vulnerable.

Rather than enslaving American Indians, the French focused on trading with them and, in some cases, forming strategic alliances and playing a role in intertribal war. French colonies in North America simply applied French law when possible, but the small number of colonists coupled with the remote, frontier society resulted in few reported crimes. New France officially ceased to be when Canada was ceded to Great Britain in 1763, and Spain and Britain divided up that portion of French territory that would later make up part of the United States.

English Law in the New World

Although England was the nation whose colonies later became the United States, Spain had a head start of more than a century. Pope Alexander VI declared in 1493 that Spain would be given the bulk of the Americas. England, which was at the time a militarily weak nation, did nothing to colonize the New World. Even after the Church of England broke with Roman Catholicism in 1534, England

Canadian and Inuit traders barter over white fox furs in this photograph from early 20th-century Montreal. The French colonies in North America, unlike the British and Spanish colonies, functioned primarily as trading posts and were generally grounded in mutually beneficial relationships with Native peoples. *(Library of Congress, Prints and Photographs Division [LC-USZ62-112764])*

did not colonize the Americas; this was due in part to ongoing conflicts with the Spanish and the power of their naval forces. The first attempt at a colony, in 1585, failed largely because transport between England and North America had been interrupted by the Spanish. It was not until 1588, when England secured a major naval victory over the Spanish Armada, that English colonization of the Americas became a realistic possibility.

The first viable English colony in North America at Jamestown, Virginia, was founded in 1607. For the rest of the 17th century, the English colonies expanded at a rapid pace—due in part to overpopulation in England—and, within a matter of decades, England became the dominant colonial empire in North America.

If harsh by contemporary standards, particularly with regard to their restrictions on religious expression, the laws of the English colonies were for the most part more lenient than the laws of England. In England, overpopulation had created an impoverished class of "masterless men"[2] who roamed the countryside sustaining themselves on lives of crime. In an effort to combat this, English law allowed the death penalty for such offenses as theft and robbery and expanded the number of capital crimes so that by the 18th century, nearly 300 offenses could potentially

In 17th-century England, robbery and other property crimes potentially carried the death penalty—an aggressive measure taken to combat poverty-related crime. In the British colonies, the death penalty was used far less frequently. *(Library of Congress, Prints and Photographs Division [LC-USZ62-2848])*

lead to execution.[3] In contrast, most English colonies allowed the death penalty for only about a dozen offenses. Imprisonment was also fairly rare in the colonies, as it was in England; the concept of penitentiaries would not emerge on a widespread basis until the 18th century. Other punishments, such as whipping, humiliation in the stocks, and banishment were generally used, though serious offenders were jailed pending trial.

English colonies essentially fell into three categories: the southern colonies (such as Virginia), which were patterned after English law; the New England colonies (such as Massachusetts), which displayed more of a Puritan colonial influence; and the middle colonies (such as Pennsylvania), which generally offered their own variations on English law. It is impossible to definitively assess the crime rate during the colonial era, because records—even of serious crimes—were not comprehensive. Nevertheless, existing records suggest an exceptionally low crime rate. In his book *Popular Justice*, historian Samuel Walker points out that during the 13-year period between 1632 and 1645, the county courts of Accomack-Northampton in Virginia recorded only 60 criminal cases, most consisting of nonpredatory crimes (such as drunkenness, cursing, and fornication).[4]

Although English colonial law was sometimes more egalitarian than the law of the empire it represented, oppressed classes certainly existed in the New World. Generally speaking, only free white heterosexual Christian males of certain social status were allowed to participate in the most important aspects of colonial life. Under colonial law, women were excluded from participation in most government functions and subject to their husbands in most legal matters. Although there were laws prohibiting spousal abuse, there was little support or protection available to women who sought to file charges against their husbands.

In most states, members of non-Christian faiths could be subject to penalties ranging from banishment to death. Gay men and lesbians were subject to prosecution and possible execution under the capital crime of sodomy. American Indians who committed crimes against English colonists were treated far more harshly than their white counterparts.

Indentured servants, England's masterless men, often traded poverty and the prospect of debtors' prison for transit overseas to the new colonies, where they could live as virtual slaves for a limited period of time—usually two to seven years—and buy their freedom through labor. Many did not survive their tenure or were forced to serve for the remainder of their lives through fraud or manipulation. As would later be the case with African-American slaves, indentured servants played a central and unrewarded role in maintaining the agricultural economy of the American colonies, particularly in the South.

The institution of slavery slowly superseded the institution of indentured servitude. Slavery dates from the earliest years of English settlement in North America, when four African-American slaves were brought to Virginia in 1619, but it remained comparatively rare for the better part of the 17th century. The final decades of the 1600s, however, saw both a codification in colonial law of what it meant to be a slave and a dramatic increase in the number of slaves in the American colonies. By the end of the 17th century, approximately 40 percent of Virginia's population was made up of slaves. Some colonies had laws against the abuse of slaves, but they were not widely enforced. Physical punishment of slaves was regarded as part of normal life, and a 1669 law in the colony of Virginia actually legalized the killing of slaves, provided that any such killing occurred during the process of punishment.[5]

The colonies most clearly patterned after the English system of crime and punishment, the middle and southern colonies, generally relied on a county system. As part of his job, the sheriff oversaw law enforcement for his county—but he was also responsible for other county issues. In some cases, he was assisted in his law enforcement responsibilities by constables, who essentially functioned as police officers but were most likely part-time employees of the county. These officials conducted little or no criminal investigation. Cases of homicide came to public attention only when someone reported a suspicious death to a sheriff or magistrate, who then called a coroner to conduct a hearing to determine the likely cause of death and the persons responsible. Under this arrangement, accused killers could rarely be tried unless they were caught at the scene of the crime or witnessed doing the deed.

The New England colonies largely abandoned the county model in favor of a town meeting system. New England towns were regarded as voluntary communities, heavily influenced by the theology of Puritanism, a movement that rejected the Anglican tradition in favor of abolishing Roman Catholic influences and establishing a stricter code of social conduct. The early New England colonies were in most respects religious communities, dominated as much by church and gossip as by law. Citizens were expected to monitor the behavior of their neighbors and report suspicious activities to the local church or, in particularly severe cases, to public officials. More often than not, however, crimes were dealt with by churches and resolved by way of public penance or other forms of retribution. Church membership was considered even more important than citizenship, and the churches of New England had immense power. They were also supported by the courts, which often banished or hanged religious dissidents, enforced laws prohibiting blasphemy and witchcraft, and took other measures to support the religious establishment.

The collusion between religious and legal interests was demonstrated clearly in the Antinomian Controversy, in which Boston's perceived social harmony—based on religious and cultural orthodoxy—was challenged by one woman. In 1636, housewife and herbalist Anne Hutchinson began holding meetings at her home to discuss the sermons of local minister John Cotton. Cotton preached that the strict moral code of the Puritans was not necessary for salvation—that salvation is determined by God alone and cannot be influenced by human behavior. This belief, sometimes referred to as *antinomianism* ("against law"), ran counter to Puritanism's emphasis on strict moral behavior. When Hutchinson's sermons began to rival Cotton's in influence, Massachusetts governor John Winthrop grew concerned that a woman preacher who railed against the religious foundations of what he called his "city upon a hill"[6] could do immense damage. He had her arrested, brought to trial, and expelled from the colony. Although he never clarified what the grounds for expulsion were, they seemed to be based on a mix of two factors: her refusal to submit to established Puritan gender roles (which called on women to minister only to other women, if at all) and her success at promoting the antinomian belief system. John Cotton, who was perceived as less dangerous (in part because of his gender), was acquitted and allowed to remain in Massachusetts.

This theocratic system was challenged and permanently transformed by the Salem witch trials of 1692, in which 19 women and one man were killed after being accused of witchcraft by witnesses who had been assembled by local minister Samuel Parris. The trials relied heavily on spectral evidence, eyewitness testimony that was accepted regardless of alibis on the basis that a witch could send her specter to appear and physically commit any act of which she had been accused. As was the case in the

This 1892 drawing of "witches" being imprisoned in the stocks evokes the 1692 Salem witch trials. *(Library of Congress, Prints and Photographs Division [LC-USZ62-476])*

Antinomian Controversy, the overall effect of the trials was to target women who did not conform to Puritan societal norms. Outraged officials soon ended the witch trials and banned the use of spectral evidence, and the backlash from the event left New Englanders suspicious of prosecutions based on religious zeal.

By the end of the 17th century, the English colonies had significantly changed their approaches toward crime and punishment. This was due partly to societal change in North America and partly to changes in domestic English law. Two pieces of English legislation enacted in 1689, the Religious Toleration Act and the Bill of Rights, significantly reduced oppression of religious minorities and protected defendants from unfair trials and cruel and unusual punishment.

New Netherland and the Problem of Smuggling

When colonists from the Netherlands settled in Manhattan in 1626, they were in most respects acting on behalf of the Dutch West India Company. The early criminal justice history of the colony was not promising. Prosecutors were paid on a commission basis, drawn from fines they were able to win on behalf of the colony. Defendants were expected to incriminate themselves, and those who were not willing to oblige were sometimes subject to torture. The situation quickly grew worse: Governor Willem Kieft, who served from 1638 to 1646, began his tenure by placing himself in complete control of New Netherland's highest judicial court.

Settlers who had grown accustomed to the Dutch tradition of a judicial council made up of nine independent justices, each with an equal vote, were horrified to confront a council comprised of two members: Kieft, who had two votes, and a token second justice, who had one.

Kieft's greatest blunder, however, was his treatment of local American Indians. In 1639, he began demanding tribute from American Indian tribes residing near the Hudson River. A year later, rumor circulated that a small group of Raritans—an American Indian tribe living near the Hudson River—had stolen hogs from colonists. Without investigating the rumor (the culprits later turned out to be Dutch traders), Kieft responded to the accusation by sending Dutch militia to a nearby Raritan village, where they destroyed property and killed four men. Seeking retribution, a group of Raritan warriors killed four Dutchmen in response. Local tribes refused to pay tribute to New Netherland and frequently came into violent conflict with Dutch settlers, but a 1642 treaty eased tensions considerably.

The situation grew far worse in February 1643, when hundreds of men, women, and children belonging to Hudson River tribes, fleeing from combat with the Mohawk, asked for the protection of the Dutch. Despite the treaty, Kieft was unwilling to give up the opportunity to decimate the river tribes; in the middle of the night, Kieft sent 120 soldiers to ambush and slaughter them, leaving the impression that the Mohawk had committed the atrocity. When it became clear that the Dutch were to blame, all 11 Hudson River tribes converged on New Netherland, burning settlements and driving the Dutch colonists into New Amsterdam for protection. When colonists learned of the massacre that provoked the conflict, they appointed eight counselors to serve in Kieft's stead and wrote a letter to Holland demanding that he be recalled. In 1647, he was sent back to the Netherlands, dying when his boat sank en route. He was replaced by Peter Stuyvesant, who reformed the colony but was largely unable to undo the damage Kieft's massacre had inflicted on the Indian-Dutch relationship. The height of the conflict, making up the years between 1641 and 1645, is remembered as Kieft's War.

The Dutch colony under Stuyvesant was much smaller than the English, French, and Spanish colonies, comprising parts of what are today the states of New York, New Jersey, and Delaware, but it foreshadowed the future United States in several important respects. The first was its diversity. In 1646 French missionary Isaac Jogues marveled at the diversity of New Netherland's most successful colony, New Amsterdam, writing that "there may well be four or five hundred men of different sects and nations: the Director General told me that there were men of eighteen different languages . . . [and] there are . . . Catholics, English Puritans, Lutherans, [and] Anabaptists, here called [Mennonites]."[7] Today, three and a half centuries later, New Amsterdam—now called New York City—is still regarded as the most diverse city in the United States.

The second was trade-related crime. Smuggling was one of the primary concerns of New Netherland, and many traders were frustrated by the invasive searches and tedious security protocols that the New Netherland government observed. When the English conquered New Amsterdam in 1664 and inherited its fur trade, they also inherited its smuggling problem. A century later, transcontinental trade would force the British to search and seize merchandise in the North American colonies with very little oversight, and tax revenue lost to smuggling would be compensated for by new taxes on luxury trade goods. These two factors would dramatically contribute to the frustration of British colonists in North America, a frustration that would culminate in the American Revolution.

Chronicle of Events

1499
- Christopher Columbus establishes New Spain's *encomienda* system when he assigns 300 American Indians to some of his companions as serfs.

1512
- *December 27:* The Spanish government implements the Laws of Burgos, placing American Indians under the jurisdiction of Spanish law.

1514
- Spain's King Charles I declares the Requerimiento ("requirement"), stating that all American Indians must submit to the authority of Spain and convert to Roman Catholicism. Those who refuse are subject to deadly force.

1521
- *August 13:* The Aztec government of Mexico City surrenders to Spanish conquistadores.

1524
- The Consejo de Indias (Council of the Indies) is created by the Spanish government to administer criminal and civil justice in New Spain.

1525
- *February 28:* The captured Aztec emperor Cuauhtemoc is tortured and executed by conquistadores.

1527
- The first *audiencia* (judicial court) in New Spain is established in Mexico City.

1534
- French explorer Jacques Cartier claims parts of Quebec and Newfoundland for France.

1538
- The Spanish government imports enslaved Africans into Brazil to replace American Indian workers, essentially beginning the African-American slave trade.

1552
- Bartolomé de Las Casas publishes his *Brevísima relación de la destrucción de las Indias (Short Account of the Destruction of the West Indies)*, which chronicles Spanish abuse of American Indians.

1562
- *October:* The British slave trade begins.

1588
- The English fleet defeats the Spanish Armada, allowing England to establish colonies in the Americas.

1607
- *May 14:* Jamestown, Virginia, the first successful English settlement in the Americas, is founded.

1608
- *July 3:* The first permanent French settlement in North America is established.

1614
- The first permanent Dutch settlement in North America is established.

1619
- *August 20:* A trading ship docking in Jamestown, Virginia, sells four African-American passengers into indentured servitude in exchange for supplies.

1620
- *November 11:* The Plymouth Colony of Massachusetts is founded.

1626
- The Netherlands establishes a colony on Manhattan island.

1634
- *March 25:* The colony of Maryland is founded.

1637
- *November 12:* Religious leader Anne Hutchinson is banished from Massachusetts for stating the belief that salvation occurs by grace and that obeying religious laws is not necessary in order to achieve salvation.

1638
- Four indentured servants escape from their master in Massachusetts and encounter and murder a member of the Narragansett tribe. One of the four dies at the hands of Narragansett law enforcement representatives, one escapes, and the other two are tried and executed by the English government.

1639
- Nepaupuck, a member of the Quillipieck tribe, is captured by his leader and accused of murdering an

Englishman named Abraham Finch. He is turned over to the English government, which finds him guilty and promptly executes him.

• New Netherland governor Willem Kieft abolishes the colony's judicial council and places himself in control of its criminal justice system.

1640

• *July 9:* African-American indentured servant John Punch is declared a "slave for life" by the colony of Virginia, an incident that marks the official beginning of racial slavery in the English colonies.

1641

• The Massachusetts General Court approves the Massachusetts Body of Liberties, which promotes jury trials and freedom from unlawful search and seizure but applies the death penalty in cases of homosexuality, adultery, bestiality, polytheism, witchcraft, and blasphemy.

1643

• *February:* New Netherland governor Willem Kieft's attack on nearby American Indian villages prompts retaliatory attacks that destroy several Dutch settlements near New Amsterdam.

1649

• *September 21:* The colony of Maryland passes the ironically titled Toleration Act, which guarantees religious freedom for all Christians but mandates the death penalty for non-Christians.

In this 1906 photographic re-creation of a 17th-century Puritan home, a woman sits at a spinning wheel by a fireplace. Colonial Massachusetts was governed by a strict social code that required neighbors to monitor one another's activities and was more likely to address unacceptable behavior in church than through codified legal standards. *(Library of Congress, Prints and Photographs Division [LC-USZ62-90823])*

1660

• *June 1:* Quaker evangelist Mary Dyer is executed for attempting to spread Quakerism in Massachusetts.

1663

• *September 13:* Slaves revolt in Gloucester County, Virginia, marking the first organized slave rebellion in North American history.

1664

• *September 8:* England assumes control of New Amsterdam (modern-day New York).

1669

• The Virginia Assembly passes a law that declares slaveholders may legally kill their slaves in the process of punishment.

1670

• *September 5:* Future Pennsylvania governor William Penn is acquitted in London on charges of disturbing the peace. He had been arrested for meeting with other Quakers, a persecuted group in England at the time.

1674

• *November 10:* In the Treaty of Westminster, the Netherlands officially cedes New Netherland (now New York and New Jersey) to England.

1681

• *April 2:* The colony of Pennsylvania is founded.

1689

• *May 24:* The English Toleration Act is passed, promoting religious toleration in England and the colonies.
• *December 16:* The English Bill of Rights, which prohibits cruel and unusual punishment and punishments without trial, takes effect.

1690

• John Locke's *Two Treatises on Government*, which will heavily influence U.S. civil rights law, is published.

1692

• During the infamous Salem witch trials, local officials in Salem, Massachusetts, try and execute 20 people for witchcraft.

1693

• *May:* Massachusetts governor William Phips pardons all accused witches.

1697

• The Massachusetts General Court declares a day of fasting and penance in response to the Salem Witch Trials.
• Samuel Parris, the Salem minister who led the witch hunt, is fired by his congregation.

Eyewitness Testimony

The American Indian Experience

After the wars and killings had ended, when usually there survived only some boys, some women, and children, these survivors were distributed among the Christians to be slaves. The *repartimiento* or distribution was made according to the rank and importance of the Christian to whom the Indians were allocated, one of them being given thirty, another forty, still another, one or two hundred, and besides the rank of the Christian there was also to be considered in what favor he stood with the tyrant they called Governor. The pretext was that these allocated Indians were to be instructed in the articles of the Christian faith. As if those Christians who were as a rule foolish and cruel and greedy and vicious could be caretakers of souls! And the care they took was to send the men to the mines to dig for gold, which is intolerable labor, and to send the women into the fields of the big ranches to hoe and till the land, work suitable for strong men. Nor to either the men or the women did they give any food except herbs and legumes, things of little substance. The milk in the breasts of the women with infants dried up and thus in a short while the infants perished. And since men and women were separated, there could be no marital relations. And the men died in the mines and the women died on the ranches from the same causes, exhaustion and hunger.

Jesuit priest Bartolomé de Las Casas, writing on the effects of the encomienda *system, 1552 quoted in Zinn and Arnove,* Voices of a People's History of the United States, *p. 39.*

I am now grown old, and must soon die; and the succession must descend, in order, to my brothers . . . and then to my two sisters, and their two daughters. I wish their experience was equal to mine; and that your love to us might not be less than ours to you.

Why should you take by force that from us which you can have by love? Why should you destroy us, who have provided you with food? . . . We can hide our provisions, and fly into the woods; and then you must consequently famish by wronging your friends. What is the cause of your jealousy? You see us unarmed, and willing to supply your wants, if you will come in a friendly manner, and not with swords and guns, as to invade an enemy.

I am not so simple, as not to know it is better to eat good meat, lie well, and sleep quietly with my women and children; to laugh and be merry with the English; and, being their friend, to have copper, hatchets, and whatever else I want, than to fly from all, to lie cold in the woods, feed upon acorns, roots, and such trash, and to be so hunted, that I cannot rest, eat, or sleep. In such circumstances, my men must watch, and if a twig should but break, all would cry out, "Here comes Captain [John] Smith"; and so, in this miserable manner, to end my miserable life; and, Captain Smith, this might be soon your fate too, through your rashness and unadvisedness.

I, therefore, exhort you to peaceable councils; and, above all, I insist that the guns and swords, the cause of all our jealousy and uneasiness, be removed and sent away.

Wahunsonacock ("King Powhatan"), leader of the Powhatan confederacy, writing to Virginia colonist John Smith in a winter 1607 letter, quoted in Nabokov, Native American Testimony, *pp. 72–73.*

France and Spain in the New World

The Indians must be made to work for wages in the fields or in the cities, so that they have no excuse for idleness . . . This order must be enforced by our justices; private Spaniards must not be allowed to bring pressure upon the Indians, even within their own encomiendas. You are to give orders for proper daily wages to be paid to the Indians themselves, and not to their chiefs, or to any other intermediaries. They are not to be overworked; and it must be made clear that Spaniards who disregard these orders will be severely punished . . .

You are to do justice, and to see to it that the grievances of the Indians are removed, and their tributes lightened; observing and enforcing in all things the provisions made by the New Laws for the good government of the Indies.

Instructions to Luis de Velasco, second viceroy of New Spain, 1550, quoted in J. H. Parry, The Audiencia of New Galicia in the Sixteenth Century: A Study in Spanish Colonial Government, *pp. 65–66.*

The encomenderos, who have only been encomenderos, and not conquistadors, be not deceived, Your Excellency . . . they are tyrants . . . because those people are free by right and natural law and do not owe the Spaniards anything . . . Encomiendas in themselves are bad, wicked, and intrinsically depraved, not in harmony with any law or reason, because to give or apportion free men against their will, commanding them for the good and usefulness [of the Spaniards] . . . and behind their backs to deprive kings of their kingdoms and princes and natural lords of their domains—is there greater infernal depravity, wickedness and inequity, impiety and tyranny?

Bartolemé de Las Casas, writing in a reply to Fray Matías de San Martín, bishop of Charcas, quoted in Luis N. Rivera, A Violent Evangelism: The Political and Religious Conquest of the Americas, *p. 119.*

I asked the savages for an Iroquois prisoner, whom they gave me. I saved him from a good many tortures that he would have suffered, such as they inflicted upon his companions . . .

Some days afterward this Iroquois prisoner, whom I had under guard, on account of the excess of liberty that I allowed him, got away and escaped, because of the fear and terror that he felt, in spite of the assurances given him by a woman of his tribe, whom we had at our settlement.

Samuel de Champlain, The Voyages and Explorations of Samuel de Champlain *(1632), v. 1, pp. 226, 229.*

All punishment of innocent subjects, be they great or little, are against the law of nature . . . But the infliction of what evil soever on an innocent man that is not a subject, if it be for the benefit of the Commonwealth, and without violation of any former covenant, is no breach of the law of nature. For all men that are not subjects are either enemies, or else they have ceased from being so by some precedent covenants. But against enemies, whom the Commonwealth judgeth capable to do them hurt, it is lawful by the original right of nature to make war; wherein the sword judgeth not, nor doth the victor make distinction of nocent and innocent as to the time past, nor has other respect of mercy than as it conduceth to the good of his own people. And upon this ground it is that also in subjects who deliberately deny the authority of the Commonwealth established, the vengeance is lawfully extended, not only to the fathers, but also to the third and fourth generation not yet in being, and consequently innocent of the fact for which they are afflicted: because the nature of this offense consisteth in the renouncing of subjection, which is a relapse into the condition of war commonly called rebellion; and they that so offend, suffer not as subjects, but as enemies. For rebellion is but war renewed.

Thomas Hobbes, from Leviathan *(1660), The University of Adelaide. Available online at URL: http://etext.library. adelaide.edu.au/h/hobbes/thomas.*

The petition of Phillip Corven, a Negro, in all humility showeth: That your petitioner being a servant to Mrs.

Anne Beazley, late of James City County, widow, dead. The said Mrs. Beazley made her last will and testament in writing . . . and, amongst other things, did order, will appoint that your petitioner by the then name of Negro boy Phillip, should serve her cousin, Mr. Humphrey Stafford, the term of eight years, then next ensuing, and then should enjoy his freedom and be paid three barrels of corn and a suit of clothes, as by the said will appears.

Soon after the making of which will, the said Mrs. Beazley departed this life, your petitioner did continue and abide with the said Mr. Stafford . . . some years, and the said Mr. Stafford sold the remainder of your petitioner's time to one Mr. Charles Lucas, with whom your petitioner also continued, doing true and faithful service; but the said Mr. Lucas, coveting your petitioner's service longer than of right it was due, did not at the expiration of the said eight years, discharge your petitioner from his service, but compelled him to serve three years longer than the time set by the said Mrs. Beazley's will, and then not being willing your petitioner should enjoy his freedom, did, contrary to all honesty and good conscience with threats and a high hand, in the time of your petitioner's service with him, and by his confederacy with some persons compel your petitioner to set his hand to a writing, which the said Mr. Lucas now saith is an Indenture for twenty years, and forced your petitioner to acknowledge in the same County Court of Warwick . . .

Your Petitioner therefore most humbly prayeth your honors to order that the said Mr. Lucas make him satisfaction for the said three years service above his time, and pay him corn and clothes, with costs of suit.

A civil petition against slavery fraud (1675), addressed to William Berkeley, governor of Virginia, quoted in Aptheker, A Documentary History of the Negro People in the United States, *v. 1, pp. 2–3.*

Crime in the English Colonies

And I have nothing to comfort me, nor is there nothing to be gotten here but sickness and death, except [in the event] that one had money to lay out in some things for profit. But I have nothing at all—no, not a shirt to my back but two rags, nor clothes but one poor suit, nor but one pair of shoes, but one pair of stockings, but one cap, but two bands. My cloak is stolen by one of my fellows, and to his dying hour would not tell me what he did with it; but some of my fellows saw him have butter and beef out of a ship, which my cloak, I doubt [not], paid for . . . I am not half a quarter as strong as I was in England, and all is for want of victuals; for I do protest unto you that I have eaten more in a day at home than I have allowed me here for a week.

Indentured servant Richard Frethorne, writing to his father in England in March and April 1623, quoted in Zinn and Arnove, Voices from a People's History of the United States, *pp. 64–65.*

WINTHROP: Mrs. Hutchinson, you are called here as one of those that have troubled the peace of the commonwealth and the churches here; you are known to be a woman that hath had a great share in the promoting and divulging of those [theological] opinions that are causes of this trouble, and to be nearly joined not only

In 1637, Anne Hutchinson was banished from the Massachusetts Bay Colony for preaching in her home. She was excommunicated from the church and moved to what later became Rhode Island and New York. *(Library of Congress, Prints and Photographs Division [LC-USZ62-53343])*

in affinity and affection with some of those the court had taken notice of and passed censure upon, but you have spoken diverse things . . . and you have maintained a meeting and an assembly in your house that hath been condemned by the general assembly as a thing not tolerable nor comely in the sight of God nor fitting for your sex . . . therefore I would intreat to you to express whether you do not hold and assent in practice to those opinions and factions that have been handled in court already . . .

HUTCHINSON: I am called here to answer before you but I hear no things laid to my charge.

W: I have told you already and more I can tell you.

H: Name one Sir.

W: Have I not named some already?

H: What have I said or done?

W: Why, for your doings, this you did harbour and countenance those that are parties in this faction you have heard of.

H: That's matter of conscience, Sir.

W: Your conscience you must keep or it must be kept for you.

H: Must not I then entertain the saints because I must keep my conscience . . .

W: You have joined with them in the faction.

H: In what faction have I joined with them?

W: In presenting the [Antinomian theological] petition . . .

H: Wherein?

W: Why in entertaining [the Antinomians].

H: What breach of law is that Sir?

W: Why dishonouring of parents . . . If [the Antinomians] be . . . of another religion, if you entertain them then you dishonour your parents and are justly punishable . . .

H: I may put honor upon them as the children of God as they do honor the Lord.

W: We do not mean to discourse with those of your sex but only this; you do adhere unto them and do endeavour to set forward this faction and so you do dishonour us . . .

Mrs. Hutchinson, the sentence of the court you hear is that you are banished from out of our jurisdiction as being a woman not fit for our society, and are to be imprisoned till the court shall send you away.

H: I desire to know [why] I am banished?

W: Say no more, the court knows [why] and is satisfied.

Interrogation of accused heretic Anne Hutchinson by Governor John Winthrop of Massachusetts, November 7, 1637, quoted in Hall, The Antimonian Controversy, *pp. 312–348.*

Master Ambros Marten, for calling the church covenant a stinking carrion and a human invention, and saying he wondered at God's patience, feared it would end in the sharp and said the ministers did dethrone Christ, and set up themselves: he was fined 10 pounds, and counseled to go to Master [Richard] Mather to be instructed by him.

An account of a 1639 trial in colonial Massachusetts, quoted in Powers, Crime and Punishment in Early Massachusetts, *p. 204.*

At this court one Margaret Jones of Charlestown was indicted and found guilty of witchcraft, and hanged for it. The evidence against her was,

1. that she was found to have such a malignant touch, as many persons (men, women, and children) whom she stroked with any affection or displeasure, or, etc., were taken with deafness, or vomiting, or other violent pains or sickness,
2. she practicing [medicine], and her medicines being such things as (by her own confession) were harmless . . . yet had extraordinarily violent effects,
3. she would use to tell such as would not make use of her [medicine], that they would never be healed, and accordingly their diseases and hurts continued, with relapse against the ordinary course, and beyond the apprehension of all physicians and surgeons,
4. some things which she foretold came to pass accordingly; other things she could tell of (as secret speeches, etc.) which she had no ordinary means to come to the knowledge of,
5. she had (upon search) an apparent [nipple] in her secret parts as fresh as if it had been newly sucked, and after it had been scanned, upon a forced search, that was withered, and another began on the opposite side,
6. in the prison, in the clear day-light, there was seen in her arms, she sitting on the floor, and her clothes up, etc., a [ghostly] little child, which ran from her into another room, and the officer following it, it was vanished. The like child was seen in two other places, to which [Jones] had relation; and one made that saw it, fell sick upon it, and was cured by the

said Margaret, who used means to be employed to that end.

Her behavior at her trial was very intemperate, lying notoriously, and railing upon the jury and witness, etc., and in the like distemper she died. The same day and hour she was executed, there was a very great tempest at Connecticut, which blew down many trees, etc.

Governor John Winthrop, describing a capital witchcraft case in Massachusetts in his journal of June 4, 1648, quoted in Powers, Crime and Punishment in Early Massachusetts, *p. 460.*

Philip Veren was ordered to be set by the heels in the stocks one hour for disowning the country's power, in open court, about forcing any to come to the public worship.

From court records of Essex County, Massachusetts (1663), quoted in Powers, Crime and Punishment in Early Massachusetts, *p. 151.*

Smuggling and Thievery in New Netherland

[S]ome Christians attempted . . . to steal maize from these Indians, out of their cabins, which they perceiving endeavored to prevent, thereupon three Indians were shot dead, two houses standing opposite the fort were in return forthwith set on fire . . . Imagining that the Director had accused him [of stealing the corn], he [Maryn Adriaenzen] being one of the signers of the petition he determined to revenge himself. With this resolution he proceeded to the Director's house armed with a pistol, loaded and cocked, and a hanger by his side; coming unawares into the Director's room, he presents his pistol at him, saying, "What devilish lies art thou reporting of me?" but by the promptness of one of the bystanders, the shot was prevented, and he himself immediately confined . . . Shortly afterwards some of the commonalty collected before the Director, riotously demanding the prisoner; they were answered that their request should be presented in order and in writing, which about 25 men did; they therein asked the Director to pardon the criminal. The matters were referred to them to decide conscientiously thereupon, in such wise that they immediately went forth, without hearing parties or seeing any complaints or documents. They condemn him in a fine of five hundred guilders, and to remain three months away from the Manhatens, but on account of the importance of the affair and some considerations, it was resolved to send the criminal with his trial to Holland.

From The Journal of New Netherland *(1647), quoted in J. Franklin Jameson,* Narratives of New Netherland, 1609–1664, *The Cumorah Project. Available online at URL: http://www.cumorah.com/etexts/nwnth10.txt.*

This contraband trade has ruined the country, and contraband goods are now sent to every part of it . . . [O]f inspection and confiscation there is no lack; hence legitimate trade is entirely diverted, except a little, which exists *pro forma*, as a cloak for carrying on illicit trading . . . Now the Company itself carries on the forbidden trade, the people think they too can do so without guilt, if they can do so without damage; and this causes smuggling and frauds to an incredible extent, though not so great this year as heretofore.

Adrian van der Donk, from The Representation of New Netherland *(1650), reprinted in J. Franklin Jameson,* Narratives of New Netherland, 1609–1664, *The Cumorah Project. Available online at URL: http://www.cumorah.com/etexts/nwnth10.txt.*

Trade has long been free to every one, and as profitable as ever. Nobody's goods were confiscated, except those who had violated their contract, or the order by which they were bound; and if anybody thinks that injustice has been done him by confiscation, he can speak for himself.

Cornelis van Tienhoven, from Answer to the Representation of New Netherland *(1650), reprinted in J. Franklin Jameson,* Narratives of New Netherland, 1609–1664, p., *The Cumorah Project. Available online at URL: http://www.cumorah.com/etexts/nwnth10.txt.*

CHAPTER TWO

A New System of Justice
1700–1789

By the end of the 17th century, England had emerged as the dominant colonial power in North America. The British colonial presence consisted of 13 viable colonies—Connecticut, Carolina, Delaware, Maryland, Massachusetts, New Hampshire, New Jersey, New York, Pennsylvania, Rhode Island, and Virginia, plus Newfoundland and Nova Scotia—with a combined population of 275,000.[1] The Dutch colonial presence had completely collapsed with the English conquest of New Netherland in 1664, the French outposts in North America met with little success, and the Spanish colonial presence in the Americas, though considerable, was situated primarily in Central and South America.

Yet by 1790, the British Empire in North America had essentially been lost. In its place were the 13 United States of America, with a total population of 3.9 million[2] and a civilian defense force that had driven away one of the most formidable armies on Earth. With this transformation came a new attitude toward crime and punishment based not on social harmony, but instead on protecting individual rights. Most central to this shift was a combination of two factors that are not ordinarily associated with one another: international smuggling and European philosophy.

Molasses, Sugar, and Tea

The early 18th century was marked by an increasingly cosmopolitan society in the English colonies. Ethnically diverse (including Dutch, French, and German immigrants) and driven by trade, the English colonies in North America represented a kind of commercial culture that would come to define the American way of life. Importation and exportation were central to the cultural and economic survival of the English colonies.

Although smuggling had been a reality in the English colonies for many years, it became a more serious problem during the 18th century, as the colonies engaged more and more frequently in foreign trade. A major contributor to the North American colonial black market was the Molasses Act of 1733, passed by the British parliament as a means of discouraging foreign trade by levying heavy tariffs against rum, molasses, and sugar imported from non-British colonies. The legislation primarily targeted imports from French and Dutch territories in the West Indies and was to encourage trade with struggling British colonies in the West Indies, such as Barbados. Often viewed as a luxury good, molasses was a staple of 18th-century colonial America, in large part because it was instrumental to the production of rum, a vital trade item. The tariffs were a burden on colonists, and they created the first widespread objection to British taxation. "[M]olasses," John Adams would later reflect, "was an essential ingredient in American independence."[3] In response to the high cost of rum, colonists illegally imported tax-free rum from other European nations.

During the early 1760s, the British government suddenly found itself in need of revenue. The French and Indian War, in which Britain battled France in North America for control of Canada and much of the Great Lakes region and Ohio Valley, began in 1754; in 1756 it became part of the Seven Years' War, a global conflict pitting Britain, Hanover, and Prussia against France, Austria, Russia, Saxony, Spain, and Sweden. By the time Britain had achieved its victory and the Treaty of Paris was signed, it had sustained heavy losses of all kinds. The sense in Parliament was that the British military had dedicated much of its resources to the North American conflict and that the British government deserved to be compensated by the colonies that had benefited from the war.

Concerned with the increase in illegal smuggling, particularly when it involved Britain's wartime enemy the French, the British parliament passed the Sugar Act of 1764 to replace the unsuccessful Molasses Act. The Sugar Act cut foreign tariffs on molasses by half but introduced new regulations to make smuggling more difficult to hide. It also introduced new taxes on coffee, sugar, wines, and indigo dye. The response to the Sugar Act was actually harsher than the response to the Molasses Act in the North American colonies, but reaction remained relatively mild compared to what would soon follow.

In March 1765, Parliament passed the Stamp Act. This new legislation taxed all paper used for publication or official business in the North American colonies, requiring each sheet to bear a stamp as evidence that the relevant tax had been paid. Colonists viewed the Stamp Act as punitive and unfair, and it was now that the complaint against "taxation without representation" began to clearly take shape. The American colonies, accustomed to local democratic processes, operated on principles different from those of the British parliament, which did not formally represent the American colonies in its legislative decisions. The British took the position that the American colonies enjoyed "virtual representation" in Parliament, as a legislator was not expected to represent only the interests of his or her jurisdiction. The American colonists were also not the only British citizens not directly represented in Parliament—some regions of England itself had no formal representation. Still, decisions regarding taxation of the North American colonies had taken place without the consent of those colonies, and the response was immediate—both in considerable acts of arson and vandalism committed by a group of violent protestors called the Sons of Liberty and in the Stamp Act Congress, a legislative session made up of representatives from the 13 colonies who met to condemn not only the Stamp Act but also the very concept of taxation without representation.

The Boston Tea Party summed up colonial dissatisfaction with British tax and anti-smuggling laws. Ensuring the supply of affordable trade goods—such as tea, sugar, and molasses—was one objective of the American Revolution. *(National Archives and Records Administration [532892])*

Opposition to the Stamp Act grew so pronounced that the tax became impossible to enforce. Yielding to pressure, Parliament repealed the Stamp Act a year later—but also passed the Declaratory Act, stating that the British government wielded authority over the North American colonies and could tax or regulate them at its own discretion.

In June 1767, Parliament made good on its promise through the Townshend Revenue Act, which taxed imports on tea, paper, lead, paint, and certain kinds of glass. Once again, the American colonists fiercely objected—and once again Parliament caved in, leaving only the tax on tea intact. American colonists, now thoroughly incensed, refused to drink English tea and instead drank slightly less expensive, illegally smuggled Dutch tea. British lawmakers, not unaware of this practice, passed the Tea Act in 1773, granting the East India Company—a British tea company subject to the tea tax—freedom to import its tea directly to North America without passing through Britain, which would grant it relief from most tariffs and result in a price that, even after the tax, would be lower than the smuggled Dutch tea. The end result would be a near-monopoly for the East India Company and near-universal payment of what many colonists regarded as an unfair tax. A small group of colonists responded with the Boston Tea Party in December 1773, attacking a docked East India Company transport and destroying almost 100,000 pounds of British tea by depositing it in Massachusetts Bay.

Because the individual perpetrators could not be found, Parliament decided to punish the North American colonies as a whole. The American Revolution came in response to the five so-called Intolerable Acts, all in 1774 and 1775: the Boston Port Act (closing all Boston trading ports until the Massachusetts colony agreed to pay the cost of the East India Company's destroyed tea), the Impartial Administration of Justice Act (granting British soldiers the liberty to be tried in England if accused of a crime related to riot suppression—a new policy colonists associated with the 1770 Boston Massacre, in which a small group of British soldiers fired into a crowd of protesters), the Massachusetts Government Act (abolishing town meetings and giving the British government more direct control over Massachusetts), the Quartering Act (holding colonists responsible for feeding and housing soldiers), and the Quebec Act (granting greater land rights in the former French colony and endorsing its Roman Catholic culture). Although new British legislation directed against smugglers led to growing anti-British sentiment in the colonies, equally offensive to many were the means the British government used to enforce existing legislation.

Writs of Assistance and Bills of Attainder

The Fourth Amendment to the U.S. Constitution states that "no Warrants shall issue, except upon probable cause . . . and particularly describing the place to be searched, and the persons or things to be seized."[4] Likewise, Article I, Section 9, states that "No Bill of Attainder . . . shall be passed."[5] These restrictions were based on realistic concerns surrounding British policies that were actually put to use in the years preceding the American Revolution.

Writs of assistance, or general search warrants, were royal orders issued to customs officials and other law enforcement officers granting them the authority to search any house for any suspected evidence or contraband goods without making any sort of formal request or establishing probable cause. During the mid-18th century, they were used primarily as part of a failed effort to prevent the widespread smuggling that had become common among the North American colonists, but due to the lack of oversight, abuses were rampant. Customs officials were allowed to seize material they suspected to be smuggled, sell them, and keep a portion of the profits.

Because they were royal orders, writs of assistance were effective for the life of the reigning monarch but expired upon his or her death. After King George II's death in 1760, colonial officials were eager to renew the writs of assistance themselves under the principle of royal assent, by which royal orders could be made by government officials acting on behalf of the monarch. When British officials in Massachusetts attempted to renew the writs of assistance for their customs officials in 1761, colonial prosecutor James Otis resigned from his post and argued that the writs of assistance violated the most fundamental principles of British law. Regardless of whether royal assent granted officials the authority to renew the writs, a larger issue for Otis was that he believed that they violated the natural rights of British citizens—the first time a highly visible argument based on natural rights had been made against British policies in North America. "Every man, merely natural, was an independent sovereign, subject to no law but the law written on his heart and revealed to him by his Maker," Otis argued. "His right to his life, his liberty, no created being could rightfully contest. Nor was his right to his property less contestable."[6] The loyal British justices of the court were not persuaded by Otis's argument, but one person in attendance—future U.S. president John Adams—was inspired by the natural rights argument, later remarking that "American independence was then and there born."[7]

Equally offensive to the concept of natural rights were the bills of attainder ("taintedness"), which granted Parliament the ability to "stain" an individual by declaring him or her to be guilty of a crime, claim that individual's property for the state, and punish him or her for the alleged offense or offenses without the benefit of a trial. Although bills of attainder were not frequently used, they essentially gave Parliament the authority to execute any specific person without trial merely by accusing him or her of treason. Although many North American colonists were outraged that this concept existed, the American revolutionaries themselves used bills of attainder to claim the land of colonists loyal to Britain.

We Hold These Truths to Be Self-Evident . . .

British abuses of power contributed to American policies and declarations protecting the rights of the accused, but the process behind these policies occurred in a more complex and organic, and less reactionary, manner.

The most significant factor in the overall philosophy behind U.S. human rights was the Enlightenment, a European philosophical movement that began in the 17th century and ended in the 18th. The Enlightenment favored a conscious return to the rationalism of the Greek philosophers and a new system of thought favorable to science and to individual rights. In his *Second Treatise of Government* (1690), British philosopher John Locke argued that human beings possess natural rights and that legitimate governmental power comes not from the divine right of kings but rather from the "consent of the governed."[8] In his *Discourse on the Origin and Basis of Inequality Among Men* (1754), French philosopher Jean-Jacques Rousseau argued that human beings are equal in their natural state and become unequal only when society makes them so; eight years later, in his *The Social Contract* (1762), he argued that the ideal government is a direct democracy, controlled by the general will of its citizens.

The Enlightenment philosopher who had the greatest influence on the American philosophy of crime and punishment was the Italian thinker Cesaré Beccaria. His work *On Crimes and Punishments* (1764) was a favorite of Thomas Jefferson, who copied quotations from it for easy reference. Most central to Beccaria's thesis was that the purpose of punishment is always to deter future crime, not to punish past crime. Revenge, from Beccaria's perspective, is useless for purposes of criminal justice. Because the purpose of punishment is to deter future crime, punishments should be known by the public, be rendered as swiftly as reasonably possible, and be of a similar character as the crime, so that the people will quickly associate the idea of the crime with the idea of the penalty.

Beccaria was also a staunch opponent of the death penalty, arguing that it desensitizes people to the value of human life, violates the natural right to life, and is less effective as a deterrent than a lifetime of public supervised hard labor. A dead prisoner, Beccaria reasoned, is of no value to the community; he or she can contribute nothing, and the deterrent effect of his or her execution will fade almost immediately as the offender is simply forgotten. But a prisoner serving public hard labor will never be forgotten—he or she will always be a visible sign of the original offense—and the fruits of the prisoner's labor will also serve to benefit the larger community. In his *Notes on the State of Virginia* (1785), Jefferson proposed a new law code for Virginia based on a modified form of Beccaria's system. Jefferson was not as strict an opponent of the death penalty as Beccaria, but he believed that the death penalty should be restricted to cases of murder and treason. At the time Beccaria wrote, death penalties for property crimes were commonplace in England,

Thomas Jefferson advocated a reformed criminal justice system with fewer capital crimes and more systematic punishments. *(National Archives and Records Administration [532932])*

and death penalties for religious offenses were not unheard of. Jefferson's proposed strict limits on the death penalty were considered radical and were never adopted by Virginia's legislature. Nevertheless, the broader principles of Beccaria's system became the principles of the American constitutional framers, and Jefferson himself would be given the opportunity to implement some of Beccaria's suggested reforms when he became president in 1801.

The ideas of the Enlightenment were considered highly controversial, but the writings of early American thinkers became part of the Enlightenment movement; the framers of American government would base the entire system on the principles established by philosophers of the European Enlightenment. The Declaration of Independence was itself a short work of Enlightenment philosophy, proposing that "all men are created equal"; that "life, liberty, and the pursuit of happiness" are basic rights, worth more than social harmony or the alleged natural or divine authority of kings; that governments are social contracts and should be controlled by the governed; and that the sole purpose of government is to protect the rights of individuals.[9] These general principles would inform the later constitutional debates.

If the Enlightenment influenced the rhetorical broad strokes and philosophical emphases of the American revolutionary movement, more practical concerns determined its specific philosophy of criminal justice. Several weeks before the Declaration of Independence was approved by the Second Continental Congress, Virginia legislator George Mason drafted a Virginia Declaration of Rights, a document that guaranteed specific rights to citizens of Virginia. These rights included the right to a jury trial and a ban on writs of assistance (general search warrants). Both were practical concerns for Virginians: Jury trials had been threatened by the Massachusetts Government Act (which gave sheriffs the power to appoint juries), and customs officials used—and frequently abused—writs of assistance in the process of conducting their work.

The Enlightenment also highlighted the paradox of slavery. The 18th century had been characterized by the slow consolidation of slave labor as slaves participated in both the agricultural economy of the southern colonies and the more mixed economies of the middle and northern colonies. The early part of the century experienced overt resistance by slaves. In 1739, the Stono Rebellion created widespread upheaval in South Carolina when more than 20 slaves captured weapons from a store near the Stono River Bridge, declared themselves free, burned at least seven plantations, and headed toward an anticipated refuge in the unsettled swamps of Florida. Militias, however, apprehended and executed the main group of rebel slaves before they could escape. Slave rebellions were not confined to the South, however. In 1712, slaves in New York City murdered nine whites, and in 1741 a series of mysterious fires in New York City prompted rumors of an organized and widespread slave rebellion. In each case, officials arrested and then deported or executed dozens of slaves and suspected accomplices. In each case, the revolts provoked fear among slave owners and prompted new legislation designed to restrict the behavior of slaves and free black people. Moreover, the violent reprisals helped reinforce the power structure upon which slavery was built.

By the end of the 18th century, Enlightenment discourse about rights helped change the ways in which opponents challenged slavery. Free black people adopted the language and political strategies of the Enlightenment and the Revolutionary movement and petitioned legislatures for their own rights and the freedom of others still enslaved. Beginning with Vermont, six states (all northern) abolished slavery or provided for gradual emancipation between 1777 and 1784. In many ways, Enlightenment thinking about rights and liberties provided a vehicle that could have ended racial slavery during the Revolutionary Era—although it only in fact did so in states where growing commercial economies were already minimizing slavery's usefulness.

The United States of America

In the Declaration of Independence of July 1776, the Second Continental Congress declared all 13 colonies to be independent states. Virginia had already passed its Declaration of Rights several months prior to independence, and Connecticut and Rhode Island simply adopted modified forms of their colonial charters. The other 10 states established constitutional conventions to draft new constitutions—and, in most cases, new declarations of rights—influenced, in most cases, by their predecessors.

Chief among these predecessors was the English Bill of Rights of 1689, passed by Parliament in response to the short but turbulent reign of King James II. This act, the first major British rights declaration since the Magna Carta of 1215, prohibited cruel and unusual punishment as well as punishment prior to conviction. Several months before the Declaration of Independence was signed, the Virginia Declaration of Rights built on this tradition but went much further, granting freedom of speech, press, and religion, among other liberties, and in most respects foreshadowing the general protections granted by the U.S. Bill of Rights. In terms of criminal justice, it guaranteed jury trials and prohibited writs of assistance.

Other state constitutional conventions were inspired by the Virginia example and attempted to improve on it. The constitution of New Jersey and the Pennsylvania Declaration of Rights, passed later that year, showed the influence of the Virginia declaration but also guaranteed the right to counsel. The Delaware Declaration of Rights built on the Virginia and Pennsylvania rights declarations but also included a clause banning all ex post facto laws (laws calling for the punishment of crimes after the fact). The Maryland Declaration of Rights included all of the criminal justice provisions found in the Virginia, Pennsylvania, and Delaware declarations and added a clause banning bills of attainder. North Carolina's declaration was patterned after Virginia's but included a clause establishing indictments, formal written statements provided by prosecutors to grand juries establishing a case against a suspect, as a central part of the criminal justice process. By the time the last of the constitutional conventions, Massachusetts, passed its rights declaration in March 1780, all of the basic aspects of U.S. defendant rights had been written into law in one or more states (though they were not always observed).

When the Articles of Confederation were adopted in November 1781 and the United States of America was officially founded, federal law became an issue. The very fact that the states were no longer subject to British law meant that new laws regarding extradition needed to be written, and the articles included a clause guaranteeing extradition in cases of high crimes and misdemeanors.

In September 1787, the U.S. constitutional convention approved the Constitution of the United States of America. After significant debate, the Constitution included clauses guaranteeing trials by jury and granting protection from both ex post facto legislation and bills of attainder, but the Constitution was lacking in other respects. There were no prohibitions against general warrants nor against cruel and unusual punishment, no statements granting right to counsel, and none of the other protections that had gradually evolved during the state-by-state constitutional convention process. George Mason, the author of the original Virginia Declaration of Rights, refused to support the finished Constitution—as did many other veterans of the American Revolution. It was ratified by Virginia's legislature in July 1788 only after significant debate and by a slim 89-79 margin.[10] North Carolina and Rhode Island still declined to ratify the Constitution.

The establishment of a strong national government alone had distressed many state legislators who supported the idea of 13 independent states, and the prospect of leaving this national government free to pass laws that would violate state declarations of rights seemed unfathomable. Pennsylvania legislator John Smilie echoed the concerns of many when he argued that "unless some criterion is established by which it could be easily and constitutionally ascertained how far our [federal] governors may proceed, and by which it might appear when they transgress their jurisdiction, this idea of altering and abolishing government is a mere sound without substance."[11] The lack of a bill of rights did not go unnoticed by the former colonial administrators either. "This being the beginning of American Freedom," predicted one 1788 *London Times* editorial, "it is very clear the ending will be Slavery."[12] When Thomas Jefferson, author of the Declaration of Independence, also became a strong supporter of the Bill of Rights, James Madison—the principal leader of the U.S. constitutional convention—took it upon himself to propose a full Bill of Rights in June 1789. It was adopted three months later.

James Madison proposed the Bill of Rights in 1789, providing basic due process protection to U.S. citizens. *(Library of Congress, Prints and Photographs Division [LC-USZ62-13004]*

Emerging Issues in the New Republic

The 18th century marked the collapse of the British colonial empire in North America and the beginning of the United States. It represented the first government ever founded according to Enlightenment principles. While John Winthrop's model of Massachusetts as a socially harmonious enterprise, a "city upon a hill,"[13] was in most respects the ideal of the colonial system, the ideal of the new U.S. system was protection of individual rights. In the centuries since the American Revolution, the tension between these two ideals—the social harmony ideal of the colonies and the individualistic ideal of the Declaration of Independence—has defined almost every major U.S. domestic policy controversy, including (and perhaps especially) those controversies that deal with criminal justice.

It is still important, however, to note just how young the United States was in 1790. The Bill of Rights was reassuring but completely unenforceable. The Supreme Court had never been granted the power to strike down any piece of legislation for violating the Constitution, so the U.S. Congress was free to violate—or reinterpret—the Bill of Rights however it chose. None of the Bill of Rights' provisions were applicable to the states, which were governed only by their own constitutions and rights declarations. In many respects, the 13 states had 13 different systems of criminal justice. There was no true federal law enforcement system. In particular, because most criminal offenses fell under state and local jurisdictions, states and counties operated most courts hearing criminal cases, and federal protections were seldom relevant.

Old controversies continued to eat away at the fledgling republic. The issue of American Indian relations became more pronounced, as U.S. government officials

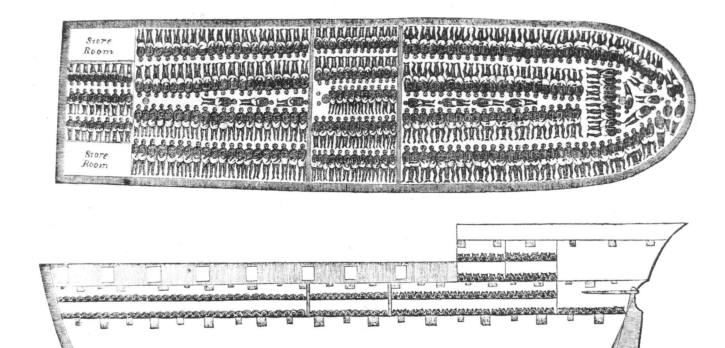

This sketch depicts a British slave ship. Legislators debating the text of the new Constitution were divided over slavery, and ultimately decided on a compromise: The import of new slaves would end in 1808, but the domestic slave trade would continue indefinitely. *(Library of Congress, Prints and Photographs Division [LC-USZ62-44000])*

signed treaties with local tribes and reserved ever-shrinking regions of the country for American Indian use. The issue of slavery sometimes threatened to tear the republic apart and would literally do so 70 years later. Banned in many northern states but essential to the southern agricultural economy, slavery was abhorred by some of the most influential constitutional framers—including Benjamin Franklin, who dedicated the last few years of his life to the abolitionist cause—but most often was regarded as an insoluble dilemma and swept under the rug. Slave revolts and alleged slave conspiracies resulted in dozens of deaths as well as state laws legalizing the killing of slaves and forcing even free African Americans into an oppressive, exploitative system. The U.S. Constitution included a provision permitting Congress to ban the international slave trade in 1808, but the end of the foreign slave trade would contribute to the emergence of new generations of African-American slaves born in the United States. Both issues—American Indian relations and slavery—would dominate the 19th century, resulting in large, violent conflicts that would dwarf the American Revolution in scope and human cost.

Chronicle of Events

1701
- *October 28:* Governor William Penn signs the Pennsylvania Charter of Privileges.

1705
- *October:* Virginia passes the slave codes of 1705, which states that all slaves are "held to be real estate" and can legally be killed by their masters, who are to be "free of all punishment . . . as if such [an] accident never happened"; that runaway slaves can legally be killed by anyone, using any means they choose; and that marriage between whites and nonwhites is illegal to be paid by six months in prison for the offender and a fine of 10,000 pounds of tobacco for the minister performing the wedding.

1712
- *April 7:* In New York City, 27 abused slaves rebel against their masters, killing nine whites. Twenty-one of the slaves are captured and executed.

1733
- *May 17:* Parliament passes the Molasses Act.

1739
- More than 20 slaves in South Carolina burn plantations and attempt to escape to Florida in the Stono Rebellion before being captured and executed.

1740
- Fifty slaves living in Charleston, South Carolina, are accused of plotting a slave revolt and summarily executed. South Carolina passes the Anti-Literacy Act, which makes it illegal to teach slaves to read and write.

1741
- A series of mysterious fires in New York City generates rumors of a slave conspiracy and leads to arrests and executions of slaves suspected to be involved.

1748
- French political philosopher Charles de Montesquieu publishes his masterpiece, *The Spirit of the Laws,* which advocates separation of powers, civil rights protections, and other concepts that will influence the U.S. Constitution.

1754
- French philosopher Jean-Jacques Rousseau publishes his *Discourse on the Origin and Basis of Inequality Among Men,* which argues that human beings are equal in nature and become unequal only when civilized.

1761
- *February 24:* James Otis, who had recently resigned as prosecutor for the British government, represents Boston citizens who object to British writs of assistance (general warrants).

1762
- Rousseau publishes *The Social Contract,* which argues that the ideal government is controlled by the general will of its people.

1764
- Italian philosopher Cesare Beccaria publishes *On Crimes and Punishments,* which influences the political philosophy of many early American thinkers, such as Thomas Jefferson.
- *April 5:* Facing the expiration of the largely unenforced Molasses Act of 1733, the British government passes the Sugar Act, which reduces the taxes on molasses by half but adds new taxes to sugar, coffee, and miscellaneous other luxury goods.

1765
- *March 22:* The British government passes the Stamp Act, which charges a tax on all individual printed sheets of paper used in Britain's North American colonies, with no North American representation.
- *October:* Representatives from nine North American colonies assemble for the Stamp Act Congress, where they draft a resolution condemning the Stamp Act and stating that taxes should not be levied against colonies that are not represented in the legislature.

1766
- The British government repeals the Stamp Act but passes a new resolution, the Declaratory Act, stating that it has the liberty to "make laws and statutes . . . to bind the colonies . . . in all cases whatsoever."

1767
- *June 29:* The British government passes the Townshend Revenue Act, which levies taxes on paper, lead, paint, certain types of glass, and tea.

The 1770 Boston Massacre heightened tensions between the British government and American colonists in the years prior to the American Revolution. *(National Archives and Records Administration [518263])*

1770

- *March 5:* A crowd of protesters gather to heckle a British soldier who had been accused of striking a young colonist. Nine British soldiers rush to his aid. When one is struck in the head, the soldiers fire into the rowdy crowd, killing five and wounding six. The event will be referred to by colonists as the Boston Massacre.
- *June 29:* As it had previously with the Stamp Act, the British government caves in on the Townshend Revenue Act, leaving the tax on tea, however, as a symbol of the British government's authority to tax the colonists. Many colonists drink smuggled Dutch tea instead, paying a slightly lower rate and symbolically rejecting the British government's authority to tax them.

1773

- *April 27:* The British government passes the Tea Act, allowing the East India Company to ship tea directly from India without paying tariff fees through British wholesalers.
- *December 16:* Dozens of American colonists disguised as Mohawk Indians board a docked East India Company tea shipment and, in protest against the Tea Act, proceed to pour nearly 100,000 pounds of tea into the Atlantic Ocean in an event referred to as the Boston Tea Party.

1774

- *March 31:* The British government passes the Boston Port Act, the first of the Five Intolerable Acts (also known as the Coercion Acts), ordering the Boston trading ports closed until the American colonists pay for the tea destroyed in the Boston Tea Party.
- *May 20:* The British government passes the Impartial Administration of Justice Act, the second of the five Intolerable Acts. The Impartial Administration of Justice Act grants the governor of Massachusetts the authority

to send British soldiers and others responsible for quelling protests to Britain to stand trial if they are accused of a crime in the process of performing their duties.

The British government passes the Massachusetts Government Act, third of the five Intolerable Acts, which abolishes town meetings, grants sheriffs the sole power to appoint juries, and places Massachusetts government officials under the direct authority of King George III.

- *June 2:* The British government passes the Quartering Act (the fourth of the Five Intolerable Acts), holding American colonists responsible for feeding and lodging British soldiers.
- *June 22:* The British government passes the Quebec Act, granting citizens of Quebec—which had been a French colony until 1763—the option of using French civil law in local affairs, formally recognizing the Roman Catholic faith (as the French government was Catholic and the British government Anglican), and expanding the province's borders south to the Ohio and Mississippi rivers. American colonists regard this as the fifth of the Five Intolerable Acts, as some of the land newly granted to Quebec had already been claimed by investors.
- *September 5–October 26:* The First Continental Congress blocks trade with Britain.

1775

- *April 19:* The American Revolution begins.
- *May 10:* The Second Continental Congress assembles.

1776

- *June 12:* The Virginia legislature adopts George Mason's Virginia Declaration of Rights, which includes numerous civil rights protections later protected in the U.S. Constitution and the Bill of Rights, including jury trials and a ban on general search warrants.
- *July 2:* The State of New Jersey adopts a new constitution, which is less extensive than the Virginia Declaration of Rights in most respects but includes the right to counsel.
- *July 4:* The Second Continental Congress approves the Declaration of Independence.
- *September 11:* The constitutional convention of Delaware adopts a new rights declaration, which is patterned after the Virginia and draft Pennsylvania declarations but includes a provision banning all ex post facto laws.
- *September 28:* Pennsylvania officially adopts its rights declaration, which is largely similar to the Virginia declaration but includes the right to counsel.
- *November 3:* Maryland adopts a rights declaration, which protects all rights of the accused specified in previous

state rights declarations and includes a new provision specifically banning bills of attainder.
- *December 17:* North Carolina adopts a declaration of rights, which is modeled on previous rights declarations but includes a provision granting the right to an indictment.

1777

- *July 8:* Vermont adopts a declaration of rights and, through Article I of the new declaration, becomes the first state to outlaw slavery.

1780

- *March 2:* Massachusetts adopts its declaration of rights, which includes most of the civil rights protections granted in previous rights declarations.

1781

- *November 15:* The Articles of Confederation are ratified, and the United States of America is founded. The articles include a clause stating that extradition among the states will be honored for all felonies and high misdemeanors.

1787

- *July 13:* Physician Benjamin Rush publishes his pamphlet "An Enquiry Into the Effects of Public Punishments Upon Criminals and Upon Society," which argues against the public punishments that had dominated English and colonial American criminal justice for centuries.
- *September 17:* The Constitutional Convention approves the U.S. Constitution, which guarantees trials by jury and includes protections against ex post facto legislation and bills of attainder but does not include a declaration of rights.

1788

- James Madison, who had been nicknamed "the father of the Constitution" for his role in drafting and securing votes for the original U.S. Constitution and had initially regarded a constitutional rights declaration as unnecessary, changes his mind and joins Thomas Jefferson in advocating a federal Bill of Rights.

1789

- *September 25:* James Madison's proposed 10 amendments to the U.S. Constitution—the U.S. Bill of Rights—are adopted by Congress and sent to the states for ratification.

Eyewitness Testimony

Smuggling and Free Trade in the North American Colonies

Had the colonies been fully heard before the last act had been passed, no reasonable man can suppose it ever would have passed at all, in the manner it now stands. For what good reason can possibly be given for making a law to cramp the trade and interest of many of the colonies, and at the same time lessen in a prodigious manner the consumption of the British manufactures in them? These are certainly the effects this act must produce.

The duty of three pence per gallon on foreign molasses is well-known to every man in the least acquainted with it to be much higher than that article can possibly bear, and therefore must operate as an absolute prohibition. This will put a total stop to the exportation of lumber, horses, flour, and fish to the French and Dutch sugar-colonies . . .

Putting an end to the importation of foreign molasses at the same time puts an end to all the costly distilleries in these colonies and to the rum trade with the coast of Africa, and throws it into the hands of the French? With the loss of the foreign molasses trade the cod-fishing in America must also be lost and thrown also into the hands of the French. That this is the real state of the whole business is not mere fancy; neither this nor any part of it is an exaggeration, but a sober and most melancholy truth.

View this duty of three pence per gallon on foreign molasses, not in the light of prohibition, but supposing the trade to continue and the duty to be paid. Heretofore hath been imported into the colony of Rhode Island only about one million, two hundred and fifty thousand gallons annually; the duty on this quantity is £14,375 sterling, to be paid yearly by this little colony; a larger sum than was ever in it at any one time. This money is to be sent away, and never to return; and yet the payment is to be repeated every year. Can this possibly be done? Can a new colony, compelled by necessity to purchase all its clothing, furniture, and utensils from England, to support the expenses of its own internal government, obliged by duty to comply with every call from the Crown, to raise money in emergencies; after all this, can every man in it pay twenty-four shillings a year for the duties of a single article only? There is surely no man in his right mind believes this possible.

Stephen Foster, "The Grievances of the American Colonies," July 30, 1764, quoted in Peabody, American Patriotism, pp. 9–10.

What should we think of a companion who, having supped with his friends at a tavern, and partaken equally of the joys of the evening with the rest of us, would nevertheless contrive by some artifice to shift his share of the reckoning upon others, in order to go off scot-free? If a man who practiced this would, when detected, be deemed and called a scoundrel, what ought he to be to be called who can enjoy all the inestimable benefits of public society, and yet by smuggling, or dealing with smugglers, contrive to evade paying his just share of the expense, as settled by his own representatives in Parliament, and wrongfully throw it upon his honester and perhaps much poorer neighbours?

He will perhaps be ready to tell me that he does not wrong his neighbours; he scorns the imputation; he only cheats the King a little, who is very able to bear it. This, however, is a mistake. The public treasure is the treasure of the nation, to be applied to national purposes. And when a duty is laid for a particular public and necessary purpose, if, through smuggling, that duty falls short of raising the sum required, and other duties must therefore be laid to make up the deficiency, all the additional sum laid by the new duties and paid by other people, though it should amount to no more than a half-penny or a farthing per head, is so much actually picked out of the pockets of those other people by the smugglers and their abettors and encouragers.

And what mean, low, rascally pickpockets must those be, that can pick pockets for half-pence and for farthings!

Benjamin Franklin, "On Smuggling and Its Various Species" (1767), quoted in Bigelow, The Works of Benjamin Franklin, pp. 326–327.

Much hath been said of the united strength of Britain and the colonies, that in conjunction they might bid defiance to the world. But this is mere presumption . . .

Besides what have we to do with setting the world at defiance? Our plan is commerce, and that, well attended to, will secure us the peace and friendship of all Europe; because, it is the interest of all Europe to have America a FREE PORT. Her trade will always be a protection, and her barrenness of gold and silver secure her from invaders.

I challenge the warmest advocate for reconciliation, to shew, a single advantage that this continent can reap, by being connected with Great Britain. I repeat the challenge, not a single advantage is derived. Our corn will fetch its price in any market in Europe, and our imported goods must be paid for, buy them where we will.

Thomas Paine, Common Sense (1776), p. 13.

Philosophy of Crime During the Early Enlightenment

[M]ankind, notwithstanding all the privileges of the state of Nature, being but in an ill condition while they remain in it are quickly driven into society. Hence it comes to pass, that we seldom find any number of men live any time together in this state. The inconveniences that they are therein exposed to by the irregular and uncertain exercise of the power every man has of punishing the transgressions of others, make them take sanctuary under the established laws of government . . .

For in the state of Nature to omit the liberty he has of innocent delights, a man has two powers. The first is to do whatsoever he thinks fit for the preservation of himself and others within the permission of the law of Nature; by which law, common to them all, he and all the rest of mankind are one community . . . The other power a man has in the state of Nature is the power to punish the crimes committed against that law. Both of these he gives up when he joins in a private, if I may so call it, or particular political society, and incorporates into any commonwealth separate from the rest of mankind.

The first power—viz., of doing whatsoever he thought fit for the preservation of himself and the rest of mankind, he gives up to be regulated by the laws made by the society, so far forth as the preservation of himself and the rest of that society shall require; which laws of the society in many things confine the liberty he had by the law of Nature.

Secondly, the power of punishing he wholly gives up, and engages his natural force, which he might before employ in the execution of the laws of Nature, by his own single authority, as he thought fit, to assist the executive power of the society as the law shall require. For being now in a new state, wherein he is to enjoy many conveniences from the labour, assistance, and society of others in the same community, as well as protection from its whole strength, he is to part also with as much of his natural liberty, in providing for himself, as the good, prosperity, and safety of the society shall require, which is not only necessary but just, since the other members of the society do the like.

But though men when they enter into society give up the equality, liberty, and executive power they had in the state of Nature into the hands of the society . . . yet it being only with an intention in every one the better to preserve himself, his liberty and property (for no rational creature can be supposed to change his condition with an intention to be worse), the power of the society or legislative constituted by them can never be supposed to extend farther than the common good, but is obliged to secure every one's

The English philosopher John Locke profoundly influenced early U.S. political philosophy. *(Library of Congress, Prints and Photographs Division [LC-USZ62-59655])*

property by providing against those [defects] that made the state of Nature so unsafe and uneasy. And so, whoever has the legislative or supreme power of any commonwealth, is bound to govern by established standing laws, promulgated and known to the people, and not by extemporary decrees, by indifferent and upright judges, who are to decide controversies by those laws; and to employ the force of the community at home only in the execution of such laws . . . And all this to be directed to no other end but the peace, safety, and public good of the people.

John Locke, from The Second Treatise of Government *(1690), pp. 76–78.*

Rights of the Accused

As you last week were disappointed of my *Journal*, I think it incumbent upon me, to publish my apology which is this. On the Lord's Day, the Seventeenth of this [month], I was arrested, taken and imprisoned in the common gaol of this city by virtue of a warrant from the Governor, and the Honorable Francis Harrison, Esq., and others in Council of which (God willing) you have a copy, whereupon I was put under such restraint that I had not the liberty of pen, ink, or paper, or to see or speak with people . . . I have since that time the liberty of speaking through the hole of the door, to my wife and servants . . . and I hope for the future by the liberty of speaking to my servant thro' the hole in the door of the prison, to entertain you with my weekly *Journal* as formerly.

Newspaper publisher John Zenger (who had been imprisoned for criticizing the governor of New York), New York Weekly Journal, *June 3, 1735, p. 1.*

[The general warrant] appears to me the worst instrument of arbitrary power, the most destructive of English liberty and the fundamental principles of law, that was ever found in an English law-book . . . Your Honors will find in the old books concerning the office of a justice of the peace precedents of general warrants to search suspected houses. But in more modern books you will find only special warrants to search such and such houses, specially named, in which the complainant has before sworn that he suspects his goods are concealed; and will find it adjudged that special warrants only are legal.

In the same manner I rely on it, that the writ [warrant] prayed for in this petition, being general, is illegal. It is a power that places the liberty of every man in the hands of every petty officer . . . In the first place, the writ is universal . . . so that, in short, it is directed to every subject in the King's dominions. Every one with this writ may be a tyrant; if this commission be legal, a tyrant in a legal manner, also, may control, imprison, or murder any one within this realm. In the next place, it is perpetual; there is no return. A man is accountable to no persons for his doings. Every man may reign secure in his petty tyranny, and spread terror and desolation around him . . . In the third place, a person with this writ, in the daytime, may enter all houses, shops, etc., at will, and command all to assist him. Fourthly, by this writ not only deputies, etc., but even their menial servants, are allowed to lord it over us . . .

[O]ne of the most essential branches of English liberty is the freedom of one's house. A man's house is his castle; and whilst he is quiet, he is as well guarded as a prince in his castle. This writ, if it should be declared legal, would totally annihilate this privilege.

English colonial prosecutor James Otis, from his argument against writs of assistance (general warrants) given before the Superior Court of Massachusetts, February 24, 1761. Opposition to general warrants would later form the basis of the Fourth Amendment. Constitution Society. Available online at URL: http://www.constitution.org/bor/otis_against_writs.htm.

. . . [James] Otis was a flame of fire!—with his promptitude of classical allusions, a depth of research, a rapid summary of historical events and dates, a profusion of legal authorities, a prophetic glance of his eye into futurity, and a torrent of impestuous eloquence, he hurried away every thing before him. American independence was then and there born; the seeds of patriots and heroes were then and there sown, to defend the vigorous youth, the *non sine Diis animosus infans* ["an adventurous child, thanks to the gods"]. Every man of a crowded audience appeared to me to go away, as I did, ready to take arms against writs of assistance. Then and there was the first scene and first act of opposition to the arbitrary claims of Great Britain. Then and there the child Independence was born. In fifteen years, namely in 1776, he grew up to manhood, and declared himself free.

John Adams, describing James Otis's argument against writs of assistance delivered on February 24, 1761, in a letter to William Tudor, March 29, 1817, quoted in Tyler, Literary History of the American Revolution, *p. 36.*

Criminal Justice

It is an essential point, that there should be a certain proportion in punishments, because it is essential that a great crime should be avoided rather than a smaller, and that which is more pernicious to society rather than that which is less . . . It is a great abuse amongst us to condemn to the same punishment a person that only robs on the highway and another who robs and murders.

In China, those who add murder to robbery are cut in pieces: but not the others; to this difference it is owing that though they rob in that country they never murder. In Russia, where the punishment of robbery and murder is the same, they always murder. The dead, say they, tell no tales.

French philosopher Charles de Montesquieu, from The Spirit of the Laws, *1748, the Founders' Constitution at the University of Chicago. Available online at URL: http://press-pubs.uchicago.edu/founders/print_documents/amendVIIIs3.html.*

The power of the laws depends still more on their wisdom than on the severity of their administrators, and the public will derive its greatest weight from the reason which has dictated it . . . In fact, the first of all laws is to respect the laws: the severity of penalties is only a vain resource invented by little minds in order to substitute terror for the respect which they have no means of obtaining. It has constantly been observed that in those countries where legal punishments are most severe, they are also most frequent; so that the cruelty of such punishments is a proof only of the multitude of criminals, and, punishing everything with equal severity, induces those who are guilty to commit crimes, in order to escape being punished for their faults.

But though the government be not master of the law, it is much to be its guarantor, and to possess a thousand means of inspiring the love of it. In this alone the talent of reigning consists . . . A fool, if he be obeyed, may punish crimes as well as another: but the true statesman is he who knows how to prevent them: it is over the wills, even more than the actions, of his subjects that the honourable rule is extended. If he could secure that every one should act aright, he would no longer have anything to do; and the masterpiece of his labours would be to be able to remain unemployed. It is certain, at least, that the greatest talent a ruler can possess is to disguise his power, in order to render it less odious, and to conduct the State so peaceably as to make it seem to have no need of conductors.

French philosopher Jean-Jacques Rousseau, from A Discourse on Political Economy *(1755), the Constitution Society. Available online at URL: http://www.constitution. org/jjr/polecon.htm.*

Let us consult the human heart, and there we shall find the foundation of the sovereign's right to punish; for no advantage in moral policy can be lasting which is not founded on the indelible sentiments of the heart of man. Whatever law deviates from this principle will always meet with resistance which will destroy it in the end; for the smallest force continually applied will overcome the most violent motion communicated to bodies . . .

The multiplication of mankind, though slow, being too great, for the means which the earth, in its natural state, offered to satisfy necessities which every day became more numerous, obliged men to separate again, and form new societies. These naturally opposed the first, and a state of war was transferred from individuals to nations.

Thus it was necessity that forced men to give up a part of their liberty. It is certain, then, that every individual would choose to put into the public stock the smallest portion possible, as much only as sufficient to engage others to defend it. The aggregate of these, the smallest portions possible, forms the right of punishing; all that extends beyond this is abuse, not justice.

Observe that by *justice* I understand nothing more than that bond which is necessary to keep the interest of individuals united, without which men would return to their original state of barbarity . . .

The end of punishment, therefore, is no other than to prevent the criminal from doing further injury to society,

The execution of Beatrice Cenci (1577–99), beheaded for helping her siblings kill her abusive father, horrified Italian observers and influenced the philosophy of 18th-century Italian thinker Cesare Beccaria. *(Library of Congress, Prints and Photographs Division [LC-USZ62-84765])*

and to prevent others from committing the like offence. Such punishments, therefore, and such a mode of inflicting them, ought to be chosen, as will make the strongest and most lasting impressions on the minds of others, with the least torment to the body of the criminal.

Italian philosopher Cesare Beccaria, from Of Crimes and Punishments *(1764), the Constitution Society. Available online at URL: http://www.constitution.org/cb/crim_pun.htm.*

The Bill of Rights Debate

If the men who at different times have been entrusted to form plans of government for the world, had been really actuated by no other motives than the public good, the condition of human nature in all ages would have been widely different from that which has been exhibited to us in history. In this country perhaps we are possessed of more than our share of political virtue. If we will exercise a little patience and bestow our best endeavors on the business, I do not think it impossible, that we may yet form a federal constitution much superior to any form of government which has ever existed in the world. But whenever this important work shall be accomplished, I venture to pronounce that it will not be done without a careful attention to the framing of a bill of rights . . .

[T]he people of this country, at the revolution, having all power in their own hands, in forming the constitutions of the several states, took care to secure themselves, by bills of rights, so as to prevent as far as possible the encroachments of their future rulers upon the rights of the people. Some of these rights are said to be *unalienable,* such as the rights of conscience. Yet even these have been often invaded, where they have not been carefully secured, by express and solemn bills and declarations in their favor.

Before we establish a government, whose acts will be the supreme law of the land, and whose power will extend to almost every case without exception, we ought carefully to guard ourselves by a bill of rights, against the invasion of these liberties which it is essential for us to retain, which it is of no real use for government to deprive us of; but which, in the course of human events, have been too often insulted with all the wantonness of an idle barbarity.

Anonymous newspaper contributor ("An Old Whig"),
November 27, 1787, quoted in Borden, The Antifederalist
Papers, *p. 47.*

Rouse up, my friends, a matter of infinite importance is before you on the carpet, soon to be decided in your convention: The New Constitution. Seize the happy moment. Secure to yourselves and your posterity the jewel Liberty, which has cost you so much blood and treasure, by a well regulated Bill of Rights, from the encroachments of men in power . . .

My friends and countrymen, let us pause for a moment and consider. We are not driven to such great straits as to be obliged to swallow down every potion offered us by wholesale, or else die immediately by our disease. We can form a Constitution at our leisure; and guard and secure it on all sides.

Anonymous newspaper contributor ("A Farmer"), "The
Expense of the New Government," *January 11, 1788,*
quoted in Borden, The Antifederalist Papers, *p. 34.*

It is a maxim universally admitted, *that the safety of the subject consists in having a right to a trial as free and impartial as the lot of humanity will admit of.* Does the Constitution make provisions for such a trial? I think not: For in a criminal process a person

shall not have a right to insist on a trial in the vicinity where the fact was committed, where a jury of the peers would, from their local situation, have an opportunity to form a judgment of the *character* of the person charged with the crime, and also to judge the *credibility* of the witnesses . . .

These circumstances, as horrid as they are, are rendered still more dark and gloomy, as there is no provision made in the Constitution to prevent the Attorney-General from filing information against any person, whether he is indicted by the grand jury or not; in consequence of which the most innocent person in the Commonwealth may be taken by virtue of a warrant issued in consequence of such information, and dragged from his home, his friends, his acquaintance, and confined in prison, until the next session of the court, which has jurisdiction of the crime with which he is charged (and how frequent those sessions are to be, we are not yet informed of) and after long, tedious and painful imprisonment, though acquitted on trial, may have no possibility to obtain any kind of satisfaction for the loss of his liberty, the loss of his time, great expenses and perhaps cruel sufferings.

But what makes the matter still more alarming is that as the model of criminal process is to be pointed out by Congress, and they have no constitutional check on them, except that the trial is to be by a *jury;* but who this jury is to be, how qualified, where to live, how appointed, or by what rules to regulate their procedure, we are ignorant as of yet . . . The mode of trial is altogether indetermined—whether the criminal is to be allowed the benefit of council; whether he is to be allowed to meet his accuser face to face; whether he is to be allowed to confront the witnesses and have the advantages of cross examination we are not yet told.

These are matters of by no means small consequence, yet we have not the smallest constitutional security, that we shall be allowed the exercise of these privileges, neither is it made certain in the Constitution, that a person charged with a crime, shall have the privileges of appearing before the court or jury which is to try them.

On the whole, when we fully consider this matter . . . we shall find Congress possessed of powers enabling them to institute judicatories, little less inauspicious than a certain tribunal in Spain, which has long been the disgrace of Christendom—I mean that diabolical institution the INQUISITION.

What gives the additional glare of horrour to these gloomy circumstances, is the consideration that Congress have to ascertain, point out, and determine what kind of punishments shall be inflicted on persons convicted of crimes; they are nowhere restrained from inventing the most cruel and unheard of punishments, and annexing them to crimes, and there is no constitutional check on them, but that RACKS and GIBBETS, may be amongst the most mild instruments of their discipline.

There is nothing to prevent Congress from passing laws which shall compel a man who is accused or suspected of a crime, to furnish evidence against himself, and even from establishing laws which shall order the court to take the charge exhibited against a man for truth, unless he can furnish evidence of his innocence.

I do not pretend to say Congress *will* do this, but sir, I undertake that Congress (according to the powers proposed to be given to them by the Constitution) *may* do it; and if they do not, it will be owing *entirely*—I repeat it, it will be owing *entirely* to the GOODNESS of the MEN, and not in the *least degree* owing to the GOODNESS of the CONSTITUTION.

Massachusetts legislator Abraham Holmes, arguing against ratification of the unamended U.S. Constitution during the Massachusetts Ratifying Convention's debates, January 30, 1788, quoted in Madison, The Debates, *pp. 104–111.*

In the new constitution for the future Government of the Thirteen United States of America, the President and Senate have all the executive, and two thirds of the legislative power.

This is a material deviation from those principles of the English Constitution for which they fought. With us, and in all good Governments, it should be a fundamental maxim, that, to give a proper balance to the political system, the different branches of the Legislature should be *unconnected*, and the legislative and executive powers should be *separate*.

By the *new constitution of America*, this *Union* of the executive bodies operates in the most weighty matters of the State . . .

In this formidable combination of power, there is no *responsibility*; and there is *power* without *responsibility*, how can there be *liberty?* . . .

Trial by Jury has already been materially injured.

The trial in criminal cases is not by twelve men of the *vicinage*, or of the *county*, but of the *State*;—and the *States* are from fifty to seven hundred miles in extent!

In criminal cases this *new System* says, the Trial shall be by Jury;—On civil cases it is silent. There it is fair to infer, that as in criminal cases it has been materially impaired, in civil cases it may be altogether omitted. But it is in truth strongly discountenanced in civil cases; for this New System gives the Supreme Court, in matters of appeal, jurisdiction both of *law* and *fact*.

This being the beginning of *American Freedom*, it is very clear the ending will be *Slavery*. For it can not be denied, that this constitution is, in its *first principle*, highly and dangerously Oligarchic;—and it is every where agreed that a Government administered by a few, is, of all Governments, the *worst*.

Leonidas, "New Government of America," The (London) Times, *April 1, 1788, p. 2.*

The most considerable of these remaining objections [to the Constitution] is that the plan of the convention contains no bill of rights . . .

It has been several times truly remarked that bills of rights are, in their origin, stipulations between kings and their subjects, abridgments of prerogative in favor of privilege, reservations of rights not surrendered to the prince . . . It is evident, therefore, that, according to their primitive significance, they have no application to constitutions, professedly founded upon the power of the people and executed by their immediate representatives and servants. Here, in strictness, the people surrender nothing; and as they retain everything they have no need of particular reservations . . .

I go further and affirm that bills of rights, in the sense and to the extent in which they are contended for, are not only unnecessary in the proposed Constitution but would even be dangerous. They would contain various exceptions to powers which are not granted; and, on this very account, would afford a colorable pretext to claim more than were granted. For why declare that things shall not be done which there is no power to do? Why, for instance, should it be said that the liberty of the press shall not be restrained, when no power is given by which restrictions may be imposed?

I will not contend that such a provision would confer a regulating power; but it is evident that it would furnish, to men disposed to usurp, a plausible pretense for claiming that power. They might urge with a semblance of reason that the Constitution ought not to be charged with the absurdity of providing against the abuse of an authority which was not given, and that the provision against restraining the liberty of the press afforded a clear implication that a power to prescribe proper regulations concerning it was intended to be vested in the national government. This may serve as a specimen of the numerous handles which would be given to the doctrine of constructive powers, by the indulgence of an injudicious zeal for bills of rights.

"Publius" (Alexander Hamilton), responding to antifederalist critics of the draft Constitution, May 28, 1788, The Federalist Papers, *pp. 510, 512–514.*

I shall take the liberty of declaring, that . . . all *public* punishments tend to make bad men worse, and to increase crimes, by their influence upon society.

Issues and Controversies

I.   The reformation of a criminal can never be affected by a public punishment, for the following reasons.

1st. As it is always connected with infamy, it destroys in him the sense of shame, which is one of the strongest out-posts of virtue.

2nd. It is generally of such short duration, as to produce none of those changes in body or mind, which are absolutely necessary to reform obstinate habits of vice.

3rdly. Experience proves, that public punishments have increased propensities to crimes . . . The criminals, who were sentenced to work in the presence of the City of London, upon the Thames, during the late war, were prepared by it, for the perpetration of every crime, as soon as they were set at liberty from their confinement . . .

II. To shew, that public punishments, so far from preventing crimes . . . are directly calculated to produce them.

All men, when they suffer, discover either fortitude, insensibility, or distress . . .

Fortitude is a virtue, that seizes so forcible upon our esteem, that whenever we see it, it never fails to weaken, or to obliterate, our detestation of the crimes with which it is connected in criminals . . .

2ndly. If criminals discover insensibility under their punishments, the effect of it must be still more fatal upon society. It removes, instead of exciting terror . . .

3dly. The effects of distress in criminals, though less obvious, are not less injurious to society, than

fortitude or insensibility . . . [T]he sympathy of the spectator is rendered abortive, and returns empty to the bosom in which it was awakened . . . It is sufficient to observe, that [sympathy] is the vicegerent of divine benevolence in our world . . . If such are the advantages of sensibility, now what must be the consequences to society, of extirpating or weakening it in the human breast? But public punishments are calculated to produce this effect.

Benjamin Rush, "An Enquiry Into the Effects of Public Punishments Upon Criminals and Upon Society," in Essays, Literary, Moral, and Philosophical, *1787, pp. 138–142.*

To the Honorable, the Senate and House of Representatives of the commonwealth of Massachusetts Bay in general court assembled February 27, 1788:

The petition of great number of black freemen of this commonwealth humbly sheweth that your petitioners are justly alarmed at the inhuman and cruel treatment that three of our brethren, free citizens of the town of Boston, lately received. The captain, under a pretense that his vessel was in distress on a island below in this harbor, having got them on board put them in irons and carried them off, from their wives and children, to be sold for slaves. This being the unhappy state of these poor men, what can your petitioners expect but to be treated in the same manner by the same sort of men? What then are our lives and liberties worth if they may be taken away in such a cruel and unjust manner as these? . . .

One thing more we would beg leave to hint, that is that your petitioners have for some time past beheld with grief ships cleared out from this harbor for Africa and there they either steal or cause others to steal our brothers and sisters, fill their ships' hulls full of unhappy men and women crowded together, then set out to find the best markets, seal them there like sheep for the slaughter and then return near like honest men; after having sported with the lives and liberties of fellow men and at the same time calling themselves Christians: blush, oh heavens, at this.

A petition against kidnapping and the slave trade, February 27, 1788, reprinted in Aptheker, A Documentary History of the Negro People in the United States, *pp. 20–21.*

CHAPTER THREE

The American Experiment
1790-1829

By early 1790, the United States of America was an independent nation with a population of almost 4 million.[1] It had a strong federal government with a Constitution, Bill of Rights, and Supreme Court, and its 13 states had begun to move beyond the British system of criminal justice and develop new ways of addressing crime. Influenced by philosophers of the Enlightenment and led by veterans of a revolution, it was a new and untested nation that had not yet developed a distinctive character of its own. The phrase "the American experiment" was never more applicable than during the final years of the 18th century and the first decades of the 19th, as Congress and state governments worked to create a new nation based on untested philosophical principles and make it work.

The weaknesses of the early American system were considerable. Although there was a Constitution and Bill of Rights and there was a Supreme Court, the power of the former was limited by the powerlessness of the latter—the Supreme Court had the power only to interpret law, not to actually strike down unconstitutional legislation, rendering the human rights guarantees of the United States's founding documents little more than legislative guidelines. Crimes were punished based on widely divergent state laws, and penalties were based primarily on torture, fines, and humiliation. No prison system existed in which to house criminals, nor did police forces exist to capture them, and the ways that crimes were punished varied considerably from state to state.

Other societal factors also challenged the new American system, the chief among them slavery. The U.S. Constitution had given Congress the authority to outlaw the international slave trade in 1808, and it banned the import of slaves that year. The 1793 invention of the cotton gin, however, helped make large-scale cotton growing in the South profitable for the first time and gave new life to slavery; it was clear that abolition would not be forthcoming. Slave codes in states such as Virginia and Maryland denied slaves (and sometimes free African Americans) literacy, civil liberties, and other rights and privileges accorded white citizens as a matter of course.

The cotton gin transformed the shape of the southern agricultural economy. Because it dramatically increased cotton yields, it increased southern plantation owners' demand for unpaid slave labor. *(Library of Congress Prints and Photographs Division [LC-USF33-011617-M3])*

But one of the most challenging criminal justice controversies of the early republic was political. Politics—foreign and domestic—presented the first new challenge to the American experiment, as the nation's first truly contentious presidential election occurred at nearly the same time as an international controversy between the United States and its revolutionary ally, France. Although little more than a footnote today, the resulting legislation—and the controversy it generated—came very close to radically transforming several important aspects of U.S. law.

Politics and Justice

During the American Revolution, the colonial revolutionaries benefited from the assistance of France, which forced Great Britain into a two-pronged war that it could not win and that was instrumental in guaranteeing an independent United States. When France faced its own revolution, the British government supported its traditional enemies by affirming the legitimacy of the French monarchy and refusing to recognize the revolutionaries. U.S. politics soon hinged on the conflict between Britain and revolutionary France: The Federalists, led by John Adams, supported the British position, while the Democratic Republicans, supported by Thomas Jefferson, supported the French. But when France experienced its own violent revolution, the United States declined to intervene. The Jay Treaty of 1795, which the pro-British Federalist government of the United States negotiated with Great Britain, establishing most-favored-nation trading status between the two countries, further offended France as well as the pro-French Jeffersonian Republicans in the United States. As French privateers began to capture U.S. ships at sea, President John Adams and members of Congress began to look for means to reduce tensions, but when a U.S. ambassador was confronted—through the machinations of French spies identified by Adams only as "X," "Y," and "Z"—with a demand that the United States give $250,000 to the French government before resuming diplomatic talks, the U.S. Federalist majority began to discuss punishing the French for demanding a bribe. One method used was an unofficial naval war against French privateers—the event that essentially created both the U.S. Navy and, to protect the homeland in the event of a French attack, the U.S. Army. The other method was to enact the controversial Alien Acts, based on Great Britain's Alien Act of 1792.

Congress passed a total of three Alien Acts in 1798: the Alien Friends Act (which gave the U.S. government the authority to expel without trial any resident alien considered dangerous), the Alien Enemies Act (which gave the U.S. government the authority to expel or imprison all resident aliens who held citizenship in a nation at war with the United States), and the Naturalization Act (which increased the number of years of residency required for U.S. citizenship from 5 to 14).

Adams faced increasing scrutiny from the Jeffersonian Republicans, who were likely to field candidate Thomas Jefferson to run against him in the 1800 presidential election. The author of the Declaration of Independence and a crucial early advocate for the Bill of Rights, Jefferson was a formidable candidate whom Adams had defeated in the 1796 election by only three electoral votes. Worse, from Adams's perspective, a legion of newspaper publishers supported Jefferson, and they wrote editorials, sometimes fair and sometimes unfair, highly critical of Adams and the majority Federalists. To combat this, Congress passed—and Adams signed—another piece of legislation based on recent British law (in this case the Seditious Meetings Act of 1795): the Sedition Act, which criminalized all "false, scandalous, and malicious writing"[2] directed against government officials. In practice, it allowed the U.S. government to arrest anyone who wrote editorials critical of the administration and put them on trial, forcing them to prove the truth of their allegations or face hefty fines and up to two years' imprisonment. Curiously, the act was written to expire in March 1801—mere months after the conclusion of the presidential election that those subject to the act had hoped to influence. The Naturalization Act could also impact the 1800 election, as French and Irish immigrants constituted a core Republican constituency—and noncitizens were, of course, ineligible to vote. Because the Alien Acts and the Sedition Act were passed together in July 1798, they are generally referred to collectively as the Alien and Sedition Acts.

The legislatures of Virginia and Kentucky responded with resolutions condemning the acts, arguing that they violated the Bill of Rights—especially the Tenth Amendment, which guarantees states' rights. These resolutions introduced the "nullification" doctrine, the idea that the Constitution was merely a compact between sovereign states and that the individual states had the power to "nullify" unconstitutional laws. Of course, these resolutions also represented political interests: Thomas Jefferson himself drafted the Virginia Resolution and Jefferson's political collaborator James Madison drafted the Kentucky Resolution. Because of their fierce language pertaining to the dangers of federal encroachment, the

Virginia and Kentucky Resolutions would be cited 70 years later, in the weeks leading up to the Civil War, by southern legislatures to justify secession on the basis of "nullification."

As important as the Virginia and Kentucky Resolutions was the application of the Sedition Act itself, which was used to arrest 25 newspaper writers, a large figure, considering the relatively small number of newspapers published at the time. Among those arrested was Benjamin Franklin's grandson Benjamin Franklin Bache, editor of the newspaper *Aurora*, on the grounds that he had once ridiculed Adams by calling him "blind, crippled, [and] toothless."[3] Public outcry against federalism and the Sedition Act, coupled with Federalist attempts to end the naval conflict with France (which lost it the support of pro-British loyalists), helped win for Jefferson a victory in the very close and contentious 1800 presidential election and permanently undermine the Federalists as a national party. John Adams would become the second and final Federalist president, and the Republicans—or, as they were later known, the Democratic-Republican Party—controlled the presidency until the party split in 1828, becoming the Democratic Party and the Whig Party. Tensions between the United States and France largely dissipated following the

Duels, such as that between Alexander Hamilton and Aaron Burr, were a common—albeit illegal—means of resolving disputes in the late 18th and early 19th centuries. *(Library of Congress Prints and Photographs Division [LC-USZ62-75928])*

1800 Treaty of Montefontaine, a gesture of peace and goodwill that had cost Adams his party's support and arguably the election.

Jefferson would later pardon all those convicted under the Sedition Act, which expired in 1801 as planned; the Alien Acts were never renewed by Congress, and they too were no longer in effect by the end of 1802. Still, strikingly absent from this constitutional crisis was the U.S. Supreme Court, which had never ruled on the constitutionality of the Alien and Sedition Acts—because it had never given itself the authority to do so.

Adams and Jefferson would later bury their differences and resume their friendship. The same cannot be said for political rivals Aaron Burr and Alexander Hamilton; when Jefferson and Burr received a tie vote and faced a runoff in Congress, Hamilton, a Federalist, convinced those of his party to support Jefferson over the ambitious Burr, whom Hamilton called a "cold-blooded Cataline."[4] Burr never forgave him, and soon—after Hamilton arguably cost Burr the governorship of New York in 1804—their mutual hatred had become so pronounced that they felt only a duel could settle their differences. Duels were almost universally illegal—treated, on paper, as if they were any other kind of murder—but in practice, few people were arrested for winning a fair duel. This changed in July 1804, when Burr and Hamilton met on the shores of the Hudson River armed with pistols. The more popular Hamilton was shot dead, and the far less popular Burr went on to approach various disgruntled generals about the possibility of overthrowing the United States and establishing himself as leader of a new government. His treason trial in 1807 acquitted him in the eyes of the court but completely destroyed his credibility, the injustice of Hamilton's death fresh in the minds of many Americans. Soon duelists were considered murderers and were more likely to be prosecuted as such.

The Rule of Law

For the first 20 years after the passage of the U.S. Constitution in 1787, U.S. law was new and somewhat controversial. Initially, federal law did not provide adequately for infractions such as piracy, treason, and common crimes that occurred within the borders of the United States but outside the jurisdiction of any specific state—and immediately after laws were passed to address this lapse, they were tested by a large-scale rebellion. Also significant was the role of the Supreme Court; the Constitution and its first 10 amendments, the Bill of Rights of 1789, prohibited Congress from creating various laws but provided no means by which they could be struck down. The authority that governed interpretation of the Constitution was the same authority that governed passage of laws in the first place: legislative assent.

The Supreme Court established its authority to strike down unconstitutional legislation in *Marbury v. Madison* in 1803. The backdrop to the case, as in the case of the Alien and Sedition Acts, centered on the conflict between the Federalist administration of John Adams and the incoming Republican administration of Thomas Jefferson. Adams, on his last day in office—March 3, 1801—appointed judge James Marbury to the federal bench. At the time, commissions for judicial appointments were hand-delivered by the U.S. secretary of state. Incoming president Thomas Jefferson noted that the appointment took place after sunset, and he declared it null and void, ordering his new secretary of state, James Madison, not to deliver the commissions. James Marbury sued, citing the 1789 Judiciary Act, which gave the U.S. Supreme Court direct authority to issue writs of *mandamus* (mandate) to

During the early years of the Supreme Court, justices had no designated chambers and often met at one another's homes to debate rulings. As the power of the Court grew, so did its architecture. By the time this Supreme Court building was constructed during the 1930s, the judiciary had achieved parity with the executive and legislative branches of government. *(National Archives and Records Administration [594954])*

any federal officeholders. Ironically, the chief justice of the Supreme Court, John Marshall, had served simultaneously as Adams's secretary of state and had himself signed the commissions supporting the appointees.

On February 24, 1803, the Supreme Court under Marshall chose neither to obey the Judiciary Act nor to oppose the Adams administration's judicial appointments. The U.S. Constitution, Marshall argued in his unanimous 6-0 ruling, technically gave the Supreme Court only appellate jurisdictions in cases such as Marbury's—and the Judiciary Act, by giving the Court direct jurisdiction and skipping lower federal courts, violated the Constitution. This left him with only one option: to declare the Judiciary Act to be in conflict with the Constitution—to be unconstitutional—and therefore to be struck down. By seeking a compromise, Marshall gave the Supreme Court immense power and established its authority as a full branch of the U.S. government. Virtually all landmark Supreme Court rulings are vested in the authority Marshall asserted in *Marbury v. Madison*.

At the same time that the U.S. judiciary began to establish its power to strike down unconstitutional legislation, the federal government began to establish its power to prosecute crime. In 1790, Congress passed An Act for the Punishment of Certain Crimes against the United States, also known as the Crimes Act of 1790. It was the first federal criminal justice legislation to pass Congress and included charges for treason, counterfeiting of federal records, piracy, and serious crimes taking place in federal jurisdictions. The law called for the death penalty in cases of murder, treason, and piracy and further mandated that the criminals' bodies could be surgically dissected after their deaths.

The Crimes Act was passed largely in response to piracy and armed revolt. Treason, in particular, was seen as a potential threat to the U.S. government. The new nation had only recently revolted against its own colonial overlord, and some revolutionaries were still fighting. One such revolutionary was Captain Daniel Shays. Shays was frustrated by the poverty that he and other Americans faced immediately following the war, a poverty that denied them the right to vote (as property ownership was a prerequisite to voting) and occasionally resulted in arrest. In September 1786, Shays led 600 farmers—many of them veterans of the American Revolution, who assembled to protest wearing their Continental army uniforms—in revolt. They successfully occupied the courthouse of Springfield, Massachusetts, for four days, preventing the Supreme Judicial Court from holding sessions. After they were driven away by a larger state militia, they abandoned the courthouse but regrouped several months later—this time 2,000 strong—in an attempt to occupy Springfield's military arsenal. A smaller but very well-armed militia successfully drove Shays's forces away, and, one week later, another group of Massachusetts militiamen routed his army and essentially ended Shays's revolt. Shays and his high-ranking accomplices were arrested for treason, but most were eventually pardoned. It was hoped that the new Crimes Act would discourage rebellions such as those of Shays by providing a penalty for treason that included both death and mutilation of the body.

The first serious test of the new laws arose, as the American Revolution itself had, in response to taxes. The U.S. Excise Act of 1791 levied fairly heavy taxes on rye whiskey, a major commodity in rural Pennsylvania. During the summer of 1794, several thousand disgruntled grain farmers burned down the home of the regional tax inspector and marched into Pittsburgh in open revolt against the U.S. government. The federal response was swift: For the first time since establishing its independence, the U.S. government assembled an army. President George Washington himself served as general of 13,000 soldiers (becoming the only sitting president ever to lead his own troops into battle), who marched into rural Pennsylvania and sent the would-be revolutionaries fleeing. Twenty leaders were arrested and taken to Philadelphia for trial, although one of the primary leaders—David Bradford—fled to Louisiana. All 20 were convicted but, as in the case of Shays' Rebellion, eventually pardoned by Washington, including two who had been convicted of treason and sentenced to death. The event demonstrated the emerging republic's strength. Thomas Jefferson's administration later ended the whiskey taxes in 1802.

As was generally the case at the time, slaves were treated less generously than free whites, a fact clearly evident in the case of a planned rebellion led by 24-year-old slave Gabriel Prosser. Inspired by the Haitian rebellion, in which slaves overtook their masters and won their freedom, Prosser planned to amass a large group of armed slaves outside Richmond, Virginia, and launch an uprising. The revolt was planned for August 30, 1800, but heavy rains produced flooding that prevented the attack. When news of the conspiracy leaked to Virginia authorities, they rounded up and arrested Prosser and an unknown number of other slaves. Unlike Shays and the leader of the Whiskey Rebellion, Prosser was hanged—as were at least 34 other slaves who had participated in his hypothetical rebellion. When David Walker, a free African American living in Boston, published his *Appeal* in 1829 calling for an end to slavery (by revolt, if necessary), the public outcry was overwhelming. The fear of slave revolts would become even more pronounced in the coming decades, leading to laws restricting the movements of

African Americans, slave and free, and especially to laws encouraging the capture of—and discouraging aid to—fugitive slaves.

The new federal mechanisms of criminal justice, designed primarily to address issues that threatened the stability of the United States, constituted only one of many innovations that occurred during the early years of the republic. Influenced by thinkers such as President Thomas Jefferson, who opposed the death penalty in all but the most extreme cases, state legislatures began to adopt laws against capital punishment, which increasingly became applicable only in the most severe cases, such as murder and treason. Punishments based on humiliation and physical torture were still common, but they became less prevalent as a new type of sentence became more widely accepted: imprisonment.

The First Modern Penitentiaries

Jails in North America were common, even during the colonial era. They served as holding areas for suspects awaiting trial, who would then be punished with torture, public humiliation, fines, or death. Jails were also used to house debtors while they made arrangements to repay their debts. The jail itself was not a form of punishment—it was merely a means of temporary storage.

During the late 18th century, philosophers of the European Enlightenment, particularly Italian philosopher Cesare Beccaria, helped foster new ideas among American thinkers that criminals were not inherently sinful but instead malleable; with proper treatment and discipline, they might eventually become law-abiding members of society. Local and state governments in the early republic began to regard punishment, not only as a means of incapacitating the offender and exacting retribution, but also of reforming the prisoner and thereby preventing future crimes, and new models of punishment became popular. Forced labor prisons represented an early experiment in this direction. In 1786, Pennsylvania passed a "wheelbarrow law" calling for hard labor as punishment instead of the death penalty in most capital cases. The concept of hard labor varied from setting to setting, but Connecticut's Newgate Prison, established in 1773, was typical. Prisoners worked underground in a copper mine under extremely harsh conditions as a means to atone for their crimes. Punishment was based on reform, deterrence, and retribution, and hard labor—particularly hard labor in public view—seemed to serve all three purposes. Hard labor became more common and physical and emotional punishments less common among the white, free population. Among the slave population, whipping remained the most common form of punishment; government officials worried that sentencing slaves to hard labor would deprive their masters of laborers. Still, the late 18th century saw a gradual shift away from quick punishments—a few lashes of the whip or an hour in the stocks or on the old, reliable gallows—and toward longer punishments, such as imprisonment at hard labor.

Pennsylvania Quakers, however, were not always satisfied with the hard labor approach, and they certainly were not satisfied with widespread use of the death penalty. Founding father and physician Benjamin Rush became a harsh critic of the prison system, joining with Quaker leaders to found the Philadelphia Society for Assisting Distressed Prisoners (later known as the Philadelphia Society for Alleviating the Miseries of Public Prisons) in 1776. Rush was dissatisfied with many aspects of the criminal justice system: the death penalty, the use of public punishments, and the nature of prisons as they existed at the time, which often

Dr. Benjamin Rush, a signer of the Declaration of Independence, was a staunch critic of public punishments and an early advocate for the penitentiary system. *(National Archives and Records Administration [532855])*

housed debtors and murderers, men, women, and children, together with minimal supervision. Rush and the Philadelphia Society took aim at Philadelphia's squalid Walnut Street Jail with some success, and it was completely redesigned in 1790 to function as a *penitentiary,* an institution designed to make people repent of their sins (become penitent) through "unremitting solitude at hard labor."[5] The concept of the penitentiary was simple: Offenders became prisoners sentenced to live in the penitentiary for a given period of time as punishment for their offenses. In the new, reformed Walnut Street Jail, prisoners lived silently, largely in isolation from one another, received religious instruction on a regular basis, and were given work (though the level of work was not generally as strenuous as that of many earlier hard labor prisons). Debtors were held separately and dealt with in a less harsh manner. Children were not imprisoned at Walnut Street at all, and during the late 1820s several special reform institutions were established for juvenile delinquents.

The reformed Walnut Street Jail served as a model for future penitentiaries and the first example of what became known as the Pennsylvania system. This system was exemplified by Philadelphia's Eastern State Penitentiary, which applied the system on a much larger scale. By emphasizing rehabilitation over punishment, the Pennsylvania system constituted a practical example of the abstract Enlightenment focus on humanitarian prisons. Still, it was itself in need of reform. The prison administrators were not aware of the psychological effects of solitary confinement, and its universal application left many residents mentally ill. Some early prison administrators saw a problem that they regarded as more immediate: Prisoners in the Pennsylvania system were expected to spend a great deal of time in solitude and religious contemplation, time that could be spent reimbursing the state for their keep.

In 1821, Elam Lynds became warden of Auburn Prison in Auburn, New York, and he created what became known as the Auburn system. The Auburn system combined the Pennsylvania penitentiary concept with the earlier idea of hard labor and was sometimes more psychologically beneficial as prisoners were allowed to associate with each other while working, albeit in near-total silence. Over time the Auburn system would become more popular than the Pennsylvania system, due in part to the practical benefit to society of prison labor.

Although the Auburn system was more successful than the Pennsylvania system, the prototype created by Lynds was based on extremely hard labor, enforced silence, physical punishment, and strict, fearsome discipline. Lynds established his system at Auburn and "perfected" it at Sing Sing, which Lynds ordered built by convict labor during the 1820s. Located in Westchester County, New York, Sing Sing was the first prison to use the famous black-and-white striped uniforms that became emblematic of convict status. Lynds deliberately underfed prisoners so that he could sell most of the food provided by the state as surplus, ordered the prisoners to produce brickwork, which he then sold at a profit, and sometimes allowed prisoners to escape in exchange for bribes—corruption that would eventually force him into resignation and a comfortable early retirement in 1845.

Elam Lynds is most infamous, however, for imposing strict labor discipline at Auburn and Sing Sing. He helped develop a contract labor system in which local manufacturers set up shop within the prisons, using inmates as workers. To make this system function, Lynds prohibited communication among workers and instituted military-style discipline.

"I don't believe in reformation of an adult criminal," Lynds once said. "He's a coward, a willful lawbreaker whose spirit must be broken by the lash."[6] Lynds's idea of criminal justice was built on using hard labor and physical coercion to achieve prison discipline. Both the Auburn and Pennsylvania systems assumed that criminals often became wicked through social influences alone and could be reformed through supervision, honest work, and religious instruction.

The Auburn system, like the Pennsylvania system, sought to transform prisoners into productive members of society, but while the Pennsylvania system attempted to do this by encouraging a solitary life of personal reflection and transformation, the Auburn system attempted to do this by communal labor. The two competing systems would continue to define the U.S. penitentiary system for most of the 19th century, but the contrast between Lynds's concept of criminal justice as pure punishment and the reform movement's emphasis on the redemptive effects of imprisonment informs the debate over criminal justice to this day.

Chronicle of Events

1790

- The renovated Walnut Street Jail in Philadelphia, Pennsylvania, becomes the first modern penitentiary.
- *January 4:* The Crimes Act (titled "An Act for the Punishment of Certain Crimes Against the United States"), which establishes federal law enforcement authority over treason, federal counterfeiting, and serious crimes taking place in federal jurisdictions or at sea, is passed by Congress.
- *July 22:* The Trade and Intercourse Act (titled "An Act to Regulate Trade and Intercourse with the Indian Tribes") is passed by Congress. It calls on states to hold whites accountable for crimes committed against American Indians under the same terms that would be applied if the American Indian victims were citizens of the relevant state.

1791

- *March 3:* Congress passes the Duties on Distilled Spirits Act, also known as the Excise Act, which taxes whiskey.
- *December 15:* The Bill of Rights (passed by Congress in 1789) is ratified and formally takes effect.

1793

- *January:* Conflicts between Britain and postrevolutionary France begin to affect U.S. trade, as privateers from both nations interfere with U.S. cargo.
- *February 12:* President Washington signs the Fugitive Slave Act (titled "An Act Respecting Fugitives from Justice, and Persons Escaping from the Service of Their Masters"), which clarifies laws regarding the capture of runaway slaves and levels penalties against those who provide aid to them.

1794

- *August 7–11:* A group of 13,000 soldiers personally led by President George Washington quashes a revolt of several thousand Pennsylvania farmers who object to federal taxes on whiskey as a result of the Excise Act.

1796

- President George Washington's vice president, Federalist presidential candidate John Adams, defeats (by a 71 to 68 electoral vote margin) secretary of state and Republican candidate Thomas Jefferson, who becomes vice president.

1798

- *July 6:* Congress passes An Act Respecting Alien Enemies, which allows for the expulsion (without trial) of all male citizens belonging to a foreign country with which the United States is engaged in war.
- *July 14:* Congress passes the Sedition Act, which allows for the arrest of those who criticize U.S. government officials and the imprisonment of those who cannot prove those criticisms to be true in a court of law.
- *December 24:* The Virginia Resolution, condemning the Alien and Sedition Acts as a violation of multiple constitutional amendments, is approved by the state legislature.

1799

- *December 3:* The Kentucky Resolution, condemning the Alien and Sedition Acts, is approved by the state legislature.

1800

- *August 30:* Approximately 1,000 armed slaves assemble six miles outside of Richmond, Virginia, led by Gabriel

The Sedition Act, championed and signed by President John Adams in 1798, restricted political dissent. *(National Archives and Records Administration [532843])*

Prosser with plans to overtake the city. The slaves are unable to mount an attack on the city due to flooding.

- *August 31:* Virginia authorities arrest Prosser and the other leaders of the planned slave revolt. Prosser and 34 other slaves are later executed for conspiracy.
- *December 3:* President John Adams, a Federalist, is soundly defeated. Republican candidates Thomas Jefferson and Aaron Burr tie for first place with 73 electoral votes each (Adams received 65).

1801

- *February 17:* The U.S. House of Representatives, which is dominated by Federalists, breaks an electoral tie between Thomas Jefferson and Aaron Burr by electing Jefferson as president and Burr as vice president.

1803

- *February 24:* In *Marbury v. Madison,* the U.S. Supreme Court establishes the power to strike down unconstitutional laws.

1804

- *July 11:* Aaron Burr kills Alexander Hamilton in a duel.

1807

- *September 1:* Former vice president Aaron Burr is acquitted of treason after conspiring to take control of the Louisiana Territory and establish it as a nation under his own rule.

1808

- *January 1:* A new federal law banning the importation of slaves into the United States takes effect.

1821

- Pennsylvania authorizes construction of Eastern State Penitentiary at Cherry Hill in Philadelphia. It becomes the first large-scale effort to implement the "Pennsylvania System" in corrections.
- *December:* Elam Lynds becomes warden of Auburn prison in Auburn, New York.

1825

- Sing Sing prison is founded in New York State by Elam Lynds, who constructs the prison using convict labor.
- New York House of Refuge, the first major reform institution for juveniles, opens under the private auspices of the New York Society for the Prevention of Poverty.

1826

- The Boston House of Reformation, another early institution for juveniles, is opened by the Boston City Council.

1828

- The Philadelphia House of Refuge, the third major juvenile institution of the decade, opens its doors.

1829

- Eastern State Penitentiary opens in Philadelphia.
- *September 28:* Massachusetts free African American David Walker publishes *Appeal,* a widely distributed pamphlet calling on slaves to rebel.

Eyewitness Testimony

Challenges to the Rule of Law

Had the constitution of the United States a foundation equally firm and equitable [with that of France], we should not at this day witness the laws of the Union stained with,

1st, Mercantile regulations, impolitic in themselves, and highly injurious to the agricultural interests of our country.

2d, With funding systems, by which the property and rights of poor, but meritorious citizens, are sacrificed to wealthy gamesters and speculators,

3d, With the establishment of banks, authorizing a few men to create a fictitious money, by which they may acquire rapid fortunes without industry.

4th, With excise laws, which violate the tranquility of domestic retirement, and which prevent the farmer from enjoying the fruits of his care and industry.

"The Farmer," as quoted in "Observations on the Letters of 'A Farmer,' Addressed, Number III," The Pennsylvania Gazette, *September 19, 1792, p. 2.*

Whereas combinations to defeat the execution of the laws laying duties upon spirits distilled within the United States and upon stills, have from the time of the commencement of those laws existed in some of the western parts of Pennsylvania:

And whereas the said combinations, proceeding in a manner subversive equally of the just authority of government and of the rights of individuals to have hitherto effected their dangerous and criminal purpose; by the influence of certain irregular meetings whose proceedings have tended to encourage and uphold the spirit of opposition, by misrepresentations of the laws calculated to render them odious, by endeavours to deter those who might be so disposed from accepting offices under them, through fear of public resentment and of injury to person and property, and to compel those who had accepted such offices by actual violence to surrender or forbear the execution of them; by circulating vindictive menaces against all those who should otherwise directly or indirectly aid in the execution of the said laws, or who, yielding to the dictates of conscience and to a sense of obligation, should themselves comply therewith, by actually injuring and destroying the property of persons who were understood to have so complied;

by inflicting cruel and humiliating punishments upon private citizens for no other cause than that of appearing to be friends of the laws; by intercepting the public officers on the high ways, abusing, assaulting, and otherwise ill treat-

ing them; by going to their houses in the night, gaining admittance by force, taking away their papers, and committing other outrages; employing for these unwarrantable purposes the agency of armed banditti disguised in such manner as for the most part to escape discovery:

And whereas, the endeavors of Legislature to obviate objections to the said laws, by lowering the duties and other alterations conducive to the convenience to whom they immediately effect (though they have given satisfaction in other quarters) and the endeavors of the executive officers to conciliate a compliance with the laws, by explanation, by forbearance, and even by particular accommodations, founded on the suggestion of local considerations have been disappointed of their effect by the machinations of persons whose industry to excite resistance has increased with every appearance of a disposition among the people to relax in their opposition and to acquiesce in the laws insomuch that many persons in the said western parts of Pennsylvania have at length been hardy:

enough to perpetrate acts which I am advised amount to treason, being overt acts of levying war against the [United] States; the said persons having on the sixteenth and seventeenth of July last proceeded in arms (on the second day amounting to several hundreds) to the house of John Neville inspector of the revenue for the fourth survey of the district of Pennsylvania, having repeatedly attacked the said house with the persons therein, wounding some of them; having seized David Lenox, marshal of the district of Pennsylvania, who previous thereto had been fired upon, while in the execution of his duty, by a party of armed men detaining him for some time prisoner, till for the preservation of his life and the obtaining of his liberty he found it necessary to enter into stipulations to forbear the execution of certain official duties touching protests issuing out of a Court of the United States—and having finally obliged the said inspector of the revenue, and the said Marshal from considerations of personal safety to fly from that part of the country, in order by a circuitous route to proceed to the seat of government; avowing as the motives of these outrageous proceedings in intention to prevent by force of arms the execution of the said laws, to oblige the said inspector of the revenue to renounce his said office to withstand by open violence the lawful authority of government of the United States, and to compel thereby an alteration in the measures of the legislature and a repeal of the laws aforesaid.

And whereas by a law of the United States initiated "An act to provide for calling forth the militia to execute the laws of the Union, suppress insurrections and repel invasions," it is enacted "that whenever the laws of the United

States shall be opposed or the execution thereof obstructed in any State by combinations too powerful to be suppressed by the ordinary course of judicial proceedings, or by the powers vested in the Marshals by that act, the same being notified by an Associate Justice or a District Judge, it shall be lawful for the President of the United States to call forth the militia of such State to suppress such combinations, and to cause the laws to be duly executed.

"And if the militia of a State where such combinations may happen shall refuse or be insufficient to suppress the same it shall be lawful for the President, if the Legislature of the United States shall not be in session, to call forth and employ such numbers of the militia of any other State or States, most convenient thereto, as may be necessary; and the use of the militia so to be called forth may be continued, if necessary, until the expiration of thirty days after the commencement of the ensuing session:

"Provided always that whenever it may be necessary, in the judgment of the President, to use the military force hereby directed to be called forth the President shall forthwith and previous thereto, by proclamation, command such insurgents to disperse and retire peaceably to their respective abodes within a limited time" . . .

And whereas it is, in my judgment, necessary, under the circumstances of the case, to take measures for calling forth the militia in order to suppress the combinations aforesaid and to cause the laws to be duly executed, and I have accordingly determined so to do, feeling the deepest regret for the occasion, but withal the most solemn conviction that the essential interests of the Union demand it, that the very existence of government and the fundamental principles of social order are materially involved in this issue, and that the patriotism and firmness of all good citizens are seriously called upon, as occasion may require, to aid in the effectual oppression of so fatal a spirit.

Wherefore, and in pursuance of the proviso above recited, I George Washington, President of the United States, do hereby command all persons, being insurgents as aforesaid, and all others whom it may concern, on or before the first day of September next to disperse and

President George Washington personally led troops to help dispel the Whiskey Rebellion in 1794, becoming the only sitting U.S. president to directly command military forces. *(National Archives and Records Administration [532881])*

retire peaceably to their respective abodes. And I do moreover warn all persons whomsoever against aiding, abetting or comforting the perpetrators of the aforesaid treasonable acts; and do require all officers and other citizens, according to their respective duties and the laws of the land, to exert their utmost endeavors to prevent and suppress such dangerous proceedings.

George Washington, "By Authority by the President of the United States of America, a Proclamation," Daily Advertiser, August 11, 1794, p. 1.

That the people have an original right to establish, for their future government, such principles as, in their opinion, shall most conduce to their own happiness, is the basis on which the whole American fabric has been erected. The exercise of this original right is a very great exertion; nor can it nor ought it to be frequently repeated. The principles, therefore, so established are deemed fundamental. And as the authority, from which they proceed, is supreme, and can seldom act, they are designed to be permanent . . .

Certainly all those who have framed written constitutions contemplate them as forming the fundamental and paramount law of the nation, and consequently the theory of every such government must be, that an act of the legislature repugnant to the constitution is void . . .

It is emphatically the province and duty of the judicial department to say what the law is. Those who apply the rule to particular cases, must of necessity expound and interpret that rule. If two laws conflict with each other, the courts must decide on the operation of each. So if a law be in opposition to the constitution: if both the law and the constitution apply to a particular case, so that the court must either decide that case conformably to the law, disregarding the constitution; or conformably to the constitution, disregarding the law: the court must determine which of these conflicting rules governs the case. This is of the very essence of judicial duty . . .

The constitution declares that 'no bill of attainder or ex post facto law shall be passed.'

If, however, such a bill should be passed and a person should be prosecuted under it, must the court condemn to death those victims whom the constitution endeavours to preserve?

'No person,' says the constitution, 'shall be convicted of treason unless on the testimony of two witnesses to the same overt act, or on confession in open court' . . .

From these and many other selections which might be made, it is apparent, that the framers of the constitution contemplated that instrument as a rule for the government of courts, as well as of the legislature . . .

It is also not entirely unworthy of observation, that in declaring what shall be the supreme law of the land, the constitution itself is first mentioned; and not the laws of the United States generally, but those only which shall be made in pursuance of the constitution, have that rank.

Thus, the particular phraseology of the constitution of the United States confirms and strengthens the principle, supposed to be essential to all written constitutions, that a law repugnant to the constitution is void, and that courts, as well as other departments, are bound by that instrument.

John Marshall, from his majority opinion in Marbury v. Madison, 1803, FindLaw.com. Available online at URL: http://laws.lp.findlaw.com/getcase/us/5/137.html.

The parties being placed at their stations—The second who gives the word shall ask them whether they are ready—being answered in the affirmative, he shall say *"present"* after which the parties shall present & fire when they please. If one fires before, the opposite second shall say, one, two, three, fire, and he shall fire or loose his fire.

And asked if they were prepared, being answered in the affirmative he gave the word *present* as had been agreed on, and both of the parties took aim & fired in succession. The intervening time is not expressed, as the seconds do not precisely agree on that point. The pistols were discharged within a few seconds of each other and the fire of Col. Burr took effect; Gen. Hamilton almost instantly fell, Col. Burr then advanced toward Genl H____n with a manner and gesture that appeared to Gen. Hamilton's friend to be expressive of regret, but without speaking turned & withdrew—Being urged from the field by his friend as has been subsequently stated, with a view to prevent his being recognized by the surgeon and bargemen who were then approaching. No further communication took place between the principals, and the barge that carried Col. Burr immediately returned to the city.

Nathaniel Pendleton and William P. Van Ness, seconds of Alexander Hamilton and Aaron Burr, providing an account of the infamous duel for the press, quoted in Hofstadter and Wallace, American Violence, p. 388.

O Burr, oh Burr, what hast thou done,
Thou hast shooted dead great Hamilton!
You hid among a bunch of thistle,
And shooted him dead with a great hoss pistol!
An anonymous poem chiding Aaron Burr for killing Alexander Hamilton in an 1804 duel, quoted in Chernov, Alexander Hamilton, p. 721.

Walnut Street Jail in Philadelphia became the first penitentiary in the United States in 1790. *(Library of Congress Prints and Photographs Division [LC-USZ62-45561])*

I saw a paragraph, a few years since, in a South Carolina paper, which, speaking of the barbarity of the Turks, it said "The Turks are the most barbarous people in the world—they treat the Greeks more like *brutes* than human beings." And in the same paper was an advertisement, which said: "Eight well built Virginia and Maryland *Negro fellows* and four *wenches* will positively be *sold* this day, to *the highest bidder*!" And what astonished me still more was, to see in this same *humane* paper!! the cuts of three men, with clubs and budgets on their backs, and an advertisement offering a considerable sum of money for their apprehension and delivery. I declare, it is really so amusing to hear the Southerners and Westerners of this country talk about *barbarity*, that it is positively enough to make a man *smile*.

David Walker, Appeal, *September 28, 1829, Documenting the American South at the University of North Carolina—Chapel Hill. Available online at URL: http://docsouth.unc. edu/nc/walker/walker.html.*

The Early Penitentiary System

The labor performed in the workshops, of Auburn Prison, is of various descriptions; all however useful and profitable . . . For several years after the erection of this Prison, the agent purchased all the raw materials, caused them to be

manufactured in this prison, and sold them from the Prison stores, on account of the State. Very serious losses resulted from this system, in consequence of which the Legislature abolished it, and adopted the plan of hiring by contract, which is now pursued with decided advantage. The contractors furnish the materials, pay a certain fixed sum per diem for the labor of the convicts, and dispose of the articles manufactured exclusively on their own account . . .

The discipline of the Prison is enforced by the punishment of stripes, inflicted by the assistant keepers, upon the back of the prisoners, in such manner as to produce personal suffering in the delinquent, without danger to the health or any vital part. We say that the rules of the prison are thus enforced, because such is the authority given to the officers; but . . . in point of fact the power is rarely exercised.

From the First Annual Report of the Board of Managers of the Prison Discipline Society, *Boston, June 2, 1826, p. 51.*

The building at the corner of Walnut and Sixth streets was commenced in 1774, in pursuance of an act of the legislature. The lot on which it stands is about 200 feet on Walnut street, by 400 feet on Sixth street. The principal building is of stone, fronting on Walnut street, and occupies nearly the entire front. It is built in the most substantial manner, and divided into rooms of equal dimensions, 20 by 18 feet, while a passage, eleven and a half feet wide in width, extends the whole length of the building. In another adjoining building are contained the solitary cells, which are so constructed as to admit light and air, but totally to exclude communication.

On the admission of a convict he is externally cleansed, his former attire is taken from him, and he is clothed in the uniform of the jail, which consists of gray cloth, made by the prisoners, and adapted to the season. Work suited to the age, capacity, and former employment of the convict, is then assigned to him, and an account opened with him. He is charged with the expenses of his board, clothes, the fine imposed on his conviction, and the costs of prosecution, and credited with the proceeds of his labor. At the expiration of the term of servitude, half the amount of the surplus, if any, after deducting those charges, is paid to him. The hours for work, for meals, and for repose are stated, and announced by the ringing of a bell. The prisoners eat at the same time—the blacks at a separate table from the whites. Divine service is performed in the chapel of the prison twice each Sunday, and religious instruction is occasionally administered at other times.

The Prune street department of this prison, which was formerly appointed to untried prisoners, is now used as a penitentiary for youthful delinquents, in order to keep them apart from convicts confirmed in vice, and thus, as far as practicable, obviate the injurious consequences arising from that glaring defect in our prison system—pernicious intercourse within the jail walls.

The management of the prison is committed to a board of inspectors, a portion of whom are elected every six months by the councils of Philadelphia, the commissioners of Southwark, the Northern Liberties, and Spring Garden. The inspectors are themselves governed by certain regulations laid down by act of assembly.

From Philadelphia in 1830-1 *(1830), pp. 133–134.*

I do not believe in a complete reform, except with young delinquents. Nothing, in my opinion, is rarer than to see a convict of mature age become a religious and virtuous man. I do not put much faith in the sanctity of those who leave the prison. I do not believe that the counsels of the chaplain, or the meditations of the prisoner, make a good Christian of him. But my opinion is that a great number of old convicts do not commit new crimes, and that they have even become useful citizens, having learned in prison a useful art, and contracted habits of constant labor. This is the only reform which I ever have expected to produce, and I believe it is the only one which society has a right to expect.

Sing Sing warden Elam Lynds, from an 1833 interview, quoted in Beaumont and de Tocqueville, On the Penitentiary System in the United States and Its Application in France, *pp. 163–164.*

There is another prison in New York which is a house of correction. The convicts labour in stone-quarries near at hand, but the jail has no covered yards or shops, so that when the weather is wet (as it was when I was there) each man is shut up in his own little cell, all the live-long day . . .

Imagine [these cells] in number 400, and in every one a man locked up; this one with his hands through the bars of his grate, this one in bed (in the middle of the day, remember), and this one flung down in a heap upon the ground with his head against the bars like a wild beast. Make the rain pour down in torrents outside. Put the everlasting stove in the midst; hot, suffocating, and vaporous, as a witch's cauldron. Add a smell like that of a thousand old mildewed umbrellas wet through, and a thousand dirty clothes-bags musty, moist, and fusty, and you will have some idea—a very feeble one, my dear friend, on my word—of this place yesterday week.

Charles Dickens, describing the Auburn-style penitentiary on Blackwell's Island in a letter to John Forster, March 6, 1842, quoted in House et al., The Letters of Charles Dickens, *v. 3, p. 104.*

CHAPTER FOUR

The American City
1830–1854

The mid-19th century radically transformed the character of the United States as a more diverse urban culture began to emerge. The population multiplied almost tenfold over a period of 70 years—increasing from 3.9 million in 1790 to 31.4 million in 1860[1]—and the predominantly native-born population of English ancestry found itself confronted by millions of immigrants from Ireland, Germany, and numerous other countries. It can be said that the 18th century determined the basic framework of American government, but the 19th century determined the country's national character. The cities of the United States soon became massive, multicultural environments made up of numerous ethnicities, lifestyles, religions, and demographics. The 17th-century Puritan ideal of America as a single homogenous culture began to die, and a new ideal began to take shape. The process was as turbulent as it was transformative.

To meet the challenges presented by population growth and urbanization, a new tradition of U.S. law enforcement and criminal justice began to emerge. During the 1830s, riots became increasingly common. In the major cities, informal night patrols began to give way to organized municipal police departments. Juveniles, dealt with on an informal basis or treated as adults by law enforcers, began to be seen as a new class of offenders. Newspapers, the medium of the time, began to focus on celebrity trials, and the sensationalistic media coverage led to a new genre of fiction: the detective story. By 1854, the core attributes of U.S. law enforcement as it is most commonly known today—a regulated police force confronting crime generally rooted in impoverished minority subcultures—were in place.

As the U.S. criminal justice system in the cities became more modernized, national problems began to loom on the horizon. Increasingly strict fugitive slave laws led to a southern criminal justice system that focused on the capture of slaves, while violence against slaves, slave owners, and abolitionists led to an increasingly tense national environment. By the 1850s, it had already become clear that the United States was on the brink of civil war. This is why the period during the mid-19th century that brought about the birth of the American city is more commonly known by another name, the antebellum period: the period before the war.

The Gathering Storm

The issue of slavery had divided the nation since the late 18th century, and the controversy grew increasingly more severe as more northern states banned slavery and southern states built their entire economies around slave-supported agriculture. By 1830, slavery had become a regional issue: Southerners generally supported it, while northerners generally opposed it. How to handle slavery in the new states being created in the West was becoming the critical question of the day.

Slave owners did find one immediate use for the West: It was a good place to ship American Indians who owned fertile southern land. During the 1830s, the U.S. federal government under Andrew Jackson's presidency negotiated treaties with numerous tribes in the southeastern United States. In the case of the Treaty of New Echota, signed by a progovernment Cherokee faction in 1835, there was no real need to negotiate terms; approximately 15,000 Cherokee were simply shipped out by force on what would later become known as the "Trail of Tears" from Georgia

President Andrew Jackson forced more than 15,000 Cherokee to migrate from Georgia to Oklahoma. One-quarter of the migrants died during the trek. *(National Archives and Records Administration [528352])*

to Oklahoma. Roughly 4,000 Cherokee—more than one-quarter of the displaced Cherokee population—died during the arduous journey, and the rest were forced to resettle on faraway land that they had never wanted. Southern agriculturalists used the old land to plant crops, which slaves in turn worked. Both cases involved the government-sponsored exploitation of nonwhites by whites and benefited the southern economy.

One of the disadvantages of forced human labor for whites, however, was that laborers could potentially leave or even rebel against their masters. Rumors of slave revolts swept the southeastern United States and terrified whites, especially in the wake of the 1831 Nat Turner Rebellion—one of the strangest and bloodiest insurrections of the early 19th century. Virginia slave Nat Turner acted as a preacher for other slaves on his and surrounding farms, assuming an influential position in the spiritual and daily lives of nearby African Americans. Claiming to have been visited by a "Spirit" that "spoke to the prophets in former days" and to have received visions of "white spirits and black spirits engaged in battle,"[2] he proclaimed that God had called on him to lead a slave uprising and gathered 70 to 80 slaves together into a makeshift army in August 1831. The human cost was terrible: Turner's followers, upon his orders, found and murdered 57 whites. Turner's followers attacked whites as representatives of the slave system in general. They killed armed men on their front porches and slaughtered frightened young children in their homes. Although Turner's orders were explicit, he left most of the actual killing to others.

The illegal horror of Turner's Rebellion quickly met with government-sanctioned horror in response: Virginia assembled a militia of nearly 3,000 troops, and they took it upon themselves to kill any African Americans who happened to be walking about in the same general area as Turner—regardless of whether they were complicit in, or even aware of, Turner's violence. The militia killed between 100 and 200 African Americans at random—far more than Turner had actually led—and mounted many of their heads on posts by busy roads as a warning to slaves who might consider assisting Turner. The monstrous strategy worked. Turner himself was captured two months later, hiding in a nearby swamp, and he and several dozen accomplices were executed.[3]

Turner's Rebellion terrified southern slave owners, who had already grown concerned about the possibility of slave revolts. The antiabolitionist riots that peppered the United States during the 1830s and early 1840s used Turner as a pretense for inflicting violence against African Americans and abolitionists, as white mobs did during the Philadelphia riots of 1834 and the attempted lynching of abolitionist William Lloyd Garrison in 1835. Usually, violence against abolitionists consisted of destroying the presses used to publish antislavery newspapers, but in Alton, Illinois, the tactics of slavery advocates gave the abolitionist movement its first well-known martyr.

On November 7, 1837, Elijah P. Lovejoy—editor of the antislavery *Alton Observer*—received his new printing press. It was his third; pro-slavery rioters had destroyed his previous two. As he noticed an angry mob outside his office, he called out to them that he and his colleagues did not wish to harm them but would do so in self-defense if attacked. The mob obliged; they set fire to the roof, forcing evacuation, and then shot Lovejoy five times as he tried to lead his friends to safety. They took the new press, carried it outside, and threw it in the nearest river. Then they came back for Lovejoy's corpse, which they mutilated and dragged through the streets the next day in front of a cheering crowd of slavery supporters.

Lovejoy was the first well-known casualty of the abolitionist movement, but he was far from the last. Slavery supporters grew increasingly angry at the highly vocal culture of New England reformers who frowned on the institution, which had become the lifeblood of the southern economy. They especially frowned on the attempts slaves made to flee north, hiding in the homes of the abolitionists as they traveled—a network of safe houses that would later become known as the Underground Railroad.

When President George Washington signed the Fugitive Slave Act in 1793, its purpose was clear: to provide uniform national standards for the capture and extradition of slaves. By the mid-19th century, however, regional differences made this policy difficult to enforce. Northern officials seldom felt inclined to spend resources capturing escaped southern slaves—a process that consumed the southern criminal justice system, creating Charleston, South Carolina's massive 100-member slave patrol—and the U.S. Supreme Court ruling in *Prigg v. Pennsylvania* (1842) stated that northern states, though obliged to turn over fugitive slaves in accordance with the 1793 act, were not obligated to actually capture them. Some northern states began passing laws prohibiting their law enforcement officials from capturing fugitive slaves, which infuriated southern slavery advocates.

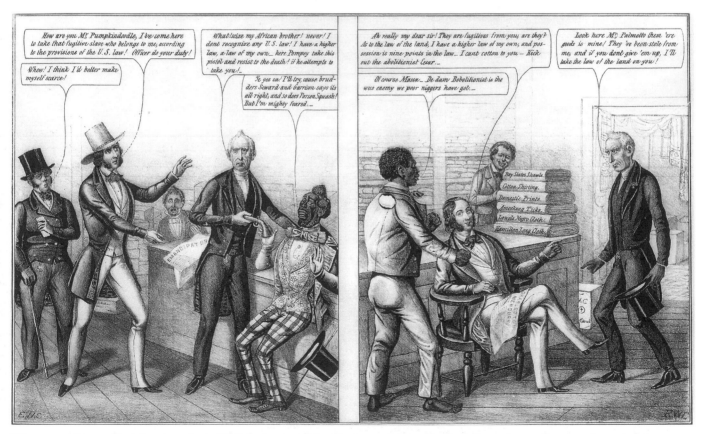

This pro-southern editorial cartoon from 1851 features racist caricatures of slaves. In the left panel, a northerner refuses to return an escaped slave, in defiance of the Fugitive Slave Act. In the right panel, a southerner refuses to return stolen goods to their northern owner. *(Library of Congress Prints and Photographs Division [LC-USZ62-89722])*

As tensions over slavery grew, Congress was pressured to find a solution. The Compromise of 1850 was intended to give both parties the best of both worlds. To satisfy abolitionists, California was declared a free state, and the slave trade was banned in Washington, D.C.; to satisfy slave owners, Congress passed the Fugitive Slave Act of 1850. The new bill required northern states to participate in the capture of slaves—and, most remarkably, also declared that slaves would not be eligible to a trial of any kind. The owner's affidavit attesting ownership of the slave would be sufficient to bring about the slave's arrest and extradition. The bill also leveled stiff penalties against free persons who assisted slaves in escaping—a clause that specifically targeted the Underground Railroad. President Millard Fillmore even attempted to bring the charge of treason against a group of Quakers who had refused to assist the government in capturing fugitive slaves, but they were acquitted on the grounds that their actions, though illegal, did not constitute treason.

The effects of the new Fugitive Slave Act were significant. Because the North was not seen as a permanent safe zone for fugitives, Canada became the new destination of slaves escaping on the Underground Railroad. The new law also hardened abolitionists' opposition to what they perceived as the growing southern "slave power." Northern states continued to pass laws requiring that state officials not participate in the capture of slaves; one Massachusetts law automatically vacated the office of any state official who cleared the capture of a fugitive slave. Although these state bills were declared unconstitutional in *Ableman v. Booth* (1859), the Civil War commenced soon afterward, and the question of fugitive southern slaves quickly became moot. Most northern states never completely cooperated with the new Fugitive Slave Act.

As the national debate over the institution of slavery continued, the major cities of the North faced other challenges. They reacted to these challenges by making radical changes in the way they conducted law enforcement and in so doing created the quintessential law enforcement institution: the police department.

Law and Order

The first professional police force in North America was established by the Dutch in New Amsterdam, the future New York City, in 1658. Essentially night watchmen, this city patrol—known as the *ratelwacht* for the loud rattles patrolmen carried, which essentially served the same function as police whistles—was small (made up of only 10 patrolmen), poorly trained, and not terribly well organized, but it functioned reasonably well according to the low expectations of the time. During the colonial era and the early years of the United States, night watchmen were paid to patrol cities to serve essentially the same function that private security guards serve today.

During the early years of the 18th century, southern states began to also hire professional slave patrollers whose duty was to capture fugitive slaves and send them back to their masters. New Orleans had its own professional slave patrol in 1809, and by 1822 the city of Charleston, South Carolina, had more than 100 officers dedicated to tracking the movements of African Americans and recovering fugitive slaves. The use of night watchmen also became more widespread in the North during the early decades of the 19th century, but the programs were generally smaller and less ambitious than the slave patrols of the South. It was not until the 1830s that larger northern cities began to see a need for a bigger, more disciplined police force.

The mass immigration of the mid-19th century led to poverty and urban growth, creating circumstances in which crime thrives. London had faced this problem for centuries; it was the impoverished "masterless men" of the previous century who had been locked in debtors' prisons or shipped off to the colonies as servants. Britain had tried a number of approaches over the centuries—including making property offenses punishable by death—but the problem of crime in London continued to grow. In 1829, legislator Robert Peel culminated 50 years of debate over the best method of managing crime and disorder by proposing the creation of the London Metropolitan Police, a consolidated—and, at the time, unprecedented—police force. Instead of hiring part-time underpaid night watchmen, London would hire salaried full-time officers to operate in a quasi-military fashion and to provide 24 hours of continuous coverage on specified "beats." Officers finally had a chain of command and reasons to do their jobs well; with promotion came a much higher salary. The end result was the first modern, centralized police force, one that would serve as the model for U.S. police departments in the decades to come.

But in the years leading up to the creation of the major U.S. urban police forces, lawlessness had become so severe that the stability of the government sometimes came into question. In the Charlestown, Massachusetts, riots of August 1834, a Pennsylvania anti-Catholic mob burned down the Mt. Benedict School for Girls based on vague allegations of unspecified improper behavior. Riots were most commonly based on deep-seated ethnic or religious conflicts, but sometimes factors were far more mundane. In 1834, for instance, the collapse of the Bank of Maryland inspired the bank's patrons to hunt down bankers and destroy their homes. In 1839, rioters attacked a medical school in Worthington, Ohio, for using cadavers. In 1841, unemployed whites in Cincinnati grew jealous of the economically stable African-American community and burned down numerous homes and shops. These ethnic divisions resulted in conflicts that are difficult to comprehend today, as when in May 1849, nativist, pro-American rioters stormed the Astor Place Opera House in New York City over the management's decision to replace an American actor with a rising British star. The resulting violence led to 22 deaths. Like poverty, rioting had become a part of American urban life—an attempt to impose popular will on a society that appeared to be increasingly fragmented and chaotic. But clearly there was no single popular will.

Emerging riots and vigilantism seemed to demand a new approach to law enforcement, and U.S. city leaders turned to the London Metropolitan Police as a model. In 1838, Boston organized the first police

Antislavery activist Harriet Tubman traveled to the South 19 times and personally freed more than 300 slaves in the years leading up to the American Civil War. *(National Archives and Records Administration [559120])*

department in the United States. Over the coming years, every major city in the northeastern United States would follow. Initially, the Boston police were very much like the night watchmen who had preceded them, except that they offered 24-hour patrols and centralized leadership, but when Boston reorganized its police force 16 years later, it gave its officers badges, guns, and uniforms.

Unlike the London Metropolitan Police, police in American cities needed to base their existence on American democratic traditions. For that reason, they were consciously incorporated into American urban politics. For example, when the city of New York created the New York Municipal Police in 1845, the new legislation provided that each ward would be a separate patrol district and that officers must be residents of that ward. In this way, patrolmen were expected to represent the views of local residents and to enforce the laws based on local interests. For example, police in some affluent wards might enforce the laws requiring saloons to close on Sundays, and other officers in immigrant wards might not. Only in 1853 were the New York police outfitted with uniforms distinguishing them from the general public. With this arrangement, police fell under the control of local politicians and particularly the Democratic Party. Seeking to separate policing from local politics, in 1857 the Republican-dominated New York State legislature created the Metropolitan Police for the City of New York and legally abolished the Municipal Police. Democratic mayor Fernando Woods resisted, and the two forces coexisted (sometimes violently) for several months. The state government

In May 1849, an angry mob of nationalists burned down the Astor Place Opera House in New York City in response to a rivalry between two actors—one English and one American. *(Library of Congress Prints and Photographs Division [LC-USZ62-42326])*

eventually prevailed. In 1870, the Metropolitan Police were abolished, and control over policing was returned to the local level. Regardless of who was in charge, the creation of full-time police forces—especially regular beat patrols by armed and uniformed officers—changed urban life in the United States. The American police officer had arrived.

Criminal Justice Reform

The period also witnessed improvements in the way criminals were treated, including some early and tentative prison reform, the emergence of the insanity defense, and a significant shift away from public punishments based on humiliation, such as the pillory and stocks.

Among the most significant developments were new institutions for juvenile offenders. During the colonial period, children were often regarded as if they were little adults. For example, 12-year-old Hannah Ocuish was hanged in Connecticut in 1786 for killing a six-year-old girl in a fight. Even in the case of Ocuish, however, the murder was seen as tragic and blamed on external circumstances. The Rev. Henry Channing, pastor of the Congregational Church at New London, delivered a stirring execution sermon using Ocuish's actions as a case study in what happens when children do not receive sufficient religious instruction.

As American culture developed further, philanthropists and reformers increasingly saw poverty and city life as causes for delinquency. In 1817, New York's Society for the Prevention of Pauperism was founded to improve the lot of poor and neglected children. During the late 1820s, these same philanthropists established houses of refuge to house, educate, and discipline poor and disorderly youth. Founded in New York in 1825, Boston in 1826, and Philadelphia in 1828, these institutions functioned as juvenile detention centers, orphanages, children's homeless shelters, and, in a sense, foster homes. Children were admitted to houses of refuge, not only for criminal offenses, but also for poverty, vagrancy, or other conditions that were not illegal but were thought to lead to crime. In 1838, when the father of Mary Ann Crouse attempted to free her from the Philadelphia House of Refuge on a writ of habeas corpus, the Pennsylvania Supreme Court affirmed in the case of *Ex parte Crouse* that houses of refuge could take children away from home for their own good. This decision established the legal doctrine of *parens patrie* in American law; the state can step in and act as a parent to a child if authorities believe that they are at risk. Houses of refuge offered discipline and regimentation as a means of treatment. Life in houses of refuge was fairly strict; children woke early, and, compelled to pray and forbidden to talk to each other, they lived under a strict code of silence, schedule, and religious instruction.

In spite of these new institutions, popular concern with juvenile crime and delinquency continued to grow in the 1840s and 1850s. George W. Matsell, the New York City chief of police during this period, in 1848 famously called attention to an apparent epidemic of "children who are growing up in ignorance and profligacy, only destined to a life of misery, shame, and crime."[4] In response, governments and private agencies sought new ways to address the problem. In the early 1850s many states and cities began to establish their own publicly funded correctional institutions for children. Like houses of refuge, most of them centralized all activities in a single, prisonlike building, but public institutions also differed from the earlier model. They characteristically were located in rural, not urban, locations, and they typically were called "reform schools" in order to stress their educational goals.

Other reformers believed that cities themselves represented the key source of corruption for children and that institutions were no better. Charles Loring Brace, for example, founded the Children's Aid Society (CAS) in 1853. Believing that urban life contributed to delinquency and that a rural lifestyle would teach children obedience and discipline, the CAS sought to remove unsupervised youths from American cities and relocate them to farms in the rural heartland where they could learn a strong work ethic. By 1890, more than 90,000 children were shuttled off to rural farm families on Brace's "orphan trains."[5]

No single figure was more crucial to criminal justice reform than Dorothea Dix. When she visited East Cambridge Jail in Massachusetts in 1841 to teach a Sunday School class, she was shocked at what she found: men and women, prostitutes, violent criminals, the mentally handicapped, and the insane, all locked together in cold, filthy, barren rooms. Some severely mentally handicapped prisoners were kept in cages and ignored, left alone to tear at their skin and eat their own feces. Dix began an international asylum movement to provide separate facilities for the mentally handicapped. In addition to creating 32 asylums of her own, she established precedents that would expand the system to the point of ubiquity. There were only 13 asylums in the entire United States in 1843; by 1880, as a direct result of Dix's work, there were 123—almost 10 times as many. Dix also investigated the abuse of other prisoners, visiting a total of 318 jails and prisons between 1843 and 1847 and summing up her thoughts in her *Remarks on Prisons and Prison Discipline* (1845).

The period between 1830 and 1854 witnessed the emergence of an increasingly fragmented urban culture, the beginning of the modern U.S. law enforcement system, and the birth of the modern juvenile justice movement. Though this period is usually discussed in relation to the Civil War, the profound changes that took place in urban life during these years would have lasting national implications. The major cities of the young nation were no longer relics of British colonial influence; instead, they presented a new and distinctly American way of life.

Heroes and Villains

Although American newspapers did not invent sensationalism, they certainly refined it. During the mid-19th century, Americans were captivated by tales of gruesome murders, diabolically ingenious murderers, and the brilliant detectives who connected the two. The stories were compelling and—as novelists quickly discovered—did not need to be true in order to draw readers' attention.

Two of the most widely known murder victims of the period were both women of questionable repute whose suspected killers were wealthy and respectable members of the community. The first victim was Helen Jewett, who at the time of her death in 1836 was one of the most prominent prostitutes in New York. Jewett represented the elite class of prostitutes of her day. Like a courtesan, she established lasting relationships with clients built on intellect and romance. Unlike other prostitutes of her time, she refused to tolerate physical abuse; clients who treated her badly could expect to end up in court. She was also more likely to hunt down her own clients—meeting them at social gatherings, at the theater, or through mutual acquaintances and offering conversation to be followed by discreet offers. And, in the tradition of the courtesan, she was a gifted conversationalist and writer; she was raised and educated in the household of a leading Maine judge and could dazzle her prospective customers with literary allusions and witty banter.

But she was still a prostitute and certainly not an appropriate wife for Richard P. Robinson, a young New York clerk with possibilities and pretensions of achieving more. Robinson had begun seeing Jewett in 1835, and the two of them carried on an extended, complicated, and emotionally tumultuous affair. As he became increasingly manipulative of her, she became increasingly possessive of him, on the one hand breaking off the relationship a number of times and on the other threatening black-mail to expose white-collar crimes he had committed at work if he did not remain faithful to her. On the morning of April 10, 1836, brothel manager Rosina Townsend smelled smoke and went upstairs to find Jewett's corpse, killed by an axe blow to the head and disfigured by a fire apparently intended to obscure the crime.

Although initial newspaper reports all but convicted Robinson on their own, they quickly grew sympathetic to his cause. "No man should hang for the murder of a whore,"[7] chanted a group of men marching down Broadway. Robinson was acquitted and quickly left the state, changing his name and living out his life in relative obscurity in Texas. Still, media coverage of the trial—with every new, lurid detail printed in local newspapers—was unprecedented, and the public appetite for news on the story was enormous. The murder helped establish "penny papers"—cheap newspapers sold on the streets—as the most viable medium of the day, papers noted for their sensational contents.

Nine years later, Boston newspapers reported on a similar case when the body of prostitute Maria Bickford was discovered on October 27, 1845. Her throat had been cut, and, as in the earlier case, an attempt had been made to burn down the scene of the crime. Also present was a prominent suspect—Albert Tirrell, whose family, the Weymouth Tirrells, was one of the richest and most respectable in Boston. Tirrell was married, and he had very recently been caught having an af-fair with Bickford. His wife brought charges of adultery against him, a charge that carried a six-month prison sentence and no small amount of social stigma, but he was able to convince her to drop the charges after begging her forgiveness in public and signing an oath to "observe propriety in his behavior."[8]

After returning home to his wife, he left again for Bickford's brothel. After resuming their sexual activities, Tirrell and Bickford had a heated argument. Her body was found a few hours later, and both physical evidence and eyewitness testi-mony left no doubt that Tirrell had killed Bickford. Nevertheless, he was acquitted under remarkable circumstances: His attorney admitted that Tirrell had caused Bickford's death but claimed that he did so while sleepwalking and was able to pro-duce numerous witnesses testifying to a litany of Tirrell's sleepwalking experiences dating to his childhood. After his acquittal, his family had him institutionalized so that he would not harm others.

Still, neither of these cases attracted the same level of attention as the mys-terious death of Mary Rogers. Unlike the other victims, Rogers was not a pros-titute—she was a cigar clerk, well liked by the literati of New York City, and had engaged in many conversations with the likes of Washington Irving and James Fenimore Cooper. On July 28, 1841, her body was found floating in the Hudson River. The coroner suspected that sexual assault was involved but could not oth-erwise determine the cause of death. Although most historians now attribute her death to a botched abortion, her unexplained death terrified young women in the city, who feared a similar fate, galvanized city authorities, who saw her death as a direct failure of the New York police, and saddened the many cigar patrons who had grown fond of her. One of those patrons was a young writer named Edgar Allan Poe.

Poe had written the first modern detective story, "The Murders in the Rue Morgue," in 1841, the year of Rogers's death. In that story, he adopted the same general style used by reporters who had covered the death of Jewett, Bickford, and Rogers in telling a gruesome story involving the discovery of women's bodies stuffed in a morgue chimney. Poe's fictional detective, Auguste Dupin, would eventually determine that the culprit was an orangutan. Could Dupin solve Rogers's murder as well? Poe asked this question in November 1842's "The Mystery of Marie Roget," a very thinly veiled attempt to ascertain the details of Rogers's death from Dupin's perspective based on the available evidence. Although a masterpiece of detective fiction, it did not solve the mystery. In the final analysis, no one did.

Other mystery writers followed Poe, including the British novelist Charles Dickens, whose novel *Bleak House* (1853) features an enigmatic detective known only as Inspector Bucket, and Dickens's protégé, the mystery writer Wilkie Collins. Collins's *The Moonstone* (1868) is widely regarded as the first modern mystery novel, involving many elements that would occur in most later formula mysteries: false suspects, re-creations of the crime scene, and, of course, a famous detective on the order of Auguste Dupin. The charisma of the detective was always crucial to detective fiction, because readers needed to be more impressed with the craftiness of the person solving the crime than with the craftiness of the person who committed it. Newspaper reports of murders—with bungling detectives unable to track down villains of the worst order—left readers starving for some stories, at least, in which an intellectual hero could be counted on to inevitably bring the villain to justice. This formula was perfected in Arthur Conan Doyle's character of Sherlock Holmes, who only met his match in the nearly unstoppable villain, Professor Moriarty, who, with his intellect and apparent invulnerability to the law, symbolized the many unsolved crimes that had gripped England in the preceding years.

Chronicle of Events

1831

- William Lloyd Garrison begins publishing *The Liberator*, which will become the best-known abolitionist newspaper in the country.
- *August 22–24:* Nat Turner, a 31-year-old Virginia slave, leads 70 to 80 other slaves on a killing spree, murdering 57 white men, women, and children. A local militia of 3,000 responds by killing 100 to 200 African Americans.
- *November:* Nat Turner and several dozen accomplices are captured and soon executed.

1832

- An antiabolitionist mob attacks the post office in Charleston, South Carolina, in hopes of stopping the distribution of abolitionist literature.

1833

- *August 28:* Parliament bans slavery in Great Britain.

1834

- New York and Philadelphia are plagued by a series of riots, a trend that will continue throughout the 1830s in every major U.S. city. Motives for riots vary but generally involve either immigration or slavery. In Philadelphia pro-slavery rioters sometimes target individual free African Americans.
- *March:* In Baltimore, angry clients of the collapsing Bank of Maryland riot and attack the homes of bank owners.
- *August:* In Charlestown, Massachusetts, anti-Catholic rioters burn down the Mt. Benedict School for Girls.

1835

- A Cherokee faction signs the Treaty of New Echota, relocating the Cherokee tribe to Oklahoma.
- *October:* Pro-slavery rioters attack a meeting of the Massachusetts Anti-Slavery Society and nearly lynch abolitionist William Lloyd Garrison. The mayor of Boston imprisons Garrison for his own protection.
- *November 24:* The Texas Rangers police force is founded.
- *December 7:* In his State of the Union address, President Andrew Jackson unsuccessfully asks Congress to ban the mailing of abolitionist literature.

Kentucky abolitionist James Birney was regularly subject to assaults and death threats. *(LIbrary of Congress Prints and Photographs Division [LC-USZ62-15298])*

1836

- *April 10:* New York prostitute Helen Jewett is murdered, apparently by clerk Richard P. Robinson, in what would become one of the most highly publicized cases in American history.
- *July 30:* A pro-slavery mob in Cincinnati destroys the press used by James Birney to publish his abolitionist newspaper *The Philanthropist*. The mob's anger then turns against the city at large, focusing on areas where blacks and whites are known to associate with each other. The city government is forced to impose martial law and sends armed volunteers into the streets to quell the riots.

1837

- *January 27:* In an address before the Young Men's Lyceum in Springfield, Illinois, 28-year-old future president Abraham Lincoln refers to major city riots as he speaks of the "increasing disregard for law which pervades the country."

• *November 7:* Illinois abolitionist Elijah Lovejoy is murdered by a mob of slavery supporters.

1838

• The first modern police department in the United States is founded in the city of Boston.
• In *Ex parte Crouse*, the Pennsylvania Supreme Court rules that the government has the right and responsibility to intervene in family relations when children are at risk, establishing the legal doctrine of *parens patrie* in American law regarding children and young offenders.
• *May 15:* An angry mob attempts to disrupt the Anti-Slavery Convention of American Women in Philadelphia.
• *May 17:* The meeting hall the Anti-Slavery Convention of American Women had rented is burned to the ground.
• *September 3:* Frederick Douglass escapes slavery in Maryland.

1839

• Protesters opposed to the use of cadavers riot against a medical college in Worthington, Ohio.
• *August 1:* A group of 53 slaves overthrow the Spanish slave ship *Amistad* and steer it into the harbor of New Haven, Connecticut.

1841

• Solomon Northup, a free African American living in New York, is kidnapped by slave traders and forced into slavery in Louisiana.
• *March:* A young schoolteacher named Dorothea Dix visits East Cambridge Jail to teach a Sunday School class for women inmates and is appalled to find criminals and the insane housed together in squalid conditions. She will dedicate the rest of her life to improving treatment of the incarcerated and institutionalized in the United States and Europe.
• *April:* Edgar Allan Poe's "Murders in the Rue Morgue," widely considered the first modern detective story, is published.
• *July 28:* The body of New York cigar clerk Mary Rogers is found floating in the Hudson River. Although most initially believe that she was murdered, her death is later suspected to be the result of a botched abortion.
• *September:* In Cincinnati, Ohio, approximately 1,500 unemployed whites riot against a local African-American community, burning down homes and shops.

1842

• *January:* In *Prigg v. Pennsylvania*, the U.S. Supreme Court rules that the federal government cannot compel states to assist in the capture of fugitive slaves. Subsequently, several free states pass laws barring state officials from assisting in the capture of slaves.

1843

• In Massachusetts, humanitarian reformer Dorothea Dix asks the Massachusetts legislature to create separate institutions for the mentally ill rather than housing them with prisoners.

1845

• The New York City Municipal Police Department is founded.
• Elam Lynds, the brutal warden of New York's Sing Sing Prison, is forced into retirement by a corruption scandal.
• Dorothea Dix's *Remarks on Prisons and Prison Discipline in the United States*, criticizing U.S. prison conditions, is published.

1846

• *March 28:* Massachusetts gentleman Albert Tirrell is acquitted for the murder of his lover Maria Bickford. Although eyewitness testimony and physical evidence prove that Tirrell had slashed her throat, attorney Rufus Choate successfully argues that Tirrell had killed Bickford while he was sleepwalking and should not be held responsible for the crime.

1849

• Harriet Tubman escapes from slavery in Maryland.
• *May 10:* Thousands of nativist protesters surround the Astor Place Opera House in New York City demanding the firing of British actor William Macready and the reinstatement of American actor Edwin Forrest. The protests turn violent, leading to 22 dead and more than 100 wounded.

1850

• The city of Philadelphia creates a police department. Less than a decade later, it will have more than 700 officers.
• *September 18:* Congress passes a new Fugitive Slave Act, which states that fugitive slaves are to be convicted without trial and establishes harsh penalties for anyone who assists fugitive slaves.

1852

• The cities of Cincinnati and New Orleans establish police departments.

1853

• The New York City Municipal Police Department adopts uniforms—one standard for an "official" policing department.
• Charles Loring Brace founds the Children's Aid Society, which relocates neglected urban juvenile delinquents to farm families.

1854

• The Boston Police Department is reorganized. Boston officers become the first American police to serve under a police chief or carry a badge.
• Philadelphia police become the first officers in the country required to carry guns. Up until this time, most American police officers were supplied with "night sticks" similar to those used in England.
• *May 24:* When fugitive slave Anthony Burns is arrested in Boston under the Fugitive Slave Act of 1850, abolitionists riot in protest.

Eyewitness Testimony

Slavery and Criminal Justice

No assailants being in sight Mr. Lovejoy stood, and was looking round. Yet, though he saw no assailant, the eye of his murderer was on him. The object of hatred, deep, malignant, and long continued, was fully before him—and the bloody tragedy was consummated. Five balls were lodged in his body, and he soon breathed his last. Yet after his mortal wound he had strength remaining to return to the building and ascend one flight of stairs before he fell and expired . . . All but two or three marched out and ran down Water Street, being fired on by the mob as they went. Two, who were wounded, were left in the building, and one, who was not, remained to take care of the body of their murdered brother. The mob then entered, destroyed the press, and retired.

An account of the murder of abolitionist Elijah Lovejoy, published in Edward Beecher's Narrative of the Riots at Alton *(1838), quoted in Hofstadter and Wallace,* American Violence, *pp. 408–409.*

The [Fugitive Slave Act of 1793] punishes those who interfere with the rights of the slave-holder; but is silent as to the rights of negroes wrongfully seized, and of the states whose territory is entered by persons, under pretext of right, to violate the laws and carry forcibly away those who are living under their protection. These cases are clearly left to the guardianship of the states themselves. The tenth article of the amendments to the constitution secures this right; and self-respect, if not self-protection, demands its exercise.

Justice Joseph Story, from his majority opinion in Prigg v. Pennsylvania *(1842). Available online at URL: http://laws.findlaw.com/us/41/539.html.*

I speak advisedly when I say this,—that killing a slave, or any colored person, in Talbot county, Maryland, is not treated as a crime, either by the courts or the community. Mr. Thomas Lanman, of St. Michael's, killed two slaves, one of whom he killed with a hatchet, by knocking his brains out. He used to boast of the commission of the awful and bloody deed. I have heard him do so laughingly, saying, among other things, that he was the only benefactor of his country in the company, and that when others would do as much as he had done, we should be relieved of "the d——d n——s."

The wife of Mr. Giles Hicks, living but a short distance from where I used to live, murdered my wife's cousin, a young girl between fifteen and sixteen years of age, mangling her person in the most horrible manner, breaking her nose and breastbone with a stick, so that the poor girl expired in a few hours afterward. She was immediately buried, but had not been in her untimely grave but a few hours before she was taken up and examined by the coroner, who decided that she had come to her death by severe beating. The offence for which this girl was thus murdered was this:—She had been set that night to mind Mrs. Hicks's baby, and during the night she fell asleep, and the baby cried. She, having lost her rest for several nights previous, did not hear the crying. They were both in the room with Mrs. Hicks. Mrs. Hicks, finding the girl slow to move, jumped from her bed, seized an oak stick of wood by the fireplace, and with it broke the girl's nose and breastbone, and thus ended her life. I will not say that this most horrid murder produced no sensation in the community. It did produce sensation, but not enough to bring the murderess to punishment. There was a warrant issued for her arrest, but it was never served. Thus she escaped not only punishment, but even the pain of being arraigned before a court for her horrid crime . . .

Colonel Lloyd's slaves were in the habit of spending a part of their nights and Sundays in fishing for oysters, and in this way made up the deficiency of their scanty allowance. An old man belonging to Colonel Lloyd, while thus engaged, happened to get beyond the limits of Colonel Lloyd's, and on the premises of Mr. Beal Bondly. At this trespass, Mr. Bondly took offence, and with his musket came down to the shore, and blew its deadly contents into the poor old man.

Mr. Bondly came over to see Colonel Lloyd the next day, whether to pay him for his property, or to justify himself in what he had done, I know not. At any rate, this whole fiendish transaction was soon hushed up. There was very little said about it at all, and nothing done. It was a common saying, even among little white boys, that it was worth a half-cent to kill a "n——r," and a half-cent to bury one.

Frederick Douglass, from Narrative of the Life of Frederick Douglass, *1845, republished by Project Gutenberg. Available online at URL: http://www.gutenberg.org/etext/23.*

Riots and Slave Revolts

[A]s we approached the house we discovered Mr. Richard Whitehead standing in the cotton patch, near the lane fence; we called him over into the lane, and Will, the executioner, was near at hand, with his fatal axe, to send him to an untimely grave. As we pushed on to the house, I discovered some one run round the garden, and thinking it was some of the white family, I pursued them, but finding it was a servant girl belonging to the house, I returned to commence the work of death, but they whom I left, had not been idle; all the family were already murdered, but Mrs. Whitehead and her daughter Margaret. As I came round to the door I saw Will pulling Mrs. Whitehead out of the house, and at the step he nearly severed her head from her body, with his broad axe. Miss Margaret, when I discovered her, had concealed herself in the corner, formed by the projection of the cellar cap from the house; on my approach she fled, but was soon overtaken, and after repeated blows with a sword, I killed her by a blow on the head, with a fence rail. By this time, the six who had gone by Mr. Bryant's, rejoined us, and informed me they had done the work of death assigned them.

Lawyer Thomas R. Gray, recounting how slave insurrectionist Nat Turner described his murder of a young local woman, Margaret Whitehead Greenberg, in The Confessions of Nat Turner *(1831), p. 50.*

It is with much gratification we inform the public, that the sole contriver and leader of the late insurrection in Southampton, concerning whom such a hue and cry has been kept up for months, and so many false reports circulated—the murderer *Nat Turner,* has at last been taken and safely lodged in prison.

It appears that on Sunday morning last, Mr. Phipps, having his gun, and going over the lands of Mr. Francis, (one of the first victims of the hellish crew,) came to a place where a number of pines had been cut down, and perceiving a slight motion among them, cautiously approached, and when within a few yards, discovered the villain who had so long eluded pursuit, endeavoring to ensconce himself in a kind of cave, the mouth of which was concealed with brush. Mr. P. raised his gun to fire, but Nat hailed him and offered to surrender. Mr. P. ordered him to give up his arms: Nat then threw away an old sword, which it seems was the only weapon he had. The prisoner, as his captor came up, submissively laid himself on the ground and was thus securely tied—not making the least resistance!

Mr. P. took Nat to his own residence, where he kept him until Monday morning—and having apprised his neighbors of his success, a considerable party accompanied him and his prisoner to Jerusalem, where, after a brief examination, the culprit was committed to jail.

Our informant (one of our own citizens, who happened to be in the country at the time) awards much

BLOW FOR BLOW.

This 19th-century abolitionist sketch indicates how the possibility of slave revolts struck fear into slave owners throughout the South. *(Library of Congress Prints and Photographs Division [LC-USZ62-53189])*

praise to the people of Southampton for their forbearance on this occasion. He says that not the least personal violence was offered to Nat—who seemed, indeed, one of the most miserable objects he had ever beheld—dejected, emaciated and ragged. The poor wretch, we learn, admits all that has been alleged against him—says that he has at no time been five miles from the scene of his atrocities; and that he has frequently wished to give himself up, but could never summon sufficient resolution!

A newspaper account of the capture of Nat Turner, from "Capture of Nat Turner," Petersburg Intelligencer *(November 4, 1831), reprinted in* The Liberator *(November 12, 1831), p. 1.*

Leave not one stone upon another, of this worst nunnery that prostitutes female virtue and liberty under the garb of holy religion. When Bonaparte opened the nunnerys of Europe, he found crowds of Infant skulls!

An anonymous sign appearing in Charlestown, Massachusetts, on August 10, 1834, shortly before anti-Catholic rioters burned down the Mt. Benedict School for Girls, quoted in Schultz, "Burning Down the House," Sextant (1993). Available online at URL: http://www.salemstate.edu/sextant/v4n2/schultz.html.

To the Selectmen of Charlestown!! Gentlemen—it is currently reported that a mysterious affair has lately happened at the Nunnery in Charlestown, now it is your duty gentlemen to have this affair investigated *immediately*, if not the *Truckmen* of *Boston* will demolish the Nunnery Thursday night—August 14.

An anonymous sign appearing in Charlestown, Massachusetts, on August 10, 1834, quoted in Schultz, "Burning Down the House," Sextant (1993). Available online at URL: http://www.salemstate.edu/sextant/v4n2/schultz.html.

All persons giving information in any shape or testifying in court against any one concerned in the late affair at Charlestown may expect assassination according to the oath which bound the party to each other.

Anonymous sign appearing on the old Charlestown Bridge in Charlestown, Massachusetts, following the torching of the Mt. Benedict School for Girls in August 1834, quoted in a letter from Mother St. Augustine O'Keeffe to Rev. F. Flynn, June 17, 1887, reprinted in Jeanne Hamilton, "The Nunnery as Menace," EWTN Libraries, June 12, 1996. Available online at URL: http://www.ewtn.com/library/HUMANITY/BURNING.TXT.

The city has been in a most alarming condition for several days, and from about eight o'clock on Friday evening until about three o'clock yesterday morning, almost entirely at the mercy of a lawless mob, ranging in number from two to fifteen hundred.

On Tuesday evening last, a quarrel took place near the corner of Sixth Street and Broadway, between a party of Irishmen and some Negroes, in which blows were exchanged and other weapons, if not firearms, used. Some two or three of each party were wounded.

On Wednesday night the quarrel was renewed in some way, and some time after midnight a party of excited men, armed with clubs, etc., attacked a house occupied as a negro boarding house, on McAllister Street,

demanding the surrender of a Negro who they said had fled into the house . . . Several of the adjoining houses were occupied by Negro families, including women and children . . . The interference of some gentlemen from the neighborhood succeeded in restoring quiet . . .

On Friday, during the day, there was considerable excitement, threats of violence and lawless outbreaking were indicated in various ways, and came to the ears of the police and of the Negroes. Attacks were expected upon the Negro residences in McAllister, Sixth, and New Streets. The Negroes armed themselves, and the knowledge of this increased the excitement. But we do not know that it produced any known measure of precaution on the part of the police to preserve the peace of the city.

Before eight o'clock in the evening, a mob, the principal organization of which, we understand, was arranged in Kentucky, openly assembled in Fifth Street Market, unmolested by the police or citizens. The number of this mob, as they deliberately marched from their rendezvous toward Broadway and Sixth Street, is variously estimated, but the number increased as they progressed. They were armed with clubs, stones, etc. Reaching the scene of operations, with shouts and blasphemous imprecations, they attacked a negro confectionery on Broadway, and demolished the doors and windows. This attracted an immense crowd. Savage yells were uttered to encourage the mob onward to the general attack upon the Negroes. About this time the Mayor came up and addressed the people, exhorting them to peace and obedience to law. The savage yell was instantly raised, "Down with him." "Run him off," was shouted, intermixed with horrid imprecations, and exhortations to the mob to move onward.

They advanced to attack with stones, etc., and were repeatedly fired upon by the Negroes. The mob scattered, but immediately rallied again, and again were in like manner, repulsed . . . These things were repeated until past one o'clock, when a party procured an iron six-pounder from near the river, loaded it with boiler punchings, etc., and hauled it to the ground, against the exhortations of the Mayor and others. It was posted on Broadway, and pointed down Sixth Street. The yells continued, but there was a partial cessation of firing. Many of the Negroes had fled to the hills. The attack upon houses was recommenced with firing of guns on both sides, which continued during most of the night, and exaggerated rumors of the killed and wounded filled the streets. The cannon was discharged several times. About two o'clock a portion of the military, upon the call of the Mayor, proceeded to the scene of disorder and succeeded at keeping the mob at bay. In the morning, and throughout the day, several blocks, including the battle-ground, were surrounded by sentinels, and kept under martial law . . .

It was resolved to embody the male Negroes and march them to jail for security, under the protection of the military and civil authorities.

From two hundred and fifty to three hundred Negroes, including sound and maimed, were with some difficulty marched off to jail, surrounded by the military and officers; and a dense mass of men, women and boys, confounding all distinction between the orderly and disorderly, accompanied with deafening yells . . .

The crowd was in that way dispersed. Some then supposed that we should have a quiet night, but others, more observing, discovered that the lawless mob had determined on further violence, to be enacted immediately after nightfall. Citizens disposed to aid the authorities were invited to assemble, enroll themselves, and organize for action. The military were ordered out, firemen were out, clothed with authority as a police band. About eighty citizens enrolled themselves as assistants of the marshal, and acted during the night under his direction . . . As was anticipated, the mob, efficiently organized, early commenced operations, dividing their force and making attacks at different points, thus distracting the attention of the police. The first successful onset was made upon the printing establishment of the *Philanthropist* [an abolitionist newspaper]. They succeeded in entering the establishment, breaking up the press, and running with it, amid savage yells, down through Main Street to the river, into which it was thrown.

The military appeared in the alley near the office, interrupting the mob for a short time. They escaped through byways, and, when the military retired, returned to their work of destruction in the office, which they completed. Several houses were broken open in different parts of the city, occupied by Negroes, and the windows, doors, and furniture totally destroyed. From this work they were driven by the police, and finally dispersed from mere exhaustion . . .

A report of the 1841 Cincinnati riots, published in the Cincinnati Daily Gazette, *September 6, 1841, quoted in Hofstadter and Wallace,* American Violence, *pp. 208–210.*

Law and Order

If a foreign journalist had visited the condition of the metropolis, as respected crime, and the organization of its police, and if, without tracing the circumstances from which that organization arose, he had inferred design,

from the ends to which it appeared to conduce, he might have brought forward plausible reasons for believing that it was craftily framed by a body of professional depredators, upon a calculation of the best means of obtaining from society, with security to themselves, the greatest quantity of plunder. He would have found the metropolis divided and subdivided into petty jurisdictions, each independent of every other, each having sufficiently distinct interests to engender perpetual jealousies and animosities, and being sufficiently free from any general control to prevent any intercommunity of information or any unity of action.

An 1829 report on the state of criminal justice months prior to the implementation of the highly successful London Metropolitan Police program, which would become the model for U.S. police departments in the following decades, quoted in "The Report of the Select Committee on the Metropolitan Police," The Times *(October 7, 1834), p. 2.*

The new police force is on the eve of being brought into action, and of putting to an immediate test the justice of those complaints which have been made by all classes of individuals for more than two centuries against the inefficiency of our "ancient and most reverend watchmen."

The principle on which English Police (as it is called) has hitherto invariably proceeded, is congenial to our national prejudices, leaving men's free agency in a great measure uninterrupted, until it ripens into the actual perpetration of crime. This respect and deference for the freedom of the subject, has nevertheless overshot one purpose, while it served a worse: it has forgotten to protect the innocent, and has transferred all its real benefits to the wrong-doer. The instructions to the new police . . . set out with a formal abandonment of the rule that it should be the sole aim of justice to punish guilt,—a policy the inevitable effect of which was to permit every species of outrage upon the unoffending, that the criminal might be hanged upon "satisfactory evidence," instead of restrained by the interposition of public authority, upon reasonable suspicion of his atrocious purpose: the result of which delicate system has been, that the honest or helpless has been sacrificed to the villain, and the villain himself to the vengeance of the law.

The theory taught by the new regulations, is that the power about to act under them ought to have for its main object *the prevention of crime*—not the execution of the criminal.

It is true that the forthcoming system may be productive of considerable, though partial evil; if the abuse of such a right and practice as that of interference before the fact be not guarded against with great vigilance and discretion. But if the right be in general exercised on fair grounds of apprehended crime, and from a *bona fide* zeal on behalf of the public safety, we do not see that, as a whole, any rational objection can be made to it. Undoubtedly, officers of a much more enlarged degree of attainment and intelligence than those to whom the humbler functions of the police have hitherto been intrusted must be sought out for the performance of this more complicated service; and, indeed, the instructions which have been prepared, and the duties imposed upon the new guardians of the public peace, would have been quite ludicrous under the ancient regime . . . A hierarchy is established, of which the most lucrative and confidential offices are held forth to the ambition of its humblest members. A superintendence is provided for, which must bring the qualifications of every individual police-man to the intimate knowledge of his superiors at the head of the corps, which creates a solid responsibility every where, and affixes the strongest sanctions by which human nature can be influenced to the obligations entailed upon each person appertaining to the service . . .

The pay of the lowest rank is very moderate, being only 3*s.* [shillings] per day; and that small salary liable to specific deductions. The inspectors, however, are said to have 100 £ [pounds] per annum, and the superintendents 200*l.*; and to these offices, through the intermediate rank of sergeant, every zealous police constable is, by the formal conditions of the service, told that he might reasonably aspire. If the system be not jobbed, it is one which promises advantageously for the public safety.

A London Times *editorial on the new London Metropolitan Police, one day before they began their duties, published in "The New Police Force is on the Eve of Being Brought Into Action. . . ,"* The Times *(September 25, 1829), p. 2.*

A large concourse, numbering from a thousand to fifteen hundred persons, assembled in the Park at 5 1/2 o'clock yesterday afternoon, in accordance with a call issued by order of a previous meeting of the members of the Police.

The objects of the meeting were stated in the following notice, which were posted prominently in the streets and published in the mornings papers:

"A meeting of citizens, and all others who feel aggrieved at the ridiculous and oppressive rules, and regulations of the Commissioners of Police and especially that portion of the late order imposing an expensive and fantastical uniform, will be held in the Park" . . .

CHARLES S. SPENCER, Esq., was the next speaker . . . MR. SPENCER spoke of the course of the *Tribune* and *Herald* in advocating the use of the proposed uniform . . . The *Tribune* had said that if the officers did not like the uniform they could resign, and that plenty of men would be ready to fill their places . . . But what could be expected of such men? Of what good would a policeman be who possessed no self-respect?

A New York Daily Times *editorial on 1854 protests against new police uniforms, quoted in Vila and Morris,* The Role of Police in American Society, *pp. 38–39.*

Criminal Justice Reform

For [boys brought up in crime] there should be an establishment on an extensive scale in the country, where they should be brought up to useful labour for terms not less than from five to seven years . . . For . . . (incidental juvenile offenders,) there should be a town penitentiary, where rigid discipline for one year might be usefully applied, their parents being called on to enter into security for their future good conduct.

Anonymous, Old Bailey Experience: Criminal Jurisprudence and the Actual Working of Our Penal Code of Laws *(1833), quoted in Sanders,* Juvenile Offenders for a Thousand Years, *p. 146.*

Long before reaching the house, wild shouts, snatches of rude songs, imprecations and obscene language, fell upon the ear, proceeding from the occupant of a low building, rather remote from the principal building to which my course was directed. Found the mistress, and was conducted to the place which was called "the home" of the forlorn maniac, a young woman, exhibiting a condition of neglect and misery blotting out the faintest idea of comfort, and outraging every sentiment of decency. She had been, I learnt, "a respectable person, industrious and worthy. Disappointments and trials shook her mind, and, finally, laid prostrate reason and self-control. She became a maniac for life. She had been at Worcester Hospital for a considerable time, and had been returned as incurable." The mistress told me she understood that, "while there, she was comfortable and decent." Alas, what a change was here exhibited! She had passed from one degree of violence to another, in swift progress. There she stood, clinging to or beating upon the bars of her caged apartment, the contracted size of which afforded space only for increasing accumulations of filth, a foul spectacle. There she stood with naked arms and dishevelled hair, the unwashed frame invested with fragments of unclean garments, the air so extremely offensive, though ventilation was afforded on all sides save one, that it was not possible to remain beyond a few moments without retreating for recovery to the outward air. Irritation of body, produced by utter filth and exposure, incited her to the horrid process of tearing off her skin by inches. Her face, neck, and person were thus disfigured to hideousness. She held up a fragment just rent off. To my exclamation of horror, the mistress replied: "Oh, we can't help it. Half the skin is off sometimes. We can do nothing with her; and it makes no difference what she eats, for she consumes her own filth as readily as the food which is brought her."

Men of Massachusetts, I beg, I implore, I demand pity and protection for these of my suffering, outraged sex. Fathers, husbands, brothers, I would supplicate you for this boon; but what do I say? I dishonor you, divest you at once of Christianity and humanity, does this appeal imply distrust. If it comes burdened with a doubt of your righteousness in this legislation, then blot it out; while I declare confidence in your honor, not less than your humanity. Here you will put away the cold, calculating spirit of selfishness and self-seeking; lay off the armor of local strife and political opposition; here and now, for once, forgetful of the earthly and perishable, come up to these halls and consecrate them with one heart and one mind to works of righteousness and just judgment.

Become the benefactors of your race, the just guardians of the solemn rights you hold in trust. Raise up the fallen, succor the desolate, restore the outcast, defend the helpless, and for your eternal and great reward receive the benediction, "Well done, good and faithful servants, become rulers over many things!"

Injustice is also done to the convicts: it is certainly very wrong that they should be doomed day after day and night after night to listen to the ravings of madmen and madwomen. This is a kind of punishment that is not recognized by our statutes, and is what the criminal ought not to be called upon to undergo. The confinement of the criminal and of the insane in the same building is subversive of that good order and discipline which should be observed in every well-regulated prison. I do most sincerely hope that more permanent provision will be made for the pauper insane by the State, either to restore Worcester Insane Asylum to what it was originally designed to be or else make some just appropriation for the benefit of this very unfortunate class of our "fellow-beings."

Gentlemen, I commit to you this sacred cause. Your action upon this subject will affect the present and future condition of hundreds and of thousands.

Humanitarian reformer Dorothea Dix, addressing the Massachusetts legislature, demanding that the mentally ill be housed in separate facilities, 1843, "Memorial to the Massachusetts Legislature," USINFO at the U.S. Department of State. Available online at URL: http://usinfo.state.gov/ usa/infousa/facts/democrac/15.htm.

In connection with this report I deem it to be my duty to call the attention of your Honor to a deplorable and growing evil which exists amid this community, and which is spread over the principal business parts of the city. It is an evil and a reproach to our municipality, for which the laws and ordinances afford no adequate remedy.

I allude to the constantly increasing numbers of vagrant, idle, and vicious children of both sexes, who infest our public thoroughfares, hotels, docks, &c. Children who are growing up in ignorance and profligacy, only destined to a life of misery, shame, and crime, and ultimately to a felon's doom. Their numbers are almost incredible, and to those whose business and habits do not permit them a searching scrutiny, the degrading and disgusting practices of these almost infants in the schools of vice, prostitution and rowdyism, would certainly be beyond belief. The offspring of always careless, generally intemperate, and oftentimes immoral and dishonest parents, they never see the inside of a school-room, and so far as our excellent system of public education is concerned, (and which may be truly said to be the foundation of our free institutions,) it is to them an entire nullity. Left, in many instances, to roam day and night wherever their inclination leads them, a large proportion of these juvenile vagrants are in the daily practice of pilfering wherever opportunity offers, and begging where they cannot steal. In addition to which, the female portion of the youngest class, those who have only seen some eight or twelve summers, are addicted to immoralities of the most loathsome description. Each year makes fearful additions to the ranks of these prospective recruits of infamy and sin, and from this corrupt and festering fountain flows on a ceaseless stream to our lowest brothels—to the Penitentiary and the State Prison.

George W. Matsell, "Report of the Chief of Police Concerning Destitution and Crime among Children in the City" (1849), quoted in Sanders, Juvenile Offenders for a Thousand Years, *p. 379.*

To the friends of the Children's Aid Society:

The first year of our efforts among the poor and vagrant children of New-York has been mainly one of experiment. We have been explorers, seeking the way to go, and the means to act. In this year we have done no inconsiderable service, though very little in comparison to what we propose.

1. We have sent out of the City to good country homes more than two hundred neglected children.
2. We have sustained a workshop, in which 115 poor boys have been profitably employed.
3. We have cooperated with benevolent Women in establishing Industrial Schools for Girls, through which this unfortunate class may be trained for the Public Schools, or for some useful employment in the City or the country.
4. We have enlisted churches and individuals to organize Sunday meetings for boys in various quarters of City.
5. We have opened a Lodging-house for Newsboys.
6. We have directed the attention of the public to this suffering class.

To enable us to do this, We have received from the generous and spontaneous benevolence of our friends here and elsewhere, donations amounting to nearly $5,000.

We are at the present time sending children into the country at the rate of 800 per annum. The poor girls under the daily charge of the various Industrial Schools in cooperation with the Society number more than 400.

From an article written on the first anniversary of the Children's Aid Society, announcing the previous year's work and seeking further donations, published in "New-York City: The Children's Aid Society," New York Daily Times (June 28, 1854), p. 3.

Crime and Popular Culture

One of the most cold-blooded, atrocious, and, as far as is known, unprovoked murders that has ever been recorded in the annals of crime, took place during the night of Saturday, or early yesterday morning, at a house of ill-fame, No. 41 Thomas street, kept by a woman named Rosina Townsend.

The following are the particulars: Between the hours of eight and ten o'clock on Saturday evening, a young man named Francis P. Robinson, the son of a highly respectable gentleman . . . called at the house of Mrs. Townsend, for the purpose of visiting one of the female inmates, a young girl named Ellen Jewett, with whom he was on terms of intimacy, having frequently been with her on former occasions. This girl, who was of prepossessing appearance, and only about 21 years of age, was much attached to him, and, since her first acquaintance with him (which commenced at a house of ill-fame in Duane street, kept by a Mrs. Berry), she has given frequent evidences of it.

On accosting him on Saturday night, she expressed herself much pleased to see him, and he accompanied her up stairs to her chamber, and supped with her, after which, as Mrs. Townsend swears, they went to bed together for the night. About three o'clock in the morning, the latter female, who keeps the key of the front door under her pillow after a certain hour of the night, and suffers no one to leave or enter the house without her knowledge, heard, or thought that she heard, some persons in the yard. She thereupon opened her room door, and asked who was there, but received no answer.

She was about to retire to rest again, when she was alarmed at smelling fire in the house, and perceived a dense body of smoke coming from some of the up stairs rooms. She called some of the inmates from their beds, and, on going up stairs, they discovered the room in which the girl Jewett slept to be in flames, and she laid upon the bed, which had been set on fire in different places, horribly butchered.

The watch was called, and the first thing that was done was to extinguish the fire, which was evidently the work of an incendiary and was burning in several different places. This being, with some difficulty, accomplished, the body of the unfortunate girl was examined, when it was found that she was quite dead, having a dreadful wound on the right side of the head, penetrating to the brain, which had been inflicted with some heavy weapon. The demoniac perpetrator of the murder had, it was apparent, after accomplishing this horrible purpose, set fire to the bed upon which his victim lay "in the stillness of death," for the purpose of hiding the dark deed, and shielding himself from the consequences of exposure. And but for the timely discovery of the fire by the owner of the premises, his designs might have been successful, although the lives of other persons who were sleeping in the house, unconscious of the demon who was within it, and the danger which surrounded them, might have been, like that of this unfortunate creature, inhumanly sacrificed; inasmuch as that the flames had already made considerable progress, and had began their havoc upon the inanimate body, some parts of which were frightfully blackened . . .

Intelligence of the monstrous atrocity was soon spread abroad, and Mr. Brink, the first police officer to whom it was communicated, set about to ferret out the author. Little doubt was entertained that young Robinson, who is but nineteen years of age, was the murderer, because it was known by the persons in the house that he had not left the deceased up to the time that the street door was locked for the night. Mrs. Townsend had no doubt that it was he whom she had heard in the yard on the preceding night, and Mr. Brink went to ascertain how he could by that way have made his exit. While examining the back premises, he found . . . a cloak, which, on being shown to some of the deceased's acquaintances . . . was recognized as belonging to [Robinson], and had, no doubt, been left by him in his haste to get away.

From this place his route was traced over another fence leading into Hudson St., and close to this was found a small hatchet, clotted with blood, with which the fatal act had evidently been committed, and which was yesterday recognized as having been in Robinson's possession on Saturday evening previous to his visiting the deceased, thus making out a *prima facia* case of murder against the accused, of the most deliberate and diabolical description . . .

The causes assigned for the commission of this dreadful crime by Robinson—if he indeed be the guilty individual—are various. One is, that he was jealous of the deceased. Another is, that he was about to get married to a beautiful and wealthy young lady, and that the deceased, determined that he should not desert her (Ellen) threatened that, if he did get married, she would annoy him, and expose his previous habits, and that, therefore he destroyed her.

"Most Horrible Murder and Arson," The New York Transcript, *April 25, 1836, reprinted in* Huron Reflector, *April 26, 1836, p. 1.*

The terrible mystery which for more than a year has hung over the fate of Mary Rogers, whose body was found, as our readers will remember, in the North river, under circumstances such as convinced every one that she was a victim of hellish lust and then of murder, is at least explained, to the satisfaction, we doubt not, of all . . . On the Sunday of Mrs. Rogers's disappearance, she came to her house from this city, in company with a young physician, who undertook to procure for her a premature delivery.

While in the hands of the physician she died, and a consultation was then held as to the disposal of the body. It was finally taken at night . . . and sunk in the river, where it was found. Her clothes were first tied up in a bundle, and sunk in a pond . . . in that neighborhood; but it was afterwards thought they were not safe there, and they were accordingly taken and scattered through the woods as they were found. The name of the physician is unknown to us, nor do we know whether it was divulged or not. The Mayor has been made acquainted with these facts . . . and we doubt not an immediate inquiry after the guilty wretch will be made . . . It explains many things connected with the affair which before were wrapped in mystery—especially the apathy of the mother of Miss Rogers upon the discovery of the body. It will be remembered, that she did not even go to identify it, and made no inquiries concerning the affair.

"The Mary Rogers' Mystery Explained," New York Tribune, *November 9, 1842, reprinted in* The Ohio Statesman, *November 10, 1842.*

The mental features discoursed of as the analytical are, in themselves, but little susceptible of analysis. We appreciate

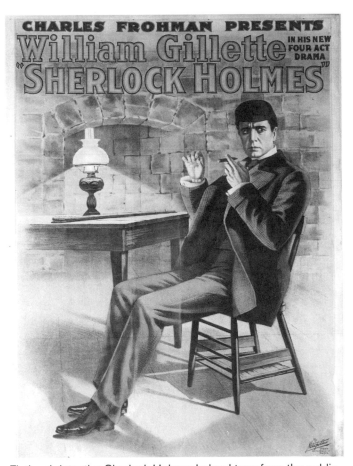

Fictional detective Sherlock Holmes helped transform the public perception of law enforcement. *(Library of Congress Prints and Photographs Division [LC-USZ6-497])*

them only in their effects. We know of them, among other things, that they are always to their possessor, when inordinately possessed, a source of the liveliest enjoyment. As the strong man exults in his physical ability, delighting in such exercises as call his muscles into action, so glories the analyst in that moral activity which *disentangles*. He derives pleasure from even the most trivial occupations bringing his talent into play. He is fond of enigmas, of conundrums, of hieroglyphics; exhibiting in his solutions of each a degree of *acumen* which appears to the ordinary apprehension praeternatural. His results, brought about by the very soul and essence of method, have, in truth, the whole air of intuition.

First paragraph from Edgar Allan Poe's "The Murders in the Rue Morgue," widely regarded as the first modern detective story, Graham's Magazine, *April 1841, republished in* Edgar A. Poe, Tales, *1845, p. 119.*

Refreshed by sleep, Mr. Bucket rises betimes in the morning and prepares for a field-day. Smartened up by the aid of a clean shirt and a wet hairbrush, with which instrument, on occasions of ceremony, he lubricates such thin locks as remain to him after his life of severe study, Mr. Bucket lays in a breakfast of two mutton chops as a foundation to work upon, together with tea, eggs, toast, and marmalade on a corresponding scale. Having much enjoyed these strengthening matters and having held subtle conference with his familiar demon, he confidently instructs Mercury "just to mention quietly to Sir Leicester Dedlock, Baronet, that whenever he's ready for me, I'm ready for him." A gracious message being returned that Sir Leicester will expedite his dressing and join Mr. Bucket in the library within ten minutes, Mr. Bucket repairs to that apartment and stands before the fire with his finger on his chin, looking at the blazing coals.

Thoughtful Mr. Bucket is, as a man may be with weighty work to do, but composed, sure, confident. From the expression of his face he might be a famous whist-player for a large stake—say a hundred guineas certain—with the game in his hand, but with a high reputation involved in his playing his hand out to the last card in a masterly way. Not in the least anxious or disturbed is Mr. Bucket when Sir Leicester appears, but he eyes the baronet aside as he comes slowly to his easy-chair with that observant gravity of yesterday in which there might have been yesterday, but for the audacity of the idea, a touch of compassion.

Inspector Bucket prepares to inform Sir Leicester Dedlock that his wife is a murderer in Charles Dickens's Bleak House *(1853), republished by Project Gutenberg. Available online at URL: http://www.gutenberg.org/etext/1023.*

CHAPTER FIVE

A Nation Dissolved
1855-1869

Criminal justice in the period between 1855 and 1869 was dominated by two issues: the American Civil War and the institution of slavery. Abolitionists were largely successful in banning slavery in the North, while southerners were equally successful in keeping it legal in the South. Their dispute therefore hinged on the western territories, and the presence or absence of slavery in those new states was seen as a bellwether for the direction the government would take. When Abraham Lincoln was elected president in 1860 partly on a platform of not expanding slavery into the western territories, it was clear that the conflict had become unsustainable. Although slavery was not the only cause of the Civil War, it was the most pronounced. No other issue more clearly distinguished the northern perspective from the southern.

As the war began, it became clear that the new criminal justice system established over the preceding decades would not be enough to restore order. Riots broke out throughout the country, and interference with troop activity became common. Both Union president Lincoln and Confederate president Jefferson Davis dealt with this problem by suspending the practice of habeas corpus in particularly vulnerable areas—and Lincoln would officially suspend it nationally. Meanwhile, a nightmarish Confederate military prison called Andersonville in Sumter County, Georgia, housed tens of thousands of starving, diseased Union soldiers—and, at any given time, dozens or hundreds of their corpses.

After the war, the criminal justice challenges were in many ways equally imposing. The abolition of slavery provoked southern laws designed to maintain the institution in everything but name by giving white employers immense power over the lives of their black employees. And as the Fourteenth Amendment was proposed to combat these policies, the Ku Klux Klan—the "Invisible Empire of the South"[1]—emerged to spread fear among African Americans and their white supporters. As the federal government faced a large, powerful, and anonymous secret society, it would once again suspend habeas corpus to deal with the threat. In the Civil War's aftermath—as was the case during the war itself and in the years leading up to it—U.S. leaders faced a critical challenge in attempting to impose order on an overwhelmingly disordered society.

Half Slave, Half Free

From the arrival of African-American slaves in Jamestown, Virginia, in 1619 until the final abolition of slavery by the Thirteenth Amendment in 1865, chattel slavery brought with it a unique set of criminal justice dilemmas. For purposes of law, slaves were human property—sometimes treated like human beings and sometimes treated strictly as property.

How slaves were treated seems to have depended primarily on the role they played in the local economy. In northern states, where the slave population was small (with fewer than 4,000 slaves reported in all of New England by the first U.S. census in 1790)[2] and the institution of slavery was not crucial to the economy, slaves primarily worked in homes or on small farms. This meant that they generally reported directly to their masters, who sometimes bonded with them and came to see

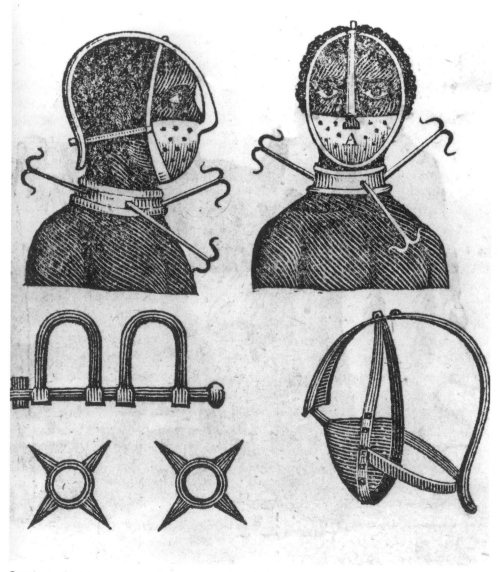

Southern slave owners sometimes used torture instruments, such as these, on slaves they regarded as disobedient. *(Library of Congress Prints and Photographs Division [LC-USZ62-31864])*

them as full human beings. The relatively close master-slave relationship, operating within the framework of an economy that did not depend on slavery, allowed many slaves to earn their freedom and live as free persons, who would sometimes in turn purchase slaves of their own. By the time of the Civil War, most northern states did not allow slavery, either because it had recently been outlawed or because it had never been introduced in the first place.

In the South, on the other hand, the economy was based less on trade and industry and more on agricultural commodities. Although fewer than one-fourth of southerners actually owned slaves, they cumulatively owned more than 4 million in 1860, most of them working on massive cotton plantations owned by fewer than 2 percent of southerners.[3] On these large plantations slave owners and slaves did not generally spend much time together. Instead, slave owners were more likely to hire poor whites, called overseers, to manage the slave population. For the southern aristocracy, slaves were essentially livestock—means by which cotton could be produced. Free African Americans were rare in the cotton-growing regions of the Deep South and were subject to kidnapping by slave traders who could effortlessly pass them off as slaves. The southern attitude toward slavery was determined primarily by fear: fear of violence at the hands of slaves and of economic collapse at the hands of abolitionists.

The threat of violence seemed very real to southern slave owners; reports of planned slave revolts peppered newspapers during the early to mid-19th century, and violent examples, such as Nat Turner's rebellion in 1831, were sometimes carried out. Southern slave owners knew that they could not survive an attack from even a fraction of their slave population; if only 1 percent of slaves rebelled, the force would still be several times larger than any colonial or state militia that could be quickly mustered. The abolition of slavery was also seen as a dire economic threat—the southern economy thrived on agriculture only because maintaining millions of slave laborers was relatively inexpensive. Hiring paid laborers instead would have threatened the agricultural profit margin and with it the financial security of the southern cotton barons.

The combination of distance and fear led southern opinion makers to favor laws that treated slaves strictly as property and kept them under tight rein. The Virginia slave codes of 1705, for example, stated that slaves were human real estate and allowed that masters who killed their slaves while physically disciplining them could not be subsequently charged with murder, manslaughter, or any related crime in a court of law.[4] Most slaves were not educated, and some states enforced laws that made it a crime to teach slaves to read and write or to allow literate slaves to practice their skills.[5]

The difference between northern and southern culture on the issue of slavery became most clear when the issue of fugitive slaves emerged. The Fugitive Slave Act of 1793 established parameters by which slaves who escaped across state lines could be captured and returned to their masters, but northern abolitionists seldom cooperated in enforcing the law. The updated Fugitive Slave Act of 1850 attempted to compel cooperation with the law by establishing strict penalties for anyone who attempted to aid a runaway slave or who refused to participate in his or her recapture. In 1854, the Supreme Court of Wisconsin declared the new Fugitive Slave Act unconstitutional and released runaway slaves captured under its provisions. The defendant in the case was abolitionist Sherman M. Booth, who argued against the imprisonment of a fugitive slave in his newspaper, the *Free Democrat*. When a mob actually freed the slave, Booth was prosecuted under the Fugitive Slave Act on the basis that his complaint was responsible for the mob's actions. The Wisconsin ruling was overturned, however, and the Wisconsin court chastised by the U.S. Supreme Court in *Ableman v. Booth* (1859). Still, legal opposition to the Fugitive Slave Act remained: Northern legislatures defied it by passing laws that leveled penalties against those following the Fugitive Slave Act's mandate,[6] while southern legislators appealed to the federal government for support.[7] The conflict was exacerbated by the tendency of southern slave traders to kidnap free northern African Americans and sell them to southern plantations as unclaimed runaway slaves and by an 1857 Supreme Court case that both horrified and galvanized the abolitionist cause.

Dred Scott was a slave serving the Emerson family of St. Louis, Missouri, during the 1830s. When the Emersons moved to the free state of Illinois and later to the Wisconsin Territory, spending several years at each, Scott made no attempt to challenge for his freedom. After the family returned to St. Louis and Scott's master died, however, Emerson's widow hired out the Scotts to other families in the community. Aware of the fact that court precedents had established that long-term residency in a free state could revoke slave status, Scott and his family sued for their freedom. The case was appealed to the Supreme Court, which in *Dred Scott v. Sandford* (1857) not only struck down Scott's claim to freedom but made a point of ruling that African Americans—slave or free—were not citizens and had no have legal standing to file suits on the basis of civil rights. The judgment had a ripple effect on the free African-American and abolitionist communities and established a judicial precedent that was more radically pro-slavery than any before it.

Slaves could not expect much success in courts, but they had access to another means of escape: the Underground Railroad, an informal network of safe houses operated by free African Americans and white abolitionists from roughly 1810 until slavery was abolished at the end of the Civil War. Underground Railroad "conductors" kept runaway slaves hidden from the authorities as they escaped north—to the northern free states or all the way to Canada. No definite figures are available on the number of slaves who escaped north using the Underground Railroad, but historians have estimated that as many as 100,000 may have successfully completed the dangerous journey north between 1810 and 1850.[8]

Extralegal violence over the issue of slavery hardened divisions between North and South in the 1850s. When Congress passed the Kansas-Nebraska Act in 1854, allowing the newly organized Kansas territory to decide whether to permit slavery on the basis of a popular vote, it virtually invited radical abolitionists and proslavery advocates to flood into the state to try to shape the outcome of the election. In March 1855, thousands of proslavery Missourians entered Kansas to vote for a proslavery legislature. Slavery opponents responded by establishing a rival government in Topeka and began organizing an armed militia in the town of Lawrence. In May 1856, however, a proslavery mob burned several buildings in Lawrence and destroyed the printing presses. At this point, radical abolitionist John Brown decided that force would be necessary to achieve antislavery goals. Three days after the burning of Lawrence, he led seven men to a group of cabins near the Pottawatomie Creek outside of Lawrence. There, they attacked and killed five men affiliated with the proslavery forces. Brown fled Kansas to avoid prosecution for the murders, but the so-called Pottawatomie massacre initiated two years of intermittent guerilla warfare between pro- and antislavery forces.

This 1893 illustration depicts slaves escaping on the Underground Railroad. *(Library of Congress Prints and Photographs Division [LC-USZ62-28860])*

In 1859, Brown resurfaced. On the night of October 16, he led 21 men in an attack on the U.S. military arsenal at Harpers Ferry, Virginia. His goal was to capture the armory, take the weapons stored there, and initiate a slave rebellion. Brown's force seized the armory, but slaves in the surrounding area did not rally to his cause. Rather than retreating, Brown and his men occupied the armory and waited. On October 18, a force of U.S. Marines under the command of Robert E. Lee stormed the armory, wounding or killing most of Brown's force and capturing Brown. Brown used the ensuing trial as a public opportunity to condemn slavery, proclaiming his guilt and preaching in favor of abolition. He was hanged on December 2, 1859. Brown's death, however, made him a martyr for the abolitionist cause. At the same time, his actions also heightened southerners' fears that slaves might rebel and that abolitionists would use force to end slavery.

By 1860, when Abraham Lincoln was elected president, the dispute over slavery dominated the national discourse. Lincoln, who had been elected under the banner of the new Republican Party and promised not to expand slavery into the western territories, was extremely unpopular with the slave owners who controlled the South Carolina state legislature. Advocates of slavery saw him as a menace. They understood restrictions of slavery even in the territories to represent an implicit danger to their way of life. After months of threats, South Carolina formally seceded from the United States on December 20, 1860. Between Lincoln's election in November 1860 and his inauguration in March 1861, a total of seven southern states in the Lower South—South Carolina, Georgia, Alabama, Mississippi, Louisiana, Texas, and Florida—left the Union and formed the Confederate States of America. To prevent the Union from supplying Fort Sumter—a Union military base located in Charleston, South Carolina's harbor—Confederate batteries on the shore fired on the fort on April 12 and forced it to surrender 36 hours later. This battle represented the start of the American Civil War. Following the capture of Fort Sumter, four more states—Virginia, North Carolina, Tennessee, and Arkansas—seceded from the Union and joined the Confederacy in rapid succession. By the end of May 1861, the Confederacy had drafted a constitution and elected its own president in former Mississippi senator Jefferson Davis. The Civil War between North and South was underway.

Criminal Justice in Wartime

"The privilege of the writ of habeas corpus shall not be suspended," reads Article I, Section 9 of the Constitution, "unless when in cases of rebellion or invasion the public safety may require it."[9] The tradition of habeas corpus ("you have the body") allows citizens to appear before judges before imprisonment and challenge the validity of their arrest; it prevents secret detentions and imprisonment without trial. This tradition is a hallmark of civil liberties law, without which it is extremely difficult to guarantee that other due process rights are protected. Lincoln's decision to suspend habeas corpus during the Civil War was extremely controversial at the time and remains so today.

Lincoln's first exemption to habeas corpus took place in April 1861, after pro-Confederate protesters in Baltimore, Maryland, attempted to interfere with Union troop movements. Maryland, one of only four slave states that had remained loyal to the Union, was a potential gain for the Confederacy—its location, nestled adjacent to the borders of Confederate Virginia and Union Washington, D.C., was of great strategic importance; if Maryland were to secede, it would make the Union capital an island in Confederate territory. In an attempt to keep Maryland in Union hands, Lincoln imposed a limited form of martial law by declaring, in a letter to General Winfield Scott, that habeas corpus need not be observed on the Washington-Maryland border.[10] In October, Lincoln expanded the order to include the entire area surrounding Washington in an attempt to prevent more pro-Confederate uprisings. After Lincoln signed the first draft law in July 1862 (which provided for 300,000 additional troops to be called up from state militias), concern about possible draft riots led him to suspend habeas corpus nationally.[11] Military and law enforcement officers abused this policy on a somewhat regular basis, frequently arresting citizens for criticizing Lincoln or the policies of the government. Still, for the time being, the possibility of large-scale draft riots seemed to have been averted.

This changed in March 1863 with the Enrollment Act (passed alongside the Habeas Corpus Act, which endorsed Lincoln's decision to suspend habeas corpus in territories affected by the Civil War). The Enrollment Act replaced the state militia drafts with a general national civilian draft. Potential draftees could either serve, pay $300, or hire a replacement, which ensured that any wealthy draftee who did not want to serve would not be forced to do so and that poor draftees had almost no means of avoiding military service. The Enrollment Act paralleled a draft law enacted in the Confederacy in 1862. With military service came the strong possibility of death from disease or from one of the many massive battles such as Antietam or Gettysburg. Coming on the heels of the Emancipation Proclamation, which took effect on New Year's Day in 1863 and declared all southern slaves to be free, the message to poor whites was that they would be forced to serve against their will, fighting and risking death in an army devoted to ending the institution of slavery. Racist sentiment in the North was not as pronounced as it was in the South, but it still existed under the surface. The new legislation brought it out into the open. "The nation is at the time in a state of Revolution," according to one *Washington Times* editorial: "North, South, East, and West."[12]

The threat of military conscription exacerbated tensions that already existed in U.S. cities in the middle of the 19th century. In particular, urban populations were divided by ethnicity and origin. As Irish workers migrated to the United States in the 1840s and 1850s, white native-born workers often regarded them as competitors for a limited number of jobs. In addition, many white workers regarded Irish immigrants' Catholic faith as unacceptable in what was at the time a primarily Protestant nation. In big cities, gangs coalesced among young men along these lines of ethnicity and religion, pitting the Irish Dead Rabbits against native-born Bowery Boys. The depth of feeling is evident in the murder of William "Butcher Bill" Poole in 1855. An Irish-born assailant shot Poole, a prominent gambler and leader of a group of native-born toughs, in a New York City saloon on February 24, 1855. He died eight days later. The death of Poole—a man prominent in the subculture of saloons and gambling dens, the basis for the character "Bill the Butcher" in the 2002 motion picture *Gangs of New York*, but no public figure—generated a tremendous public response. A reported 6,000 people marched in his funeral parade. In death, the New York City press transformed him into a paragon of American values, widely repeating his dying words, "Goodbye boys, I die a true American."[13] By contrast, the press portrayed his killer, Lewis Baker, as representing all that they claimed was wrong with U.S. cities. In their depiction Poole was an Irish immigrant who had taken a job away from a deserving American worker and who had assassinated an American champion. In reality both men were members of a violent subculture, but in light of the hostility that existed between native-born and Irish workers at this time, their confrontation was elevated in the public eye to the level of a symbolic conflict between natives and newcomers. With the coming of the Civil War, however, native-born and Irish urban workers often directed their hostilities less against one another than against the draft that threatened to pull them into the conflict.

The Detroit riot of March 6, 1863, was the first large-scale northern draft riot of the Civil War, but (as was generally true with other riots) the

President Abraham Lincoln took forceful measures to preserve order during the Civil War. *(National Archives and Records Administration [528325])*

draft was not the only factor. Thomas Faulkner, a mixed-race man who was permitted to vote and usually passed as white, was accused of raping two girls—one white, one African American—and was jailed for it. An angry mob of poor whites, frustrated by the draft policy and full of rage against the city's African-American community, marched down the streets of Detroit to attack black-owned businesses and burn them to the ground, beating any men, and in some cases beating any women and children, who had attempted to flee. Although only one man—Joshua Boyd, an African American—died from the attacks, injuries and maimings were widespread throughout the city's black community, and 15 black-owned businesses were destroyed.

Far more costly were the New York City draft riots, and, unlike the case with the Detroit riot, the instigating factor was the draft itself. On July 13, 1863, the names of draftees were drawn; they were published in the newspapers the next day. New York City's poor—particularly in the Irish-American community, which tended to be prejudiced against African Americans due to competition over low-paying jobs—gathered in the streets and soon became a violent mob. The throng roamed through New York's Lower East Side, burning down black-owned institutions (not only businesses but also in one case a black church and in another a black orphanage), beating and lynching many who fled from them. When the riots came to a close, entire neighborhoods had been completely decimated. The number of casualties remains unknown, but it is likely that roughly 100 people were killed.[14]

Due in part to the draft riots and in part to an already overworked criminal justice system, enforcing the draft code became nearly impossible. The Union government had drafted 300,000 people; of those, only about 150,000 (most of them paid substitutes) actually served in the Union army of more than 2 million.[15] The Union drafts were, by and large, a failure; they did not meet the personnel needs of the Union army, and they raised considerable northern resentment against the Union cause.

Lincoln's suspension of habeas corpus was also controversial and resulted in a Supreme Court verdict that was—in a rare case—completely ignored by Lincoln's administration. On May 25, 1861, Maryland secessionist John Merryman was arrested by Union military forces and held without charge (though there is some evidence that military officials suspected that he had sabotaged bridges used by the Union military). When a complaint was filed before the Supreme Court on his behalf, they ruled in *Ex Parte Merryman* (1861) that only Congress has power to suspend habeas corpus and that the U.S. government must allow Merryman to appear before a judge to determine what crime he had been accused of committing. Military officers refused to release Merryman to a court, and Lincoln took no action to put the Court's ruling into effect. Later, after seven weeks of imprisonment, Merryman was abruptly released, no charges having ever been filed to justify his arrest in the first place.

It was only after the war, in December 1866, that the Supreme Court registered an objection to habeas corpus that was honored by other branches of government. In October 1864, Lambden Milligan was arrested by Union military officers in Indiana and brought forward to a military tribunal. According to prosecutors, he had attempted to conspire with others to arm Confederate prisoners and establish a movement to take over Indiana by force and claim it for the Confederacy. Charged before a tribunal, he was found guilty in May 1865 and sentenced to hang. Although the new president, Andrew Johnson, commuted his sentence to life in prison, Milligan felt that his rights had been violated by Lincoln's suspension of habeas corpus. In *Ex Parte Milligan* (1866), the Supreme Court agreed, reaffirming the *Merryman* precedent that left the decision to suspend habeas corpus in the hands of Congress and pointing out that the act applied only to territory directly affected by the Civil War, a category that did not include Indiana, where little actual fighting took place. He was released, as ordered.

Although Confederate president Jefferson Davis complained of Lincoln's "[b]astiles filled with prisoners, arrested without civil process or indictment duly found; the writ of habeas corpus suspended by Executive mandate" in an address on February 22, 1862,[16] he approved suspension of habeas corpus throughout several major Virginia cities only three days later. Still, Davis's suspension of habeas corpus was not nearly as extensive as Lincoln's; unlike the Union, the Confederacy never formally suspended habeas corpus throughout its territory, though the actions of specific military commanders were frequently tantamount to a suspension of habeas corpus.

The Confederacy was also subject to frequent wartime riots. Bread riots, in particular, were a serious problem, as the poor in the Confederacy often had little access to food, due in part to difficulty in transporting supplies and in part to merchants who sometimes raised the price of goods in order to stay in business. The most well-known upheaval was the Richmond Bread Riot of April 1863 in Virginia, in which protesters—primarily women—ransacked grocery stores, looting food and leaving. These riots were seldom violent, but they had a crippling effect on merchants.

The most infamous criminal justice scandal of the Confederacy was the Andersonville prison in Sumter County, Georgia, which accepted 49,485 Union soldiers as prisoners—and caused the deaths of approximately 13,000 of them.[17] When Henry Wirz was placed in charge of the prison in April 1864, he began to use starvation as a means of imposing discipline. Because of inadequate nutrition, disease also became a serious concern. As the end of the war began to approach, Andersonville had turned into a horrific concentration camp; tens of thousands of skeletal, scurvy-ridden soldiers, very few able to walk without assistance and many unable to walk at all, could be found alongside 13 months' worth of urine and feces and hundreds of rotting corpses—representative of the 100 to 200 prisoners who died every day during the prison's worst period. Although Andersonville was a unique case, Union and Confederate military prisons often treated their prisoners harshly. Northerners, who had seen photographs of the emaciated soldiers in *Harper's Weekly*, were horrified at the treatment their soldiers had received and called for retribution.[18] Wirz was sentenced to death on November 6 1865. When his executioner stated that he "deplored this duty," Wirz responded: "I know what orders are, major. And I am being hanged for obeying them."[19]

Rebuilding the Nation

When Robert E. Lee surrendered on behalf of the Confederacy to Ulysses S. Grant in April 1865, the surrender terms were clear: Each Confederate soldier or officer would, upon turning over his weapons, "be allowed to return to his home, not to be disturbed by the United States authorities so long as they observe their paroles ['not to take up arms against the Government of the United States'], and the laws in force where they may reside."[20] Even Confederate president Jefferson Davis, briefly arrested for treason at the end of the war, was set free and lived to an old age, dying in 1889 after writing his memoirs. The American Civil War did, however, destroy the autonomy of the South as it was understood in the preceding years. While in the early 1860s Lincoln expressed little interest in abolishing slavery in the South, the Emancipation Proclamation of January 1863 and the Thirteenth Amendment, proposed in January 1865, formally abolished chattel slavery in the United States. In response to the abolition of slavery, southern legislators passed "Black Codes," legislation designed to restore the social norms associated with slavery as much as possible. Louisiana's Black Codes prohibited African Americans from entering or exiting cities without permissory notes from a white employer and from living in cities at all—except in cases where their employers were willing to grant permission in writing.[21] Mississippi's Black Codes made it a crime for whites to fraternize with African Americans unless they had an official reason for doing so.[22] Although federal officials put an end to the Black Codes as such by way of the Fourteenth Amendment (which promises that "No state shall make or enforce any law which shall abridge the privileges or immunities of citizens of the United States"), they would form the basis of a new kind of discrimination.

In addition to the official racism of southern governments, unofficial racist groups began to emerge. The Ku Klux Klan was founded in 1865 in Pulaski, Tennessee, as a fraternal order for Confederate veterans unhappy with the outcome of the Civil War. It quickly expanded to include hundreds of thousands of

The Battle of Gettysburg left 8,000 dead. *(National Archives and Records Administration [533310])*

This 1872 illustration depicts an attack by the Ku Klux Klan on an African-American family. *(Library of Congress Prints and Photographs Division [LC-USZ62-127756])*

mostly anonymous members dedicated to white supremacy. Billing itself "The Invisible Empire of the South," the Klan soon turned to violence. Members donned white hoods and interrupted political rallies protesting the Black Codes and other forms of discrimination in the South. Whites who supported African Americans would find anonymous, threatening letters signed with a skull and crossbones—and, if they ignored these warnings (as few did), death. Successful black businessmen were often lynched or faced torture and the destruction of their property. The Klan quickly faded from view soon vanished from the national culture, but its influence would be felt in the 1870s and the organization would emerge again decades later under new leadership, picking up where it had left off.

Chronicle of Events

1855
• *February 24:* William "Butcher Bill" Poole is fatally shot in a New York City saloon by Lewis Baker.

1856
• *May 21:* Pro-slavery rioters burn and pillage the town of Lawrence, Kansas, a city that serves as the antislavery capital of Kansas.
• *May 22:* After delivering a passionate speech condemning slavery and ridiculing pro-slavery South Carolina senator Andrew Butler, Massachusetts senator Charles Sumner is beaten into unconsciousness by Butler's nephew, South Carolina representative Preston Brooks.
• *May 24:* In retaliation for the destruction of Lawrence, Kansas, abolitionist John Brown and his followers murder five Kansas pro-slavery activists. Brown never publicly admits to the crime and is never charged.

1857
• *March 7:* In *Dred Scott v. Sandford*, the Supreme Court rules that African Americans are not citizens and are therefore not protected by the Constitution. As part of its ruling, it also holds that Congress did not have the power to pass the Missouri Compromise and rescinds the federal ban on slavery in the western territories.

1859
• *March 7:* In *Ableman v. Booth*, the Supreme Court rules that the Fugitive Slave Act is constitutional and that states do not have the authority to release federal prisoners under any circumstances.
• *October 16:* Abolitionist John Brown leads 21 men into Harpers Ferry, Virginia, where they seize the city's federal arsenal in an attempt to establish Harpers Ferry as a haven for escaped slaves.
• *October 18:* John Brown is captured.
• *December 2:* John Brown is hanged for treason.

1860
• *December 20:* South Carolina secedes from the United States.

1861
• *February 8:* The Constitution of the Confederate States of America is approved in Montgomery, Alabama. It establishes slave ownership as a legal right and includes

Confederate president Jefferson Davis initially advocated in favor of criminal due process, but most of these protections vanished by the end of the war. *(National Archives and Records Administration [529264])*

constitutional provisions that specify a strengthened fugitive slave act.
• *February 9:* Jefferson Davis is elected president of the Confederacy.
• *April 12:* Confederate forces bombard Fort Sumter in South Carolina, beginning the American Civil War.
• *April 19:* Pro-Confederate protesters in the border state of Maryland riot in Baltimore in an attempt to block Union troop movements.
• *April 27:* In a letter to General Winfield Scott, President Abraham Lincoln grants permission for military leaders to suspend habeas corpus along the Maryland-Washington border when arresting suspects for rebellion.
• *May 20:* North Carolina secedes from the Union. The Confederacy is now made up of 11 states—the largest it will ever become.
• *May 25:* Maryland secessionist John Merryman is arrested without charge by the military and detained for several days.
• *May 28:* U.S. Supreme Court Chief Justice Roger Taney, sitting as a circuit court judge, rules in *Ex Par-*

te Merryman that John Merryman's imprisonment is unconstitutional.

• *October 14:* President Lincoln expands suspension of habeas corpus to include all territory between Bangor, Maine, and Washington, D.C.

1862

• *February 27:* Confederate president Jefferson Davis declares martial law and suspends habeas corpus in several Virginia cities.

• *April 16:* Confederate president Jefferson Davis declares that all healthy white men between 18 and 35 years old may be drafted for up to three years of military service.

• *July 17:* President Lincoln signs the first Union draft law, calling on 300,000 state militia members to transfer to the Union army.

• *September 24:* Facing opposition to the federal draft, President Lincoln suspends habeas corpus for all rebels, insurgents, and draft protesters nationwide and decrees that they may be subject to military tribunals rather than civilian trials.

1863

• *January 1:* President Lincoln issues the Emancipation Proclamation, declaring that all slaves living in Confederate territories will be "forever free."

• *March 3:* Congress passes the Enrollment Act (also known as the Federal Draft Act), the first compulsory draft of civilians in U.S. history. A special loophole allows draftees to avoid service by contributing $300 to the Union cause or hiring a replacement, making the already unpopular legislation even less popular among the poor.

• *March 6:* Incensed by the draft policy and rape accusations leveled against a local African-American man, white mobs riot in Detroit, Michigan, destroying at least 15 African-American businesses and private homes.

• *April 2:* Men, women, and children plunder the city of Richmond, Virginia, during the "bread riot," complaining that food is too expensive and too difficult to obtain.

• *July 13:* In response to the federal draft, thousands of poor New Yorkers instigate a violent riot. Although estimates vary, most historians agree that up to 100 people were killed during the insurrection.

• *August 21:* Pro-slavery terrorists led by William C. Quantrill attack the community of Lawrence, Kansas, slaughtering 150 men and boys.

• *December 8:* President Lincoln issues a Proclamation of Amnesty and Reconstruction, declaring that all Confederates who swear an oath to the Union will be pardoned.

1864

• *April:* Henry Wirz is appointed commandant of the Andersonville Confederate military prison in Sumter County, Georgia.

1865

• *April 9:* General Robert E. Lee surrenders to General Ulysses S. Grant at Appomattox Courthouse in Virginia, ending the American Civil War.

• *May:* Union soldiers take control of the Andersonville military prison and are shocked to find tens of thousands of horribly starved, diseased soldiers lying in agony—and nearly 13,000 dead and buried in mass graves nearby.

• *November 6:* Henry Wirz, commandant of the Andersonville Confederate military prison, is sentenced to death for "wanton cruelty."

• *December 18:* The Thirteenth Amendment, banning slavery in the United States, is ratified.

1866

• *May:* The Ku Klux Klan is founded in Pulaski, Tennessee.

• *June:* The Fourteenth Amendment passes both houses of Congress.

1867

• *January:* Humanitarian reformers Enoch Wines and Theodore Dwight report to the New York Legislature on the conditions of prisons and reformatories in the United States and Canada.

1868

• *July 28:* The Fourteenth Amendment is ratified and goes into effect.

Eyewitness Testimony

The Final Years of American Slavery

Dear Sir: I came from Virginia in March, and was at your office the last of March. My object in writing you, is to inquire what I can do, or what can be done to help my wife to escape from the same bondage that I was in. You will know by your books that I was from Petersburg, Va., and that is where my wife now is. I have received two or three letters from a lady in that place and the last one says, that my wife's mistress is dead, and that she expects to be sold. I am very anxious to do what I can for her before it is too late, and beg of you to devise some means to get her away. Capt. The man that brought me away, knows the colored agent at Petersburg, and will do all he can to forward my wife. The Capt. Promised, that when I could raise one hundred dollars for him that he would deliver her in Philadelphia. Tell him that I can now raise the money, and will forward it to you at any day that he thinks that he can bring her. Please see the Captain and find when he will undertake it, and then let me know when to forward the money to you. I am at work for the Hon. Charles Cook, and can send the money any day. My wife's name is Harriet Robertson, and the agent at Petersburg knows her.

Please direct your answer, with all necessary directions, to N. Coryell, of this village, and he will see that all is right.

Former slave Daniel Robertson, writing to William Still,
director of the Underground Railroad in Philadelphia,
August 11, 1856, quoted in Aptheker, A Documentary
History of the Negro People in the United States, *p. 389.*

The words "people of the United States" and "citizens" are synonymous terms, and mean the same thing. They both describe the political body who, according to our republican institutions, form the sovereignty, and who hold the power and conduct the Government through their representatives . . . The question before us is, whether the class of persons described in this plea in abatement compose a portion of this sovereignty? We think they are not, and that they are not included, and were not intended to be included, under the word "citizens" in the Constitution, and can therefore claim none of the rights and privileges which that instrument provides for and secures to citizens of the United States. On the contrary, they were at that time considered as a subordinate and inferior class of beings, who had been subjugated by the dominant race, and, whether emancipated or not, yet remained subject to their authority, and had no rights or privileges but such as those who held the power and the Government might choose to grant them.

It is not the province of the court to decide upon the justice or injustice, the policy or impolicy, of these laws. The decision of that question belonged to the political or law-making power; to those who formed the sovereignty and framed the Constitution. The duty of the court is, to interpret the instrument they have framed, with the best lights we can obtain on the subject, and to administer it as we find it, according to its true intent and meaning when it was adopted . . .

It is difficult at this day to realize the state of public opinion in relation to that unfortunate race, which prevailed in the civilized and enlightened portions of the world at the time of the Declaration of Independence, and when the Constitution of the United States was framed and adopted. But the public history of every European nation displays it in a manner too plain to be mistaken.

They had for more than a century before been regarded as beings of an inferior order, and altogether unfit to associate with the white race, either in social or political relations; and so far inferior, that they had no rights which the right man was bound to respect; and that the negro might justly and lawfully be reduced to slavery for his benefit. He was bought and sold, and treated as an ordinary article of merchandise and traffic, whenever a profit could be made by it. This opinion was at that time fixed and universal in the civilized portion of the white race. It was regarded as an axiom in morals as well as in politics, which no one thought of disputing, or supposed to be open to dispute; and men in every grade and position in society daily and habitually acted upon it in their private pursuits, as well as in matters of public concern, without doubting for a moment the correctness of this opinion . . .

The legislation of the different colonies furnishes positive and indisputable proof of this fact.

It would be tedious, in this opinion, to enumerate the various laws they passed upon this subject. It will be sufficient, as a sample of the legislation which then generally prevailed throughout the British colonies, to give the laws of two of them; one being still a large slaveholding state, and the other the first State in which slavery ceased to exist.

The province of Maryland, in 1717, passed a law declaring "that if any free negro or mulatto intermarry with any white woman, or if any white man shall intermarry with any negro or mulatto woman, such negro or mulatto shall become a slave during life, excepting mulattoes born of white women . . . And any white man or woman who shall intermarry as aforesaid, with any negro or mulatto, such white man or white woman shall become servants during the term of seven years . . ."

The other colonial law to which we refer was passed by Massachusetts in 1705. It is entitled "An act for the better preventing of a spurious and mixed issue," &c.; and it provides, that "if any negro or mulatto shall presume to smite or strike any person of the English or other Christian nation, such negro or mulatto shall be severely whipped . . ."

We give both of these laws in the words used by the respective legislative bodies, because the language in which they are framed, as well as the provisions contained in them, show, too plainly to be misunderstood, the degraded condition of this unhappy race. They were still in force when the Revolution began, and are a faithful index to the state of feeling towards the class of persons of whom they speak, and of the position they occupied throughout the thirteen colonies, in the eyes and thoughts of the men who framed the Declaration of Independence . . . They show that a perpetual and impassable barrier was intended to be erected between the white race and the one which they had reduced to slavery, and governed as subjects with absolute and despotic power, and which they then looked upon as so far below them in the scale of created beings, that intermarriages between white persons and negroes or mulattoes were regarded as unnatural and immoral, and punished as crimes, not only in the parties, but in the person who joined them in marriage. And no distinction in this respect was made between the free negro or mulatto and the slave, but this stigma, of the deepest degradation, was fixed upon the whole race.

U.S. Chief Justice Robert B. Taney, from his ruling in Dred Scott v. Sandford *(1857), FindLaw.com. Available online at URL: http://laws.findlaw.com/us/60/393.html.*

Whereas, The Supreme Court of the United States has decided in the case of Dred Scott, that *people of African descent are not and cannot be citizens of the United States, and cannot sue in any of the United States courts* . . . and whereas, this Supreme Court is the constitutionally approved tribunal to determine all such questions; therefore,

Resolved, That this atrocious decision furnishes final confirmation of the already well known fact that under the Constitution and Government of the United States, the colored people are nothing, and can be nothing but an alien, disfranchised and degraded class.

Resolved, That to attempt, as some do, to prove that there is no support given to Slavery in the Constitution and essential structure of the American Government, is to argue against reason and common sense, to ignore history and shut our eyes against palpable facts; and that while it may suit white men who do not feel the iron heel, to please themselves with such theories, it ill becomes the man of color whose daily experience refutes the absurdity, to indulge in any such idle phantasies.

Resolved, That to persist in supporting a Government which holds and exercises the power, as distinctly set forth by a tribunal from which there is no appeal, to trample a class under foot as an inferior and degraded race, is on the part of the colored man at once the height of folly and the depth of pusillanimity.

Resolved, That no allegiance is due from any man, or any class of men, to a Government founded and administered in iniquity, and that the only duty the colored man owes to a Constitution under which he is declared to be an inferior and degraded being, having no rights which white men are bound to respect, is to denounce and repudiate it, and to do what he can by all proper means to bring it into contempt.

Robert Purvis, speaking against the Supreme Court's decision in Dred Scott v. Sandford *in Philadelphia's Israel Church on April 3, 1857, less than one month after the ruling was delivered, quoted in Aptheker,* A Documentary History of the Negro People in the United States, *p. 392.*

I walked towards my office, then just within the armory inclosure, and not more than a hundred yards from my dwelling. As I proceeded I saw a man come out of an alley near me, then another, and another, all coming towards me. When they came up to me I inquired what all this meant; they said, nothing, only they had taken possession of the Government works.

I told them they talked like crazy men. They answered, "Not so crazy as you think, as you will soon see." Up to this time I had not seen any arms; presently, however, the men threw back the short cloaks they wore, and displayed Sharpes's rifles, pistols, and knives. Seeing these, and fearing something serious was going on, I told the men I believed I would return to my quarters. They at once cocked their guns, and told me I was a prisoner . . .

Up to this time the citizens had hardly begun to move about, and knew nothing of the raid.

When they learned what was going on, some came out armed with old shot-guns, and were themselves shot by concealed men. All the stores, as well as the arsenal, were in the hands of Brown's men, and it was impossible to get either arms or ammunition, there being hardly any private arms owned by citizens. At least, however, a few weapons were obtained, and a body of citizens crossed the river and advanced from the Maryland side. They made a vigorous attack, and in a few minutes caused all the invaders who were not killed to retreat to Brown inside of the armory gate. Then he entered the engine-house, carrying his prisoners along . . .

When Lieutenant Stuart came in the morning for the final reply to the demand to surrender, I got up and went to Brown's side to hear his answer.

Stuart asked, "Are you ready to surrender, and trust to the mercy of the Government?"

Brown answered promptly, "No! I prefer to die here."

His manner did not betray the least fear.

Stuart stepped aside and made the signal for the attack, which was instantly begun with sledge-hammers to break down the door.

Finding it would not yield, the soldiers seized a long ladder for a battering-ram, and commenced beating the door with that, the party within firing incessantly . . . [A]fter two or three strokes of the ladder the engine rolled partially back, making a small aperture, through which Lieutenant Green of the marines forced himself, jumped on top of the engine, and stood a second in the midst of a shower of balls, looking for John Brown. When he saw Brown he sprang about twelve feet at him, and gave an under-thrust of his sword, striking him about midway the body and raising him completely from the ground. Brown fell forward with his head between his knees, and Green struck him several times over the head . . .

I was not two feet from Brown at the time. Of course I got out of the building as soon as possible, and did not know until some time later that Brown was not killed. It seems that in making the thrust Green's sword struck Brown's belt and did not penetrate the body. The sword was bent double. The reason that Brown was not killed when struck on the head was that Green was holding the sword in the middle, striking with the hilt and making only scalp wounds.

When Governor Wise came and was examining Brown, I heard the questions and answers; and no lawyer could have used more careful reserve, while at the same time he showed no disrespect. Governor Wise was astonished at the answers he received from Brown.

After some controversy between the United States and the State of Virginia as to which had jurisdiction over the prisoners, Brown was carried to the Charlestown jail and, after a fair trial, was hanged.

John E. Daingerfield, hostage of John Brown, writing of the July 1859 raid on Harpers Ferry, quoted in Hofstader and Wallace, American Violence, *pp. 98–101.*

Dear Brother: . . . It was a sense of the wrongs which we have suffered that prompted the noble but unfortunate Captain John Brown and his associates to attempt to give freedom to a small number, at least, of those who are now held by cruel and unjust laws, and by no less cruel and unjust men. To this freedom they were entitled by every known principle of justice and humanity, and for the enjoyment of it God created them. And now, dear brother, could I die in a more noble cause? Could I, brother, die in a manner and for a cause which would induce true and honest men more to honor me, and the angels more readily to receive me into their happy home of everlasting joy above? I imagine that I hear you, and all of you, mother, father, sisters and brothers, say—"No, there is not a cause for which we, with less sorrow, could see you die." Believe me when I tell you, that though shut up in prison and under sentence of death, I have spent some very happy hours here. And were it not that I know that the hearts of those to whom I am attached by the nearest and most enduring ties of blood-relationship—yea, by the closest and strongest ties that God has instituted—will be filled with sorrow, I would almost as life die now as at any time, for I feel that I am now prepared to meet my Maker . . .

Fugitive slave John A. Copeland, who assisted in John Brown's rebellion, from a letter to his brother, December 10, 1859, quoted in Aptheker, A Documentary History of the Negro People in the United States, *p. 443.*

Dear Sir—I am happy to think, that the time has come when we no doubt can open our correspondence with one another again. Also I am in hopes, that these few lines may find you and your family well and in the enjoyment of good health, as it leaves me and my family the same. I want you to know, that I feel as much determined to work in this glorious cause, as ever I did in all my life, and I have some very good hams on hand that I would like very much for you to have. I have nothing of interest to write about just now, only that the politics of the day is in a high rage, and I don't know of the result, therefore, I want you to be one of those wide-a-wakes as is mentioned from your section of country now-a-days, &c. Also, if you wish to write to me, Mr. J. Brown will inform you how to direct a letter to me.

No more at present, until I hear from you; but I want you to be a wide-awake.

A letter addressed to Philadelphia director of the Underground Railroad, William Still, signed "Ham & Eggs" and written in code ("hams" meaning slaves seeking liberty). October 17, 1860, quoted in Aptheker, A Documentary History of the Negro People in the United States, *p. 419.*

Criminal Justice in Wartime

You are engaged in repressing an insurrection against the laws of the United States. If at any point on or in the vicinity of the military line which is now used between the city of Philadelphia via Perryville, Annapolis City and Annapolis Junction you find resistance which renders it necessary to suspend the writ of habeas corpus for the public safety, you personally or through the officer in command at the point where resistance occurs are authorized to suspend the writ.

Abraham Lincoln, letter to General Winfield Scott, April 27, 1861, quoted in Neely, The Fate of Liberty, *p. 8.*

The mob, in its first appearance to me, was a parcel of fellows running up Lafayette street after two or three colored men. They then returned back, and in a short time I saw a tremendous crowd coming up Croghan street on drays, wagons, and foot, with kegs of beer on their wagons, and rushed for the prison. Here they crowded thick and heavy. After this, while I was standing on the corner, with a half dozen other gentlemen, a rifle ball came whistling over our heads. After which we heard several shots, but only one ball passing us. In a short time after this there came one fellow down saying, "I am shot in the thigh." And another came with his finger partly shot off. A few minutes after that another ruffian came down, saying: "If we are got to be killed up for Negroes then we will kill every one in this town." A very little while after this we could hear them speaking up near the jail, and appeared to be drinking, but I was unable to hear what they said. This done, they gave a most fiendish yell and started down Beaubien street. On reaching Croghan street, a couple of houses west on Beaubien street, they commenced throwing, and before they reached my residence, clubs, brick, and missiles of every description flew like hail. Myself and several others were standing on the side-walk, but were compelled to hasten in and close our

This illustration depicts the burning of a black orphanage by Irish rioters during the New York City draft riots of 1863. *(Library of Congress Prints and Photographs Division [LC-USZ62-126179])*

doors, while the mob passed my house with their clubs and bricks flying into my windows and doors, sweeping out light and sash!

They then approached my door in large numbers, where I stood with my gun, and another friend with an axe, but on seeing us, they fell back. They approached four times determined to enter my door, but I raised my gun at each time and they fell back. In the meantime part of the mob passed on down Beaubien street. After the principle part had passed, I rushed up my stairs looking to see what they were doing, and heard the shattering of windows and slashing of boards. In a few moments I saw them at Whitney Reynolds, a few doors below Lafayette street. Mr. Reynolds is a cooper; had his shop and residence on the same lot, and was the largest colored cooper establishment in the city—employing a number of hands regular.

I could see from the windows men striking with axe, spade, clubs, &c., just as you could see men thrashing wheat. A sight the most revolting, to see innocent men, women, and children, all without respect to age or sex, being pounded in the most brutal manner.

Sickened with the sight, I sat down in deep solicitude in relation to what the night would bring forth; for to human appearance it seemed as if Satan was loose, and his children were free to do whatever he might direct without fear of the city authority.

Thomas Buckner, describing the Detroit race riots of March 6, 1863, quoted in Aptheker, A Documentary History of the Negro People in the United States, *v. 1 pp. 501–502.*

This photograph shows a mass grave at Andersonville Prison. *(National Archives and Records Administration [533035])*

Early in the morning men began to assemble here in separate groups, as if in accordance with a previous arrangement, and at last moved quietly north along the various avenues. Women, also, like camp followers, took the same direction in crowds. They were thus divided into separate gangs, apparently to take each avenue in their progress, and make a clean sweep. The factories and workshops were visited, and the men compelled to knock off work and join them, while the proprietors were threatened with the destruction of their property, if they made any opposition. The separate crowds were thus swelled at almost every step, and armed with sticks, and clubs, and every conceivable weapon they could lay hands on, they moved north towards some point which had evidently been selected as a place of rendezvous. This proved to be a vacant lot near Central Park, and soon the living streams began to flow into it, and a more

wild, savage, and heterogeneous-looking mass could not be imagined . . .

A ragged, coatless, heterogeneously weaponed army, it heaved tumultuously along toward Third Avenue. Tearing down the telegraph poles as it crossed the Harlem and New Haven railroad track, it surged angrily up around the building where the drafting was going on. The small squad of police stationed there to repress disorder looked on bewildered, feeling they were powerless in the presence of such a host. Soon a stone went crashing through a window, which was the signal for a general assault on the doors. These giving way before the immense pressure, the foremost rushed in, followed by shouts and yells from those behind . . .

Journalist and historian Joel Tyler Headley, describing the New York draft riots of July 13, 1863, quoted in Zinn and Arnove, Voices of a People's History of the United States, *pp. 204–205.*

Would that I was an artist and had the material to paint this camp and all its horrors, or the tongue of some eloquent Statesman and had the privilege of expressing my mind to our honorable rulers in Washington, I should glory to describe this hell on earth where it takes seven of its occupants to make a shadow.

Sgt. David Kennedy of the 9th Ohio Cavalry, describing his imprisonment in Andersonville Prison in a July 27, 1864, diary entry, quoted in Lois Barber, "A Veterans Day Remembrance," The Times News, November 10, 2001.

Reconstruction and the Birth of Jim Crow

On the corner where I was standing I saw the police from Dauphin Street turning up Canal Street, and running with pistols in their hands . . . As they passed Dryades Street they were firing in the street there, and the loafers that were there were throwing bricks at the Negroes, and the Negroes, too, were throwing bricks; and as the people came up they commenced. They fired to scare the people, but they fired with bullets. After firing some time the street got a little clear . . . When they got to the Mechanics' Institute they found the door fastened and they could not get in; then they backed out and fired several times through the windows . . .

[A]s they fired they broke the glass. Then the fire bells began to ring and the firemen began to come. The policemen then succeeded in bursting open the doors and went inside. What they did inside I do not know, but in about a quarter of an hour after there were a good many came out wounded, cut up, shot in the face and head; and there were police taking them to the calaboose; as they passed with them the crowd would knock them down and kill them, and some of the police were helping them kill them on the street. I spoke to the lieutenant of police, with whom I am acquainted . . . and I begged him "For God's sake, stop your men from killing these men so." He gave me no answer, but walked away to the Mechanics' Institute. After a while I spoke to him again; said I, "For God's sake, stop these men from this; I could arrest them all myself." His reply was, "Yes, God damn them; I'll set fire to the building and burn them all." I said no more, but went away.

J. B. Jourdain, describing the New Orleans Massacre of July 30, 1866, quoted in Aptheker, A Documentary History of the Negro People in the United States, v. 2 p. 555.

CHAPTER SIX

East and West
1870–1889

The American Civil War and the debate over slavery had overwhelmed almost every reform movement and drained almost every national law enforcement institution of its power. As Reconstruction began in the South and settlement increased in the western territories, however, the culture of the United States began to change in very radical ways.

One of the most notable changes dealt with population growth. Due to widespread immigration from Europe and smaller scale immigration from Asia, the U.S. population grew from 38.6 million in 1870 to 63 million in 1890.[1] In settled areas, police departments and prisons became ubiquitous; in more sparsely settled areas, lawlessness often reigned, and corruption was a fact of life. But as Americans moved west, their social movements eventually moved west with them. As frontier lawmen became obsolete, replaced by more tightly regulated law enforcement agencies, the U.S. criminal justice system began to show early signs of an emerging national standard of criminal justice. Although the United States was still a divided nation in many ways, the period of Reconstruction and western expansion represented an awkward adolescence in the development of the U.S. criminal justice system—one that preceded the wave of reforms that would create the modern United States.

The Laws of White Men

Racism was a central issue in the years following the American Civil War, just as it had been in the years preceding it. In the 11 states that had only recently made up the Confederacy, fear of a large and suddenly liberated African-American population led to oppression—of both the legal and the illegal varieties—as whites attempted to protect their privileged status.

One significant sign of privilege was the right to vote. The Fifteenth Amendment, which was ratified in March 1870, granted voting rights to African Americans. Enforcing this policy in southern states, which had only accepted the amendment on the threat of being denied readmission to the United States, proved to be almost impossible. Opponents of African-American civil rights, such as the Ku Klux Klan, the White League, the White Man's Party, and the Knights of the White Camellia, used fraud, threats, and violence to keep African Americans away from the polls and to silence white liberals. Interviews conducted by the Joint Select Committee to Inquire into the Conditions of Affairs in the Late Insurrectionary States, established by Congress in 1871, revealed the almost ubiquitous threat of violence against the African-American community. Assaults, rapes, and even murders sometimes went ignored by local law enforcement authorities. Congress initially responded with the Force Act of May 1870, which made it a federal crime to interfere with a citizen's right to vote, and the Ku Klux Klan Act of April 1871, which suspended habeas corpus in cases involving the Klan. Still, these groups—made up of thousands of whites (anonymous and hooded in the case of the Klan), many of them well-armed military veterans—were generally tolerated and sometimes actively supported by local southern law enforcement officials.

When racist paramilitary groups did encounter resistance, they were often so powerful that they were able to overwhelm law enforcement authorities. In Vicksburg, Mississippi, in December 1874, white supremacist city officials and paramilitary supporters demanded the resignation of African-American sheriff Peter Crosby. When Crosby refused, the mayor declared martial law and had Crosby arrested. A predominantly African-American militia gathered to demand Crosby's release and reinstatement but found itself confronted by a company of armed white men commanded by Colonel Horace Miller, a Confederate veteran. As the black militia turned to retreat, the white company fired upon them, killing dozens.[2] The event was remarkable for its scope but not particularly unusual for the time. During Reconstruction the use of organized violence to impose white political power over African Americans was commonplace. This persistent violence sufficiently reduced the African-American and Republican vote in that 1875 Mississippi state elections that white supremacist Democratic politicians regained control of the governor's office and state legislature.

In the wake of the contested 1872 Louisiana gubernatorial elections, rumors circulated that pro-Confederate whites would attempt to seize power by force. In April 1873, predominantly black officers of the Louisiana state militia attempted to hold the courthouse in Colfax, Louisiana, but were outnumbered by an attacking White League force. The militia surrendered, and the White League took advantage of the opportunity to shoot as many black militiamen as they could, killing approximately 100 and scattering the rest. Only U.S. military intervention prevented a wider scale rampage.[3]

The White League became even more ambitious in September 1874 in a (briefly) successful coup that would become known as the Battle of Liberty Place. Facing down an army of police officers and black militiamen led by former Confederate general James Longstreet, the White League attacked Louisiana's seat of government in New Orleans, successfully deposed the governor, captured Longstreet (who was seen as a traitor for abandoning the Confederate cause and leading black soldiers into battle), and took control of the city for three days. Federal troops arrived and sent the White League fleeing. Longstreet was rescued and the previous governor reinstated, but it became clear that the government of Louisiana did not have the resources to protect itself from the organized white supremacist movement. Federal troops would occupy the city for two and a half years, until they withdrew following the election of former Confederate general and civil rights opponent Francis T. Nicholls as governor in 1877 and the emergence of Jim Crow. The White League rebellion was short-lived, but its attitude toward civil rights would be reflected in the policies of the Louisiana state government for decades to come.

A portrait of Sitting Bull, chief of the Hunkpapa Lakota. *(National Archives and Records Administration [530896])*

As oppression of African Americans continued in the South, racism in the western territories focused to a greater extent on American Indians and Hispanics. In March 1871, Congress passed the Indian Appropriations Act and made American Indians wards of the federal government, ending the possibility of treaties and other measures that would have protected the autonomy of individual tribes. The U.S. government then began violating the treaties that had already been signed, instigating a series of small wars, the most remarkable being the Black Hills War of 1874–76, in which soldiers led by Lakota chiefs Sitting Bull and Crazy Horse proved fierce and deadly adversaries to U.S. military forces. Large-scale conflicts between the U.S. military and American Indian tribes largely ended with the massacre at Wounded Knee in South Dakota in December 1890, where U.S. soldiers responded to an accidentally discharged firearm by killing 153 Lakota men, women, and children. As many as 150 additional Lakota, who fled the carnage, died of starvation or exposure.[4]

Small-scale abuses of American Indian and Hispanic Americans were common in the western territories. One of the most chilling was the lynching of a young pregnant California woman known only as Juanita. In 1851, the newly married Juanita was approached by a white laborer named Jack Cannon, who offered her a bag of gold dust in exchange for sexual relations. When she refused, he beat the door down and attempted to rape her. She stabbed him in self-defense and was immediately carried off by a crowd of protesters who gave her an impromptu "trial." A defense attorney appeared to defend her case pro bono but was physically attacked and thrown out in the streets before he could argue on her behalf. Without examining the evidence, the crowd immediately declared her guilty, and she was hanged from a bridge overlooking the Yuba River. Her case sparked international protest, but lynchings of American Indians and Hispanics continued unabated on the western frontier, where the rule of law applied only if local authorities wanted it to.

The Wild West in Myth and Reality

No era in American history has been used to convey the spirit of rugged American individualism, fierce masculine determination, and chivalry like the early decades of western expansion. The western genre in novels and films tells us of a time when honorable lawmen fought outlaws in the streets of western towns, defending the helpless with kindness and charm. According to this tradition, good triumphed over evil in the West; it stands as a symbol of determination, a sign that Americans who respect justice can triumph over evil even in lawless lands.

In reality, criminal justice in the Old West was a far less admirable process. Towns were often little better than temporary camps that sprang up almost overnight to serve the needs of those involved in mining claims or cattle drives. People came and went, stopping briefly to buy and sell, to drink, and to blow off steam. Lawmen were often corrupt to the point of villainy. Outlaws were common criminals—nothing more, nothing less—and enjoyed notoriety only because, in the wide open spaces of the Old West, it took longer to catch them. Because of the lack of investigation and limits of forensic technology (even fingerprints were not available as a means of identification until 1905),[5] many crimes went unpunished, and many abuses of power were successfully covered up. It was not a glamorous period in U.S. history, and the larger problems of criminal justice on the western frontier were solved only as settlement increased. Life on the western frontier was remote from the protections and social structures that those in more settled regions of the country—even rural areas—enjoyed. Western frontier towns were like islands in a massive ocean, and criminal justice—when it did exist—stood a small chance of conforming to American norms.

One case in point was Judge Roy Bean. In 1884, the grizzled, middle-aged former Confederate guerrilla became judge of the tiny railroad stopover town of Langtry, Texas, where he opened up a saloon that doubled as a courthouse. His sign read: "JUDGE ROY BEAN, Notary Public—Justice of the Peace—Law West of the Pecos—Ice Beer."[6] For 20 years, he ruled the town with an iron shot glass. One of his favorite tricks was to serve drinks to anxious customers awaiting the train but take his time delivering the change—then fine the customer the exact amount for cursing when the train showed up. Marriages were two dollars; divorces cost five. Trials took place in the saloon itself, and drinks were offered to everyone. As charming as Judge Bean was, even he had his dark side: He once dismissed the murder of a Chinese laborer by flipping through his law book and remarking "There ain't a damn line here nowheres that makes it illegal to kill a Chinaman,"[7] and the odds for Hispanics were seldom better. Still, he was reasonably effective at keeping road gangs at bay and was consistently reelected by his constituency.

Although Judge Bean was sometimes called a "hangin' judge," he did not impose a particularly high number of death sentences. The judge who earned the moniker—and more or less invented it—was Isaac C. Parker, better known as "Hangin' Judge" Parker, a judge in the largely unsettled western regions and American Indian Territory of Arkansas. Appointed in 1875, Parker ordered 172 death sentences during his 21-year tenure (though 84 would be overturned on appeal).[8] As nearby settlement grew, popular sentiment turned against his excesses. Congress stripped him of his power in 1895, and he died before the transfer of power was completed.

But the justice meted out by gunslinging lawmen was at times so brutal and unprovoked that it would have made the "Hangin' Judge" look like a sweet-natured pacifist by comparison. James "Wild Bill" Hickok earned his place in the Old West mythos by allegedly participating in an 1861 gunfight with the "McCanles gang," which was purported to be a courageous and impressive showdown between a noble sharpshooter and a gang of hardened criminals. The truth was far more alarming. Hickock had been working for Russel, Majors, and Waddell, a freighting company that owed rancher Dave McCanles money, or so McCanles believed. When McCanles showed up at the Nebraska business office with two ranch hands outside and his 12-year-old son in tow, Hickock shot McCanles in the back, and other employees

At this saloon Judge Roy Bean dispensed his unique brand of justice. *(National Archives and Records Administration [530985])*

helped him dispatch the two ranch hands. The 12-year-old boy was allowed to leave unharmed, but he was not allowed to testify in Hickok's murder trial. The removal of the only witness willing to talk resulted in Hickok's acquittal (on the grounds of self-defense) and left dime store novelists free to tell his story for him.[9] McCanles was transformed into a fearsome outlaw, his two unarmed ranch hands into eight heavily armed stooges, and Hickok into a brilliant marksman who had single-handedly outgunned all nine of them after being shot 11 times. The legend of "Wild Bill" was born. Hickok went off to fight in the Civil War and assist in operations against American Indians in the late 1860s. He served with distinction, which bolstered his image even further (though some of the stories that were told about his military career, such as the claim that he shot 50 Confederate soldiers with 50 consecutive bullets, were fabricated).

Hickok's heavily embellished war record and victory over the "McCanles gang" won him election as sheriff of Ellis County, Texas, in 1869 and appointment as U.S. marshal in the county seat of Hays City soon afterward, where he proved that he actually was fairly handy with a revolver. A marked man, Hickok was hunted down by local outlaws who wanted to make a name for themselves by killing him, and he dispatched them all. Hickok moved on to a position as city marshal of Abilene, Kansas, in 1871, where he confronted numerous outlaws, including the notorious killer John Wesley Hardin (who would later vex the Texas Rangers). Hickok accidentally shot his own deputy to death during a gunfight, however, and left after only six months. Although his tenure at Abilene would not have qualified as successful by most standards, storytellers transformed it into an amazing and dramatic success. Hickok's end came in August 1876, when his reputation finally caught up with him. Jack McCall, who believed that Hickok had shot his brother, snuck up behind the legendary gunslinger when he was playing poker and shot him in the head. Hickok's hand was a pair of aces and a pair of eights—known, from that point onward, as the "dead man's hand."

Famed lawman Wyatt Earp was no more savory a character. After being arrested for horse stealing in California, Earp moved on to Wichita, Kansas, in 1874, where he served as city marshal for three years until he was fired for corruption. In 1876, Earp moved on to Dodge City, Kansas, where he served as a deputy marshal for five years under the leadership of fellow legend William "Bat" Masterson. Earp and Masterson were reasonably effective lawmen, at least when it came to the laws they enforced.[10] In 1879, Earp moved on to Tombstone, Arizona, where his legend would be made.

This photograph depicts the 1884 hanging of accused bandit John Heith in Tombstone, Arizona. With no prisons and little supervision, frontier law enforcement officials often dealt with accused criminals in an extralegal manner. *(National Archives and Records Administration [530989])*

Wyatt Earp and his brother Morgan were appointed deputy town marshals of Tombstone, serving under their brother, town marshal Virgil Earp. They had clashed on many occasions with the Clanton gang—Ike and Billy Clanton, Frank and Tom McLaury, and Billy Claiborne. None were particularly handy with firearms, but the Clantons had been implicated in a local bank robbery. Eager to become sheriff of a nearby county and recognizing that capturing the Clanton gang could ensure him the position, Wyatt Earp turned his attention to catching the Clantons. He met with Ike Clanton, offering to give Clanton all of the reward money if he would implicate other members of his gang. Clanton seemed willing, but the death of several members of his gang in other states made it impossible to build a convincing case. Concerned that word of the deal could harm his reputation, Earp attempted to prejudice local outlaws against Ike by spreading a rumor that he had tried to sell out other members of his gang. The conflict escalated, reaching its climax on October 26, 1881, at the O.K. Corral.

Wyatt, Morgan, and Virgil Earp deputized a local tough called Doc Holliday and began stalking the Clantons. Sheriff John Behan begged the Earps to give him time to persuade the Clantons to leave town, but they ignored his pleas and continued on their way. In lot 2, block 17, behind the O.K. Corral, the Earps and Holliday confronted five members of the Clanton gang and called on them to disarm, then opened fire. In the ensuing gunfight, three of the five members of the Clanton gang—Billy Clanton and the McLaury brothers—were killed, and all of the Earp gang except for Wyatt were injured by gunfire. Although Old West folklore has it that the shootout was a fair fight, most historians believe that the Clanton gang was caught by surprise and that several members were not even armed when the gunfight began. The Earps were accused of murder and ultimately driven out of town.

Men in Black Hats

On the other side of the law, another set of brothers would become even more well known than the Earps. The outlaws Frank and Jesse James had been "bushwhackers" during the Civil War—guerrillas who fought an irregular campaign on behalf of the Confederacy in Union-dominated Missouri. The James brothers continued their campaign after the war ended. During that time, they participated in William Quantrill's burning of Lawrence, Kansas, in 1863. From 1866 until 1882, they were America's most famous outlaws, praised as persecuted Robin Hoods by Confederate sympathizers and frustrated antirailroad westerners and cursed as brutal criminals by northerners but always watched, discussed, and, in their own way, celebrated. The James brothers robbed their first bank, Liberty, Missouri's Clay County Savings Bank, in February 1866 and murdered a bystander while they were at it. They added train robberies to their repertoire in 1873 when they derailed an Iowa train, resulting in the death of the engineer.[11]

As their string of bank and train robberies (and murders) increased, law enforcement authorities grew more focused on capturing them. In January 1875, private police officers employed by the Pinkerton National Detective Agency staked out the James's mother's house and, believing that the outlaws were inside, threw an explosive device of some kind into the house. The Pinkertons and their supporters would later argue that it was either a flare or a smoke bomb, but whatever they threw managed to kill the James's nine-year-old stepbrother and maim their mother. The brothers themselves were not actually in the house. The event generated support for Frank and Jesse James and contributed to their status as sympathetic outlaws. As the reward money for the capture of the James brothers—dead or alive—increased, their criminal associates gradually found it more difficult to resist the obvious temptation. On April 3, 1882, accomplice Bob Ford snuck up behind his friend Jesse, shot him in the back of the head, and fled to claim his $10,000 reward. Frank James turned himself in soon afterward, was acquitted of all charges, and retired from his life of crime, living a largely quiet and uneventful life until his death in 1915.

No discussion of Old West outlaws would be complete without some mention of Billy the Kid, whose real name (either William B. Bonney or Henry McCarty) remains shrouded in mystery.[12] Devoted to his mother, he snapped after her death in 1874 and turned to a life of crime. The Kid shot his first victim, Frank Cahill, in 1877 (when he would have been 15 or 16 years old); Cahill had made the mistake of calling him "a pimp and a son of a bitch"[13] and paid for it with his life. After a brief stint with an outlaw gang called "The Boys," the Kid worked as a cowboy under rancher John Tunstall, a kindly English immigrant living in Lincoln County, New Mexico, who quickly became the father the Kid had never had. Tunstall was a central participant in the Lincoln County War of 1878, where conflicts between wealthy ranchers such as Tunstall and a monopolistic general store called The House grew violent. When Tunstall refused to pay a debt, he was confronted by gunmen—who had theoretically been deputized but were working for The

House—and shot in the head. The tragedy devastated the Kid, who swore revenge on Tunstall's killer, William Morton. Deputized by a sympathetic constable, who also happened to be Tunstall's foreman, the Kid and several accomplices formed a gang called the Regulators and began hunting down Morton. When they found and arrested him on March 6, 1878, they faced a dilemma: Should they take him back to the pro-House sheriff, where he would very likely be released immediately, or kill him on the spot? They chose the latter option, and Tunstall's death was avenged. The Kid and his Regulators still wanted to claim one more target: Sheriff William Brady, who had deputized Tunstall's killers in the first place. They hunted him down and killed him in April 1878, and with that act the Kid had secured his status as an outlaw.

In March 1879, the Kid had lived on the run for 11 months and was generally dissatisfied with the experience. Hoping to start over with a clean slate, the Kid offered the governor of New Mexico a deal: a full pardon in exchange for testimony against other local outlaws. The governor accepted his deal but ultimately betrayed him, allowing him to go on trial for the sheriff's murder. An angry Kid escaped from prison in June 1879 and picked up where he had left off, making his living as a cattle rustler. By this time, the Kid's notoriety had begun to catch up with him. The newly minted sheriff of Lincoln County, New Mexico, Pat Garrett, made it his personal mission to track down the nationally famous outlaw and bring him to justice. The Kid was arrested in December 1880 and sentenced to death, but he escaped weeks before his execution in April 1881 by killing two guards. His end came just a few months later, when Garrett found him. On July 14, 1881, Pat Garrett ambushed the Kid and shot him dead.

The Golden Age of the Texas Rangers

In 1823, Texas governor Stephen F. Austin called on 10 "rangers" to help monitor American Indian attacks. The Rangers served as scouts and special militia for the state until they disbanded during the American Civil War because they individually enlisted in the Confederate army and state militia ranks.

In 1874, the Democratic Party came to power in Texas and, concerned with crime and eager to reaffirm its antebellum past, recommissioned the Texas Rangers as a new, highly trained force structured to address peacekeeping, militia, and law enforcement needs. For the next 15 years, the Texas Rangers were the most elite law enforcement unit in the western territories. They shut down riots and feuds, brought a law enforcement presence to areas of the state that had none, and crossed the Mexican border to reclaim stolen cattle. But what brought the Rangers the most acclaim was their uncanny ability to track down fugitives—more than 3,000 between 1874 and 1882,[14] including some of the deadliest outlaws in the country. Two outlaws, in particular, stand out: Sam Bass and John Wesley Hardin. Sam Bass was remarkable because he was nearly impossible to catch; John Wesley Hardin, because he was exceptionally vicious and competent with firearms.

Today Sam Bass is eulogized with a ballad that states in part: "A kinder-hearted fellow you seldom ever see."[15] Bass got this reputation by spreading his stolen loot thick, inspiring loyalty with his generosity, but he was an exceptionally effective stagecoach robber. His largest heist came in September 1877, when he managed to rake in $60,000 in a single robbery—an amazing sum of money at the time. To supplement his robbery income, Bass stole cattle and operated houses of prostitution. Law enforcement had no real luck capturing this allegedly kind-hearted fellow because he had a large circle of well-paid friends who were fiercely devoted to him. One of

This photograph depicts a dress parade at New York State Reformatory in Elmira, New York. *(Library of Congress Prints and Photographs Division [LC-USZ62-83739])*

those friends was not Jim Murphy, an accomplice who informed the Rangers about a bank robbery Bass had been planning. The Rangers caught up with the outlaw on July 20, 1878, and shot him as he rode away. He died of his injuries the next day—on his 27th birthday.

Although Bass was clever, he was not exceptionally dangerous; there is no evidence that he ever actually killed anyone. The same cannot be said for John Wesley Hardin, one of the most prolific murderers of the Old West, who claimed he killed 44 people—not counting victims he had shot in the back. There is little reason to doubt his claim, as at least 35 of his murders can be documented.[16] The son of a Methodist minister, Hardin began his career in 1868 at age 15 by shooting a newly freed slave to death and then picking off the three U.S. soldiers who had attempted to capture him for the crime. After shooting a deputy sheriff to death in 1874, Hardin's notoriety increased, as did the price on his head. To save his own life, he fled from his native Texas to Florida, taking care to keep a low profile and avoid killing people en route. It did him no good; the Rangers caught up with him in August 1877 and brought him back to Texas to stand trial. Hardin received a 25-year prison sentence, studied law in prison, and began practicing law upon his release in 1894, but he was ambushed and shot to death the next year by an aging constable who felt he had it coming.

The Rangers' success in capturing outlaws was remarkable, but occasional allegations of racism against Hispanics, American Indians, and African Americans became more pronounced. Following the 1910 Mexican revolution, the Rangers engaged in a series of border skirmishes with Mexican militias and bandits. Between the years 1914 and 1919, the Rangers killed about 5,000 Hispanics.[17] But for those 15 magical years between 1874 and 1889, the Texas Rangers were as free of abuse and corruption as any comparably sized law enforcement agency in the western territories could be.

Reforming Criminals and Prisons

As criminal justice expanded into the western territories, the existing system in the more densely settled eastern states faced a process of change. Prison reformers, who had begun their work in the years leading up to the Civil War, used Reconstruction and the climate of reform it created to fix an often broken and inhumane prison system.

In 1866, the New York Prison Association commissioned minister Enoch Wines and professor Theodore Dwight to produce a study of prisons in the United States and Canada, to be delivered to the New York state legislature. When the report—arguing that the prison system emphasized retribution over rehabilitation and that "not one of the state prisons in the United States was seeking the reformation of its inmates as a primary goal"[18]—was published, the effects were monumental.

Reformers accepted the report as a call to arms, assembling the National Congress on Penitentiary and Reformatory Discipline in Cincinnati in October 1870 to discuss means of improving the national prison system. Leading penologists including Wines and Zebulon Brockway, the superintendent of the Detroit House of Correction, argued for innovations such as parole and time off for good behavior, coupled with the threat of additional time for poor behavior. The sense was that if imprisonment became more flexible, relying on indefinite sentences contingent on prisoner reform and behavior, then they could more effectively serve as a means of socially conditioning criminals to behave as productive members of society. "[T]he prisoner's destiny," according to a declaration issued by the Cincinnati Congress, "should be placed, measurably, in his own hands.[19]

When Brockway became superintendent of New York's Elmira Reformatory in 1877, he put his theory to the test. He graded each prisoner on three categories: school (attendance of and participation in educational programs offered by the prison), work (performance in the prison labor system), and general behavior. Prisoners whose behavior consistently improved received increasingly comfortable clothing and beds; prisoners whose behavior grew worse were demoted to less comfortable clothing and beds. A "first grade" prisoner—one who consistently received a perfect score in all three categories—could be subject to early release by parole after as little as one year of imprisonment. Although the system was not widely adopted at the time (and although prisoner abuse, including abuse that took place specifically under Brockway's direction, marred the reformatory system's progressive flavor), it served as an early model for a parole system that would become almost ubiquitous during the 20th century.

As social reformers focused on transforming prisoners, an increasing number of scientists, influenced by Charles Darwin's theory of evolution and the prospect of reducing human behavior to biological causes, began to look for ways of determining the sort of people who might become criminals by nature. This new field, called criminal anthropology, was pioneered by Italian penologist Cesare Lombroso, who argued in his magnum opus *L'Uomo Delinquente (The Criminal Man)* that some human beings are atavistic, or represent a step toward evolutionary regression to a lower form of life. He believed that this tendency could be pointed out based on study of specific physical characteristics, called stigmata (signs), which were exceptionally common in the criminal population but less common in the general population. These stigmata included unusual jaw size, asymmetrical facial features, and other features.

Meanwhile, the United States had produced a like-minded thinker. While conducting studies for the New York Prison Association in 1874, Richard L. Dugdale found an entire family of criminals and paupers, all descended from a common ancestor. In his study *The Jukes*, he argued that the inability to function in society was genetic and led to pauperdom, inevitably resulting in an "idiotic adult unable to help himself, who may be justly called a living embodiment of death."[20] Paupers who had vigor and would not be satisfied with life as an "idiotic adult" became even more dysfunctional criminals. Dugdale felt that paupers and criminals bred faster than more genetically gifted persons, "breeding like rats in their alleys and hovels" and threatening "to overwhelm the well-bred classes of society."[21] Decades later, this would lead to a full-scale eugenics movement based on preventing alleged genetically inferior persons from reproducing.

At this point in history, however, the conflict between the criminal anthropology of Lombroso and Dugdale and the "new penology" of Brockway and the Cincinnati Congress was ultimately a debate over the proper goals of criminal justice. If criminal behavior was inborn, then prisoner reform would have largely been a waste of time; if criminal behavior was not inborn, then dismissing the possibility of reform and redemption would have been cruel. The conflict between these two extremes would dominate the debate over criminal justice throughout the 20th century.

Chronicle of Events

1870

- *March 30:* The Fifteenth Amendment grants suffrage to African Americans and authorizes Congress to pass "appropriate legislation" to protect this right.
- *May 31:* Congress passes the Force Act, making it a federal crime to interfere with a citizen's right to vote.
- *October:* The National Congress on Penitentiary and Reformatory Discipline, a group of penologists and prison experts, meets in Cincinnati for the first time to discuss prison reform. Their "Declaration of Principles" articulates the ideas that will become known as the "new penology."

1871

- *March 3:* Congress passes the Indian Appropriations Act, declaring that American Indians will be treated as wards of the federal government and not as members of autonomous nations. This effectively removes the possibility of future treaties between the U.S. government and the governments of American Indian tribes.
- *April 20:* Congress passes the Ku Klux Klan Act, allowing the suspension of habeas corpus in cases involving the KKK.
- *April 20:* Congress establishes the Joint Select Committee to Inquire into the Condition of Affairs into the Late Insurrectionary States, which is initially formed to investigate claims of lawlessness in the former Confederacy.

1872

- The 13-volume results of the Joint Select Committee's work are published, revealing reports of widespread violence directed against African Americans.

This photograph shows the Watertown, New York, branch of the Ku Klux Klan in 1870. Klan groups of the 19th century ranged from relatively harmless fraternal orders to violent domestic terrorist groups. *(Library of Congress Prints and Photographs Division [LC-USZ62-122392])*

1873

- *April 13:* Members of the White League, a white supremacist paramilitary group, massacre about 100 African-American men in Colfax, Louisiana.
- *July 21:* Frank and Jesse James rob their first train, taking $3,000. They leave behind terrified passengers and a dead engineer.
- *October 8:* The first women's prison in the country, Indiana Women's Prison, receives its first inmate.

1874

- The Texas Rangers, formerly a state militia, are recommissioned to address law enforcement needs.
- *July 1:* Four-year-old Charley Ross, the son of a wealthy Philadelphia man, is kidnapped. Charley is never found. The kidnappers demand a ransom but refuse to show up to collect it. Later confessions and rumors connect his kidnapping to several known criminals and a corrupt former New York City police officer, but his ultimate fate will remain a mystery.
- *August 30:* The White League lynches four Republican politicians in Coushatta, Louisiana.
- *September 14–17:* The White League attempts to take over the Louisiana state government in New Orleans. They face former Confederate general James Longstreet, who leads a small group of police officers and black militiamen in defense of the governor. Longstreet loses what will become known as the Battle of Liberty Place, and the White League installs its own white supremacist government.
- *September 17:* The U.S. military reclaims New Orleans from the White League, rescues Longstreet, and reinstates the previous government.
- *December 21:* White supremacists massacre an African-American militia in Vicksburg, Mississippi.

1875

- *January 26:* Pinkertons detectives stalking outlaws Frank and Jesse James throw a smoke bomb into their mother's house, blowing her right arm off and killing Jesse's nine-year-old stepbrother. Neither of the James brothers was actually in the house at the time.

1876

- Criminal anthropologist Cesare Lombroso publishes the first edition of his *L'Uomo Delinquente (The Criminal Man)*, which argues that hardened criminals are lawbreakers by nature and that criminal tendencies can be determined based on physical characteristics such as facial asymmetry and jaw size.

- *May:* Prison reformer Zebulon Brockway becomes superintendent of the Elmira Reformatory in New York, establishing a new prison system of indeterminate sentences based on rewards and punishment.
- *August 2:* Western lawman "Wild Bill" Hickok is assassinated while playing poker. His hand—a pair of aces and a pair of eights—will become known as the "dead man's hand.
- *September 7:* After murdering a bank cashier in Northfield, Minnesota, the James-Younger gang is met with a hail of gunfire from angry citizens. The gang is effectively destroyed.

1877

- Criminal anthropologist Richard Dugdale publishes his study *The Jukes*, which argues that criminal tendencies are inborn traits passed on from generation to generation.
- *August 23:* Notorious Texas outlaw John Wesley Hardin is captured by the Texas Rangers.
- *September 19:* Texas outlaw Sam Bass and his gang rob a Union Pacific train of $60,000.

1878

- *July 20:* Texas Rangers pursue outlaw Sam Bass. Bass's gang kills a deputy sheriff, at which point a Texas Ranger named Richard Clayton Ware runs outside and shoots Bass as he rides away.
- *July 21:* Sam Bass dies on his 27th birthday from wounds inflicted by Texas Ranger Richard Clayton Ware.

1880

- Scottish missionary Henry Faulds suggests fingerprints as a possible means of identification in his paper "On the Skin-Furrows of the Hand," published in the science journal *Nature.*

1881

- *July 14:* Pat Garrett, sheriff of Lincoln County, New Mexico, tracks down and kills Billy the Kid.
- *October 26:* At the O.K. Corral in Tombstone, Arizona, the Earp brothers and Doc Holliday ambush and slaughter the local Clanton outlaw gang.

1882

- *April 3:* Enticed by the promise of a $10,000 reward, James gang accomplice Bob Ford shoots and kills outlaw Jesse James.
- *August 2:* Judge Roy Bean sets up shop as justice of the peace in the remote city of Vinegaroon, Texas.

- *October 5:* Outlaw Frank James surrenders to authorities.

1883
- French scientist Alphonse Bertillon develops a means of suspect identification based on precise body measurements.
- Judge Roy Bean moves on to the remote city of Langtry, Texas, where he will spend 20 years dispensing odd justice and collecting odder fines in his courthouse saloon, which will bear a sign that reads: "JUDGE ROY BEAN, Notary Public—Justice of the Peace—Law West of the Pecos—Ice Beer."
- *September 6:* Frank James is acquitted on all charges.

1887
- *November 23:* An unknown number of African-American workers—at least 30—are killed while on strike in Thibodaux, Louisiana.

Eyewitness Testimony

Race and Colonialism

To President Board of Supervisors:
Do you want any men? Can raise good crowd within twenty-four hours to kill out your negroes.

A December 12, 1874, telegram from J. G. Gates and A. H. Mason in Trinity, Texas, offering volunteers to resume racist attacks in Vicksburg, Mississippi, following the race riots of December 7, in which at least 30 African Americans were killed, quoted in Hofstadter and Wallace, American Violence, *p. 227.*

The police force of Indians mentioned in my last report has been continued through the year, and has rendered most efficient service. They have been faithful and vigilant, prompt to quell all disturbances, to arrest criminals, and to give full information regarding all cases that might come under their jurisdiction. So effective have they been in the discharge of their duties that only on special occasions has it been necessary for me or an employee to accompany them when sent to arrest a criminal.

After the arrival of the Rio Verde Indians the number of policemen was increased to eight. On the 31 of July, after the removal of the White Mountain Indians, I increased the number to twenty-five. They were carefully chosen from the various tribes and bands, armed with needle-guns [a new type of rifle that had been issued to the U.S. Army in the 1870s] and fixed ammunition, and placed under the command of Mr. Clay Beauford, who has been guide and scout in this country for several years.

Such is the latest organization of the San Carlos Police Force. The duties of this force are to patrol the Indian camps, to quell disturbances, to arrest offenders, to report any signs of disorder or mutiny, to scour the entire reservation and arrest Indians who are absent from the agency without a pass, and also to arrest whites who trespass contrary to the rules of the reservation. My intention is to mount the police as soon as possible, as a mounted force is far more effective, while the extra expense is but a trifle.

I wish to state further that the police force has entirely superseded the necessity of a military force. I have never yet found it necessary to ask for a single soldier to act as escort, guard, or to do any police duty.

John P. Clum, U.S. agent for the Apaches on the San Carlos reservation in Arizona, describing the first postcolonial tribal police force in a report to the Commissioner of Indian Affairs, September 1, 1875, quoted in Vila and Morris, The Role of Police in American Society, *pp. 46–47.*

Murder, foul murder has been committed and the victims were inoffensive and law-abiding Negroes. Assassins more cruel, more desperate, more wanton than any who had hitherto practiced their nefarious business in Louisiana have been shooting down, like so many cattle, the Negroes in and around Thibodaux, Lafourche parish, La.

For three weeks past the public has been regaled, daily, with garbled reports of the troubles existing between the laborers and planters in the sugar district . . . Militia from different portions of the State have been on duty in the threatened section, and during all of this time the only acts and crimes of an outrageous character committed were so committed by either the troops, sugar planters or those in their hire. The Negroes during all of the time behaving peaceably, quietly and within the limits of the law, desiring only to secure what they asked and demanding what they had and have a perfect right to do—an increase of wages.

With an obstinacy worthy of the righteousness of their cause the Negroes quartered in Thibodaux refused to acceded to the planters.

Such being the case, the planters determined to kill a number of them, thus endeavoring to force the balance into submission. The militia was withdrawn to better accomplish this purpose, and no sooner had they departed for home than the preparation for the killing of the Negroes began. Last Sunday night, about 11 o'clock, plantation wagons containing strange men fully armed were driven into Thibodaux and to Frost's restaurant and hotel and there the strangers were quartered. Who they were and where they came from, no one, with the exception of the planters and Judge Taylor Beattie, seemed to know; but it is a fact that next day, Monday, [martial] law was declared and these cavalcades of armed men put on patrol duty and no Negro allowed to either leave or enter the town without shooters, insolent and overbearing toward the Negroes, doing all in their power to provoke a disturbance . . . Finding that the Negroes could not be provoked from their usual quiet, it was resolved that some pretext or other should be given so that a massacre might ensue.

It came: Tuesday night the patrol shot two of their number, Gorman and Molaison, and the cry went forth "to arms, to arms! The Negroes are killing the whites!" This was enough. The unknown men who by this time had turned out to be Shreveport guerrillas, well versed in the Ouachita and Red River plan of killing "niggers," assisted by Lafourche's oldest and best, came forth and fired volley after volley, into the houses, the churches, and wherever a Negro could be found.

"Six killed and five wounded" is what the daily papers here say, but from an eye witness to the whole transaction we learn that no less than thirty-five Negroes were killed outright. Lame men and blind women shot; children and hoary-headed grandsires ruthlessly swept down! The Negroes offered no resistance; they could not, as the killing was unexpected. Those of them not killed took to the woods, a majority of them finding refuge in this city . . .

Citizens of the United States killed by a mob directed by a State judge, and no redress for the same! Laboring men seeking an advance in wages, treated as if they were dogs! Black men whose equality before the law was secured at the point of the bayonet shown less consideration than serfs? . . . At such times and upon such occasions, words of condemnation falls like snowflakes upon molten lead. The blacks should defend their lives, and if they needs must die, die with their faces toward their persecutors fighting for their homes, their children and their lawful rights.

An anonymous report of the 1887 Thibodaux massacre, in which a militia of angry whites shot or lynched dozens, possibly hundreds, of working-class black protesters, published in The Weekly Pelican, *November 26, 1887, p. 2, quoted in Zinn and Arnove,* Voices of a People's History of the United States, *pp. 221–223.*

The proud spirit of the original owners of these vast prairies, inherited through centuries of fierce and bloody wars for their possession, lingered last in the bosom of Sitting Bull. With this fall the nobility of the redskin is extinguished, and what few are left are a pack of whining curs.

The whites, by law of conquest, by justice of civilization, are masters of the American continent, and the best safety of the frontier settlements will be secured by the total annihilation of the few remaining Indians.

Why not annihilation? Their glory has fled, their spirit broken, their manhood effaced; better that they die than live the miserable wretches that they are. We cannot honestly regret their extermination.

This 1870 *Harper's Weekly* sketch depicts American Indians traveling under U.S.-enforced migration. *(Library of Congress Prints and Photographs Division [LC-USZ62-102450])*

Aberdeen Saturday Pioneer *editor and future author of* The Wizard of Oz *L. Frank Baum, in an 1890 editorial, quoted in Tim Carpenter, "'Oz' Author Sought Indian Holocaust,"* Lawrence Journal-World. *Available online at URL: http://www.ljworld.com/section/frontpage/story/29224.*

Criminal Justice on the Western Frontier

"Wild Bill" was a strange character, just the one which a novelist might gloat over. He was a Plainsman in every sense of the word, yet unlike any other of his class. In person he was about six feet one in height, straight as the straightest of the warriors whose implacable foe he was; broad shoulders, well-formed chest and limbs, and a face strikingly handsome; a sharp, clear, blue eye, which stared you straight in the face when in conversation; a finely-shaped nose, inclined to be aquiline; a well-turned mouth, with lips only partially concealed by a handsome moustache. His hair and complexion were those of the perfect blond. The former was worn in uncut ringlets falling carelessly over his powerfully formed shoulders. Add to this figure a costume blending the immaculate neatness of the dandy with the extravagant taste and style of the frontiersman, and you have Wild Bill, then as now the most famous scout on the Plains.

Whether on foot or on horseback, he was one of the most perfect types of physical manhood I ever saw. Of his courage there could be no question; it had been brought to the test on too many occasions to admit of a doubt. His skill in the use of the rifle and pistol was unerring; while his deportment was exactly the opposite of what might be expected from a man of his surroundings. It was entirely free from all bluster or bravado. He seldom spoke of himself unless requested to do so. His conversation, strange to say, never bordered either on the vulgar or blasphemous. His influence among the frontiersmen was unbounded, his word was law; and many are the personal quarrels and disturbances which he has checked among his comrades by his simple announcement that "this has gone far enough," if need be followed by the ominous warning that when persisted in or renewed the quarreller "must settle it with me."

"Wild Bill" is anything but a quarrelsome man; yet no one but himself can enumerate the many conflicts in which he has been engaged, and which have almost invariably resulted in the death of his adversary. I have a personal knowledge of at least half a dozen men whom he

has at various times killed, one of these being at the time a member of my command. Others have been severely wounded, yet he always escapes unhurt. On the Plains every man openly carries his belt with its invariable appendages, knife and revolver, often two of the latter. Wild Bill always carried two handsome ivory-handled revolvers of the large size; he was never seen without them. Where this is the common custom, brawls or personal difficulties are seldom if ever settled by blows. The quarrel is not from a word to a blow, but from a word to the revolver, and he who can draw and fire first is the best man.

No civil law reaches him; none is applied for. In fact there is no law recognized beyond the frontier but that of "might makes right." Should death result from the quarrel, as it usually does, no coroner's jury is impanelled to learn the cause of death, and the survivor is not arrested. But instead of these old-fashioned proceedings, a meeting of citizens takes place, the survivor is requested to be present when the circumstances of the homicide are inquired into, and the unfailing verdict of "justifiable," "self-defence," etc., is pronounced, and the law stands vindicated. That justice is often deprived of a victim there is not a doubt. Yet in all of the many affairs of this kind in which "Wild Bill" has performed a part, and which have come to my knowledge, there is not a single instance in which the verdict of twelve fair-minded men would not be pronounced in his favor.

That the even tenor of his way continues to be disturbed by little events of this description may be inferred from an item which has been floating lately through the columns of the press, and which states that "the funeral of 'Jim Bludso,' who was killed the other day by 'Wild Bill,' took place to-day." It then adds: "The funeral expenses were borne by 'Wild Bill.'" What could be more thoughtful than this? Not only to send a fellow mortal out of the world, but to pay the expenses of the transit.

General George Custer, describing Wild West legend "Wild Bill" Hickok in his serial memoirs "My Life on the Plains" (part four), published in Galaxy, *April 1872, pp. 473–474.*

The notorious outlaw, "Bill the Kid," who was killed last Saturday morning at Fort Sumner, had been stopping with the Mexicans in that vicinity disguised as one of them ever since his escape from the Lincoln county jail. Pat Garrett, sheriff of Lincoln county, has been on his track for some time, and on the day above mentioned arrived at Fort Sumner, having been put on the track by some Mexicans. He had to threaten their lives in order to get them to divulge the Kid's whereabouts.

About midnight Sheriff Garrett entered the room of one Pete Maxwell, a large stock owner residing at the fort, and supposed to have knowledge of the fugitive's exact whereabouts. Garrett had not been in the room over twenty minutes when the Kid entered in his stocking feet, knife in hand, and ostensibly for the purpose of buying some meat. He immediately observed Garrett crouching at the head of the bed, and asking Maxwell what that was, drew his revolver. Maxwell made no answer, but proceeded to crawl toward the foot of the bed. Had he answered, giving Garrett's name, Billy would have killed him at once as he is a dead shot.

Billy moved slightly, getting into the moonlight then shining in at the window. Garrett recognizing him, fired, the ball passing through his heart. He fell backward, his knife in one hand and revolver in the other. Garrett, thinking him not dead, fired again but missed. Had his first shot failed, he would have been riddled with bullets, as the Kid is coolly desperate and very accurate in aim when in close quarters. His death is hailed with great joy throughout this section of the country, as he had sworn that he would kill several prominent citizens, and had already slain fifteen or eighteen men.

A report of Pat Garrett's ambush of Billy the Kid, published in the Fort Wayne Daily Gazette, *July 26, 1881, p. 4.*

This photograph depicts train robber Jesse James (1847–82). *(Library of Congress Prints and Photographs Division [LC-USZ62-3855])*

We are once more pained to announce the death of Hon. Jesse James. We speak of him as Honorable Jesse James because it is possible that he may not be dead yet, and we do not want any personalities raked up in case he should be still at large. The regular semi-annual death of Jesse James has been the cause of national sorrow for some time. His obituary has been written seven or eight times by the faltering hands that pen these lines, and we are still young. Death has claimed Mr. James for its own a good many times, and now he has once again been butchered to make a Missouri holiday. The soil from Maine to California has been drenched with his gore, and the green grass waves above his ashes in every portion of our great land. No man has perished from the face of the earth so ubiquitously as Mr. James, and no other American citizen has yielded up his young life under such varied and peculiar circumstances. Lay him low where the bobolink blossoms on the sweet potato vine, and plant him in the valley where the pecan waves.

Born of humble and obscure parents, he rapidly rose to the proud eminence of America's leading thief and murderer. When death marked him as its victim the last time, he was as prominent a man as Henry Ward Beecher or Roscoe Conkling. His genius took a different shoot, it is true, but he won a name as a plunderer which throws the achievements of our modern bank cashiers back into the cold and calmy oblivion. Death has once more stilled the pulse of a man who, were it not for his little eccentricities as a human butcher and grand larceny connoisseur, would have made an elegant humorist or statesman. Had he been less of an enthusiast, and less radical as a murderer, he might have shone in the best society. Had he pleaded emotional insanity the first time he got up a surprise funeral, instead of making an outlaw of himself, he might not be alive, loved and respected. But he was ignorant of the law and thought that when a man murdered all the first-class passengers on a train, he would be dealt with harshly and ostracized.

Bill Nye's final obituary for the legendary outlaw Jesse James, published in Daily Nevada State Journal, *April 9, 1882, p. 1.*

Sam Bass was born in Indiana, it was his native home,
    And at the age of seventeen young Sam began to roam.
Sam first came out to Texas a cowboy for to be—
    A kinder-hearted fellow you seldom ever see.

Sam used to deal in race stock, one called the Denton mare,
    He matched her in scrub races, and took her to the Fair.
Sam used to coin the money and spend it just as free,
    He always drank good whiskey wherever he might be.

Sam left the Collin's ranch in the merry month of May
    With a herd of Texas cattle the Black Hills for us to see,
Sold out in Custer City and then got on a spree—
    A harder set of cowboys you seldom ever see.

On their way back to Texas they robbed the U. P. train,
    And then split up in couples and started out again.
Joe Collins and his partner were overtaken soon,
    With all their hard-earned money they had to meet their doom.

Sam made it back to Texas all right side up with care;
    Rode into the town of Denton with all his friends to share.
Sam's life was short in Texas; three robberies did he do,
    He robbed all the passenger, mail, and express cars too.

Sam had four companions—four bold and daring lads—
    They were Richardson, Jackson, Joe Collins, and Old Dad;
Four more bold and daring cowboys the Rangers never knew,
    They whipped the Texas Rangers and ran the boys in blue.

Sam had another companion, called Arkansas for short,

Was shot by a Texas Ranger by the name of Thomas Floyd;
Oh, Tom is a big six-footer and thinks he's mighty fly,
    But I can tell you his racket—he's a deadbeat on the sly.

Jim Murphy was arrested, and then released on bail;
    He jumped his bond at Tyler and then took the train for Terrell;
But Mayor Jones had posted Jim and that was all a stall,
    'Twas only a plan to capture Sam before the coming fall.

Sam met his fate at Round Rock, July the twenty-first,
    They pierced poor Sam with rifle balls and emptied out his purse.
Poor Sam he is a corpse and six feet under clay,
    And Jackson's in the bushes trying to get away.
Jim had borrowed Sam's good gold and didn't want to pay,
    The only shot he saw was to give poor Sam away.
He sold out Sam and Barnes and left their friends to mourn—
    Oh, what a scorching Jim will get when Gabriel blows his horn.

And so he sold out Sam and Barnes and left their friends to mourn,
    Oh, what a scorching Jim will get when Gabriel blows his horn.
Perhaps he's got to heaven, there's none of us can say,
    But if I'm right in my surmise he's gone the other way.
    "The Ballad of Sam Bass," compiled in John A. Lomax,
    Cowboy Songs and Other Frontier Ballads, 1929,
    quoted in Jesse Sublett, "Lone on the Range: Texas Lawmen of
    Lore," Texas Monthly. *Available online at URL: http://*
    www.texasmonthly.com/1000-01-01/webextra49-5.php

Criminal Justice Reform, Eugenics, and the New Penology

The appearance of the [Cincinnati] Congress is striking and has been the subject of favorable comment by the press of this city. Many of the members are men of large heads and of highly intellectual and benevolent countenances. Their refinement and culture have been obtained rather in the schools of experience, than in the learned universities. Yet they are not mere philanthropic, much less mawkish enthusiasts. They are able, I might say sharp men of business, believers in facts rather than theories, aware of the magnitude of the evils with which they have to deal, and desirous, as well as for the sake of society as from love to the inmates of our adult prisons and our juvenile refuges, to bring about the thorough reformation of these unfortunate classes and, if possible, to bridge over the great gulf which separates them from society; to do so with mutual advantage to them and to society . . .

A large number of the questions raised and treated as arising out of the papers read or suggested by them might be included under the "end and the means of prison discipline." What is the end and what are the means most conducive to it? . . . [Scholars] substantially agree that the supreme end of prison discipline is the reformation of the criminal, and the protection of society by that means; that punishment, in so far as used of necessity—the prisoner's liberty and privileges being necessarily abridged—or of choice as a means to the end in view, should be reformatory and not retributive. That principle being once admitted, and it also being admitted, as it must be—for if not self-evident it is proved by fact and experience—that kindness and culture are more powerful reform agents than force and prevention, the principal prison systems of the world stand condemned. They have been for the most part framed and administered with a view to punishment mainly, if not exclusively. They deprive the prisoner of rights and privileges, the denial of which are not necessary to his safe keeping, still less to his reformation.

Indeed, it was generally conceded that reformation was utterly impossible as long as the prisoner feels that he is treated with unnecessary severity, and thereby irritated; so long as his feelings of self-respect and manhood are being lessened or destroyed, thereby lessening his willpower . . . and striking at the very crisis of reformation. It was held that a prisoner by crime and incarceration only loses such rights and privileges as by their withdrawal are necessary in order to ensure his safe-keeping and to promote his reformation, and, as a rule, his restoration to society.

But, if this be, whence the narrow cell, the wretched bed, the comparative deprivation by night (as in many prisons) before the hour of sleep arrives, filling the mind with gloom and preventing opportunities of reading? Whence the traditional striped prison garb, the tin dippers and other degrading substitutes for respectable Christian crockery? Whence the enforced silence, destroying speech

and even reason, when long continued? Whence the refusal to communicate freely with their families and receive letters from them, often of the best tendencies? . . . Mr. [Zebulon] Brockway, in particular, in his paper on the subject, would sweep all these away, and seek elevation by amelioration and kindness from the very first.

A report on the Cincinnati Congress of October 1870, "Our Criminal Classes," New York Herald, *October 20, 1870, p. 5.*

In July 1874, the New York Prison Association having deputed me to visit thirteen of the county jails of this State and report thereupon, I made a tour of inspection in pursuance of that appointment. No specially striking cases of career criminals, traceable through several generations, presented themselves till [not included] county was reached. Here, however, were found six persons, under four family names, who turned out to be blood relations in some degree. The oldest, a man of fifty-five, was waiting trial for receiving stolen goods; his daughter, aged eighteen, held as witness against him; her uncle, aged forty-two, burglary in the first degree; the illegitimate daughter of the latter's wife, aged twelve years, upon which child the latter had attempted rape, to be sent to the reformatory for vagrancy; and two brothers in another branch of the family, aged respectively nineteen and fourteen, accused of an assault with intent to kill, they having maliciously pushed a child over a high cliff and nearly killed him . . .

These six persons belonged to a long lineage, reaching back to the early colonists, and had intermarried so slightly with the emigrant population of the old world that they may be called a strictly American family. They had lived in the same locality for generations, and were so despised by the reputable community that their family name had come to be used generically as a term of reproach.

That this was deserved became manifest on slight inquiry. It was found that out of twenty-nine males, in ages ranging from fifteen to seventy-five, the immediate blood relations of these six persons, seventeen of them were criminals, or fifty-eight percent; while fifteen were convicted of some degree of offense, and received seventy-one years of sentence . . .

The crimes and misdemeanors they committed were assault and battery, assault with intent to kill, murder, attempt at rape, petit larceny, grand larceny, burglary, forgery, cruelty to animals. With these facts in hand, it was thought wise to extend the investigation to other branches of the family, and explore it more thoroughly . . .

Observation discloses that any given series of social phenomena—as honest childhood, criminal maturity and pauper old age, which sometimes occurs in the life of a single individual—may be stretched over several generations, each step being removed from the other by a generation, and in some cases two. Consequently, the nature of the investigation necessitated the study of families through successive generations, to master the full sequence of phenomena and include the entire facts embraced in the two main branches of inquire into which the subject necessarily divides itself; THE HEREDITY that fixes the organic characteristics of the individual, and THE ENVIRONMENT which affects modifications in that heredity. It reduces the method of study, then to one of historico-biographical synthesis united to statistical analysis, enabling us to estimate the cumulative effects of any condition which has operated through successive generations: heredity giving us those elements of character which are derived from the parent as a birthright, environment all the events and conditions occurring after birth which have contributed to shape the individual career or deflect its primitive tendency.

Heredity and environment, then, are the parallels between which the questions of crime and public dependence and their judicious treatment extend: the objective point is to determine how much of each results from heredity, how much from environment. The answer to these determines the limits of possibility in amending vicious lives, and the scrutiny will reveal some of the methods which the present organization of society automatically sets in motion, which, without conscious design nevertheless convert harmful careers into useful ones. The discovery of such spontaneous social activities will furnish models to be followed in dealing with the unbalanced.

Richard Dugdale, The Jukes: A Study in Crime, Pauperism, Disease, and Heredity, *4th ed. 1877; reprint, 1970, pp. 7–8, 11–12.*

Let us imagine an institution in which the guardian of the peace can learn to make a pleasant bow, to walk with grace, to shake hands with dignity, to lift his hat in a courtly way, or to extend his protecting arm to a lady with Chesterfieldian decorum. Such arts are teachable, and could be eloquently lectured upon and illustrated by some great actor, famous for his grace of manner . . . and with what unctuous humor and fine rhetoric could our distinguished senator, Wm. M. Evarts, unfold the mystery of how to crack a pleasant joke . . .

Imagine a policeman so trained! Why, the transaction of business with him by the average citizen would be both a pleasure and an instruction. A request for the locality of a certain street would be cheerfully answered with a pleasant bow, that would send the citizen on his way refreshed and light of heart. A lady compelled to cross Broadway amid a throng of jostling vehicles, would find herself escorted with a courteous consideration that would land her on the opposite side-walk positively pleased with her perilous trip; and the unfortunate gentleman who should have worshipped too long and too often at the rosy shrine of Bacchus would find himself guided to his home, or when too far "gone," to the nearest police-station, with a dignified and shocked formality that would not only make him feel perfectly safe, but would positively shame him into a better line of conduct, because, for the moment at least, he would be the churl and the officer the gentleman. I do not know whether, in surprising a burglar at his nefarious occupation, a police-officer so schooled could stop to consider how the burglar should be accosted; but I can imagine a policeman brought to such a fine pitch of mental equilibrium that even then he would carefully weigh his words and actions, with a view not only to effect the capture of the burglar, but to preach to him in his person and bearing an effective moral lesson . . .

There are certain districts in New York, as in all great cities, where life is seen in its crudest and most revolting forms. If the police squads that perform such districts were living specimens of all that is lovely and courteous in mankind, they would breathe out an atmosphere about them that could not fail to impregnate the minds of the dullest of the denizens . . . and in due course of time it might come to pass that Mulberry and Baxter streets would begin to rival Rotten Row and the *Bois de Boulogne* in the exchange of courtesies and the practice of politeness; and every philosopher who has ever written bears testimony to the fact that good manners breed good morals . . . The development of the Kindergarten system demonstrates that no lessons are so powerful as object lessons; and what more striking and delightful daily instruction can be imagined than the perpetual appearance and reappearance of a corps of policeman so admirably trained as to be positively fascinating.

George W. Walling, a former superintendent and 38-year veteran of the New York police department, writing in his 1887 memoirs about the role of the police officer, quoted in Vila and Morris, The Role of Police in American Society, *pp. 50–52.*

CHAPTER SEVEN

The Gilded Age and Progressive Era
1890–1913

The late 19th and early 20th centuries are sometimes called "the birth of modern America."[1] These decades saw a profound transformation of life in the United States. The later stages of the Industrial Revolution drove the growth of the American economy, big businesses in fields such as steel and oil consolidated into massive corporations in efforts to operate more efficiently and control their markets, and new industries such as automobile manufacturing sprang up to market new technologies.

In addition, America became a much more urban nation; large cities such as Chicago nearly doubled in population each decade between 1870 and 1920, the number of towns and cities in the United States grew rapidly, and by 1920 the U.S. Census Bureau would report that more than half of all Americans lived in urban places.[2] Immigration also transformed the American population. In the decade between 1890 and 1900, nearly 4 million foreign immigrants came to the United States; between 1900 and 1910, nearly 9 million did.[3] These immigrants, moreover, came from different sources than their predecessors. Whereas the bulk of "old" immigrants prior to 1890 came from northern and western European countries such as Britain, Ireland, and Germany, the majority of "new" immigrants after 1890 came from southern and eastern European countries such as Italy, Poland, and Russia. The "new" immigrants were more likely to speak foreign languages, to have darker complexions, and to be Catholic or Jewish. These changes were profoundly disturbing for many Americans, and they helped generate two sets of reactions. First, on a broad level, many Americans—particularly those drawn from a growing middle class—would become involved in a wide range of "progressive" reform movements to address the consequences of these changes and to reestablish some sort of social order. And second, on a more narrow level, many would become particularly concerned about problems of crime and disorder and consider new ways to make the justice system more responsive to a changing America.

The period between 1890 and 1914 saw the birth of modern crime and punishment. On the one hand, these years saw new, widespread public attention to

Chicago's South Water Street was already a busy center of regional commerce by the time this photo was taken in 1915. (National Archives and Records Administration [521051])

spectacular crimes and trials. Even though the best-known cases (such as that of Lizzie Borden) had very little in common with the most pervasive crimes of the day, public fascination with them reflected a more general concern with crime and social change. On the other hand, these years also saw the completion of the 19th-century process of building criminal justice institutions. Police, courts, and corrections began to assume modern forms, and new institutions such as juvenile courts were created to fill gaps in the system. Justice in the American South, however, was affected less by these national trends. Instead, the emergence of rigid racial segregation in the late 19th and early 20th centuries helped to shape a system of criminal justice institutionally similar to that elsewhere but defined by legal and extralegal mechanisms of racial control.

Crime in the Public Eye

Since the 1830s, coverage of crime and justice had been a staple of newspapers. In the 1890s and 1900s, however, a series of spectacular crimes and trials dominated public attention in an unprecedented fashion. In some ways, this simply reflected the growth of the print medium, but it also reflected one way that popular concerns about larger social changes manifested themselves.

The trial of Lizzie Borden, for example, would become the most famous murder case in American history (at least until the O. J. Simpson trial of the 1990s). On August 4, 1892, the body of a leading local banker, Andrew Borden, was found in the sitting room of his locked home in Fall River, Massachusetts; soon after, his wife, Abby, would be found dead in an upstairs spare bedroom. Both had been killed by multiple axe blows to the face and head. Suspicion immediately fell upon Borden's 32-year-old unmarried daughter, Lizzie, who lived at home with her father and stepmother. Other than a maid, who was immediately cleared, no one else had been near or had access to the house that day. Although circumstances strongly suggested that Lizzie (who had been at home that morning) was responsible, no direct evidence linked her to the crime. No one had seen her do it, no murder weapon was ever found, and she did not have blood on her person or her clothing. Plus the morning's timing was so tight that it was hard to imagine how she could have accomplished the killing without detection (or, conversely, how anyone else could have done it without encountering her).

When Borden was arrested and her case came to trial in 1893, it generated a sensation. The image of a genteel, church-going, middle-class woman who did charity work on trial for murder attracted the national press to Fall River for daily coverage. In the end, the court found her not guilty. Lacking physical evidence tying her to the crime, the jury apparently could not imagine a woman of her standing committing such a heinous act. Borden's case attracted such publicity, and she went free—at least in part—because the American public and her jury clung to an image of pure, moral, and unchanging womanhood even in the midst of the massive changes going on around them.

Other murders attracted public attention because they involved celebrities. In 1906, for example, Harry K. Thaw, the son of a wealthy Pittsburgh family and a fixture of New York gossip columns, walked up to Stanford White, a well-known architect who had designed New York City's Madison Square Garden, during a nightclub show on that building's roof and shot White three times in the head. Thaw announced that White had "ruined" Thaw's wife, Evelyn Nesbit, a former actress and famed beauty. Thaw claimed that White, who had helped Nesbit get her start on the stage, had seduced her (prior to their marriage) and that he was merely taking appropriate revenge. Although there was no doubt that Thaw had committed the crime—dozens of eyewitnesses at the club saw him do it—his 1907 trial became another national sensation, generating daily front page stories in newspapers coast to coast. The combination of celebrity, sex, and violence attracted widespread interest. In addition, Thaw's lawyers, facing a difficult case, mounted a novel defense. They claimed "temporary insanity" and implicitly suggested that Thaw had been justified in killing his wife's seducer. In the end, the case was not resolved in a particularly decisive way. Thaw's first, three-month-long trial ended with a hung jury; a second trial found him not guilty by reason of insanity and sent him to the Matteawan Asylum for the Criminally Insane, from which he would be released in 1915.

The turn of the 20th century also saw a new breed of murderer capture the public's attention: America's first known serial killers. In November 1894, a man whose given name was Herman Mudgett but who lived most of his life under various aliases, including Dr. H. H. Holmes, was arrested in an elaborate insurance scam. Mudgett had arranged with a partner, Benjamin Pitezel, to fake Pitezel's death, substitute a different body, and then collect a $10,000 insurance policy. Mudgett really did kill Pitezel, though, and then kidnapped Pitezel's three children in an effort to deceive his wife and steal her share of the insurance money, traveled around the country with them, and eventually killed them all. In the end, private detectives hired by Pitezel's wife caught up with Mudgett in Philadelphia and had him arrested. During his trial and following his conviction, it became apparent that the Pitezel killings represented only the most recent of Mudgett's crimes. Throughout the early 1890s, he had posed as a doctor in Chicago, operating a drug store on the first floor of a hotel building that he owned and had designed as a castle. There, he had apparently killed a number of people, mostly women—wives and mistresses attracted to his magnetic personality or boarders attracted to Chicago by the city's 1893 World's Fair. Between his 1895 conviction and 1896 hanging, Mudgett gave a number of often-contradictory confessions to reporters, printed in lurid detail in the press, chronicling his killing spree and claiming responsibility for the death of as many as 27 people.[4] While it is difficult to separate Mudgett's crimes from his inventions, many people associated with him did disappear, and his "castle" did contain crematoria and evidence of burned human remains.

Less widely known but comparably horrific were the crimes of Belle Gunness, probably America's first female serial killer. After her farmhouse in LaPorte, Indiana, burned to the ground in April 1908, authorities found 11 bodies: two females in the house, perhaps Gunness and her daughter, and nine adult males in graves scattered around the property. Gunness had apparently advertised for husbands in Norwegian-language newspapers on the Great Plains, encouraging bachelor farmers to liquidate their assets and join her in Indiana, and then killed them. She was suspected of murdering two husbands, all of her children, and a number of other men seen around the farm over the years. Her crimes were suspected only when the brother of one of her victims arrived in LaPorte the week after the fire, looking for him. In the end, Gunness's fate remains uncertain. She was presumed dead in the fire, but the body thought to be hers was badly disfigured and was never definitively identified, so she may have slipped away.

As is the case today, popular attention to these spectacular crimes proved to be somewhat ironic because they were in no way representative of the routine offenses of the time. Middle-class female killers, celebrity killers, and serial killers were all exceptions to the rule. Instead, members of the working and lower classes committed most crimes—and particularly violent crimes. Murderers tended to be younger men, usually acted on impulse, and often killed in relatively public places under the influence of alcohol and in response to seemingly trivial disputes.

Furthermore, there is no evidence that the murder rate increased between 1890 and 1914.[5] Given the lack of nationally recorded homicide data during this period, generalization is hazardous, but the available evidence from local studies of large cities suggests that the incidence of murder was relatively unchanged during this period. In Philadelphia, homicide rates may have actually decreased at the turn of the century.[6] In spite of the rapidity of change, urban-industrial society may have produced a more disciplined population where more people had become accustomed to working regular hours, sitting in school and absorbing lessons, and absorbing values of thrift and deferred gratification—thereby becoming less likely to act impulsively and kill one another.[7] In New York City, the nation's largest city, homicide rates remained surprisingly stable in these years.[8] And in Chicago, the nation's fastest growing city, homicide rates increased sharply, but a large portion of this increase can be explained not by a change in criminal behavior but by changes in enforcement and prosecution practices. Police in Chicago devoted more effort to investigating crimes, and prosecutors started handling offenses differently, charging suspects with homicide in marginal cases (such as vehicular deaths) that would have been considered accidents earlier. These changes in legal practices suggest that even though the incidence of killing remained more or less stable, the public was becoming more concerned and increasingly expecting prosecutors and courts to do something about it.[9]

One other pattern deserves note: Throughout American cities, rates of homicide by and against African Americans remained far higher than those among whites. These disparities increased at the turn of the 20th century as southern blacks began migrating to northern cities. In Chicago the nature of homicide among blacks also began to shift as the traditional impulsive violence among young men gradually came to coexist with increased violence among families and acquaintances. As southern blacks moved to northern cities looking for freedom and often found only new forms of discrimination in jobs and housing, a small number demonstrated their frustration through violence against friends and loved ones.[10]

Progressive Police Reform

The transformation of American social conditions and the emergence of movements for progressive reform fostered calls for a more professional, more methodical system of criminal justice. Among the first targets for reform were big-city police departments.

Urban police departments of the late 19th century were notoriously tied to urban politics. Officers sometimes owed their jobs to political connections, and they frequently accepted payoffs to ignore the vice and illegal economic enterprise that characterized American cities. In addition, their methods of enforcing the law were often rough. With limited legal authority, loose structures of command and control, and courts that they felt could not be relied upon to punish offenders, many urban police used their personal discretion to maintain public order. Sometimes they mediated disputes, sometimes they disciplined offenders on their own, and sometimes they brutally beat citizens whom they believed had done something to deserve it. These patterns of policing attracted public attention and the concern of urban reformers by the 1890s. Most famously, Republican legislators in New York convened the Lexow Committee in 1894 to investigate police corruption and brutality in New York City. They discovered that police appointments were routinely bought and sold, much like many other appointments to municipal government, because they represented opportunities to make money.[11]

Moreover, the Lexow Committee focused its attention on the routine exercise of police brutality by officers such as Alexander "Clubber" Williams. Williams, against whom more than 350 public complaints had been filed by 1890, was notorious among New York police officers, widely known for his dictum, "There is more law in the end of a nightstick than in a decision of the Supreme Court.[12] The Lexow Committee forced Williams into retirement in 1895 and gave police brutality a bad reputation, but it could not effect fundamental changes in New York policing. When the crusading young legislator (and future president) Theodore Roosevelt served as co-commissioner of the New York City Police Department between 1895 and 1897, he discovered ongoing corruption and sought to remove or reassign offending officers, but ultimately failed to overcome the entrenched system.

After the turn of the 20th century, a rising generation of police leaders seeking to make their vocations more professional initiated a new wave of reform. The annual meeting of their professional organization, the International Association of Chiefs of Police (IACP), which first met in 1893 under the name of the National Police Chiefs Union, became a forum for discussing the best ways to improve policing, particularly after Washington, D.C., police chief Richard Sylvester became their president in 1901. Sylvester and the IACP advocated separating policing from politics, providing longer tenure and more job security for police administrators, centralizing control of police operations, raising the minimum educational standards for officers, and establishing training programs for new recruits.[13] While some of their goals were self-serving, they also exemplified the ideal of a more professional, efficient, and autonomous police force.

August Vollmer, who led the Berkeley, California, police department between 1905 and 1932, did more than any other police chief to make these ideals a reality. In order to attract better-qualified recruits, he established rigorous standards for job applicants and eventually recruited students from the University of California to serve as police officers. Vollmer also established a permanent training program in 1908, one of the first in the United States. While the few police schools elsewhere trained recruits primarily in military drill and firearms, Berkeley's school taught the principles of public service and scientific crime detection. Vollmer implemented technological innovations, making Berkeley's police one of the first departments to respond to radio calls from a central headquarters and drive automobiles to reach crime scenes quickly. Many of these innovations soon became standard operating procedures for police in other cities. Automobiles in particular replaced walking patrols by the 1920s.

Early 20th-century police also began to implement new methods of criminal investigation and identification. Nineteenth-century police had done very little to investigate crime; unless detectives already knew who was responsible or happened to round up a known criminal, they had few means to solve mysteries, recover stolen property, or catch killers. Moreover, in an era before systematic record keeping and information sharing, criminals could simply move from place to place to stay ahead of the law (this anonymity is one reason that killers like Mudgett could operate freely). This began to change at the end of the century, when a wave of European "criminal scientists" such as Alphonse Bertillon developed new ways of tracking offenders. Bertillon, a Frenchman, created a system of precise physical measurements of criminals, notations of distinguishing features such as scars, and photographs, all to standardize criminal investigations. By 1890, criminal scientists in Great Britain, most notably the Scottish missionary Henry Faulds, had formulated new methods of capturing and organizing fingerprints as a method of criminal identification as well. American police departments, which had used "rogue's galleries" of photographs to identify criminals since the 1890s, adopted both the Bertillon system and fingerprinting after 1900.

Police administrators also reconsidered the relationship of the police to the public. In Berkeley, Vollmer implemented programs specifically aimed at redirecting young offenders. By the late 1910s and early 1920s, he had begun to argue that police should serve as social workers, identifying boys and girls at risk for "predelinquency" and referring them to appropriate social agencies. In addition, he established a citywide "coordinating committee" to integrate the work of police, courts, schools, and social welfare agencies in dealing with troubled youths. In Cleveland, Ohio, Police Chief Fred J. Kohler implemented a different approach beginning in 1907. He tried to apply the "golden rule" to minor offenses, asking his officers to warn and release men, women, and children whom they might otherwise have arrested for drunkenness, disorderly conduct, vagrancy, or delinquency. At a time when these "public order" offenses constituted the large majority of arrests in American cities, Kohler considered the cure—arrest, exposure to the courts, and a permanent criminal record—worse than the disease. Kohler's policies generated a

The FBI recorded its 100 millionth fingerprint, that of child actor Margaret O'Brien, in 1947. *(National Archives and Records Administration [518186])*

sharp drop in arrests in Cleveland but also sharp criticism; he was forced to resign in 1909.

Police departments also became a vehicle for social reform. Social workers had urged police to exercise wider powers to protect young women and girls from what they perceived to be the moral hazards of the modern city and, in particular, the new commercial amusements that it offered. In 1905, the city of Portland, Oregon, authorized Lola Baldwin to serve as a police "operative" for the duration of that city's World's Fair. In 1910, at the urging of social welfare advocates such as the Woman's Christian Temperance Union, the Los Angeles Police Department hired social worker Alice Stebbins Wells to serve as a full-time policewoman. Wells became a tireless leader of the movement to hire policewomen in departments nationwide. These officers, however, did not serve on conventional patrols. Instead, they exemplified a particular form of "crime prevention," defined by moral concerns. They patrolled amusement parks, dance halls, and places of commercial entertainment seeking to protect young women and girls from moral corruption and thereby to prevent them from falling into lives of crime. Policewomen became fairly standard additions to big-city departments by the end of the 1910s.

New police agencies were also created during the Progressive Era. In particular, President Theodore Roosevelt created one of the first federal law enforcement agencies, the Bureau of Investigation (the forerunner of today's Federal Bureau of Investigation), by executive order in 1908. Federal law enforcers did not have much to do because most criminal offenses fell under local and state jurisdiction until Congress passed the Mann Act in 1910. This law, making it illegal to transport a person of the opposite sex across state lines for "immoral purposes," had been intended to combat interstate prostitution. In its application, however, it became a tool (enforced arbitrarily) for applying criminal sanctions to enforce the morality of unmarried consenting couples. The Harrison Act of 1914, criminalizing the possession of certain narcotics, further expanded the scope of federal criminal justice.

Prisons, Courts, and Social Reform

Like the police, courts and the routine operations of justice became more professional at the turn of the 20th century, or at least more systematic. For most of the 19th century, which arrests and cases were prosecuted depended largely on the whims of police and the demands of complainants, and defendants in routine cases usually represented themselves. At the end of the century, however, public prosecutors or district attorneys became more common, better trained, and better paid. They exercised more power over which cases proceeded and how they would be prosecuted. More or less simultaneously, defense attorneys also became more common. Serving as a criminal defense attorney became a way for young lawyers to gain reputations and clients and also to make money from court appointments. As court personnel became more professional at the end of the 19th century, court procedures became more systematized as well. In particular, plea bargaining became a common way to settle cases; the jury trial had already become less common in the 1890s. In Alameda County, California, for example, 41 percent of defendants prosecuted in the 1880s and 1890s plead guilty prior to trial.[14]

New courts exclusively for juveniles exemplify a Progressive Era ideal of using the legal system to achieve social reform. Prior to the 20th century children, and adolescents who got into trouble with the law were treated the same as adults. In Illinois, for example, the 1827 criminal code set the age of criminal responsibility at 10 years. By the end of the 19th century, however, a new concept that adolescents were different from adults, more vulnerable and more malleable, became increasingly widespread. Not surprisingly, child-welfare reformers criticized courts and penal institutions for treating adolescents like adults, arguing that sending young offenders to courts or jails was unduly punitive or that courts might be reluctant

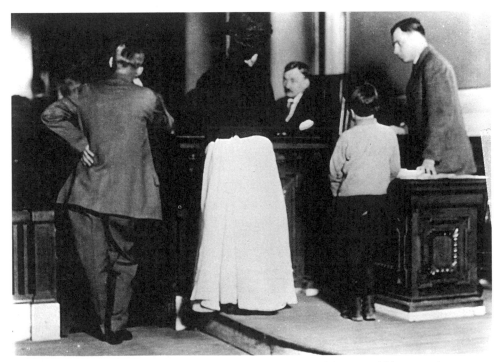

In this 1910 juvenile court hearing in St. Louis, Missouri, an eight-year-old boy stands accused of stealing a bicycle. *(Library of Congress Prints and Photographs Division [LC-USZ62-29156])*

to punish them because of their age and therefore let them off entirely. To address these concerns, turn-of-the-century social reformers—concentrated initially in Chicago—advocated the creation of special courts for juveniles separate from those for adults. By 1899, a coalition of reformers led by the Chicago Women's Club, the Chicago Bar Association, and members of Catholic and Protestant charities convinced the Illinois state legislature to pass a Juvenile Court Act establishing a juvenile court for Cook County (Chicago). This institution, which began operating on July 1, 1899, under Judge Richard Tuthill, represented the world's first juvenile court. The idea spread rapidly, however, and by 1920 almost every state provided for some sort of juvenile justice.

Under juvenile court laws, young offenders—typically boys age 16 and younger and girls age 17 and under—were to be excluded from normal criminal proceedings and processed in courts designed exclusively for them. As articulated by their most famous advocate of the early 1900s, Judge Ben B. Lindsey of Denver, Colorado, juvenile courts had a very different purpose than did criminal courts. They intended to help, not punish, young offenders. Not only would they segregate juveniles from adult offenders by providing separate detention facilities, transportation, court hearings, and correctional options, but courts would also try to diagnose the sources of delinquency and to prevent its recurrence. To do so, courts would send probation officers to investigate children's homes, discover the social and familial sources of the problems, and prescribe solutions.[15] In many ways, juvenile courts best exemplify Progressive Era optimism about using the criminal justice system to achieve social good.

In practice, juvenile courts did not fully live up to their ideals. On the one hand, their resources to achieve social change were limited. In Chicago, for example, the juvenile court only gradually accumulated mechanisms to implement its goals. Only in 1905 (six years after the court's founding) did the state permit Cook County to appropriate moneys to pay probation officers (up until that point they had been volunteers or police officers), only in 1907 did the court build a permanent detention facility, and only in 1915 did it establish a psychiatric clinic to evaluate and treat young offenders. It never had enough personnel or resources to properly manage its caseload. On the other hand, courts also expanded the power of the state over young offenders. Not only did juvenile courts hear cases involving crimes (such as theft or assault), but they also heard cases involving status offenses (such as running away, skipping school to work, or playing in the streets). For girls in an era shaped by Victorian morality and respectability, status offense charges often became an excuse for authorities and parents to intervene if girls asserted too much independence or engaged in precocious sexuality. Moreover, in city after city juvenile courts increased the numbers of children and youth under court authority and pulled the children of immigrants and African Americans disproportionately into the juvenile justice system.

While juvenile courts attempted to reform young delinquents through individual treatment, indeterminate sentences and parole were intended to do the same for adults. Around the turn of the 20th century, legislatures in state after state created broad but indeterminate sentencing guidelines for each crime, giving judges the authority to set minimum and maximum sentences and granting parole boards discretion to determine the actual release date. The logic of these new sentencing practices derived from the "new penology" of the 1870s. Indeterminate sentences would allow judges to set punishments that fit not only the crime but also the criminal, and they would allow officials in the prisons and on parole boards to determine whether an offender had been rehabilitated and was ready for release. As with

In this photograph from 1909 Boston, two children steal newspapers as a police officer's back is turned. *(Library of Congress Prints and Photographs Division [LC-USZ62-58925])*

juvenile courts, indeterminate sentences and parole faced difficulties in practice. In order to fight criticism that these new arrangements were too lenient, judges tended to oversentence and parole boards tended to stiffen release dates. As a result, the actual time prisoners served often increased under indeterminate sentencing.

More generally, the Progressive Era also saw calls for penal reform. Critics pointed out the harshness of conditions inside America's prisons and suggested that prisons could be used for not only punishment but also rehabilitation. In New York State, former businessman and public official Thomas Mott Osborne highlighted the condition of America's prisons by going undercover as convict "Tom Brown" and spending a week in Auburn Penitentiary in 1913. His 1914 account of his experiences, *Within Prison Walls*, became a focal point for the prison reform movement and earned Osborne an appointment as the warden of Sing Sing prison. Osborne's brief administration at Sing Sing is best remembered for experiments with prison democracy; the mixed results there and the glare of publicity led to his resignation. In the larger context, however, Osborne's short foray into prison administration highlights a larger transition in how prisons operated. Between the early 19th and early 20th centuries, most American prisons had concentrated on controlling their inmates and using prison industries to support the cost of their operations. Beginning in the 1910s and in 1917 at Sing Sing, prisons were increasingly influenced by the reformist and rehabilitative ethos of the Progressive Era and sought to replace their industrial-labor regimes with penal practices aimed at treating inmates.

Women's prisons also saw experiments with reform and treatment. Dr. Katherine B. Davis, who directed New York's Women's Reformatory at Bedford between 1901 and 1914, established innovative programs based on the psychiatric diagnosis of individual offenders. Like other reforms, these efforts reflected a Progressive Era optimism that the sources of crime could be identified and treated. Also like other reforms, however, Davis's efforts at Bedford reflected the difficulty of using correctional institutions to try to achieve social change. Davis's acclaimed tenure at Bedford ended in the midst of scandals over the ways that her administration mingled treatment with brutal punishments of prisoners who did not cooperate.

Progressive Era thinking about humanitarianism and reform generated somewhat contradictory results involving capital punishment and the death penalty. On the one hand, a humanitarian impulse together with a fascination with the technology of the new era fostered a movement in the 1880s and 1890s to replace hanging with a more modern and seemingly humanitarian method: the electric chair. Appeals by convicts such as Willie Kemmler, sentenced to be the first man to die in New York's electric chair, failed when the courts determined that death by electricity, while perhaps unusual, was by no means cruel. Kemmler's actual execution in 1890 gave lie to that decision, however, when he required two extended and gruesome applications of electricity before he died.

On the other hand, the reformist impulse of the Progressive Era also generated a movement to abolish the death penalty entirely. Criminal defense lawyer Clarence Darrow, for example, argued in his 1902 examination of the criminal justice system, *Resist Not Evil,* that capital punishment defeated one of the major premises of modern justice, rehabilitation of the offender. These sentiments led seven states to abolish the death penalty during the Progressive Era: Kansas in 1907, Minnesota in 1911, Washington in 1913, South Dakota and Oregon in 1914, Arizona in 1916, and Missouri in 1917.

Southern Justice

Justice in the turn-of-the-century South did not follow the same patterns as it did in the rest of the United States. Elsewhere, urbanization and progressive reform were the driving forces in reshaping the criminal justice system. Reform had its place in the South also, but that reform was distorted by the emergence of the Jim Crow system of segregation.

Legal segregation by race became the norm in most states of the former Confederacy in the 1890s. States and localities passed laws providing for separate public accommodations such as schools, public transportation, and even restrooms and drinking fountains. Furthermore, the U.S. Supreme Court upheld the constitutionality of these new restrictions in its infamous 1896 decision *Plessy v. Ferguson:* As long as accommodations of equal quality were provided for both blacks and whites, they could remain segregated. This decision established the doctrine of "separate but equal."[16] In reality, of course, "separate" very rarely meant equal, and nowhere was this more true than in the area of criminal justice. Throughout the South, states passed various statutes, or "black codes," making violations of agreements between landowners (often white) and tenant farmers (usually black) criminal, rather than just civil, matters and requiring workers (again, as it was applied, usually black) to demonstrate that they had gainful employment for fear

The body of lynching victim Jesse Washington who was burned to death by a mob in Waco, Texas, in 1916. *(Library Congress Prints and Photographs Division [LC-USZ62-35740])*

of criminal prosecutions. Measures of these types helped fill southern courts and correctional institutions with African-American men.

The racial hierarchy in the South was also maintained by extralegal means. In particular, lynchings peaked in the decades around the turn of the 20th century, with 3,700 recorded nationwide between 1889 and 1930.[17] Although lynching was a nationwide phenomenon, 80 percent of the lynchings in these decades occurred in the South.[18] And while the victims of vigilante justice had historically included people of all races, in the turn-of-the-century South they were overwhelmingly African-American.[19] Southern white defenders of lynching argued that they sought to maintain order and propriety; frequently they would explicitly maintain that the victims of lynchings were black males who had sexually assaulted white women. In contrast, opponents of lynching, such as the crusading African-American journalist Ida B. Wells, argued that lynchings almost never involved sexual assaults and that victims were rarely even accused of such crimes. Instead, victims were often African-American men who had achieved some sort of economic or political success or who refused to accept the existing racial hierarchy and who therefore represented an implicit threat to southern whites.

The South's racial system also shaped its legal punishments. As early as 1868, entrepreneurs needing labor to help rebuild the southern infrastructure after the Civil War struck deals with Mississippi state officials to work inmates outside prison walls. In 1876, Mississippi passed a "Leasing Act," making this practice of convict leasing official. While the law was race-neutral, it was clearly designed to lease African-American prisoners. Only inmates serving less than 10-year sentences could be leased. Hence, it applied to blacks victimized by the "black codes," not so much to whites whom Mississippi courts would only convict for heinous crimes carrying longer sentences. With Mississippi in the lead, most southern states established convict leasing systems in the late 19th century whereby they rented out their overwhelmingly African-American convicts to contractors needing labor for the most grueling and dangerous jobs. The practice of convict leasing faded away in the early 20th century, in part due to scandals resulting from the horrifying conditions under which these convicts lived and worked, but also in part due to protests by organized labor that leased convicts might be taking away jobs that should more legitimately go to free workers.

The emergence of a new set of prisons in the South to take the place of convict leasing also followed a trajectory shaped by race. In 1904, Mississippi again established a model for the region when it opened the Parchman State Penitentiary on a 20,000-acre cotton plantation. As conceived by Governor James K. Vardaman, Parchman was an example of penal reform. Vardaman, who had written extensively about criminal justice issues in the 1890s prior to assuming office, understood that most inmates would be released eventually and thus saw prison as a socializing agent. Parchman was thus designed to socialize its overwhelmingly African-American inmates (90 percent in 1917)[20] to be good workers in a system of tenant cotton farming and sharecropping. The prison was organized as a plantation, with no walls or cells. Instead, inmates were divided into camps surrounded by barbed wire and put to work farming under the supervision of other prisoners (called "trusties") and a sergeant, or overseer. Parchman farm resembled nothing more than a plantation, and it reproduced the racial hierarchies and sharecropping agricultural economy that existed on the outside. In the South as elsewhere, the reform of the criminal justice system was shaped by the larger dynamics of the society in which it operated.

Chronicle of Events

1890
- *August 6:* Convicted murderer William (Willie) Kemmler is executed at Auburn Penitentiary, but it does not go smoothly; he dies only after two extended applications of electricity.

1892
- *May 21:* Ida B. Wells's editorial condemning southern "lynch law" as a mechanism for whites to establish political power appears in *Free Speech,* a weekly newspaper in Memphis, Tennessee.
- *May–June:* In response to Ida B. Wells's editorial condemning lynching, white supremacists destroy the presses at *Free Speech* and force Wells to leave Memphis, launching her on a journalistic crusade against lynching in the American South.
- *August 4:* Andrew Borden and his wife, Abby, are brutally murdered at their home in Fall River, Massachusetts.

1893
- The National Police Chiefs Union (later known as the International Association of Chiefs of Police) meets for the first time in Chicago.
- *June 20:* Lizzie Borden is found not guilty for the murder of her parents Andrew and Abby Borden.

1894
- The Lexow Committee conducts a systematic investigation of the New York City Police Department, discovering systematic corruption and brutality.
- *November 20:* Herman Mudgett (alias Dr. H. H. Holmes) is arrested in Philadelphia for an insurance scam involving his partner, Benjamin Pitezel, who, along with his three children, has disappeared. Authorities suspect Mudgett of killing Pitezel, then kidnapping and later murdering the family.

1895
- Theodore Roosevelt is appointed one of four commissioners of the New York City Police Department and attempts to clean up widespread corruption.
- *September 12:* A grand jury in Philadelphia indicts Herman Mudgett for the murder of Benjamin Pitezel.

1896
- *May 7:* Herman Mudgett is executed at Moyamensing Prison, outside of Philadelphia.

Theodore Roosevelt served as New York's police commissioner before he was elected governor, and later president. *(National Archives and Records Administration [298098])*

1897
- Theodore Roosevelt resigns as co-commissioner of the New York Police Department, having achieved limited success.

1899
- Judge Ben B. Lindsey begins to operate a juvenile court unofficially in Denver, Colorado.
- *July 1:* Cook County (Chicago) Juvenile Court, established earlier that year by the Illinois state assembly, begins operations. It becomes the world's first court to officially segregate juvenile offenders from adults.

1900
- Dr. Katherine B. Davis is appointed director of New York Women's Reformatory at Bedford.

1902
- Defense attorney Clarence Darrow publishes his critique of the criminal justice system and especially capital punishment, *Resist Not Evil.*

1904

• Mississippi opens the Parchman State Penitentiary, a 20,000-acre prison farm modeled on a cotton plantation.

1905

• August Vollmer is elected town marshal for Berkeley, California, where he will serve as either town marshal or police chief until 1932.

1906

• *June 25:* Harry K. Thaw, son of a wealthy and prominent Pittsburgh family, shoots and kills well-known architect Stanford White in front of dozens of witnesses at New York's Madison Square Garden.

1907

• Cleveland, Ohio, police chief Fred J. Kohler initiates a new policy of "golden rule" policing, encouraging his men *not* to arrest people for violating public order via drunkenness or vagrancy (the most common source of arrests at the turn of the 20th century) and instead to send them home and give them a chance to reform themselves.

1908

• *April 28:* The LaPorte, Indiana, home of Belle Gunness burns to the ground. As authorities investigate the scene, they discover 11 bodies, apparently including that of Mrs. Gunness, but also those of nine previously deceased adult males.

1909

• Leonhard Felix Fuld publishes *Police Administration,* the first serious study of the subject.

This photograph shows Harry K. Thaw leaving the courtroom during his first trial. *(Library of Congress Prints and Photographs Division [LC-DIG-GGBAIN-04039])*

1910

• Alice Stebbins Wells, a trained social worker, is hired as a policewoman by the Los Angeles Police Department.
• The U.S. Congress passes the Mann Act, or White-Slave Traffic Act, of 1910, prohibiting the transport of any woman or girl across state lines for prostitution or other immoral purposes.

1913

• *September 29–October 6:* Thomas Mott Osborne, a retired businessman and former mayor of Auburn, New York, spends one week undercover as Prisoner No. 33333x at the Auburn penitentiary. The experience converts him into a leading advocate of prison reform.

Eyewitness Testimony

Spectacular Crimes

A young woman, thirty-two years of age, up to that time of spotless character and reputation, who had spent her life nearly in that immediate neighborhood, who had moved in and out of that old house for twenty or twenty-one years, living there with her father and with her stepmother and with her sister. This crime that shocked the whole civilized world, Mr. Foreman and gentlemen, seemed from the very first to be laid at her door by those who represented the Government in the investigation of the case.

We shall show you that this young woman, as I have said, had apparently led an honorable, spotless life; she was a member of the church; she was interested in church matters; she was connected with various organizations for charitable work; she was ever ready to help in any good thing, in any good deed; and yet for some reason or other the Government in its investigation seemed to fasten the crime upon her.

. . . there is not one particle of direct evidence in this case, from beginning to end, against Lizzie Andrew Borden. There is not a spot of blood, there is not a weapon that they have connected with her in any way, shape or fashion. They have not had her hand touch it or her eye see it or her ear hear of it. There is not, I say, a particle of direct testimony in the case connecting her with this crime. It is wholly and absolutely circumstantial . . .

Opening statement by A. J. Jennings for the defense in the trial of Lizzie Borden, June 15, 1893, Famous Trials: The Trial of Lizzie Borden. Available online at URL: http://www.law.umkc.edu/faculty/projects/ftrials/LizzieBorden/bordenhome.html.

FRANK LESLIE'S ILLUSTRATED WEEKLY

NEW YORK, JUNE 29, 1893.

THE BORDEN MURDER TRIAL.

A SCENE IN THE COURT-ROOM BEFORE THE ACQUITTAL—LIZZIE BORDEN, THE ACCUSED, AND HER COUNSEL, EX-GOVERNOR ROBINSON.

This 1893 issue of *Frank Leslie's Illustrated Weekly* focused largely on the lurid Lizzie Borden trial. *(Library of Congress Prints and Photographs Division [LC-USZ62-123237])*

THAW MURDERS STANFORD WHITE; SHOOTS HIM ON THE MADISON SQUARE GARDEN ROOF; ABOUT EVELYN NESBIT; "HE RUINED MY WIFE," WITNESSES SAY HE SAID; AUDIENCE IN A PANIC; CHAIRS AND TABLES ARE OVERTURNED IN WILD SCRAMBLE FOR THE EXITS

Harry Kendal Thaw of Pittsburg, husband of Florence Evelyn Nesbit, former actress and artist's model, shot and killed Stanford White, the architect, on the roof of Madison Square Garden at 11:05 last night, just as the first performance of the musical comedy "Mamzelle Champagne" was drawing to a close. Thaw, who is a brother of the Countess of Yarmouth and a member of a well known and wealthy family, left his seat near the stage, passed between a number of tables, and, in full view of the players and of scores of persons, shot White through the head. Mr. White was the designer of the building on the roof of which he was killed. He it was who put Miss Nesbit, now Mrs. Thaw, on the stage.

Thaw, who was in evening clothes, had evidently been waiting for Mr. White's appearance. The latter entered the Garden at 10:55 and took a seat at a table five rows from the stage. He rested his chin in his right hand and seemed lost in contemplation. Thaw had a pistol concealed under his coat. His face was deathly white. According to A. L. Belstone, who sat near, White must have seen Thaw approaching. But he made no move. Thaw placed the pistol almost against the head of the sitting man and fired three shots in quick succession . . .

An account of the murder of Stanford White, published in New York Times, June 26, 1906, pg. 1

Police Reform

It would seem clear without argument that with a police force so concededly efficient in the protection of life and property in all other respects, the fact of such glaring omission of duty in reference to what may be called "protected" vice and crime, presents a sufficiently strong and convincing inference of a corrupt motive, one sufficient in itself to indict the Police Department as a whole, not only of flagrant and inexcusable omission of duty, but of a corrupt purpose as well. It is inconceivable that a department, ranking with the best in the world, with a detective bureau unsurpassed by any, with superior officers conceded to be the inferiors of none in the enforcement of law and order and the protection of life and property in all other respects, should have been so phenomenally inefficient in the respects here considered, except for a corrupt purpose. Just so long, however, as the actual existence of the fact of corruption remained unproven by direct and positive evidence, just so long as the indisputable efficiency of the police in other respects enabled the department to defy criticism and thus perpetuate a condition of affairs the disclosure of which by direct evidence has caused a sensation throughout the world. . . .

It was proven by a stream of witnesses who poured continuously into the sessions of the committee that many of the members of the force, and even superior officers, have abused the resources of physical power which have been provided for them and their use only in cases of necessity in the making of arrests and the restraints of disorder, to gratify personal spite and brutal instincts, and to reduce their victims to a condition of servility. This condition has gone to such an extent that even in the eyes of our foreign-born residents our institutions have been so degraded, and those who have fled from oppression abroad, have come here to be doubly oppressed in a professedly free and liberal country. The harm thus done by engendering bitterness and hatred in the minds of multitudes of those people who look upon the police as the highest expression of governmental power, and their consequent inducement to phases of radicalism thus forced upon them cannot be estimated.

An excerpt from the Lexow Committee's 1894–1895 investigation of the New York City Police Department, reprinted in the New York Times, *January 17, 1895.*

How changed is the work of the policeman in these later days of telegraph, telephone and a thousand and one appliances of that marvelous force, electricity! When I first became a patrolman and thirty years is not so long ago, the work was vastly different. Nobody dreamed of telephones and patrol wagons then. Posts were three times as long as they are now in the cities and an officer was forced to lug his tipsy prisoner on a wheelbarrow for miles sometimes to the station. Now under the approved methods the division of labor system holds good. A policeman takes his prisoner to the nearest patrol box, a few blocks at the farthest, presses a button, says a word or two through the telephone and in a jiffy the patrol wagon with two men as a crew is at his service. In Brooklyn we are making the roundsmen keep track of their men through the patrol boxes. It is more sure, it seems to me, than the old system of going the "rounds." While I am in this branch of the topic which has been assigned to me I might say that in every way the police force has kept abreast of the march of progress.

W. J. McKelvey, "Improvements in Police Work," in Proceedings of the Third Annual Convention of the National Association of Chiefs of Police of the United States and Canada, *Atlanta, Ga., May 12–14, 1896, reprinted in Vila and Morris,* The Role of Police in American Society, *p. 60.*

If imprints of the whole ten fingers . . . of convicted criminals are kept on official record, as in England as they are now, any system of indexing them, however crude and imperfect, which enables the fresh imprint of a suspect to be confronted with that of his actual former record, must inevitably lead to prompt and unerring recognition, however large the number of resembling cases that may be classed along with it. . . .

Now that the system is no longer the fad of scientific monomaniacs, as it was supposed to be a few years ago, it has succeeded far beyond official anticipation, gives the police effective control of the great and dangerous class of professional criminals such as had never been dreamed of before the advent of finger-prints. Its institution has cost the country nothing—of even a word of thanks—and even in local police districts it has effected much saving of time and money. . . .

It has been laid down with every superfluity of emphasis that—not one finger-print but—four points of agreement in a possible forty or so which an average single finger-print contains, is enough to secure an infallible identification by the "experts" of Scotland Yard.

Henry Faulds, advocating the use of fingerprint identification and explaining its technical application, in Guide to Finger-Print Identification *(1905), pp. 70–71.*

For a great many years in Cleveland—practically always; certainly throughout the period of my service on the force—the police have done as the police do everywhere with drunks and disorderly persons, petty thieves, bad boys and small offenders generally—we ran them in. It was the custom in Cleveland; it is still the custom of practically the whole world, and customs—ground as they are into the fibre of men's minds—are hard to break. But we have broken the custom of the world and ages in Cleveland. We are treating men as men, even when they are drunk; even when they disturb the peace; even when they insult the dignity of a policeman. We often make arrests, but even then we deal with our prisoners as citizens, as human beings. And we all like the change, not only the offenders, but the police. It works, humanity does—the results of our so-called Golden Rule Policy are good . . .

I know, and you know men who have erred thus in youth, and yet late have become good citizens; yes, some of them are the leading citizens of the country. Some of them are chiefs of police. As we all know, with some, crime is a disease; with others it is a lack of proper education, training, and healthy environments, and with others, it is weakness—inability to resist temptation. Now, I finally concluded that it was our duty not to help these unfortunates on their downward course, but to save them. It seemed to me it was up to the police to learn to know the difference between a thief, a mischievous man or boy. And why not? Of all men, who is so able to judge whether an arrest is necessary as a policeman if given the opportunity? Who knows the neighborhood? Who is first on the scene? Who has all the facts and circumstances at first hand—before there has been time to destroy or make up evidence?

Upon these observations and thoughts my policy is formed. Firm in the belief that some remedy was necessary, I decided to experiment. I determined to have my policemen use their best human instincts. I proposed that my men should exercise that discretion that judges did not always exercise . . .

First—Juveniles were never to be placed in city prisons. They were to be taken home or the parents sent for and the child turned over to them with a warning for parental correction.

Second—Intoxicated persons were to be taken or sent home, unless it seemed necessary for the protection of their lives or their property to confine them until sober. And in that case they were to be allowed to plead guilty, and, by signing a waiver of trial, let go without appearing in court . . .

Third—Juveniles and intoxicated persons are cited only because they appear to be in the majority, but apparent offenders of any misdemeanor charges are warned and released by simply taking their names and address, unless it can be shown that the offense was committed with malice and forethought—with the intention to injure the person or property of another . . .

Chief Fred J. Kohler, "Arrests of First Offenders," International Association of Chiefs of Police, 15th Annual Session, *Detroit, Michigan, June 2–5, 1908, reprinted in* Proceedings of the Annual Conventions of the International Association of Chiefs of Police, 1906–1912, *vol. 2, pp. 30–32.*

In considering the qualifications required of candidates for appointment as police patrolmen, we noticed with what scrupulous care the examiners inquire into the candidate's physical efficiency, and we also learned that the inquiry into the candidate's intellectual fitness is generally confined to a short examination in the common branches. In the professional training received by the policemen during their probationary period, and the intellectual training is confined to instruction in the rules and regulations of the department by the obsolete method of catechetical instruction. It is certainly true that the police officer must possess physical powers rather than intellectual powers, that he must first act rather than think, but a moment's reflection will convince anyone that he must think as well as act.

It is this element of individual discretion which distinguishes the police officer from the soldier. The soldier is merely a part of a great military machine; it is his duty to obey the orders of his superior without individual reflection. The policeman, on the other hand, does not always nor even generally act under the immediate supervision of his superior officer and, accordingly, he must himself determine by the exercise of a sound discretion whether he shall act or not, and if he decides to act, what he shall do and how he shall do it. To fit him for the performance of this important function the ideal police officer ought to receive a professional training similar in some respects to that now required of applicants for the position of probation officer,—a good secondary education followed by a special course of study in sociology and the special problems of police duty. It is probably impracticable to demand of policemen such an education at the present time as a condition precedent to appointment, but, bearing this ideal in mind, we can improve the present unsatisfactory intellectual ability of the police officer in two respects,—by supplying the police officers during their probationary period suitable instruction by competent teachers in place of the old-fashioned catechetical instruction, and by offering inducements to men of good general education, high school graduates and college-bred men, to enter the higher ranks of the uniformed force and make the police business their lifework.

Leonhard Felix Fuld, Police Administration, *1909, quoted in Vila and Morris,* The Role of Police in American Society, *p. 81.*

The prime advantage of the automobile over this horse-drawn vehicle is its economy. Consider the economy of time in a suburban run of twelve miles from the city as compared with the time consumed by a horse-drawn vehicle over the same distance, and you will find a difference of several hours. Can you tell me where time is more truly money than in this great department of police service? I think each of us can readily recall numerous instances where, if we had been just a few minutes earlier in getting to the scene of trouble, we might have saved later on endless hours of work in our efforts to locate and apprehend fugitives.

With the now common use of telephones, there are now many instances where police stations are called up at all hours of the night by female members of households who may hear noises or see suspicious persons lurking about their places. Since almost every home is now provided with a telephone, the quick response of the automobile has resulted in much good and general satisfaction to our people. On several occasions we were able to reach residences and surround the house before the burglars came out with their loot, whereas, if response had been made to these calls in the old-fashioned way, I am quite sure the birds would have flown long before the wagon reached the scene . . .

The horse as a means of locomotion is restricted in strength, speed and endurance, but the automobile never tires, and in my opinion it will only be a short time when it will be universally adopted for patrol service in all of the police departments in the country.

J. H. Hager, "The Automobile as a Police Department Adjunct," in International Association of Chiefs of Police: Sixteenth Annual Session, *Buffalo, N.Y., June 15–18, 1909, reprinted in Vila and Morris,* The Role of Police in American Society, *pp. 82–84.*

There are some who are criminals by inheritance and some who are made so through domestic neglect. While the function of the police in past has been to deal with criminals as they find them, in this progressive age those who, in addition to preventing a crime or solving a mystery, exercise an influence for the eradication of criminal instincts where they may be early brought to their attention, whether they be hereditary or the result of environment, are rendering a service to humanity.

The value of such service has been practically demonstrated by the heads of police departments in some of our cities, who have led in eliminating slum resorts, reducing overcrowded tenements, furnishing and protecting public playgrounds, protecting children against dissipated and criminal parents, enforcing the gambling and cigarette laws, rescuing girls under age from evil resorts, excluding youth from disreputable localities and aiding in the maintenance of houses of detention and juvenile courts . . .

These improvements in the police service are in line with the prevailing sentiment that there is no necessity for maltreatment of prisoners. Antiquated methods were those where violators received severe penalties at the hands of the police force before they were arraigned in court, where they were dragged through the streets and, in some instances, first intimidated by a good clubbing. The patrol wagon and signal service have been devised as remedial agents for such practices, but, more than all else, the improved standard of the American policeman has contributed to humane methods. While physical strength is essential, members of the force should be taught to realize that intelligence and tact are more far reaching and effective in the securing of prisoners. As conditions have improved and enlightened methods been introduced, the treatment of the law-breaker must keep pace with surroundings so that his overtaking and punishment call for study and skill. An officer of the law should know that he is not only the instrument of apprehension and arrest, but that his duty is to accomplish the work with the least amount of friction . . .

Richard Sylvester, chief of the Washington, D.C., police and president of the International Association of Chiefs of Police, arguing in 1910's "Principles of Police Administration" for a more professional model of policing. Journal of Criminal Law and Criminology *1 (September 1910): 410–416.*

The arrival of the Woman Police Officer is a striking commentary upon the changed conditions of our day.

During the last half century the world has been frequently reminded that women could not be police officers and could not be soldiers . . . The battles of the future will be intellectual and moral battles, and a vast army of women have been studying and working to prepare themselves as no body of soldiers has ever done before to help wage victorious warfare against the forces that would destroy the race.

Out of the many which might be named, two generally inclusive reasons for the woman police officer center our attention.

1st—The police department is the great peace army. Its province is to keep the peace, to prevent crime through maintaining law and order.

During the last 25 years an active spirit of prevention has manifested itself in every line of human activity. A spirit based, no doubt, upon two deepest promptings—the quickening sense of brotherhood, of mutual responsibility, and the very self-preservation of the race under our increasing social complications. The woman officer is an emphasis upon the prevention spirit of police work.

2nd—To-day men, women and children face together industrial vicissitudes and society commingle. Therefore, it now requires the best that both men and women can give, in the police department as elsewhere, to adequately meet the needs and properly handle men, women, and children. Naturally, then, the woman's work concerns itself mostly with women and children . . .

Coming naturally under the domain of the woman officer are the places of amusement where the young gather—dance halls, skating rinks, picture shows, penny arcades, amusement parks, etc. Whenever it is necessary to make an arrest, the woman officer can make it, and carry the case through the court just as her brother officer would.

Alice Stebbins Wells, "Women on the Police Force," The American City 8 (April 1913), p. 401.

Criminal Justice and Social Reform

Punishments are cruel when they involve torture or a lingering death; but the punishment of death is not cruel within the meaning of that word as used in the constitution. It implies there is something inhuman and barbarous,—something more than the mere extinguishment of life. The courts of New York held that the mode adopted in this instance might be said to be unusual because it was new, but that it could not be assumed to be cruel in the light of that common knowledge which has stamped certain punishments as such; that it was for the legislature to say in what manner sentence of death should be executed; that this act was passed in the effort to devise a more human method of reaching the result; that the courts were bound to presume that the legislature was possessed of the facts upon which it took action; and that by evidence taken *aliunde* [from elsewhere] the statute that presumption could not be overthrown. They went further, and expressed the opinion that upon the evidence the legislature had attained by the act the object had in view in its passage. The decision of the state courts sustaining the validity of the act under the state constitution is not re-examinable here, nor was that decision against any title, right, privilege, or immunity specially set up or claimed by the petitioner under the constitution of the United States.

C. J. Fuller, delivering the opinion of the New York State Supreme Court in In re Kemmler *(1890), reprinted in Vila and Morris,* Capital Punishment in the United States, *pp. 68–69.*

FAR WORSE THAN HANGING; KEMMLER'S DEATH PROVES AN AWFUL SPECTACLE; THE ELECTRIC CURRENT HAD TO BE TURNED ON TWICE BEFORE THE DEED WAS FULLY ACCOMPLISHED.

Auburn, NY, Aug. 6 [1890]—A sacrifice to the whims and theories of the coterie of cranks and politicians who induced the Legislature of this State to pass a law supplanting hanging by electrical execution was offered to-day in the person of William Kemmler, the Buffalo murderer. He died this morning under the most revolting circumstances, and with his death there was placed to the discredit of the State of New York an execution that was a disgrace to civilization.

Probably no convicted murderer of modern times has been made to suffer as Kemmler suffered. Unfortunate enough to be the first man convicted after the passage of the new execution law, his life has been used as the bone of contention between the alleged humanitarians who supported the law, on one side, and the electric-light interests, who hated to see the commodity in which they deal reduced to such a use as that. For fifteen months they have been fighting as to whether he should be killed or not, and the question has been dragged through every court. He has been sentenced and resentenced to death, only to be dragged back from the abyss by some intricacy of the law.

The uncertainty in which he has lived so long would have driven any ordinary man insane. That suffering has culminated in a death so fearful that people throughout the country will read of it with horror and disgust.

The execution cannot merely be characterized as unsuccessful. It was so terrible that word fails to convey the idea. It was, as those who advocated it desired that it should be, attended by men eminent in science and in medicine, and they almost unanimously say that this single experiment warrants the prompt repeal of the law. The opinion is further expressed that the public will demand its repeal, and that it is the first and last electrical execution that this State will ever witness. As might be expected, such of the so-called humanitarians as witnessed Kemmler's fearful death still insist that their hobby will be a success "under proper conditions." The publication of the scenes that were enacted in the death room will probably prevent them from having an opportunity to prove their assertion . . .

"Goodbye, William," said [Warden] Durston, and a click was heard. The "good-bye" was the signal to the men at the lever. The great experiment of electrical execution had been launched. New York State had thrown off forever the barbarities, the inhumanities of hanging its criminals. But had it? Words will not keep pace with what followed. Simultaneously with the click of the lever the body of the man in the chair straightened. Every muscle of it seemed to be drawn to its highest tension. It seemed as though it might have been thrown across the chamber were it not for the straps which held it. There was no movement of the eyes. The body was as rigid as though cast in bronze, save for the index finger of the right hand, which was closed up so tightly that the nail penetrated the flesh on the first joint, and the blood trickled out on the arm of the chair . . .

After the first convulsion there was not the slightest movement of Kemmler's body. An ashen pallor had overspread his features. What physicians know as the "death spots" appeared on his skin. Five seconds passed, ten seconds, fifteen seconds, sixteen, and seventeen. It was just 6:43 when Dr. [E. C.] Spikzka, shaking his head, said: "He is dead." Warden Durston pressed the signal button, and at once the dynamo was stopped. The assembled witnesses who sat as still as mutes up to this point gave breath to a sigh. The great strain was over. Then the eyes that had been momentarily turned from Kemmler's body returned to it and gazed with horror on what they saw. The men rose from their chairs impulsively and groaned at the agony. "Great God! He is alive! . . .

Again came that click as before, and again the body of the unconscious wretch in the chair became as rigid as one of bronze. It was awful, and the witnesses were as horrified by the ghastly sight that they could not take their eyes off it. The dynamo did not seem to run smoothly. The current could be heard sharply snapping. Blood began to appear on the face of the wretch in the chair. It stood on the face like sweat.

A report on the execution of William Kemmler, published in New York Times, *August 7, 1890, p. 1.*

All punishment and violence is largely mixed with the feeling of revenge,—from the brutal father who strikes his helpless child, to the hangman who obeys the orders of the judge; with every man who lays violent unkind hands upon his fellow the prime feeling is that of hatred and revenge. Some human being has shed his neighbor's blood; the state must take his life. In no other way can the crime be wiped away. In some inconceivable manner it is believed that when this punishment follows, justice has been done. But by no method of reasoning can it be shown that the injustice of killing one man is retrieved by the execution of another, or that the forcible taking of property is made right by confining some human being in a pen. If the law knew some method to restore a life or make good a loss to the real victim, it might be urged that justice has been done. But if taking life, or blaspheming or destroying the property of another be an injustice, as in our short vision it seems to be, than punishing him who is supposed to be guilty of the act, in no way makes just the act already done. To punish a human being simply because he has continued a wrongful act, without any thought of good to follow, is vengeance pure and simple, and more detestable and harmful than any casual isolated crime.

Defense attorney Clarence S. Darrow, writing in his 1902 book Resist Not Evil, *pp. 56–57.*

I do not know how to explain what may be done with the juvenile court and its offices better than to tell what has been done in the court over which I have the honor to preside and to refer to some of the principles underlying the methods pursued.

Its purpose is of course to prevent crime before crime is actually committed; to correct, to aid, and assist those who might be criminals, or who might do a criminal act, to avoid falling into either misfortune. It deals only with children and those responsible for the faults of children. It realizes that we can not have good men and women unless we start with good children. Because of infancy both the constitution and laws of the State and public sentiment will justify methods of dealing with children which would not be tolerated in dealing with adults. It believes in which statistics show, that the inception of crime is in the waywardness of misdirected children. It would take care of these children in adolescence, when character is plastic and can be molded as clay in the potter's hands. It would help to form character and not postpone the evil day in a bungling attempt to reform it. All of this is easily said. It is not so easily done. It can be done. It is being done in some cities. It is a strenuous life. It requires men and women of intelligence, tact, skill, and enthusiasm. It is not so much the law as the work. It is not so much the statute as those who administer it. But I do not want to underestimate the importance of the law. Without it we would be fearfully handicapped; and yet without any statutory law, but invoking the principles of the chancery courts for hundreds of years in dealing with the welfare of children of the State, and with intelligent, earnest effort much can be accomplished in any city in this land to relieve some of the distressing conditions imposed by the criminal law . . .

The result of this system has been to encourage boys to assist the court not only in helping them, but in helping other boys who are disposed to evil ways. Let me illustrate the idea with a few cases in point: one evening five boys came to my chambers at the courthouse to see me. I had never seen but one of the boys before. This particular boy was what we might class as a "street boy," in fact, originally a very difficult and dangerous case. He said to me, "Judge, I told dese kids that they was sure to get caught by the cops for swipin' wheels, and we's been talkin' it over, and just concluded that the best thing to do was to come up here and snitch up. I told de kids dey would get a square deal." I soon became acquainted with these boys, although I was amused at first to notice the apparent fear or trepidation, mixed with doubt and misgivings, upon the countenances of the four new ones. They were not yet satisfied that the assurances of their friends were as safe as represented. We were not long in becoming fast friends, however, and those boys, in a free and easy fashion, gave me the history of their pilferings, which disclosed that I had upon my hands a very serious case. The result was a free, easy, and friendly talk which did not involve either preaching, cross words, or threats. I just talked with those boys as though I was one of them, a companion and a friend in trouble, and advising the best way out, and the best way to keep out for all time. Four of those boys are to this day voluntary probationers. They have never even been charged or tried for any offense, although they had thirteen stolen bicycles to their credit, or rather discredit. I personally investigated at the police station, and found complaints that fitted exactly the number they admitted. The wheels had been discharged and shifted around, and either sold or destroyed.

I remember telling this incident to a police officer, a good man at heart, and he did not exactly agree with me in my method of treating the case. He thought the boys should have been arrested, and an effort made to return the wheels. This was very impracticable under the circumstances. I told him that I thought more of the boys than I did of the wheels; that I believed there was an even greater duty to save those boys than to save the bicycles, notwithstanding that I respected the rights of the owners. I haven't a particle of doubt that

the result of that incident was to save many citizens' property which would otherwise have been stolen . . . I have been entirely satisfied with the result. For over a year these boys have been reporting to me on an average once every two weeks . . . during that time, I am sure their lives have been entirely free from thefts or other serious improprieties. Had any of these boys shown a disposition to return to their former bad habits, it was thoroughly understood between us that I retained the privilege to have them charged with the offense they had voluntarily confessed.

Ben B. Lindsey, "The Reformation of Juvenile Delinquents through the Juvenile Court," in Barrow, Children's Courts in the United States, (1904), pp. 30–31, 34–35.

Why is it not just and proper to treat these juvenile offenders, as we deal with the neglected children, as a wise and merciful father handles his own child whose errors are not discovered by the authorities? Why is it not the duty of the state, instead of asking merely whether a boy or a girl has committed a specific offense, to find out what he is, physically, mentally, morally, and then if it learns that he is treading a path that leads to criminality, to take him in charge, not so much to punish as to reform, not to degrade but to uplift, not to crush but to develop, not to make him a criminal but a worthy citizen.

And it is this thought—the thought that the child who has begun to go wrong, who is incorrigible, who has broken a law or an ordinance, is to be taken in hand by the state, not as an enemy but as a protector, as the ultimate guardian, because either the unwillingness or inability of the natural parents to guide it toward good citizenship has compelled the intervention of the public authorities; it is this principle, which, to some extent theretofore applied in Australia and a few American states, was first fully and clearly declared, in the Act under which the Juvenile Court of Cook County, Illinois, was opened in Chicago on July 1, 1899, the Hon. R. S. Tuthill presiding.

Julian W. Mack, "The Juvenile Court," Harvard Law Review 23 (December 1909–10), p. 107.

Thus I was drawn to the prison almost in spite of myself; and, becoming more and more interested, I felt that there was a great need of some one's making a study at first hand—some one sympathetic but not sentimental—of the thoughts and habits of the men whom the state holds in confinement. It is easy to read a textbook on civil government and then fancy we know exactly how the administration of a state is conducted; but the actual facts of practical politics are often miles asunder from textbook theory. In the same way "the Criminal" has been extensively studied, and deductions as to his instincts, habits, and character drawn from the measurements of his ears and nose; but I wanted to get acquainted with the man himself, the man behind the statistics.

So the idea of some day entering prison and actually living the life of a convict first occurred to me more than three years ago. Talking with a friend, after his release from prison, concerning his own experience and the need of changes in the System, I brought forward the idea that it was impossible for those of us on the outside to deal in full sympathy and understanding with the man within the walls until we had come in close personal contact with him, and had had something like a physical experience of similar conditions . . .

. . . there were in Auburn Prison two types of punishment cells: the jail, and screen cells . . . The jail at Auburn is at present the place where all offenders against prison discipline are sent for punishment.

Whether the offense is whispering in the shop or a murderous assault upon an inmate or a keeper, the punishment is exactly the same, varying only in length. So far as I can learn, there is no specific term for any offense; so that when a man goes to the jail, he never knows how long he may be kept there. The official view, as I understand it, is that no matter what the cause for which the man is sent to the jail, he had better stay there until "his spirit is broken."

. . . Now I truly am a prisoner; I can not possibly get myself out of this iron cage, and there is no one to let me out. There is no one except my fellow prisoners within hearing, no matter how loud I might cry for help. This is at any rate the real thing, whatever can be said of the rest of my bit. And now that all chance of escape is gone I begin to feel more than before the pressure of the horror of this place; the close confinement, the bad air, the terrible darkness, the bodily discomforts, the uncleanness, the lack of water. My throat is parched, but I dare not drink more than a sip at a time, for my one gill—what is left of it—must last until morning. And then there is the constant whirr-whirr-whirring of the dynamo next door, and the death chamber at our backs . . .

Is it imagination that the very air here seems to be tainted with unseen but malign and potent influences, bred of the cruelty and suffering—the hatred and madness which these cells have harbored? If ever there was a spot haunted by spirits of evil, this must surely be the

place. I have been shown through dungeons that seemed to reek with the misery and wretchedness with which some lawless medieval tyrant had filled them; but here is a dungeon where the tyrant is an unreasoning, unreachable System, based upon the law and tolerated by good, respectable, religious men and women. Even more than the dungeons of Naples is this "the negation of God"; for its foundation is not the brutal whim of a degenerate despot, but the ignorance and indifference of a free and civilized people. Or rather, this is worse than a negation of God, it is a betrayal of God.

Prison reformer Thomas Mott Osborne, Within Prison Walls: Being a Narrative of Personal Experience during a Week of Voluntary Confinement in the State Prison at Auburn New York, *(1914), pp. 3, 204–205, 231–232, 240–241.*

Lynching and Racial Discrimination

All the tables for various states and cities confirm the census data, and show without exception that the criminality of the negro exceeds that of any other race of any numerical importance in this country. Only a very searching inquiry can fully disclose the most important phases of this subject, but it has been shown that in this respect education has utterly failed to raise the negro to a higher level of citizenship, the first duty of which is to obey the laws and respect the lives and property of others . . .

The crime of lynching is the effect of a cause, the removal of which lies in the power of the colored race. Rape is only one of the many manifestations of an increasing tendency on the part of the negro to misconstrue personal freedom into sexual license, and this tendency, persisted in, must tend toward creating a still wider separation of the races. The fact that lynchings should be frequent is a natural consequence of a social and political condition under which the frequent commission of the crime of rape is possible. Until the negro learns to respect life, property, and chastity, until he learns to believe in the values of a personal morality operating in his everyday life, the criminal tendencies brought out in the foregoing tables will increase, and by so much the social and economic efficiency of the race will be decreased.

. . . in the statistics of crime and the data of illegitimacy the proof is furnished that neither religion nor education has influenced to an appreciable degree the moral progress of *the race.* Whatever benefit the individual colored man may have gained from the extension of

Ida B. Wells was the leading antilynching activist of her time. *(Library of Congress Prints and Photographs Division [LC-USZ62-107756)]*

religious worship and educational processes, *the race* as a whole has gone backwards rather than forwards. While it is not possible to prove by statistics that the moral condition of the slaves was exceptionally good, all the data at my command show that physically the race was superior to the present generation, and no physical health is possible without a fair degree of sexual morality. It is true that the sexual relations were as law as they are not, but they were lax in the nature of concubinage or irregular sexual intercourse, in which affection played at least a small if not an important part. In the irregular sexual relations of the present day prostitution for gain is the prevailing rule, and one of the determining causes of the inordinate mortality and high degree of criminality.

Statistician Frederick L. Hoffman, offering a partial defense of lynching in his book Race Traits of the American Negro, *(1896), pp. 228, 234–236.*

Our country's national crime is lynching. It is not the creature of an hour, the sudden outburst of uncontrolled fury, or the unspeakable brutality of an insane mob. It represents the cool, calculating deliberation of an intelligent people who openly avow that there is an "unwritten law" that justifies them in putting to death without complaint under oath, without trial by jury, without opportunity to make defense, without right of appeal . . .

The alleged menace of universal suffrage having been avoided by the absolute suppression of the negro vote, the spirit of mob murder should have been satisfied and the butchery of negroes should have ceased. But men, women, and children were the victims of murder by individuals and murder by mobs, just as they had been killed at the demands of the "unwritten law" to prevent "negro domination." Negroes were killed for disputing over terms of contracts with their employers. If a few barns were burned some colored man was killed to stop it. If a colored man resented the imposition of a white man and the two come to blows, the colored man had to die, either at the hands of the white man then and there or later at the hands of the mob that speedily gathered. If he showed a spirit of courageous manhood he was hanged for his pains, and the killing was justified by the declaration that he was a "saucy nigger." Colored women have been murdered because they refuse to tell the mobs where relatives could be found for "lynching bees." Boys of fourteen years have been lynched by white representatives of American civilization. In fact, for all kinds of offenses—and for no offenses—from murders to misdemeanors, men and women are put to death without judge or jury; so that, although the political excuse was no longer necessary, the wholesale murder of human beings went on just the same. A new name was given to the killings and a new excuse was invented for doing so.

Again the aid of the "unwritten law" is invoked, and again it comes to the rescue. During the last ten years a new statute has been added to the "unwritten law." This statute proclaims that for certain crimes or alleged crimes no negro shall be allowed a trial; that no white woman shall be compelled to charge an assault under oath or to submit any such charge to the investigation of a court of law. The result is that many men have been put to death whose innocence was afterward established; and today, under the reign of the "unwritten law," no colored man, no matter what his reputation, is safe from lynching if a white woman, no matter her standing or motive, cares to charge him with insult or assault.

Ida B. Wells, "Lynch Law in America," Arena *23 (January 1900), pp. 15–24, quoted in Shi and Mayer,* For the Record, *pp. 138–139.*

CHAPTER EIGHT

Bootleggers and G-Men

1914–1933

The first few decades of the 20th century brought to life a new, nationalized United States. For much of the 19th century, even through the Progressive Era, criminal justice was primarily a state matter. It was only with World War I and the fear of dissent, with the Nineteenth Amendment and the emergence of Prohibition, and

Louisiana governor Huey "Kingfish" Long, like many immensely popular isolationist politicians, condemned U.S. involvement in World War I as a failure of foreign policy. *(Library of Congress Prints and Photographs Division [LC-USZ62-111014])*

with interstate crime and the Federal Bureau of Investigation (FBI) that an important and clearly defined national criminal justice system began to take shape. Other, more specific concerns also called for a more nationalized approach. The horrific Parker and Lindbergh child murder-kidnapping cases, which the newspapers of the time covered in every excruciating detail, tore at the sympathies of the U.S. public and seemed to demand a dramatic response. Interstate bandits such as John Dillinger, Bonnie and Clyde, and Pretty Boy Floyd used automobiles in their crimes and achieved a notoriety rivaling that of 19th-century frontier outlaws. And a 1931 federal commission report highlighted both abuses and inadequacies of local law enforcement systems—inadequacies that, over time, demanded more federal intervention.

During the period between 1914 and 1933, the most visible question facing U.S. criminal justice was how the growing federal criminal justice system would combat the dangers presented by modern society. How would the nascent structure deal with the problems of World War I, Prohibition, and Great Depression banditry? The federal system's awkward first steps, some wildly successful, some wildly unsuccessful, have defined its role ever since.

The Wartime Crisis of Order

At the time of his arrest in 1914, Gavrilo Princip was a meek, sad-looking young man. He had always been; his years of struggling with tuberculosis had nearly taken his life, and despite military aspirations, his less-than-intimidating appearance had prevented him from ever becoming the heroic soldier he wanted to be. He wanted to fight for his Serbian homeland during the First Balkan War of 1912, but he was rejected for being too small, weak, and frail. The teenage Princip decided that he would one day commit an act of great courage—an act that would show that he meant something. He began to enthusiastically participate in the Serbian nationalist movement, which proposed expanding the newly independent state of Serbia to include ethnic Serbs living in regions under the political control of the powerful Austro-Hungarian Empire. Although Princip had never affiliated himself with terrorist organizations, he somehow caught the eye of organizers in the Black Hand, a violent Serbian revolutionary movement. The organizers came to him with a bold assignment: help terrorists kill Archduke Franz Ferdinand, heir to the throne of Austria-Hungary.

Franz Ferdinand had always been a voice of moderation and peace, urging calm during the Balkan War. An unpretentious man, Ferdinand traveled to the Bosnian city of Sarajevo to meet with a population many of whom were hostile toward Austrian rule. When he arrived on the morning of June 28, 1914, Sarajevo proved to be even more hostile than he had expected. One of the Black Hand terrorists working with Princip threw a grenade at Franz Ferdinand's carriage, hitting the carriage behind it and sending two members of the entourage to the hospital. Although Franz Ferdinand was shaken, he was very much alive. The planned assassination attempt was unsuccessful. Princip and his companions went their separate ways, convinced that they had failed.

As the archduke's carriage rode through Franz Josef Street, Franz Ferdinand instructed his driver to stop and drive to the hospital so that he could visit his injured companions. Through a strange twist of fate, the unimposing, 19-year-old Princip was walking toward a restaurant and saw the vehicle halt. Spying his opportunity to make history, he rushed up to the vulnerable carriage, shooting Franz Ferdinand in the neck and the archduke's pregnant wife, Sophie, in the stomach. Both died within minutes. Princip was quickly arrested. Although he would succumb to tuberculosis in prison just four years later, he had achieved his goal. Although the Black Hand and not the Serbian government had ordered the assassination, anti-Serbian sentiment in Austria was fierce, and its government used Franz Ferdinand's death as an excuse to declare war on Serbia—instigating World War I, which would bring defeat to the Austro-Hungarian Empire. And Princip had finally transcended his physical limitations. From that point onward, artistic renderings of the assassination depicted a tough, frightening-looking killer, not the feeble young man who had shot the archduke.

In this 1914 photograph, early feminist Emmeline Pankhurst is carried away by police officers. *(Library of Congress Prints and Photographs Division [LC-USZ62-133006])*

Between 1914 and 1918, World War I resulted in the deaths of more than 8.5 million soldiers as Europe's great powers clashed, leading to the collapse of four dominant empires.[1] Meanwhile, at home, most Americans opposed U.S. involvement in the bloody war, and the U.S. government delayed entry for more than two and one half years. President Woodrow Wilson's reelection in 1916 was largely due to his success in preventing the United States from intervening. But as German submarines sank U.S. merchant ships and the German government unsuccessfully attempted to convince Mexican leaders to become allies against the United States, both congressional and public sentiment gradually turned in favor of the war. The United States declared war on Germany in April 1917, and the role of the country suddenly changed.

Meanwhile, two social forces began to converge in the United States. The first was the antiwar movement, as many Americans remained unconvinced that entering the war was the correct decision. The second was hostility toward immigrants, most notably those with either connections to wartime enemies or who held radical political leanings. President Wilson's willingness to question the patriotism of those whom he termed "hyphenated Americans" helped convince the public to express hostility toward German Americans and other immigrants as well.[2] Americans demonstrated their antipathy in ways both innocuous (schools ceased to teach the German language, and communities renamed sauerkraut "liberty cabbage") and violent (in April 1918 a mob near St. Louis captured a German immigrant named Robert Prager, wrapped him in a U.S. flag, and hanged him).[3] This antipathy came to include Russians and radicals as well when, in November 1917, the Bolshevik Revolution placed communists in control of Russia, allowing that nation to withdraw from the U.S.-supported alliance and negotiate peace with Germany.

Congress responded to the antiwar movement with the Espionage Act of June 1917 and the Sedition Act of May 1918, which made it a crime to aid U.S. enemies in wartime, obstruct military recruiting, or cause insubordination or disloyalty in the armed forces.[4] In practice, these new laws were used to silence war critics—some 2,000 of them—with up to 20 years in prison or (in some cases) with deportation.[5] Most famously, Eugene V. Debs, the leader of the American Socialist Party and five-time candidate for president, was arrested and convicted under the revised Espionage Act after delivering a pro-Bolshevik, antiwar speech in Canton, Ohio, on June 16, 1918. Debs ultimately made his final run for the presidency in 1920 from the Atlanta Federal Prison, garnering more than 900,000 votes.[6] Although these laws were only temporarily enforced, they helped discourage antiwar activism for much longer.

Private organizations also assumed a role in repressing wartime dissent. More than a quarter million citizens joined the American Protective League (APL), founded in March 1917, with the express goal of spying on other citizens and organizations. The APL's activities, geared largely toward illegally harassing labor unions, not only went unpunished but also were praised by many in the Wilson administration. "Its membership, which is carefully guarded," Attorney General Thomas Watt Gregory wrote in a 1917 letter, "includes leading men in various localities . . . This organization has been of the greatest possible aid in thousands of cases in the principal cities of the United States."[7] Sometimes the APL engaged in its own vigilante protection of American values. In July 1917, APL members in Bisbee, Arizona—together with the local sheriff and on behalf of a local mining company—swept through the town, arrested more than 1,000 striking copper mine workers on the premise that their labor action undermined the war effort, forced them onto a freight train, and left them in the New Mexico desert without food or water.[8]

Wartime tensions also contributed to racial conflicts. As white workers left for war and as the war stopped the flow of immigrant laborers from Europe to the United States, industrial jobs in northern cities became available to African Americans. Beginning in 1916, blacks, who overwhelmingly lived in the U.S. South, migrated to northern urban places in search of opportunities. While many found new freedom and created new lives for themselves, they also encountered hostility from white populations who viewed the newcomers as flooding their cities and competing for employment. Lynching of African Americans remained common in the South. Race relations deteriorated as southern whites dimly perceived that the foundations of their livelihoods were changing and as African American activists began to demand equal justice in the courts and a federal law against lynching. The Ku Klux Klan experienced a revival not only in the South but also in northern states such as Indiana, Ohio, and Michigan. In the North, this hostility also manifested itself in the form of race riots. In July 1917, striking white workers in East St. Louis, Illinois, lashed out violently against black migrants whom the rioters feared would take their jobs. These tensions continued after the war: In 1919, Washington, D.C., experienced a major race riot, and in July of that year, Chicago underwent five days of bloody rioting after a white crowd killed a black youth for crossing an unmarked racial division at a Lake Michigan beach; in the end, 38 people died and hundreds were injured.[9]

The Red Scare

Tensions between native-born U.S. citizens and European immigrants, particularly those with proradical or prosocialist tendencies, blossomed after the war. The situation became more dire with the "Red Summer" of 1919, a year in which more than 4 million workers nationwide engaged in more than 3,300 strikes.[10] It seemed as if all of America's predominantly foreign-born labor force demanded better wages and job conditions that summer. Some 350,000 steel workers, 450,000 coal miners, and the entire Boston police force walked off the job that year. These agitations generated widespread fears of chaos and disorder. Adding to the tensions, on May 1, 1919 (International Labor Day), U.S. postal workers discovered more than three dozen mail bombs addressed to government officials. In June, a bomb exploded outside the home of U.S. Attorney General A. Mitchell Palmer.[11]

Aggravated by the bombings, growing anti-immigrant and antisocialist factions created a "Red Scare": a period during which anti-immigrant and antisocialist

In this 1927 photograph, Bartolomeo Vanzetti (left) and Nicola Sacco (to his right) return to the courthouse. *(Library of Congress Prints and Photographs Division [LC-USZ62-124547])*

sentiment reached hysterical proportions and dominated the public policy debate. Palmer, aspiring to the presidency in 1920, led the charge against the perceived threat of a communist revolution. He established an antiradical division in the Justice Department under the direction of a young attorney named J. Edgar Hoover. In November 1919, Hoover began a campaign to arrest and deport "alien" (non–U.S. citizen) radicals by targeting more than 300 members of the Union of Russian Workers, as well as prominent anarchist leader Emma Goldman, eventually deporting them to the Soviet Union on a ship dubbed the "Soviet Ark." Buoyed by this initial success, Palmer and Hoover engaged in a nationwide roundup of suspected radicals and agitators in January 1920 called the "Palmer Raids." While these arrests dealt a grievous blow to radical organizations such as the Industrial Workers of the World (IWW)and the Socialist Party, they also proved to be Palmer's undoing and the end of the Red Scare. Relying on local law enforcement agencies, the Justice Department could not prevent the frequent apprehension of U.S. citizens nor widespread abuses of detainees' civil rights. Accused of gross violations of human rights by other cabinet members and proven wrong in his predictions of a nationwide communist uprising, Palmer was disgraced by the summer of 1920.[12]

During these years of tension, local criminal justice authorities acted in a comparably discriminatory fashion and faced minimal oversight. Just as the U.S. Supreme Court found the Sedition Act of 1918 to be constitutional, lower courts also bent to the anti-immigrant, antiradical political pressures of the time.[13] No case better demonstrates this than the 1921 trial of Italian anarchists Nicola Sacco and Bartolomeo Vanzetti, who were accused of capital murder in the April 15, 1920, robbery of the Slater and Morrill Shoe Factory in South Braintree, Massachusetts. Although witnesses did not identify Sacco or Vanzetti as the perpetrators—the robbery was committed by five men, whom witnesses were able to identify only as Italian-American—the pair showed up at a nearby auto repair shop asking about a similar vehicle three weeks later. They carried loaded revolvers, and that was deemed sufficient ground for their arrest.

At their 1921 trial, evidence for their guilt was extremely scant. Fortunately for the prosecution, the only witnesses who could vouch for the defendants' alibis were also poor and Italian-American, and, in many cases, they were connected to the same anarchist causes as Sacco and Vanzetti. The all-white native-born jury did not believe their testimony, and the prosecution, relying as it did on the anti-immigrant and antiradical sentiment of the time, was able to get a conviction without making a substantial case. In the years following their convictions, Sacco and Vanzetti's case became a cause célèbre among civil rights activists who supported numerous appeals and challenges. Sacco and, particularly, Vanzetti, contributed to this interest by arguing articulately that they faced death not because of any crimes they may have committed but due to their political beliefs. Sacco and Vanzetti were executed in 1927, over the protests of numerous prominent celebrities and intellectuals.

As the terror of the Red Summer began to diminish in 1920, however, the Red Scare came to an end. Even when a wagon containing dynamite and steel shrapnel exploded in front of the J. P. Morgan Building on Wall Street in New York City during the lunch hour on September 16, 1920, killing 38 people and injuring more than 200, the public reaction did not compare with that of a few months earlier. In November 1920, Republican candidate Warren G. Harding won the presidency in part by offering a "return to normalcy," shifting the public policy debate away from foreign policy and toward domestic issues. The Sedition Act was repealed in 1921, and Harding commuted Debs's sentence, releasing him from prison on Christmas Day.[14] The Red Scare dominated the national mood, but only briefly. It would reemerge after World War II, most notably manifested in the accusations leveled by Wisconsin senator Joseph McCarthy, but it never achieved the same degree of influence over U.S. public policy debate as it had in the immediate aftermath of World War I.

The Rise of Organized Crime

In 1917, Congress passed the Eighteenth Amendment, which laid the groundwork for a national ban on "the manufacture, sale, or transportation of intoxicating liquors."[15] The amendment was ratified in 1919 and went into effect in 1920. But this was no abrupt legislative coup: By time Prohibition was made federal law, 26 states had already outlawed the sale of alcoholic beverages. The prohibition movement can be best understood as a social movement 50 years in the making, led by Americans frustrated with the social effects of alcoholism, the illegal criminal enterprises that tended to crop up around saloons, and—perhaps most importantly of all—the chaos and decadence that many Americans felt that saloons represented. Prohibiting alcohol did not eliminate its demand, however, and new, better-organized criminal enterprises emerged to meet that demand.

Although organized crime gangs have always been a part of American life and come from a diverse range of ethnicities, no organized crime tradition has had a greater impact on the American popular imagination than the Mafia ("honorable

This photograph shows a Prohibition-era underground still. *(National Archives and Records Administration [541928])*

men"), a general term used to describe Italian (particularly Sicilian) and Italian-American crime gangs (often, but not always, family-run). The concept of the Mafia served as both a realistic summary of Italian-American crime families and as an excuse for prejudice against Italian-American immigrants. When New Orleans police chief David C. Hennessy was assassinated in 1890, for example, the crime was blamed on the Mafia and used to justify lynchings of prominent local Italian-American immigrants, none of whom had been definitively associated with organized crime. Nonetheless, organized criminal operations controlled illegal enterprises such as prostitution and gambling in many U.S. cities throughout the late 19th and early 20th centuries, and Italian Black Hand societies became notorious for kidnappings and murders in the 1910s.

Prohibition provided new and more extensive opportunities for organized crime. Soon legal saloons were replaced by secret illegal "speakeasies" where liquor was served. A staggering amount of money could be made selling contraband liquor, and bootlegging (illegally producing, distributing, and retailing alcoholic beverages) allowed organized criminal operations to expand their businesses in ways that they never had before. No figure in organized crime was more infamous than Al Capone, who controlled the city of Chicago, Illinois, through bribery, intimidation, violence, and brilliant public relations. His criminal career started to take shape in the early 1910s, when as a teenager he began to run errands for criminal gangs operating in his Brooklyn, New York, neighborhood under the leadership of Johnny Torrio. After leaving school at age 14, marrying at age 15, and fathering a son, Capone worked as a saloon bouncer and gunman for the Five Points Gang in New York. But he remained loyal to Torrio, who had been a father figure of sorts to him. When in 1919 Torrio asked the 21-year-old Capone to help him build his criminal enterprise in Chicago, Capone accepted his offer.

Torrio was no ordinary underworld thug; he was a shrewd criminal entrepreneur who realized that because of Prohibition, a great deal of money could be made from the bootlegging business. Despite Torrio's assurances, Chicago's crime boss, Big Jim Colosimo, refused to even give bootlegging a try, preferring to manage his prostitution franchise. After Colosimo was gunned down in the vestibule of one of his cabarets on May 11, 1920—possibly by Capone acting on Torrio's orders—Torrio was left as leader of the gang, and Capone became his lieutenant.[16]

But Torrio did not run the only gang in Chicago, and he had a long-standing conflict with the North Side Gang, a predominantly Irish organized crime syndicate operated by Dion O'Banion. The situation was exacerbated in 1924, when Torrio's men assassinated O'Banion, and a year later O'Banion's men ambushed and wounded Torrio in revenge. Weakened and facing his own mortality, Torrio decided to retire to New York and leave his gang in the hands of Capone. Capone wasted little time, murdering the most powerful leaders of the North Side Gang and establishing himself as the undisputed master of the Chicago criminal underworld.

Al Capone was remarkably popular for a man who was strongly identified with Chicago's homicidal gang wars of the late 1920s. His criminal enterprises focused on bootlegging, gambling, and prostitution—three crimes that were regarded as victimless and were in demand among otherwise law-abiding citizens. Capone also spent time and money conducting charitable endeavors in Chicago, which included funding and supervising a soup kitchen. Seen by many in the city as a voice of defiance against the establishment, an advocate for the poor and marginalized, he allowed his reputation to shield him from trouble when violence and bribery could not, prompting one frustrated *Chicago Tribune* writer to sarcastically refer to him as "Al Capone of Sherwood forest."[17] But violence and bribes were certainly helpful, too; Capone apparently controlled many police officers in Chicago and helped influence the policies of the department.

Violent, influential, and as popular as a criminal overlord could be, Al Capone had become nearly invincible by 1929. But he had still not been able to eliminate the North Side Gang, which had made several bold and well-planned attempts on his life. Although Dion O'Banion himself had been gunned down in 1924, his criminal organization was still doing quite well under the leadership of George "Bugs" Moran and remained the only serious contender to Capone's status as king of Chicago.

On February 14, 1929, seven of Moran's top lieutenants arrived at 2122 North Clark Street to meet with an out-of-town gangster, who had offered to sell them a large shipment of bootleg liquor. Suddenly, men in police uniforms showed up and ordered Moran's lieutenants to stand facing the wall, which was standard procedure. With the lieutenants turned facing the other way, the five "police officers" opened fire with machine guns, slaughtering Moran's men. Although initial public suspicion was that actual police officers were responsible for the killings, it soon became obvious, particularly to law enforcement authorities, that Capone's men had been behind the murders. The federal government heightened its investigation of Capone's activities. In 1931, federal agents—most notably "untouchable" (ostensibly bribery-proof) U.S. Treasury agents under the leadership of Eliot Ness—successfully arrested and convicted Capone on tax evasion charges based on unreported gambling revenue, sentencing him to 11 years in federal prison. By the time of Capone's early release in 1939, his brain had become so inflamed due to syphilis that he was both mentally ill and partially paralyzed. He retired quietly to Florida and died eight years later.

By then, Prohibition was dead too. Public sentiment had turned against it, and it proved to be unenforceable. In New York State alone, Prohibition replaced 15,000 legal saloons with 32,000 illegal speakeasies.[18] The Twenty-first Amendment, passed and ratified in 1933, destroyed the bootlegging industry by legalizing alcohol, but by then the damage had been done. Organized crime had exploited a lucrative new source of revenue for 13 years, and that was enough time for criminal gangs to increase their leverage in the United States.

Crime Commissions

At the same time, the Prohibition era also brought progressive, business-oriented reform to city and state governments. Nowhere was this more apparent than in the field of criminal justice. Beginning in Cleveland, Ohio, in 1921, reform-minded businessmen and lawyers, worried about the apparent lawlessness of the time, formed commissions to investigate the nature of crime and the workings of law enforcement in their jurisdictions. The results—crime commission reports for Cleveland, Missouri, Illinois, and elsewhere—analyzed how criminals evaded the justice system and how law enforcement operations could become more efficient in order to better control crime.

This trend culminated in the late 1920s and early 1930s with the recommendations of the National Commission on Law Observance and Enforcement.

This photograph of George W. Wickersham was taken during the final days of his commission's work. *(Library of Congress Prints and Photographs Division [LC-USZ62-107698])*

Established by President Herbert Hoover in 1929 and led by former attorney general George Wickersham, the purpose of the commission was to explore the impact of Prohibition, to investigate the factors that led to crime, and to suggest policy changes that would reduce crime's effects. In 1931, the commission, popularly known as the Wickersham Commission, issued its findings in 14 volumes. Its most significant recommendations were threefold. First, it recommended that Prohibition not be repealed, a recommendation that would be summarily ignored two years later when the Twenty-first Amendment ended Prohibition. Second, it made a variety of practical suggestions regarding the goals and function of local law enforcement agencies, thereby leading to more uniform standards and increased federal influence over local law enforcement policies. Third and perhaps most crucially, its report *Lawlessness in Law Enforcement* highlighted corruption and abuse perpetrated by local police departments. It particularly drew attention to the seemingly ubiquitous police use of the "third degree," the practice of using psychological pressure and violence to extort confessions from criminal suspects. This finding did not generate immediate change, but it did contribute to a gradual move toward professionalization and restraint in law enforcement.

Kidnapping and the Lindbergh Law

Kidnapping was certainly not a new crime, but the kidnapping of young children for ransom, particularly when murder was suspected, was a horrible thought to contemplate for American parents. Even as early as 1874, the kidnapping, disappearance, and probable murder of four-year-old Charley Ross captured the American imagination in a way that few crimes had, driven as it was by both wall-to-wall media coverage and the father's desperate and ultimately futile search for his son as he traveled to 300 cities and put up more than 700,000 posters pleading for information.[19] The May 21, 1924, kidnapping of 14-year-old Bobby Franks in Chicago, Illinois, also filled the newspapers, both as police desperately tried to recover the youth and, after his dead body was recovered, as the public learned that 18-year-old Richard A. Loeb and 19-year-old Nathan Leopold had killed him. The case remained in the public eye as Leopold and Loeb's families hired the most prominent defense attorney of the time, Clarence Darrow. Darrow convinced a judge to sentence the accused to life in prison rather than the death penalty.[20] Other child kidnappings and disappearances captured the American public's imagination, but the Parker and Lindbergh cases were uniquely disturbing.

In December 1926 in Los Angeles, California, 19-year-old William Hickman kidnapped 12-year-old Marion Parker from school after convincing administrators that her father had been in a terrible accident. After sedating her with ether or chloroform, he took her home and began writing ransom notes to her father, a wealthy bank magnate. "Use good judgment," his letter read. "You are the loser." Following a demand for $1,500, he added: "Failure to comply with these requests means no one will ever see the girl again except the angels in heaven.[21] When Parker's father arrived with the money, Hickman accepted it, drove ahead a little bit, and then pushed a blanket-wrapped human form out of the car door before speeding off. The anxious father ran ahead and opened the blanket to find his daughter's mutilated body. The rest of her body was discovered the next day. Hickman was arrested and later hanged. The brutal sadism of the crime left an indelible imprint on the American consciousness, but it was only the second most infamous child kidnapping and murder of its era.

Charles Lindbergh was seen as an American hero and almost unquestionably the most famous American of the 1920s. The son of a respected congressman, the bold young stunt pilot achieved international fame in May 1927, when he became the first person to fly solo across the Atlantic Ocean. Two years later he married Anne Morrow, an author and, like Charles, the child of a politician. They settled down and began raising a family but faced tragedy when their 20-month-old son, Charles Lindbergh, Jr., vanished from their New Jersey home on the evening of March 1, 1932. When they received a $50,000 ransom demand, President Herbert Hoover promised to "move Heaven and Earth" to find the child but had no authority to do so.[22] Multiple local law enforcement agencies, confused over both jurisdiction and proper investigative techniques, provided little assistance. Lindbergh passed $50,000 to the kidnappers (the serial numbers having been recorded in advance), then received erroneous instructions as to the child's location. On May 12, 1932, over two months into the ordeal, the infant's body was found less than five miles from the Lindbergh's home, and it appeared he had been killed the night of the kidnapping. In 1934, serial numbers on the bills traced the money to German carpenter Bruno Hauptmann, who was hastily tried and found guilty. He was executed in 1936, although many observers at the time and historians since have doubted his guilt.[23]

The Lindbergh case received unprecedented newspaper coverage and contributed to a wave of public support for new federal antikidnapping legislation. The Federal Kidnapping Act, proposed in late February 1932, less than a week before the Lindbergh kidnapping, was quickly championed as the "Lindbergh law."[24] This new bill, passed four months later, made it a federal crime punishable by life in prison to transport a kidnapping victim across state lines and presumed that a victim had been taken across state lines if missing for more than seven days. In May 1934, a provision was added allowing for the death penalty in cases in which physical harm had been inflicted on the victim, though the death penalty clause was seldom enforced, and the U.S. Supreme Court found it to be unconstitutionally vague in 1968.[25] Perhaps the most significant aspect of the law was that it allowed federal law enforcement authorities to participate in kidnapping investigations rather than leaving such matters strictly to local police departments—crucial, given the mobility of kidnappers in the age of automobiles.

The Emergence of Federal Crime Control

Interstate bandits, such as kidnappers, relied on automobiles, traveling from state to state and robbing banks and other businesses as they went. Jurisdictional limitations made a strictly local response impractical, eventually transforming the Bureau of Investigation from a minor agency to a central and robust part of the U.S. criminal justice system. By the middle of the 1930s, the Bureau of Investigation would become the Federal Bureau of Investigation (FBI), complete with a nationwide fingerprinting laboratory and a large staff of trained agents, but this did not happen overnight; the origins of the FBI were rooted in the U.S. law enforcement system's relative failure to capture interstate bandits, who managed to elude authorities in such a daring way that they often achieved the same level of folk hero status accorded to outlaws in the Old West.

Perhaps the most famous, or infamous, of the depression-era interstate bandits was John Dillinger. Although his career as an interstate bank robber lasted only about a year—from June 1933 to July 1934—he robbed between 11 and 20 banks (as far west as Sioux Falls, South Dakota, and as far east as central Ohio), murdered at least 10 people, freed his entire gang from jail by force, and escaped from jail twice.[26] Every time authorities seemed close to catching him, he slipped away. His status as the Department of Justice's "Public Enemy No. 1" only seemed to enhance his fame. He was perceived as attractive, charming, and—in an era when the government had become unpopular—surprisingly well liked by the U.S. public. When law enforcement agents gunned him down on July 22, 1934, many found it difficult to believe. Even after newsreel footage showed Dillinger's body lying in an open casket, many suspected that it had been a double of some kind, perhaps due in part to the fact that Dillinger had at one point undergone surgery to alter his appearance in an effort to evade law enforcement.

Less infamous but more homicidal were Bonnie Parker, Clyde Barrow, and the Barrow Gang that they led. Responsible for 13 murders and a string of bank robberies between January 1930 and May 1934, Bonnie and Clyde were, like Dillinger, frequently idolized by the U.S. public.[27] Only three years after they were ambushed and killed by former Texas Highway Patrol officers in 1934 (based on a tip from a man they believed to be one of their last remaining loyal criminal associates), Fritz Lang's film *You Only Live Once* (1937), starring Sylvia Sidney and Henry Fonda, achieved box office success by loosely modeling its heroes on Bonnie and Clyde. The 1967 film *Bonnie and Clyde* starring Faye Dunaway and Warren Beatty transformed them into symbols of Vietnam-era rebellion. The romantic idea of two outlaws brought together by love and standing alone together against the world nonetheless clashed with their callously violent behavior.

Dillinger and the Barrow Gang represented only a small number of the interstate bandits that plagued the United States during the era of the Great Depression. Among many others were Charles Arthur "Pretty Boy" Floyd, who became almost a Robin Hood figure in the public's consciousness; George "Machine Gun" Kelly, a southern bandit known for his gentle demeanor; and the hot-tempered George "Baby Face" Nelson, who by all accounts genuinely enjoyed killing. Interstate bandits had become a serious, widespread problem. In addition to the crimes they committed themselves, they projected an image of lawlessness and made the police appear weak and ineffectual.

In 1933, newly elected president Franklin D. Roosevelt and Attorney General Homer S. Cummings responded by instigating an unofficial war on crime. They devoted new resources to the Bureau of Investigation, opening new field offices, hiring more agents, and bolstering its fingerprinting and scientific investigation capacities. The agency was initially called the Division of Investigation, but in 1935 it became known by a new name: the Federal Bureau of Investigation. J. Edgar Hoover, who had directed the Bureau of Investigation since 1924, remained in that position.

J. Edgar Hoover was founding director of the FBI, and he remained its leader until his death in 1972. *(National Archives and Records Administration [518187])*

Although it would continue to develop over the coming years, the FBI's basic role had been established. It would deal primarily with multijurisdictional crime, which local law enforcement agencies were generally ill-equipped to handle. It served as an information clearinghouse for local police. In effect, it became the closest thing the United States had to a federal police agency.

By 1934, moreover, the FBI had successfully targeted the interstate bandits so pervasive in the early depression era. FBI agents conducted a wide-ranging manhunt for John Dillinger in 1934 and, in spite of early difficulties, were instrumental in his death. Later that same year, FBI agents killed Pretty Boy Floyd near East Liverpool, Ohio, and Baby Face Nelson near Chicago. In January 1935, FBI agents gunned down key figures in the Barker-Karpis Gang: Fred Barker and his mother, Kate "Ma" Barker, in Florida. Before the month was over, FBI agents also apprehended Alvin Karpis, the mastermind of the gang and the last major bandit still free. With camera crews filming, J. Edgar Hoover personally arrested Karpis in Atlantic City, New Jersey. The year 1934 also marked a watershed in the rise of federal criminal justice. In that year, the Alcatraz Federal Penitentiary opened on an island in San Francisco Bay as a high-security prison for major criminals and repeat escapees. By the middle of the 1930s, the federal government had established a new, active, and effective presence in criminal justice nationwide.

Chronicle of Events

1914

- *April 20:* Private security officers and National Guard troops attack coal miners on strike against the Colorado Fuel and Mine Company. As many as 32 strikers and family members die in the confrontation known as the Ludlow Massacre.
- *June 28:* Serbian terrorist Gavrilo Princip kills Archduke Franz Ferdinand of Austria and his wife, Sophie. Tensions between Austria and Serbia increase, leading to World War I.
- *December 17:* Congress passes the Harrison Narcotics Tax Act, the first comprehensive federal law restricting the import and distribution of cocaine and opiates.

1915

- *September 8:* After accidentally entering a white woman's hotel room in Greenfield, Tennessee, a black man named Mallie Wilson is arrested and then kidnapped from jail and lynched by a white mob.
- *August 17:* Leo Frank, an American Jew, is lynched in Marietta, Georgia, for the 1913 murder of his 13-year-old factory employee Mary Phagan after first being convicted on circumstantial evidence and then being granted clemency by the Georgia governor.

1916

- *June 5:* In *United States v. Jin Fuey Moy,* the Supreme Court rules in favor of physicians who sold opiates to addicted patients, determining that the government should not interfere in the practice of medicine.
- *July 22:* A terrorist bomb goes off at San Francisco's Preparedness Day Parade, killing 10 people and wounding 40.

1917

- *April 6:* The United States declares war on Germany, entering World War I.
- *June 15:* Congress passes the Espionage Act, outlawing any act that could be construed as interfering with the U.S. armed forces or passing information to an enemy.
- *July:* White workers in East St. Louis, Illinois, riot against African-American migrants who they fear have come to take their jobs. Estimates of the number of dead range between 40 and 200; approximately 6,000 blacks are forced to leave their homes.
- *July 12:* More than 1,000 striking copper miners, linked to the Industrial Workers of the World and antiwar ac-

tivists, are arrested and deported from Bisbee, Arizona, to the New Mexico desert.

1918

- *April 5:* Accused of making disloyal statements, German-born Robert Prager is lynched by a mob of more than 300 men and boys in Collinsville, Illinois.
- *June 30:* Perennial Socialist Party presidential candidate Eugene V. Debs is arrested under the 1917 Espionage Act for giving a speech two weeks earlier in Canton, Ohio, criticizing the U.S. war effort.
- *September 16: New York Evening World* editor Charles Chapin murders his wife. He is arrested and sentenced to life in Sing Sing prison, where his beautiful gardens earn him the nickname "The Rose Man of Sing Sing."
- *November 11:* Germany and the Allies agree to an armistice, effectively ending World War I.

1919

- *January 16:* The Eighteenth Amendment is ratified, prohibiting the manufacture, sale, and distribution of alcoholic beverages.
- *March 3:* The Supreme Court hands down two rulings pertaining to the Harrison Narcotics Tax Act of 1914: *United States v. Doremus* and *Webb v. United States.* In *Doremus,* the Court rules that the act is constitutional even though its primary intended purpose is not to raise revenue. In *Webb,* the Court rules that physicians who knowingly provide unlimited amounts of cocaine or narcotics to satisfy the needs of addicts and are paid for the service may be prosecuted under the act.
- *March 10:* In *Debs v. United States,* the U.S. Supreme Court upholds Eugene Debs's conviction under the Espionage Act, ruling that his intention to obstruct the draft and recruitment for the war superseded his rights to free speech.
- *May 1:* Socialists parading in Cleveland, Ohio, to protest the imprisonment of Eugene V. Debs meet with opposition from antisocialists, and violence ensues. Two people are killed, 116 injured, and 40 arrested.
- *May 1:* U.S. postal workers discover 36 mail bombs addressed to various government officials.
- *June 2:* Bombs explode in eight U.S. cities, including one in Washington, D.C., in front of the home of Attorney General A. Mitchell Palmer.
- *July 27:* Following the drowning of a black youth at a Lake Michigan beach, white mobs rampage through Chicago Illinois's "Black Belt" while police reportedly stand aside. These riots result in 38 deaths and more than 500 injuries.

- *July 30:* The Chicago riots end after 6,000 National Guard troops are deployed to control the violence.
- *December:* Under orders from Attorney General A. Mitchell Palmer, 249 pro-socialist immigrants are apprehended, placed on the army transport *Buford* (nicknamed the "Soviet Ark"), and forcibly deported to the Soviet Union.

1920

- *January 1:* The Volstead Act, or National Prohibition Act, goes into effect, beginning the enforcement of Prohibition.
- *January 2–6:* The U.S. Justice Department, in coordination with local law enforcement and under the leadership of A. Mitchell Palmer, conducts a roundup of more than 5,000 suspected radicals in 33 cities.
- *April 15:* In Braintree, Massachusetts, a shoe manufacturer's paymaster and his guard are murdered during an armed robbery in broad daylight.

- *May 8:* After African-American railroad porter Henry Scott is accused of insulting a white woman, she notifies the sheriff of Lakeland, Florida, who arrests Scott. White residents of Lakeland subsequently abduct and kill Scott.
- *May 11:* Chicago crime boss Big Jim Colosimo is murdered—possibly by Al Capone—allowing Colosimo's lieutenant, Johnny Torrio, to take over the operation, with Capone as his own second-in-command.
- *September 16:* A bomb carried by a horse-drawn wagon explodes on Wall Street in New York City outside the headquarters of J.P. Morgan, Inc. Thirty-eight people are killed and more than 200 injured.

1921

- *July 14:* Sacco and Vanzetti are convicted of first-degree murder in the South Braintree robbery and sentenced to death.
- *October 11:* More than 500 whites in Leesburg, Texas, lynch, burn, and dismember an African-American man

Notorious gangster Al Capone attempted to redeem his reputation through charitable enterprises. In this photograph from 1931, men wait in line outside a soup kitchen that Capone established in Chicago during the Great Depression. *(National Archives and Records Administration [541927])*

named Wylie McNeely accused of assaulting an 18-year-old white woman.

- *December 25:* President Warren Harding orders that Eugene V. Debs be released from prison, commuting his sentence to time served.

1922

- The Cleveland Survey of Criminal Justice releases its report, *Criminal Justice in Cleveland.* It becomes a model for crime surveys in other cities and states, as well as the national Wickersham Commission study.
- *March 27:* The U.S. Supreme Court rules in *United States v. Behrman* that physicians who knowingly prescribe large quantities of narcotics or cocaine to drug addicts may be prosecuted under the Harrison Act of 1914, even if a medical need is claimed.
- *June:* The Anti-Lynching Crusaders, a group of female activists advocating antilynching legislation, is founded under the auspices of the NAACP.
- *July 28:* Rep. Leonidas Dyer (R-MO) proposes federal antilynching legislation in the U.S. Congress at the behest of African-American female activists including the Anti-Lynching Crusaders. A well-organized filibuster led by southern legislators blocks it.

1923

- *February 19:* The U.S. Supreme Court in *Moore v. Dempsey* overturns the conviction of 12 African-American farmers who had been convicted in an Arkansas courtroom of killing five white men in a 1919 riot.

1924

- *February 8:* Gee Jon becomes the first man executed in a U.S. gas chamber.
- *May 10:* J. Edgar Hoover is appointed director of the Bureau of Investigation, the predecessor to the FBI.
- *May 21:* Bobby Franks, 14-year-old, is kidnapped and murdered by 18-year-old Richard A. Loeb and 19-year-old Nathan F. Leopold, Jr.
- *August 24:* Attorney Clarence Darrow, defending Leopold and Loeb, agrees to plead them guilty but argues that that they should be sentenced to life in prison rather than the death penalty.
- *November 10:* Chicago organized crime figure Dion O'Banion is gunned down in his florist shop by rival gangsters.

1925

- *April 13:* In *Linder v. United States,* the Supreme Court rules that the Harrison Act of 1914 cannot be used to prosecute physicians who prescribe normal amounts of narcotics to patients to serve a stated medical need, even if the patients are known to be addicts.
- *June 8:* In *Gitlow v. New York,* the Supreme Court declares that state laws cannot violate the free speech clause of the First Amendment. This ruling establishes the incorporation doctrine, an interpretation of the Fourteenth Amendment allowing federal courts to strike down state laws.
- *September 9:* Two white men are killed after a mob of angry whites surround the home that an African-American physician, Dr. Ossian Sweet, has recently purchased in a previously all-white neighborhood in Detroit, Michigan. Detroit police arrest Dr. Sweet and 10 other black men inside the house, charging them with murder.

1926

- *May 13:* Defended by Clarence Darrow, Ossian Sweet is found not guilty in his second murder trial.
- *September 20:* A group of Chicago North Side Gang assassins unsuccessfully attempts to kill Al Capone.
- *October 11:* Al Capone's assassins kill North Side Gang leader Hymie Weiss.

1927

- *August 22:* Sacco and Vanzetti are executed at Massachusetts's Charlestown prison.
- *December 15:* Edward Hickman kidnaps and murders 12-year-old banking heir Marion Parker, then writes notes to her father demanding a ransom payment.
- *December 22:* Following a nationwide manhunt, Hickman is arrested in Oregon for killing Marion Parker.

1928

- *July 6:* The first feature-length film with synchronous dialogue throughout the entire movie, *The Lights of New York,* is released by Warner Brothers. This fictional portrayal of life in a New York organized crime syndicate helps launch the gangster movie genre.
- *October 19:* Edward Hickman is executed for the murder of Marion Parker.

1929

- The Illinois Crime Survey, the most ambitious regional criminal justice investigation of the decade, is published.
- *February 14:* Seven members of Chicago's North Side Gang are killed by Al Capone's lieutenants in what becomes known as the St. Valentine's Day Massacre.

- *May 20:* President Herbert Hoover appoints former attorney general George W. Wickersham to lead the National Commission on Law Observance and Enforcement (Wickersham Commission) to investigate the root causes of crime and propose public policy changes likely to reduce the crime rate.
- *October 24:* The U.S. stock market crashes, starting the Great Depression.

1930

- *January:* Bonnie Parker meets Clyde Barrow for the first time.
- *March 8:* Bonnie Parker supplies a pistol that allows Clyde Barrow to escape from McLennan County Jail in Waco, Texas.
- *June 30:* The U.S. Bureau of Narcotics is formed, headed by commissioner Harry J. Anslinger.

1931

- *January 9: Little Caesar,* an influential gangster movie starring Edward G. Robinson, is released.
- *January 19:* The Wickersham Commission completes its report, noting widespread police misconduct, recommending that Prohibition not be repealed, and suggesting a wide array of changes to law enforcement practices.
- *March 25:* Nine African-American youths hitching a ride on a Great Southern Railroad train become involved in a confrontation with a group of white youths. The subsequent arrest of the African-American youths for rape leads to the "Scottsboro Boys" trials.
- *April 9:* Eight of the nine defendants in the first Scottsboro Boys trial are convicted and sentenced to death.
- *April 23:* Warner Brothers releases *The Public Enemy* starring James Cagney. It becomes one of the most influential gangster movies.
- *October 18:* Al Capone is convicted of tax evasion charges, sentenced to 11 years in prison, and fined $272,692.

1932

- *March:* On appeal, the Alabama Supreme Court upholds the convictions of seven of the Scottsboro Boys,

overturning that of Eugene Williams because he was a minor.
- *March 1:* Charles Lindbergh, Jr., the 20-month-old son of famed aviator Charles Lindbergh, is kidnapped between 8 P.M. and 10 P.M.
- *April 9: Scarface,* another seminal gangster movie, is released.
- *May 12:* The body of Charles Lindbergh, Jr., is discovered in the woods of Hopewell, New Jersey, less than five miles from the house where he was kidnapped.
- *June 17:* Congress passes the Lindbergh Law, making it a federal crime to transport a kidnap victim across state lines for ransom.
- *November 7:* The U.S. Supreme Court issues its first ruling involving the Scottsboro case, *Powell v. Alabama.* The ruling finds that the defendants' lack of adequate legal counsel violated their civil rights and returns the case to the state courts.

1933

- *May 20:* The FBI begins its hunt for Bonnie Parker and Clyde Barrow on the grounds that they transported a stolen automobile across state lines.
- *June 10:* John Dillinger commits his first bank robbery, in New Carlisle, Ohio.
- *June 17:* A gang of interstate bandits, widely believed to be led by Charles Arthur "Pretty Boy" Floyd, attempts to free fellow outlaw Frank Nash from federal authorities in Kansas City, Missouri. In what will become known as the Kansas City Massacre, they shoot to death four law enforcement officers—and inadvertently kill Nash as well.
- *July 27:* President Franklin D. Roosevelt and Attorney General Homer S. Cumming discuss transforming the Bureau of Investigation into a federal "super police force" that could be used to fight interstate crime.
- *October 12:* Infamous bank robber John Dillinger is freed from prison by three members of his gang, who murder the county sheriff in the process.
- *December 5:* The Twenty-First Amendment becomes law, striking down the Eighteenth Amendment and ending Prohibition.

Eyewitness Testimony

World War I, Social Disorder, and the First Red Scare

The master class has always declared the wars; the subject class has always fought the battles. The master class has had all to gain and nothing to lose, while the subject class has had nothing to gain and all to lose—especially their lives . . .

And here let me emphasize the fact—and it cannot be repeated too often—that the working class who fight all the battles, the working class who make the supreme sacrifices, the working class who freely shed their blood and furnish the corpses, have never yet had a voice in either declaring war or making peace. It is the ruling class that invariably does both. They alone declare war and they alone make peace . . .

What a compliment it is to the Socialist movement to be persecuted for the sake of truth! The truth alone will make the people free. And for this reason the truth must be permitted to reach the people. The truth has always been dangerous to the rule of the rogue, the exploiter, the robber. So the truth must be ruthlessly suppressed. That is why they are trying to destroy the Socialist movement; and every time they strike a blow they add a thousand new voices to the hosts proclaiming that Socialism is the hope of humanity . . .

Eugene V. Debs's June 16, 1918, speech at Canton, Ohio, for which he was arrested, tried, and convicted for violating the Sedition Act. Reprinted in Lorence, Enduring Voices, *vol. 2, pp. 169–170.*

The lightning that set Chicago's race antagonisms aflame did not strike out of a clear sky. Only those who did not care or want to see could have failed to be aware that the storm clouds had been gathering a long while, and that the very air was charged with electricity . . .

Thus somewhat thrown off their guard, the Negro workers continued steadily at work, and great crowds of them resorted to the bathing beaches where sections of the shore were informally set apart for their use, although without any warrant for segregation either by ordinance or statute. Across this watery line a Negro boy on a raft drifted Sunday afternoon, July 27, when the beach was thronged both by whites and blacks immediately adjacent to each other. A white man threw a stone at the lad which knocked him into the water. Some of the Negroes demanded the arrest of the assailant and, when a white patrolman refused, he was beaten, and later suspended by the chief of police. The fugitive was captured by other Negroes, placed under arrest by other officers, and held under $50,000 bail, to be tried for murder. Meanwhile those seeking to save the boy from drowning were prevented by the whites from rescuing him. Then and there came the first clash which led to the week of rioting . . .

The fury spread like wild-fire, first back in the "black belt" where safeguards disappeared as rapidly as the perils to life and property increased. Workers in the stockyards, 10,000 or more of whom are Negroes, were at first guarded as they entered and left, but few of them could get to their work when rioting made passage through the streets unsafe and the street-cars were completely stopped by the carmen's strike. Groups and crowds gathered, grew, and loitered. Gangs of white and black hoodlums appeared and ran amuck. Armed men of either color dashed through the district in automobiles and beyond, firing as they flew. Two white men, wounded while shooting up the district, were found to carry official badges, one being thus identified as in the United States civil service and the other as a Chicago policeman. White men firing machine guns from a truck were killed. White and Negro policemen were in turn attacked and badly beaten by mobs of the opposite color. The torch followed attacks upon Negro stores and dwellings, scores of which were set on fire.

White reformer Graham Taylor, describing the 1919 Chicago race riots, in the August 9, 1919, issue of the social work journal, The Survey, *reprinted in Arneson,* Black Protest and the Great Migration, *pp. 169–170.*

I have already say that I not only am not guilty of these two crimes, but I never committed a crime in my life—I have never stolen and I have never killed and I have never spilt blood, and I have fought against crime, and I have fought and I have sacrificed myself even to eliminate the crimes that the law and the church legitimate and sanctify.

This is what I say: I would not wish to a dog or to a snake, to the most low and misfortunate creature of the earth—I would not wish to any of them what I have had to suffer for things that I am not guilty of. I am suffering because I am a radical and indeed I am a radical; I have suffered because I was an Italian, and indeed I am an Italian; I have suffered more for my family and for my beloved than for myself; but I am so convinced to be right that you can only kill me once but if you could execute me two times, and if I could be reborn two other times, I would live again to do what I have done already.

Bartolomeo Vanzetti, speaking immediately before he was sentenced to death in Dedham Court House in Dedham, Massachusetts, on April 9, 1927, quoted in Linder, The Trial of Sacco and Vanzetti. *Available online at URL: http://www.law.umkc.edu/faculty/projects/ftrials/SaccoV/SaccoV.htm.*

Prohibition and Organized Crime

The criminal is not an outlaw in this community. If he has any relation to the law it is as a superlaw. His political connections are much more important than the connections of the average law abiding citizen. He is supported and protected by men in politics. . . .

Corrupt politics uses the criminal in political work. In return, he gets immunity so far as politics is able to grant it. He can get a pardon or parole if he fails to evade punishment in any other way. There is a chain extending from important men of good character down through politics until it reaches the gunman, criminal, and murderer.

So long as there are compromises with political leaders who make politics a corrupt business there will be successful raids of the public by criminals. A dulled conscience will make a record of active crime. When responsibility is brought home all along the line there will be a change.

The criminal cannot stand alone. Take away from him the political system which defends and protects him and he can be exterminated. Until then he will do the exterminating. That is the situation. It cannot be reached by hushing it. It must be attacked by publicity.

"Immune Criminals and the Why of It," Chicago Daily Tribune, *January 27, 1925.*

"Body No. 2," sings out Lieut. Sullivan, and cards give it the name of Albert Weinshank, and someone asks if it is the former state representative and is told it is his cousin.

Weinshank had only $18 in cash on him when he was killed, but he had a fine diamond ring and a bankbook showing his account in the name of A. R. Shanks.

The scene of this gruesome job is to be cleared space in the middle of the long and narrow garage that fronts on Clark Street and runs a hundred feet or more west to the alley. Over along the north wall are the bodies. All around are trucks and automobiles.

Back in the rear is a big [German shepherd], chained beneath a truck that Pat Roche of the United States special intelligence service says is a typical beer truck. The dog looks vicious, but he looks scared, too.

"Seven men died like dogs, but the dog lives," a detective says as he warns others against getting too close to the dog. But the dog does not even bark; he seems mystified that so many strange men dare walk back and forth within his reach.

An account of the aftermath of the St. Valentine's Day Massacre of 1929, in which seven associates of the Moran gang in Chicago were killed by Al Capone's henchmen. "Slay Doctor in Massacre," Chicago Daily Tribune, *February 15, 1929, p. 1.*

The weapons that have made Chicago infamous are the machine gun, the pistol, and the sawed-off shotgun. These weapons leave death in their trail, and it is with human killing that this report is concerned. These killings, of course, are a serious reflection upon the law enforcing agencies and no one will be heard to deny that they constitute a grave menace to the peace and dignity of the city and state. As advertised to the world, however, the citizens of Chicago going about their daily tasks and visitors coming to the city on business or pleasure are actually in danger, while upon the streets, of being killed by gangsters' bullets. Nothing could be more untrue. In the two years last passed only two innocent bystanders were killed in Cook County and neither was killed by gangsters. When gangsters kill, they kill each other . . .

Gang killings, of course, are spectacular, mysterious, and dramatic; they possess all of the elements of intense human interest and therefore have great news value. Plays have been written and "movie" scenarios woven around Chicago's gangs, and there has been so much exploitation of these events that when a Chicago gunman's weapon "barks" its echo is heard around the world; while if the same weapon were discharged in any other city in the country it would hardly be heard around the block. It is a fact that there was a substantial reduction in gang killings during 1927. While such crimes have been reduced, there has been a slight increase in other murders . . .

A discussion of homicide in Chicago, from the Illinois Association for Criminal Justice, The Illinois Crime Survey, *1929, pp. 593–594.*

Crime and the reign of the captains of crime have entered the field of otherwise legitimate business. The "racketeer" is merely a captain of gunmen and a man who undertakes by force to accomplish and guarantee the trade regulations and the freedom from competition in the lesser industries, which in the higher and wealthier callings are accomplished by means of the trade association and the "gentleman's agreement." He

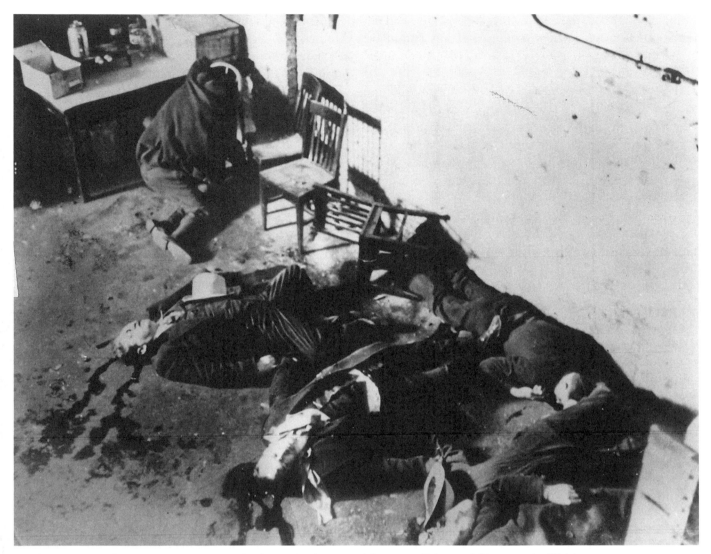

The St. Valentine's Day Massacre left a bloody aftermath. *(Library of Congress Prints and Photographs Division [LC-USZ62-123252])*

is a captain of the gunmen whom organized vice and organized gambling and liquor selling have brought among us and have maintained.

We have tolerated in Chicago a medieval feudal system. We have our warlords. We have had our small armies of mercenaries. These armies have been recruited by the gambling, the vice, and the liquor interests, but their services may be obtained by anyone who will pay the price. Vice, gambling, and liquor selling can hardly call on the public for protection, but often the gambler and the liquor seller is the victim of the "hi-jacker" and himself needs defending. He always desires to rid himself of competitors and obnoxious rivals. He, therefore, hires mercenaries and these mercenaries have been allowed to be maintained because a large number of our policemen have been bootleggers or connivers with bootleggers, and

only too often public officers have profited from the lawlessness which they have protected.

A discussion of organized crime in Chicago, from the Illinois Association for Criminal Justice, The Illinois Crime Survey, *1929, p. 816.*

Kidnapping, Banditry, and Murder

Now, your Honor, I have spoken about the war. I believed in it. I don't know whether I was crazy or not. Sometimes I think perhaps I was. I approved of it; I joined in the general cry of madness and despair. I urged men to fight. I was safe because I was too old to go. I was like the rest . . .

We read of killing one hundred thousand men in a day. We read about it and we rejoiced in it—if it was the other fellows who were killed. We were fed on flesh and drank blood. Even down to the prattling babe. I need not tell you how many upright, honorable young boys have come into this court charged with murder, some saved and some sent to their death, boys who fought in this war and learned to place a cheap value on human life. You know it and I know it. These boys were brought up in it. The tales of death were in their homes, their playgrounds, their schools; they were in the newspapers that they read; it was a part of the common frenzy—what was a life? It was nothing. It was the least sacred thing in existence and these boys were trained to this cruelty . . .

I protest against the crimes and mistakes of society being visited upon them. All of us have a share in it. I have mine. I cannot tell and I shall never know how many words of mine might have given birth to cruelty in place of love and kindness and charity . . .

I do not know how much salvage there is in these two boys. I hate to say it in their presence, but what is there to look forward to? I do not know but what your Honor would be merciful to them, but not merciful to civilization, and not merciful if you tied a rope around their necks and let them die; merciful to them, but not merciful to civilization, and not merciful to those who would be left behind. To spend the balance of their days in prison is mighty little to look forward to, if anything. Is it anything? They may have the hope that as the years roll around they might be released. I do not know. I do not know. I will be honest with this court as I have tried to be from the beginning. I know that these boys are not fit to be at large. I believe they will not be until they pass through the next stage of life, at forty-five or fifty. Whether they will then, I cannot tell. I am sure of this; that I will not be here to help them. So far as I am concerned, it is over . . .

I care not, your Honor, whether the march begins at the gallows or when the gates of Joliet close upon them, there is nothing but the night, and that is little for any human being to expect.

But there are others to consider. Here are these two families, who have led honest lives, who will bear the name that they bear, and future generations must carry it on.

Here is Leopold's father—and this boy was the pride of his life. He watched him, he cared for him, he worked for him; the boy was brilliant and accomplished, he educated him, and he thought that fame and position awaited him, as it should have awaited. It is a hard thing for a father to see his life's hopes crumble into dust. Should he be considered? Should his brothers be considered? Will it do society any good or make your life safer, or any human being's life safer, if it should be handed down from generation to generation, that this boy, their kin, died upon the scaffold?

And Loeb's the same. Here are the faithful uncle and brother, who have watched here day by day, while Dickie's father and his mother are too ill to stand this terrific strain, and shall be waiting for a message which means more to them than it can mean to you or me. Shall these be taken into account in this general bereavement? Have they any rights? Is there any reason, your Honor, why their proud names and all the future generations that bear them shall have this bar sinister written across them? How many boys and girls, how many unborn children will feel it? It is bad enough as it is, God knows. It is bad enough, however it is. But it's not yet death on the scaffold. It's not that. And I ask your Honor, in addition to all that I have said to save two honorable families from a disgrace that never ends, and which could be of no avail to help any human being that lives.

Now, I must say a word more and then I will leave this with you where I should have left it long ago. None of us are unmindful of the public; courts are not, and juries are not. We placed our fate in the hands of a trained court, thinking that he would be more mindful and considerate than a jury. I cannot say how people feel. I have stood here for three months as one might stand at the ocean trying to sweep back the tide. I hope the seas are subsiding and the wind is falling, and I believe they are, but I wish to make no false pretense to this court. The easy thing and the popular thing to do is to hang my clients. I know it. Men and women who do not think will applaud. The cruel and thoughtless will approve. It will be easy to-day; but in Chicago, and reaching out over the length and breadth of the land, more and more fathers and mothers, the humane, the kind and the hopeful, who are gaining an understanding and asking questions not only about these poor boys, but about their own—these will join in no acclaim at the death of my clients.

These would ask that the shedding of blood be stopped, and that the normal feelings of man resume their sway. And as the days and the months and the years go on, they will ask it more and more. But, your Honor, what they shall ask may not count. I know the easy way. I know the future is with me, and what I stand for here; not merely for the lives of these two unfortunate lads, but for all boys and all girls; for all of the young, and as far as possible, for all of the old. I am pleading for life, understanding, charity, kindness, and the infinite mercy that considers all. I am pleading that we overcome cruelty with kindness and hatred with love. I know the future is on my side. Your Honor stands between the past and the future. You may hang these boys; you may hang them by the neck until they are dead. But in doing it you will turn your face toward the past. In doing it you are making it harder for every other boy who in ignorance and darkness must grope his way through the mazes which only childhood knows. In doing it you will make it harder for unborn children. You may save them and make it easier for every child that sometime may stand where these boys stand. You will make it easier for every human being with an aspiration and a vision and a hope and a fate. I am pleading for the future; I am pleading for a time when hatred and cruelty will not control the hearts of men. When we can learn by reason and judgment and understanding and faith that all life is worth saving, and that mercy is the highest attribute of man.

Defense attorney Clarence Darrow, pleading for the lives of the young murderers Nathan Leopold and Richard Loeb, in his closing statement in Illinois v. Leopold and Loeb *(1924).*

Shortly after 9 A.M. the lookouts recognized the eight-cylinder sedan approaching at terrific speed. Some of the officers coolly walked out and into the roadway, motioning and shouting for the driver to halt, while those in the ambuscade trained their weapons on the criminals.

[Clyde] Barrow answered by stepping on the accelerator and reaching for a sawed-off shotgun. In a split second the officers of the law, spurred by the knowledge of Barrow's ruthlessness, opened up their death-dealing barrage.

The first volley appeared to have the effect of a bolt of lightning, and the uncontrolled car shot with its topmost speed into the embankment. The law had settled its score with Barrow and his quick-shooting woman accomplice.

The ambush of Bonnie Parker and Clyde Barrow, as recounted in "Barrow and Woman Are Slain by Police," New York Times, *May 24, 1934, pp. 1–2.*

The whole topic of conversation at the present time seems to be the Hauptmann trial in New Jersey. It was not so much so at first, but since the trial has really started, we can hardly meet a person on the street who does not want to know what you think of the Hauptmann case and whether you think he will be convicted, even before they ask about the weather. . . .

It is not that murders have not been committed before, many of them quite as horrible as the Lindbergh kidnapping and killing. The victims have often been innocent little children, which makes the matter so much the worse, but this seems to be different . . . It is said that there are more reporters in the little town in New Jersey watching this trial than were employed in the World War. It seems as though not a single angle of the case—not a

single word has been dropped that is not being reported and the great American public is morbidly picking it up and reading it. But, it is presumed we are like that, so what is there to be done?

A commentary on the trial of Bruno Hauptmann, accused killer of 20-month-old Charles Lindbergh, Jr., from "Topics of Conversation," Adirondack Record-Elizabethtown Post, *January 10, 1935, p. 10.*

Federal Law Enforcement Reform

The defendant was arrested by a police officer, so far as the record shows, without warrant, at the Union Station in Kansas City, Missouri, where he was employed by an express company. Other police officers had gone to the house of the defendant, and being told by a neighbor where the key was kept, found it and entered the house. They searched the defendant's room and took possession of various papers and articles found there, which were afterwards turned over to the United States marshal. Later in the same day police officers returned with the marshal, who thought he might find additional evidence, and, being admitted by someone in the house, probably a boarder, in response to a rap, the marshal searched the defendant's room and carried away certain letters and envelopes found in the drawer of a chiffonier. Neither the marshal nor the police officer had a search warrant . . .

It is thus apparent that the question presented involves the determination of the duty of the court with reference to the motion made by the defendant for the return of certain letters, as well as other papers, taken from his room by the United States marshal, who, without authority of process, if any such could have been legally issued, visited the room of the defendant for the declared purpose of obtaining additional testimony to support the charge against the accused, and, having gained admission to the house, took from the drawer of a chiffonier there found certain letters written to the defendant, tending to show his guilt. These letters were placed in the control of the district attorney, and were subsequently produced by him and offered in evidence against the accused at the trial. The defendant contends that such appropriation of his private correspondence was in violation of rights secured to him by the 4th and 5th Amendments to the Constitution of the United States. We shall deal with the 4th Amendment, which provides:

'The right of the people to be secure in their persons, houses, papers, and effects, against unreasonable searches and seizures, shall not be violated, and no warrants shall issue but upon probable cause, supported by oath or affirmation, and particularly describing the place to be searched, and the persons or things to be seized' . . .

The effect of the 4th Amendment is to put the courts of the United States and Federal officials, in the exercise of their power and authority, under limitations and restraints as to the exercise of such power and authority, and to forever secure the people, their persons, houses, papers, and effects, against all unreasonable searches and seizures under the guise of law. This protection reaches all alike, whether accused of crime or not, and the duty of giving to it force and effect is obligatory upon all intrusted under our Federal system with the enforcement of the laws. The tendency of those who execute the criminal laws of the country to obtain conviction by means of unlawful seizures and enforced confessions, the latter often obtained after subjecting accused persons to unwarranted practices destructive of rights secured by the Federal Constitution, should find no sanction in the judgments of the courts, which are charged at all times with the support of the Constitution, and to which people of all conditions have a right to appeal for the maintenance of such fundamental rights.

What, then, is the present case? Before answering that inquiry specifically, it may be well by a process of exclusion to state what it is not. It is not an assertion of the right on the part of the government always recognized under English and American law, to search the person of the accused when legally arrested, to discover and seize the fruits or evidences of crime. This right has been uniformly maintained in many cases . . . Nor is it the case of burglar's tools or other proofs of guilt found upon his arrest within his control. The case in the aspect in which we are dealing with it involves the right of the court in a criminal prosecution to retain for the purposes of evidence the letters and correspondence of the accused, seized in his house in his absence and without his authority, by a United States marshal holding no warrant for his arrest and none for the search of his premises. The accused, without awaiting his trial, made timely application to the court for an order for the return of these letters, as well as other property. This application was denied, the letters retained and put in evidence, after a further application at the beginning of the trial, both applications asserting the rights of the accused under the 4th and 5th Amendments to the Constitution.

If letters and private documents can thus be seized and held and used in evidence against a citizen accused of an offense, the protection of the 4th Amendment, de-claring his right to be secure against such searches and seizures, is of no value, and, so far as those thus placed are concerned, might as well be stricken from the Constitution. The efforts of the courts and their officials to bring the guilty to punishment, praiseworthy as they are, are not to be aided by the sacrifice of those great principles established by years of endeavor and suffering which have resulted in their embodiment in the fundamental law of the land. The United States marshal could only have invaded the house of the accused when armed with a warrant issued as required by the Constitution, upon sworn information, and describing with reasonable particularity the thing for which the search was to be made. Instead, he acted without sanction of law, doubtless prompted by the desire to bring further proof to the aid of the government, and under color of his office undertook to make a seizure of private papers in direct violation of the constitutional prohibition against such action. Under such circumstances, without sworn information and particular description, not even an order of court would have justified such procedure; much less was it within the authority of the United States marshal to thus invade the house and privacy of the accused. In *Adams v. New York* (1904), this court said that the 4th Amendment was intended to secure the citizen in person and property against unlawful invasion of the sanctity of his home by officers of the law, acting under legislative or judicial sanction. This protection is equally extended to the action of the government and officers of the law acting under it . . . To sanction such proceedings would be to affirm by judicial decision a manifest neglect, if not an open defiance, of the prohibitions of the Constitution, intended for the protection of the people against such unauthorized action. . . .

We therefore reach the conclusion that the letters in question were taken from the house of the accused by an official of the United States, acting under color of his office, in direct violation of the constitutional rights of the defendant; that having made a seasonable application for their return, which was heard and passed upon by the court, there was involved in the order refusing the application a denial of the constitutional rights of the accused, and that the court should have restored these letters to the accused. In holding them and permitting their use upon the trial, we think prejudicial error was committed.

U.S. Supreme Court justice William R. Day, writing for the unanimous Court in Weeks v. United States *(1914). This ruling definitively established the exclusionary rule, which holds that evidence obtained illegally may not be used at trial.*

1. The corrupting influence of politics should be removed from the police organization.
2. The head of the department should be selected at large for competence, a leader, preferably a man of considerable police experience, and removable from office only after a preferment of charges and a public hearing.
3. Patrolmen should be able to rate a "B" on the Alpha test, be able-bodied and of good character, weigh [at least] 150 pounds, measure [at least] 5 feet 9 inches tall, and be between 21 and 31 years of age. These requirements may be disregarded by the chief for good and sufficient reasons.
4. Salaries should permit decent living standards, housing should be adequate, eight hours of work, one day off weekly, annual vacation, fair sick leave with pay, just accident and death benefits when in performance of duty, reasonable pension provisions on an actuarial basis.
5. Adequate training for recruits, officers, and those already on the roll is imperative.
6. The communication system should provide for call boxes, telephones, recall system, and . . . teletype and radio.
7. Records should be complete, adequate, but as simple as possible. They should be used to secure administrative control of investigations and of department units in the interest of efficiency.
8. A crime-prevention unit should be established if circumstances warrant this action and qualified women police should be engaged to handle juvenile delinquents' and women's cases.
9. State police forces should be established in States where rural protection of this character is required.
10. State bureaus of criminal investigation and information should be established in every State.

The National Commission on Law Observance and Enforcement (the Wickersham Commission), from the conclusion of its Report on Police *(1931), quoted in Vila and Morris,* The Role of Police in American Society, *p. 141.*

CHAPTER NINE

World War II and the Cold War
1934–1957

The United States suffered through the hardest year of the Great Depression in 1933. Unemployment reached levels never seen before or since, gradually rising from what had been a stable 3.2 percent in 1929 to a peak of 24.9 percent. The jobs that were available generally paid poorly, and basic needs such as food and shelter became increasingly difficult to afford. The economy had improved slightly by 1934, which can be credited in large part to the New Deal policies of President Franklin D. Roosevelt. Unemployment dropped in 1934 to 21.7 percent, the lowest level since 1931 and the first drop in unemployment since the Great Depression began. But the economy was still in dismal condition, and it would not reach pre-1929 levels until World War II.[1]

In the midst of this economic crisis, interstate crime posed a mounting challenge to U.S. law enforcement. The Federal Bureau of Investigation (FBI), under the leadership of J. Edgar Hoover, continued to expand its role of addressing interstate crime and federal offenses. Likewise, the Federal Bureau of Narcotics (FBN), under Harry J. Anslinger, initiated an ongoing campaign against drug trafficking. By this time, U.S. law enforcement achieved the form that it still holds to this day: municipal, county, and state officers investigating crimes within their jurisdictions and federal agencies investigating cross-jurisdictional offenses. The federal agencies advanced a model of crime control through active enforcement and harsh penalties rather than crime prevention.

The Great Depression, World War II, and the cold war dominated American life between 1934 and 1957, and these overarching historical events had an impact in the arenas of crime and justice. Moreover, many of the ongoing issues that shape American life began to come to a head at mid-century. Discrimination based on race, youth, nationality, and political affiliation had always been present in the United States, but increased newspaper, magazine, newsreel, and television coverage made it more visible to the American people. New movements formed as activists demanded equality for all Americans, galvanized by the conviction and sentencing under highly suspicious circumstances of nine young African-American men in Alabama.

The Southern Way

During the era of segregation, the U.S. South operated under an informal racial code that was often rendered formal by state legislatures. Black men and women were regarded as second-class citizens, and those who did not accept this treatment were often the targets of violence. Although the incidence of lynching decreased during the 1920s, southern courts remained willing to convict and sentence African Americans based on minimal evidence. Public lynchings were also supplemented by an unknown number of quieter racially motivated killings. Between 1934 and 1957, these southern practices, represented by the Scottsboro trials and the Emmett Till murder, revealed the stark racial dimensions of southern life to the rest of the country. Both events demonstrated the low premium many southern law enforcement authorities placed on African-American lives, and they began to galvanize support for the strong national Civil Rights movement that would emerge during the coming decades.

On March 25, 1931, an African-American teenager named Haywood Patterson did something that Alabama youths frequently did during the 1930s. He hitched a free ride on a Great Southern Railroad freight train bound for Memphis, Tennessee, riding the rails in search of work. As Patterson held on to the roof of a tank car on the moving train, a white stowaway standing on the roof mischievously stepped on his hand, attempting to dislodge Patterson. When eight young black stowaways stepped in to defend Patterson, a group of whites stood in opposition and a fight broke out. The small group of black youths, ranging in age between 12 and 20, threw most of their white assailants off the train, and the fight ended as

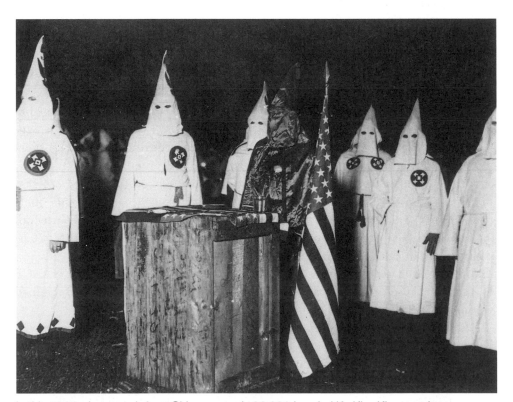

In this 1920 photograph from Chicago, nearly 30,000 hooded Ku Klux Klan members assemble for a massive rally. *(Library of Congress Prints and Photographs Division [LC-USZ62-64768])*

the train accelerated. As soon as the displaced whites dusted themselves off and reported being assaulted by a gang of black youths, the train was stopped by a group of armed whites in Paint Rock, Alabama. The nine blacks were tied up and thrown in the back of a flatbed truck, then driven to a jail in Scottsboro, Alabama. Soon they would become known in national newspapers as the "Scottsboro Boys." As was typical of the time, none of their white attackers were arrested.[2]

It was common knowledge in 1930s Alabama that one of the most reliable ways to send a black man to the electric chair was to accuse him of raping a white woman. At the time of the trial, no black man in Alabama had ever been convicted of raping a white woman and *not* sentenced to death. So when two young white women on the train, 19-year-old Victoria Price and 17-year-old Ruby Bates, claimed that the nine black youths had raped them at knifepoint, the "boys" were quickly charged. Public sentiment rose against them to such a degree that the governor of Alabama had to call out the National Guard to protect the jail where they were held from a crowd of several thousand angry white people.

The trial, however, was little more than a legally valid lynching. The state-appointed defense attorneys did not mount a defense; they called no defense witnesses other than the teenagers themselves, did not point out inconsistencies in the prosecution's case, and did not cross-examine any of the prosecution's witnesses. On April 9, 1931, slightly more than two weeks after the alleged attack, eight of the nine defendants were summarily sentenced to death as a white mob cheered outside the courtroom. Twelve-year-old defendant Roy Wright escaped the death penalty by mistrial; the prosecutor had refused to seek the execution of a child, but 11 jurors refused to enforce any lesser sentence against him. Thirteen-year-old Eugene Williams received no such protection, and he was sentenced to die along with the others.

The quick verdict shocked many northerners, particularly those in the National Association for the Advancement of Colored People (NAACP) and International Labor Defense (ILD), a workers' rights organization. The Scottsboro boys were provided competent defense attorneys for their March 1932 appeal to the Alabama Supreme Court, which overturned Williams's conviction on account of his age but upheld the conviction and sentencing of the other seven. Even the blatant irregularities of the first Scottsboro trial were not enough to convince Alabama justices to order a retrial. The ILD appealed the case to the Supreme Court.

On November 7, 1932, the U.S. Supreme Court ruled on the Scottsboro case in *Powell v. Alabama*. In a 7-2 decision, the Court held that by providing inadequate counsel the state of Alabama had violated the due process clause of the Fourteenth Amendment. New trials were ordered, and Haywood Patterson was the first to face trial in front of another all-white Alabama jury in early March 1933, slightly less than two years after a white teenager fatefully stepped on his hand. The NAACP had distanced itself from the case due to the controversy involved, but ILD retained world-class defense attorney Samuel Liebowitz to represent Patterson.

Liebowitz decimated the prosecution's case. Testimony from the doctor who had examined Price established that while a vaginal examination turned up evidence of a sexual encounter, there was no bruising, tearing, or other physical damage consistent with a struggle of any kind, much less a violent gang rape as she had alleged. The doctor also stated that the sperm he had found in her vagina was nonmotile, indicating that the sexual encounter had occurred at least a day before the alleged rape. In cross-examining various friends and associates of Price who had been present with her in the days leading up to the incident, Liebowitz unearthed a possible explanation for the biological evidence. Price had very recently had a sexual encounter with one of the whites who had been involved in the altercation on the train.

The most dramatic moment came at the end of the trial, when Liebowitz called Ruby Bates to the stand. Bates confessed that none of the defendants had even touched her or Price and that the pair had concocted the rape story to avoid being arrested for vagrancy or crossing state lines with a man for sexual purposes. Having discredited the prosecution's evidence, Liebowitz rested his case. The all-white Alabama jury deliberated and then delivered their verdict the next day. Walking out of the jury room laughing and slapping each other on the back, they declared that they had found Patterson guilty, and they sentenced him for a second time to death in the electric chair. "If you ever saw those creatures, those bigots whose mouths are slits in their faces," an angry and exhausted Liebowitz told the press after leaving the courtroom, "whose eyes pop out like a frog's, whose chins drip tobacco juice, bewhiskered and filthy, you would not ask how they could do it."[3] The presiding judge, James Horton, later set aside the jury's verdict and ordered a new trial, although this would likely end his judicial career. This proved accurate; Horton, who had not even faced a challenger in the previous election, was soundly defeated when he ran for reelection in 1933.

The new trial—this time for the oldest seven Scottsboro "boys"—was held in November 1934 under Judge William Callahan, who made no secret of his biases against the defendants. He declared most of Liebowitz's central arguments inadmissible, refusing, for example, to allow him to introduce the possibility that the biological evidence from Victoria Price had come from anyone but one of the nine black youths. For a third time, Patterson was found guilty and sentenced to death. Clarence Norris, another of the Scottsboro defendants, was also sentenced to death. Callahan agreed to suspend trials of the other defendants until these convictions were appealed to a higher court.

On April 1, 1935, the U.S. Supreme Court ruled unanimously in *Norris v. Alabama* that procedural irregularities warranted new trials. No black had served on a jury in Decatur, Alabama, in more than 60 years. Liebowitz was able to show that in this particular case, the prosecution had forged documents to make it appear that African Americans had been part of the jury pool when, in fact, the list had been illegally pared down to guarantee an all-white jury. The forgery was so sloppy that the verdict was not particularly difficult for the Supreme Court. In January 1936, Haywood Patterson went to trial for a fourth time and was found guilty for a fourth time—but this time the jury sentenced him to 75 years in prison rather than to death. It was the first time in Alabama history that a black man found guilty of raping a white woman did not receive the death penalty.

Although the Patterson verdict was unjustly harsh, it marked a shift in direction for the Scottsboro trials. The prosecution, having lost an immeasurable amount of money and time on the case, agreed to drop charges against four of the nine Scottsboro youths. The remaining five were all sentenced to what amounted to life imprisonment, but all of them were out of prison by 1950. Four were paroled, and Haywood Patterson escaped and fled to Michigan. The state of Michigan located Patterson and promptly released him, refusing to send him back to Alabama.

The story of the Scottsboro boys did not end happily. Even the four defendants who were never formally sentenced spent six formative years of their lives in Alabama's brutal and poorly regulated prison system, and the other five were not released until they were well into their 30s. Once free, most died soon afterward; Patterson, for example, in 1952. The Alabama criminal justice system had destroyed the lives of nine young black men, but this was nothing unusual. Perhaps the most tragic fact about the case is that what made it uncommon was its scale: nine men being tried for one offense demanded national media attention. Most of the countless similar stories of young black men arrested and prodded through equally phony trials toward an unearned punishment may never be told.

A National Approach to Law Enforcement

The Scottsboro case made it clear to national observers that the governments of southern states were mostly incapable of dealing with criminal justice issues affecting African Americans and brought more federal attention to what had historically been regarded as state law enforcement priorities. The two landmark Supreme Court cases that resulted from the Scottsboro trials, *Powell v. Alabama* (1932) and *Norris v. Alabama* (1935), established precedents for federal intervention in cases in which defendants were given inadequate representation and African Americans were illegally excluded from the jury pool, respectively. Although the cases did not resolve the problem of racism in southern courts, they served as notice that rigged trials against African-American defendants could be overturned on appeal in the rare instances when sufficient representation was available.

National attention to the Scottsboro trials came at the end of the Prohibition era, a time when the federal law enforcement presence had already become more pronounced in response to organized crime, interstate banditry, and kidnapping. As the attention of law enforcement agents began to turn away from banning the manufacture and sale of alcoholic beverages, national interest in restricting other mood-altering substances increased. The first federal laws against drug trafficking, such as the 1914 Harrison Narcotic Act, focused narrowly on hard drugs: opiates such as heroin and morphine and the powerful stimulant cocaine (which was incorrectly labeled a narcotic, or central nervous system depressant, in early antidrug legislation). However, during the 1930s, the U.S. government found a new target: marijuana.

In the 1930s, marijuana was becoming popular among subcultures in the U.S. population—migrant agricultural laborers and jazz musicians—and disproportionately used by Latinos and African Americans.[4] Newspapers and magazines published exposés of marijuana throughout the 1930s, and states passed laws restricting its use. At the behest of state governors, the U.S. Treasury Department's Bureau of Narcotics became involved as well. Harry K. Anslinger, the commissioner of the Narcotics Bureau from 1930 to 1962, had spent much of his career in the ongoing struggle against the most dangerous drug of the day, heroin. In the mid-1930s, he also focused public attention on marijuana and what he regarded as its insanity-inducing properties. In a July 1937 article for *The American Magazine* titled "Marijuana: Assassin of Youth!" Anslinger wrote a lengthy and graphic account of various purportedly marijuana-inspired actions ranging from suicide to murder to child molestation.[5]

Tell Your Children, the 1936 film created by director Louis Gasnier for use in church youth programs, captures the tone of the day's discourse about drugs. Gasnier was a veteran of the silent film era who still employed the technique of using exaggerated facial expressions and dramatic shifts in body language to convey emotion. Without sound this effect creates dramatic tension; with sound it conveys comical overacting. The overacting, coupled with the plot, in which marijuana use quickly creates a downward spiral of rape, suicide, and murder, made it an ineffective cautionary tale but an extremely promising 1930s camp-horror movie. Recognizing its commercial potential, a producer bought the rights to the film, retitled it *Reefer Madness,* and distributed it nationally. It generated a modest financial return and was forgotten for several decades until it was rediscovered in the 1970s by those who regarded it as a camp comedy, a reductio ad absurdum of antidrug rhetoric.

"Bugsy" Siegel, like many who had made money as bootleggers during the Prohibition era, moved on to other lucrative rackets after Prohibition was repealed. *(Library of Congress Prints and Photographs Division [LC-USZ62-120865])*

The federal government effectively outlawed marijuana with the Marihuana Tax Act of 1937 (*marihuana* was the customary spelling in the 1930s). Supported by Anslinger, the bill theoretically required nothing more than that all persons who grew, sold, or distributed marijuana register with the federal government and pay a tax—between one dollar and 24 dollars per year, depending on how the marijuana was to be used, plus one dollar per ounce each time physicians transferred the drug and 100 dollars per ounce for each transfer by nonphysicians. Every state had outlawed marijuana, however, so registering and paying the tax invited arrest by local authorities and state prosecution; failing to register and pay the tax risked arrest by federal authorities, with penalties of up to five years imprisonment and a $2,000 fine (almost $29,000 in 2007 dollars) per offense.[6]

Drugs fell off the national agenda during World War II, in part because the conflict disrupted international distribution, but returned with a vengeance in the late 1940s and early 1950s. A new drug culture concentrated around marijuana emerged among urban hipsters, artists, and musicians, and heroin use became increasingly prevalent among disengaged urban youth, particularly African Americans and Latinos. Although the problem tended to be concentrated among minority subcultures, much of the discourse about drugs in the media and government in the early 1950s focused on the perceived threat to white middle-class youths. The U.S. Senate's Special Committee to Investigate Organized Crime in Interstate Commerce, chaired by Estes Kefauver of Tennessee, conducted hearings on drug use in 1951 and heard testimony from addicts explaining how they had succumbed to the allure of drugs.[7]

With Anslinger still the leading figure shaping drug policy, the federal government responded to the new wave of heroin use by enacting tougher penalties for drug trafficking. The 1951 Boggs Act, passed in the months following the Kefauver committee's hearings, instituted mandatory minimum sentences for drug violations starting with two to five years in prison for first-time offenders in possession of marijuana, opiates, or cocaine. In November 1954, President Dwight D. Eisenhower announced a "war on drugs" and appointed a special committee of cabinet members to investigate the narcotics problem. Congress responded by passing the Narcotics Control Act of 1956, further toughening the federal drug penalties. Under this new law, first-time offenders convicted of possessing marijuana, opiates, or cocaine were required to be sentenced to between two and 10 years in prison. Still, the tougher penalties did not seem to curtail drug use. The Bureau of Narcotics reported that the number of heroin addicts in the United States increased to approximately 45,000 by 1960, and casual drug use would only expand in the 1960s.[8]

World War II and the Cold War

More than any other event, World War II shaped America at mid-century. The war impacted the areas of the law, criminal justice, and violence.

The rise of fascist powers in Europe and Japan in the years leading up to World War II focused U.S. fears on international threats. As the United States entered the war in December 1941 following the Japanese attack on Pearl Harbor, Americans living on the West Coast became concerned about the threats of attack and of domestic subversion. The Franklin D. Roosevelt administration responded by issuing Executive Order 9066 on February 19, 1942, ultimately forcing more than 110,000 Japanese Americans on the West Coast to leave their homes, careers, and possessions behind as they were herded into inland internment camps.[9] The same regulation also justified surveillance, forced relocation, and deportation of German and Italian Americans, albeit less extensive. Wartime laws mandated that approximately 600,000 Italian Americans carry "identity cards" clearly listing their status.[10] These regulations, upheld by the Supreme Court in *Hirabayashi v. United States* (1943) and *Korematsu v. United States* (1944), granted official sanction to growing nativist sentiment.

The war also caused broad dislocations on the home front as millions of Americans joined the military and took defense jobs. In some cases, the resulting stresses erupted in violence, especially in the industrial boomtowns. In Los Angeles, California, months of small-scale conflicts between Mexican-American youths and U.S. Navy personnel stationed in their neighborhoods erupted into full-scale rioting in June 1943 called the "zoot suit" riots. No specific event is known to have precipitated the confrontations, but they emerged from a context of hostility between groups occupying the same territory. Latino youths perceived servicemen as interlopers in their neighborhoods, whereas servicemen perceived Latino youths as unpatriotic because many were not enlisted in the armed forces and wore flamboyant zoot suits (very baggy pants and oversized, almost knee-length coats with wide lapels and heavy shoulder pads) at a time when cloth was conserved for the war effort. In addition, in 1942 and 1943, Los Angeles newspapers blamed Latino youths for a perceived wartime outbreak of crime and violence, heightening public hostility toward them. During the riots, servicemen attacked Latino youths, tearing off their zoot suits from their backs and giving the outbreak its name. The Los Angeles Police Department (LAPD) did little to quell the attacks, instead arresting more than 600 Mexican-American youths. Eight nights of violence ended only when the U.S. Navy ordered its personnel to leave the city of Los Angeles and return to their bases. Barely two weeks later, similar violence broke out in Detroit, the so-called arsenal of democracy, as young white city residents fought African Americans who had moved to the city to work in defense factories.

The conclusion of World War II restored some stability in the United States and brought an end to the wartime German, Italian, and Japanese governments abroad. More Americans began to understand that the leaders of these nations did not completely represent the will of the people. This was expressed in a particularly dramatic way by the hanging and mutilation of Italian dictator Benito Mussolini at the hands of that country's citizens, a high-profile sign of the contempt that many Axis citizens felt toward their former leaders at the end of the war. With the Axis powers defeated, U.S. fears turned to a new target: the Soviet Union.

The American people had already begun to fear communists following Russia's Bolshevik Revolution of 1917, which contributed to the first Red Scare, from about 1919 to 1921, in which popular opinion raged against communists and those who held foreign ideologies. In the aftermath of World War II, the Soviet Union, which had joined the Allied forces in 1941, emerged with control over much of Eastern Europe, one of the world's strongest militaries, and an ideological orientation distinctly different from that of the United States. Until its collapse in 1991, it represented America's main rival for influence on the world stage.

The cold war between the United States and the Soviet Union dates from the end of World War II. By 1946, the Soviet Union clearly intended to maintain its military occupation over eastern Europe, while the United States and its main allies, Britain and France, intended to rebuild the nations of western Europe along the lines of capitalist democracies. In 1946, former British prime minister Winston Churchill described the situation by asserting that "an iron curtain has descended across the [European] continent."[11] Earlier that year, U.S. diplomat George Kennan had set

Japanese-American detainees eat in a dining area at California's Manzanar Relocation Camp. This photograph is by Ansel Adams. *(National Archives and Records Administration [536863])*

the terms for the cold war from the U.S. perspective by arguing in a famous memo to his superiors in the U.S. State Department that the Soviet Union was expansionist by its very nature and that the United States should do everything in its power to contain the spread of communism.[12]

The Second Red Scare

This concern over the spread of communism moved from foreign policy to U.S. domestic policy as well. By late 1946, Harry Truman's White House faced considerable pressure to root out federal employees who harbored communist, socialist, or unacceptably liberal political beliefs. In response, in March 1947, Truman issued Executive Order 9835, authorizing executive agencies to identify potential subversives working for the federal government. Under the resulting Loyalty-Security program, approximately 2,700 federal workers lost their jobs between 1947 and 1956.[13] Also in 1947, the U.S. House of Representatives' House Un-American Activities Committee (HUAC) traveled to Hollywood to conduct hearings on the film industry, particularly the question of whether communists had infiltrated the Screen Writers' Guild and thereby exercised control over U.S. cinema. It was not a safe time to disagree with popular opinion.[14]

In 1949, two events further heightened the tensions of the cold war. The first, in August, was the detonation of the first Soviet nuclear bomb. Until that time, the United States was the only nation in the world with nuclear capabilities, but this Soviet display of strength sent a clear message that the United States could be both a nuclear aggressor and a nuclear victim. The sobering prospect of annihilation was suddenly very real.

The second event, China's communist revolution, established that the world's most populous nation was willing to embrace communism and that it represented a valid alternative to liberal democracy. Fear of nuclear annihilation was certainly potent enough on its own, but coupled with fear of irrelevance, fear that the democratic way of life might have actually become overshadowed by the new communist ideology, made the situation even worse. The Korean War, which began in 1950 as a conflict between the U.S.-backed South Korean democracy and the Chinese-backed North Korean communist republic, was emblematic of the relationship between the United States and the communist world and the relationship between the philosophies upon which their governments were based. Perceived betrayal of the United States by direct espionage or even by mere affiliation with communist groups became a Manichaean struggle between good and evil.

Trials and Hearings

Such was the fate of Alger Hiss, who had clerked for Supreme Court justice Oliver Wendell Holmes, worked for the U.S. State Department during World War II, and served as a temporary secretary-general of the fledgling United Nations. While president of the Carnegie Endowment for International Peace in 1948, Hiss was accused by Whittaker Chambers, a former senior editor at *Time* magazine, of passing documents to the Soviets. Chambers claimed that he knew this because he had been a Soviet spy from 1934 to 1938 and had used Hiss as a go-between. An outraged Hiss volunteered to appear before the U.S. House of Representatives to defend himself and later sued Chambers for libel. In the course of these experiences, he declared under oath that he had never been a Soviet spy. After Chambers produced microfilm of State Department documents and copies that government officials claimed had been transcribed on Hiss's family typewriter, Hiss was convicted of perjury—the statute of limitations on espionage having already expired—and spent 44 months in prison. In later years some scholars questioned the authenticity of the government's analysis and suggested that Hiss had been railroaded by his critics, although intercepted Soviet communications first released to the public in the 1990s—the VENOMA documents—reinforced the position that Hiss had passed information to the Soviet Union.[15]

Julius and Ethel Rosenberg would pay a much higher price for their alleged espionage activities. Julius, the son of Polish immigrants, became active in the Communist Party while studying engineering at the City University of New York. There he met Ethel Greenglass, a shipping clerk and union organizer whose activities routinely put her in conflict with her employers. The Rosenbergs were married in 1939. During World War II, Julius Rosenberg worked as an inspector in the U.S. Signal Corps while also serving as a member and branch chairman in the American Communist Party, an affiliation that cost him his job in 1945.

In July 1950, Julius Rosenberg was arrested on espionage charges; Ethel Rosenberg was arrested a month later. Both had been accused of passing nuclear secrets to the Soviet Union, allowing that country to develop its nuclear weapons in 1949. The linchpin of the case was the testimony of Ethel Rosenberg's younger brother, David Greenglass, who had worked on the Manhattan Project, the top-secret U.S. nuclear weapons program. Greenglass confessed to spying on behalf of the Soviets and agreed to testify against the Rosenbergs in exchange for a reduced sentence for himself and immunity for his wife. Central to the prosecution's case and the judge's decision to sentence the Rosenbergs to death was the belief that it was the Rosenbergs' alleged espionage that had allowed the Soviets to build the bomb. The Rosenbergs were both executed in June 1953.

Intercepted Soviet spy communications released to the public in 1995 told a very different story. Julius Rosenberg had never delivered especially useful information on the U.S. atomic bomb to the Soviets, though he had given them a proximity fuse, a crucial piece of conventional missile technology, in 1944—at a time when the United States and Soviet Union were allied against the Axis powers.

No one better exemplified the accusatory atmosphere of the late 1940s and early 1950s than Senator Joseph McCarthy of Wisconsin. Anticommunism existed earlier than McCarthy, but McCarthy provided the movement its form and substance when, on February 9, 1950, he declared before the Republican Women's Club of Wheeling, West Virginia, that "I have in my hand fifty-seven cases of individuals who would appear to be either card carrying members or certainly loyal to the Communist Party, but who nevertheless are still helping to shape our foreign policy [by working in the U.S. State Department]."[16]

McCarthy's speech inaugurated four years of accusations and congressional investigations of whether any communists actually worked for the federal government. McCarthy stood at center stage, conducting congressional hearings over whether perceived communist influence within the government may have contributed to the success of communists in China and elsewhere. Charges of communism were applied widely, used to constrain the civil liberties and free thinking of government employees, intellectuals, and artists. McCarthy's influence began to wane only in 1954, when a more moderate Republican president, Dwight D. Eisenhower, sought to rein him in and McCarthy himself overreached, accusing the U.S. Army of harboring communist sympathizers.

Postwar Crime and Justice

The years following World War II were full of contradictions in the United States and in the history of crime and justice. These were years of widespread economic growth and prosperity. Following brief uncertainty immediately following the war, the United States experienced sustained economic expansion. Returning service members took advantage of the G.I. Bill of Rights to attend college, buy homes, and start businesses. U.S. corporations benefited from the new prosperity and consumer demand to buy products at unprecedented levels. Middle-class families increasingly moved away from crowded cities into their own homes in the suburbs. Many Americans embraced a domestic ideology centered on home, family, and childrearing. After nearly a century of declining birthrates and smaller family sizes, the U.S. birthrate increased sharply in the mid-1940s, leading to a so-called baby boom that lasted until the early 1960s.

Ordinary crime was rare. The U.S. homicide rate declined through World War II, turned upward in 1946 as soldiers returned from war and faced uncertainty, then fell to its 20th-century low in the late 1940s and 1950s, dropping to just 4.5 murders per 100,000 people in 1955.[17] The incarceration rate—measuring people held in federal and state prisons—also remained essentially flat during this period, hovering at just over 100 inmates per 100,000 people in the U.S. population.[18] This period, however, also marked unusually vociferous concerns about crime. The emergence of new youth cultures helped generate renewed fears of juvenile delinquency and youth gangs, while the transformation of U.S. cities helped create concerns about crime more generally. The criminal justice system and, in particular, police responded to these concerns by engaging in a new wave of reform and professionalization.

The Delinquency Scare

Juvenile delinquency—crimes or status offenses committed by people ages 17 or younger—became a major public issue during World War II and the postwar era. In the war years, the absence of parents due to war work or military service and the increased responsibilities that teenagers assumed were widely expected to generate an increase in delinquency. Boys might steal cars, while "khaki-mad" girls were perceived more likely to commit sexual improprieties with men in uniform. While crime statistics from this period are notoriously unreliable, the numbers seemed to support this concern. On a national level, the FBI's Uniform Crime Reports showed a sharp national increase in arrests of juveniles during the war years.[19] On a local level the Los Angeles Police Department's annual reports stated that juvenile arrests increased from roughly 3,500 in 1940 to more than 9,000 in 1944.[20]

After a relative lull in the late 1940s, juvenile delinquency reemerged as a major public issue throughout the 1950s. How much juvenile crime actually increased is unclear. Both the FBI's count of juvenile arrests and the U.S. Children's Bureau's count of juvenile court cases showed sharp increases, but officials at these agencies privately expressed concerns about their completeness and reliability.[21] What is clear is that delinquency became a substantial public concern. Magazines such as the *Saturday Evening Post* and newspapers such as the *New York Times* published major stories on juvenile misbehavior. The number of articles in mass-circulation magazines, as counted in the *Reader's Guide to Periodical Literature*, spiked between 1953 and 1958.[22] Hollywood filmmakers, sensing both a timely issue and an opportunity to market to a new audience of young people, produced films dealing with delinquency such as *The Wild One* (1953), *Blackboard Jungle* (1955), and *Rebel Without a Cause* (1955), as well as dozens of lesser-known films such as *Teenage Crime Wave* (1955). Committees of concerned adults ranging from local school boards and chambers of commerce to the U.S. Senate conducted investigations of delinquency.

These Senate hearings provided a national forum for discussions of possible connections between delinquency and the mass media. A Senate subcommittee first looked into the delinquency question in 1950, but the 1953 creation of the Senate Subcommittee to Investigate the Causes of Delinquency gave the issue its greatest public prominence. Spearheaded by Democratic senator Estes Kefauver of Tennessee, the subcommittee heard testimony on delinquency through the end of the 1950s and gained a national spotlight in 1954 when it turned its attention to comic books. At the time, comics were extremely popular, largely aimed toward a young male readership and often quite sensational in their content. Child psychologist Frederic Wertham spent his career studying links between media and youth violence and campaigning against comic books. His 1954 book, *The Seduction of the Innocent*, documented the graphic violence pervasive in horror and crime comics, and argued strongly that these images contributed to juvenile violence. When in New York City in April 1954 the Senate subcommittee heard testimony on comics Wertham acted as the lead witness, detailing numerous examples of gore and brutality in comics. When comic book publishers such as William M. Gaines of EC Comics aggressively defended themselves, they succeeded only in turning the public against them. By October 1954, the comic book industry, fearing federal regulation or an outright ban, voluntarily adopted a new code of standards and agreed to self-censor its content.[23]

The worst-case scenario that Kefauver and Wertham had in mind probably involved urban gangs. Gangs of criminal adults had existed in urban centers such as New York and Chicago since the mid-19th century, and groups of delinquent youths had routinely called themselves gangs since at the least the 1920s. In the years following World War II, however, gangs of youths in their teens and early 20s became more pervasive and violent. As cities, including New York, experienced the constriction of old ethnic neighborhoods concurrently with African-American migration and Puerto Rican immigration in the 1940s and 1950s, Irish and Italians youths fought to (in their minds) protect their neighborhood territories from newcomers. New York gangs made national headlines in 1959 when 15-year-old Puerto Rican immigrant Salvador Agron, known as the "Capeman" (for the black cape he wore), was arrested and convicted for the murders of two youths in a fight to control a neighborhood playground. Agron had gone to the playground with his gang, the Vampires, confronted two teenage boys, and apparently stabbed them to death in the ensuing fight. His subsequent trial and conviction helped make gangs a national concern in the late 1950s.[24] Conflicts between ethnic gangs sank so deeply into the national consciousness that *West Side Story*—a musical derived from Shakespeare's *Romeo and Juliet* about rival Puerto Rican and white gangs in New York—became a major hit as a Broadway show in 1957 and as a film in 1961.

What caused this sudden concern with juvenile delinquency? To some extent, crimes by teenagers did increase in the 1950s. Also, law enforcement treated delinquency more seriously in the 1950s than it had in earlier decades, thereby increasing arrest counts and the public attention paid to the problem. Finally, teenagers themselves fully emerged as a distinct social group in the 1940s and 1950s. The very word *teenager* was first used in print in 1941 (in an article in *Popular Science*) and came into common use during World War II.[25] Popular concerns about teenage crime intertwined with more general concerns about the music teenagers danced to, how teenagers dressed, and the ways in which schools and social institutions mixed teenagers of different classes and races. In Buffalo, New York, for example, public school administrators campaigned against delinquency in the mid-1950s by encouraging teenagers to "dress right," to trade in their blue jeans and leather jackets for respectable sweater sets and skirts for girls and coats and ties for boys. The schools also used vocational education programs to help diverse groups of students, but then denied African Americans access to the vocational schools, thereby creating barriers to them joining skilled trades as adults.[26]

Given the public concern with delinquency in the 1940s and 1950s, it is no surprise that new agencies to handle young offenders emerged in this period as well. California established the innovative California Youth Authority (CYA) in 1941, creating a central state-level clearinghouse for all juvenile justice administration. By 1943, the CYA assumed control of the state's juvenile reform schools, and in the postwar years it established policies for classifying youths as they entered the system and monitoring them on parole as they left it.[27] At the local level, settlement houses, churches, and public agencies sought to prevent delinquency and violence in the streets. They hired what they called "street workers" or "detached workers" to intervene with youth gangs. Taking their cue from the innovative Chicago Area Project founded in 1934, young street workers tried to meet delinquent youths in public, befriend them, determine their interests, and direct them to productive, or at least noncriminal, activities. Sponsored by the mayor's office, the New York City Youth Board opened in 1947 and directed more than 40 gang workers by 1955.[28]

Police Professionalization

Concerns about crime also fostered increased professionalism and efficiency by the police. The stage for police professionalization had been set in the 1920s, when reformers such as August Vollmer, the chief of police in Berkeley, California, began to streamline policing and in the 1930s, when the FBI pioneered scientific crime investigation. Professionalization continued to advance in the 1930s and 1940s as figures such as Vollmer's protégé, Orlando W. Wilson, chief of the Kansas City, Missouri, police and later a professor of criminal justice at the University of California, Berkeley, developed police administration into a more systematic practice. Wilson led the movement to shift police officers from walking a beat to patrolling in automobiles—one officer per car. In this way, police could respond to calls more quickly and efficiently. However, the shift to automobiles reduced the presence of police officers in people's daily lives; rather than being figures whom ordinary citizens would run into casually as they walked the streets, police officers became figures whom people would call for service and avoid otherwise.

In the years following World War II, increased funding, improved technology, and underlying concerns about social change all helped spur police professionalization. William H. Parker, chief of the Los Angeles Police Department (LAPD) between 1950 and 1966, exemplified this process. Moreover, Parker's influence extended even beyond his tenure because three of his protégés followed him as chief, leading the LAPD between 1966 and 1992.

In sharp contrast to the 19th-century police focus on maintaining public order, Parker's LAPD concentrated overwhelmingly on fighting crime, still a relatively new goal for police in the postwar era. Parker's administration stamped out the financial corruption and graft that had earlier pervaded the LAPD. Instead, he promoted a very professional image for the LAPD through his own public statements, through his officers' demeanor, and through the media, especially the radio and television program *Dragnet*. *Dragnet* began in 1949 as a radio show produced by and starring actor Jack Webb. It moved to television as a movie in late 1951, became a regular series that aired on NBC from 1952 until 1959, and was revived between 1967 and 1970. During the 1953–54 season *Dragnet* was the second highest rated show on television. When Webb asked for the LAPD's formal cooperation to produce the show, Parker provided it, but in return he demanded a contract giving the LAPD absolute script approval. Webb gained authenticity for his show; Parker gained a weekly televised forum to promote his model of policing.[29]

Parker's model of policing involved authoritative, interventionist law enforcement suited to managing a sprawling city with the smallest per capita urban police force in the United States. Parker called it "proactive policing."[30] Under his leadership LAPD officers were encouraged to use tactics such as stopping and frisking suspicious persons and conducting intensive patrols of high-crime neighborhoods. Parker's administration tolerated police violence against suspected criminals. LAPD-style policing, adopted widely by police elsewhere in the 1950s and 1960s, helped protect people whom Parker considered the respectable public, but it also brought the weight of police authority down on the people who lived in high-crime neighborhoods. The people who most needed police protection instead received police authoritarianism. This disconnect contributed to the tensions that increasingly emerged between urban police forces and urban residents in the postwar decades.

The Murder of Emmett Till

In many ways, the factors that shaped southern life before World War II persisted in the postwar years. In August 1955, a 14-year-old Chicago boy named Emmett Till was sent to his great-uncle's home in Money, Mississippi, to spend the rest of the summer picking cotton. After a long day of working, Emmett and a small group of other black youths went to a grocery store owned by a local white couple, Roy and Carolyn Bryant, for refreshments. Walking to the counter with a pack of bubble gum in his hand, Emmett committed what would turn out to be a fatal mistake. He whistled at Carolyn Bryant, who was working alone in the store. When Roy Bryant came back to town a few days later, he became enraged and sought vengeance. He explained the situation to his half brother J. W. Milam, and the pair decided to kidnap and murder the boy.

When Till's mutilated body was pulled from the Tallahatchie River on August 31, national newspapers could only attempt to express the horror of the crime. Till had been beaten beyond recognition. His murderers shot him in the head with a .45-caliber pistol, then tied his body to a cotton gin fan with barbed wire and dumped it in the river. Till's uncle wasn't able to identify him—only a ring with Emmett's father's initials, "L. T.," gave any clue as to the body's identity. Although the condition of the body would ordinarily warrant a closed-casket funeral, Emmett's mother chose to hold an open-casket ceremony instead, so that the American people would be able to see what Mississippi racism had done to her son. The iconic photograph of Till's body, originally published in the African-American magazine *Jet* and reprinted many times since, speaks to the jarring violence of Bryant and Milam.

Nevertheless, the white officials who operated Mississippi's criminal justice system demonstrated casual indifference toward Till's death. The Mississippi attorney general's office conducted no serious investigation into the murder. No autopsy was performed, and state prosecutors rebuffed witness-gathering efforts by committed law enforcement agents, local reporters, and the NAACP (in which Medgar Evers, the organization's state field secretary, went undercover as a cotton worker in an attempt to gather information). When the case came to trial, Bryant and Milam were acquitted by an all-white jury in just over an hour. Jurors bragged that they would have acquitted the defendants even more quickly had they not taken a soda break.

Upon hearing the verdict, Bryant and Milam stood up and passionately kissed their wives—historically interpreted as their way of displaying to the world that, in killing Till, they had defended white womanhood from black manhood. They exited the courtroom to laughter, broad grins, and congratulations. A few months later, after being offered $4,000 and assured that double jeopardy laws would prevent them from ever being tried again, Bryant and Milam cheerfully confessed to the killing in an issue of *Look* magazine. "I just decided it was time a few people got put on notice," Milam boasted.[31] Bryant and Milam were never convicted of the murder and spent the rest of their lives as free men. Milam died in 1981, and Bryant died in 1994, both of natural causes.

It seemed to some that southern racial relations would never change. Till's murder occurred more than 20 years after the Scottsboro cases and seemed to reflect the same willingness to use violence and the legal system to maintain white dominance. Till's murder, however, also happened just one year after the U.S. Supreme Court's historic decision in *Brown v. Board of Topeka* declared racial segregation of schools unconstitutional and just months before the beginning of the Montgomery, Alabama, bus boycott that is often considered the beginning of the modern mass movement for African-American civil rights. The violence of Till's death reflected a new defensiveness on the part of southern white racial hard-liners in the face of change, a defensiveness that would be manifested in violence throughout the late 1950s and 1960s. Till's death also helped to mobilize that nascent Civil Rights movement. The widely distributed images of Till's mutilated body became a symbol of what activists would fight against.

Chronicle of Events

1933

- *March:* Haywood Patterson is retried in the Scottsboro case. He is again convicted, despite an effective defense attorney and a supportive judge.

1934

- Alcatraz Federal Penitentiary, a former military prison on an island in San Francisco Bay, is reopened as a new state-of-the-art federal prison for high-profile inmates.
- *May 23:* Bonnie Parker and Clyde Barrow are killed by a posse of law enforcement officers on a roadside near Bienville Parish, Louisiana.
- *July 22:* At the end of a months-long manhunt, FBI agents gun down John Dillinger outside of a Chicago movie theater.
- *September 19:* Bruno Richard Hauptmann is arrested for the Lindbergh baby kidnapping and murder.
- *October 22:* FBI agents shoot and kill Pretty Boy Floyd near East Liverpool, Ohio.
- *November:* In the third trial of the Scottsboro Boys, Haywood Patterson and Clarence Norris are again convicted and sentenced to death.
- *November 27:* Baby Face Nelson is killed in a shoot-out with FBI officers outside of Chicago.

1935

- *January 15:* FBI agents surround a house in Ocklawaha, Florida, occupied by bandits Fred and Kate "Ma" Barker. The Barkers refuse to surrender and are killed in a hail of gunfire.
- *January 20:* After FBI agents track down bandit Alvin Karpis, FBI director J. Edgar Hoover personally arrests him in Atlantic City, New Jersey.
- *February 14:* Bruno Richard Hauptmann is convicted in the Lindbergh kidnapping and sentenced to death.
- *April 1:* The U.S. Supreme Court issues its second ruling relating to the Scottsboro case, *Norris v. Alabama,* indicating that the exclusion of African Americans from jury pools constituted a violation of civil rights and returned the cases to state courts.

1936

- The anti-marijuana film *Tell Your Children* is produced. It becomes better known as *Reefer Madness.*
- *January:* Haywood Patterson is tried for a fourth time in relation to the Scottsboro case and again convicted, but this time sentenced to 75 years in prison.
- *April 3:* Bruno Hauptmann is executed.

1937

- *July:* U.S. Narcotics Commissioner Harry J. Anslinger's article "Marijuana, Assassin of Youth" is published in *The American Magazine.*
- *October 1:* The Marihuana Tax Act of 1937 becomes federal law.

1941

- *December 7:* The Japanese attack on American forces at Pearl Harbor leads the United States to enter World War II.

1942

- *February 19:* The Roosevelt administration issues Executive Order 9066, requiring the internment of Japanese-American people living on the West Coast.

1943

- *June 3:* Sailors and soldiers attack Mexican-American youths in Los Angeles, reflecting months of growing tensions between the two groups. The conflicts last for eight days and become known as the zoot suit riots.
- *June 20:* Confrontations between blacks and whites on Detroit's Belle Isle spread to the rest of the city and devolve into a race riot lasting two days.

1945

- *August 13:* Japan surrenders to the United States, ending World War II.

1947

- *March 21:* The Truman administration issues Executive Order 9835, creating a loyalty-security program for federal employees.
- *October 27–30:* The House Un-American Activities Committee (HUAC) takes testimony from Hollywood screenwriters and directors.

1948

- *August:* Whittaker Chambers and Alger Hiss testify before HUAC as part of an investigation of communists in the U.S. government.
- *December 15:* Alger Hiss is indicted for committing perjury in his testimony before HUAC.

1949

- *July:* Alger Hiss's first perjury trial ends in a hung jury.
- *Summer:* Chinese communists win a civil war and assume government power.
- *August:* The Soviet Union tests its first nuclear weapon.

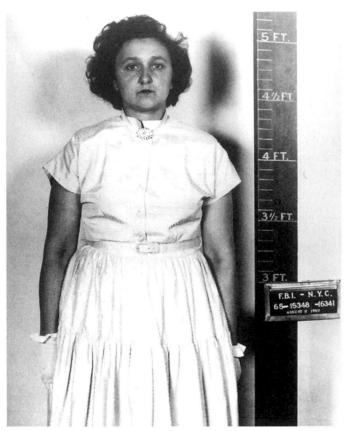

This mug shot of Ethel Rosenberg was taken by federal officials in 1950. *(National Archives and Records Administration [596909])*

1950

- *January 21:* Alger Hiss is found guilty of perjury in his second trial.
- *February 9:* Senator Joseph McCarthy delivers his famous speech in Wheeling, West Virginia, accusing the U.S. State Department of harboring communist agents.
- *July 17:* Having been named a participant in a conspiracy that had passed nuclear secrets to the Soviet Union, Julius Rosenberg is arrested for espionage.
- *August 9:* William H. Parker is appointed chief of the Los Angeles Police Department (LAPD).

1951

- Senator Estes Kefauver's Special Committee to Investigate Organized Crime in Interstate Commerce conducts hearings on drug addiction.
- *March 6:* The trial of Julius and Ethel Rosenberg on charges of atomic espionage begins.
- *April 5:* Judge Irving Kaufman sentences the convicted Julius and Ethel Rosenberg to death.

- *November 2:* Congress passes the Boggs Act, establishing mandatory minimum prison sentences for violations of federal drug laws.

1953

- *June 19:* Julius and Ethel Rosenberg are executed.

1954

- Fredric Wertham's *Seduction of the Innocent* is published.
- *April 21:* The Senate Subcommittee to Investigate the Causes of Juvenile Delinquency begins to hear testimony in New York City on the links between comic books and juvenile crime.
- *April–June:* During the Army-McCarthy hearings, the U.S. Senate redirects its attention to alleged improper actions by Joseph McCarthy.
- *May 17:* The U.S. Supreme Court issues its historic decision in *Brown v. Board of Education of Topeka, Kansas,* declaring unanimously that racial segregation in schools is unconstitutional.
- *October 26:* A newly formed comic book industry trade group, the Comics Magazine Association of America, publishes a code of standards that comic book publishers agree to accept voluntarily.
- *November 27:* President Dwight D. Eisenhower announces his war on drugs.
- *December 2:* The U.S. Senate censures Joseph McCarthy.

1955

- *August 28:* Emmett Till, a 14-year-old African-American youth from Chicago, is kidnapped from his uncle's home in rural Mississippi.
- *August 29:* Roy Bryant and J. W. Milam, two white men, are arrested in relation to Till's kidnapping.
- *August 31:* Till's beaten and mutilated body is found in Mississippi's Tallahatchie River.
- *September 23:* Roy Bryant and J. W. Milam are tried but acquitted for the murder of Emmett Till.

1956

- *January 24:* Bryant and Milam's confession to killing Emmett Till is published in *Look* magazine.
- *July 18:* President Eisenhower signs the Narcotics Control Act of 1956.

1957

- *September 27:* The musical *West Side Story,* about rival New York City gangs, opens at Broadway's Winter Garden Theater.

Eyewitness Testimony

Racism and Lynchings

Officials and residents of Scottsboro maintained that the crowd was peaceful and showed no evidence of lynching spirit . . . Chance conversation with residents of the town, however, did not tend to substantiate this view of the officials. A kind-faced, elderly woman selling tickets at the railroad station, for instance, said to me that if they re-tried the Negroes in Scottsboro, she hoped they would leave the soldiers home next time. When I asked why, she replied that the next time they would finish off the "black fiends" and save the bother of a second trial. Then she told me a lurid story of the mistreatment suffered by the two white girls at the hands of those "horrible black brutes," one of whom had had her breast chewed off by one of the Negroes.

When I called to her attention that the doctor's testimony for the prosecution was to the effect that neither of the girls showed signs of any rough handling on their bodies, it made no impression upon her. Her faith in her atrocity story, which had been told to her "by one who ought to know what he was talking about," remained unshaken.

Teacher and civil rights activist Hollace Ransdall, reporting on the atmosphere surrounding the first Scottsboro trials, May 27, 1931, quoted in Famous American Trials: The "Scottsboro Boys" Trial. *Available online at URL: http://www.law.umkc.edu/faculty/projects/FTrials/scottsboro/scottsb.html.*

In the light of the facts outlined in the forepart of this opinion—the ignorance and illiteracy of the defendants, their youth, the circumstances of public hostility, the imprisonment and the close surveillance of the defendants by the military forces, the fact that their friends and families were all in other states and communication with them necessarily difficult, and above all that they stood in deadly peril of their lives—we think the failure of the trial court to give them reasonable time and opportunity to secure counsel was a clear denial of due process . . .

Let us suppose the extreme case of a prisoner charged with a capital offence, who is deaf and dumb, illiterate and feeble minded, unable to employ counsel, with the whole power of the state arrayed against him, prosecuted by counsel for the state without assignment of counsel for his defense, tried, convicted and sentenced to death. Such a result, which, if carried into execution, would be little short of judicial murder, it cannot be doubted would be a gross violation of the guarantee of due process of law;

and we venture to think that no appellate court, state or federal, would hesitate so to decide . . . The duty of the trial court to appoint counsel under such circumstances is clear, as it is clear under circumstances such as are disclosed by the record here; and its power to do so, even in the absence of a statute, can not be questioned. Attorneys are officers of the court, and are bound to render service when required by such an appointment . . .

The United States by statute and every state in the Union by express provision of law, or by the determination of its courts, make it the duty of the trial judge, where the accused is unable to employ counsel, to appoint counsel for him. In most states the rule applies broadly to all criminal prosecutions, in others it is limited to the more serious crimes, and in a very limited number, to capital cases. A rule adopted with such unanimous accord reflects, if it does not establish, the inherent right to have counsel appointed, at least in cases like the present, and lends convincing support to the conclusion we have reached as to the fundamental nature of that right.

Justice George Sutherland, writing for the U.S. Supreme Court from his majority opinion in Powell v. Alabama *(287 U.S. 45), overturning the convictions of the Scottsboro defendants based on the trial judge's failure to allow adequate legal representation, November 7, 1932.*

Till had been shot in the head and severely beaten. The body was weighted down with a gin pulley, a cast iron wheel used to operate a cotton gin. The wheel, approximately a foot and a half in diameter, weighed 150 to 200 pounds. It was attached to the boy's body with barbed wire wrapped around his waist . . .

Sheriff H. C. Strider of Tallahatchie County, in which the body was found, said, . . . "We found a bullet hole one inch above his right ear. The left side of his face had been cut up or beat up—plumb into the skull". . .

Till was visiting his uncle and aunt, Moses and Elizabeth Wright, a farm couple living at Money . . . [A]nother Negro who was visiting the Wrights has said that Till whistled at a "pretty lady" at the store, and that this may have been the cause of the trouble . . .

"I think you're making a big to-do about this," [an official] told a reporter seeking to learn routine facts about the case.

A newspaper account describing the discovery of the body of Emmett Till, a 14-year-old Chicago native who was lynched while visiting relatives in rural Mississippi. From "Find Kidnapped Chicago Boy's Body in River," Chicago Tribune, *September 1, 1955, p. 1.*

I'm no bully; I never hurt a n____r in my life. I like n____rs—in their place—I know how to work 'em. But I just decided it was time a few people got put on notice. As long as I live and can do anything about it, n____rs are gonna stay in their place. N____rs ain't gonna vote where I live. If they did, they'd control the government. They ain't gonna go to school with my kids. And when a n____r gets close to mentioning sex with a white woman, he's tired o' livin'. I'm likely to kill him. Me and my folks fought for this country, and we got some rights. I stood there in that shed and listened to that n____r throw that poison at me, and I just made up my mind. "Chicago boy," I said, "I'm tired of 'em sending your kind down here to stir up trouble. Goddam you, I'm going to make an example of you—just so everybody can know how me and my folks stand."

J. W. Milam, admitting that he had helped kidnap and murder Emmett Till in 1955. From William Bradford Hule, "The Shocking Story of Approved Killing in Mississippi," Look, January 24, 1956, reproduced in The American Experience: The Murder of Emmett Till. *Available online at URL: http://www.pbs.org/wgbh/amex/till/sfeature/sf_look_confession.html.*

Refocusing U.S. Drug Policy

We can stop teen-age drug addiction now. To do it, we must recognize this dread curse for what it is. It is not just another form of delinquency. It is the deliberate exploitation of naïve boys and girls by drug traffickers who aim to open up a rich new market, to raise a huge new crop of addicts.

What crime is worse, more villainous than addicting teen-age boys and girls to narcotics? "You might as well shoot them in the back," remarked Senator Estes Kefauver in Washington. "It might even be kinder."

The teen-age victims themselves call it the "white death." I have seen their rueful faces and probed into the wreckage of young lives ruined—possibly for good—at sixteen, seventeen, eighteen. They call it the "white death" because of the powdered white opiate with which the drug merchants have enslaved them.

What are we going to do about it?

Are we going to sit back and accept it? Are we going to wring our hands in surrender and admit that henceforth one of the hazards of growing up—even for our own children—may be enslavement to narcotic drugs?

Or are we ready to beat the dope merchants at their own game, to make the teen-age drug traffic (as we once made kidnapping) too hot to handle? Do we have the vitality, the determination to stamp out this curse here and now?

Howard Whitman, "How We Can Stop Narcotic Sales," Woman's Home Companion, June 1951, reprinted in Belenko, Drugs and Drug Policy in America, p. 191.

President Eisenhower called today for a new war on narcotic addiction at the local, national, and international level.

He appointed a special Cabinet committee of five members to coordinate the campaign against illegal narcotics and enjoined them to "omit no practical step to minimize and stamp out narcotic addiction."

James C. Hagerty, White House press secretary, said that new legislation might be asked from the next Congress to step up the drive against the narcotics traffic and to aid the rehabilitation of those who have become addicts.

President Dwight D. Eisenhower initiates his "war on drugs." From W. H. Lawrence, "President Launches Drive on Narcotics." New York Times, November 28, 1954, pp. 1–2.

The Red Scare

Citizens of this country who betray their fellow-countrymen can be under none of the delusions about the benignity of Soviet power that they might have been prior to World War II. The nature of Russian terrorism is now self-evident. Idealism as a rationale dissolves . . .

I consider your crime worse than murder. Plain deliberate contemplated murder is dwarfed in magnitude by comparison with the crime you have committed. In committing the act of murder, the criminal kills only his victim. The immediate family is brought to grief and when justice is meted out the chapter is closed. But in your case, I believe your conduct is putting into the hands of the Russians the A-bomb years before our best scientists predicted would perfect the bomb has already caused, in my opinion, the Communist aggression in Korea, with the resultant casualties exceeding 50,000 and who knows but that millions more of innocent people may pay the price of your treason. Indeed, by your betrayal you undoubtedly have altered the course of history to the disadvantage of our country.

No one can say that we do not live in a constant state of tension. We have evidence of your treachery all around us every day—for the civilian defense activities throughout the nation are aimed at preparing us for an atom bomb attack. Nor can it be said in mitigation of the offense that the power which set the conspiracy in motion and profited from it was not openly hostile to the United States at the time of the conspiracy. If this was your excuse the error of your ways in setting yourselves above our properly constituted authorities and the decision of those authorities not to share the information with Russia must now be obvious . . .

The statute of which the defendants at the bar stand convicted is clear. I have previously stated my view that the verdict of guilty was amply justified by the evidence. In the light of the circumstances, I feel that I must pass such sentence upon the principals in this diabolical conspiracy to destroy a God-fearing nation, which will demonstrate with finality that this nation's security must remain inviolate . . .

The evidence indicated quite clearly that Julius Rosenberg was the prime mover in this conspiracy. However, let no mistake be made about the role which his wife, Ethel Rosenberg, played in this conspiracy. Instead of deterring him from pursuing his ignoble cause, she encouraged and assisted the cause. She was a mature woman—almost three years older than her husband and almost seven years older than her younger brother. She was a full-fledged partner in this crime.

Indeed the defendants Julius and Ethel Rosenberg placed their devotion to their cause above their own personal safety and were conscious that they were sacrificing their own children, should their misdeeds be detected—all of which did not deter them from pursing their course. Love for their cause dominated their lives—it was even greater than their love for their children.

Judge Irving Kaufman, from his ruling sentencing the Rosenbergs to death, April 5, 1951, quoted in Famous Trials: The Rosenberg Trial. *Available online at URL: http://www.law.umkc.edu/faculty/projects/ftrials/rosenb/ROSENB.HTM.*

Buds are beginning to appear on the forsythia, and welts on Joe McCarthy. The early arrival of spring and a series of humiliations for our would-be Fuehrer have made this a most pleasant week in the capital.

The events of the week are worth savoring. Blunt Charlie Wilson called McCarthy's charges against the army "tommyrot" and for once Joe had no comeback. Next day came the ignominious announcement that he was dropping that $2,000,000 suit against former Senator Benton for calling McCarthy a crook and a liar; the lame excuse promised to launch a nationwide "I Believe Benton" movement. [Adlai] Stevenson followed with a speech calculated to impress those decent conservatives who had grown disgusted with the Eisenhower Administration's cowardice in the Zwicker affair.

When McCarthy sought to answer Stevenson, the Republican National Committee turned up in Ike's corner and grabbed the radio and TV time away from him . . . Next day, a Republican albeit a liberal Republican, Flanders of Vermont, actually got up on the floor of the Senate and delivered a speech against McCarthy. That same night Ed Murrow telecast a brilliant TV attack on McCarthy.

Under Stevenson's leadership, Eisenhower rallied. At a press conference he endorsed the Flanders attack . . . Like an escaped prisoner, flexing cramped muscles in freedom, the President . . . even had the temerity to suggest that it might be a good idea to swap butter and other surplus farm commodities with Russia.

Investigative journalist I. F. Stone, reporting on the early phase of Senator Joseph McCarthy's fall from grace during the Army-McCarthy hearings, March 15, 1954, reprinted in Zinn and Arnove, Voices from a People's History of the United States, *pp. 384–385.*

McCarthy: (Mr. Chairman) . . . in view of Mr. Welch's request that the information be given once we know of anyone who might be performing any work for the Communist Party, I think we should tell him that he has in his law firm a young man named Fisher whom he recommended, incidentally, to do the work on this Committee, who has been, for a number of years, a member of an organization which is named, oh, years and years ago, as the legal bulwark of the Communist Party . . .

Whether you knew that he was a member of that Communist organization or not, I don't know. I assume you did not, Mr. Welch, because I get the impression that while you are quite an actor, you play for a laugh, I don't think you have any conception of the danger of the Communist Party. I don't think you, yourself, would ever knowingly aid the Communist cause. I think you're unknowingly aiding it when you try to burlesque this hearing in which we're attempting to bring out the facts.

Welch: Mr. Chairman . . .

Mundt: The Chair may say that he has no recognition or no memory of Mr. Welch recommending either Mr. Fisher or anybody else as counsel for this Committee.

McCarthy: I refer to the record, Mr. Chairman . . . to the news story on that . . .

Welch: Senator McCarthy, I did not know, Senator—Senator, sometimes you say may I have your attention—

McCarthy: I'm listening . . .

Welch: May I have your attention?

McCarthy: I can listen with one ear and talk with—

Welch: No, this time, sir, I want you to listen with both. Senator McCarthy, I think until this moment—

McCarthy: Good. Just a minute. Jim, Jim, will you get the news story to the effect that this man belongs to the—to this Communist front organization . . .

Welch: I will tell you that he belonged to it.

McCarthy: Jim, will you get the citation, one of the citations showing that this was the legal arm of the Communist Party, and the length of time that he belonged, and the fact that he was recommended by Mr. Welch. I think that should be in the record . . .

Welch: Senator, you won't need anything in the record when I finish telling you this. Until this moment, Senator, I think I never really gauged your cruelty, or your recklessness. Fred Fisher is a young man who went to the Harvard Law School and came into my firm and is starting what looks to be a brilliant career with us. When I decided to work for this Committee, I asked Jim St. Clair, who sits on my right, to be my first assistant. I said to Jim, "Pick somebody in the firm to work under you that you would like." He chose Fred Fisher, and they came down on an afternoon plane. That night, when we had taken a little stab at trying to see what the case is about, Fred Fisher and Jim St. Clair and I went to dinner together. I then said to these two young men, "Boys, I don't know anything about you, except I've always liked you, but if there's anything funny in the life of either one of you that would hurt anybody in this case, you speak up quick."

And Fred Fisher said, "Mr. Welch, when I was in the law school, and for a period of months after, I belonged to the Lawyers' Guild," as you have suggested, Senator. He went on to say, "I am Secretary of the Young Republican's League in Newton with the son of [the] Massachusetts governor, and I have the respect and admiration of my community, and I'm sure I have the respect and admiration of the twenty-five lawyers or so in Hale & Dorr." And I said, "Fred, I just don't think I'm going to ask you to work on the case. If I do, one of these days that will come out, and go over national television, and it will just hurt like the dickens." And so, Senator, I asked him to go back to Boston. Little did I dream you could be so reckless and so cruel as to do an injury to that lad. It is, I regret to say, equally true that I fear he shall always bear a scar needlessly inflicted by you. If it were in my power to forgive you for

your reckless cruelty, I would do so. I like to think I'm a gentle man, but your forgiveness will have to come from someone other than me . . .

McCarthy: Mr. Chairman, may I say that Mr. Welch talks about this being cruel and reckless. He was just baiting . . . Now, I just give this man's record and I want to say, Mr. Welch, that it had been labeled long before he became a member, as early as 1944—

Welch: Senator, may we not drop this? We know he belonged to the Lawyers' Guild.

McCarthy: Let me finish . . .

Welch: And Mr. Cohn nods his head at me. I did you, I think, no personal injury, Mr. Cohn?

Cohn: No, sir.

Welch: I meant to do you no personal injury.

Cohn: No, sir.

Welch: And if I did, I beg your pardon. Let us not assassinate this lad further, Senator.

McCarthy: Let's, let's—

Welch: You've done enough. Have you no sense of decency, sir, at long last? Have you left no sense of decency?

An exchange between Senator Joseph McCarthy (R-WI) and defense attorney Joseph Welch, representing the U.S. Army, during the Army-McCarthy hearings, June 9, 1954, reproduced in American Rhetoric. *Available online at URL: http://www.americanrhetoric.com/speeches/welch-mccarthy.html.*

The Delinquency Scare

In peacetime a main cause of youngsters' getting into trouble, as every juvenile court judge knows, is "broken homes"—homes disrupted by separation or divorce, by poverty, illness, or death. The children suffer. In the vast upheaval of war, there are a multitude of new causes of broken homes.

Fathers leave their families to work in the big war-production centers. Older brothers go into the services. Older sisters go into war work. Mothers are busy with civilian defense activities or take places on the assembly lines. The friendly home which cherished the youngsters has become a lonely place, where older members of the family appears only on hurried excursions, at irregular hours . . .

If the violence among boys is alarming, the increasing wartime waywardness of teen-age girls is tragic. Again, the neglect of parents is a primary cause, but wartime conditions have a direct effect . . .

Anne is lonesome, bewildered, and restless. Her world has changed. The boys have gone away, may never come back. She thinks she will never be able to get married. She might as well try to have a good time. She gets into the habit of strolling downtown at night with a girl-friend and picking up the acquaintances of soldiers on leave and war workers. Far from home, with money in their pockets, they, too, are eager for excitement. Result: trouble.

FBI director J. Edgar Hoover on juvenile delinquency during World War II, from "Wild Children," American Magazine, July 1943, pp. 103–104.

1) Crimes shall never be presented in such a way as to create sympathy for the criminal, to promote distrust of the forces of law and justice, or to inspire others with a desire to imitate criminals.
2) No comics shall explicitly present the unique details and methods of a crime.
3) Policemen, judges, government officials, and respected institutions shall never be presented in such a way as to create disrespect for established authority.
4) If crime is depicted it shall be as a sordid and unpleasant activity.
5) Criminals shall not be presented so as to be rendered glamorous or to occupy a position which creates the desire for emulation.
6) In every instance good shall triumph over evil and the criminal punished for his misdeeds.
7) Scenes of excessive violence shall be prohibited. Scenes of brutal torture, excessive and unnecessary knife and gun play, physical agony, gory and gruesome crime shall be eliminated.
8) No unique or unusual methods of concealing weapons shall be shown.
9) Instances of law enforcement officers dying as a result of a criminal's activities should be discouraged.
10) The crime of kidnapping shall never be portrayed in any detail, nor shall any profit accrue to the abductor or kidnapper. The criminal or the kidnapper must be punished in every case.

The original 1954 Standards of the Comics Code Authority, established in the wake of Fredric Wertham's work on comic books and juvenile delinquency, quoted in "The Comics Code" in Lambiek's Comiclopedia. Available online at URL: http://lambiek.net/comics/code_text.htm.

Agron, 16 years old, has admitted, according to the police, that he wore a strange, Dracula-like cape to the playground and that he "cut" someone. . . .

"How do you feel about killing those boys," a newsman called to Agron. The sloping shoulders shrugged. "Like I always feel. Like this," came the words, indifferently.

"Are you sorry?"

"That's for me to know and you to find out."

"Do you feel like a big man?" another newsman pressed Agron.

"Do you?" the youth parried.

There was a series of similar exchanges and then this question: "Was it worth killing a kid to be here today talking on a mike?"

"I feel like killing you; that's what I feel like," Agron lashed out.

As the two prisoners entered the wagon, someone wanted to know if Agron was "sorry about your father and mother?"

"Yeah," came the reply. "That, yeah. But nothing else."

A newspaper account of the indictment of youth gang members Salvador Agron and Antonio Hernandez on homicide charges, from Milton Bracker, "2 Gang Suspects Are Denied Bail," New York Times, September 4, 1959, pp. 1–2.

Police Reform

We're trying to play fact and not fiction. We try to make cops human beings, guys doing a job for low pay, but we're trying to get away from the 'dumb-cop' idea. They aren't dumb; they're pretty smart. The average law officer has a handful of law books in the back of his car. The officer's job is not to make an arrest, but to get a conviction. We try to combine the best qualities of the men I've seen downtown [at the police station] . . . try to incorporate the way of speaking, make a composite.

Television producer and actor Jack Webb, on the portrayal of police officers in his show Dragnet, *quoted in Richard Tregaskis, "The Cops' Favorite Make-Believe Cop," Saturday Evening Post, September 26, 1953, p. 25.*

No matter how well a police department is organized or how efficient and honest is its administration, it is judged by individual citizens, and consequently by the nature of its public contacts. Good public relations involve far more than *saying*—they involve *doing*. It is the policeman out on his beat, the police officer in a radio car or on a motorcycle, and the desk officer or jailer in the station who make friends or enemies for the department. Though there are other influences involved, *the police themselves are the most important factor in determining public attitudes.*

Los Angeles police commander G. Douglas Gourley, "Police Public Relations," Annals of the American Academy of Political and Social Science, *no. 291, January 1954, p. 135.*

We put out forty-one million dollars a year to operate a police department in the city of Los Angeles, and I think that's horrible . . . We have become inured to criminality and are doing nothing about it. We accept it as part of the American scene.

The police have unjustly become a symbol of oppression. People cry out against us when we want to use wire taps or other devices to catch known offenders, and they yell about civil rights if we stop a car on suspicion and just happen to find it full of stolen goods. Even the courts are going along with this trend, and are coming up with one decision after another to make it easier for the criminal. But let these same crusaders become the victims in a crime, and the whole picture changes. Now they call the police in a hurry, and they want the villains put away for life.

Los Angeles police chief William H. Parker, quoted in Dean Jennings, "Portrait of a Police Chief," Saturday Evening Post, *May 7, 1960, p. 88.*

CHAPTER TEN

Civil Disobedience and Civic Reform
1958–1970

The 1960s represent a transition in modern American history. Decades of activism for social change culminated in the triumphs of the Civil Rights movement, in a judicial revolution in the federal courts that widened individual rights, and in Great Society programs that expanded the social safety net provided by the federal government. At the same time, these changes met resistance on all sides. Social activists, spurred on by the passion of the baby boom generation born in the decades after World War II and now in their teens and 20s, often believed that these changes did not go far enough and in many cases lashed out violently in frustration. By contrast, social changes met resistance from traditionalists who believed that the United States had been transformed too much already. Traditionalists' resistance often became violent, whether it appeared in the form of police beatings of protesters, surveillance of radical groups, or white supremacist attacks on civil rights activists. And in the midst of these changes, ordinary crime increased sharply after decades of relative calm. The criminal justice system—always a reflection of larger society and culture, found itself forced to transform quickly in order to keep pace with the rapidity of change.

An Era of Change

Political assassination shaped the 1960s. At least in the public mind, the presidency of John F. Kennedy, between 1961 and 1963, represented a sort of Camelot, a golden age in which a distinguished and beautiful family led the nation in a time of prosperity. Moreover, by its final year, Kennedy's administration had begun to commit itself to redressing the social and racial inequalities that still characterized American life. Camelot was shattered, however, by Kennedy's murder on November 22, 1963. As Kennedy waved to surrounding crowds from the back of an open convertible driving in a motorcade through Dallas, Texas, a sniper in the Texas Book Depository building shot the president. He was rushed to Parkland Memorial Hospital but died within hours. A certain sense of American security and complacency died with him.

President John F. Kennedy appointed his younger brother Robert to serve as U.S. attorney general. *(National Archives and Records Administration [194255])*

Lee Harvey Oswald, a former marine drawn to political extremist groups, was seen leaving the depository building. When a Dallas police officer stopped Oswald and sought to question him, he shot the officer dead and fled into a nearby movie theater. There, police arrested him. The investigation, however, had been botched from the beginning. Doctors seeking to save the president had destroyed key forensic evidence. Law enforcement agencies—city and county police, the Texas Rangers, the FBI, and the Secret Service—had competed over jurisdiction and ended up interrogating Oswald together without either a plan or a stenographer. Finally, as Oswald was being transferred from the city lock-up to the more secure county jail, a Dallas nightclub owner named Jack Ruby slipped through the crowd and shoot Oswald to death in front of national television cameras. Rather than stand trial in open court, Oswald took the truth about his role in the assassination with him to the grave.

Lacking answers, much of the American public was inclined to believe wild speculation about Kennedy's death. Kennedy's successor, Lyndon B. Johnson, appointed a special commission led by Earl Warren, the chief justice of the U.S. Supreme Court, to conduct an investigation. In September 1964, the Warren Commission issued its report, concluding that Oswald had acted alone in killing the president. Despite 26 volumes of evidence, the commission failed to explain key disparities, lacked access to crucial information, and failed ultimately to convince many people that no larger conspiracy had been involved. Lacking a definite alternative, much of the public found it easy to believe that unknown shadowy conspirators, including the Soviet Union, Cuba, organized crime bosses, and even the Central Intelligence Agency (CIA), had been behind Kennedy's death. With the assassination, the optimism of Kennedy's Camelot gave way to paranoia and distrust.[1]

This public sense of disorder was exacerbated five years later with the killing of John Kennedy's younger brother, Robert. Robert Kennedy, the U.S. attorney general during his brother's administration, had emerged as a political leader in his own right, winning election as a U.S. senator from New York in 1964 and leading the race for the Democratic Party's presidential nomination in 1968. On the night of June 5, as Kennedy celebrated his victory in the California primary at the Los Angeles Ambassador Hotel, a young second-generation Palestinian American named Sirhan Sirhan shot him in the head; Kennedy died the next day. Sirhan claimed that he had committed the crime for ideological reasons, as a protest against Kennedy's support for Israel in its conflicts in the Middle East. As a practical matter, Robert Kennedy's death eliminated another national political leader capable of following through on the decade's promise of positive social change.

Crime and violence also injured the Civil Rights movement with the assassination of Martin Luther King, Jr., on April 4, 1968. King, still the best known advocate of civil rights and the movement's most prominent leader, had been visiting Memphis, Tennessee, in support of a garbage workers' strike. Standing on the balcony of the Lorraine Motel, he was felled by a sniper's bullet. Authorities quickly recovered the murder weapon and used it to identify the shooter as James Earl Ray, a small-time thief and con man. Ray escaped arrest, however, and fled to Canada, England, and Portugal; he was apprehended two months after the killing on June 8 in London. Charged with King's murder, Ray pleaded guilty in March 1969 in order to avoid the death penalty. He soon recanted, suggesting that he had been set up to take the blame for a wider conspiracy to kill King. The question of how an impoverished ex-convict managed to elude an international manhunt and become a fugitive in Europe continued to linger over the case until Ray's 1998 death.[2] In the more immediate context of the late 1960s, King's assassination represented one more blow to peaceful change. As was so often the case during the decade, political violence robbed a reform movement of its leader and generated yet more frustration with the slow pace of social progress.

America also found itself increasingly divided over the conflict in Vietnam. A low-level struggle in the early 1960s in which the United States had supplied a few thousand military advisers, the conflict escalated sharply in 1964. In the aftermath of reported attacks on U.S. naval vessels operating off the coast of North Vietnam, President Johnson asked Congress to authorize the Gulf of Tonkin Resolution (named for the site of the attacks) granting him the power to expand America's military commitment to the war. U.S. military personnel in Vietnam increased from roughly 25,000 troops at the end of 1964 to 184,000 at the end of 1965 and peaked at nearly 550,000 in the middle of 1969.[3] As U.S. participation in the war assumed an alternating cycle of setbacks followed by expanded military operations and troop commitments, the war generated increased opposition from the U.S. public. In late January 1968, popular confidence in the war effort was shattered by the Tet offensive, in which North Vietnamese regular army forces and Vietcong insurgents struck against U.S. forces deep in South Vietnam. By 1969, polling showed that a majority of Americans believed that the United States had made a mistake sending troops to fight in Vietnam.[4]

Youth Activism and the Government's Response

The escalation of the Vietnam conflict paralleled the growth of youthful radicalism and antiwar sentiment. In the early 1960s, the large cohort of Americans born during and after World War II began to reach adulthood, and a vocal minority of them began to express dissatisfaction with the world as they found it, characterizing themselves as a "New Left." The founders of Students for a Democratic Society (SDS), which would become the largest youth activist group on college campuses in the 1960s, argued in their 1962 manifesto, the Port Huron Statement, that "we are people of this generation, bred in at least moderate comfort, housed now in universities, looking uncomfortably at the world we inherit."[5] The movement for African-American civil rights fanned the flames of idealism for many young people. When in 1964 the University of California banned recruiting and fundraising for civil rights groups on its Berkeley campus, students responded with a massive, wide-ranging movement advocating the cause of free speech. By 1965 and 1966, the expansion of the Vietnam War swelled the ranks of groups like SDS, which became the most convenient forum for antiwar activism.

These groups also became increasingly divided over the question of whether to use nonviolent methods to achieve their goals or to adopt more confrontational tactics. While a majority embraced peaceful means, violence garnered more public attention. As early as October 1967, protesters declared a "Stop the Draft Week" in Oakland, California, proposing to shut down that city's induction center for recruits and draftees for all of northern California. After the Oakland police drove off protesters early in the week using clubs and tear gas, a larger and better-prepared crowd returned later in the week and managed to block off a portion of downtown Oakland near the induction center using cars, buses, trucks, newspaper racks, benches, and anything else they could move; at least temporarily, they stopped the draft. The movement was shifting toward confrontation.[6]

By 1968, this pattern of defiance was reaching a climax. In April, students at New York City's Columbia University occupied the main administration building and many classroom facilities to protest the university's complicity in both the Vietnam War abroad (as evidenced by the school's contracts with the Defense Department) and racism at home (as evidenced by the school's plan to build a new recreation facility inaccessible to the adjoining predominantly African-American neighborhood, Morningside Heights). Similarly, students at Harvard University, Berkeley, Cornell University, and San Francisco State University all occupied university facilities that spring to protest both local policies and the war.

In each case they were met with police repression as local law enforcement agencies served as a bulwark against change. Columbia University administrators ended their school's occupation by calling in hundreds of New York City police officers who brutally beat students, protesters, and bystanders. Likewise, in California Governor Ronald Reagan used police and the National Guard to evict radicals from a "people's park" they had created on vacant university property. Similar scenarios played out at Harvard, Cornell, and elsewhere.[7]

This cycle of confrontation and resistance peaked in August 1968 at the Democratic National Convention in Chicago. Antiwar protesters were determined to use the presidential nomination of Johnson's vice president, Hubert H. Humphrey, as occasion to denounce the administration's policies in Vietnam. Tens of thousands of activists converged to camp in the city's lakeside parks and to protest against the war. Mayor Richard J. Daley's administration responded by denying them permits to camp or to conduct demonstrations, fortifying the city, and mobilizing more than 12,000 police officers. This situation was ripe for disaster. The police were on edge, and many protesters had come with an intention of taunting and provoking them. Beginning on August 25, when police broke up a rally in Chicago's Lincoln Park, they responded to protesters' insults with tear gas and billy clubs. On August 28, the final night of the convention, police attacked a peaceful protest march near Grant Park, indiscriminately beating participants and onlookers and forcing many to flee into Chicago's most prestigious hotels for safety. Although this was later characterized as a "police riot," antiwar activists suffered the worst consequences. Public opinion polls indicated greater support for Chicago authorities than for the protesters, and in March 1969 Daley convinced a federal judge to summon a grand jury to consider charges against organizers of the protests. Eight—Abbie Hoffman, Jerry Rubin, David Dellinger, Rennie Davis, Tom Hayden, John Froines, Lee Weinter, and Bobby Seale—were ultimately indicted for violating a new federal law making it a crime to cross state lines with the intention of inciting a riot. Seale's case was severed from the others, but the trial of the "Chicago Seven" lasted

Police officers and demonstrators fill the streets of Chicago, Illinois, during the 1968 Democratic National Convention. Anti–Vietnam War protesters converged on the city to protest Democratic nominee Hubert Humphrey's support for the war. Chicago mayor Richard Daley refused to grant the protesters the right to march through the streets. Demonstrators decided to march anyway and were attacked by police officers. *(AP Photo)*

through late 1969 and early 1970. All were convicted, but each had his conviction reversed on appeal in 1971 or 1972. The trial, however, consumed the time, energy, and resources of leaders of the antiwar movement. In a more subtle way than police violence, the criminal courts system also served as a bulwark against change.[8]

Law enforcement agencies targeted 1960s activists in other ways as well. Most prominently, the FBI operated five "counterintelligence" programs—each called COINTELPRO—between 1956 and 1971. Initiated during the Red Scare of the 1950s to monitor the American Communist Party, the program expanded in the 1960s to encompass new groups perceived as threats, such as the New Left, black nationalists, and white hate groups. The shadowy COINTELPROs fell under the intelligence, not the investigative, arm of the FBI. Rather than investigate specific crimes, their mission was to maintain surveillance on activist groups, infiltrate them with double agents, and discredit them in the public eye.[9] In a manner similar to the

FBI, local police, such as the Chicago Police Department, also maintained "Red Squads" tasked with infiltrating radical groups. By 1968, the membership of many activist groups was laced with police officers acting as spies or agents provocateurs. Many veterans of the Chicago protests believed strongly that efforts by police agents in their midst helped to generate the confrontational atmosphere that led to the violence at the Democratic National Convention. Regardless, by the end of the 1960s many public officials were clearly willing to use the mechanisms of the criminal justice system to repress dissent and maintain the status quo.

Violent Reaction to the Civil Rights Movement

The movement for African-American civil rights also peaked in the late 1950s and 1960s. Both the American public and criminal justice institutions, however, were divided over the Civil Rights movement. Many people and agencies applauded its gains and worked actively for its success. Others, in contrast, fought to slow racial change. Resistance to civil rights often came from ordinary people violently exercising what they perceived to be the popular will to maintain white privilege. And criminal justice agencies often stood by idly, failing to conduct thorough investigations or trials or, worse, actively participating in the popular resistance. The slow progress of the Civil Rights movement ultimately drove some of its supporters to embrace violent rhetoric and action as well.

Just after midnight on June 12, 1963, Medgar Evers, the Mississippi field secretary of the National Association for the Advancement of Colored People (NAACP), was returning home when a group of men waiting in his driveway shot him in the back. He died within the hour. His death helped to mobilize the Civil Rights movement in Mississippi and even generated reward offers from the governor and white newspapers. A subsequent investigation by the FBI used fingerprints found on the murder weapon to identify a suspect, Byron De La Beckwith, a leader in Mississippi's White Citizens' Council, a white supremacist group. De La Beckwith's January 1964 trial ended with a mistrial; although the local district attorney mounted a vigorous case, the jury was deadlocked. A second trial ended in the same fashion. A significant portion of the Mississippi population that formed the jury pool apparently harbored the idea that a white man could not be convicted for killing a black man; the prosecutor determined that further attempts would be pointless. Only in 1990 was the case reopened, and in February 1994 73-year-old De La Beckwith was convicted for a crime committed more than 30 years earlier.

Whites working for the Civil Rights movement were victims of violence as well. On June 21, 1964, three civil rights workers—Michael Schwermer, Andrew Goodman (both white), and James Chaney (black)—disappeared while investigating a church burning in Neshoba County, Mississippi. Their burned car was found outside of Philadelphia, Mississippi. Although Sheriff Lawrence Rainey suggested that, "if they're missing, they just hid somewhere, trying to get a lot of publicity,"[10] their disappearance prompted President Lyndon Johnson to order the FBI to lead a massive search. Their bodies were discovered six weeks later. Later investigations revealed that the three had been jailed on fictitious charges of speeding. After dark a sheriff's deputy took them to a deserted road where they were met by three carloads of Ku Klux Klan members. The attackers killed Schwermer and Goodman, each with a single shot, and beat Chaney before murdering him as well. In

December, a tip from a paid informant helped the FBI arrest 21 men, including the sheriff and deputy. Voting rights activists in Mississippi that summer nonetheless complained that the substantial FBI presence did little to prevent harassment by Klansmen and arbitrary arrest by local law enforcement.[11]

As with protests against the Vietnam War, law enforcement agencies also often acted as bulwarks against racial change in the 1960s. When, in the spring of 1961, activists associated with the Congress of Racial Equality (CORE) engaged in "Freedom Rides," travels on public buses in Mississippi to test the application of recent Supreme Court decisions desegregating public transportation and terminals, they often found themselves arrested for "breach of the peace." When demonstrators refused to pay the $200 fine, they were incarcerated in Mississippi's Parchman Farm Penitentiary. While protestors did not experience the harshest treatment afforded to normal convicts, their time at the notorious work farm steeled them for the ongoing civil rights battle.[12]

In other cases, law enforcement officials openly led the resistance to the Civil Rights movement. In 1963, Martin Luther King, Jr.'s Southern Christian Leadership Conference (SCLC) targeted the city of Birmingham, Alabama—reputed to be the most segregated big city in America—in part because its sheriff, Eugene T. "Bull" Connor, was an outspoken racist who could be counted upon to respond to provocation. When King led a Good Friday protest march, Connor ordered his arrest. On May 2, when King organized more than 1,000 children to engage in a protest march from the Sixteenth Street Baptist Church, Connor had them arrested as well. When yet another protest occurred on the following day, Connor ordered his officers to prevent demonstrators from leaving the church and to apprehend those who escaped; the police beat demonstrators and fired on them with water cannons. Even with SCLC's victory in the eyes of the public, the conflict did not end. Later that year, on a Sunday morning in September, a bomb destroyed the Sixteenth Street Baptist Church, killing four teenage girls.[13]

These outrages—publicized in newspapers and on television news—helped generate widespread public opposition to police violence and support for the Civil Rights movement. The events in Birmingham built political momentum for the passage of the 1964 Civil Rights Act, which outlawed racial segregation in all places of public accommodation. In addition, even though FBI director J. Edgar Hoover publicly decried the Civil Rights movement, the 1964 events in Mississippi led the FBI to open investigations of violence against civil rights workers and to establish a new COINTELPRO to infiltrate and undermine white supremacist groups.

Race Riots and Violent Resistance

For many people fighting for civil rights, however, federal laws and federal intervention were not enough. These people remained frustrated with the slow pace of change, the lack of protection that civil rights workers received from police and law enforcement, and the persistent racial inequality visible in both southern and northern U.S. cities. Many responded to this frustration by issuing violent statements and, increasingly, taking violent action. For many people, Malcolm X came to embody these views. Malcolm X had come to prominence in the late 1950s as the spokesman for a predominantly African-American religious group based in northern cities, the Nation of Islam. In his public statements, he had openly condemned whites, argued for black separatism, and demanded that African Americans gain rights by any means necessary, implicitly endorsing violence. Although Malcolm X moderated his views and broke from the Nation of Islam in his later years, he remained a symbol of black resistance. Moreover, his February 1965 murder (apparently at the hands of former Nation of Islam colleagues) and the posthumous publication of his manifesto, *The Autobiography of Malcolm X,* transformed him into a martyr for the cause of black nationalism.

The spirit of violent resistance hung over race riots that tore apart U.S. cities in the mid-1960s. Between 1964 and 1967, urban black communities across the country erupted in distressingly similar patterns of violence. Often, confrontations between police officers and African Americans provided the spark for violence that destroyed much of the physical infrastructure of black communities. On July 16, 1964, for example, an off-duty New York City police officer intervened in a confrontation between a group of black teenage boys and an apartment building superintendent in Harlem. Witnesses disagree about how the confrontation escalated, but it ended when the officer drew his weapon, fired three shots, and killed 15-year-old James Powell. After a crowd surrounded the officer, the NYPD sent 75 officers to restore calm. That night, a protest march near the police station erupted into violence, which expanded into six nights of rioting throughout predominantly black neighborhoods in Manhattan and Brooklyn. The NYPD avoided tactics used in Birmingham such as fire hoses and tear gas, but they still earned widespread criticism for firing warning shots and using violence to control the riots.[14] The following summer, a similar scenario occurred in Los Angeles, California. On August 11, 1965, the arrest of a black motorist in the predominantly black Watts neighborhood by a white police officer exploded into six days of rioting that engulfed 45 square miles, destroyed $200 million worth of property, led to more than 4,000 arrests, and killed 34 people.[15] The summer of 1966 saw similar riots in Chicago, Illinois; Cleveland, Ohio; Omaha, Nebraska; Dayton, Ohio; San Francisco, California; Atlanta, Georgia; and 38 other cities. The summer of 1967—the most violent yet—witnessed massive riots in Detroit, Michigan, and Newark, New Jersey, as well as conflagrations in more than 100 additional locations.[16] Lacking concrete progress in combating racial discrimination in housing and jobs, many African Americans in cities expressed their frustration through violence. Impartial investigations of the riots found that these were not isolated events or the work of a small number of agitators. Instead, they were results of deep-seated inequalities in U.S. society. The National Advisory Commission on Civil Disorders—appointed by President Johnson and called "the Kerner Commission" after its chair, former Illinois governor Otto Kerner—famously reported that "our nation is moving toward two societies, one black, one white—separate and unequal."[17]

This frustration helped shift the direction of the Civil Rights movement as well. In the mid-1960s, organizations such as CORE and the Student Nonviolent Coordinating Committee (SNCC) gradually moved away from their earlier focus on desegregation and instead began to advocate more drastic social change. In 1966, each chose new, young, vibrant leaders—Floyd McKissick in CORE and Stokely Carmichael in SNCC—to help develop plans to organize northern cities. Carmichael in particular rejected older integrationist strategies and articulated a new approach. "We been saying freedom for six years and we ain't got nothin'. What we gonna start saying now is Black Power."[18] Carmichael's "Black Power" slogan came to represent a new direction for the movement, one that celebrated black pride and cultural autonomy, one that demanded rights rather than requesting integration.

In 1965, numerous riots occurred in predominantly African-American neighborhoods across the United States. In this photograph, a California Highway Patrol officer orders a group of African Americans suspected of looting to stand against a store wall in Watts, a neighborhood in Los Angeles. *(AP Photo)*

The Black Panther Party, founded in Oakland, California, in October 1966 by Huey Newton and Bobby Seale, most visibly articulated the new "Black Power" orientation. Decrying police brutality against African Americans, the Black Panthers armed themselves with shotguns and followed police officers on their patrols, looking for discriminatory treatment of black suspects, arbitrary arrests, and police brutality. Styling themselves a revolutionary party and dressing in black leather and berets, the Black Panthers attracted enormous media attention. They sought to use the nation's fascination with violence to advance their own cause. FBI director J. Edgar Hoover reportedly characterized them as "the greatest threat to the internal security of the United States."[19] They also became the target of an FBI COIN-TELPRO program. The Black Panthers' confrontational stance, however, also alienated mainstream opinion; many white Americans shied away from black calls for violent resistance. Moreover, a series of confrontations between the Panthers and police in Los Angeles, Chicago, and New York in late 1969 and early 1970 left the organization in disarray.

In the late 1960s, other ethnic groups also adopted more confrontational tactics in pursuit of civil rights. On November 9, 1969, American Indian protesters sailed in San Francisco Bay to Alcatraz Island, the site of the former federal prison, and took control of the facility. Symbolically claiming the island for displaced Indian people, they maintained possession of it for 19 months until federal marshals and FBI agents removed the handful of remaining protesters. The dramatic tactic of occupying a famous federal prison, built on what had once been Native American land, highlighted the modern plight of Native peoples.

Civil Liberties and the Supreme Court

The 1960s also represented a watershed in terms of the ways that criminal justice institutions dealt with civil rights and civil liberties. This transition is most evident in two areas: a judicial revolution implemented by the U.S. Supreme Court, and law enforcement reforms driven largely by President Lyndon Johnson's Great Society programs. In each case, the federal government brought change from the top down to local law enforcement agencies.

Chief Justice Earl Warren's Supreme Court issued a series of decisions in the 1960s in cases dealing specifically with criminal procedure. In 1961, the Court ruled in *Mapp v. Ohio* that criminal evidence obtained via police searches and seizures conducted without a warrant was inadmissible in court. This "exclusionary rule" extended the federal protections embodied in the Fourth Amendment to local criminal cases. In 1963, the Supreme Court ruled in *Gideon v. Wainwright* that, under the Sixth Amendment, every felony defendant had the right to an attorney. This decision forced city and county governments to establish or to expand public defender systems for indigent offenders. And most famously, in 1966, the Court ruled in *Miranda v. Arizona* that police needed to inform all arrested suspects of their rights to an attorney and against self-incrimination. All of these decisions demanded a higher standard of conduct by police and courts in conducting and justifying their investigations and trials. They helped to replace an arcane system in which police and prosecutors had all of the power over criminal suspects with one in which each side operated on a more even and predictable playing field.[20]

The Supreme Court also extended to juvenile courts many of these same due process protections. In particular, in the 1967 case of Gerald Gault, a 15-year-old Arizona boy committed to a state reform school until age 21 for making an obscene phone call, the Court ruled that juvenile procedures routinely disregarded constitutional rights. Specifically, it determined that courts had to provide juveniles with adequate notice of the charges against them, legal counsel, the right to confront witnesses, and protections against self-incrimination. Like the other decisions, the *Gault* case clarified and protected defendants' rights. More broadly, this case all but overturned the legal premise of juvenile courts. Rather than seeing juvenile courts as institutions that operated under the doctrine of *parens patrie*, protecting the best interests of the child, the Supreme Court acknowledged that juvenile court hearings could result in a youth's confinement, and should therefore provide many of the protections that would be found in adult courts. Intentionally or not, it challenged the distinctive premise of juvenile courts that young offenders were different from adults.[21]

As a whole, these Supreme Court decisions constituted a judicial revolution because they applied a single national standard to criminal courts operated by the states, counties, and localities. These decisions represent a broad use of the incorporation doctrine, the legal theory that the Fourteenth Amendment to the U.S. Constitution incorporates all of the civil protections explicated in the first ten amendments, and therefore applies the federal protections in the Bill of Rights to state and local governments. Many states had already adhered to these rules to some degree. But following the judicial revolution, they were required to. And the consistent thrust of these decisions was to define the rights of criminal defendants and to protect them against abuses by law enforcement officials. These legal changes embodied the reform-minded spirit of the 1960s and represent one of the era's most powerful legacies.

Legislative Criminal Justice Reforms

President Lyndon Johnson's programs to enact a Great Society in the United States also brought far-reaching changes to the criminal justice system. In particular, the new initiatives that emerged between 1965 and 1968 represented the culmination of both the emerging academic discipline of criminology and the era's liberal reform-minded impulses. In March 1965, Johnson announced the President's Commission on Law Enforcement and Administration of Justice, a major investigative body charged with analyzing the nature of both crime and criminal justice in the United States. In an effort to discover the extent of unreported crime, it launched a novel survey of Americans assessing how often they had been victims of offenses. This evolved into the U.S. Census Bureau's annual National Crime Victimization Survey, which began in 1973 and is still regarded as the most accurate measure of the extent of crime. The commission also conducted detailed investigations of routine police work and the operations of criminal courts and corrections. Its 1967 report *The Challenge of Crime in a Free Society* explained crime as a result of limited social and economic opportunities for the poor and for racial minorities. Having diagnosed the problem, it proposed solutions built on positive action by the federal government. These included establishing preventive measures premised on creating greater economic opportunity; developing more flexible and rehabilitative modes of correction for individual offenders; eliminating systematic unfairness within the criminal justice system in the hopes of generating more legitimacy among the populations policed; hiring personnel who were both more qualified and more diverse; conducting systematic research into crime and justice; allocating more federal funding for state and local law enforcement; and encouraging greater engagement in crime prevention by social service agencies, civic groups, religious organizations, and individual citizens. As practical consequences, the commission strongly endorsed the expanded use of probation and parole as a means of correction rather than incarceration and justified a dramatic expansion of federal spending on law enforcement.[22]

In June 1968, Congress responded to the commission by passing the Omnibus Crime Control and Safe Streets Act. Among its many provisions, this established the Law Enforcement Assistance Administration (LEAA) to make grants to state and local governments for planning, recruitment, and training of law enforcement personnel; public education relating to crime prevention; education and training of special law enforcement units to combat organized crime; and the organization, education, and training of police officers for the prevention and detection of riots and other civil disorders. The act also established a National Institute of Law Enforcement and Criminal Justice to make grants for training, education, and research to improve law enforcement and develop new methods to prevent and to reduce crime. In essence, the act dramatically expanded the federal government's support for and involvement in day-to-day law enforcement. LEAA was widely criticized both for its heavy spending on riot equipment and for its limited effectiveness in reducing crime, and it was phased out after 12 years. Nonetheless, it established the enduring practice of federal support for local law enforcement.[23]

Urban police departments, the targets of much criticism in the 1960s, made very gradual efforts to improve relations with their communities. Municipal police forces faced pressure from civil rights activists and the small number of black police officers to hire more African Americans; activists argued that black officers would be more attuned than whites to black communities. Progress was slow, however. Even though the Civil Rights Act of 1964 prohibited discrimination in hiring, most cities began to employ substantial numbers of blacks only in the late 1960s and early 1970s. Likewise, it took the 1972 amendments to the Civil Rights Act to force police departments to hire women in any numbers and to eliminate gender-specific duties for them. A number of police departments also experimented with civilian review boards that investigated complaints against police. Convinced that police officers systematically covered up their brother officers' misconduct and brutality, many civil rights activists maintained that only civilians could impartially examine complaints. The mayors of Philadelphia and New York—both liberal Republicans—came to agree and established civilian review boards in 1958 and 1966, respectively. In each case, however, police rank-and-file officers resisted and ultimately generated enough political momentum to eliminate the boards. Regardless of slow progress and setbacks, the political circumstances of the 1960s propelled police on a trajectory toward closer connections with their communities.[24]

In short, the 1960s in general and Lyndon Johnson's presidency in particular represented the heyday of liberal criminal justice reform. This era saw a clarification and expansion of rights for criminal defendants, a reconsideration of the nature of crime and justice from the perspective of academic sociologists and criminologists, and gradual changes in the actual practice of justice that extended the role of the federal government in local law enforcement.

The Upturn in Crime

In the midst of the dramatic changes in American society between 1958 and 1970, ordinary crime increased dramatically as well. Since a peak in the early years of the Great Depression, the rate of homicide in the United States—measured in terms of victims of murder compared to the U.S. population—had experienced a long decline between the mid-1930s and the mid-1950s. At the end of the relatively peaceful years following World War II, the U.S. homicide rate reached a historic low of 4.5 murders per 100,000 people in 1955, 1957, and 1958. Beginning in the late 1950s and accelerating in the 1960s, however, the U.S. homicide rate turned sharply upward; it reached 8.3 per 100,000 by 1970 and peaked at more than 10 per 100,000 in 1974.[25]

Other crimes also increased sharply. The rate of "index crimes" reported by the FBI—murder and non-negligent manslaughter, forcible rape, robbery, aggravated assault, burglary, larceny/theft, and motor vehicle theft—more than doubled between 1960 (the first year for which reliable figures are available) and 1970.[26]

Crime became increasingly associated with cities. Americans had long believed that crime was an urban phenomenon, but the reality was that for much of American history controlling for population, rural areas tended to be more dangerous than urban ones. This, too, changed in the late 1950s and 1960s. In 1958, for the first time, New York City's homicide rate exceeded that of the United States as a whole. Since then, New York City's homicide rates have surpassed those of the United States every year, often by large margins in the 1970s, 1980s, and 1990s.[27]

Why the dramatic change? Scholars tend to explain the increase in crime in terms of the confluence of race, economic opportunity, and the deindustrialization of U.S. cities. The arguments of the Kerner Commission and the President's Crime Commission emerged from the academic thinking of the 1960s, which tended to link crime to limits on economic opportunity; these commissions, in turn, provided further evidence for the thinking that helped generate them. Specifically, in the decades after World War II, northern U.S. cities had been transformed by the massive migration of African Americans from the U.S. South and Latinos from Mexico and Central America. At the same time, however, American industry—the historical engine of jobs—began to relocate outside the cities and, increasingly, outside the United States entirely. As a result, migrants arrived in urban America at precisely the same time as economic opportunities for them departed. Moreover, in an era of emerging mass consumer culture, people who had few chances to get ahead were very aware of those who did. They experienced "relative deprivation," a sense that they needed more and more material goods to enjoy the standards of living that other people experienced and that they saw on television and in the movies. As the modern economy placed greater demands on them for skills and education that they did not have, many people responded instead with frustration, crime, and violence.[28]

Much of the American public, however, tended to focus simplistically on one element of this explanation: race. As more African Americans arrived in cities and cities became more crime-ridden, popular opinion often tended to associate blacks and crime. This fear of cities as being filled with crime encouraged many of those who could afford it to relocate to the suburbs. The shorthand term for this process describes it in explicitly racial terms: *white flight*.

Popular Terror

Popular fears of crime were also exacerbated by a number of high-profile cases in the 1960s. The "Boston Strangler," for example, terrorized eastern Massachusetts, raping and killing 13 women between 1962 and 1964. The Strangler broke into locked homes and attacked women ranging between 19 and 85 years of age. The case was only partly resolved. In 1965, a mental asylum inmate named Albert DeSalvo was identified as the Strangler but never put on trial. Already committed to a psychiatric institution, the Commonwealth of Massachusetts simply transferred him to a state prison. In a similar fashion, a drifter named Richard Speck also contributed to public fears of crime. In July 1966, Speck broke into a townhouse occupied by student nurses from South Chicago Community Hospital and killed eight of them.[29] Mere weeks later, on August 1, the American public's sense that they were safe in their ordinary lives was further undermined when Charles Whitman climbed to the observation deck of the University of Texas at Austin's Tower and Main Building and began shooting people on the campus below. Firing unimpeded for more than an hour and a half, he killed 16 people and wounded 31 before being shot to death by police officers. While public fears concentrated on African-American crime, all three of these prominent killers were white.

No figure better encapsulated public fears than Charles Manson. In the late 1960s, Manson, a white ex-convict in his early 30s, gathered what he called a "family" of young followers attracted by a combination of hallucinogenic drugs, sexual orgies, and apocalyptic visions of a coming racial upheaval inspired by the music of the Beatles. On the night of August 9 and 10, 1969, four of Manson's followers broke into the Beverly Hills mansion rented by film director Roman Polanski and slaughtered Polanski's pregnant wife, the actress Sharon Tate, as well as four guests. The following night, the same four, in addition to Manson himself, invaded the home of supermarket executive Leno LaBianca and his wife, Rosemary, and brutally murdered them as well. This time, they used the victims' blood to scrawl slogans such as "Death to Pigs," "War," and "Healter Skelter" on the walls. Hollywood's rich and famous were terrified; prominent members of the film community reportedly went into hiding, avoided Tate's funeral, and bought out nearby sporting goods stores' stocks of shotguns in order to defend themselves. Only months later did police trace the killings back to Manson and his followers. And even Manson's arrest did little to reassure the public. His trial and ultimate conviction made headline news throughout 1970 and 1971, and during his moment of fame his personal charisma simultaneously seduced and repulsed the American public. He seemed to embody a twisted version of sex-and-drug aided counterculture increasingly visible in the late 1960s and early 1970s. For many observers, his very existence suggested that the cultural changes of the era represented a threat to the established social order.[30]

In this context, crime increasingly became a hot-button political issue. Lyndon Johnson's decision to create the President's Crime Commission resulted in part from the success that his Republican challenger, Barry Goldwater, had in the 1964 presidential campaign by raising the issue of "law and order." The liberal orientation of crime commission investigations and the civil liberties emphasis of the Supreme Court's decisions under Earl Warren, however, helped generate a backlash in the late 1960s. Critics blamed the rise in crime on the increased permissiveness of American society in general and on the civil rights orientation of the Warren Court in particular. Many argued that rulings such as *Mapp* and *Miranda* tied the hands of police, making it more difficult for them to conduct effective investigations and to apprehend and convict offenders. It was not uncommon to see cars bearing bumper stickers that read "Impeach Earl Warren." Rank-and-file police officers, angered by new criticisms, public pressure to integrate their ranks, and new rules imposed by the courts, fought back in the court of public opinion. They used lobbying, picketing, and the threat of strikes to push local governments to accept police unions and engage in collective bargaining; these unions, in turn, became the voice of police officers defending their own turf and autonomy. By the 1968 presidential election, Republican candidate Richard M. Nixon successfully made the issue of maintaining law and order his own and used it to attract substantial numbers of votes from working-class white males, a traditionally Democratic constituency. Nixon's victory over Democratic rival Hubert Humphrey changed the nature of federal intervention in local law enforcement. For most of the 1960s, the federal government had approached crime as a problem that could be remedied by social reform, but after 1968 the federal government put greater emphasis on vigorous law enforcement and crime fighting. At the close of the 1960s, that decade's increase in crime helped to slow the momentum of that decade's push for social change.[31]

The debates over crime and criminal justice in the 1960s reflected the cultural divisions that wracked the nation as a whole in this period. In many different forums, activists for social change arrayed themselves against defenders of the status quo. The results were mixed. The period witnessed tremendous progress, particularly in terms of the expansion and clarification of civil rights and civil liberties. At the same time, on many different fronts, the decade closed on a note of reaction and backlash against the changes that had been made.

Chronicle of Events

1956

- The FBI initiates a formal counterintelligence program against the Communist Party-USA officially called COINTELPRO.

1957

- *January 23:* The Ku Klux Klan murders 25-year-old Willie Edwards by forcing him to jump into the Alabama River. No charges are filed.

1958

- *April 4:* Mobster Joey Stompanato, abusive husband of actress Lana Turner, threatens to disfigure Turner but is fatally stabbed by the actress's 14-year-old daughter. The death is ruled a justifiable homicide. The incident will inspire the film *L.A. Confidential.*

1959

- *August 29:* Two white New York City teenagers are killed in a scuffle with five Puerto Rican youths, including 15-year-old Salvador Agron, dubbed the "Capeman" by the press.

1960

- *June 16:* Alfred Hitchcock's most successful thriller, *Psycho,* is released in the United States. The deranged murderer in the film is loosely based on serial killer Ed Gein.

1961

- The FBI establishes a second formal counterintelligence program (COINTELPRO) targeting the Socialist Workers Party.
- *June 19:* U.S. Supreme Court decision in *Mapp v. Ohio* establishes a new federal precedent that criminal evidence obtained through illegal search and seizure cannot be admitted into courts.

1962

- *June 11:* Three men—John and Clarence Anglin and Frank Morris—become the only prisoners to successfully escape from Alcatraz Prison, though there is no evidence that they were able to swim to shore.

1963

- *March 18:* The U.S. Supreme Court decision in *Gideon v. Wainwright* establishes that in order to guarantee Sixth Amendment protections that felony defendants have attorneys at trial, each criminal jurisdiction must provide legal counsel in the form of public defenders.
- *April–May:* In Birmingham, Alabama, a series of civil rights protests led by Martin Luther King, Jr.'s Southern Christian Leadership Conference (SCLC) meet public confrontation with law enforcement officials under the command of Sheriff Eugene "Bull" Connor. Connor's use of excessive force helps to generate nationwide public sympathy for the civil rights cause.
- *June 12:* Medgar Evers, field secretary of the National Association for the Advancement of Colored People (NAACP), is murdered in Mississippi, becoming one of the first martyrs to the cause of African-American civil rights.
- *September 15:* The bombing of the Sixteenth Street Baptist Church in Birmingham, Alabama, by white segregationists kills four teenage African-American girls.
- *November 22:* President John F. Kennedy is shot and killed in Dallas, Texas. Later that day, Lee Harvey Oswald is arrested for the assassination.
- *November 24:* Jack Ruby murders Lee Harvey Oswald.

1964

- The FBI establishes a third COINTELPRO aimed at white hate groups such as the Ku Klux Klan.
- *June 21:* Three civil rights workers—two white, one black—engaged in a voter registration project disappear in Mississippi, leading to a massive search and FBI investigation.
- *June 22:* The U.S. Supreme Court decision in *Cooper v. Pate* establishes the principle that prison inmates have constitutional rights.
- *July 16–22:* Race riots occur in New York City's Harlem neighborhood after the fatal shooting of a 15-year-old African-American boy by a white police officer.
- *August 7:* The U.S. Congress passes the Gulf of Tonkin Resolution, authorizing President Lyndon B. Johnson to dramatically expand the American military commitment in the Vietnam conflict.

1965

- *February 21:* Malcolm X, civil rights leader and former spokesman for the Nation of Islam, is murdered in New York City.
- *August 11–15:* Following a confrontation between a white police officer and a black motorist, five days of rioting convulse the predominately African-American Watts neighborhood of Los Angeles.

1966

- *June 13:* The U.S. Supreme Court decision in *Miranda v. Arizona* establishes new legal guidelines that in order to protect Fifth Amendment protections against self-incrimination, criminal suspects must be informed of their rights to remain silent and to have a defense attorney.
- *July 14:* Richard Speck murders eight student nurses from the South Chicago Community Hospital.
- *August 1:* Charles Whitman shoots dozens of people from the observation deck of the University of Texas at Austin's Tower and Main Building, killing 16 people and wounding 31.
- *October:* The Black Panther Party for Self-Defense is founded in Oakland, California, by Huey P. Newton and Bobby Seale.

1967

- The FBI establishes a fourth COINTELPRO targeting black nationalist organizations such as the Black Panther Party.
- *February:* The report of the President's Commission on Law Enforcement and Administration of Justice, *The Challenge of Crime in a Free Society,* is published.
- *May 15:* The U.S. Supreme Court decision *In re Gault* requires juvenile courts to provide many of the same due process protections as criminal courts and rejects the long-standing legal doctrine of *parens patrie* (that juvenile courts acted as "parents" for their young charges).
- *July 14–27:* Race riots convulse the cities of Newark, New Jersey, and Detroit, Michigan, the two largest among hundreds of civil disorders in U.S. cities during that summer.
- *October 16:* "Stop the Draft Week" protests in Oakland, California, lead to the first violent confrontations between anti–Vietnam War activists and police.

1968

- The FBI establishes a fifth and final COINTELPRO aimed at infiltrating student radical, and groups associated with the New Left.
- *January 30:* Offensive action by North Vietnamese regular army forces and Vietcong insurgents during a truce for the Tet holiday strikes a major blow to U.S. military forces in Vietnam and undermines American popular support for the war.
- *March 1:* The National Advisory Commission on Civil Disorders—popularly known as the Kerner Commission—issues its landmark report analyzing the sources of racial upheavals in American cities.

The Reverend Dr. Martin Luther King, Jr., preached nonviolence but was nevertheless a target of government surveillance. *(Library of Congress Prints and Photographs Division [LC-USZ62-122990])*

- *April 4:* Civil rights leader Martin Luther King, Jr., is fatally shot in Memphis, Tennessee.
- *April 23–30:* Student radicals' occupation of administrative and classroom buildings at Columbia University concludes with their forcible eviction by the New York City Police Department; 139 students are injured.
- *June:* Passage of the Omnibus Crime Control and Safe Streets Act helps to establish a permanent federal role in criminal justice.
- *June 5:* U.S. senator and Democratic presidential candidate Robert F. Kennedy is shot to death in Los Angeles, California, by Sirhan Sirhan.
- *June 8:* James Earl Ray is arrested in London for killing Martin Luther King, Jr., after traveling to Europe and eluding authorities for more than two months.
- *August 25–28:* Anti–Vietnam War protesters at the Democratic National Convention in Chicago engage in a series of violent confrontations with the Chicago Police Department. On the fourth night of the convention, police brutally attack protesters outside the convention

hotel in what an investigating commission would term a "police riot."

1969

- *March 10:* James Earl Ray pleads guilty to the murder of Martin Luther King, Jr., receiving a 99-year prison sentence but avoiding a trial that could have resulted in the death penalty.
- *March 20:* A federal judge indicts eight leaders of the protests at the Chicago Democratic National Convention the previous August for violating the Anti-Riot Act of 1968.
- *August 9:* Members of Charles Manson's cult (or "family") murder five people (including the actress Sharon Tate) at a Beverly Hills, California, estate, stabbing the victims more than 100 times.
- *August 10:* Members of Manson's cult kill supermarket executive Leno LaBianca and his wife, Rosemary, in their Los Angeles home.
- *November 9:* American Indian protesters begin an "occupation" of Alcatraz Island in San Francisco Bay, the site of the former federal prison.

1970

- *February 18:* A jury finds five of the defendants guilty in the Chicago Seven trial.
- *June 24:* Manson and three others are put on trial in Los Angeles for the Tate-LaBianca murders.

1971

- *January 15:* Manson and his codefendants are convicted of first-degree murder in the Tate-LaBianca case.
- *June 11:* American Indian protesters end their occupation of Alcatraz Island.

1972

- *November 21:* The Seventh Circuit Court of Appeals overturns the convictions in the Chicago Seven trial.

Eyewitness Testimony

An Era of Change

The Dallas motorcade, it was hoped, would evoke a demonstration of the President's personal popularity in a city which he had lost in the 1960 election. Once it had been decided that the trip to Texas would span 2 days, those responsible for planning, primarily Governor Connally and Kenneth O'Donnell, a special assistant to the President, agreed that a motorcade through Dallas would be desirable. The Secret Service was told on November 8 that 45 minutes had been allotted to a motorcade procession from Love Field to the site of a luncheon planned by Dallas business and civic leaders in honor of the President. After considering the facilities and security problems of several buildings, the Trade Mart was chosen as the luncheon site. Given this selection, and in accordance with the customary practice of affording the greatest number of people an opportunity to see the President, the motorcade route selected was a natural one. The route was approved by the local host committee and White House representatives on November 18 and publicized in the local papers starting on November 19. This advance publicity made it clear that the motorcade would leave Main Street and pass the intersection of Elm and Houston Streets as it proceeded to the Trade Mart by way of the Stemmons Freeway.

By midmorning of November 22, clearing skies in Dallas dispelled the threat of rain and the President greeted the crowds from his open limousine without the "bubbletop," which was at that time a plastic shield furnishing protection only against inclement weather. To the left of the President in the rear seat was Mrs. Kennedy. In the jump seats were Governor Connally, who was in front of the President, and Mrs. Connally at the Governor's left. Agent William R. Greer of the Secret Service was driving, and Agent Roy H. Kellerman was sitting to his right.

Directly behind the Presidential limousine was an open "follow-up" car with eight Secret Service agents, two in the front seat, two in the rear, and two on each running board. These agents, in accordance with normal Secret Service procedures, were instructed to scan the crowds, the roofs, and windows of buildings, overpasses, and crossings for signs of trouble. Behind the "follow-up" car was the Vice-Presidential car carrying the Vice President and Mrs. Johnson and Senator Ralph W. Yarborough. Next were a Vice-Presidential "follow-up" car and several cars and buses for additional dignitaries, press representatives, and others.

The motorcade left Love Field shortly after 11:50 A.M., and proceeded through residential neighborhoods, stopping twice at the President's request to greet well-wishers among the friendly crowds. Each time the President's car halted, Secret Service agents from the "follow-up" car moved forward to assume a protective stance near the President and Mrs. Kennedy. As the motorcade reached Main Street, a principal east-west artery in downtown Dallas, the welcome became tumultuous. At the extreme west end of Main Street the motorcade turned right on Houston Street and proceeded north for one block in order to make a left turn on Elm Street, the most direct and convenient approach to the Stemmons Freeway and the Trade Mart. As the President's car approached the intersection of Houston and Elm Streets, there loomed directly ahead on the intersection's northwest corner a seven-story, orange brick warehouse and office building, the Texas School Book Depository. Riding in the Vice President's car, Agent Rufus W. Youngblood of the Secret Service noticed that the clock atop the building indicated 12:30 P.M., the scheduled arrival time at the Trade Mart.

The President's car, which had been going north, made a sharp turn toward the southwest onto Elm Street. At a speed of about 11 miles per hour, it started down the gradual descent toward a railroad overpass under which the motorcade would proceed before reaching the Stemmons Freeway. The front of the Texas School Book Depository was now on the President's right, and he waved to the crowd assembled there as he passed the building. Dealey Plaza—an open, landscaped area marking the western end of downtown Dallas stretched out to the President's left. A Secret Service agent riding in the motorcade radioed the Trade Mart that the President would arrive in 5 minutes.

Seconds later shots resounded in rapid succession. The President's hands moved to his neck. He appeared to stiffen momentarily and lurch slightly forward in his seat. A bullet had entered the base of the back of his neck slightly to the right of the spine. It traveled downward and exited from the front of the neck, causing a nick in the left lower portion of the knot in the President's necktie. Before the shooting started, Governor Connally had been facing toward the crowd on the right. He started to turn toward the left and suddenly felt a blow on his back. The Governor had been hit by a bullet which entered at the extreme right side of his back at a point below his right armpit. The bullet traveled through his chest in a downward and forward direction, exited below his right nipple, passed through his right wrist which had been in his lap, and then caused a wound to his left thigh. The force of the bullet's impact appeared to spin the Governor to his right, and Mrs. Connally pulled him down into her lap. Another bullet then struck President Kennedy in the rear portion of his head, causing a massive and fatal wound. The President fell to the left into Mrs. Kennedy's lap.

Secret Service Agent Clinton J. Hill, riding on the left running board of the "follow-up" car, heard a noise which sounded like a firecracker and saw the President suddenly lean forward and to the left. Hill jumped off the car and raced toward the President's limousine. In the front seat of the Vice-Presidential car, Agent Young-blood heard an explosion and noticed unusual movements in the crowd. He vaulted into the rear seat and sat on the Vice President in order to protect him. At the same time Agent Kellerman in the front seat of the Presidential limousine turned to observe the President. Seeing that the President was struck, Kellerman instructed the driver, "Let's get out of here; we are hit." He radioed ahead to the lead car, "Get us to the hospital immediately." Agent Greer immediately accelerated the Presidential car. As it gained speed, Agent Hill managed to pull himself onto the back of the car where Mrs. Kennedy had climbed. Hill pushed her back into the rear seat and shielded the stricken President and Mrs. Kennedy as the President's car proceeded at high speed to Parkland Memorial Hospital, 4 miles away.

The Warren Commission, Report of the President's Commission on the Assassination of President Kennedy, *pp. 2–3.*

. . . [It] is felt that the following suggestions for counterintelligence action can be utilized by all offices:

1. Preparation of a leaflet designed to counteract that Students for a Democratic Society (SDS) and other minority groups speak for the majority of students at universities. The leaflet should contain photographs of New Left leadership at the respective universities. Naturally, the most obnoxious pictures should be used.
2. The instigating of or the taking advantage of personal conflicts or animosities existing between New Left leaders.
3. The creating of impressions that certain New Left leaders are informants for the Bureau or other law enforcement agencies.
4. The use of articles from student newspapers and/or the underground press to show the depravity of New Left leaders and members. In this connection, articles showing advocation of the use of narcotics and free sex are ideal to send to university officials, wealthy donors, members of the legislature and parents of students who are active in New Left matters.
5. Since the use of marijuana and other narcotics is widespread among members of the New Left, you should be alert to opportunities to have them arrested by local police authorities on drug charges . . .
6. The drawing up of anonymous letters regarding individuals active in the New Left. These letters should set out their activities and should be sent to their parents, neighbors and the parents' employers. This could have the effect of forcing the parents to take action.
7. Anonymous letters and leaflets describing faculty members and graduate assistants in the various institutions of learning who are active in New Left matters . . . Anonymous mailings should be made out to university officials, members of the state legislature, Board of Regents, and to the press. Such letters should be signed "A Concerned Alumni" or "A Concerned Taxpayer" . . .

Suggested methods to be employed by COINTELPRO against antiwar liberals on college campuses, July 17, 1968, from the U.S. Senate, 94th Congress, 1st Session, Select Committee to Study Governmental Operations with Respect to Intelligence Activities, Hearings, quoted in Fried, McCarthyism, p. 219.

. . . at 7:57 P.M., with two groups of club-wielding police converging simultaneous and independently, the battle was joined. The portions of the throng out of the immediate area of conflict largely stayed put and took up the chant, "The whole world is watching." but the intersection fragmented into a collage of violence.

. . . A Milwaukee Journal reporter says in his statement, "when the police managed to break up groups of protesters they pursued individuals and beat them with clubs. Some police pursued individual demonstrators as far as a block . . . and beat them . . . In many cases it appeared to me that when police had finished beating the protesters they were pursuing they then attacked, indiscriminately, any civilian who happened to be standing nearby. Many of these were not involved in the demonstrations."

"It seemed to me," an observer says, "That only a saint could have swallowed the vile remarks to the officers.

However, they went to extremes in clubbing the Yippies. I saw them move into the park, swatting away with clubs at boys and girls lying in the grass. More than once I witnessed two officers pulling at the arms of a Yippie until the arms almost left their sockets, then, as the officers put the Yippie in a police van, a third jabbed a riot stick into the groin of the youth being arrested. It was evident that the Yippie was not resisting arrest."

A description of confrontations between Chicago police and anti–Vietnam War protesters outside the Democratic Party's 1968 National Convention, from the Walker Report, Rights in Conflict: The Violent Confrontation of Demonstrators and Police in the Parks and Streets of Chicago during the Week of the Democratic National Convention of 1968. *A report submitted by Daniel Walker, director of the Chicago Study Team, to the National Commission on the Causes and Prevention of Violence (1968); reprinted in Hofstadter and Wallace, eds.,* American Violence, *pp. 378, 380.*

Violent Resistance to Civil Rights and Violence as a Tool of Civil Rights

The Rev. J. H. Cross, pastor of the church, was standing near his pulpit when the blast went off beneath him and he was shaken up. He [later] rushed outside to calm the crowd, grabbing a police megaphone and urging people to keep their heads and refrain from violence.

"The police are doing everything they can. Please go home," he urged.

"The Lord is our shepherd," he sobbed. "We shall not want."

The dead were identified as Cynthia Wesley, 14, who had been directly in the path of the blast and was identified only by clothing and a ring; Denise McNair, who was found crushed under a pile of stone; Carol Robertson, 14, and Addie Mae Collis, 14.

An account of the Sixteenth Street Baptist Church bombing in Birmingham, Alabama, from "Bomb Negro Church; Birmingham Children Victims; 21 Injured," Chicago Tribune, *September 16, 1963, p. 1.*

A second mistrial was declared today in the murder case against Byron De La Beckwith, the accused killer of Medgar W. Evers, after the jury of white men reported it was unable to agree on a verdict.

Two hours later the 43-year-old defendant was freed, under $10,000 bond, for the first time since his arrest last June 22. He slipped into an unmarked car

from the side door of the Hinds County Courthouse and was taken away under police guard to his home in Greenwood . . .

District Attorney William L. Waller, who has vigorously prosecuted the case, said he was undecided whether he would seek a third trial.

"I think the defense case was much better this time," Mr. Waller told reporters. "I don't see any reason to assume we can put on a better case; I don't know what my attitude will be in the future."

A newspaper account of the second 1964 trial of Byron De La Beckwith. John Herbers, "Beckwith's 2d Trial Ends in Hung Jury," New York Times, *April 19, 1964, p. 1.*

There is definitely a minority-police problem, not only in New York City, but elsewhere. Every police officer and every newspaper police reporter in any city knows that police brutality has been a fact of life for years. The late Walter White, whose skin was white, wrote in his lynching investigations of being deputized in a certain Southern city and told, "Now you can go out and kill niggers."

Pictures of the gassing and beating of Selma demonstrators last March 7 show a state trooper about to kick a Negro woman who already is blinded, choking and completely helpless from the tear gas.

Forty years ago while covering police news for a Kansas City weekly I found a wounded Negro "burglar" at a filling station who was not yet dead after being shot by a policeman. He told the almost incredible story of being planted by the policeman to rob the filling station of cans of oil at night so the policeman could make a capture and win a promotion. The dupe was not told that he was to be executed by police bullets . . .

Give some policemen a gun, a club, a blackjack and the authority of the law and they sometimes confuse their personal likes and dislikes with what the law provides.

Roy Wilkins, "Viewing the Charges of Police Brutality," Los Angeles Times, *May 31, 1965, p. A5.*

The statement of an acknowledged flogger that "they were alive when we left them in the woods" shocked spectators today as House investigators told the story of the flogging victims, whose decapitated bodies were found in the Mississippi river . . .

The murder victims, young Negro students, were Charles Moore and Henry Dee of Meadville, Miss. Klansman Charles Edwards of Meadville was invoking the 5th amendment when he was confronted with a hitherto secret statement that he gave the Mississippi state police . . .

Appell read the statement, which quoted Edwards as saying that he and another Meadville klansman, James Ford Seale, picked up the victims in a truck, with the help of other unnamed klansmen, took them to a woods and administered the flogging.

When the police interviewed Edwards on Nov. 6, 1964, he told the story, according to Appell, and insisted that the flogging victims were alive the last time he saw them. When found the victims were chained to an automobile engine at the bottom of the river.

Journalist William Moore, from "Bare Tale of Negro Beatings," Chicago Tribune, January 15, 1966, p. 4.

Events of August 12, 1965

By 12:20 A.M. approximately 50 to 75 youths were on either side of Avalon Blvd. at Imperial Highway, throwing missiles at passing cars and the police used vehicles with red lights and sirens within the riot area perimeter in an effort to disperse the crowd. As they did so, the rock throwing crowd dispersed, only to return as the police left the scene. Some of the older citizens in the area were inquiring, "What are those crazy kids doing?" A number of adult Negroes expressed the opinion that the police should open fire on the rock throwers to stop their activities. The police did not discharge firearms at the rioters. It was estimated that by 12:30 A.M. 70% of the rioters were children and the remainder were young adults and adults. Their major activity was throwing missiles at passing vehicles driven by Caucasians. One rioter stationed himself a block from the intersection of Avalon Blvd. and Imperial Highway, where the major group of rioters were centered, and signaled to this group, whenever a vehicle driven by a Caucasian approached the intersection, so that it could be stoned. . . .

Witnesses stated at this time, young Negro rioters said: "I'm throwing rocks because I'm tired of a white man misusing me." "Man this is the part of town they have given us, and if they don't want to be killed they had better keep their————out of here." "The cops think we are scared of them because they got guns, but you can only die once; if I get a few of them I don't mind dying."

. . . Sunrise disclosed five burned automobiles, amidst a large amount of rubble, broken bricks, stones, and shattered glass, in the vicinity of the intersection of Imperial Highway and Avalon Blvd.

As an indication of the mood of the crowd of approximately 400 persons who had gathered . . . on Thursday morning, the following comment of the youths in the crowd are quoted:

"Like why, man, should I go home? These———— cops have been pushin' me 'round all my life. Kickin' my————and things like that. Whitey ain't no good. He talked 'bout law and order, its his law and his order it ain't mine . . ."

"If I've got to die, I ain't dyin' in Vietnam, I'm going to die here . . ."

"I don't have no job. I ain't worked for two years. He, the white man, got everything, I ain't got nothing. What you expect me to do? I get my kids when I see Whitey running. If they come in here tonight I'm going to kill me one."

"They always————with the Blood—beatin' them with stocks, handcuffing women, I saw one of them— ————go up side a cat's head and split it wide open. They treat the Blood like dirt—they've been doing it for years. Look how they treated us when we were slaves—we still slaves . . ."

"Whitey uses his cops to keep us here. We are like hogs in a pen—then they come in with those silly helmets sticks and guns and things—Who the————[Police Chief William] Parker think he is, God?"

Excerpt from California state commission headed by John McCone to investigate the 1965 riots in the Watts section of Los Angeles. California Governor's Commission on the Los Angeles Riots, Transcripts, Depositions, Consultants' Reports, and Selected Documents, *II,* Chronology of the Los Angeles Riots; *reprinted in Hofstadter and Wallace, eds.,* American Violence, *pp. 264–265.*

The summer of 1967 again brought racial disorders to American cities, and with them shock, fear and bewilderment to the nation.

The worst came during a two-week period in July, first in Newark and then in Detroit. Each set off a chain reaction in neighboring communities.

On July 28, 1967, the President of the United States established this Commission and directed us to answer three basic questions:

What happened?

Why did it happen?

What can be done to prevent it from happening again?

To respond to these questions, we have undertaken a broad range of studies and investigations. We have visited the riot cities; we have heard many witnesses; we have sought the counsel of experts across the country.

Left to right: Hosea Williams, Jesse Jackson, Martin Luther King, Jr., and Ralph Abernathy stand on a balcony at the Lorraine Motel in Memphis, Tennessee, on April 3, 1968, one day before King was assassinated. *(AP Images)*

This is our basic conclusion: Our nation is moving toward two societies, one black, one white—separate and unequal.

Reaction to last summer's disorders has quickened the movement and deepened the division. Discrimination and segregation have long permeated much of American life; they now threaten the future of every American.

This deepening racial division is not inevitable. The movement apart can be reversed. Choice is still possible. Our principal task is to define that choice and to press for a national resolution.

To pursue our present course will involve the continuing polarization of the American community and, ultimately, the destruction of basic democratic values.

The alternative is not blind repression or capitulation to lawlessness. It is the realization of common opportunities for all within a single society.

This alternative will require a commitment to national action—compassionate, massive and sustained, backed by the resources of the most powerful and the richest nation on this earth. From every American it will require new attitudes, new understanding, and, above all, new will.

The vital needs of the nation must be met; hard choices must be made, and, if necessary, new taxes enacted.

Violence cannot build a better society. Disruption and disorder nourish repression, not justice. They strike at the freedom of every citizen. The community cannot—it will not—tolerate coercion and mob rule.

Violence and destruction must be ended—in the streets of the ghetto and in the lives of people.

Segregation and poverty have created in the racial ghetto a destructive environment totally unknown to most white Americans.

What white Americans have never fully understood but what the Negro can never forget—is that white society is deeply implicated in the ghetto. White institutions created it, white institutions maintain it, and white society condones it.

It is time now to turn with all the purpose at our command to the major unfinished business of this nation. It is time to adopt strategies for action that will produce quick and visible progress. It is time to make good the promises of American democracy to all citizens—urban and rural, white and black, Spanish-surname, American Indian, and every minority group.

Our recommendations embrace three basic principles:

- To mount programs on a scale equal to the dimension of the problems;
- To aim these programs for high impact in the immediate future in order to close the gap between promise and performance;
- To undertake new initiatives and experiments that can change the system of failure and frustration that now dominates the ghetto and weakens our society.

These programs will require unprecedented levels of funding and performance, but they neither probe deeper nor demand more than the problems which called them forth. There can be no higher priority for national action and no higher claim on the nation's conscience.

The opening statement of the Report *issued by the National Advisory Commission on Civil Disorders (1968), pp. 1–2.*

"Martin Luther King is dead," said Henry Lux, assistant police chief, in announcing his death.

Paul Hess, assistant administrator of St. Joseph hospital, confirmed later that Dr. King died at 7 P.M. of a bullet wound in the neck.

The Rev. Jesse Jackson said he and others in the King party were getting ready to go to dinner when the shooting occurred.

Dr. King had been in his second-floor room in the Lorraine motel throughout the day until just before 6 P.M.

Then he emerged, wearing a black suit and white shirt. He paused, leaned over the green iron railing and started chatting with an associate, the Rev. Mr. Jackson, who was standing just below him.

The Rev. Mr. Jackson introduced him to Ben Branch, of Chicago, a musician who was to play at the rally King was to address two hours later . . . [T]he aid asked King:

"Do you know Ben?"

"Yes, that's my man!" Dr. King glowed.

They said King then asked if Branch would play a spiritual, "Precious Lord, Take My Hand," at the night meeting.

"I really want you to play that tonight," King said.

Then there was a shot.

An account of the final moments of Martin Luther King, Jr.'s life, from "Martin Luther King Slain," Chicago Tribune, *August 5, 1968, p. 1.*

Judicial Revolution, Law Enforcement Reform, and Civil Liberties

Since the Fourth Amendment's right of privacy has been declared enforceable against the States through the Due Process Clause of the Fourteenth, it is enforceable against them by the same sanction of exclusion as is used against the Federal Government. Were it otherwise, then just as without the [1914] *Weeks* rule the assurance against unreasonable federal searches and seizures would be "a form of words," valueless and undeserving of mention in a perpetual charter of inestimable human liberties, so too, without that rule the freedom from state invasions of privacy would be so ephemeral and so neatly severed from its conceptual nexus with the freedom from all brutish means of coercing evidence as not to merit this Court's high regard as a freedom "implicit in the concept of ordered liberty" . . . Only last year the Court itself recognized that the purpose of the exclusionary rule "is to deter—to compel respect for the constitutional guaranty in the only effectively available way—by removing the incentive to disregard it" [*Elkins v. United States*, 1960] . . .

The right to privacy, no less important than any other right carefully and particularly reserved to the people, would stand in marked contrast to all other rights declared as "basic to a free society." This Court has not hesitated to enforce as strictly against the States as it does against the Federal Government the rights of free speech and of a free press, the rights to notice and to a fair, public trial, including, as it does, the right not to be convicted by use of a coerced confession, however logically relevant it be, and without regard to its reliability . . . And nothing could be more certain than that when a coerced confession is involved, "the relevant rules of evidence" are overridden without regard to "the incidence of such conduct by the police," slight or frequent. Why should not the same rule apply to what is tantamount to coerced testimony by way of unconstitutional seizure of goods, papers, effects, documents, etc.?

Justice Tom Clark, from his majority ruling in Mapp v. Ohio *(1961), expanding the exclusionary rule to include state law under the Fourteenth Amendment.*

If policewomen are here to stay, which seems today to be an established fact, not only in the United States but all over the world, it is not because they have tried to compete against men in work that always has been and will always be predominantly a man's job. It is because they have brought to their work talents that are generally considered peculiarly feminine—an unusually highly developed interest in human relationships—and have accentuated, rather than subordinated, their femininity.

Lois Lundell Higgins, from the introduction to her Policewoman's Manual *(1961), defending the then-predominant distinctions in the way by which male and female officers performed their duties, quoted in Vila and Morris,* The Role of Police in American Society, *p. 171.*

In the cases before us today, given this background, we concern ourselves primarily with this interrogation atmosphere and the evils it can bring. In No. 759, *Miranda v. Arizona,* the police arrested the defendant and took him to a special interrogation room where they secured a confession. In No. 760, *Vignera v. New York,* the defendant made oral admissions to the police after interrogation in the afternoon, and then signed an inculpatory statement upon being questioned by an assistant district attorney later the same evening. In No. 761, *Westover v. United States,* the defendant was handed over to the Federal Bureau of Investigation by local authorities after they had detained and interrogated him for a lengthy period, both at night and the following morning. After some two hours of questioning, the federal officers had obtained signed statements from the defendant. Lastly, in No. 584, *California v. Stewart,* the local police held the defendant five days in the station and interrogated him on nine separate occasions before they secured his inculpatory statement.

In these cases, we might not find the defendants' statements to have been involuntary in traditional terms. Our concern for adequate safeguards to protect precious Fifth Amendment rights is, of course, not lessened in the slightest. In each of the cases, the defendant was thrust into an unfamiliar atmosphere and run through menacing police interrogation procedures. The potentiality for compulsion is forcefully apparent, for example, in *Miranda,* where the

indigent Mexican defendant was a seriously disturbed individual with pronounced sexual fantasies, and in *Stewart,* in which the defendant was an indigent Los Angeles Negro who had dropped out of school in the sixth grade. To be sure, the records do not evince overt physical coercion or patent psychological ploys. The fact remains that in none of these cases did the officers undertake to afford appropriate safeguards at the outset of the interrogation to insure that the statements were truly the product of free choice.

It is obvious that such an interrogation environment is created for no purpose other than to subjugate the individual to the will of his examiner. This atmosphere carries its own badge of intimidation. To be sure, this is not physical intimidation, but it is equally destructive of human dignity. The current practice of incommunicado interrogation is at odds with one of our Nation's most cherished principles—that the individual may not be compelled to incriminate himself. Unless adequate protective devices are employed to dispel the compulsion inherent in custodial surroundings, no statement obtained from the defendant can truly be the product of his free choice.

Chief Justice Earl Warren, from his majority ruling in Miranda v. Arizona, et al. *(1966).*

Increased Crime and the Law Enforcement Response

At about 11 P.M., six of the women were in the building. Miss Amurao and one other woman were asleep in a bedroom. They were awakened by a knock on the bedroom door.

A man came into the room with a knife. Altho he later displayed a revolver, he did not have it in his hand when he entered their bedroom. He ordered Miss Amurao and the other woman to walk ahead of him into an adjoining bedroom. He awakened four women asleep there, and herded them all into the rear bedroom.

In the rear bedroom, the man took a sheet from a bed, cut it into strips with his knife, and bound the women's hands behind their backs.

While he was at this task, three more women came into the building and walked into the bedroom. He bound their hands also . . .

The night was one of confused horror for Miss Amurao. She recalled hearing the alarm clock sound at 5 A.M. She knew the time because it was set for that hour.

"I thought, if the man was still in the house that would scare him off," she told police. "But I wasn't sure he had left. I waited, and when I didn't hear anything, after a while I crawled out."

[A homicide detective] said she related how she had worked her hands free, left the bedroom, and found the other women dead.

An account of Richard Speck's murder of eight student nurses in Chicago, from "Search for Mass Slayer," Chicago Tribune, July 15, 1966.

[Ramiro] Martinez was at home cooking a steak when he heard a radio report about a sniper shooting up the University of Texas campus.

Martinez, 29, and a 5-year police veteran, left his steak, pulled on his uniform and sped to the campus . . .

[Police Chief Robert A. Miles] said that Martinez, acting on his own initiative, crawled and ran to the tower's building entrance.

There, the chief said, Martinez deputized Allen Crum, an employee of the University Co-operative Store.

Crum armed himself with a rifle and the two then took the elevator and the stairs to the southeast entrance to the observation deck . . . When the officer came to the northeast corner of the platform, he saw Whitman with a rifle aimed at the southwest corner of the deck.

"Martinez knew Crum was coming around that corner," Miles said.

The officer immediately fired his service revolver at Whitman, Miles said, and Whitman fired back once. Martinez then emptied his revolver at Whitman.

Officer [Houston] McCoy, 26, had followed Martinez and rushed out onto the platform with a shotgun when he heard the shots.

McCoy, Miles said, shot Whitman twice with the shotgun.

An account of the police response to University of Texas tower sniper Charles Whitman, who shot 42 bystanders (killing 10) before he was gunned down by Officers Martinez and McCoy, from Paul Recer, "Officer Left His Steak; Later Shot Tower Sniper," Dallas Morning News, August 2, 1966, p. 8.

Many Americans take comfort in the view that crime is the vice of a handful of people. This view is inaccurate. In the United States today, one boy in six is referred to the juvenile court. A Commission survey shows that in 1965 more than two million Americans were received in prisons or juvenile training schools, or placed on probation. Another Commission study suggests that about 40 percent of all male children now living in the United States will be arrested for a nontraffic offense during their lives. An independent survey of 1,700 persons found that 91 percent of the sample admitted they had committed acts for which they might have received jail or prison sentences.

Many Americans also think of crime as a very narrow range of behavior. It is not. An enormous variety of acts make up the "crime problem." Crime is not just a tough teenager snatching a lady's purse. It is a professional thief stealing cars "on order." It is a well-heeled loan shark taking over a previously legitimate business for organized crime. It is a polite young man who suddenly and inexplicably murders his family. It is a corporation executive conspiring with competitors to keep prices high. No single formula, no single theory, no single generalization can explain the vast range of behavior called crime.

Many Americans think controlling crime is solely the task of the police, the courts, and correction agencies. In fact, as the Commission's report makes clear, crime cannot be controlled without the interest and participation of schools, businesses, social agencies, private groups, and individual citizens. . . .

An important finding of the survey is that for the Nation as a whole there is far more crime than ever is reported. Burglaries occur about three times more often than they are reported to the police. Aggravated assaults and larcenies over $50 occur twice as often as they are reported. There are 50 percent more robberies than are reported. In some areas, only one-tenth of the total number of certain kinds of crimes are reported to the police. Seventy-four percent of the neighborhood commercial establishments surveyed do not report to police the thefts committed by their employees.

The existence of crime, the talk of crime, the reports of crime, and the fear of crime have eroded the basic quality of life of many Americans . . . One-third of a representative sample of all Americans say it is unsafe to walk alone at night in their neighborhoods. Slightly more than one-third say they keep firearms in the house for protection against criminals. Twenty-eight percent say they keep watchdogs for the same reason.

Under any circumstance, developing an effective response to the problem of crime in America is exceedingly difficult. And because of the changes expected in the population in the next decade, in years to come it will be more difficult. Young people commit a disproportionate share of crime and the number of young people in our society is growing at a much faster rate than the total population. Although the 15- to 17-year-old age group represents only 5.4 percent of the population, it accounts for 12.8 percent of all arrests. Fifteen and sixteen year olds have the highest arrest rate in the United States. The problem in the years ahead is dramatically foretold by the fact that 23 percent of the population is 10 or younger.

Despite the seriousness of the problem today and the increasing challenge in the years ahead, the central conclusion of the Commission is that a significant reduction in crime is possible if the following objectives are vigorously pursued:

First, society must seek to prevent crime before it happens by assuring all Americans a stake in the benefits and responsibilities of American life, by strengthening law enforcement, and by reducing criminal opportunities.

Second, society's aim of reducing crime would be better served if the system of criminal justice developed a far broader range of techniques with which to deal with individual offenders.

Third, the system of criminal justice must eliminate existing injustices if it is to achieve its ideals and win the respect and cooperation of all citizens.

Fourth, the system of criminal justice must attract more people and better people—police, prosecutors, judges, defense attorneys, probation and parole officers, and corrections officials with more knowledge, expertise, initiative, and integrity.

Fifth, There must be much more operational and basic research into the problems of crime and criminal administration, by those both within and without the system of criminal justice.

Sixth, the police, courts, and correctional agencies must be given substantially greater amounts of money if they are to improve their ability to fight crime.

Seventh, individual citizens, civic and business organizations, religious institutions, and all levels of government must take responsibility for planning and implementing the changes that must be made in the criminal justice system if crime is to be reduced.

An excerpt from the President's Commission on Law Enforcement and Administration of Justice, The Challenge of Crime in a Free Society *(1967), pp. v–vi.*

CHAPTER ELEVEN

A Crisis of Confidence
1971–1981

During the 1970s, crime seemed to have become a constant element of the American condition. In spite—or perhaps because—of the public policy attention devoted to the issue throughout the previous decade, crime rates remained extremely high. The homicide rate hovered near a historic peak of 10 homicides per 100,000 people for the entire decade.[1] The rate of serious "index" crimes known to police rose by more than 40 percent between 1971 and 1981.[2] And the National Crime Victimization Survey, a new set of statistics based on reliable survey data and first issued in 1973, suggested that Americans were victims of twice as many serious violent crimes than they reported to police and three times as many as had been recorded in earlier measures.[3] With cities associated with crime and already losing manufacturing jobs, many affluent people moved to the suburbs and beyond, reinforcing urban poverty and leaving struggling urban infrastructures that were more vulnerable to crime. New York City, for example, earned a reputation as one of America's most dangerous places, with drugs and prostitution rampant in Times Square, muggers in alleys, and looting during the 1977 blackout.

This sense that crime was pervasive might be seen as one symptom of larger changes taking place in U.S. society. The 1970s can be regarded as a transitional decade in which the United States came to terms with its changing place in the world, changing political alignments, and changing economic structures. During the first half of the decade, the Vietnam War slowly wound down. Protests against the war peaked in 1970 and 1971 even as the Nixon administration gradually reduced troop levels; the last U.S. combat troops left Vietnam in 1973. As the divisive conflict came to an end, the American people suffered through the trial of Lieutenant William Calley. Accused of leading a massacre of several hundred men, women, and children in the Vietnamese village of My Lai, Calley was court-martialed in 1971, sentenced to life in prison, then pardoned by President Richard Nixon. A war crimes trial against a U.S. serviceman made it difficult for Americans to see their nation as wholly innocent in the conflict.

The nation suffered through an even greater crisis centered on President Nixon following the burglary of the Democratic Party's national headquarters in Washington's Watergate Hotel in 1972. The burglars, it turned out, had been clandestine operatives affiliated with Nixon's reelection campaign. The subsequent investigation revealed that Nixon himself had been at the heart of a conspiracy to cover up widespread illegal activities on behalf of his administration. Nixon resigned in disgrace on August 9, 1974, as the American people's faith in their leaders deteriorated further.

Americans in the 1970s also suffered some of the worst effects of structural changes in the economy. In the early part of the decade, the Nixon administration fought a long and ineffective battle against "stagflation," an unprecedented combination of slow economic growth and sharp monetary inflation. An oil embargo by petroleum exporting countries in 1973, and a renewed energy crisis in 1979, each led to long lines at gasoline stations and highlighted for many Americans that the United States had become vulnerable to changes in the world's markets. By 1979, President Jimmy Carter warned the American people that the United States faced "a crisis of confidence" evident in "the growing doubt about the meaning of our own lives and in the loss of a unity of purpose for our Nation."[4]

This same crisis of confidence also affected the operations of criminal justice in the 1970s. For law enforcement agencies, the long-accepted mission of catching criminals by whatever means possible faced serious challenges. The FBI, for example, retreated from acting as a beacon of tough-minded crime control after the 1972 death of J. Edgar Hoover ended his administration, which had dated to the Prohibition era. Hoover's successor, L. Patrick Gray, was forced to resign in 1973, following the revelation of his cooperation in Nixon White House cover-ups. Then, between 1973 and 1976, Freedom of Information Act (FOIA) lawsuits and inquiries by the House and Senate Select Committees on Intelligence disclosed the long history of COINTELPRO and Hoover's other secret investigations. The FBI found itself reduced to acting as just another bureaucratic agency.[5]

The fundamental assumptions behind the operations of criminal justice also began to shift in the 1970s. On the one hand, the early part of the decade witnessed the greatest successes of a movement toward respecting the civil rights of criminals and providing treatment outside correctional institutions. Community-based corrections represented one of the grand experiments of the era, as the number of adults on parole increased from approximately 62,000 in 1965 to more than 156,000 in 1975 and the number of adults on probation increased from approximately 144,000 to 923,000 in the same period.[6]

On the other hand, the concept of rehabilitation came under attack from academic criminologists. Most notably, a team led by Robert Martinson concluded in a 1974 study that, with few exceptions, the many rehabilitative criminal justice programs operating in the 1950s and 1960s had little appreciable impact. Although Martinson's report acknowledged a variety of outcomes, it was widely interpreted as demonstrating that when it comes to criminal rehabilitation nothing works.[7] The resulting "nothing works" controversy granted greater authority to voices arguing that the most effective mission for criminal justice institutions was deterring crime. Criminologist James Q. Wilson's 1975 analysis *Thinking about Crime*, claimed that imposing mandatory prison sentences on each person convicted of a serious crime would dramatically reduce the overall crime rate.[8] Wilson's emphasis on deterrence and selective incapacitation helped provide an intellectual rationale for policy shifts toward tougher sentencing and increased incarceration in the late 1970s and early 1980s.

Local police departments were also forced to change in the wake of urban crises and civil rights activism of the late 1960s. In the 1970s, rank-and-file officers

A female police officer directs traffic in 1974 Washington, D.C. *(National Archives and Records Administration [556737])*

gained more say in decision making through police unions, educational and professional standards for police increased, and African Americans and women attained greater representation and influence within police departments.[9] The criminal justice system found itself pulled in different directions in the 1970s, moving toward greater attention to civil rights on the one hand, beginning to get tougher on crime on the other hand, and all the while dealing with increasingly extensive and complicated problems of crime.

The Soledad Brothers and Attica's Children

If the 1960s represented the golden age of the Civil Rights movement, the 1970s represented the decade during which the majority white culture took it all in. As is true of most social justice movements, the most visible and appealing figures are the first to benefit, and the least visible and appealing figures are the last to gain. The Civil Rights movement vastly improved conditions for upper- and middle-class blacks, but those who were poor, imprisoned, or otherwise invisible were the last to benefit from improving human rights standards in the United States.

As race riots and the Black Power movement gradually undermined the popularity of the Civil Rights movement among whites and the successes of the movement made it seem less relevant during the late 1960s and early 1970s, mainstream condemnation of civil rights abuses became less common. Prisoners, in particular, were opportune victims of white racism. In 1959, 18-year-old George Jackson was sentenced to one year to life in prison for robbing $70 from a convenience store at gunpoint under the indeterminate sentencing laws prevailing in California. Jackson, who saw himself as a political prisoner, was not a model inmate; he spent 12 years in prison, seven of them in solitary confinement. During that time he educated himself, became a committed Marxist, and achieved national prominence in 1970 with the publication of *Soledad Brother*, a collection of his political writings.

Jackson was in Soledad Prison in January 1970 when eight white prisoners attempted to forcibly claim Soledad Prison's basketball court from seven black prisoners. The violence escalated when black prisoner W. L. Nolen resisted the white inmates and was gunned down by a white prison guard. When two other black prisoners ran to his side and attempted to help him to his feet, they were also quickly shot to death. After a quiet three-day hearing before an all-white coroner's jury, the guard's decision to shoot an unarmed black prisoner was deemed acceptable, and he was allowed to return to work.

In retaliation, Jackson and two other prisoners allegedly tracked down and murdered a white prison guard. The three assailants, nicknamed the Soledad Brothers (after Jackson's book), were all placed in solitary confinement while awaiting trial. In August 1971, George Jackson was shot to death during an alleged escape attempt. In spite of an official story, in which guards claimed that Jackson was armed, prison officials were never able to produce a credible account of exactly how Jackson managed to get a gun in the first place. His attorney, Stephen Bingham, was accused of smuggling it into prison but later acquitted after a jury was unable to accept the state's account.[10]

Regardless of the actual sequence of events, one fact was clear: George Jackson, the nation's best-known imprisoned black militant, had been shot dead by a white guard. The news resonated in New York's Attica Correctional Facility, where prisoners wore black armbands and sat in a silent fast on August 22, 1971. New York's prisons were already riddled with tensions. The previous year, Attica inmates went on strike for two days to protest the brutal prison conditions, and inmates at Auburn temporarily took control of the prison yard until their demands were met. In early 1971, New York's Department of Correctional Services was reorganized under the leadership of new commissioner Russell G. Oswald. While Oswald made changes such as expanding mail and visiting privileges and offering pork-free meals for Muslim inmates, these changes also raised expectations. Cell searches revealed that prisoners had been communicating with inmates in California about coordinating protests against prison conditions.[11] When word of Jackson's death reached Attica, the prison was ready for revolt.

On September 9, 1971, more than 1,200 inmates rebelled and took over the prison, beating guard William Quinn to death and holding 39 guards and employees hostage in the exercise yard. The resulting standoff lasted for four days and became a major media event. Celebrities such as *New York Times* columnist Tom Wicker and Black Panther Party chairman Bobby Seale arrived to act as observers, and television and radio journalists entered the prison to cover the negotiations and interview inmates. On the fourth day, state officials under the direction of Governor Nelson Rockefeller decided to recapture Attica. Police helicopters dropped tear gas into the exercise yard, and hundreds of state police fired indiscriminately into the prison. When the dust settled, 43 people had died in the Attica uprising: prison guard William Quinn, 10 hostages, and 32 inmates. After the prison was retaken, the families of the 10 slain hostages were told that the hostages' throats had been cut by inmates and were encouraged to sign workers' compensation agreements waiving their right to sue. Later, the official state autopsy revealed that all 10 hostages had been shot by state police. The state refused to acknowledge its culpability until 2006, when families of the slain hostages won a $12 million settlement in court.[12]

If the treatment of hostages' families was unjust, the treatment of the surviving inmates was worse. In the weeks following the Attica uprising, prison guards attempted to restore "order" by forcibly stripping and beating inmates, requiring them to crawl on broken glass and dramatically increasing the already intolerable levels of harassment and abuse that had preceded the riot. The post-riot torture was so severe and so gratuitous that inmates and their families also successfully sued New York State—to the tune of $8 million in 2000.[13] In 1972, the New York State Special Commission on Attica—called the McKay Commission after its chairman, New York University law school dean Robert B. McKay—issued a full report on the Attica uprising and the state's response to it. The decision by state officials to assault the prison with tear gas, helicopters, and live weapons was roundly condemned.

Modern Drug Enforcement

The election of President Richard Nixon brought with it a sharp change in U.S. drug policy. Nixon's drug policies were highly innovative, combining increased enforcement and tougher sentences with law enforcement reorganization, more effective international diplomacy, and a dramatic increase in federal funding for drug treatment programs. Nixon also increased the overall drug enforcement budget elevenfold, from $65 million in 1969 to $719 million in 1974.[14]

The centerpiece of the Nixon antidrug agenda was the Comprehensive Drug Abuse Prevention and Control Act (CDAPCA) of 1970, which expanded the authority of the federal government vis-à-vis drug prosecution. One of the components of the CDAPCA, the Controlled Substances Act, reduced the emphasis in federal law on controlling marijuana but targeted more dangerous and addictive drugs such as heroin. It also established strict regulations pertaining to the distribution of prescription drugs. In July 1973, the Nixon administration consolidated a half dozen federal agencies working on drug issues—including the successor to Harry Anslinger's old Bureau of Narcotics—into one bureaucratic giant, the Drug Enforcement Agency (DEA).

Nixon's emphasis on the treatment of drug addiction exceeded that of any president before or since. In mid-1971, he issued an executive order establishing the Special Action Office for Drug Abuse Prevention (SAODAP) and appointed Jerome Jaffe, a psychiatrist specializing in methadone treatment programs, to facilitate a network of federally funded drug treatment programs that continued to exist for decades. In 1974, SAODAP was reconstituted under the supervision of the National Institutes of Health (NIH) and became the National Institute on Drug Abuse (NIDA).

The Nixon administration's record on international drug trafficking was punctuated by a humiliating failure followed by a dramatic success. The humiliating failure was Operation Intercept, an attempt in September 1969 to block marijuana traffic by performing rudimentary two-minute searches of vehicles crossing the Mexican border. The searches were just brief enough to render them impractically superficial and just long enough to create unpopular traffic jams at border cities. Over an 11-day period, the operation generated an average of five arrests per day—all involving small amounts of contraband—despite the fact that nearly 2 million vehicles were searched.[15] Mexico's attempt at drug enforcement, Operation Condor, launched in 1975, was far more successful at

This print of a marijuana leaf was produced by the U.S. Treasury Department for use by law enforcement officials attempting to identify marijuana plants. *(Library of Congress Prints and Photographs Division [LC-USZ62-104029])*

reducing Mexican-U.S. drug trafficking. By crop-dusting marijuana and opium fields with herbicide, the Mexican government reduced its percentage of the U.S. drug supply substantially over a five-year period. In 1976, approximately 75 percent of the U.S. marijuana supply came from Mexico; by 1981, only 4 percent did.[16]

Until 1972, as much as 95 percent of the U.S. heroin supply came into the country by way of the "French Connection," in which Turkish heroin was smuggled into the United States by international smugglers operating out of Marseilles, France.[17] The United States sought to fight the heroin epidemic by putting dramatic international pressure on Turkey, demanding that it ban opium production. If Turkey complied, the United States would assist the Turkish government in helping opium farmers transition to other crops; if Turkey did not comply, U.S. foreign aid would be cut dramatically. Turkey complied, and the French Connection dried up, creating a short-term heroin shortage in the United States and forcing traffickers to look elsewhere for their supply, which had the net long-term effect of diversifying the international heroin trafficking industry.

The Rockefeller Drug Laws

State responses to illegal drugs varied, but one state's approach to the drug war is still emblematic of tough drug policy. In the aftermath of the Attica prison uprising, New York governor Nelson Rockefeller increasingly committed himself to law and order. In particular, he championed new state drug laws that rejected the treatment inherent in federal drug policy under the Nixon administration and instead emphasized harsh criminal penalties to deter drug use. The Rockefeller drug laws, which he signed into law on May 8, 1973, established tough mandatory minimum sentences for drug-related crimes: 15 years to life for the possession of four ounces or more of cocaine, heroin, or marijuana or for the sale of two ounces. The penalty was the same as the penalty for second-degree murder, marking the first time that a state had raised the penalties for drug-related crimes to match or exceed penalties for violent crimes. These laws established a precedent adopted by other states, and eventually the federal government, of applying strict mandatory minimum sentences to drug crimes.

The Rockefeller laws do not seem to have had a significant impact on the drug problem in New York, but they did have an extremely significant impact on the prison population—more than 150,000 New Yorkers were imprisoned between 1973 and 2002 under the Rockefeller statutes.[18] Perhaps most distressingly, African Americans and Latinos, who collectively made up only one-third of the New York population, composed 94 percent of those arrested under the Rockefeller drug laws.[19] Due to the rapidly growing inmate population, New York, like other states that adopted similar sentencing rules, found itself forced to engage in massive construction of new prisons in the 1980s and 1990s.[20]

By the late 1990s, the mass incarceration resulting from the Rockefeller laws seemed to have provoked a reaction against them among New Yorkers. In an April 1999 Zogby poll, 83 percent of New York respondents stated that they would support a more rehabilitation-oriented and less incarceration-based response to drug possession, and 50 percent of respondents stated that they would be more likely to vote for a candidate who supported drug policy reform.[21] In 2004, the state government abolished the mandatory character of the Rockefeller sentences, allowing those convicted under Rockefeller statutes to petition for early release, sometimes after serving as little as three years. Nonetheless, the Rockefeller laws represented a key turning point in U.S. drug policy. Applying mandatory minimum sentences to drug offenses influenced other state legislatures around the country and established a model that would be adopted under the ensuing federal war on drugs in the 1980s.

The Mafia in Popular Culture and Reality

When Mario Puzo's *The Godfather* became a bestselling book in 1969 and two Academy Award–winning films in 1972 and 1974, it changed the way Americans saw organized crime. Televised federal hearings and investigations had made organized crime increasingly visible in the 1960s, but *The Godfather* helped replace its public image as a highly organized national conspiracy with that of a much more human grouping of criminal entrepreneurs rooted in an ethnic subculture and living by a strange and complex code of family honor. New words began to enter the American vocabulary. *Omertà*, an Italian word that can be loosely translated as both "masculinity" and "code of silence," was perceived as the standard of manly self-sufficiency—a commitment to dealing with disputes independently without bringing in law enforcement authorities, even when it might seem beneficial to do so. A respected adviser, standing at or near the top of the power hierarchy but outside the core family group, might be known as a *consigliere*. These and other Italian words contributed to an intricate, hagiographic portrayal of Italian-American crime families as representative of a unique underworld power structure. This portrayal, in turn, resonated with a U.S. public that had grown increasingly suspicious of established political power. As an unpopular war continued to rage and the century's defining presidential scandal took shape, Americans found comfort in the belief that, in at least some contexts, honor existed among thieves.

From a criminal justice perspective, of course, organized crime looked far less admirable. Driven by drug distributing, prostitution, fraud, theft, racketeering, and violence, organized crime was dangerous in its own right and contributed to an intricate, mysterious underworld culture that made particular offenses easier to hide. Organized crime also posed considerable difficulties for prosecutors because it allowed ample opportunity for criminals to work more or less anonymously, running afoul of specific laws from time to time but largely relying on intimidation and the code of silence to protect themselves from prosecution. Jurisdictional challenges also came with prosecuting organized crime cases. Most criminal acts connected to racketeering were initially violations of state law, not federal law, which left police departments and prosecutors with the uncomfortable prospect of investigating criminal enterprises whose territorial jurisdiction exceeded their own.

This changed in October 1970, when Congress passed the Organized Crime Control Act, which included the Racketeer Influenced and Corrupt Organizations (RICO) statute. The RICO Act targeted the structure and leadership of organized crime. It expanded federal wiretapping authority and established witness protection programs to encourage informers to cooperate with law enforcement, directly challenging the *omertà*. Under it, leaders of organized crime could be prosecuted for the federal crime of racketeering if they could be linked to a pattern of specific offenses including murder, witness intimidation, or money laundering. Regardless of whether they personally committed a particular crime, bosses could be prosecuted if the action was construed as part of a larger criminal enterprise. The RICO Act forced criminal organizations to maintain an even more rigorous code of silence in order to insulate their most powerful members from prosecution, and they did so with mixed success. Frank Tieri, the 76-year-old head of the Genovese crime family (one of the infamous "five families" of New York City), was successfully convicted under RICO statutes in 1980, striking fear into the hearts of other criminal overlords. This fear proved to be well founded. In 1986, the then-current heads of four out of the "five families" were convicted on charges related to the RICO Act. For the first time in U.S. history, organized crime families had become deeply vulnerable on a national level, and that vulnerability would limit their power for decades to come.

Defining Serial Murder

FBI profiler Robert Ressler first coined the term "serial murder" in 1976. Although serial killers in the United States date to at least the late 19th century, increased media attention—coupled with advances in forensic technology and information sharing between law enforcement agencies, allowing for more frequent identification of multiple offenders—brought the concept of serial murder into the American consciousness as a specific kind of deeply disturbed behavior that would come to personify human evil in the popular imagination.

According to most authorities, serial murder is the murder of three victims by one individual over a period of one month or longer, with a significant "cooling-off" period between murders.[22] This "cooling-off" period, which distinguishes serial killers from spree killers, makes a serial killer a particularly frightening figure, because it establishes that a serial killer could be almost anyone, anywhere. Also significant is the fact that murder is generally associated in U.S. culture with low-income members of minority groups, yet serial killers have historically been far more likely to be white, financially solvent, and to have little or no criminal history. Thus, those who felt sheltered from crime by race and class segregation felt extremely vulnerable to serial killers because of this.

No single serial killer defined this Jekyll-and-Hyde dynamic more clearly than Ted Bundy. A charming young man who had earned a psychology degree with honors from the University of Washington, volunteered as a crisis line counselor, worked to reelect a popular Republican governor, and had even once saved a three-year-old from drowning in a lake, Bundy was attractive, well groomed, well liked, and well spoken, but under his disarming exterior existed a violent psychopath. The exact number of Bundy's victims is unknown, but it is clear that he raped, murdered, and mutilated between 30 and 40 women between 1974 and 1978. Like most serial killers, he had a "type"—all of his victims were young, white, middle-class women and girls—and a violent sexual fixation. His primary reason for murdering women was to achieve total sexual dominance by mutilating and raping the corpses, his revenge for being rejected by various women as a young man. In every respect, Bundy was a typical serial killer: a white, middle-class male psychopath with an overwhelming personal desire to achieve dominance over others.

Less typical was the case of David Berkowitz, better known as the "Son of Sam," who killed six New Yorkers between summer 1976 and spring 1977. Originally dubbed "the .44-caliber killer" for his pattern of sneaking up on couples parked in cars and shooting them with his revolver, Berkowitz confessed to the crimes upon arrest, claiming that his drive to kill was based on demonic messages delivered by his neighbor's dog. In the years after the killings, Berkowitz converted to Christianity and came to deny having killed anyone, attributing the "Son of Sam" slayings to members of a violent cult with whom he shared membership. This is not to say that Berkowitz believed that he should be freed from prison. He repeatedly stated that he did not wish to be paroled, even to the point of skipping his own parole hearings, and that acting as an accomplice to the killings justified his life term. Although it was in Berkowitz's self-interest to deny responsibility for the killings and convicted serial killers are not generally regarded as credible witnesses, some journalists who have investigated the killings share his belief that he did not act alone. The "Son of Sam" murder cases remained unsolved despite Berkowitz's arrest and conviction.

Perhaps the most frightening serial killer of the 1970s was convicted child molester John Wayne Gacy. By day, he tended to his Chicago construction business and entertained children's birthday parties as "Pogo the Clown." By night, he raped and murdered at least 33 men and boys, some as young as nine years old. Police learned about Gacy's activities while investigating him in 1978 regarding the disappearance of a 15-year-old boy. After noticing a disturbing smell in his home, they investigated further and found 29 badly decomposed bodies stuffed under the stairway. Nine of Gacy's victims remained unidentified.

Cult leader Jim Jones speaks to a group of followers. *(AP Photo/str/Greg Robinson)*

The most shocking mass killing of the decade was not the work of a serial killer at all, but instead of a religious cult leader, the Reverend Jim Jones. Jones had attracted a large following mainly consisting of Americans to his "People's Temple" in the jungles of Guyana, but reports filtered back to the United States of human rights violations and of members being forced to stay against their will. When Congressman Leo J. Ryan, accompanied by print and television reporters, traveled to Guyana in 1978 to investigate, they met with Jones and members of his temple. The decision of 15 of Jones's followers to defect, prompted him to take action. On November 18, Ryan and four members of his party were gunned down at the Port Kaituma airstrip as they prepared to leave. Simultaneously, Jones convinced almost his entire following—more than 900 people—to commit mass suicide by consuming poisoned drinks. The scale of the resulting deaths dwarfed that of any other single crime of the era.

While unusual killings have long been a staple of sensational journalism, the new concept of serial murder seemed tailor-made for lurid media coverage. Just as the penny papers of the 19th century covered graphic details of sensational crimes, newspapers such as the *New York Post* provided wall-to-wall coverage of serial murderers' macabre careers. Coverage would peak in the 1980s, but it was the serial murderers of the 1970s whose behavior defined the parameters of the serial killer as villain.

The Death Penalty

During the 1970s, the U.S. criminal justice system examined fundamental issues pertaining to capital punishment: racial disparities in its enforcement, whether to enforce the penalty at all, and which punishments, if any, could be regarded as humane.

In 1966, the Gallup Organization conducted a poll that found that only 42 percent of Americans supported the death penalty.[23] The share of people in favor of the death penalty had been declining since the 1950s, and several states had abolished it in the late 1950s and 1960s. Reasons for this attitude were clear and understandable. More than 50 percent of executions performed between 1930 and 1967 involved African-American defendants, including hundreds of executions for rape—executions that took place primarily in southern states. During the era in which the Civil Rights movement focused public attention on discrimination, this racial disparity seemed increasingly unacceptable, a throwback to the days of lynching. Furthermore, the United States of the 1960s was undergoing a period of criminal justice reform that emphasized the rights of defendants and the need to focus on constructive methods of punishment. Capital punishment, which by definition can have no restorative value, ran contrary to the prevailing attitudes of the time. In this context, the number of executions actually carried out declined steadily in the 1960s. Beginning in 1967, no states conducted executions, maintaining an unofficial moratorium until the issue was resolved.

In 1972, the Supreme Court effectively abolished the death penalty in *Furman v. Georgia*. The ruling found that the death penalty of the time was, in the words of Justice Potter Stewart, "cruel and unusual in the same way that being struck by lightning is cruel and unusual" and that "if any basis can be discerned for the selection of these few sentenced to death, it is the constitutionally impermissible basis of race."[24] The ruling commuted all 629 state death penalty sentences to life imprisonment and banned all new death sentences.

In particular, *Furman* ended the use of the death penalty in cases of rape, although the Court would not explicitly do so until its ruling in *Coker v. Georgia* (1977). The application of capital punishment in rape cases was both racially charged and arbitrary. It was racially charged because rape had long been a pretense used by those who practiced lynching against African-American men who broke the southern racial code, and African-American defendants living in much of the South found themselves facing a similar lynching scenario in the criminal justice system. Southern courts, bolstered by local public pressure, inadequate counsel, and all-white juries, easily railroaded low-income black defendants into rape convictions and death sentences without granting them the same protections available to white defendants. Second, it was arbitrary because, while many cases of murder did not seem to warrant the death penalty, many cases of rape did. The only reliable indicator, as Justice Stewart pointed out, seemed to be race.

Regardless of the impact of the ruling, the Supreme Court was, in fact, divided deeply over the death penalty. All nine justices wrote separate opinions in *Furman*. Two, William J. Brennan and Thurgood Marshall, went so far as to say that the death penalty was necessarily incompatible with the Eighth Amendment and always constituted cruel and unusual punishment. The other three making up the narrow 5-4 majority were willing to entertain new death penalty laws provided that they were written in such a way as to reduce the arbitrariness of the sentence. This latter position offered guidance to states that wished to retain a death penalty. Executions were not necessarily unconstitutional per se, just the current application of the death penalty, so if states could develop more rigorous rules and procedures, the death penalty might pass muster with the Supreme Court.

Following the *Furman* ruling, 34 states attempted to achieve just that by revising their criminal codes to generate less arbitrary executions. At the center of the debate stood Georgia, whose sloppy death penalty statutes had brought about the moratorium in the first place. The new standards established that judges could not impose the death penalty and that juries could not impose the death penalty during the conviction phase of the trial. Instead, juries in capital cases would—after convicting the defendant—face a separate sentencing phase in which the defendant's eligibility for the death penalty would be debated by both the prosecution and the defense considering mitigating and aggravating factors. The defendant would also be entitled to a rigorous appeals process. In *Gregg v. Georgia* (1976), the Supreme Court ruled by a 7-2 margin that the new guidelines fulfilled the criteria set out in *Furman* and that the death penalty could be in force once again. The first man executed under the new standards was Utah convicted killer Gary Gilmore in 1977, who had dropped his appeals and asked to be killed quickly by firing squad.

Chronicle of Events

1970

- *October 15:* Congress enacts the Organized Crime and Control Act, which includes the Racketeer Influenced and Corrupt Organizations (RICO) Act.
- *October 27:* The Comprehensive Drug Abuse Prevention and Control Act is enacted by the federal government. One element, the Controlled Substances Act, places the emphasis of federal drug interdiction on controlling dangerous drugs such as heroin.

1971

- *March 29:* Lieutenant William Calley is convicted on 22 counts of first-degree murder for his role in the My Lai massacre.
- *April 3:* President Richard Nixon announces that he will personally review Calley's conviction.
- *August 21:* Radical California inmate George Jackson is killed in the prison yard at San Quentin, reportedly during an attempted escape.
- *September 9:* Inmates riot at the Attica Correctional Facility in Attica, New York, taking control of the prison.

- *September 13:* New York state police violently recapture Attica prison, killing 39 people.

1972

- The New York State Special Commission on Attica under the leadership of New York University law school dean Robert B. McKay issues its report, condemning the state's response to the prison uprising.
- *March 24:* Francis Ford Coppola's film *The Godfather* is released in the United States.
- *June 29:* In *Furman v. Georgia,* the U.S. Supreme Court rules that arbitrary enforcement of the death penalty violates the Eighth Amendment, temporarily abolishing capital punishment in the United States.
- *June 29:* The Turkish government bans opium production, effectively shutting down the international heroin trafficking ring known as the "French Connection."
- *May 2:* FBI founding director J. Edgar Hoover dies while still in office.
- *June 17:* Five Republican operatives are arrested while trying to bug the Watergate Hotel offices of the Democratic National Committee.
- *August 1:* The *Washington Post* reports that a $25,000 check, originally made out to the Nixon campaign, had somehow

President Richard Nixon used the federal criminal justice system for overtly political purposes. *(National Archives and Records Administration [194576])*

been deposited in the bank account of one of the five Watergate burglars.

- *September 29:* The *Washington Post* reports that Nixon re-election chair and former U.S. attorney general John Mitchell had once operated a secret surveillance program targeting Democratic Party officials.
- *October 10:* According to the *Washington Post,* FBI agents discovered evidence of a massive illegal Republican surveillance operation orchestrated by the Nixon reelection campaign.
- *November 7:* President Richard Nixon is reelected by a landslide.

1973

- *January 30:* Two of the Watergate burglars, G. Gordon Liddy and James McCord, are convicted for their role in the Watergate break-in.
- *April 27:* L. Patrick Gray, successor to J. Edgar Hoover and only the second FBI director in U.S. history, resigns after his role in the Watergate cover-up is revealed.
- *May 8:* New York governor Nelson Rockefeller signs strict drug enforcement measures into law.
- *May 18:* The Senate Watergate hearings begin. A special prosecutor is appointed to investigate possible White House involvement in the break-in and subsequent cover-up.
- *July 10:* The federal government consolidates all offices responsible for drug control into one agency, the Drug Enforcement Administration (DEA).
- *October 20:* President Nixon fires the special prosecutor responsible for investigating the Watergate scandal and abolishes the office of special prosecutor. Both the U.S. attorney general and deputy attorney general resign in protest.

1974

- Douglas Lipton, Robert Martinson, and Judith Wilks's study, *The Effectiveness of Correctional Treatment: A Survey of Treatment Evaluation Studies,* is published, articulating the controversial position that "nothing works" in correctional treatment.
- Various federal offices dealing with drug treatment and education are consolidated into a new agency, the National Institute on Drug Abuse (NIDA).
- *July 27:* The U.S. House Judiciary Committee approves impeachment charges against President Nixon.
- *August 9:* President Richard Nixon resigns.

1975

- James Q. Wilson's *Thinking about Crime* is published.

- *September 10:* The Secretary of the Army announces that William Calley will be paroled after serving just over three years of his sentence.

1976

- *July 2:* In *Gregg v. Georgia,* the U.S. Supreme Court ends a four-year moratorium on the death penalty.

1977

- *January 17:* Murderer Gary Gilmore is executed by firing squad in Utah and becomes the first person to be put to death under revised capital punishment statutes.
- *June 29:* The Supreme Court decides in *Coker v. Georgia* that the death penalty cannot be applied in cases of rape.
- *July 13:* New York City experiences a major blackout, which is soon accompanied by looting and violence.
- *August 10:* Serial killer David Berkowitz, also known as the "Son of Sam," is arrested in Yonkers, New York.

1978

- *February 15:* Serial killer Ted Bundy is arrested in Pensacola, Florida.
- *November 18:* More than 900 people—most of them U.S. citizens—are discovered to have committed suicide at a communal village in northwest Guyana at the behest of their religious leader, Jim Jones.
- *December 22:* Serial killer John Wayne Gacy is arrested in Chicago, Illinois.

1979

- *July 15:* President Jimmy Carter delivers his "crisis of confidence" speech.

1980

- *February 2:* A riot at the New Mexico State Penitentiary results in the deaths of 33 inmates.
- *February 7:* Ted Bundy is convicted on murder charges for the death of his final victim, 12-year-old Kimberly Leach. He receives a third death sentence.

1980

- *November 21:* Crime boss Frank Tieri is convicted under the RICO Act.

1981

- *May 5:* Three high-ranking operatives in the Bonanno crime family are murdered. An investigation by FBI agent Joseph Pistone (Donnie Brasco) reveals that Bonanno crime boss Joe Massino is responsible.

Eyewitness Testimony

Prison Life and Prison Riots

CTF-Central at Soledad, California is a prison under the control of the California Department of Corrections . . . However, by the 1960s the prison had earned the label in the system of "Gladiator School"; this was, primarily, because of the never-ending race wars and general personal violence which destroyed any illusions about CTF-Central being an institution of rehabilitation . . .

Two of the wings—O and X—are operated under maximum custody under the care of armed guards. There is no conflict between policy, intent and reality here: these are the specially segregated areas where murder, insanity and the destruction of men is accepted as a daily way of life. It is within the wings that the race wars become the most irrational, where the atmosphere of paranoia and loneliness congeal to create a day-to-day existence composed of terror.

A prisoner at CTF-Soledad, quoted in Micha Maguire, "Racism II," in Minton, Inside: Prison American Style, *p. 84.*

First psychiatry had the answer, then education was the answer, now it's environment—what made the prisoner the way he is? We're no longer trying to force a prisoner into a particular mold, so we have no criteria any more for running a prison. The only criterion is to keep it trouble free.

But maybe it's trouble free because the lid is on tight, who knows? You don't know when to join them or what side to take—and the nature of everything today is taking sides. The same thing that happened in Attica could happen to me . . .

J. Leland Casscles, warden of Sing Sing, quoted in Roberts, "Prisons Feel a Mood of Protest," New York Times, *September 19, 1971, p. 58.*

The Attica prison riot was not planned in advance by any group of militant inmates and began as a spontaneous burst of violent anger, a blue ribbon investigating commission concluded Tuesday, a year after the four-day insurrection was put down.

The nine-member New York State Special Commission on Attica . . . reported "the conclusion is inescapable" that state troopers and guards engaged in much unnecessary shooting in retaking the prison.

"Troopers shot into tents, trenches and barricades without looking first," the commission found. To justify their actions, some state police, the panel said, later "exaggerated, embellished and even fabricated" hostile acts by inmates.

Thirty-nine persons were killed and more than 80 were wounded by gunfire during the recapture last Sept. 13. In all, 43 persons died in the rebellion . . .

It was probably chance that a prison tragedy of such magnitude occurred first at Attica, the commission asserted, but it warned that the elements needed for a repetition "are all around us. Attica is every prison and every prison is Attica."

John J. Goldman, "Attica Uprising Not Preplanned, Blue-Ribbon Inquiry Concludes," Los Angeles Times, *September 13, 1972, p. A1.*

One inmate is dead of stab wounds and state officials said 10 other inmates were shot by guards during a riot at the Tennessee State Prison. Another 26 persons were injured, two of them guards.

The disturbance was sparked by the substitution of bologna for pork chops on the prison menu. Asked if guards shot the 10 inmates, Corrections Department spokesman James Gilchrist said, "I think unquestionably they did. The city police were not armed, no firearms were found among the inmates and I think all of those who suffered gunshot wounds were shot by about a dozen guards who had shotguns."

Quoted from "Inmate Killed in Prison Riot," Dallas Morning News, *September 13, 1975, p. A15.*

Drug Policy and the Drug Trade

President Nixon said yesterday that the drug menace has reached the dimensions of "a national emergency" and that an all-out effort is needed to prevent it from destroying the country.

In a special message to Congress, he asked for an additional $155 million to fight drug abuse and for authority to establish a central office in the White House to direct national attack on the problem.

While the emphasis in the past has been on law enforcement, the President said that the major portion of the new funds, which would bring the total to $370 million in the fiscal year beginning July 1, would be for rehabilitation programs.

Another principal aim is to enlist more cooperation from foreign governments since heroin used by American addicts is produced abroad.

"If we cannot destroy the drug menace in America," the President said, "then it will surely in time destroy us."

Carroll Kilpatrick, "Nixon Seeks National War on Drug Use," Washington Post, *June 18, 1971, p. A1.*

The original Rockefeller plan—regarded as too sweeping and simplistic by many legislators—had called for mandatory life sentences for dealing in dangerous drugs—such as heroin, cocaine, morphine, opium, LSD or amphetamines—and for drug sellers who commit violent crimes. There would have been no opportunity for plea bargaining and no possibility of parole under the original plan.

The amendments given a final vote today in the Senate would, among other things, for example, save from a life sentence a dieting housewife who gave a diet pill containing amphetamines to a friend. Instead, she would be subject to a maximum of seven years in prison. . . .

Some senators who voted for [the bill] said they had some misgivings but, as the deputy majority leader, William Conklin, Republican of Brooklyn, put it, "We have to do something."

During the negotiations on the compromise version, Mr. Rockefeller was tenacious about retaining the concept of mandatory life sentences because, as he put it in an interview some weeks ago, "It's symbolically the toughest thing we've got today."

William E. Farrell, "Senate Passes Assembly's Version of Antidrug Bill," New York Times, *May 8, 1973, p. 28.*

Any society wishing to reduce the consumption of an "undesirable" item, such as illegal drugs, has available two available strategies: reducing demand, by harassing buyers, or reducing supply, by harassing sellers. Law enforcement agencies in the United States, presumably with the approval of the voting public, seem to have opted largely for the latter strategy ("we're not really interested in users; we want the pushers"), and yet ex-addict William S. Burroughs . . . advises: "If we wish to annihilate the junk pyramid, we must start with the bottom of the pyramid: *the Addict in the Street,* and stop tilting quixotically for the 'higher ups' so called, all of whom are immediately replaceable" . . .

[E]nforcement strategy directed against drug sellers tends to enhance a natural accord between illegal business firms and the police based upon their common interest in civil order. After visiting Harlem in May 1968, [Democratic policy analyst] Harry McPherson . . . reported hearing of a conversation between [Black Panther leader] Rap Brown and a Harlem rackets boss. Brown had made a strong

U.S. narcotics agents pose with 400 pounds of recently confiscated marijuana. *(Library of Congress Prints and Photographs Division [LC-USZ62-121457])*

speech. The boss told him: "I agree with a lot of what you said. Except I don't want any riots. I've got to raise $60,000 to buy off some people downtown on a narcotics rap. I can't do that if there's a riot. You start a riot and I'll kill you." Brown is rumored to have left town the next day.

Economist Billy J. Eartherly, "Drug-Law Enforcement: Should We Arrest Pushers or Users?" American Economic Review, May 1973, pp. 210, 213–214.

The Federal Response to Organized Crime

[Undercover agent Joseph] Pistone described a 1981 conversation with Dominick "Sonny Black" Napolitano, who was a captain in the Bonanno organization.

"We took care of those three guys; they're gone," Pistone quoted Napolitano as having said. Then, he said, Napolitano told him to kill a man who had apparently fled to Florida.

"If you find him, hit him," the agent quoted Napolitano . . . Pistone told the jury that he had pretended he would search for the intended target in Miami.

The undercover work of Pistone, who used the name Donnie Brasco while posing as a gangster, has been described by the authorities as the deepest infiltration of organized crime ever achieved by the FBI . . .

Pistone testified that he was wearing a concealed transmitter during his conversation with Napolitano on May 14, 1981. The jury then put on large black earphones to listen to the tape-recorded conversation.

On the tape, a voice identified as Napolitano tells the undercover agent, "You get the chance to take him, you take him, and you can leave right on the street."

Quoted from "Undercover Agent Tells of N.Y. Mafia Killings," Chicago Tribune, August 4, 1982, p. 5.

The Mafia is a dying organization and will cease to be a major threat within the next 10 years, the United States Attorney in Manhattan, Rudolph W. Giuliani, said at a news conference last night after a Federal jury convicted a former chief of the Sicilian Mafia and 16 other defendants of running an international drug ring.

"Five or six years ago, nobody would have believed we could convict the head of the Sicilian Mafia in New York," Mr. Giuliani said in his office at One St. Andrew's Plaza in lower Manhattan. "If we continue our efforts, there's not going to be a Mafia in 5 to 10 years" . . .

Mr. Giuliani attributed what he said was the demise of the Mafia to two factors: the vigorous prosecution un-der strengthened racketeering laws and the shifting demographics that have made it difficult for Mafia leaders to recruit new members from an upwardly mobile Italian-American community.

Michael Oreskes, "Giuliani Says Trials Weaken the Mob," New York Times, March 3, 1987, p. A1.

Serial Killers

I am deeply hurt by your calling me a wemon [sic] hater. I am not. But I am a monster. I am the 'Son of Sam.' I am a little brat. When father Sam gets drunk he gets mean. He beats his family. Sometimes he ties me up to the back of the house. Other times he locks me in the garage. Sam loves to drink blood. 'Go out and kill,' commands father Sam.

Serial killer David Berkowitz (Son of Sam), from a letter left at the scene of one of his murders, April 1977, quoted in Leyton, Hunting Humans, p. 221.

Thirty-six-year-old John Wayne Gacy has shown the world two personalities.

First, there is the friendly, outgoing neighbor: a man who plowed the walks where he lived without being asked, the party-giver who enjoyed entertaining children in a clown costume, and the super-salesman who ran a thriving contracting business.

To many, this is the only John Gacy they know.

But, with the discovery of the remains of four bodies in the crawl space of his ranch-style house . . . another, darker personality has come into view.

John Gorman and Joan Zyda, "Murder Suspect's '2 Faces' Revealed," Chicago Tribune, December 23, 1978, p. S1.

[Theodore] Bundy, 32, is on trial for the murder of two coeds at Florida State University in Tallahassee on July 15, 1978, but more importantly, according to the FBI, he is a suspect in 37 other sex slayings. . . .

[R]eporters come from the various states that have since 1974 been terrorized by the disappearance of young women. Police say that most of the women had extraordinarily similar appearances, long dark hair, parted in the middle . . . One was on her way to her dorm at college to study for a Spanish test. Another had just put some clothes in a washer at a laundromat. Two young women were last seen sunbathing at a state park, helping a stranger named Ted, wearing an arm cast, who had asked them to help put his sailboat on his VW. One young woman disappeared from a resort hotel in Aspen on her way to her room to get a magazine. All of them died.

Madelaine Blaise and John Ketzenbach, "Courting Passion in the Camera's Eye," Washington Post, July 9, 1979, p. A1.

Capital Punishment

Those who wrote the Eighth Amendment knew what price their forebears had paid for a system based, not on equal justice, but on discrimination. In those days the target was not the blacks or the poor, but the dissenters, those who opposed absolutism in government, who struggled for a parliamentary regime, and who opposed governments' recurring efforts to foist a particular religion on the people. But the tool of capital punishment was used with vengeance against the opposition and those unpopular with the regime. One cannot read this history without realizing that the desire for equality was reflected in the ban against "cruel and unusual punishments" contained in the Eighth Amendment.

In a Nation committed to equal protection of the laws there is no permissible "caste" aspect of law enforcement. Yet we know that the discretion of judges and juries in imposing the death penalty enables the penalty to be selectively applied, feeding prejudices against the accused if he is poor and despised, and lacking political clout, or if he is a member of a suspect or unpopular minority, and saving those who by social position may be in a more protected position. In ancient Hindu law a Brahman was exempt from capital punishment, and under that law, "[g]enerally, in the law books, punishment increased in severity as social status diminished." We have, I fear, taken in practice the same position, partially as a result of making the death penalty discretionary and partially as a result of the ability of the rich to purchase the services of the most respected and most resourceful legal talent in the Nation.

The high service rendered by the "cruel and unusual" punishment clause of the Eighth Amendment is to require legislatures to write penal laws that are evenhanded, nonselective, and nonarbitrary, and to require judges to see to it that general laws are not applied sparsely, selectively, and spottily to unpopular groups.

A law that stated that anyone making more than $50,000 would be exempt from the death penalty would plainly fall, as would a law that in terms said that blacks, those who never went beyond the fifth grade in school, those who made less than $3,000 a year, or those who were unpopular or unstable should be the only people executed. A law which in the overall view reaches that result in practice has no more sanctity than a law which in terms provides the same.

Thus, these discretionary statutes are unconstitutional in their operation. They are pregnant with discrimination and discrimination is an ingredient not compatible with the idea of equal protection of the laws that is implicit in the ban on "cruel and unusual" punishments.

Any law which is nondiscriminatory on its face may be applied in such a way as to violate the Equal Protection Clause of the Fourteenth Amendment. Such conceivably might be the fate of a mandatory death penalty, where equal or lesser sentences were imposed on the elite, a harsher one on the minorities or members of the lower castes. Whether a mandatory death penalty would otherwise be constitutional is a question I do not reach.

Justice William O. Douglas, from his concurring opinion in Furman v. Georgia *408 U.S. 238 (1972).*

Gary Gilmore died thumbing his nose at society. He gulped down some contraband whiskey and glared around the execution room. "Let's do it," he said tersely. Then a Utah firing squad did its grim duty . . .

Of course, the last has not been heard of Gary Gilmore. Promoters are preparing to immortalize him in print, on film and on T-shirts . . .

But before the legend completely transcends reality, the true story should be told. The prison records show that he ran away from home at 12, that he was busted for auto theft at 14 and that he hung out with street gangs in Portland, Ore. . . .

At age 18, he sought a new thrill by raping young girls. He also was in and out of jails. He began his suicidal theatrics in the 1960s. He slashed his wrists, tried to hang himself and took an overdose of pills. He was committed to the Oregon state hospital four times in 1963–64 . . .

He rejected group therapy and gave flippant answers to psychiatrists' questions. Yet he was not considered insane but merely "anti-social," with "severe personality disorder."

This is the folk hero who is about to be immortalized.

A description of Gary Gilmore, the first man executed in the United States under new guidelines established in the wake of Furman v. Georgia, *from Jack Anderson and Les Whitten, "Gilmore's Death Row Behavior," Washington Post, February 21, 1977, p. C15.*

CHAPTER TWELVE

Responding to Urban Crime
1982–1992

In 1980, the U.S. homicide rate peaked at 10.2 murders per 100,000 inhabitants.[1] From 1970 through 1996, the homicide rate never dropped below 7.9 per 100,000 inhabitants. This was a remarkable aberration from the pattern both before and after the urban crime era—the homicide rate rose from 5.1 per 100,000 inhabitants in 1965 and fell back to 5.5 by 2000. Public opinion rose and fell in a more or less consistent pattern with this trend. In a 1967 Gallup poll, only 31 percent of respondents said that they would be afraid to walk alone at night within one mile of their home. In 1982, the number peaked at 48 percent. By the year 2000, it had dropped to 30 percent.[2] The era of violent urban crime was long but temporary, the questions of what caused it and what resolved it provocative but for the most part unanswered.

What is clear, however, is that cities were frightening places to many during the 1970s, 1980s, and early 1990s. To some extent this can be attributed to racial anxiety, as whites responded to newly integrated schools and communities by migrating to less integrated suburbs in a migration pattern called "white flight." But crime unquestionably peaked during this period, and public anxiety peaked with it.

A series of unusual but sensational and jarring crimes contributed to a public perception of chaos. In 1981 both the U.S. president and the pope were shot and seriously injured in assassination attempts. This unprecedented violence prompted significant changes in both gun control policies and security protocols for world leaders. In 1982, seven people died in Chicago because someone snuck into stores or warehouses and deliberately laced Tylenol capsules with cyanide. This had never happened before and prompted drug companies to seal over-the-counter medications in tamper-resistant packaging. And the brutal 1989 rape and near-murder of the "Central Park Jogger," 28-year-old investment banker Trisha Meili, contributed to a public sense that Americans could be victims of vicious random attacks at any time and in any place.

Drug use also began to rise during the 1980s. Cocaine, once the drug of the wealthy elite, became an easily accessible street drug with the invention of crack, a purified, crystalline, smokable derivative, in the early 1980s. This new form of the drug was both inexpensive and highly addictive, producing an intense but brief high that users wanted to repeat. Both the desperate mood changes caused by drug addiction and the violent turf wars caused by the illegal drug trade contributed to the overall crime rate as inner-city neighborhood residents went about the business of their lives while passing by corner drug dealers every day.

During the first part of the decade, the federal government responded to the new drug crisis with moral suasion and antidrug education. Beginning in 1981, First Lady Nancy Reagan campaigned to encourage young people to "just say no" to drugs. After drugs such as marijuana and cocaine had enjoyed a degree of public toleration in the 1970s, Nancy Reagan's efforts helped

On March 30, 1981, John Hinckley shot President Ronald Reagan, who was leaving a speaking engagement in Washington, D.C. Reagan survived the assassination attempt and went on to serve a second presidential term. *(Library of Congress, Prints and Photographs Division [LC-USZ62-13040])*

reattach a social stigma to them in the 1980s. Likewise, beginning in 1983, the Los Angeles Police Department (LAPD) pioneered new antidrug education courses for fifth- and sixth-graders called Drug Abuse Resistance Education (D.A.R.E.). In these courses, which spread rapidly across the nation, police officers would come into school classrooms and teach students about the dangers of drugs and techniques for resisting peer pressure.

By the middle of the decade, more forceful action seemed necessary, particularly in the wake of the highly publicized 1986 cocaine-related deaths of star basketball player Len Bias and football player Don Rogers. In August and September 1986, President Ronald Reagan delivered a series of speeches in which he proposed that a "war on drugs" be made a national priority. This campaign culminated on September 14, when Ronald and Nancy Reagan delivered a televised address to the nation on the subject of drugs and on the following day when Reagan issued Executive Order 12564 on the Drug Free Federal Workplace, requiring federal agencies to establish drug testing programs for employees.

Both state and federal governments proceeded to enact new legislation designed to target drugs, especially crack cocaine. Also in 1986, Reagan signed a sweeping new drug law, the U.S. Anti-Drug Abuse Act of 1986. In 1989, Reagan's successor, George H. W. Bush, made drug enforcement a centerpiece of his administration, substantially expanding the federal budget for the war on drugs and appointing a new "drug czar," William J. Bennett, to oversee the campaign. The new laws mandated minimum 10-year sentences for drug possession in what the bills deemed to be "kingpin" amounts. The legislation unapologetically targeted crack cocaine. Five grams of crack would generate a minimum five-year prison sentence, but it would take 500 grams of powdered cocaine to generate the same sentence. Because powdered cocaine is primarily used and sold by wealthy whites and crack cocaine is primarily used and sold by low-income African Americans, the bill had a racially disparate effect. In 1986, before the bill was enacted, the average black defendant convicted on federal drug charges received a sentence 11 percent longer than that of the average white defendant. In 1990, the average sentence was 49 percent longer.[3]

Facing a high crime rate that they could do almost nothing to impact, national policy makers began to back away from the idea of guaranteeing civil rights protections for the accused, from the idea of rehabilitating offenders in a productive manner, and they turned toward a simpler and more aggressive response: mass imprisonment. Between 1982 and 1992, the incarcerated population more than doubled, from 610,767 in 1982 to 1,292,347 in 1992.[4] This reflected a growing national trend away from a rehabilitative model of criminal justice that was sensitive to broader civil rights concerns and toward a more retributive model aimed at deterring crime and keeping criminals off the streets.

Victims' Rights and Citizen Participation

The civil rights–related criminal justice reforms of the 1960s and 1970s expanded understandings of due process, giving the Fourteenth Amendment more of a role in the arrest, interrogation, sentencing, and punishment of alleged criminals. But as the 1970s and 1980s unfolded, the American public became frustrated with a sense that broader due process benefited criminals instead of ordinary citizens.

An entire genre of police films, beginning with *Dirty Harry* (1971), reflected a growing sentiment that a system that gives so much weight to the civil rights of suspects would provide no way to effectively prosecute crime. These films typically followed a model. The heroic police officer would investigate a crime, discover evidence of a danger to the community, clash with superior officers, be stripped of his gun and his badge, and then—only then—be able to address the problem. Westerns and other films preached vigilante justice, and they harkened to an imaginary era during which good-hearted lawmen were invariably able to separate the guilty from the innocent without having to concern themselves with such things as due process rights. This genre of films reflected growing public frustration with the escalating urban crime rate and a criminal justice system that was dry, procedural, often distressingly ineffective, and distant from the concerns of citizens.

Shocking police mismanagement of cases also impacted public sentiment. In July 1981, Reve Walsh let her six-year-old son, Adam, play video games in the toy department at a Sears store in Hollywood, Florida, while she shopped. When a fight broke out among children in the toy department, a store employee ordered the boys to leave the building without informing Walsh. Adam was abducted outside the store, and Reve Walsh and her husband, John, launched the largest missing-child manhunt in Florida history. Adam's partial remains were found two weeks later. The case went unsolved for two years, until serial killer Ottis Toole confessed to killing the child. The case was never definitively solved, however, because Toole later recanted his testimony—after police had inadvertently discarded the physical evidence that may have proved his guilt. Toole died in prison while serving multiple life terms for his other crimes.

Following Adam's death, John and Reve Walsh became dedicated lobbyists for parents with missing children, successfully persuading Congress to pass four major pieces of federal legislation aimed at improving law enforcement handling of missing child cases. In 1984, they established the National Center for Missing and Exploited Children, which includes a missing-child database. In 1988, John Walsh was hired by the Fox television network to host *America's Most Wanted,* a weekly program that issued citizen alerts on various fugitives and provided means by which callers could make fugitives' whereabouts known to law enforcement authorities. The show aired for more than 20 years and claimed to help bring more than 1,000 fugitives to justice.

America's Most Wanted became emblematic of a victims' rights movement oriented toward fighting back by working with law enforcement—a nonviolent form of citizen participation in law enforcement that is helpful to police. NBC's *Unsolved Mysteries,* which aired from 1987 until 2002 and was hosted by Robert Stack, also highlighted fugitives and encouraged viewers to contribute information about unsolved crimes or the whereabouts of suspects. Local network news affiliates used this model as well, sometimes offering rewards for information leading to an arrest. Citizens took advantage of this new opportunity to play a direct role in the criminal justice process.

A small number of citizens, however, played a direct role in the criminal justice system in a more violent and less productive way. On December 22, 1984, four black teenagers on a New York City subway confronted a 37-year-old white electrical engineer named Bernhard Goetz and asked him for five dollars. Goetz, who had been mugged and beaten four years earlier, responded by drawing a .38-caliber revolver and firing at close range. One of Goetz's shots severed teenager Darrell Cabey's spinal cord, paralyzing him for life.

Goetz was popular among some New Yorkers who saw him as a hero. His shooting of the teenagers echoed the popular 1974 Charles Bronson film *Death Wish,* in which a vigilante-hero baited and then murdered would-be muggers and carjackers. Goetz was tried and acquitted for attempted murder and assault, though he was later convicted on minor firearms charges. Cabey sued Goetz in civil court in 1985 and was awarded $43 million in damages for the injuries he had suffered as a result of the shooting.

Politicians were also acutely aware of citizens' frustration with the criminal justice system, and they moved to address some of their concerns. Three months after taking office in 1981, President Ronald Reagan declared an annual National Crime Victims' Rights Week (still observed every April) and established a Presidential Task Force on Victims of Crime. A year later the task force issued 68 recommendations for policy changes intended to better accommodate crime victims. Some, such as Federal Executive and Legislative Recommendation 3 to "establish a federally based resource center for victim and witness assistance," became law—in this case establishing an Office for Victims of Crime under the direct authority of the U.S. Department of Justice. Other suggestions, such as a proposed constitutional amendment granting that victims "shall have the right to be present and to be heard at all critical stages of judicial proceedings," proved impractical and were not implemented.

Many of these proposals aimed to increase victims' rights by decreasing the rights of the accused. One Reagan administration proposal would have allowed illegally obtained evidence to be used at trial. Another would have allowed the use of hearsay evidence in preliminary hearings. The Reagan administration also supported stricter sentences for juvenile offenders, increased bail for suspects, and

increased criminal penalties across the board. The overall trajectory of these reforms would continue throughout the Reagan, George H. W. Bush, and Bill Clinton administrations.

Domestic Abuse and Violence against Women

In addition to the general reforms proposed to address the criminal justice process
as a whole, special attention was given to domestic violence, stalking, and child
abuse during the 1980s and early 1990s. As a result of the women's movement of
the 1970s, policy makers and media figures began to see these problems as serious
issues that the state could address rather than as private matters beyond the reach
of law enforcement.

Among the most prominent anti–domestic violence initiatives was the Domestic Abuse Intervention Project (DAIP) established in 1980 by a nonprofit group in
Duluth, Minnesota. The program sought to coordinate a community response to
domestic violence by working closely with law enforcement, legal, and correctional
agencies. In particular, it encouraged law enforcement to protect survivors, emphasizing police officer training, new mandatory arrest policies in domestic abuse
cases, cooperation with domestic violence shelters, and vigorous enforcement of
court restraining orders that ordered known abusers to stay away from their targets.
The program also used aggressive prosecution, tighter enforcement of probation
terms, and rehabilitative training programs for repeat offenders. The program was
a dramatic success. In Duluth the conviction rate for domestic abusers rose from 20
percent to 82 percent during the first two years of the program.[5] The Duluth model
was quickly adopted in other municipalities and remains the defining domestic
violence prevention policy reform model in the United States.

The federal government also enacted policies directed toward the problem of
domestic violence. The most significant was the Family Violence Prevention and
Services Act of 1984, which authorized hundreds of millions of dollars in annual
grants to fund domestic violence shelters throughout the country. The legislation,
reauthorized in 2003, led to the creation of more than 2,000 domestic violence
shelters for women and children over a 20-year period and brought the shelters
movement into the mainstream.

Increasing awareness of domestic violence dovetailed with a national movement
to curb other forms of violence against women. California passed anti-stalking legislation—laws to curb continued harassing or threatening behavior that might not
otherwise be criminal—in 1990, in the wake of well-publicized stalker attacks. One
stalker murdered actress Rebecca Schaeffer in 1989, and another attempted to kill
actress Theresa Saldana, stabbing her 10 times in 1982. Anti-stalking legislation, and
increased use of restraining orders, soon became a reality in every state.

As law enforcement authorities began to focus on ordinary examples of violent
and dysfunctional men, the most extreme examples of men fitting this description
began to assume the status of a kind of twisted folk hero.

The Serial Killer as Public Figure

By the 1980s, the concept of the serial killer had already entered the public imagination. After years of media reports detailing the crimes of the Son of Sam, Ted

Bundy, John Wayne Gacy, and others, serial killers became emblematic of the most extreme kind of criminal imaginable. At the same time, the serial killer's sheer power gave him a kind of diabolical fascination, peaking with the popularity of charming fictional cannibal Hannibal Lecter, portrayed by Brian Cox in *Manhunter* (1986) and more famously by Anthony Hopkins in *The Silence of the Lambs* (1991). Although real-life serial killers were usually unimpressive middle-class white men with a desperate need for control and a desperate lack of legitimate means by which they could achieve it, some members of the new generation of serial killers attempted to achieve gravitas, at least in the manner in which they related to the media. They craved the power and attention that came with serial murder.

Dennis Rader, dubbed the "BTK killer," was arguably the most media-fixated serial killer in U.S. history. He killed at least 10 people (eight women and two men) in the Wichita, Kansas, area between 1974 and 1991. Rader was a sexual sadist who derived gratification from binding his victims, then repeatedly strangling them into unconsciousness until he decided to end their lives. He was also proud of his crimes and unable to resist the temptation to boast about them—first by anonymously inserting a graphic account of killing four members of a single family between the pages of an engineering book at Wichita Public Library, then by sending a letter to a local television station in 1978 boasting of the seven homicides he had committed by that point. He suggested multiple names that the media could use to refer to him, but the one that stuck was "BTK," an acronym representing Rader's three-part formula for murder: bind, torture, and kill. Rader boasted of possessing a violent psychological "x factor" found in earlier serial killers, indicating that he was well schooled in the lives of his predecessors and hoped to achieve similar notoriety.

Rader kept his identity a secret for three decades, but his thirst for media exposure ultimately won out: A floppy diskette he had sent to local media in 2004 was traced to his church's computer, resulting in his arrest. The identification of Rader stunned observers. A compliance officer with a degree in justice administration, Rader served as president of his 200-member Lutheran congregation. Little about him suggested that he could be a serial killer, but DNA evidence led him to plead guilty. In a bizarre and chilling display, he casually and coldly recounted the details of the 10 murders ("projects," as he called them).

In 1991, as America became enthralled with the character of Hannibal Lecter, a decidedly more real cannibal was making headlines. In the early morning hours of July 22, police patrolling the neighborhoods of Milwaukee, Wisconsin, were flagged down by 32-year-old Tracy Edwards, a short, skinny black man who had a handcuff dangling from one wrist. When Edwards told the story of a "weird dude" who had handcuffed him and threatened him with a knife, police visited the apartment of Jeffrey Dahmer. Dahmer, who had been convicted once before on child molestation charges, invited the police into his conspicuously tidy home. When an officer stumbled across photographs of dismembered corpses, obviously taken at the apartment, Dahmer was taken into custody. The case horrified the nation. Over a 13-year period, Dahmer had killed 17 boys and men ranging in age from 14 to 33, all but three of them African Americans. Among the contents of his refrigerator, shelves, and freezer were many of their dismembered remains. Dahmer's standard modus operandi involved hanging out at gay bars, finding a willing companion to take home, drugging that companion, strangling him to death, performing sexual acts on the corpse, eviscerating and photographing the corpse, and then dismembering it, eating some of the flesh

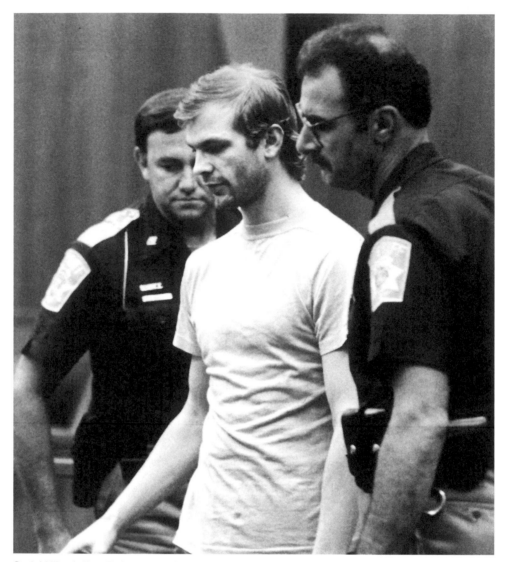

Serial killer Jeffrey Dahmer murdered 16 men and boys before he was apprehended by the police and convicted to 15 life sentences in 1991. The gruesome and grizzly details of the crimes captured the nation's attention. *(AP Photo/Bill Waugh/Pool)*

and saving some parts, most notably the heads, hands, and genitals, as souvenirs. Dahmer's behavior earned him a life sentence in a Wisconsin prison, where he was murdered by another inmate in 1994.

Rader and Dahmer were unusually prolific serial killers, but both were fairly typical in that they were self-loathing young white men obsessed with sexual fantasies centered on control, dominance, and murder. They differ from each other, however, and represent two ends of the serial killer spectrum in the role that media coverage of past serial killers played in the development of those fantasies. For Rader, it was central; he idolized past serial killers as well as his contemporaries and saw them as kindred spirits who shared with him the mysterious "x factor." For Dahmer, past serial killers played little role in his development and did not seem to influence his motives. The American public found a horrible fascination in the determination and the complete lack of conscience they displayed.

Death by Lethal Injection

During the 1970s, most U.S. executions took place by electric chair or gas chamber. Both methods presented problems. Electric chair executions were frequently botched, causing notoriously gruesome results. The gas chamber was highly expensive and put observers at risk of accidental cyanide gas poisoning. In 1977, Dr. Jay Chapman proposed a new standard: a series of three drugs, injected intravenously in large doses, that would cause death. The first, a barbiturate, would render the prisoner unconscious; the second, a paralytic, would cause muscle paralysis; and the third, potassium chloride, would stop the heart.

The first state to attempt the procedure was Texas, which executed a prisoner by lethal injection in December 1982. In the following years lethal injection gradually became the most common form of capital punishment, rendering the electric chair and gas chamber largely obsolete. In 2005, lethal injection was authorized as a method of execution by 37 of the 38 states that had a death penalty, although almost half retained alternate methods as well.

The April 22, 1983, electrocution of John Louis Evans in Alabama did as much as any single event to put the electric chair into disrepute. At 8:30 P.M. the lever was pulled, and the charge, which was supposed to be a lethal dose, was administered for 30 seconds. Sparks flew, Evans's fists clenched, smoke rose from his body, and the smell of burning flesh filled the air. A doctor examined him. He still had a pulse. A second 30-second charge was administered immediately. More smoke rose, the smell of burning flesh became more pronounced, but Evans remained alive. A third charge, administered a full 10 minutes later, finally killed him. Evans was not the only victim of an ineffective execution. Alpha Otis Stephens of Georgia breathed 23 times between his first and second two-minute charge. The mask of Jose Tafero of Florida burst into flames during the three attempts at his execution—as he continued to gasp for air. When executions went wrong, little seemed to differentiate them from the very first use of the electric chair on Willie Kemmler almost a century earlier.

The gas chamber, long hailed as the least painful form of capital punishment, also had its problems. When Mississippi executed Jimmy Lee Gray in September 1983, the scene was horrific. Prison staff cleared the room when it became clear that Gray was in pain and that the execution was not going according to plan. Gray gasped and moaned for eight minutes, continuously ramming his head into a steel pipe before he finally suffocated. If one single case ended use of the gas chamber in the United States, however, it was probably Arizona's execution of Donald Eugene Harding in April 1992. Harding gasped, turned purple, and spasmed violently for almost seven minutes before he finally asphyxiated. Reporters who witnessed the execution experienced symptoms ranging from days of psychological shock to weeks of insomnia.

By the 1990s, lethal injection had become the most widely practiced form of execution. While it, too, could go badly, it did so in a less visible way. The heavy doses of barbiturates made it highly unlikely that the condemned experienced pain, but if and when that did happen to be the case, the paralytic agent prevented prisoners from communicating that pain to onlookers.

The Beating of Rodney King

At 12:56 A.M. on March 3, 1991, Sergeant Stacey Koon of the Los Angeles Police Department (LAPD) transmitted a message to his watch commander's office:

After four Los Angeles Police Department (LAPD) officers pulled over Rodney King on suspicion of drunk driving, they beat him in an incident that was filmed and soon gained media publicity. The trial of the four officers present at the scene resulted in a "not guilty" verdict, precipitating a series of riots. In this photograph, Rodney King addresses the media. *(AP Photo/David Longstreath)*

"You just had a big time use of force," he typed. "[T]ased and beat the suspect of CHP pursuit, Big Time."[6] The suspect in question was a 25-year-old African-American man named Rodney King, and he was en route to Pacifica Hospital for treatment. "I haven't beaten anyone this bad in a long time," remarked Officer Laurence Powell, one of his assailants, minutes after the beating. "[N]ot again," his colleague responded. "I thought you agreed to chill out for a while."[7] Powell's past behavior had already been responsible for a $70,000 excessive force settlement paid out by the city of Los Angeles, and Powell was known for harassing black motorists in white neighborhoods. Several hours before the King beating, he remarked in a police transmission that a group of African-American complainants reminded him of the film *Gorillas in the Mist*.[8] By the time Powell and other attackers completed their work, King had been struck 31 times with a metal baton and kicked seven times. His skull had been fractured 11 times, which would result in permanent brain damage. His right eye socket and right cheekbone had been fractured and his right ankle broken. He sustained considerable internal injuries, including kidney damage, and his body was covered in numerous cuts, bruises, and marks, including a prominent boot print on his chest.

President George H. W. Bush ordered a federal response into the beating of Rodney King after King's assailants were acquitted by an all-white jury. *(National Archives and Records Administration [558524])*

The incident was not uncommon. When the Independent Commission on the Los Angeles Police Department (Christopher Commission), an independent commission authorized by Mayor Tom Bradley to investigate the King incident and headed by future Secretary of State Warren Christopher, issued its report in July 1991, it found evidence of widespread racism, police brutality, and cold indifference among supervisors. Even recorded electronic police transmissions indicated casual, everyday expressions of racial hatred. "I would love to drive down Slauson with a flamethrower . . . we would have a barbecue," remarked one officer, referring to a predominantly African-American, low-income neighborhood in South Central Los Angeles.[9] "I almost got me a Mexican last night," remarked an officer in another police transmission, "but he dropped the damn gun too quick."[10] Remarks such as these were not regarded as offensive within the LAPD community. They were typical and ostensibly representative of the attitude that many white officers shared. Excessive force complaints had been filed against approximately 1,800 officers; one officer, still on duty at the time of the report, had 16 separate allegations. These complaints were generally ignored without any serious investigation. Even for officers who generated the 83 successful civil lawsuits filed against the LAPD between 1986 and 1990, of which "[a] majority . . . involved clear and egregious officer misconduct resulting in serious injury or death," the penalties were "frequently light and often nonexistent."[11] It would be fair to say that the LAPD of that period generated a police culture in which violence against nonwhite suspects had made the LAPD infamous among African Americans and Latinos in Los Angeles, even as white city leaders heaped praise on the department.

When King and two friends sped down California's I-210, officers from the California Highway Patrol (CHP) began pursuit. When the car did not slow down, the CHP officers called in LAPD reinforcement and the officers, suspecting that the vehicle must be stolen given the attempt to evade law enforcement, commenced a high-speed chase. They finally caught up with the suspects in Los Angeles on Foothill Boulevard and ordered the three out of the vehicle. King's two friends immediately complied, lying face down on the ground. An officer shouted again for King to leave the vehicle, at which point the intoxicated King got out, smiling and waving at a police helicopter before he, too, lay down on the grass.

What happened next is subject to some debate. According to police testimony, King charged at an officer when he was approached. Officers, suspecting that King was high on PCP, flew into action. The beating would have been an ordinary example of LAPD violence against a nonwhite suspect were it not for the fact that George Holliday, living in a nearby apartment, heard the commotion and stepped out on his terrace with his new video camera. Oblivious to police, he filmed the attack and provided his footage to a local television station. The video later made national news, played so many times that a CNN executive referred to it as "wallpaper."[12] The immediate outrage was tangible, but it would pale in comparison to the outrage to come.

The Los Angeles Riots

At first, it appeared that the officers would face serious consequences for their actions. By April 1991, clear action had been taken. Indictments had been returned against the four officers responsible for beating King. The Christopher Commission had been formed to investigate the LAPD. Mayor Bradley had asked for the resignation of LAPD chief Daryl Gates. Low-income black and Latino residents of Los Angeles had reason to hope. After so many cases in which the LAPD had abused suspects with impunity, the department would at last be held accountable. It was inconceivable that anyone could ignore this videotaped evidence, which was so universally condemned; a poll taken shortly after the beatings reported that 92 percent of Americans believed that excessive force had been used.[13]

This optimism lasted for a year as the trial slowly proceeded to a verdict. On April 29, 1992, at 3:15 P.M., that verdict was handed down: not guilty. The jury in the trial, hailing from largely white and conservative Simi Valley, was composed of 10 whites and included no black jurors. The trial of the officers appeared to observers to be one in which white jurors simply chose to look the other way. Within two hours of the verdict, rioting erupted in predominately African-American communities around Los Angeles. Although 53 people were killed in six days of violence, the vast majority of the mainly black and Latino crowds did not attack other people. Most rioters instead targeted property, resulting in more than $1 billion in damage to the city. More than 7,000 rioters were arrested.

The administration of President George H. W. Bush responded with a middle-of-the-road approach, condemning the riots as an unacceptable display of violence while tacitly admitting that the criminal justice system in California had failed. Federal prosecutors announced charges against the four officers the day after the Los Angeles verdict, and indictments were returned three months later. On April

16, 1993, two of the four officers were convicted on charges of violating Rodney King's civil rights and received 30-month sentences; the other two were acquitted. Although the Ninth Circuit Court of Appeals would find that these sentences appeared to be excessively lenient, the U.S. Supreme Court refused to intervene. The officers were released in December 1995.

Chronicle of Events

1981
• *July 27:* Adam Walsh, an 11-year-old, disappears from a Florida shopping center.

1982
• *March 15:* Actress Theresa Saldana is stabbed 10 times by a stalker.

• *June 21:* Would-be presidential assassin John Hinckley, Jr., is found not guilty by reason of insanity and confined to a psychiatric hospital.
• *September 29–30:* Seven people are poisoned to death after an unidentified person tampers with bottled Tylenol capsules, lacing them with cyanide and placing them in drugstores throughout the Chicago area.
• *October 12:* President Ronald Reagan signs the Missing Children Act and the Victim and Witness Protection Act.

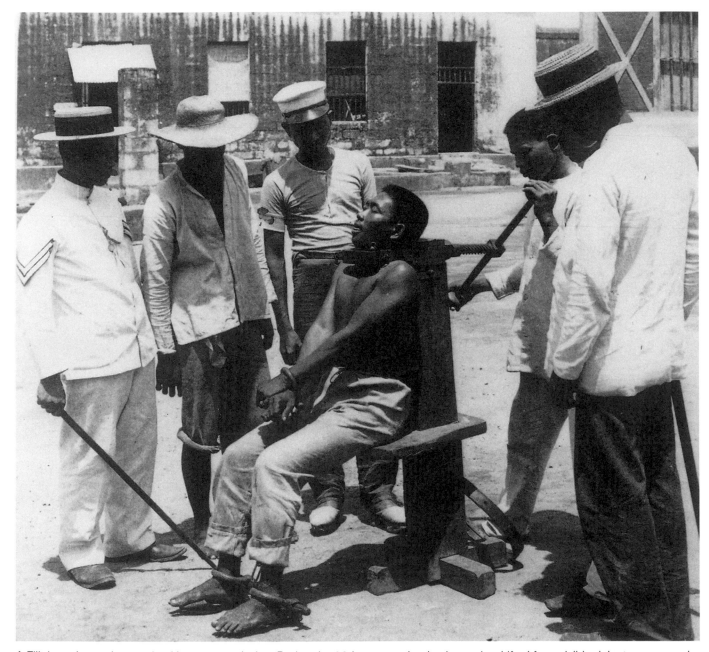

A Filipino prisoner is restrained in a garrote device. During the 20th century, the death penalty shifted from visibly violent means, such as hanging and the firing squad, to less visibly violent means, such as poison gas and lethal injection. *(Library of Congress Prints and Photographs Division [LC-USZ62-66689])*

- *December:* The Presidential Task Force on Victims of Crime releases its final report, issuing 68 policy recommendations designed to protect crime victims.
- *December 7:* The state of Texas executes Charles Brooks, Jr., by lethal injection, becoming the first U.S. state to use the procedure.

1983

- The Los Angeles Police Department (LAPD) begins its Drug Abuse Resistance Education (D.A.R.E.) program.
- *April 22:* The state of Alabama botches the execution of John Louis Evans by electric chair, slowly burning him to death in a series of three charges.
- *September 2:* The state of Mississippi botches the gas-chamber execution of Jimmy Lee Gray.
- *December 27:* Pope John Paul II meets with his would-be assassin, Mehmet Ali Agca, in an Italian prison cell. During the meeting Agca apologizes for the shooting, and the pope forgives him.

1984

- *May 25:* The National Center for Missing and Exploited Children (NCMEC) is established.
- *October 9:* President Ronald Reagan signs the Family Violence Prevention and Services Act, the first federal legislation designed to combat domestic violence.
- *December 22:* Bernhard Goetz shoots four teenage African-American muggers on a New York City subway car.

1985

- *November 29:* The *New York Times* reports that crack cocaine is being sold in New York City.

1986

- *June 19:* University of Maryland basketball star Len Bias dies of a cocaine overdose.
- *June 27:* Professional football player Don Rogers, a safety for the Cleveland Browns, dies after a cocaine overdose.
- *September 14:* President Ronald Reagan and First Lady Nancy Reagan deliver a televised speech, declaring their commitment to fighting illegal drug use.
- *September 15:* Reagan issues Executive Order 12564 on the Drug Free Federal Workplace, requiring federal agencies to establish drug-testing programs for employees.
- *October 27:* President Ronald Reagan signs the Anti-Drug Abuse Act of 1986.

1987

- *January 20:* The first NBC *Unsolved Mysteries* television special, a documentary series hosted by Raymond Burr that includes profiles of both unsolved crime cases and paranormal phenomena, debuts.

1988

- *February 7:* The Fox Television crime reality series *America's Most Wanted* debuts, hosted by National Center for Missing and Exploited Children cofounder John Walsh.
- *October 5: Unsolved Mysteries* becomes a weekly one-hour television series. Robert Stack replaces Raymond Burr as host.

1989

- *January 24:* Serial killer Ted Bundy is executed by the state of Florida.
- *April 19:* A 28-year-old female investment banker jogging in New York City's Central Park is raped and brutally beaten by a gang of youths.
- *July 18:* Actress Rebecca Schaeffer is murdered by a stalker.
- *September 5:* President George H. W. Bush delivers a nationally televised speech declaring the war on drugs a national priority and appoints William J. Bennett the first "drug czar" to coordinate federal drug control policy.

1990

- The state of California enacts the nation's first anti-stalking law.
- *December 26:* After a five-year surge, the New York Division of Substance Abuse Services reports that crack cocaine use is declining.

1991

- *January 13:* Serial killer Dennis Rader ("BTK") murders his last known victim, 63-year-old Dolores Davis.
- *February 14:* The film adaptation of Thomas Harris's thriller *The Silence of the Lambs*, centering on serial killer Hannibal Lecter (played by Anthony Hopkins), is released in the United States.
- *March 3:* Rodney King is brutally beaten by four LAPD police officers.
- *July:* The Independent Commission on the Los Angeles Police Department, known as the Christopher Commission, issues its findings, reporting widespread use of excessive force by the LAPD and pervasive problems with police management.

• *July 22:* Jeffrey Dahmer is arrested after a terrified, handcuffed man escapes from his apartment and flags down a police car. When police search Dahmer's apartment, they find the dismembered remains of 11 men.

1992

• *February 17:* In Wisconsin serial killer Jeffrey Dahmer is sentenced to 15 consecutive life sentences.

• *April 6:* The state of Arizona botches the gas chamber execution of Donald Eugene Harding.

• *April 29:* A jury acquits four LAPD officers in the beating of Rodney King.

• *April 29–May 4:* Six days of rioting in Los Angeles follow the acquittal of the LAPD officers in the Rodney King case, leading to 53 deaths and massive property damage.

Eyewitness Testimony

Drugs and Drug-Related Violence

A new form of cocaine is for sale on the streets of New York, alarming law enforcement officials because of its tendency to accelerate abuse of the drug, particularly among adolescents . . .

Since crack appeared on the streets of the Bronx last year, spreading throughout the city and its suburbs, new cocaine users have graduated more quickly from inhaling to free-basing, the most common addictive form of cocaine abuse.

Journalist Jane Gross, from "A New, Purified Form of Cocaine Causes Alarm as Abuse Increases," New York Times, *November 29, 1985, p. A1.*

America has accomplished so much in these last few years, whether it's been rebuilding our economy or serving the cause of freedom in the world. What we've been able to achieve has been done with your help—with us working together as a nation united. Now, we need your support again. Drugs are menacing our society. They're threatening our values and undercutting our institutions. They're killing our children.

From the beginning of our administration, we've taken strong steps to do something about this horror. Tonight I can report to you that we've made much progress. Thirty-seven federal agencies are working together in a vigorous national effort, and by next year our spending for drug law enforcement will have more than tripled from its 1981 levels. We have increased seizures of illegal drugs. Shortages of marijuana are now being reported. Last year alone over 10,000 drug criminals were convicted and nearly $250 million of their assets were seized by the DEA, the Drug Enforcement Administration.

And in the most important area, individual use, we see progress. In four years the number of high school seniors using marijuana on a daily basis has dropped from one in 14 to one in 20. The U.S. military has cut the use of illegal drugs among its personnel by 67 percent since 1980. These are a measure of our commitment and emerging signs that we can defeat this enemy. But we still have much to do.

Despite our best efforts, illegal cocaine is coming into our country at alarming levels, and 4 to 5 million people regularly use it. Five hundred thousand Americans are hooked on heroin. One in twelve persons smokes marijuana regularly. Regular drug use is even higher among the age group 18 to 25—most likely just entering the workforce. Today there's a new epidemic: smokable cocaine, otherwise known as crack. It is an explosively destructive and often lethal substance which is crushing its users. It is an uncontrolled fire.

And drug abuse is not a so-called victimless crime. Everyone's safety is at stake when drugs and excessive alcohol are used by people on the highways or by those transporting our citizens or operating industrial equipment. Drug abuse costs you and your fellow Americans at least $60 billion a year . . .

The job ahead of us is very clear. Nancy's personal crusade, like that of so many other wonderful individuals, should become our national crusade. It must include a combination of government and private efforts which complement one another. Last month I announced six initiatives which we believe will do just that.

First, we seek a drug-free workplace at all levels of government and in the private sector. Second, we'll work toward drug-free schools. Third, we want to ensure that the public is protected and that treatment is available to substance abusers and the chemically dependent. Our fourth goal is to expand international cooperation while treating drug trafficking as a threat to our national security. In October I will be meeting with key U.S. ambassadors to discuss what can be done to support our friends abroad. Fifth, we must move to strengthen law enforcement activities such as those initiated by Vice President Bush and Attorney General Meese. And finally, we seek to expand public awareness and prevention.

In order to further implement these six goals, I will announce tomorrow a series of new proposals for a drug-free America. Taken as a whole, these proposals will toughen our laws against drug criminals, encourage more research and treatment, and ensure that illegal drugs will not be tolerated in our schools or in our workplaces. Together with our ongoing efforts, these proposals will bring the federal commitment to fighting drugs to $3 billion. As much financing as we commit, however, we would be fooling ourselves if we thought that massive new amounts of money alone will provide the solution. Let us not forget that in America people solve problems and no national crusade has ever succeeded without human investment. Winning the crusade against drugs will not be achieved by just throwing money at the problem.

Your government will continue to act aggressively, but nothing would be more effective than for Americans simply to quit using illegal drugs. We seek to create a massive change in national attitudes which ultimately will separate the drugs from the customer, to take the user away from the supply. I believe, quite simply, that we can help them quit, and that's where you come in.

My generation will remember how America swung into action when we were attacked in World War II. The war was not just fought by the fellows flying the planes or driving the tanks. It was fought at home by a mobilized nation—men and women alike—building planes and ships, clothing sailors and soldiers, feeding marines and airmen; and it was fought by children planting victory gardens and collecting cans. Well, now we're in another war for our freedom, and it's time for all of us to pull together again. So, for example, if your friend or neighbor or a family member has a drug or alcohol problem, don't turn the other way. Go to his help or to hers. Get others involved with you—clubs, service groups, and community organizations—and provide support and strength. And, of course, many of you've been cured through treatment and self-help. Well, you're the combat veterans, and you have a critical role to play. You can help others by telling your story and providing a willing hand to those in need. Being friends to others is the best way of being friends to ourselves. It's time, as Nancy said, for America to "just say no" to drugs . . .

In this crusade, let us not forget who we are. Drug abuse is a repudiation of everything America is. The destructiveness and human wreckage mock our heritage. Think for a moment how special it is to be an American. Can we doubt that only a divine providence placed this land, this island of freedom, here as a refuge for all those people on the world who yearn to breathe free?

The revolution out of which our liberty was conceived signaled an historical call to an entire world seeking hope. Each new arrival of immigrants rode the crest of that hope. They came, millions seeking a safe harbor from the oppression of cruel regimes. They came, to escape starvation and disease. They came, those surviving the Holocaust and the Soviet gulags. They came, the boat people, chancing death for even a glimmer of hope that they could have a new life. They all came to taste the air redolent and rich with the freedom that is ours. What an insult it will be to what we are and whence we came if we do not rise up together in defiance against this cancer of drugs.

President Ronald Reagan, "Address to the Nation on the Campaign against Drug Abuse," September 14, 1986, from the Ronald Reagan Presidential Library. Available online at URL: http://www.reagan.utexas.edu/archives/speeches/1986/091486a.htm.

Lenard Hebert is an expert of sorts on America's patterns of drug abuse over the past 25 years. He hasn't studied them; he's lived them.

"I did each drug of the decade," says Hebert, a 40-year-old man now glad to be recovering in New York City's Phoenix House, one of the largest residential drug treatment centers in the world . . . [H]e recalls his time as a Marine in Vietnam in 1967: "We'd wear peace signs on our helmets and love beads around our necks. Drugs were another way to get in touch with home. And LSD was definitely the most popular drug at the time."

When he returned home in the early '70s, Hebert . . . "did strictly reefer. A good [black militant] did natural, herbal things. Then I went disco. I snorted cocaine for 10 years. It was chic because it was so expensive."

Along came crack, the smokable, highly addictive form of cocaine with its five-minute high. Hebert stopped dealing cocaine and turned his middle-class high-rise apartment into a crack den. Before he made it to Phoenix House, he was sleeping in abandoned cars and shelters for the homeless . . .

Journalist Dan Hurley, in "Cycles of Craving: Society's Drugs of Choice Appear to Come in Waves: LSD and Marijuana, Cocaine, Now Crack," Psychology Today, July/August 1989, p. 54.

Civilian Responses to Crime

4. On December 22, 1984, plaintiff [Darrell Cabey] was a passenger on a southbound No. 2 subway train on the Seventh Avenue IRT subway line, an underground rapid transit system owned by the City of New York, and operated and administered therefore by the New York City Metropolitan Transit Authority.

5. Plaintiff had earlier boarded said subway train in the company of three other Black youths, namely, Troy Canty, Barry Allen and James Ramseur.

6. At approximately 1:45 p.m. on said date, defendant [Bernhard Goetz] boarded the said subway train and took a seat in the car in which plaintiff and his companions were then riding.

7. Upon information and belief, on that date and at that time and place, defendant was carrying a fully loaded holster, in violation of the applicable laws of the City and State of New York and of the United States.

8. Upon information and belief, defendant's weapon was loaded with at least three (3) soft-nosed hollow point bullets—commonly referred to as "dum dum"

bullets—designed to cause a maximum of serious physical injury and pain to a victim. Upon information and belief, said ammunition is outlawed by both the City and State of New York and the United States, and its use is prohibited in warfare by international treaties and understandings.

9. Upon information and belief, one of plaintiff's companions, namely Troy Canty, approached defendant and asked him for five dollars ($5.00), whereupon defendant, without provocation or advance warning, drew his weapon and shot said Canty, following which he then opened fire upon the other Black youths, including plaintiff. When plaintiff attempted to flee, defendant deliberately, willfully and with malice aforethought, aimed at his back and fired his weapon thereat, severing his spinal cord.

10. Defendant then fled from the subway car in which the aforesaid incident had taken place, and left the City and State of New York, eventually arriving in Concord, New Hampshire, where, on or about December 31, 1984, he surrendered to the local authorities, and, upon information and belief, confessed and admitted to the above actions on his part.

11. At all times relevant hereto, defendant acted knowingly, willfully, deliberately, intentionally, and with malice aforethought to cause the death of or to inflict serious physical injury on plaintiff.

12. At all times relevant hereto, defendant acted with actual malice, to wit:

a. Upon information and belief, defendant later stated that he had a desire to keep on shooting plaintiff and his companions;

b. Upon information and belief, defendant later expressed regret that he had run out of ammunition;

c. Upon information and belief, defendant later stated a desire to gouge out the eyes of some or all of his victims;

d. Upon information and belief, defendant later expressed a regret that he had not taken his car keys and gouged out the eyes of some or all of his victims;

e. Upon information and belief, defendant later stated that he behaved "viciously and savagely, just like a rat" toward his victims.

f. Upon information and belief, defendant had previously publicly expressed racial epithets and slurs concerning Black and Hispanic persons.

g. Upon information and belief, defendant has stated that he has no remorse about the shooting.

From a civil complaint filed by victim Darrell Cabey against Bernhard Goetz, who shot four black youths on a subway, from Cabey v. Goetz *(Supreme Court of the State of New York, Index No. 6747–1985), January 30, 1985.*

They were too perfect, those four mischievous black children. At first Bernie Goetz didn't believe what he was seeing, I'm sure of that. Probably he thought they were a four-part hallucination—distilled, drop by drop, from his obsessive, long daydream of self-defense. It was all so opportune ... Goetz had been packing heat since 1981—the year when he was mugged and savagely beaten. Don't tell me he hadn't been rehearsing just such an encounter in his mind ...

Goetz calls himself "murderer," "coward." "My intent," he says, "was to kill." He even thought about gouging eyes out with a house key. At least one juror felt the confession was "completely and totally honest" ... After blasting those four Goetz, by his own account, went back and blew Darrell Cabey's spinal cord away. "You seem to be doing all right," he claimed to have said. "Here's another one." Damning testimony. It doesn't help sustain a self-defense plea. And yet the jury, reviewing evidence, chose not to believe Goetz's own version.

Columnist D. Keith Mano, in "The Goetz Confession," National Review, *May 13, 1988, p. 60.*

The first thing a person notices about John Walsh is his intensity. A short, handsome man, he rarely smiles—at least not in public. ... Even when the cameras stop rolling and the rest of the crew lightens up, he remains somber, completely in character ...

"America's Most Wanted" wages its war on crime every Sunday night, and the results have been astounding. ... Perhaps the most publicized capture: John Emil List, a New Jersey accountant wanted for the 1971 murder of his wife, mother, and two children. After evading the FBI for 18 years, List was captured in Richmond, Virginia, after viewers recognized a forensic bust created especially for the program ...

When Fox Broadcasting Company began in 1987 to develop a crime show based on true-to-life reenactments for its new network, a lot of names were bandied around as show host ... But when Walsh's name was suggested, Fox believed it had found the perfect match.

"I knew right then we had our guy," said Michael Linder, executive producer of "America's Most Wanted." "He looks right for the part, he has a voice that's compelling. But more than that, he's a living metaphor for what we're trying to do."

*Columnist Diane Bartley, in "John Walsh: Fighting Back,"
Saturday Evening Post, April 1990, p. 1.*

Child Abuse and Other Forms of Domestic Violence

Until recently, the millions of American women of all classes and races who are beaten annually had virtually nowhere to go. As late as 1976, New York City, with a population estimated at more than 8 million people, had 1000 beds for homeless men and 45 for homeless women. In Minneapolis-St. Paul, there were only a few beds available before the first battered women's shelter opened in 1974. A 1973 Los Angeles survey revealed 4000 beds for men and 30 for women and children—none of the 30 beds was for mothers with sons older than 4. In various states, social service or religious organizations provided minimal programs or temporary housing for displaced persons, "multi-problem" families, or the wives of alcoholics, but there was no category, "abused women." Since 1975, the ongoing struggle of the battered women's movement has been to name the hidden and private violence in women's lives, declare it public, and provide safe havens and support.

As battered women's shelters opened in hundreds of towns throughout the United States and women declared themselves sisters in a movement to end male violence, a seemingly obvious yet unprecedented challenge was hurled at centuries of male domination. In contrast to just one decade earlier, battered women are no longer invisible. Their stories . . . convey the experiences of generations of women. They also offer a painful glimpse into the lives of women, who, in 1982, are still abused and frequently find no help. Although violence against women has now been declared unacceptable, it endures pervasively. By 1981, the 5 New York City battered women's shelters, filled to capacity, turned away 85 out of every 100 callers asking for refuge.

Antiviolence activist and reformer Susan Schechter, from her book Women and Male Violence, pp. 11–12.

News stories daily remind us that children are brutally maltreated by their parents—the very persons who should be giving them love and protection. Children are beaten until their bodies no longer heal, they are scalded with boiling water, they are starved and so dehydrated that their skin shrivels around their fragile bones, they are sexually assaulted and forced to perform all sorts of perverted acts, and they are locked in closets or tied to bed posts for days on end. Abused and neglected children are in urgent need of protection—protection that can be provided only if individual citizens are willing to help . . .

Although all statistics concerning what happens in the privacy of the home must be approached with great care, we know that each year, over one million children are abused or neglected by their parents. According to the Study of National Incidence and Prevalence of Child Abuse and Neglect . . . conducted for the federal government in 1986, about 300,000 are physically abused, another 140,000 are sexually abused, and 700,000 are neglected or otherwise maltreated. Estimates vary, but it appears that at least 1,100 children die each year as a result of maltreatment. This figure would make maltreatment the sixth largest cause of death for children under age fourteen.

Douglas J. Besharov, former director of the U.S. Center on Child Abuse and Neglect, from his book Recognizing Child Abuse, pp. 1–2.

Serial Killers

Yet with each killer I met I saw a growing number of ill individuals, albeit people with no obvious disease. As a group, they all looked spent, drained but calm, as if they had recently experienced an internal storm. In the cages of the institutions where they were housed the inmates looked at peace, even though they were on trial for their lives, were serving life sentences, or were waiting on death row for their appointment with the executioner. Obviously they were physically and psychologically damaged people, some more than others. Almost all of them had scars on their bodies, missing fingers, evidence of previous contusions and multiple abrasions on and around the head and neck area. And they had permanent scars from accidents, fights, knifings, bullet and shotgun wounds, and burns; many of which had been inflicted by the killers' own family members while the killers were still at a young age. All of the killers talked about the desire for freedom even as they seemed to be "at home" in their prison environments. More than once, after a particularly grueling interview with a killer, the attending guard would put his arm around the inmate in a knowing and fatherly way and say, as he was taking the killer back to his cell, "Come on, son, let's go home."

Psychologist Joel Norris, from his book Serial Killers, *p. 3.*

"I carried it too far, that's for sure," Dahmer told police in explaining his frustrated search for a totally compliant zombie-type sex slave who would always be there for him . . .

Psychiatric testimony at Dahmer's insanity trial . . . spewed confusion over semantically similar—but differently defined—legal, psychiatric, and laymen's terms for mental disease and insanity . . .

The doctors' struggles to maintain their images as competent authorities only compounded the lunacy. One referred to "the cannibalism that we see in these sorts of cases . . ." Another said he knew of "other people with a sexual attraction to viscera." A third testified he had "seen hundreds of serial murderers in the last twenty years" . . .

The experts disagreed . . . on whether Dahmer's hoarding of heads and genitals was psychotic.

"It was very, very bizarre behavior," explained a psychologist. But you could also call it "a pretty realistic way to keep trophies."

The psychologist pointed out that hunters display animal-head trophies on the wall without being called insane or labeled paraphiliacs . . . "[T]his would not necessarily show an impaired mind."

Psychologist Joan Ullman, in "I Carried It Too Far, That's for Sure," Psychology Today, *May/June 1992, p. 28.*

Changing Methods of Capital Punishment

Two-and-a-half minutes after he had walked in, David was locked into the chair, spine straight, head tilted back, fists clenching the chair's arms. He looked like an astronaut ready for launch. I prepared to gasp when the electricity hit. But I didn't.

The switch echoed with a metallic slam and David gave a slight heave forward, like a puppet twitching at his master's pull. His thumbs tucked inside his fists, which curled into purple knots. For the next 60 seconds all we heard was the clank of the switch as the executioner altered the current. There were no cries of pain or protest, no visible signs of suffering.

The coroner waited five minutes for Martin's body to settle, so that the body noises wouldn't be confused with a heartbeat. He probed his chest with a stethoscope and his eyes with a flashlight. Finding no evidence of life in either, he walked to the execution chamber microphone. "The inmate was declared dead at 12:16 a.m.," he said . . .

David Dene Martin's death was clean and efficient, wrapped in ritual and surrounded by bureaucracy, carried out in accordance with the lawyerly dictates of Regulation 10-25. It didn't seem real. As I walked out, I half-expected him to get up and follow.

Somehow I expected the taking of a life to be something more awesome. What I saw seemed to trivialize not only his life but life in general.

Jason Deparle, "Executions Aren't News," Washington Monthly, *March 1986, p. 12.*

Electrocution may involve excruciating pain as well as physical violence, mutilation of the body, burning of the flesh, etc. Several recent executions required considerable time. In 1985 it took an executioner in Indiana 20 minutes and five surges of electricity to kill William Vandiver, who had refused to appeal his death sentence, saying only that he wished to die in peace. Alabama's 1983 execution of John Evans necessitated the better part of an hour, numerous jolts of electricity, with an electrode on the leg exploding and being destroyed in smoke and fire. Observers described it as torturing him to death.

Thirteen states have now adopted lethal injection as a means of execution—a method likely to grow in popularity. Some opponents of capital punishment have mixed feelings about this, believing that the more we sanitize and medicate the process, the easier it will be to continue with executions.

Kent S. Miller and Betty Davis Miller, quoted from To Kill and Be Killed: Case Studies from Florida's Death Row, *pp. 57–58.*

Racism and Racial Profiling

Alvin F. Poussaint, M.D., associate professor of psychiatry at Harvard Medical School, says there are two main reasons why some police officers seem to have no problem with brutalizing people or seeing them brutalized. One is that many of them, caught up in the politically inspired slogans "War on Crime" and "War on Drugs," actually see themselves as warriors in a battle against evil where the destruction—not the apprehension—of the "enemy" become the objective.

"On their jobs, some policemen develop an 'us' and 'them' attitude," Dr. Poussaint theorizes. "They begin to see 'people out there' as almost subhuman, which makes it easy for them to treat 'them' like animals." Faced with that they meticulously observe the "blue code," a conspiratorial bond of silence that is as much honored among police officers as it is among members of organized crime.

The other reason, says Dr. Poussaint, is that policemen's exposure to the world is a very negative one. "Over and over," he says, "they are confronted with a disproportionately large number of bad people. As a result, they begin to make generalizations and frequently, if they are operating in a Black community, the generalizations take on racial tones."

Managing editor Hans J. Massaquoi, in "How to Stop Police Brutality," Ebony, July 1991, p. 58.

I don't know many black people who stop policemen and ask for directions anymore. Mostly they give a wide berth, and, after yesterday's verdict in the Rodney King trial, that berth will get wider still.

I watched the verdict come in as I bounced my 8-month-old son on my knee. My mouth tightened in grim disbelief as verdict after "not guilty" verdict from a jury with no African-Americans came back. My mind's eye flashed back to tales of trials in the segregated Deep South, trials where—when they occurred at all—smirking white defendants who had assaulted or killed black people walked away, acquitted by a jury of what was indeed their peers.

Listening to the television's drone, one part of me grunted in resignation—same ol' same ol'—and the

Police officers line the sidewalk outside a store during the 1992 Los Angeles riots. After a jury returned a "not guilty" verdict for the four Los Angeles Police Department (LAPD) officers charged with the beating of Rodney King, the South Central neighborhood of Los Angeles erupted in riots. *(AP Photo/Nick It)*

other part of me just couldn't grasp it. The verdicts defied logic. Had not the jury seen the same tape I did, the one that showed the officers in question pounding away at Rodney King? Had they read—and dismissed—the computer transcripts describing we black people as animals (specifically gorillas)? Could they ignore the testimony of emergency room personnel about one officer's menacing jocularity as King lay bleeding from the injuries administered by the same officer? Obviously, they could and did.

Author and journalist Karen Grigsby Bates, quoted in Vila and Morris, The Role of Police in American Society, *p. 271.*

CHAPTER THIRTEEN

Crime and Justice as Public Issues

1993 to Present

In the 1990s, crime and justice became topics of tremendous concern to the American public. At least in the early part of the decade, this concern had a basis in quantitative fact. Between 1990 and 1994, the national homicide rate hovered around 10 victims per 100,000 residents each year, close to its 20th-century peak.[1] Likewise, the rate of serious crimes (or "index" crimes) known to police reached an all-time high in 1991 and remained substantial throughout much of the decade.[2]

It should come as little surprise that federal, state, and local governments responded with new laws and policies designed to get tough on crime and claimed credit when crime rates did fall in the late 1990s and early 2000s. This tendency to see crime as a manifestation of deeper issues also encouraged people to understand crime and justice in universal ways, however, and made it more difficult for U.S. society to come to terms with the specific situations and circumstances that shaped the day-to-day reality of crime. The peak crime years of the late 1980s and early 1990s had left Americans, and especially those Americans living in large cities, with a palpable fear of violent crime.

Yet the public concern about and fascination with crime drew on deeper issues as well. Discussions of crime seemed to be ubiquitous in the 1990s, brought into the nation's homes by the expanding media of cable television 24-hour news stations and, in particular, Court TV. The period lacked epochal wars or political tensions, and in their absence discussions of crime often became proxies for discussions of the underlying issues of the day. The murder trial of former football star O.J. Simpson transformed into a national debate about race. Moreover, crime also became a means for politically marginal extremists such as Timothy McVeigh and Theodore Kaczynski to express their antagonism toward the U.S. government and modern industrial society.

As crime decreased, so did crime-related anxiety. In a January 1994 Gallup opinion poll, 37 percent of Americans cited crime and violence as the most important problem facing the country at the time. When Gallup followed up on the same question 10 years later, only 2 percent of Americans held that view.[3] The attacks of

September 11, 2001, and the Iraq War had replaced the fear of violent domestic criminals with the fear of war and terrorism. For most of the 1990s, however, crime was the defining public issue of the day—and the lens through which larger societal problems were examined.

The O. J. Simpson Trial

Near midnight on June 12, 1994, the bodies of Nicole Brown Simpson and Ronald Goldman were discovered outside the former's home. They had been stabbed to death. Police suspected that Simpson's ex-husband, actor and football legend O. J. Simpson, was the attacker, a suspicion that appeared to be corroborated by evidence obtained at the scene. Upon the advice of his attorneys, Simpson agreed that he would turn himself in to police five days later, on the morning of June 17. Simpson did not appear. His attorney, Robert Kardashian, read a suicide note written by Simpson, in which he denied involvement in his ex-wife's death and expressed hope that the media would leave his children alone. Based on the note and Simpson's failure to surrender, it appeared that he had ended his life.

That evening 95 million viewers watched television footage of a white Ford Bronco drift slowly away from police near the junction of Interstate 5 and Interstate 405 near Los Angeles.[4] The car had already been on the road for seven hours. The Bronco, trailed by a dozen helicopters and rows upon rows of police cars, carried a suicidal O. J. Simpson driven by his longtime friend and former teammate Al Cowlings. Cowlings told police that Simpson had a gun, which he was holding to his head while threatening to end his life; police, not wanting to provoke Simpson's suicide, kept their distance and drove slowly. Finally, after nine hours on the road, the Bronco pulled up at Simpson's home in Los Angeles and remained parked in the driveway for 45 minutes. When Simpson emerged from the vehicle and surrendered, police found a passport, disguise, $8,000 in cash, and a loaded .357 Magnum revolver.

At the time of his arrest, Simpson was the most famous person ever charged with murder in the United States. The charges, which carried a possible death penalty, increased the stakes of the case tremendously. But the racial aspects overshadowed the celebrity aspects of the case. When *Time* magazine reported on the case, its cover consisted of an artificially darkened image of Simpson and the text "An American Tragedy." The LAPD, only a few years after the 1992 Rodney King beating, was still widely regarded within the civil rights community as racist and corrupt.

With this racial undercurrent, the 133-day trial began in January 1995. It would become one of the most widely watched events in television history, as Americans soon learned the names of all of the trial's central players—Judge Lance Ito, prosecutors Marcia Clark and Christopher Darden, and defense attorneys (a group dubbed "the Dream Team") F. Lee Bailey, Johnnie Cochran, Alan Dershowitz, and Robert Shapiro.

The centerpiece of the prosecution's case was DNA evidence tracing Simpson's blood to the crime scene, which prosecutors surmised came from a cut that police had discovered on Simpson's left middle finger the day after the murder. Simpson claimed that he had cut his finger on broken glass; prosecutors argued that he had been cut while murdering Ronald Goldman. This theory had several circumstantial problems, however. The first was that neither the bloody leather glove discovered at the crime scene nor the pair of clean gloves found at Simpson's home were cut, and it would have been strange for the murderer to wear gloves only to take them off during the murder. Prosecutors also failed to obtain any DNA evidence linking the bloody left glove to Simpson, calling into question the idea that he might have somehow cut his finger inside the glove. More famously, the bloody gloves found at the scene were too small to fit Simpson's hands. Prosecutors attributed this to leather shrinkage due to humidity from the blood, but that hypothesis struck jurors as questionable. The image of the undersized glove irreparably damaged the prosecution's case.

The issue of how Simpson's blood made its way to the crime scene in the first place was more difficult to resolve and required the unwitting cooperation of a perfect LAPD villain. Defense lawyers zeroed in on detective Mark Fuhrman, the LAPD officer most likely to have had the opportunity to plant the small amount of blood evidence at the scene. Fuhrman, who was white, seemed a credible witness at first—even swearing, under oath, that he had never used the "n_____" epithet to describe African Americans. When defense attorneys later uncovered audiotapes proving that Fuhrman had not only used the term, casually and with considerable frequency, but also had boasted of improper handling of African-American suspects, the prosecution's case was compromised. In the wake of the Rodney King beatings, the majority African-American jury would have had to believe beyond a reasonable doubt that an LAPD detective who had cheerfully used racial slurs and then lied about it under oath and who had boasted of acting inappropriately toward black suspects in the past had not planted evidence against a celebrity black suspect.

On October 3, 1995, the jury returned a verdict of not guilty after only three hours of deliberation. Reaction to the case divided sharply. Immediately following Simpson's arrest, 60 percent of African Americans polled believed that he was innocent, while 68 percent of whites polled believed that he had murdered his wife.[5] This trend only grew; the week before the verdict was announced, 77 percent of whites polled believed that Simpson was guilty, and 72 percent of African Americans polled believed that he was innocent.[6] The poll data reflected a massive disparity in the way that the crime had been perceived and the assumptions that were made about the relative trustworthiness of Simpson and the LAPD. White anger regarding the Simpson verdict became explosive but subsided somewhat following the 1997 civil case in which Simpson was found liable for the wrongful deaths of Nicole Brown Simpson and Ronald Goldman and ordered to pay $33.5 million in damages to the victims' families.

The Simpson trial was the most prominent example of the explosion of televised high-profile trials, but it was not by any means the first. The 1993 trial of Lyle and Erik Menendez, two brothers tried and ultimately convicted for murdering their parents, launched the success of the cable network Court TV, which offered almost limitless coverage of the Simpson trial. The 1997 trial of Louise Woodward, a British nanny convicted of involuntary manslaughter for the shaking death of an infant under her care, also attracted substantial media coverage. However, no trial, before or after, attracted the attention that the Simpson trial did.

Ruby Ridge, Waco, and the Rise of Domestic Terrorism

During the early 1990s, private militia groups flourished in the United States. The vast majority were rooted in what has been described as the patriot movement,

A group of girls, members of an early 20th-century New Jersey paramilitary club, hold rifles while standing in formation in front of a row of tents. Paramilitary clubs, long a part of American culture, often became marbled with white supremacist and other right-wing nationalist groups during the last decades of the 20th century. *(Library of Congress Prints and Photographs Division [LC-USZ62-55093])*

a right-wing populist tradition tracing back to the 1970s whose common ground includes an emphasis on the founding military principles of the American experiment (centering on the concept of a self-armed citizen militia rather than a professional army), a persistent distrust of government driven by an overriding fear of totalitarian oppression, opposition to the United Nations (UN) and other perceived instruments of world government, survivalism, hostility toward feminism and the women's liberation movement, and a profound fear of communism. Sectors of the patriot movement were also driven by Christian fundamentalism (centering on the idea of imminent global apocalypse), cultural xenophobia, and white separatism, but the movement as a whole was motivated by a general cultural backlash against the reforms brought about by the Civil Rights movement and the sexual revolution.

New domestic terrorism networks sprang from this right-wing counterculture movement during the 1990s, primarily in response to three events. The first trigger was the Ruby Ridge incident of August 1992, in which several U.S. marshals, aided by an FBI sniper, confronted white separatist Randy Weaver and shot his wife and 14-year-old son to death during an ensuing firefight and siege. Weaver was arrested following the confrontation, which had also claimed the life of a U.S. marshal. Weaver was charged with the agent's murder but ultimately acquitted on grounds of self-defense—an extremely rare outcome for a defendant prosecuted for the murder of a law enforcement official. The U.S. Department of Justice and U.S. Senate issued reports in 1994 and 1995, respectively, that roundly condemned the law enforcement response to Weaver. Twelve government agents were disciplined, one was charged with involuntary manslaughter (although ultimately acquitted), and the Weaver family was later awarded $3.1 million in damages in a wrongful death lawsuit filed against the U.S. Department of Justice.

The second trigger was the election of President Bill Clinton in November 1992. Clinton was the first Democrat to serve in the White House in 12 years and the first president who had come of age in the late 1960s. That Clinton acknowledged experimenting with marijuana and had dodged the Vietnam War draft were also extremely significant in the eyes of many right-wing paramilitarists. The effects of Clinton's election were exacerbated by the fact that both houses of Congress had been under Democratic control for the better part of the previous four decades. Right-wing paramilitarists struggled with a sense of futility and paranoia, overcome by a fear that the government was becoming larger, more invasive, and more liberal than it had ever been before. Clinton's decisions to allow closeted lesbians and gay men to serve in the military under the "don't ask, don't tell" policy and to appoint a record number of women and people of color to leadership positions within the executive branch was met with further hostility. Special criticism focused on the appointment of Attorney General Janet Reno, who was at the time the highest-ranking woman ever to serve in the executive branch.

Reno would play a central role in the third trigger: the infamous Waco incident of early 1993. At a small compound called Mount Carmel, located just outside of Waco, Texas, a 34-year-old apocalyptic cult leader named David Koresh—formerly Vernon Howell, before he had assumed his new name to signify his status as self-appointed messiah—stockpiled weapons, wives (some as young as 12), and other followers of his Branch Davidian cult in preparation for doomsday and the prophesied attack of the "Babylonians." Babylon, a literal oppressor in the Old Testament and a metaphor for Rome in the New, has traditionally been interpreted by apocalyptic theologians as referring to whatever the decadent and oppressive empire of the age happened to be. Koresh (the Hebrew transliteration of "Cyrus"), who had taken the name of the Persian emperor who liberated the Jewish people from the Babylonian captivity, regarded the United States as that empire.

Soon word spread of Koresh's activities. A local newspaper exposé published on February 27, 1993, brought public attention to the Mount Carmel compound, accusing Koresh of polygamy, statutory rape, and child abuse.[7] The Bureau of Alcohol, Tobacco, and Firearms had already been investigating Koresh based on eyewitness claims that he had converted semiautomatic weapons into fully automatic ones in violation of federal law, and on February 28 more than 70 ATF agents assembled outside the compound and prepared to storm the building. Who fired the first shot is not clear; many claim that ATF agents did, and the government did not produce evidence to the contrary. In any case, the resulting firefight, during which six ATF agents and four Branch Davidians died, convinced law enforcement officials that waiting out the Davidians would be a more reasonable strategy. The FBI took over leadership of the operation and surrounded the compound during a 51-day siege.

The burning Branch Davidian complex in Waco, Texas, was a symbol of tragedy and, in the eyes of many, of incompetent and heavy-handed law enforcement. *(AP Photo/FILE/Susan Weems)*

On April 19, 1993, the siege came to a horrifyingly tragic end. Attorney General Janet Reno, informed that the situation was rapidly getting worse and that children were being beaten, gave the go-ahead to end the siege. Tanks fired canisters of tear gas into the compound in hopes of driving out residents, the assumption being that the children, at least, would be unable to withstand the tear gas and would flee. They did not. The compound caught fire and burned, killing 76 residents, including dozens of children. It is widely regarded as the largest law enforcement failure in U.S. history. Many paramilitarists took this as a sign that the Clinton administration was waging a full-fledged assault on right-wing counterculture and was willing to slaughter human beings to assert control. On the second anniversary of the Waco tragedy, a small group of right-wing militarists exacted horrible revenge.

The Oklahoma City Bombing

Timothy McVeigh had been born to a devoutly Roman Catholic Irish-American family in New York, attended school, joined the U.S. Army, and served in the Persian Gulf War with distinction, rising to the rank of sergeant and winning the Bronze Star, among other distinctions. He was a hard-working and ambitious soldier who dreamed of becoming a Green Beret, and when opportunity presented itself after the war, he tried to take it—and failed. He was granted an honorable discharge and left his army base in Fort Riley, Kansas, to move in with his father in New York, where he worked as a security guard. At 24, McVeigh felt that his life had already peaked. He had failed at military life and had no interest in civilian life. He grew increasingly depressed. He began traveling the country trading right-wing propaganda on the gun-show circuit and living with friends from his time in the military.

Although it is difficult to trace McVeigh to any single organized terrorist group, he found like-minded associates in the paramilitary movement and new meaning in its paranoid, gun-centered culture. He grew increasingly fixated on the graphic and disturbing novel *The Turner Diaries* by white supremacist leader William Pierce, a novel that McVeigh had discovered while serving in the military. *The Turner Diaries* depicts a global race war in which a band of white supremacists fights against a "Jewish-controlled" government that restricts firearm ownership and eventually manages to exterminate nearly every nonwhite person on the planet.

According to McVeigh, the Waco incident confirmed his suspicions regarding the government. As a plan began to form in his mind, one scene from *The Turner*

On April 19, 1995, a truck bomb exploded at the Alfred P. Murrah Federal Building in downtown Oklahoma City, Oklahoma. The bombing, which killed 168 people, was orchestrated by Timothy McVeigh and Terry Nichols, right-wing militants who were angered by U.S. government actions at the Branch Davidian compound and Ruby Ridge, Idaho. *(AP Photo/Eric Draper)*

Diaries particularly inspired him: a deadly mortar attack on the U.S. Capitol Building, representing the ultimate triumph of the white paramilitary army. McVeigh could not mount such an attack on the well-defended building, but he began to see attacking the Alfred P. Murrah Federal Building in Oklahoma City on the second anniversary of the Waco incident as an acceptable alternative. In collaboration with fellow veteran Terry Nichols, McVeigh moved back to Kansas and began working on a powerful fertilizer bomb. At 9:02 A.M. on April 19, Timothy McVeigh used a rented truck full of explosives to destroy the Murrah Building.

The scale of the attack was frightening. The federal building was torn in half from the explosion. More than 300 buildings were damaged, and four nearby buildings were destroyed. All told, 168 people were killed in the attack (including 19 children), and at least 850 were injured.[8] It was the worst domestic terror attack in U.S. history until the 9/11 attacks of 2001. Americans had grown accustomed to the idea that terrorism existed but tended to see terrorists as foreigners—as was true in the attempt to bomb the World Trade Center in 1993. The prospect that paramilitary survivalists, not international terrorists, would destroy U.S. buildings was difficult to absorb. Domestic terrorism, once a vaguely defined threat, had become a reality of American life and an entirely realistic fear.

In the aftermath of the bombing, President Clinton promised a "swift, certain, and severe" response.[9] Despite the fact that law enforcement officers had nothing more than a police sketch to go on, justice would be extremely swift. At 10:20 A.M. on April 19, slightly more than an hour after the bombing, an Oklahoma Highway Patrol officer spotted McVeigh's yellow 1977 Mercury Marquis on I-35 north of Oklahoma City. At the time he had no idea who McVeigh was, but the car had no tag, and McVeigh, who had no proof of ownership, made the mistake of leaving the car with a firearm concealed under his jacket. The officer arrested McVeigh on vehicle and firearm charges and locked him in a jail in Perry, Oklahoma. Two days later the FBI ascertained McVeigh's identity and tracked him to the Oklahoma jail, where he was still awaiting trial on the misdemeanor charges. In June 1997, McVeigh was convicted of orchestrating the bombing and sentenced to death; he was executed in June 2001. Terry Nichols, a fellow veteran and paramilitary terrorist who had helped McVeigh build the bomb, was sentenced to life in prison. Michael Fortier, who helped conceal the plot but played no other direct role and later assisted in the cases against McVeigh and Nichols, was sentenced to 12 years in prison.

The Bombers

As 1993 was the year that young McVeigh fully descended into the world of domestic terrorism, it was also the year that a more experienced domestic terrorist returned to the scene. In the late 1950s, Theodore Kaczynski had been a promising student at Harvard University, which he attended after his graduation from high school at the age of 16. A lonely and socially awkward young man to begin with, Kaczynski agreed to submit to three years of experimental military stress tests that very likely loosened his tenuous grip on sanity.[10] Although he went on to earn a master's degree and Ph.D. in mathematics from the University of Michigan, where he received a fellowship from the National Science Foundation and quickly became one of the nation's leading experts on geometric function theory, his brilliance as a scholar was equaled only by his difficulties as a teacher. After accepting a position at the University of California at Berkeley, he grew frustrated and resigned after only two years, moving away in 1969 to a cabin in the Montana wilderness that would remain his home for nearly 25 years.

Kaczynski kept a low profile, so he was not a suspect in the 12 mail bomb attacks that took place between 1978 and 1987, injuring 20 people and killing one. The bombs, which initially targeted university professors and airlines, prompted law enforcement officials to refer to the attacks using the code "UNABOM" ("UNiversity and Airline BOMber")—and later to refer to the perpetrator as "the Unabomber." After he was spotted in February 1987, and a now-famous police sketch of a mustachioed man in aviator sunglasses and a hooded sweatshirt began to surface, the Unabomber vanished for six years. When he returned on June 22, 1993, his mail bomb severely injured the world-renowned University of California geneticist Charles Epstein. Two days later, Yale University computer scientist David Gelernter was also seriously injured. The bombings continued, killing New York advertising executive Thomas Mosser (targeted for his work with Exxon) in December 1994 and Gilbert Murray of the California Forestry Association in April 1995. Fear of the Unabomber was widespread and profound and clearly led Kaczynski to believe that he was in a good position to make demands.

On April 24, 1995, the same day as Murray's death, the *New York Times* and the *Washington Post* received letters from the Unabomber promising to halt the bombings if his 35,000-word manifesto was published. The newspapers printed the tract, entitled *Industrial Society and Its Future*, on September 19, 1995. The manifesto's bleak but lucid argument was that technology, and especially further advancements in computing, would eventually reduce humanity to a dependent, pointless, and utterly valueless state. David Kaczynski recognized his brother's arguments and alerted law enforcement authorities, who compared the manifesto with samples of Theodore Kaczynski's writing and concluded that they came from the same author. In April 1996, Theodore Kaczynski was arrested. After a long and convoluted trial that involved numerous client-attorney disputes and an abortive attempt at an insanity defense, Kaczynski pleaded guilty in January 1998 and was sentenced to life in prison.

After the McVeigh and Kaczynski arrests, Americans had reason to feel confident that law enforcement authorities were well situated in their attempts to combat domestic terrorism. This confidence was called into question following the bomb attack at the 1996 Summer Olympics held in Atlanta, Georgia. On July 27, 1996, a security guard named Richard Jewell discovered a pipe bomb concealed under sound equipment at Atlanta, Georgia's new Centennial Olympic Park and alerted law enforcement authorities. Partly as a result of Jewell's efforts, the death toll was relatively low for a large-scale terrorist attack—two people were killed and 111 others injured. But four days later, Jewell was identified as a "person of interest" and, implicitly, a potential suspect in the case. His personal life was scrutinized mercilessly as many Americans assumed that he was, in fact, the Olympic Park bomber. In October, the Department of Justice finally exonerated him and issued a formal apology. Jewell later sued various news organizations successfully for libel and has moved on with his life.

But in the course of exonerating Jewell, federal authorities were forced to admit that they had no viable suspects in the bombing. The real bomber, Eric Rudolph, was free to strike again. Rudolph had served in the U.S. armed forces, but he was dishonorably discharged for smoking marijuana and never rose above the rank of private. A white supremacist, he was also a religious fanatic who had associated with the right-wing Christian Identity movement and referred to himself as the Army of God.

In January 1997, a bomb exploded at the Northside Family Planning Clinic in Sandy Springs, Georgia, wounding seven. Law enforcement officials, noting similarities between this bomb and the Olympic Park pipe bomb, believed that the same criminal set both, but nobody had managed to get a good look at the suspect before he fled. A month later, a similar bomb set outside the Otherside, an Atlanta lesbian bar, yielded similar results—five injured and no description of the bomber. Rudolph vanished for 11 months, leaving many to believe that the Olympic Park bomber had gotten away with murder.

And he probably would have if his attacks had ended there, but Rudolph could not resist the opportunity to kill again. On January 29, 1998, the New Women All Woman Clinic in Birmingham, Alabama, was bombed. An off-duty police officer was killed instantly by the blast, and a nurse was maimed and crippled for life. This time, however, Rudolph would not slip away. A witness wrote down his license plate number, which was traced to his name and address, and a warrant was issued for his arrest. The Olympic Park bomber had finally been identified. Rudolph was able to evade law enforcement authorities until May 2003, when a rookie police officer spotted him scrounging through garbage behind a grocery store and a sheriff's deputy identified him from the FBI's Ten Most Wanted poster. In April 2005, Rudolph agreed to plead guilty and reveal information about other domestic terrorist activities in exchange for a sentence of four consecutive life terms.

Mandatory Sentencing

The high crime rates and high levels of public fear in the late 1980s and early 1990s prompted substantial changes in the operations of the criminal justice system. These factors contributed to ongoing efforts by politicians to deter crime by passing more punitive sentencing laws and by providing more support for police and law enforcement officials.

By 1994, almost every state as well as the federal government had adopted some form of mandatory sentencing law. These laws assumed a variety of forms, but all proposed that longer prison terms would help reduce crime. Also, all represented reactions against the more flexible indeterminate sentences characteristic of the middle of the 20th century. Most commonly, state legislatures and Congress established mandatory minimum sentences requiring that convicted offenders serve a certain number of years before becoming eligible for parole. Mandatory minimums tended to be associated with nonviolent drug offenses and often connected the required sentence with the amount of drugs involved in the case. By the mid-1990s, the federal criminal justice system had more than 100 specific mandatory minimum laws. The result has been a much more rigid sentencing system, with arbitrary "cliffs" for drug offenses. For example, in the mid-1990s federal guidelines mandated that possessing five grams of crack cocaine was punishable with no more than one year in prison, but possessing 5.01 grams was punishable with at least five years in prison.[11]

Truth-in-sentencing laws are a variation on mandatory minimums. These required that prisoners serve their full sentences before being freed. Again, they represented a reaction against indeterminate sentences, which were often perceived as allowing offenders to be released on parole and thereby get off easy or have opportunities to commit further crimes. Truth-in-sentencing laws ensured that criminals would serve the time sentenced. These laws also, however, added difficulties for corrections officials. Without the possibility of parole, prisoners no longer had an incentive to cooperate and to earn consideration for good behavior. Moreover, these new laws also contributed to prison overcrowding, because corrections officials no longer had the mechanism of parole to manage their inmate populations.

"Three strikes and you're out" rules were the most famous of these get tough initiatives. These rules varied by state, but, in essence, "three strikes" laws increased prison sentences for second major offenses and mandated life in prison for offenders who committed three felonies. In March 1994, the California assembly approved one of the first three strikes laws in the United States, sentencing any adult convicted of a third serious felony to prison for 25 years to life; by 1999 24 states had implemented similar programs. Three strikes laws remained one of the most controversial elements of the 1990s criminal justice reforms. Advocates claimed that these laws contributed to sharp drops in crime in the latter half of the decade, while opponents cited cases in which offenders who had committed comparatively minor crimes were sentenced to prison for life. More neutral scholars pointed out that three strikes laws also eliminated the incentive for defendants to plea bargain and therefore helped generate a sharp increase in the number of nonviolent third-time offenders going to trial—further glutting an already overburdened court system.

Federal Crime Policy

The federal government also became increasingly involved in criminal justice in the 1990s. In 1993, Congress enacted the Brady Handgun Violence Prevention Act, requiring a background check and five-day waiting period for all people attempting to purchase handguns. Named for James Brady, Ronald Reagan's press secretary, who had been seriously wounded during the 1981 assassination attempt on the president, the bill had been introduced numerous times in the late 1980s and early 1990s but always opposed successfully by the National Rifle Association (NRA), which claimed that the law would do little to stop criminals from acquiring guns but would hinder legitimate customers. By 1993, the early 1990s crime wave and the support of newly elected President Bill Clinton allowed the bill to become law. The law required that handguns would be denied to people with such disqualifications as criminal records and histories of mental illness. In 1998, instant background checks replaced the five-day waiting period.[12]

Clinton had made crime a core issue in his 1992 campaign for president. He promised to put 100,000 more police officers on the street if elected, and he followed through when he signed the Violent Crime Control and Law Enforcement Act in September 1994. This new law provided more than $8.8 billion in grant money to local and state law enforcement agencies to hire additional officers and strongly endorsed the principle of community policing. It also enacted a federal "three strikes" policy and substantially expanded the federal offenses that warranted the death penalty to include terrorism, organizing the international drug trade, and the murder of federal law enforcement officials; it was under this last provision that Timothy McVeigh would be executed.[13]

In the 1990s, legislators and concerned citizens also developed new ways to use criminal laws to address particular social concerns. For example, in response to a growing concern about hate crimes, Congress enacted the Hate Crime Statistics Act of 1990. This law assigned the FBI's Uniform Crime Reporting (UCR) Program to collect data about crimes that demonstrated evidence of prejudice based on race, religion, sexual orientation, or ethnicity; in 1994, the Violent Crime Control and Law Enforcement Act added disabilities to this list. Hate crimes were defined not as separate, distinct crimes but rather as traditional offenses motivated by the offender's bias. Many states sought to add additional penalties if offenses fell under the definition of a hate crime. Hate crimes statutes were controversial, however. Critics charged that they targeted behaviors that were illegal already but punished them more severely if they were based on particular motives. Hate crime laws gained national attention in 1998 following the gruesome murder of 21-year-old gay college student Matthew Shepard outside Laramie, Wyoming, by two young men who targeted him for his sexual orientation. Both attackers were convicted for murder, but the killing generated widespread demands for additional penalties based on both the horrific nature of the crime and the prejudice that generated it.

Attacks on children also became the subjects of a new wave of legislation in the 1990s. After seven-year-old Megan Kanka was raped and murdered near her Hamilton Township, New Jersey, home in July 1994 by a neighbor already twice convicted of sexual offenses, her family launched a campaign for new laws requiring states to notify communities about the presence of sex offenders. The first of these so-called Megan's Laws went into effect in New Jersey in October 1994. It required convicted sex offenders to register with local police, who then informed communities of their presence based on an evaluation of their potential threat. While the New Jersey law and its equivalents elsewhere were again controversial—critics argued that they placed additional punishments on offenders who had already paid their debts to society and thereby violated the "double jeopardy" clause of the Fifth Amendment—they withstood legal challenges. In 1996, President Clinton signed a federal Megan's Law, requiring every state to create a means of notifying the public about the location of sex offenders.

At the same time, the 1990s also saw some activists demanding a more libertarian approach to criminal justice. Critics of the ongoing war on drugs, for example, advocated relaxing some drug laws and even legalizing some drugs. Marijuana in particular, perhaps the most widespread and least dangerous illegal drug, benefited from this movement. Advocates argued that marijuana had extensive practical and medicinal uses, including providing some relief for people suffering from cancer and AIDS. In November 1996, voters in California approved Proposition 215, a statewide ballot initiative that amended state law to permit persons to grow or possess marijuana for medical use when recommended by a physician. This law inspired few imitators and contradicted federal statutes but nonetheless perhaps signaled a softening in the war on drugs.

Getting Tough on Crime

The overall thrust of criminal justice in the 1990s, however, was toward punishing more offenders more severely. Nowhere was this more evident than in corrections. Between 1990 and 2000, the number of persons incarcerated in federal and state prisons increased from about 739,000 to 1,331,000; the rate per 100,000 U.S. residents increased from 297 to 469.[14] Including local jails as well as federal and state prisons, nearly 2 million people were incarcerated in 2000, or 691 per

100,000 residents.[15] And including persons on probation or parole in this total demonstrates that nearly 6.5 million people were under some form of correctional supervision in 2000.[16] In addition, prisoners were disproportionately drawn from minority groups. In 2000, 45 percent of inmates in federal and state prisons were African Americans, and 15 percent were Hispanics.[17] Furthermore, violent crimes accounted for a comparatively small portion of this growth. Instead, at the federal level more that 56 percent of the prison population in 2000 was under sentence for drug offenses.[18]

This expansion in inmate populations fostered tremendous expansion in prisons. Most communities traditionally had opposed prisons being located near them, but in the 1990s towns in economically depressed regions such as northern New York actively lobbied for prison construction near them; prisons seemed to offer job security and economic stimulus.[19] By the mid-1990s, more than 5,000 correctional facilities operated across the United States, including more than 3,000 local jails. California alone added 21 new prisons between 1984 and 1999 and became the nation's largest correctional system, with an annual budget of more than $4 billion.[20]

Some states responded to the need for more cells and inmate beds by turning to the private sector for help. By the mid-1990s, more than 30 states used privately operated prisons to hold their inmates or contracted their inmates' labor to private companies. A fascination with privatizing and deregulating the economy dating from the 1980s helped foster this turn toward the growth of loosely regulated, for-profit prison companies in the 1990s. At the same time, some states turned toward building super maximum security, or "supermax," prisons for the most prominent and toughest offenders. These offered extraordinary security and, in many cases, 23-hour-a-day solitary confinement. In 1994, the Federal Bureau of Prisons opened its first supermax prison in Florence, Colorado; it housed prominent figures such as Timothy McVeigh, Theodore Kaczynski, and World Trade Center bomber Ramzi Yousef.[21]

The 1990s also witnessed the expanded use of the death penalty. At the time 38 states had death penalty laws, and public support for the death penalty remained strong. In 1994, a Gallup poll showed that an all-time high of 80 percent of Americans supported the death penalty.[22] The number of persons under sentence of death increased by more than 50 percent in the 1990s, from 2,356 in 1990 to 3,601 in 2000. The number of people actually executed paled in comparison to the number on death row, but even so, executions also increased rapidly in this decade, from 23 in 1990 to a post-moratorium high of 98 in 1999.[23] Across the board, the criminal justice system became much tougher in the 1990s.

Crime in the Cities

In the early 1990s, crime—particularly homicide—was concentrated in urban areas. This pattern contrasted sharply with U.S. history prior to the late 1950s, when cities generally had lower murder rates than rural areas. Nonetheless, by the end of the 20th century, U.S. cities had become much more commonly the sites for drug-related and gang-related killings, and the results are evident in the numbers. Between 1976 and 2002, more than half of all homicides in the United States occurred in cities with a population of 100,000 or more, and almost one-quarter took place in cities with a population of more than 1 million. For most of this period, the biggest cities had the highest homicide rates. In 1994, the peak year in the murder boom, cities with a population of more than 1 million had homicide rates of more than 28 per 100,000 residents, while the nation as a whole had approximately 10 killings per 100,000.[24]

Homicide trends in the early 1990s also varied according to gender, race, and age. As has been the case throughout U.S. history, men represented a large majority of both victims and perpetrators. African Americans also represented a disproportionate share of homicide victims and perpetrators. In 1994, blacks were seven times more likely than whites to be murdered and nine times more likely to commit murder. In addition, much of the spike in homicide in the early 1990s was driven by young people, particularly those between ages 14 and 24. While the homicide rate for other age groups remained flat or even declined in the early 1990s, homicide rates for these ages nearly doubled from their 1980s levels. Combining these factors, homicide rates among African-American males between ages 18 and 24 reached extraordinary levels in the early 1990s. In 1994, 176 of every 100,000 young black males became victims of murder, and 337 per 100,000 committed it.[25]

These astonishing homicide rates generated a public debate over both causes and solutions. Political scientist John J. DiIulio, Jr., famously argued in 1995 that these killers could be understood as a new generation of "superpredators," qualitatively different from anything previous. He suggested that a substantial portion of the largest generation of children in U.S. history were being raised in what he characterized as "moral poverty . . . the poverty of growing up surrounded by deviant, delinquent, and criminal adults in abusive, violence-ridden, fatherless, Godless, and jobless settings," all of which crossed racial, ethnic, and religious boundaries. DiIulio's analysis led to a conclusion that governments should, on the one hand, develop policies that encouraged two-parent families and stronger religious orientations, and on the other, expand the use of incarceration for those who had already become criminals.[26]

By contrast, Carnegie Mellon University criminologist Alfred Blumstein argued that more concrete factors were at work in the homicide boom. He maintained that the sharp increase in homicide by young males after 1985 could be correlated with "changes in illegal drug markets associated with the introduction of crack cocaine."[27] To accommodate the increased demand for the low-cost new drug in inner cities, drug distributors recruited juveniles as new sellers. These new drug dealers, often organized in gangs, carried firearms for self-protection. Firearms, according to Blumstein, rapidly diffused to other urban teenagers who had to protect themselves in an increasingly hostile environment, and these young people, already full of recklessness and bravado but lacking experience in resolving disputes, increasingly resorted to firearms to settle the conflicts that inevitably emerged among them. When homicide rates fell sharply in the late 1990s, particularly among young people, Blumstein's arguments seemed confirmed. In the late 1990s, demand for crack declined, and the drug market stabilized; the economy improved, offering more conventional job opportunities for young people; many of the original perpetrators had been incarcerated or killed; cities made extensive efforts to remove guns from the hands of juveniles; and communities rallied to recapture their neighborhoods from violent criminals.[28] By 2000, the overall U.S. homicide rate had dropped more than 40 percent from its early 1990s peak, and it was down almost 38 percent among young black males.[29]

Perhaps the most famous campaign against crime and violence in the 1990s took place in New York City under the leadership of Mayor Rudy Giuliani and Police Commissioner William J. Bratton. They derived their strategy from the thinking of criminologist George Kelling and his collaborators, who advocated what became known as the "broken windows" model of policing. According to this idea, deteriorating neighborhood conditions, such as broken windows and run-down housing, promoted fear and encouraged crime. If police, cooperating with citizens, worked to improve the neighborhood and restore order, they could also reduce crime.[30] The NYPD under Giuliani implemented these ideas by policing minor crimes that supposedly undermined New Yorkers' quality of life, enforcing laws against sleeping outdoors, jumping subway turnstiles, panhandling, jaywalking, and squeegeeing the windows of cars entering the city. Bratton also implemented a computerized program tracking incidents of crime in the city and established precinct-by-precinct goals for reducing crime. Between the early 1990s and the early 2000s, New York went from being one of the most dangerous cities in the United States to one of the safest.[31] While this could have had more to do with economic factors than policy changes, the outcome lent credibility to the "broken window" theory.

School Shootings and Tougher Juvenile Justice

In the 1990s, in the wake of this wave of crime and violence by young people, many states passed laws intended to toughen their juvenile justice systems by making it easier to transfer juveniles into adult criminal courts. Prosecutors such as San Diego's Peter Deddeh echoed the "superpredator" rhetoric of the day by arguing in 1996 that "our juvenile justice system was created at a time of 'Leave it to Beaver' type crimes, less sophisticated and not incredibly violent. But what we see now is kids who have never been socialized properly . . . who are real predators."[32] Almost every Republican gubernatorial candidate of the mid-1990s embraced the issue of juvenile justice reform, adopting the slogan that teenagers should do "adult time for adult crime."[33] At least 43 states revised their juvenile justice laws between 1995 and 1999 to facilitate transferring juveniles to adult courts. As a result, in 1998, nearly 200,000 people under age 18 were tried in adult courts, and roughly 18,000 were housed in adult prisons.[34]

Immediately upon assuming the Pennsylvania governor's office in January 1995, Tom Ridge called a special session of the state legislature to address the problem of juvenile crime. The session resulted in a series of laws revising the state's juvenile justice system and culminated in Act 33, which altered the system's fundamental assumptions. This law shifted the purpose of the state's juvenile courts from the traditional goals of prevention, treatment, and rehabilitation to a new balance of protecting the community, imposing accountability for offenses, and developing competencies in young offenders. In other words, rather than attempting mainly to reform young offenders, the 1995 law made rehabilitation one of three equal goals, along with imposing punishment and protecting potential victims. More concretely, Act 33 established mechanisms to automatically transfer offenders between ages 15 and 17 accused of one of eight violent crimes into adult criminal courts; they could still petition to return to juvenile courts, but adult criminal courts would have first jurisdiction.[35]

A variety of studies suggested that these revisions in Pennsylvania and nationwide had the typical outcomes of most efforts to make criminal justice tougher. Minorities were disproportionately represented among offenders to whom the new adult transfer rules applied, crime and recidivism were affected to negligible degrees, and a handful of offenders whose culpability for their crimes and understanding of the process were doubtful found themselves ensnared in the system. In Florida, for example, when six-year-old Tiffany Eunick died in 2000 after roughhousing with 12-year-old, 166-pound African-American Lionel Tate, a grand jury indicted Tate as an adult. After Tate's family rejected a plea bargain, the jury, who had no option of transfer to juvenile court or convicting on a lesser charge, convicted Tate of first-degree murder, which carried an automatic sentence of life in prison. The Tate verdict subsequently prompted Florida legislators to consider whether they should build more flexibility into their system. In Michigan, the October 1997 murder of 18-year-old Ronnie Greene, Jr., by 11-year-old Nathaniel Abraham forced that state also to revisit its new juvenile justice laws. Abraham, four feet nine inches tall, 65 pounds, and black, had been practicing shooting a rifle near a cluster of trees when one of his bullets fatally hit Greene in the head. Abraham claimed that the killing was an accident, but prosecutors did not believe him and put him on trial for murder, making him the youngest person in U.S. history known to be charged with homicide. In the end, Abraham was convicted, but Judge Eugene A. Moore, faced with the choice of imposing a life sentence in adult prison, referring him to juvenile corrections to be released at age 21, or imposing a blend of adult and juvenile sentences, opted to sentence Abraham as a juvenile. This decision suggested that Judge Moore, if not the public, still had faith in the capacity of the juvenile justice system to rehabilitate young offenders.[36]

By the late 1990s, public attention focused not so much on run-of-the-mill atrocities, such as those of Tate and Abraham, nor on faceless urban youths killing each other over drug deals, but on spectacular mass killings by white teenagers. Every few months, it seemed, a new tragedy would make national news and rivet the American public. In October 1997, Mississippi 16-year-old Luke Woodham killed his mother, then drove to his school and shot nine students, killing two. In December of that year, 14-year-old Michael Carneal shot eight students in Paducah, Kentucky, killing five. In March 1998, 13-year-old Mitchell Johnson and 11-year-old Drew Golden stole four handguns and three rifles from Golden's grandfather, went to their elementary school, pulled the fire alarm, and, as teachers and students marched out, began shooting from an ambush position overlooking the school. They killed four students and one teacher. Two months later, in May 1998, 16-year-old Kip Kinkel was expelled from his Springfield, Oregon, high school for possessing a firearm. That night, he used the gun to kill his parents and the next day returned to his school and shot 25 people, killing two.

This flurry culminated on April 20, 1999, when Dylan Klebold, age 17, and Eric Harris, age 18, carried out the worst school massacre in U.S. history until that time, killing 12 students and a teacher at Columbine High School in Littleton, Colorado, before taking their own lives. The two boys had been alienated at school, ostracized by the popular cliques, and had found refuge in action movies, violent video games, and goth music. They came to school that day with the intention of killing as many classmates as possible and using explosives to destroy the building, but their plans went awry; they ended up committing suicide to avoid capture. The Columbine killings riveted the nation—as with many confrontations of the 1990s, efforts by police SWAT teams to rescue trapped students and teachers were broadcast on television—and prompted tremendous public discussion about the sources of youth violence. People blamed youth culture, inattentive parenting, gender, brain chemistry, and above all the media. More so than any other event of the 1990s, the Columbine killings put the nature and sources of youthful violence on the public agenda.

At the same time, the flurry of discussion generated by Columbine was out of place. While massacres committed by white teenagers captured public attention, a disproportionate share of youth violence in the 1990s involved inner-city minority youth, as both perpetrators and victims. Moreover, while the get-tough laws of the 1990s were perhaps inspired by foreboding over young urban criminals and found their poster children in youths such as Kip Kinkel (who was prosecuted and convicted as an adult), these laws had only a marginal relationship to these spectacular crimes. Finally and most important, by the time the Columbine massacre took place, U.S. homicide rates had begun a sharp descent from their highs in the early 1990s, reaching a 30-year low in the early 2000s. At least in terms of national measures of crime, at the beginning of the 21st century, America was becoming a much safer country. American public opinion began to reflect this reality as well, perhaps because a new threat had emerged.

The Threat of International Terrorism

The United States has long been subject to international terrorist attacks, but as technology increased, so did the scale of potential damage. If regarded as a single coordinated attack, the terrorist suicide hijackings of September 11, 2001, which

In this photograph, firefighters respond to the September 11, 2001, terrorist attacks on the World Trade Center. *(Library of Congress Prints and Photographs Division [LC-DIG- PPMSCA-02139])*

claimed the lives of 2,993 people, were by far the deadliest terrorist attack in the history of the world until that time. No other earlier civilian attack even comes close. The second deadliest previous terrorist attack up to that time, the 1978 firebombing of an Iranian theater, claimed 477 lives, a horrific number of casualties, to be sure, but a figure dwarfed by the coordinated attacks that Americans came to refer to collectively as "9/11."

The 9/11 attacks were orchestrated by al-Qaeda (Arabic: "the base"), one of the most sophisticated international terrorist networks ever devised. Headed by the wealthy Saudi and former leader in the Afghan resistance Osama bin Laden, al-Qaeda's ideology represented a violent and militant branch of Wahhabism, a Sunni tradition that adheres to an extremely conservative, antimodernist ideology and emphasizes the holiness of the Saudi cities of Mecca and Medina. According to al-Qaeda, the world had been defiled by the soulless secular Western nations, which in the organization's view had oppressed the poor, threatened to dilute and ultimately eliminate traditional Muslim faith, and defiled Islamic holy sites. The chief enemy of al-Qaeda was the United States, which—because of its wealth, influence, support for Israel, and military presence in the Middle East—terrorist leaders perceived as the worst offender.

What made al-Qaeda more dangerous than any other terrorist organization was its ability to use a combination of technology and suicide bombing to coordinate intricate, sometimes simultaneous, attacks. The synchronized April 1998 bombings of U.S. embassies in Kenya and Tanzania, which claimed 303 lives, established al-Qaeda as a clear international threat; the October 2000 bombing of the USS *Cole* in Yemen, which claimed the lives of 17 U.S. Navy personnel, established that al-Qaeda would not limit its operations to vulnerable targets, but both of these attacks would be dwarfed by the ambitious coordinated 9/11 attacks.

Although the 9/11 attacks had been in the planning stages for years, they were executed in less than 90 minutes. Five terrorists armed with box-cutters hijacked American Airlines Flight 11 flying out of Boston at 8:13 A.M. Five more terrorists armed with box-cutters hijacked United Airlines Flight 175 also out of Boston at 8:43 A.M. At 8:46 A.M., just three minutes later, American Flight 11 crashed into the north tower of the World Trade Center in New York City. At 9:02 A.M., United Flight 175 crashed into the south tower of the World Trade Center. In less than an hour, 10 al-Qaeda militants had committed acts resulting in their own deaths, the deaths of 2,739 others, and the destruction of a major U.S. landmark. Within minutes, a third hijacked plane—American Airlines Flight 77 flying from Washington Dulles airport, crashed into the Pentagon, claiming 184 lives, and a fourth, United Airlines Flight 93 out of Newark, New Jersey, crashed into the ground near Shanksville, Pennsylvania, after passengers attempted to retake the plane.

Criminal Justice Reform After 9/11

The sophistication of the 9/11 attacks prompted considerable U.S. criminal justice reform. Most significant was the United and Strengthening America by Providing Appropriate Tools Required to Intercept and Obstruct Terrorism (USA PATRIOT) Act of 2001, signed into law just six weeks after the attacks. The sweeping 342-page bill passed in the Senate by a 98-1 margin and in the House by 357–66.

Many of the changes made under the USA PATRIOT Act made obvious sense. Many earlier laws governing surveillance of foreign nationals mandated that they could be investigated only if they served a nation; authorization was expanded to include terrorists not specifically serving a nation. Material support of terrorist organizations became a crime, allowing the federal government to pursue al-Qaeda's U.S.-based income streams. Federal intelligence organizations were given new channels through which they could share intelligence data. The legislation also included controversial provisions allowing warrantless search of library records, "roving wiretaps" authorized by secret courts, and relaxation of standards needed to obtain secret warrants for wiretapping. Some of these concerns were addressed in a revised version of the bill, which passed in 2006.

President George W. Bush's administration also established a massive new Department of Homeland Security (DHS) to address domestic emergencies, including (but not limited to) terrorist attacks. Although the Department of Homeland Security has been effective in many respects, it was best known in the years following the 9/11 attacks for the Homeland Security Advisory System (HEAS) alert system, which ranked the likelihood of terrorist attacks on a color-coded scale ranging from severe (red) to low (green). Homeland Security benefited from a series of funding bills, ultimately becoming the third-largest cabinet department in the executive branch (behind only the Departments of Defense and Veterans Affairs).

Many of the Bush administration's attempts to respond to the 9/11 attacks violated federal law or previously established constitutional standards. Most notable was the Terrorist Surveillance Program (TSP), its existence made public by the *New York Times* in December 2005, through which the Bush administration conducted surveillance on an unknown number of suspects without warrants or other judicial oversight, in violation of the Foreign Intelligence Surveillance Act (FISA) of 1978. In early 2007, the Bush administration discontinued the warrantless surveillance program and stated that any similar telephone surveillance would in future be conducted through legal channels.

Civil libertarians were even more concerned with the prospect of the Defense Advanced Research Project Area's Total Information Awareness (TIA) program, funded by the U.S. Department of Defense (DOD) in 2002 and 2003, which was established to create a universal information database—the equivalent of possessing FBI files on every U.S. citizen. The program was discontinued in 2003. In later years, the American Civil Liberties Union (ACLU) and other groups uncovered evidence that the FBI had been collecting extensive information on a variety of antiwar groups (including several monastic orders) under the auspices of antiterror investigations. Civil liberties groups also uncovered evidence of vast racial and religious profiling in the aftermath of 9/11, as American Muslims and Arab Americans were often targeted by law enforcement agencies.

The new emphasis on international terrorism created a new dilemma for the Bush administration: How should terrorists be classified? After the United States invaded Afghanistan in late 2001 (in response to the Taliban government's decision to host and train al-Qaeda cells), it captured 775 foreign nationals and held them at Guantánamo Bay Naval Base in Cuba. These prisoners were not considered foreign soldiers and therefore did not receive prisoner-of-war human rights protections under the Geneva Conventions, but they were also not U.S. citizens, so they did not receive protection under the Constitution. The Bush administration ultimately defined these new prisoners as "enemy combatants." The U.S. Supreme Court, however, ultimately rejected this designation in its *Hamdan v. Rumsfeld* (2006) ruling, in which it stated that enemy combatants, whether they are formally affiliated with another nation or not, are protected by international treaties agreed upon by the United States. Congress passed the Military Tribunals Act of 2006 in response to the *Hamdan* ruling, establishing a new military tribunal system to try accused terrorists. In 2008, however, the Supreme Court ruled that Guantánamo Bay detainees had the right to habeas corpus and, implicitly, to access to U.S. courts

The U.S. response was not so straightforward at times, however. In early 2006 a study by Seton Hall University law professor Mark Denbeaux determined that only 8 percent of Guantánamo Bay prisoners had actually been accused of taking up arms for al-Qaeda. The vast majority were imprisoned at Guantánamo Bay due to associations with suspected terrorists. The detention policy was, in other words, one of guilt by association.[37] The United States also came under fire for classifying two U.S. citizens, Jose Padilla and Yasser Hamdi, as enemy combatants, though they were later reclassified after several federal court rulings. Finally, and perhaps most distressingly, widespread evidence of U.S. torture directed against foreign nationals emerged, most notably at Abu Ghraib Prison in Baghdad, Iraq, in which U.S. personnel subjected an unknown number of prisoners (most arrested for offenses unrelated to terrorism) to severe physical torture and sexual humiliation. President Bush later admitted in a September 2006 speech that the CIA had held numerous suspected terrorists in secret prisons worldwide and subjected them to controversial interrogation methods, though he refused to elaborate on what the specific methods might have been.

Although post-9/11 civil liberties abuses appeared shocking by contemporary standards, they were fairly pedestrian by historical standards. Governments have traditionally responded to new threats by violating civil liberties, and the U.S. government has represented no exception to this rule. What perhaps makes the United States and other liberal democracies remarkable, in this respect, is that such civil liberties violations tend to inspire strong public resistance and ultimately prove temporary.

Internet Crime and Identity Theft

According to U.S. Census estimates, only 18 percent of U.S. households had Internet access in 1997. By 2003, the share had jumped to 55 percent. With this dramatic increase in Internet usage came a dramatic increase in Internet crime, as the number of potential victims and potential perpetrators increased.

In the early years of the Internet, computer hackers wrote and spread malicious and self-replicating code—viruses—more as a prank than as a conscious crime. Although the Blaster/LOVESAN e-mail virus of 2003 was significant in scope, infecting approximately 25 million computers, its function was ultimately to send anti-Microsoft e-mails and overload server traffic at windowsupdate.com.[38]

By the end of 2005, the function of e-mail viruses had noticeably shifted—an estimated 80 percent threatened the confidentiality of personal information.[39] The most common Internet crime in the mid-2000s was phishing, in which criminals and would-be criminals attempted to acquire personal information through the use of deceptive e-mails. Most often these e-mails appeared to match those sent by electronic vendors, banks, and other innocent third parties and request that the user "confirm" credit card, bank account, or other personal information by sending it to well-disguised criminals, who then used that information to their own advantage. According to the Symantec Internet Security Threat Report, an average of 7.9 million confirmed e-mail phishing attempts were made daily between July and December 2005.[40]

Phishing was only one of many means of identity theft, or identity fraud, in which a criminal obtained personal information—usually credit card numbers, but sometimes bank account or even social security numbers—and used that information to steal funds, to commit crimes in the victim's name, to harm the victim's financial standing, or to cause other injury. According to a 2006 study, identity theft in the United States claimed $56.6 billion dollars per year at an average of $6,383 per victim.

Because the general public became more skeptical about simple e-mail phishing attempts by the mid-2000s, some savvy thieves turned to "trojan horses," "bots," or "spyware," which infected the user's computer and recorded keystrokes, sometimes transmitting confidential information, such as bank account and credit card numbers, to criminals. One of the most notorious cases involved the 2005 arrest of a Brazilian "phishing kingpin" who allegedly stole as much as 100 million reais ($37 million) through the use of "trojan horse" spy software distributed through e-mail attachments.

The Internet has been used as a venue for countless other crimes as well. Criminal syndicates and terrorist groups frequently used the Internet to recruit new members and conduct business. Virtually all kinds of criminal mercenaries, from prostitutes to drug dealers to hit men, used the relative privacy and anonymity of Internet communication to their advantage. Pedophiles collected and distributed child pornography online, and child molesters searched online social networking sites in hopes of luring new potential victims. Although law enforcement agencies became far savvier in dealing with Internet crime during the early 2000s, the Internet's nature as a massive and largely anonymous information-based medium has provided unparalleled opportunities for many criminals. As was the case with automobiles in the early 20th century, the criminal justice system has not yet adopted the techniques needed to meet the challenges posed by criminals who use state-of-the-art technology.

Chronicle of Events

1992

Following the mandate of the Hate Crimes Statistics Act of 1990, the FBI begins tracking hate crimes.

1993

- *February 26:* A car bomb planted by the Islamic terrorist group al-Qaeda explodes in the parking garage underneath the World Trade Center in New York City, killing six people and injuring more than 1,000.
- *February 28:* The Bureau of Alcohol, Tobacco, and Firearms (ATF) raids a ranch near Waco, Texas, occupied by the Branch Davidian religious sect. Resistance leads to the deaths of four agents and six Davidians and a subsequent 51-day siege of the ranch.
- *April 19:* An FBI assault on the Branch Davidian complex in Waco, Texas, results in fires that destroy the ranch and kill 76 people inside, including 27 children.

- *November 30:* The Brady Handgun Violence Prevention Act (Brady Law) is signed into federal law by President Bill Clinton, requiring federally licensed firearms dealers to conduct background checks before selling a gun and prohibiting firearms sales to criminals, the mentally ill, drug users, and other groups.

1994

- *June 12:* Nicole Brown Simpson, former wife of football player and actor O. J. Simpson, is murdered outside her Los Angeles home together with a friend, Ronald Goldman.
- *June 17:* After an arrest warrant for the murders of Nicole Simpson and Ronald Goldman is issued against O. J. Simpson, he briefly flees in his white Ford Bronco S.U.V., only to be pursued by police in a nationally televised slow speed chase. Simpson eventually surrenders to police.
- *July 29:* Megan Kanka, age seven, is raped and murdered by a convicted sex offender living in her New Jersey neighborhood.

The Clinton (left) and Gore (right) families represented a new generation of post–World War II national politicians. *(Library of Congress Prints and Photographs Division [LC-USZ62-107301])*

- *October 31:* The first "Megan's Law" goes into effect in New Jersey, requiring public notification when a sex offender moves into a neighborhood.
- *September 13:* President Bill Clinton signs the Violent Crime Control and Law Enforcement Act of 1994 into law.

1995

- *April 19:* A truck bomb destroys the Alfred P. Murrah Federal Building in Oklahoma City, Oklahoma, killing 168 people, including 19 children. Timothy McVeigh, arrested that same day for a routine traffic stop, is later charged with the crime.
- *September 19:* The *Washington Post* and the *New York Times* jointly publish *Industrial Society and Its Future*, a manifesto by the terrorist suspect known as the Unabomber.
- *October 3:* A jury finds O. J. Simpson not guilty of killing Nicole Brown Simpson and Ronald Goldman.
- *November:* The Pennsylvania General Assembly passes Act 33, reorganizing the state's juvenile justice system so that it emphasizes balanced and restorative justice. The new law also defines specific offenses for which juvenile offenders between ages 15 and 17 would be automatically transferred to adult criminal courts.

1996

- *March 20:* Lyle and Erik Menendez are convicted for the shotgun killings of their parents after a much-publicized trial.
- *April 3:* Theodore Kaczynski is arrested in the Unabomber case.
- *May 16:* President Clinton signs a federal "Megan's Law" requiring every state to establish a mechanism to notify the public of the presence of sex offenders.
- *June 18:* A federal grand jury indicts Theodore Kaczynski on 10 charges related to bombings attributed to the Unabomber.
- *July 21:* A bombing at Centennial Olympic Park in Atlanta, Georgia, during the Summer Olympic Games kills one person and injures 111 others.
- *November:* California voters pass Proposition 215, creating an exemption from criminal penalties for medical use of marijuana. It is the first such law in the United States.

1997

- *February 4:* A jury in a civil lawsuit brought against O. J. Simpson by the families of Nicole Brown Simpson and Ronald Goldman finds Simpson liable for their deaths and awards the plaintiffs $8.5 million in damages.

- *February 9:* After eight-month-old Matthew Eappan dies in Massachusetts from injuries consistent with "shaken baby syndrome," his 19-year-old British nanny, Louise Woodward, is arrested.
- *June 2:* Timothy McVeigh is convicted of 11 federal charges resulting from the Oklahoma City bombing.
- *August 9:* Following an arrest, Haitian immigrant Abner Louima is beaten and sodomized by two New York City police officers. The incident generates widespread protest against police brutality.
- *August 14:* Timothy McVeigh is sentenced to death for his role in the Oklahoma City bombing.
- *October 1:* Luke Woodham, age 16, murders his mother in Pearl, Mississippi, then drives to school and shoots nine classmates, killing two, including an ex-girlfriend.
- *October 30:* Following a widely publicized trial, Louise Woodward is convicted of second-degree murder in the death of Matthew Eappan.
- *November 10:* Judge Hiller Zobel reduces the conviction against Louise Woodward to involuntary manslaughter and sentences her to the time she has already served in jail, effectively releasing her.
- *December 1:* Michael Carneal, age 14, shoots eight students at a high school near Paducah, Kentucky, killing five.

1998

- *January 22:* Theodore Kaczynski pleads guilty in the Unabomber case in exchange for a sentence of life in prison without parole rather than the death penalty.
- *March 24:* Mitchell Johnson, 13, and Drew Golden, 11, shoot and kill four students and a teacher at their Jonesboro, Arkansas, middle school.
- *May 20:* After being expelled from his Springfield, Oregon, high school for possessing a gun, 16-year-old Kip Kinkel kills both of his parents.
- *May 21:* Kip Kinkel, age 16, shoots 25 people (killing two) at the Springfield, Oregon, high school he had been expelled from the day before.
- *October 6:* Two men attack and beat 22-year-old Matthew Shepard in Laramie, Wyoming, in what is deemed a hate crime against Shepard on account of his sexual orientation.
- *October 12:* Matthew Shepard, age 22, dies in Laramie, Wyoming, from his injuries.

1999

- *February 4:* Amadou Diallo, an African immigrant, is killed by New York City police officers in a hail of 41 shots outside of his Bronx apartment.

- *April 20:* Teenagers Dylan Klebold and Eric Harris use automatic weapons to attack Columbine High School in Littleton, Colorado, killing 12 fellow students and one teacher before committing suicide.
- *November 16:* In Pontiac, Michigan, Nathaniel Abraham is found guilty of second-degree murder for a crime he committed at age 11 years, 9 months. He is believed to be the youngest American ever tried as an adult and convicted of murder.

2000

- *February 25:* The four New York City police officers facing charges related to the death of Amadou Diallo are found guilty on all criminal counts.

2001

- *June 11:* Timothy McVeigh is executed at the federal penitentiary in Terre Haute, Indiana, for destroying the Alfred P. Murrah Federal Building in Oklahoma City.
- *September 11:* The terrorist group known as al-Qaeda launches a series of terrorist attacks against the United States, hijacking commercial airplanes, destroying the World Trade Center in New York City, and inflicting considerable damage on the Pentagon outside of Washington, D.C. The attacks, the deadliest terrorist attacks in world history, are remembered as "the September 11th attacks" or simply "9/11."
- *October 26:* President George W. Bush signs the USA PATRIOT Act into law.

2002

- *February 7:* President George W. Bush states that he does not believe that the Geneva Conventions apply to enemy combatants who are suspected of affiliation with a terrorist organization.

2003

- *May 31:* After five years as a fugitive, Eric Rudolph is arrested in North Carolina for his role in the 1996 Atlanta Olympic Centennial Park bombing as well as a series of bombings of abortion clinics in the South.

2004

- *April 28:* The CBS television news program *60 Minutes II* reveals evidence of torture and other prisoner abuse by U.S. personnel at Abu Ghraib prison in Iraq.

2005

- *March 16:* Police arrest Brazilian "phishing" kingpin Paulo de Almeida, accused of stealing $37 million in funds from online bank accounts.

2006

- *September 7:* In a high-profile speech President George W. Bush admits that suspected terrorists had been held in secret CIA prisons and subjected to "an alternative set of [interrogation] procedures."

2007

- *December 6:* CIA director Michael V. Hayden acknowledges that the CIA had destroyed videotapes documenting the alleged torture of two suspected terrorists.

2008

- *June 12:* In *Boumediene v. Bush*, the U.S. Supreme Court rules that detainees at the Guantánamo Bay Naval Base may petition for habeas corpus.

2009

- *January 22:* President Barack Obama orders the closing of the prison camp at Guantánamo Bay.

Eyewitness Testimony

The O. J. Simpson Trial

JOHN EDWARDS (Officer): Then a woman came running out of the bushes to my left, crossed the driveway. She was a female Caucasian, blond hair. She was wearing a bra only as upper garment, and she had on a dark, I believe it was dark, light-weight sweat pants or night pajama bottoms. And she ran across and collapsed on the speaker, the identical kind of a speaker post on the inside of the gate. She collapsed on it, and started yelling, "He's going to kill me, he's going to kill me." Then she pressed the button which allowed the gate to open, and then she ran out [to me], again yelling, "He's going to kill me" . . .

CHRISTOPHER DARDEN (Prosecutor): And what was her physical demeanor and physical appearance at that time?

EDWARDS: Well, she was wet, she was shivering, she was cold. I could feel her bones, and she was real cold. And she was beat up.

DARDEN: And at some point did you identify this woman?

EDWARDS: Yes.

DARDEN: Who was this woman that you—

EDWARDS: Nicole Simpson . . .

DARDEN: What, if anything, did she say to you after she collapsed?

EDWARDS: She said, "He's going to kill me." I said, "Well, who's going to kill you?" She said, "O. J."

A police officer describing his response to a 911 call received from Nicole Simpson on January 1, 1989, from CNN's O. J. Simpson trial transcripts for January 31, 1995, TRNO 6-5, 1:27pm.

Judge [Lance] Ito's own level of impatience rose continuously and finally reached the saturation point. "Let's wind this up," he said summarily. "Let's try the Simpson case sometime today."

An account of the Simpson trial from August 14, 1995, quoted from David Margolick, "Simpson Team Reads of Officer's Slurs," New York Times, August 15, 1995, p. A12.

And so [Marcia Clark] talks about O. J. being very, very recognizable. She talks about O. J. Simpson getting dressed up to go commit these murders. Just before we break for our break, I was thinking—I was thinking last night about this case and their theory and how it didn't make any sense and how it didn't fit and how something is wrong. It occurred to me how they were going to come here, stand up here and tell you how O. J. Simpson was going to disguise himself. He was going to put on a knit cap and some dark clothes, and he was going to get in his white Bronco, this recognizable person, and go over and kill his wife. That's what they want you to believe. That's how silly their argument is. And I said to myself, maybe I can demonstrate this graphically. Let me show you something. This is a knit cap. Let me put this knit cap on. You have seen me for a year. If I put this knit cap on, who am I? I'm still Johnnie Cochran with a knit cap. And if you looked at O. J. Simpson over there—and he has a rather large head—O. J. Simpson in a knit cap from two blocks away is still O. J. Simpson. It's no disguise. It's no disguise. It makes no sense. It doesn't fit. If it doesn't fit, you must acquit.

Consider everything that Mr. Simpson would have had to have done in a very short time under their timeline. He would have had to drive over to Bundy, as they described in this little limited time frame where there is not enough time, kill two athletic people in a struggle that takes five to fifteen minutes, walk slowly from the scene, return to the scene, supposedly looking for a missing hat and glove and poking around, go back to this alley a second time, drive more than five minutes to Rockingham where nobody hears him or sees him, either stop along the way to hide these bloody clothes and knives, et cetera, or take them in the house with you where they are still hoisted by their own petard because there is no blood, there is no trace, there is no nothing. So that is why the Prosecution has had to try and push back their timeline. Even to today they are still pushing it back because it doesn't make any sense. It doesn't fit.

As I started to say before, perhaps the single most defining moment in this trial is the day they thought they would conduct this experiment on these gloves. They had this big build-up [where] . . . they were going to try to demonstrate to you that these were the killer's gloves and these gloves would fit Mr. Simpson. You don't need any photographs to understand this. I suppose that vision is indelibly imprinted in each and every one of your minds of how Mr. Simpson walked over here and stood before you and you saw four simple words, "The gloves didn't fit." And all their strategy started changing after that . . . [T]heir case from that day forward was slipping away from them and they knew it and they could never ever recapture it. We may all live to be a hundred years old, and I hope we do, but you will always remember those

In 1995, O. J. Simpson, an actor and former football star, was tried for the murders of his ex-wife Nicole Brown Simpson and her friend Ronald Goldman. The trial became the center of public and media attention. In this photograph, Simpson tries on a glove that resembles one that police investigators had found at the crime scene. *(AP Photo/Vince Bucci, Pool)*

gloves, when [Christopher] Darden asked him to try them on, didn't fit.

Defense attorney Johnnie Cochran, from his closing argument in California v. O. J. Simpson, *September 28, 1995, quoted in Linder, ed.,* Famous American Trials: The O. J. Simpson Trial. *Available online at URL: http://www.law. umkc.edu/faculty/projects/ftrials/Simpson/simpson.htm.*

Domestic Terrorism and Paramilitary Movements

In the months leading up to the bombing, McVeigh had a conversation with the owner of a copy shop in Kingman—and the topic was Waco. The owner, George Boerst, said he "mentioned something about an article [he'd] read [in a militia publication] about how an armed militia was supposed to have stormed Washington, D.C., to arrest politicians and try them in their own court."

Boerst claims that McVeigh responded by telling him, "Well, that got canceled, but something else is in the making."

This conversation reveals that the radical militia publications that McVeigh was known to read—the same publications that make leaderless resistance possible—were apparently calling for common-law courts to try officials involved with the Waco incident. Some of the ATF and FBI officials who had participated in the Waco operation had their offices in the Murrah [federal] building [in Oklahoma City]. McVeigh's response to Boerst may indicate that he was aware that the movement wanted trials for those responsible for the government's actions at Waco, and as a hard-core antigovernment adherent, McVeigh knew that a military court would dish out death sentences for those who had been involved in the deaths of the Branch Davidians . . .

Was he specifically talking about the Murrah building bombing, or was he saying that a different plan for trying officials had been determined, or both? Whatever he meant, it's clear that under the concept of leaderless resistance, McVeigh—or any other antigovernment zealot—had been given the green light to take action.

Investigative journalist Joel Dyer in Harvest of Rage *(1998), p. 233.*

[J]ust how corrupt and unfeeling do militia members believe their government is? The Internet web page of the 7th Missouri Militia states: "The 7th Missouri Militia is dedicated to fighting the true enemies of the Patriot movement—the federal and state governments and their degenerate quisling lackeys." Harold Sheil, a militia member, said, "One of the things that people really fear from the government is the idea [that] the government can ruin your life, totally destroy your life. I don't mean kill you. But they can totally destroy your life, split your family up, do the whole thing and walk off like you're a discarded banana peel, and with a ho-hum attitude" . . .

According to Richard Abanes, author of *American Militias:* "When patriots are asked why they hate their government, four answers regularly surface in varying combinations: (1) declining economic conditions; (2) unwanted social change; (3) imposition of federal authority over states' rights; and (4) environmental legislation that imposes strict regulations on what land owners can do with their property." In other words, many members of the militia movement see their lifestyles declining and believe that the government, who should be helping them, really does not care about them any longer, but instead now caters only to minority groups and special interests.

Author Robert L. Snow in Terrorists among Us *(2002), pp. 27–28.*

200. Until the industrial system has been thoroughly wrecked, the destruction of that system must be the revolutionaries' ONLY goal. Other goals would distract attention and energy from the main goal. More importantly, if the revolutionaries permit themselves to have any other goal than the destruction of technology, they will be tempted to use technology as a tool for reaching that other goal. If they give in to that temptation, they will fall right back into the technological trap, because modern technology is a unified, tightly organized system, so that, in order to retain SOME technology, one finds oneself obliged to retain MOST technology, hence one ends up sacrificing only token amounts of technology.

201. Suppose for example that the revolutionaries took "social justice" as a goal. Human nature being what it is, social justice would not come about spontaneously; it would have to be enforced. In order to enforce it the revolutionaries would have to retain central organization and control. For that they would need rapid long-distance transportation and communication, and therefore all the technology needed to support the transportation and communication systems. To feed and clothe poor people they would have to use agricultural and manufacturing technology. And so forth. So that the attempt to insure social justice would force them to retain most parts of the technological system. Not that we have anything against social justice, but it must not be allowed to interfere with the effort to get rid of the technological system.

202. It would be hopeless for revolutionaries to try to attack the system without using SOME modern technology. If nothing else they must use the communications media to spread their message. But they should use modern technology for only ONE purpose: to attack the technological system.

203. Imagine an alcoholic sitting with a barrel of wine in front of him. Suppose he starts saying to himself, "Wine isn't bad for you if used in moderation. Why, they say small amounts of wine are even good for you! It won't do me any harm if I take just one little drink . . ." Well you know what is going to happen. Never forget that the human race with technology is just like an alcoholic with a barrel of wine.

204. Revolutionaries should have as many children as they can. There is strong scientific evidence that social attitudes are to a significant extent inherited. No one suggests that a social attitude is a direct outcome of a person's genetic constitution, but it appears that personality traits tend, within the context of our society, to make a person more likely to hold this or that social attitude. Objections to these findings have been raised, but objections are feeble and seem to be ideologically motivated. In any event, no one denies that children tend on the average to hold social attitudes similar to those of their parents. From our point of view it doesn't matter all that much whether the attitudes are passed on genetically or through childhood training. In either case they ARE passed on.

205. The trouble is that many of the people who are inclined to rebel against the industrial system are also concerned about the population problems, hence they are apt to have few or no children. In this way they may be handing the world over to the sort of people who support or at least accept the industrial system. To insure the strength of the next generation of revolutionaries the present generation must reproduce itself abundantly. In doing so they will be worsening the population problem only slightly. And the most important problem is to get rid of the industrial system, because once the industrial system is gone the world's population necessarily will decrease . . . ; whereas, if the industrial system survives, it will continue developing new techniques of food production that may enable the world's population to keep increasing almost indefinitely.

From the manifesto of Theodore Kaczynski ("The Unabomber"), Industrial Society and Its Future, *originally published simultaneously in the* New York Times *and the* Washington Post *on September 19, 1995, in exchange for a promise from the suspect to end his bombing campaign, quoted in* The Courier *(Findlay, OH), special electronic edition. Available online at URL: http://www. thecourier.com/manifest.htm.*

Getting Tough on Crime

The American people have been waiting a long time for this day. In the last 25 years, half a million Americans have been killed by other Americans. For 25 years, crime has been a hot political issue, used too often to divide us while the system makes excuses for not punishing criminals and doing the job, instead of being used to unite us to prevent crime, punish criminals, and restore a sense of safety and security to the American people . . .

Not so long ago, kids grew up knowing they'd have to pay if they broke a neighbor's window playing ball. I know; I did it once. [laughter] They knew they'd be in trouble if they lied or stole because their parents and teachers and neighbors cared enough to set them straight. And everybody knew that anybody who committed a serious crime would be caught and convicted and would serve their time in jail. The rules were simple, the results were predictable, and we lived better because of it. Punishment was swift and certain for people who didn't follow the rules, and the rewards of America were considerable for those who did.

Now, too many kids don't have parents who care. Gangs and drugs have taken over our streets and undermined our schools. Every day we read about somebody else who has literally gotten away with murder. But the American people haven't forgotten the difference between right and wrong. The system has. The American people haven't stopped wanting to raise their children in lives of safety and dignity, but they've got a lot of obstacles in their way.

When I sign this crime bill, we together are taking a big step toward bringing the laws of our land back into line with the values of our people and beginning to restore the line between right and wrong. There must be no doubt about whose side we're on. People who commit crimes should be caught, convicted, and punished. This bill puts Government on the side of those who abide by the law, not those who break it; on the side of the victims, not their attackers; on the side of the brave men and women who put their lives on the line for us every day, not the criminals or those who would turn away from law enforcement. That's why police and prosecutors and preachers fought so hard for this bill and why I am so proud to sign it into law today.

When this bill is law, "three strikes and you're out" will be the law of the land; the penalty for killing a law enforcement officer will be death; we will have a significant—[applause]—we will have the means by which we can say punishment will be more certain. We will cut the Federal work force over a period of years by 270,000 positions to its lowest level in 30 years and take all that money to pay for this crime bill. The savings will be used to put 100,000 police officers on the street, a 20 percent increase. It will be used to build prisons to keep 100,000

violent criminals off the street. It will be used to give our young people something to say yes to, places where they can go after school where they are safe, where they can do constructive things that will help them to build their lives, where teachers replace gang leaders as role models. All of these things should be done and will be done.

This bill makes it illegal for juveniles to own handguns and, yes, without eroding the rights of sports men and women in this country, we will finally ban these assault weapons from our street that have no purpose other than to kill.

But my friends, let us be frank with each other: Even this great law, the toughest and smartest crime bill in our history, cannot do the job alone. By its own words, it is still a law. It must be implemented by you, and it must be supplemented by you. Even when we put a new police officer on your block, the officer can't make you safe unless you come out of your home and help the officer do his or her job. Even when we keep our schools open late and give our children an alternative to drugs and gangs, your children won't learn the difference between right and wrong unless you teach them and they're in those schools when they're open. Our country will not truly be safe again until all Americans take personal responsibility for themselves, their families, and their communities. This day is the beginning, not the end, of our effort to restore safety and security to the people of this country.

President Bill Clinton's remarks upon signing the 1994 Violent Crime Control and Law Enforcement Act, in National Archives and Records Administration, Weekly Compilation of Presidential Documents, *September 19, 1994.*

If the question is how to prevent at-risk youths from becoming stone-cold predators in the first place . . . incarceration is no solution.

But if the question is how to restrain known convicted criminals from murdering, raping, robbing, assaulting and stealing, then incarceration is a solution, and a cost-effective one.

On average, it costs $25,000 a year to keep a convicted criminal in prison. For that money, society gets four benefits: Imprisonment punishes offenders and expresses society's moral disapproval. It teaches felons and would-be felons a lesson: Do crime, do time. Prisoners get drug treatment and education. And, as the columnist Ben Wattenberg has noted, "A thug in prison can't shoot your sister."

. . . Increased incarceration explains part of the drop in crime in New York and other cities. As some recent studies show, prisons pay big dividends even if all they deliver is relief from the murder and mayhem that incarcerated felons would be committing if free.

From an editorial by political scientist John J. DiIulio, Jr., "Prisons Are a Bargain, by Any Measure," New York Times, January 16, 1996, p. A17.

School Shootings and Juvenile Crime

The Whitman administration announced today a broad overhaul of New Jersey's juvenile justice system that would make it easier for judges to lock up youthful offenders.

Now, judges may consider only a young offender's prospects for rehabilitation before sentencing. If Gov. Christine Todd Whitman gets her way—and there is every reason to believe she will in today's get-tough-on-crime-political atmosphere—judges would be permitted to lock up an offender solely because the offender is deemed dangerous to the public. . . .

Underlying today's announcement is the growing appreciation within the Whitman administration that state law now offers little deterrence to juvenile crime, that the system is held in contempt by young offenders who know that of 1,000 young people arrested for a crime in New Jersey, only 18 are even locked up, and that adult criminals are increasingly using the young in their crimes because the threat of punishment for those under 18 is so slight.

"Violent juvenile crime continues to rise in New Jersey," Mrs. Whitman said "and we continue to rank high in the number of violent crimes committed by young people."

Reporter Iver Peterson, "Big Overhaul of Juvenile Justice Planned," New York Times, May 17, 1995, p. B4.

Luke [Woodham] writes of being a "sponge of knowledge . . . Learn! Read poetry books, philosophy books, history books, science books, read biographies." In his police confession, he said that his pursuit of knowledge infuriated his mother . . .

Yet Luke was a C student at best who failed the ninth grade. In his room, police recovered only Nietzsche's *The Gay Science*, Hitler's *Mein Kampf*, and *Necronomicon*, a book of spells, chants, and incantations. Although Luke claimed to have become a student of all three, each book is still as pristine as the day it was purchased. The spines showed no signs of creasing and each page is crisp, unmarked and seemingly untouched . . .

"On Saturday of last week, I made my first kill . . . The victim was a loved one. My dear dog Sparkle." The brutal, graphic depiction of the dog's death covers two handwritten pages in his journals.

When it was read aloud at Luke's trial, several jurors covered their mouths in horror, two became physically sick. The text ended with Luke's personal assessment: "It was true beauty."

A description of the journals of Luke Woodham, a 16-year-old Pearl High School student who murdered his mother and then drove to school to shoot nine of his classmates, killing two. From Lisa Popyk, "'I Knew It Wouldn't Be Right,'" Cincinnati Post, November 9, 1998, p. 1.

My belief is that if I say something, it goes. I am the law, if you don't like it, you die. If I don't like you or I don't like what you want me to do, you die. If I do something incorrect, oh f——ing well, you die. Dead people cant do many things, like argue, whine, bitch, complain, narc, rat out, criticize, or even f——ing talk. So that's the only way to solve arguments with all you f——heads out there, I just kill! God I can't wait till I can kill you people. Ill just go to some downtown area in some big ass city and blow up and shoot everything I can. Feel no remorse, no sense of shame. Ich sage —— DU! I will rig up explosives all over a town and detonate each one of them at will after I mow down a whole f——ing area full of you snotty ass rich mother f——ing high strung godlike attitude having worthless pieces of s——whores. i don't care if I live or die in the shootout, all I want to do is kill and injure as many of you pricks as I can, especially a few people. Like [name omitted] . . .

I live in denver, and god damnit I would love to kill almost all of its residents. F——ing people with their rich snobby attitude thinking they are all high and mighty and can just come up and tell me what to do and then people I see in the streets lying their f——ing asses off about themselves. And then there is all you fitness f——heads saying s——like "yeah do 50 situps and 25 pushups each morning and run a mile every day and go to the gym and work out and just push yourself to be better and you can achieve anything and set high goals and have great expectations and be happy and be kind and treat everyone equal and give to charity and help the poor and stop violence and drive safely and don't pollute and don't litter and take shorter showers and don't waste water and eat right food and don't smoke or drink and don't sell guns and don't be a bad person"—phew. I say "f——you. shutup. and die." And then pull the trigger of a DB#3 that is in your f——ing mouth. All you f——ing people with your set standards and s——, like you have to go to college and be smart and s——, and you have to have a job and pay taxes, blah blah f——ing blah, shutup and DIE! I really don't give a god damn about what you think is "right" and what is "wrong" and what is acceptable and what isn't nice, I just don't f——ing CARE! SHUTUP AND DIE!!!!!!

Columbine shooter Eric Harris, from a blog found on his 1997 Web site, from Columbine files released by the Littleton Police Department, Littleton, Colorado, pp. JC-001-010415 and JC-001-010416.

International Terrorism

Clandestine, foreign government, and media reports indicate bin Laden since 1997 has wanted to conduct terrorist attacks in the [United States]. Bin Laden implied in U.S. television interviews in 1997 and 1998 that his followers would follow the example of World Trade Center bomber Ramzi Yousef and "bring the fighting to America."

After U.S. missile strikes on his base in Afghanistan in 1998, bin Laden told followers he wanted to retaliate in Washington . . .

Convicted plotter Ahmed Ressam has told the FBI he conceived the idea to attack Los Angeles International Airport himself, but that . . . Laden lieutenant Abu Zubaydah encouraged him and helped facilitate the operation. Ressam also said that in 1998 Abu Zubaydah was planning his own U.S. attack.

Ressam says bin Laden was aware of the Los Angeles operation. Although bin Laden has not succeeded, his attacks against the U.S. Embassies in Kenya and Tanzania in 1998 demonstrate that he prepares operations years in advance and is not deterred by setbacks. Bin Laden associates surveyed our embassies in Nairobi and Dar es Salaam as early as 1993, and some members of the Nairobi cell planning the bombings were arrested and deported in 1997.

Al Qaeda members—including some who are U.S. citizens—have resided in or traveled to the U.S. for years, and the group apparently maintains a support structure that could aid attacks.

Two al-Qaeda members found guilty in the conspiracy to bomb our embassies in East Africa were U.S. citizens, and a senior [Egyptian Islamic Jihad] member lived in California in the mid-1990s.

A clandestine source said in 1998 that a bin Laden cell in New York was recruiting Muslim-American youth for attacks.

We have not been able to corroborate some of the more sensational threat reporting, such as that . . . in 1998 saying that bin Laden wanted to hijack a U.S. aircraft to gain the release of "Blind Sheikh" Omar Abdel Rahman and other U.S.-held extremists.

Nevertheless, FBI information since that time indicates patterns of suspicious activity in this country consistent with preparations for hijackings or other types of attacks, including recent surveillance of federal buildings in New York.

The FBI is conducting approximately 70 full-field investigations throughout the U.S. that it considers bin Laden-related. CIA and the FBI are investigating a call to our embassy in the UAE in May saying that a group of bin Laden supporters was in the [United States] planning attacks with explosives.

From the daily intelligence briefing to President George W. Bush for August 6, 2001. Reprinted in "Transcript: Bin Laden Determined to Strike in US," CNN.com. Available online at URL: http://www.cnn.com/2004/ ALLPOLITICS/04/10/august6.memo/.

United Airlines Flight 175 was scheduled to depart for Los Angeles at 8:00. Captain Victor Saracini and First Officer Michael Horrocks piloted the Boeing 767, which had seven flight attendants. Fifty-six passengers boarded the flight.

United 175 pushed back from its gate at 7:58 and departed Logan Airport at 8:14. By 8:33, it had reached its assigned cruising altitude of 31,000 feet. The flight attendants would have begun their cabin service.

The flight had taken off just as American 11 [the first plane to collide with the World Trade Center] was being hijacked, and at 8:42 the United 175 flight crew completed their report on a "suspicious transmission" overheard from another plane (which turned out to have been Flight 11) just after takeoff. This was United 175's last communication with the ground.

The hijackers attacked sometime between 8:42 and 8:46. They used knives . . . , Mace . . . , and the threat of a bomb . . . They stabbed members of the flight crew . . . Both pilots had been killed . . . The eyewitness accounts came from calls made from the rear of the plane, from passengers originally seated further forward in the cabin, a sign that passengers and perhaps crew had been moved to the back of the aircraft . . .

The first operational evidence that something was abnormal on United 175 came at 8:47, when the aircraft changed beacon codes twice within a minute. At 8:51, the flight deviated from its assigned altitude, and a minute later New York air traffic controllers began repeatedly and unsuccessfully trying to contact it.

At 8:52, in Easton, Connecticut, a man named Lee Hanson received a phone call from his son Peter, a passenger on United 175. His son told him: "I think they've taken over the cockpit—An attendant has been stabbed—and someone else up front may have been killed. The plane is making strange moves. Call United Airlines—Tell them it's Flight 175, Boston to LA." Lee Hanson then called the Easton Police Department and relayed what he had heard.

Also at 8:52, a male flight attendant called a United office in San Francisco, reaching Marc Policastro. The flight attendant reported that the flight had been hijacked, both pilots had been killed, a flight attendant had been stabbed, and the hijackers were probably flying the plane. The call lasted about two minutes, after which Policastro and a colleague tried unsuccessfully to contact the flight.

At 8:58, the flight took a heading toward New York City.

At 8:59, Flight 175 passenger Brian David Sweeney tried to call his wife, Julie. He left a message on their home answering machine that the plane had been hijacked. He then called his mother, Louise Sweeney, told her the flight had been hijacked, and added that the passengers were thinking about storming the cockpit to take control of the plane away from the hijackers.

At 9:00, Lee Hanson received a second call from his son Peter:

"It's getting bad, Dad—A stewardess was stabbed—They seem to have knives and Mace—They said they have a bomb—It's getting very bad on the plane—Passengers are throwing up and getting sick—The plane is making jerky movements—I don't think the pilot is flying the plane—I think we are going down—I think they intend to go to Chicago or something and fly into a building—Don't worry, Dad—If it happens, it'll be very fast—My God, my God."

The call ended abruptly. Lee Hanson had heard a woman scream just before it cut off. He turned on a television, and in her home so did Louise Sweeney.

Both then saw the second aircraft hit the World Trade Center.

At 9:03:11, United Airlines Flight 175 struck the South Tower of the World Trade Center. All on board, along with an unknown number of people in the tower, were killed instantly.

A report of the hijacking of United Airlines Flight 175, the second plane to strike the World Trade Center on September 11, 2001, from the National Commission on Terrorist Attacks Upon the United States, The 9/11 Commission Report, *pp. 7–8.*

The forms, sometimes not much more than specks against the gleam of the skyscraper, tumbled downward almost indistinguishable from the chunks of debris, the airplane parts, the vapors of flaming aviation fuel that filled the air like fireworks. They fell at the rate of all falling bodies, thirty-two feet per second squared, slowed a certain amount by the friction of the air, so they fell for eight or nine seconds and they were going at least 125 miles an hour when they hit the pavement or crashed into the roof of the Marriott Hotel at the bottom of the World Trade Center . . .

And then everything, the towers themselves, all 110 stories of them, the entire 1,368 feet of the north tower, the 1,362 feet of the south tower with their 400,000 tons of steel and their 10 million square feet of offices, trading spaces, bathrooms, and conference rooms disintegrated into an avalanche of concrete, steel, glass, airplane parts, and thousands more bodies, all compressed into seven stories of rubble below.

New York Times *reporter Richard B. Bernstein, describing the September 11, 2001, terrorist attacks on the World Trade Center, from* Out of the Blue (2002), *p. 1.*

I witness that there is no God but God and Mohammed is His slave and Prophet.

God Almighty hit the United States at its most vulnerable spot. He destroyed its greatest buildings. Praise be to God.

Here is the United States. It was filled with terror from its north to its south and from its east to its west. Praise be to God . . .

I tell it and its people these few words: I swear by Almighty God who raised the heavens without pillars that neither the United States nor he who lives in the United States will enjoy security before we can see it as a reality in Palestine and before all the infidel armies leave the land of Mohammed, may God's peace and blessing be upon him.

God is great and glory to Islam.

May God's peace, mercy, and blessings be upon you.

Osama bin Laden, leader of the al-Qaeda international terrorism network, celebrating the attacks of September 11, 2001, quoted in "Bin Laden's Warning: Full Text," BBC News, October 7, 2001. Available online at URL: http:// news.bbc.co.uk/1/hi/world/south_asia/1585636.stm.

The War on Terror and the USA PATRIOT Act

This weekend I am engaged in extensive sessions with members of my National Security Council, as we plan a comprehensive assault on terrorism. This will be a different kind of conflict against a different kind of enemy.

This is a conflict without battlefields or beachheads, a conflict with opponents who believe they are invisible. Yet, they are mistaken. They will be exposed, and they will discover what others in the past have learned: Those who make war against the United States have chosen their own destruction. Victory against terrorism will not take place in a single battle, but in a series of decisive actions against terrorist organizations and those who harbor and support them.

We are planning a broad and sustained campaign to secure our country and eradicate the evil of terrorism. And we are determined to see this conflict through. Americans of every faith and background are committed to this goal.

Yesterday I visited the site of the destruction in New York City and saw an amazing spirit of sacrifice and patriotism and defiance. I met with rescuers who have worked past exhaustion, who cheered for our country and the great cause we have entered.

In Washington, D.C., the political parties and both Houses of Congress have shown a remarkable unity, and I'm deeply grateful. A terrorist attack designed to tear us apart has instead bound us together as a nation. Over the past few days, we have learned much about American courage—the courage of firefighters and police officers who suffered so great a loss, the courage of passengers aboard United 93 who may well have fought with the hijackers and saved many lives on the ground.

Now we honor those who died, and prepare to respond to these attacks on our nation. I will not settle for a

Osama bin Laden, leader of the al-Qaeda terrorist organization, is generally regarded as the highest-ranking architect of the 9/11 attacks. *(Library of Congress Prints and Photographs Division [LC-DIG-PPMSCA-02090])*

token act. Our response must be sweeping, sustained and effective. We have much do to, and much to ask of the American people.

President George W. Bush, from his radio address of September 15, 2001. Reprinted on www.whitehouse.gov. Available online at URL: http://www.whitehouse.gov/news/ releases/2001/09/20010915.html.

Muhammad Siddiqui is an architect in Houston, husband to a busy physician and father of two young children. When two of his family members called him to say the FBI had questioned them, he was understandably concerned. He contacted Texas ACLU attorney Annette Lamoreaux, who agreed to represent Siddiqui should the authorities contact him. On a Monday evening Siddiqui, who was home with his children, received a visit from two FBI agents.

Siddiqui opened the door to the agents and responded to their request to question him by saying, "I'd be happy to talk to you, but I'd like to have my attorney present." One of the agents told Siddiqui that he did not need an attorney and that getting an attorney would only make him look guilty ... Siddiqui repeated the phrase that Lamoreaux had advised him to say: "I'd be happy to talk to you, but I'd like to have my attorney present." When the FBI agent responded angrily, Siddiqui called Lamoreaux from his cell phone. She asked to speak to one of the agents ...

But the FBI agent on the phone did not seem to be paying attention to the rules. He screamed at Lamoreaux that Siddiqui did not have the right to counsel, to which she replied, "That is absolutely not the law" ... The agent refused to talk with her any further ...

The agents remained in the doorway of Siddiqui's apartment, one of them pulling his coat back to reveal a gun. Siddiqui, whose children were inside, was afraid ... As they were walking away, one agent turned back to Siddiqui threatening, "We will talk to you. We are watching you. Don't leave town" ...

[The next day], Lamoreaux suggested that they meet on Thursday, when Siddiqui was free from work and childcare responsibilities. The agent insisted on meeting that day and told her that he would stand outside of Siddiqui's house until he came out and talked to him. Later that day, the interview was held in Lamoreaux's office. The meeting lasted 15 minutes, and an FBI agent confirmed that Siddiqui was never a criminal target.

A report of post-9/11 Arab-American racial profiling, quoted in the American Civil Liberties Union, Sanctioned Bias, (February 26, 2004) pp. 14–15.

Striking the proper constitutional balance here is of great importance to the Nation during this period of ongoing combat. But it is equally vital that our calculus not give short shrift to the values that this country holds dear or to the privilege that is American citizenship. It is during our most challenging and uncertain moments that our Nation's commitment to due process is most severely tested; and it is in those times that we must preserve our commitment at home to the principles for which we fight abroad ...

With due recognition of these competing concerns, we believe that neither the process proposed by the Government nor the process apparently envisioned by the District Court below strikes the proper constitutional balance when a United States citizen is detained in the United States as an enemy combatant ...

We therefore hold that a citizen-detainee seeking to challenge his classification as an enemy combatant must receive notice of the factual basis for his classification, and a fair opportunity to rebut the Government's factual assertions before a neutral decisionmaker ... These essential constitutional promises may not be eroded.

At the same time, the exigencies of the circumstances may demand that, aside from these core elements, enemy combatant proceedings may be tailored to alleviate their uncommon potential to burden the Executive at a time of ongoing military conflict. Hearsay, for example, may need to be accepted as the most reliable available evidence from the Government in such a proceeding. Likewise, the Constitution would not be offended by a presumption in favor of the Government's evidence, so long as that presumption remained a rebuttable one and fair opportunity for rebuttal were provided. Thus, once the Government puts forth credible evidence that the habeas petitioner meets the enemy-combatant criteria, the onus could shift to the petitioner to rebut that evidence with more persuasive evidence that he falls outside the criteria. A burden-shifting scheme of this sort would meet the goal of ensuring that the errant tourist, embedded journalist, or local aid worker has a chance to prove military error while giving due regard to the Executive once it has put forth meaningful support for its conclusion that the detainee is in fact an enemy combatant ...

We think it unlikely that this basic process will have the dire impact on the central functions of warmaking that the Government forecasts. The parties agree that initial captures on the battlefield need not receive the process we have discussed here; that process is due only when the determination is made to continue to hold those who have been seized. The Government has made clear in its briefing that documentation regarding battlefield detainees already is kept in the ordinary course of military affairs ... Any fact-finding imposition created by requiring a knowledgeable affiant to summarize these records to an independent tribunal is a minimal one. Likewise, arguments that military officers ought not have to wage war under the threat of litigation lose much of their steam when factual disputes at enemy-combatant hearings are limited to the alleged combatant's acts. This focus meddles little, if at all, in the strategy or conduct of war, inquiring only into the appropriateness of continuing to detain an individual claimed to have taken up arms against the United States. While we accord the greatest respect and consideration to the judgments of military authorities in matters relating to the actual prosecution of a war, and recognize that the scope of that discretion necessarily is wide, it does not infringe on the core role of the military for the courts to exercise their own time-honored and constitutionally mandated roles of reviewing and resolving claims like those presented here . . .

In sum, while the full protections that accompany challenges to detentions in other settings may prove unworkable and inappropriate in the enemy-combatant setting, the threats to military operations posed by a basic system of independent review are not so weighty as to trump a citizen's core rights to challenge meaningfully the Government's case and to be heard by an impartial adjudicator.

Justice Sandra Day O'Connor, from her majority ruling in Hamdi v. Rumsfeld *(124 S. Ct. 2633).*

Internet Crime and Identity Theft

A worm that exploits a critical Remote Procedure Call (RPC) flaw to infect vulnerable Windows machines is spreading rapidly across the Internet this morning . . .

The Blaster worm (AKA Lovsan, MSBlast or Poza), which began spreading yesterday, is programmed to launch an attack against windowsupdate.com on 16 August.

Microsoft last month issued a patch to guard against the problem but uptake has been predictably slow, allowing malicious code writers to come up with software that is having a severe effect on many Windows users.

Mac, Linux and Unix computers are immune to this Microsoft-specific vulnerability. . . .

The worm launches a command shell and uses TFTP to connect to other infected systems to download the worm's executable. Blaster will scan addresses in the Internet to locate vulnerable Windows machines using TCP/TDP port 135. Once found, it will copy itself over and modify the system so the worm will be executed every time the machine is started. The worm will keep on replicating from every infected machine.

An account of the 2003 MSBlast worm, which infected an estimated 1.4 million computers. The worm's author, an 18-year-old Minnesota student, was later arrested for the crime. From John Leyden, "Blaster Worm Spreading Rapidly," The Register, *August 12, 2003.*

The Grays are a working couple with grown children . . . Like many victims of ID theft, they aren't certain how their identities were stolen. Their theory is that a credit card statement was taken from their unsecured mailbox in July 2002. However it happened, their first indication something was wrong was when they received a call in August 2002 from Consumer Fraud Control at Bank of America, the issuer of their credit card. The bank had noticed a change in the pattern of charges on the card and had received a change of address and phone number . . .

The Grays' case is a common, low-tech type of ID theft. The Web and the proliferation of e-mail have opened up new frontiers to the unscrupulous . . . Phishing (also called carding or brand spoofing) is an e-mail scam using known logos from entities such as eBay, PayPal, and America Online to "phish" for personal information. The victim receives a legitimate-looking e-mail proclaiming problems with account information: "Just click on the link and provide some additional personal and financial information to clear up a few questions." Everything looks authentic, but you're actually being redirected to a site that's here one moment and gone the next—taking your identity with it.

Janet Rubenking, from "Identity Theft: What, Me Worry?" PC Magazine *(March 2004).*

Appendix A
Documents

1. Excerpts from the Massachusetts Body of Liberties, 1641
2. Excerpts from Maryland Public Morality Codes, 1654
3. A Declaration on the Execution of Two Quaker Women, Massachusetts, 1659
4. Excerpts from an early slave law, Maryland, 1664
5. An act legalizing the killing of slaves, Virginia, 1669
6. Excerpts from the Charter of West New Jersey, 1676
7. Excerpts from the English Bill of Rights, 1689
8. Excerpts from the Pennsylvania Charter of Privileges, 1701
9. Excerpts from the Virginia Slave Codes, 1705
10. Excerpts from the Virginia Declaration of Rights, 1776
11. Excerpts from the Declaration of Independence, 1776
12. Excerpts from the Pennsylvania Declaration of Rights, 1776
13. Excerpt from the Maryland Declaration of Rights, 1776
14. Excerpt from the North Carolina Declaration of Rights, 1776
15. Excerpt from the U.S. Treaty with the Lenape Nation, 1778
16. Excerpts from the U.S. Treaty with the Cherokee Nation, 1785
17. Excerpts from the U.S. Constitution, 1787
18. Legal penalties suggested by Thomas Jefferson, *Notes on the State of Virginia*, 1785
19. Excerpts from the U.S. Bill of Rights, 1789
20. The U.S. Crimes Act, 1790
21. The Indian Tribes Act, 1790
22. The Fugitive Slave Act of 1793
23. The Alien Enemies Act, 1798
24. Excerpts from the Sedition Act of 1798
25. The Virginia Resolution of 1798
26. The Kentucky Resolution of 1799
27. Excerpts from Instructions for the London Metropolitan Police, 1829
28. Excerpts from the Fugitive Slave Act of 1850
29. The Thirteenth Amendment to the U.S. Constitution, 1865
30. Excerpts from the Mississippi Black Codes, 1865
31. Excerpts from the U.S. Civil Rights Act of 1866
32. The Fourteenth Amendment to the U.S. Constitution, 1868
33. Excerpts from the Declaration of Principles Adopted and Promulgated by National Congress on Penitentiary and Reformatory Discipline, 1870
34. Appointment, Qualification, and Duties of U.S. Marshals, 1898
35. The Illinois Juvenile Court Law of 1907
36. Excerpt from Timothy Hurley, *Origin of the Illinois Juvenile Court Law*, 1907

37. The U.S. Espionage Act of 1917, including the Sedition Act Revisions of 1918
38. The Eighteenth Amendment to the U.S. Constitution, 1919
39. Excerpts from the Wickersham Commission's *Report on Lawlessness in Law Enforcement,* 1931
40. The Twenty-first Amendment to the U.S. Constitution, 1933
41. Excerpts from the Marihuana Tax Act, 1937
42. Excerpts from the Narcotic Control Act, 1956
43. Preface to the Omnibus Crime Control Act of 1968
44. The Racketeer Influenced and Corrupt Organization (RICO) Laws of 1970
45. Excerpt from the Report of the President's Task Force on Victims of Crime, 1982
46. Excerpt from the Illinois Domestic Violence Act of 1986
47. Florida law allowing minors to be charged as adults, 1994
48. Excerpts from the USA PATRIOT Act of 2001

1. Excerpts from the Massachusetts Body of Liberties, 1641

No man's life shall be taken away, no man's honor or good name shall be stained, no man's person shall be arrested, restrained, banished, dismembered, nor in any ways punished, no man shall be deprived of his wife or children, no man's goods or estate shall be taken away from him, nor any way indamaged under color of law or countenance of authority, unless it be by virtue or equity of some express law of the country warranting the same . . . or in case of the defect of a law in any particular case by the word of God . . . Every person within the jurisdiction, whether inhabitant or foreigner, shall enjoy the same justice and law that is general for the plantation, which we constitute and execute one toward another without partiality or delay.

No man shall be twice sentenced by civil justice for one and the same crime, offense, or trespass . . . No man shall be beaten with above forty stripes . . . No man condemned to die shall be put to death within four days next after his condemnation, unless the court see special cause to the contrary, or in case of martial law . . . No man shall be forced by torture to confess any crime against himself nor to any other, unless it be in some capital case where he is first fully convicted by clear and sufficient evidence to be guilty, after which if the cause be of that nature, that it is very apparent there be other conspirators, or confederates with him, then he may be tortured, yet not with such tortures as be barbarous and inhumane . . . For bodily punishments we allow amongst us none that are inhumane, barbarous, or cruel . . .

Every married woman shall be free from bodily [harm] or stripes by her husband, unless it be in his own defense upon her assault. If there be any just cause of [punishment], complaint shall be made to authority assembled in some court, from which only she shall receive it . . . If any parents shall willfully and unreasonably deny any child timely or convenient marriage, or shall exercise any unnatural severity toward them, such children shall have free liberty to complain to authority for redress . . . If any servants shall free from the tyranny and cruelty of their masters to the house of any freeman in the same town, they shall be there protected and sustained till due order be taken for their relief . . .

If any man after legal conviction shall have or worship any other god, but the Lord God, he shall be put to death . . . If any man or woman be a witch (that is, hath or con-sulteth with a familiar spirit), they shall be put to death . . . If any man shall blaspheme the name of God, the Father, Son, or Holy Ghost, with direct, express, presumptuous, or high-handed blasphemy, or shall curse God in the like manner, he shall be put to death . . . If any man or woman shall lie with any beast or brute creature by carnal copulation, they shall surely be put to death . . . If any man lieth with mankind as he lieth with a woman . . . they both shall surely be put to death . . . If any person committeth adultery with a married or espoused wife, the adulterer and the adulteress shall surely be put to death.

Source: Massachusetts Body of Liberties (1641). The Hanover Historical Texts Project. Available online at URL: http://history.hanover.edu/texts/masslib.html.

2. Excerpts from Maryland Public Morality Codes, 1654

It is enacted, that every person or persons that shall be found drunk and lawfully convicted shall pay for such offense by him or them committed one hundred pounds of tobacco to the public use . . .

That all and every person or persons in this province that shall see any one drunk and shall not within three days make it known to the next magistrate shall be liable to the fine of one hundred pounds of tobacco . . .

It is enacted that every person or persons within the province that shall be lawfully convicted of swearing shall be liable to pay, for every oath, ten pounds of tobacco, which shall be discovered and brought to trial and punishment . . . And if any person or persons shall be known and convicted to be a common swearer, blasphemer, or curser by any imprecations whatsoever against God or man, after one admonition by a magistrate, shall be subject to such penalty or punishment as the court before whom it is presented shall determine.

No work shall be done on the Sabbath day but that which is of necessity and charity to be done; no inordinate recreations as fowling, fishing, hunting, or other, no shooting of guns be used on that day except in case of necessity. Whosoever shall be lawfully convicted of the breach of any such law shall be liable to pay one hundred pounds of tobacco, half whereof shall be to the informer and the other half to the public use.

Source: The Commonwealth of Maryland, Acts Concerning Drunkenness, Swearing, and the Sabbath (1654). The Archives of Maryland Online. Available online at URL: http://archivesofmaryland.net/.

3. A Declaration on the Execution of Two Quaker Women, Massachusetts, 1659

Although the justice of our proceedings against William Robinson, Marmaduke Stevenson, and Mary Dyer, supported by the Authority of this Court, the Laws of the country, and the Law of God, may rather persuade us to expect encouragement and commendation from all prudent and pious men, than convince us of any necessity to Apologize for the same, yet forasmuch as men of weaker parts, out of pity and commiseration (a commendable and Christian virtue yet easily abused, and susceptible to sinister and dangerous impressions) for want of full information, may be left satisfied, and men of perverser principles, may take occasion hereby to calumniate us, and render us as bloody persecutors, to falsify the one, and stop the mouths of the other, we thought it requisite to declare:

That about three Years since, diverse persons, professing themselves Quakers . . . whose persons were only secured, to be sent away by the first opportunity, without censure or punishment, although their professed tenets, turbulent and contemptuous behaviour to Authority would have justified a severer animadversion [punishment], yet the prudence of this Court was exercised, only in making provisions to secure the Peace and Order here established, against their attempts, whose design (we were well assured of by our own experience, as well as by the example of their predecessors in Munster) was to undermine and ruin the same,

And accordingly a Law was made and published, prohibiting all Masters of Ships, to bring any Quakers into this Jurisdiction . . . Notwithstanding which, by a back Door, [Quakers] found entrance, and the penalty inflicted on themselves, proving insufficient to restrain their impudent and insolent obstrusions, was increased by the loss of the ears of those that offended the second time, which also being too weak a defense against their impetuous frantic fury, necessitated us to endeavour our security, and upon furious consideration, after the former experiments, by their incessant assaults, a Law was made, that such persons could be banished, on pain of Death, according to the example of England in their provision against Jesuits . . . Mary Dyer upon the petition of her Son, and the mercy and clemency of this Court, had liberty to depart within two days, which she hath accepted of.

The consideration of our gradual proceeding, will vindicate us from the clamorous accusations of severity; our own just and necessary defense, calling upon us (other means failing) to offer the point, which these persons have violently, and willfully rushed upon, and thereby become *felons de fe*, which might have been prevented, and the Sovereign law *Salus populi* been preserved, our former proceedings, as well as the sparing of Mary Dyer, upon an inconsiderable intercession, will manifestly evince, we desire their lives absent, rather than their death present.

Source: Declaration of the General Court of Massachusetts, "Concerning the Execution of Two Quakers," October 18, 1659, quoted in Powers, *Crime and Punishment in Early Massachusetts*, p. 341.

4. Excerpts from an early slave law, Maryland, 1664

Be it enacted . . . that all Negroes or other slaves already within the province and all Negroes and other slaves to be hereafter imported into the province shall serve *durante vita* [for life]. And all children born of any Negro or other slave shall be slaves as their fathers were for the term of their lives. And forasmuch as diverse freeborn English women, forgetful of their free condition and to the disgrace of their nation, do intermarry with Negro slaves, by which also diverse suits may arise touching the issue of such women and a great damage does befall the masters of such Negroes, for prevention whereof for deterring such freeborn women from such shameful matches. Be it further enacted, by the authority, advice, and consent aforesaid, that whatsoever freeborn woman shall intermarry with any slave from and after the last day of this present Assembly shall serve the master of such slave during the life of her husband and that all the issue of such freeborn women so married shall be slaves as their fathers were. And be it further enacted that all issues of English or other freeborn women that have already married Negroes shall serve the masters of their parents till they be of thirty years of age and no longer.

Source: The Commonwealth of Maryland, Acts Concerning Negroes and Other Slaves (1664). The Archives of Maryland Online. Available online at URL: http://archivesofmaryland.net/.

5. An act legalizing the killing of slaves, Virginia, 1669

Be it enacted and declared by this Grand Assembly that if any slave resist his master, or other by his master's order [punishing] him, and by the extremity of the [punishment] should chance to die, that his death shall not be accounted a felony, but the master, or that other person appointed by the master to punish him, be [acquitted] from molestation since it cannot be presumed that prepensed malice, which alone makes murder felony, should induce any man to destroy his own estate.

Source: William Waller Heming, Statutes at Large: Being a Collection of All the Laws of Virginia from the First Session of the Legislature in the Year 1619, Vol. 2, pp. 269–271.

6. Excerpts from the Charter of West New Jersey, 1676

Chapter XVII

That no Proprietor, freeholder or inhabitant of the said Province of West New Jersey, shall be deprived or condemned of life, limb, liberty, estate, property or any ways hurt in his or their privileges, freedoms or franchises, upon any account whatsoever, without a due trial, and a Judgment passed by twelve good and lawful men of his neighborhood first hand . . .

Chapter XVIII

And that no Proprietor, freeholder, free denison, or inhabitant in the said Province, shall be attached, arrested, or imprisoned for or by reason of any debt, duty, or thing whatsoever (cases felonious criminal and treasonable excepted) before he or she have personal summon or summons, left at his or her last dwelling place, if in the said Province, by some legal authorized officer, constituted and appointed for that purpose, to appear in some court of judicature for the said Province, with a full and plain account of the cause or thing in demand, as also the name or names of the person or persons at whose suit, and the court where he is to appear, and that he hath at least fourteen days time to appear and answer the said suit, if he or she live or inhabit within forty miles English of the said court, and if at a further distance, to have for every twenty miles, two days time more . . .

Chapter XX

That in all matters and causes, civil and criminal, proof is to be made by the solemn and plain [testimony], of at least two honest and reputable persons; and in case that any person or persons shall bear false witness, and bring in his or their evidence, contrary to the truth of the matter as shall be made plainly to appear, that then every such person or persons, shall in civil causes, suffer the penalty which would

be due to the person or persons he or they bear witness against. And in case any witness or witnesses, on the behalf of any person or persons, indicted in a criminal cause, shall be found to have borne false witness for fear, gain, malice or favour, and thereby hinder the due execution of the law, and deprive the suffering person or persons of their due satisfaction, that then in all other cases of false evidence, such person or persons shall be first severely fined, and that he or they shall forever be disabled from being admitted in evidence, or into any public office, employment, or service within this Province.

Chapter XXI

That all and every person and persons whatsoever who shall prosecute or prefer any indictment or information against others for any personal injuries, or matter criminal, or shall prosecute for any other criminal cause (treason, murder, and felony only excepted) shall and may be master of his own process, and have full power to forgive and remit the person or persons offending him or herself only, as well before as after judgment, and condemnation, and pardon and remit the sentence, fine and punishment of the person or persons offending, be it personal or other whatsoever.

Chapter XXII

That the trials of all causes, civil and criminal, shall be heard and decided by the verdict or judgment of twelve honest men of the neighborhood, only to be summoned and presented by the sheriff of that division, or propriety where the fact or trespass is committed; and that no person or persons shall be compelled to fee any attorney or councilor to plead his cause, but that all persons have free liberty to plead his own cause, if he please . . .

Chapter XXIII

That in all publick courts of justice for trials of causes, civil or criminal, any person or persons, inhabitants of the said Province may freely come into, and attend the said courts, and hear and be present, at all or any such trials as shall be there had or passed, that justice may not be done in a corner nor in any covert manner, being intended and resolved, by the help of the Lord, and by these our Concessions and Fundamentals, that all and every person and persons inhabiting the said Province, shall, as far as in us lies, be free from oppression and slavery.

Source: The Charter or Fundamental Laws of West New Jersey (1676). The Avalon Project at Yale Law School. Available online at URL: http://www.yale.edu/lawweb/avalon/states/nj05.htm.

7. Excerpts from the English Bill of Rights, 1689

. . . [T]he Lords Spiritual and Temporal and Commons . . . do in the first place (as their ancestors in like case have usually done) for the vindicating and asserting their ancient rights and liberties declare . . .

That excessive bail ought not to be required, nor excessive fines imposed, nor cruel and unusual punishments inflicted;

That jurors ought to be duly impaneled and returned, and jurors which pass upon men in trials for high treason ought to be freeholders;

That all grants and promises of fines and forfeitures of particular persons before conviction are illegal and void;

And that for redress of all grievances, and for the amending, strengthening and preserving of the laws, Parliaments ought to be held frequently . . .

Source: The English Parliament, An Act Declaring the Rights and Liberties of the Subjects and Settling the Succession of the Crown (1689), most commonly known as the English Bill of Rights. The Avalon Project at Yale Law School. Available online at URL: http://www.yale.edu/lawweb/avalon/england.htm.

8. Excerpts from the Pennsylvania Charter of Privileges, 1701

That all criminals shall have the same privileges of witnesses and council as their prosecutors.

That no person or persons shall or may, at any time hereafter, be obliged to answer any complaint, matter, or thing whatsoever, relating to property, before the governor and council, or in any other place, but in ordinary course of justice, unless appeals thereto shall be hereafter by law appointed . . .

If any person, through temptation or melancholy, shall destroy himself; his estate, real and personal, shall notwithstanding descend to his wife and children, or relations, as if he had died a natural death . . .

Source: Pennsylvania governor William Penn, from articles V, VI, and VIII of the Pennsylvania Charter of Privileges (1701). The Avalon Project at Yale Law School. Available online at URL: http://www.yale.edu/lawweb/avalon/states/pa07.htm.

9. Excerpts from the Virginia Slave Codes, 1705

And for a further prevention of that abominable mixture and spurious issue [of mixed-race marriages], which hereafter may increase in this her majesty's colony and dominion . . . Be it enacted . . . That whatsoever English, or other white man or woman, being free, shall intermarry with a negro or mulatto man or woman, bond or free, shall, by judgment of the county court, be committed to prison, and there remain, during the space of six months, without bail or manprize; and shall forfeit and pay ten pounds current money of Virginia, to the use of the parish, as aforesaid.

And be it further enacted, That no minister of the church of England, or other minister, or person whatsoever, within this colony and dominion, shall hereafter wittingly presume to marry a white woman with a negro or mulatto man, upon pain of forfeiting and paying, for every such marriage the sum of ten thousand pounds of tobacco; one half to our sovereign lady the Queen, her heirs and successors, for and towards the support of the government, and the contingent charges thereof; and the other half to the informer; To be recovered, with costs, by action . . . wherein no essoin, protection, or wager of law, shall be allowed . . .

And if any slave resist his master, or owner, or other person, by his or her order, correcting such slave, and shall happen to be killed in such correction, it shall not be accounted felony; but the master, owner, and every such other person so giving correction, shall be free and acquit of all punishment and accusation for the same, as if such accident had never happened . . .

And whereas, many times, slaves run away and lie out, hid and lurking in swamps, woods, and other obscure places . . . Be it therefore enacted . . . [That] proclamation [of runaway slaves] shall be published on a Sabbath day, at the door of every church and chapel, in the said county, by the parish clerk, or reader, of the church, immediately after divine worship: And in case any slave, against whom proclamation has thus been issued, and once published at any church or chapel, as aforesaid, stay out, and do not immediately return home, it shall be lawful for any person or persons whatsoever, to kill and destroy such slaves by such ways and means as he, she, or they shall think fit, without accusation or impeachment of any crime for the same.

Source: The Virginia legislature, An Act Concerning Servants and Slaves. October 1705. Virginia Statutes on

Slaves and Servants. Available online at URL: http://www.law.du.edu/russell/lh/alh/docs/virginiaslaverystatutes.html.

10. Excerpts from the Virginia Declaration of Rights, 1776

That in all capital or criminal prosecutions a man hath a right to demand the cause and nature of his accusation, to be confronted with the accusers and witnesses, to call for evidence in his favor, and to a speedy trial by an impartial jury of his vicinage, without whose unanimous consent he cannot be found guilty, nor can be compelled to give evidence against himself; that no man be deprived of his liberty except by the law of the land or the judgment of his peers.

That excessive bail ought not to be required, nor excessive fines imposed; nor cruel and unusual punishments inflicted.

That general warrants, whereby any officer or messenger may be commanded to search suspected places without evidence of a fact committed, or to seize any person or persons not named, or whose offense is not particularly described and supported by evidence, are grievous and oppressive and ought not to be granted.

Source: Virginia legislator George Mason, from the Virginia Declaration of Rights (1776). The Avalon Project at Yale Law School. Available online at URL: http://www.yale.edu/lawweb/avalon/virginia.htm.

11. Excerpts from the Declaration of Independence, 1776

We hold these truths to be self-evident: that all men are created equal; that they are endowed, by their Creator, with certain unalienable rights; that among these are life, liberty, and the pursuit of happiness. That to secure these rights, governments are instituted among men, deriving their just powers from the consent of the governed; that whenever any form of government becomes destructive of these ends, it is the right of the people to alter or abolish it, and to institute a new government, laying its foundation on such principles, and organizing its powers in such form, as to them shall seem most likely to affect their safety and happiness . . . The history of the present King of Great Britain is a history of repeated injuries and usurpations, all having in direct object the establishment of a direct tyranny over these states. To prove this, let facts be submitted to a candid world . . .

He has obstructed the administration of justice, by refusing his assent to laws for establishing judiciary powers.

He has made judges dependent on his will alone, for the tenure of their offices, and the amount and payment of their salaries . . .

For depriving us, in many cases, of the benefits of trial by jury ;

For transporting us beyond seas to be tried for pretended offences ; . . .

In every state of these oppressions we have petitioned for redress in the most humble terms. Our repeated petitions have been answered only by repeated injury. A prince, whose character is thus marked by every act which may define a tyrant, is unfit to be the ruler of a free people.

Source: Thomas Jefferson, from the "Declaration of Independence" (1776). The National Archives Experience. Available online at URL: http://www.archives.gov/national_archives_experience/charters/declaration.html.

12. Excerpts from the Pennsylvania Declaration of Rights, 1776

That in all prosecutions for criminal offences, a man hath a right to be heard by himself and his council, to demand the cause and nature of his accusation, to be confronted with the witnesses, to call for evidence in his favour, and a speedy public trial, by an impartial jury of the country, without the unanimous consent of which jury he cannot be found guilty; nor can he be compelled to give evidence against himself; nor can any man be justly deprived of his liberty except by the laws of the land, or the judgment of his peers.

That the people have a right to hold themselves, their houses, papers, and possessions free from search and seizure, and therefore warrants without oaths or affirmations first made, affording a sufficient foundation for them, and whereby any officer or messenger may be commanded or required to search suspect places, or to seize any person or persons, his or their property, not particularly described, are contrary to that right, and ought not to be granted.

Source: From the Pennsylvania Declaration of Rights (1776). The Avalon Project at Yale Law School. Available online at URL: http://www.yale.edu/lawweb/avalon/states/pa08.htm.

13. Excerpt from the Maryland Declaration of Rights, 1776

That retrospective laws, punishing facts committed before the existence of such laws, and by them only declared criminal, are oppressive, unjust, and incompatible with liberty; wherefore no *ex post facto* law ought to be made.

That no law, to attains particular persons of treason or felony, ought to be made in any case, or at any time hereafter.

Source: The Maryland Declaration of Rights (1776), Articles XV and XVI. The Avalon Project at Yale Law School. Available online at URL: http://www.yale.edu/lawweb/avalon/states/ma02.htm.

14. Excerpt from the North Carolina Declaration of Rights, 1776

That no freeman shall be put to answer any criminal charge, but by indictment, presentment, or impeachment.

Source: The North Carolina Declaration of Rights, Article VIII (1776), quoted in Butler, *The North Carolina Experience*, p. 158.

15. Excerpt from the U.S. Treaty with the Lenape Nation, 1778

For the better security of the peace and friendship now entered into by the contracting parties, against all infractions of the same by the citizens of either party, to the prejudice of the other, neither party shall proceed to the infliction of punishments on the citizens of the other, otherwise than by securing the offender or offenders by imprisonment, or any other competent means, till a fair and impartial trial can be had by judges or juries of both parties, as near as can be to the laws, customs and usages of the contracting parties and natural justice. The mode of such trials to be hereafter fixed by the wise men of the United States in Congress assembled, with the assistance of such deputies of the Delaware nation, as may be appointed to acting in concert with them in adjusting this matter to their mutual liking. And it be further agreed between the parties aforesaid, that neither shall . . . protect in their respective states, criminal fugitives, servants or slaves, but the same to apprehend, and secure and deliver to the State or States, to which such enemies, criminals, servants or slaves respectively belong.

Source: U.S. treaty with the Delaware (Lenape tribe), Article IV. September 17, 1778. Oklahoma State University Library Electronic Publishing Center. Available online at URL: http://digital.library.okstate.edu/kappler/Vol2/treaties/del0003.htm.

16. Excerpts from the U.S. Treaty with the Cherokee Nation, 1785

If any Indian or Indians, or person residing among them, or who shall take refuge in their nation, shall commit a robbery, or murder, or other capital crime, on any citizen of the United States, or person under their protection, the nation, or the tribe to which such offender or offenders may belong, shall be bound to deliver him or them up to be punished according to the ordinances of the United States; Provided, that the punishment shall not be greater than if the robbery or murder, or other capital crime had been committed by a [U.S.] citizen on a citizen.

If any citizen of the United States, or person under their protection, shall commit a robbery or murder, or other capital crime, on any Indian, such offender or offenders shall be punished in the same manner as if the murder or robbery, or other capital crime, had been committed on a citizen of the United States; and the punishment shall be in presence of some of the Cherokees, if any shall attend at the time and place, and that they may have an opportunity to do so, due notice of the time of such intended punishment shall be sent to some one of the tribes.

It is understood that the punishment of the innocent under the idea of retaliation is unjust, and shall not be practiced on either side, except where there is a manifest violation of this treaty; and then it shall be preceded first by a demand of justice, and if refused, then by a declaration of hostilities.

Source: U.S. treaty with the Cherokee Nation, Articles VI, VII, and VIII. November 28, 1785. The New Nation, 1783–1815, at the Library of Congress. Available online at URL: http://lcweb2.loc.gov/learn/features/timeline/newnatn/nativeam/cherokee.html.

17. Excerpts from the U.S. Constitution, 1787

The Privilege of the Writ of Habeas Corpus shall not be suspended, unless when in Cases of Rebellion or Invasion of the public Safety may require it.

No Bill of Attainder or ex post facto Law shall be passed.

The judicial Power of the United States, shall be vested in one supreme Court, and in such inferior Courts as the Congress may from time to time ordain and establish. The Judges, both of the supreme and inferior Courts, shall hold their Offices during good Behaviour, and shall, at stated Times, receive for their Services, a Compensation, which shall not be diminished during their Continuance in Office . . .

The judicial Power shall extend to all Cases, in Law and Equity, arising under this Constitution, the Laws of the United States, and Treaties made, or which shall be made, under this Authority . . .

In all Cases affecting Ambassadors, other public Ministers and Consuls, and those in which a State shall be a Party, the supreme Court shall have original Jurisdiction. In all the other Cases before mentioned, the supreme Court shall have appellate Jurisdiction, both as to Law and Fact, with such Exceptions, and under such Regulations as the Congress shall make . . .

The Trial of all Crimes, except in Cases of Impeachment, shall be by Jury; and such Trial shall be held in the State where the said Crimes shall have been committed; but when not committed within any State, the Trial shall be at such Place or Places as the Congress may by Law have directed . . .

Treason against the United States, shall consist only in levying War against them, or in adhering to their Enemies, giving them Aid and Comfort. No Person shall be convicted of Treason unless on the Testimony of two Witnesses of the same overt Act, or on Confession in open Court . . .

The Congress shall have Power to declare the punishment of Treason, but no Attainder of Treason shall work Corruption of Blood, or Forfeiture except during the Life of the Person attained . . .

Source: The U.S. Constitution (1787), from Article I, Section 9, and Article III.

18. Legal penalties suggested by Thomas Jefferson, Notes on the State of Virginia, 1785

I. Crimes whose punishment extends to Life.

1. High treason.   Death by hanging. [and]
                   Forfeiture of lands and goods to the commonwealth.

2. Petty treason.   Death by hanging. Dissection. [and]
                    Forfeiture of half the lands and goods to the representatives of the party slain.

3. Murder.   1. by poison.   Death by poison. [and]
                             Forfeiture of one-half as before.

             2. in Duel.   Death by hanging. Gibbeting [public hanging], if the challenger. [and] Forfeiture of one-half as before, unless it be the party challenged, then the forfeiture is to the commonwealth.

             3. in any other way   Death by hanging. [and] Forfeiture of one-half as before.

4. Manslaughter.   The second offence is murder.

II. Crimes whose punishment goes to Limb.

1. Rape,   Dismemberment [castration].
2. [or] Sodomy,
3. Maiming,   Retaliation, and the forfeiture of half the lands and
4. [or] Disfiguring goods to the sufferer.

III. Crimes punishable by Labour.

1. Manslaughter, 1st offence.   Labour [seven] years for the public. [and] Forfeiture of half as in murder.

2. Counterfeiting money.   Labour [six] years. [and] Forfeiture of lands and goods to the commonwealth.

3. Arson.   Labour [four] years. [and] Reparation three-fold.

4. Asportation [piracy] of vessels.   Labour [four] years. [and]

5. [or] Robbery.   Reparation double.

6. [or] Burglary.

7. Housebreaking.   Labour [three] years. [and]

8. [or] Horse-stealing. Reparation.
9. Grand larceny.   Labour [two] years. Reparation.
                           Pillory.
10. Petty larceny.   Labour [one] year. Reparation.
                           Pillory.
11. Pretentions to   Ducking [dunking]. Stripes
    witchcraft, &c.   [whipping].
12. Excusable   to be pitied, not punished.
    homicide.
13. [or] Suicide.
14. [or] Apostacy. Heresy

Source: Thomas Jefferson, suggested revised legal code for the State of Virginia from *Notes on the State of Virginia* (1785). The Electronic Text Center at the University of Virginia Library. Available online at URL: http://etext. lib.virginia.edu/toc/modeng/public/ JefVirg.html.

19. Excerpts from the U.S. Bill of Rights, 1789

Amendment I
Congress shall make no law respecting an establishment of religion, or prohibiting the free exercise thereof; or abridging the freedom of speech, or of the press; or the right of the people peaceably to assemble, and to petition the government for a redress of grievances . . .

Amendment IV
The right of the people to be secure in their persons, houses, papers, and effects, against unreasonable searches and seizures, shall not be violated, and no warrants shall issue, but upon probable cause, supported by oath or affirmation, and particularly describing the place to be searched, and the persons or things to be seized.

Amendment V
No person shall be held to answer for a capital, or otherwise infamous crime, unless on a presentment or indictment of a grand jury, except in cases arising in the land or naval forces, or in the militia, when in actual service in time of war or public danger; nor shall any person be subject for the same offense to be twice put in jeopardy of life or limb; nor shall be compelled in any criminal case to be a witness against himself, nor be deprived of life, liberty, or property, without due process of law . . .

Amendment VI
In all criminal prosecutions, the accused shall enjoy the right to a speedy and public trial, by an impartial jury of the state and district wherein the crime shall have been committed, which district shall have been previously ascertained by law, and to be informed of the nature and cause of the accusation; to be confronted with the witnesses against him; to have compulsory process for obtaining witnesses in his favor, and to have the assistance of counsel for his defense . . .

Amendment VIII
Excessive bail shall not be required, nor excessive fines imposed, nor cruel and unusual punishments inflicted . . .

Source: The U.S. Constitution, Amendments I, IV–VI, and VIII (1789).

20. The U.S. Crimes Act, 1790

That if any person or persons, owing allegiance to the United States of America, shall levy war against them, or shall adhere to their enemies, giving them aid and comfort within the United States, or elsewhere, and shall be thereof convicted, on confession in open Court, or on the testimony of two witnesses to the same overt act of the treason whereof he or they shall stand indicted, such person or persons shall be adjudged guilty of treason against the United States, and shall suffer death.

And be it enacted, That if any person or persons, having knowledge of the commission of any of the treasons aforesaid, shall conceal . . . such person or persons, on conviction, shall be adjudged guilty of misprision of treason, and shall be imprisoned not exceeding seven years, and fined not exceeding one thousand dollars.

And be it enacted, That if any person or persons shall, within any fort, arsenal, dockyard, magazine, or in any other place or district of country, under the sole and exclusive jurisdiction of the United States, commit the crime of wilful murder, such person or persons, on being thereof convicted, shall suffer death.

And be it enacted, That if any person or persons, having knowledge of the actual commission of the crime of wilful murder, or other felony, upon the high seas, or within any fort, arsenal, dockyard, magazine, or other place or district of country, under the sole and exclusive jurisdiction of the United States, shall conceal . . . such person or persons shall be adjudged guilty of misprision of felony, and shall be imprisoned not exceeding three years, and fined not exceeding five hundred dollars.

And be it enacted, That if any person or persons shall, within any fort, arsenal, dockyard, magazine, or other place or district of country, under the sole and exclusive jurisdiction of the United States, commit the crime of manslaughter, and shall be thereof convicted, such person or persons shall be imprisoned not exceeding three years, and fined not exceeding one thousand dollars.

And be it enacted, That if any person or persons shall commit, upon the high seas, or in any river, haven, basin, or bay, out of the jurisdiction of any particular State, murder or robbery, or any other offence, which, if committed within the body of a county, would, by the laws of the United States, be punishable with death; or, if any captain or mariner of any ship or other vessel, shall piratically and feloniously run away with such ship or vessel, or any goods or merchandize, to the value of fifty dollars, or yield up such ship or vessel voluntarily to any pirate; or if any seaman shall lay violent hands upon his commander, thereby to hinder and prevent his fighting in defence of his ship, or goods committed to his trust, or shall make a revolt in the ship; every such offender shall be deemed, taken, and adjudged to be, a pirate and felon, and being thereof convicted, shall suffer death: and the trial of crimes committed on the high seas, or in any place out of the jurisdiction of any particular State, shall be in the district where the offender is apprehended, or into which he may first be brought.

And be it enacted, That if any citizen shall commit any piracy or robbery, aforesaid, or any act of hostility against the United States, or any citizen thereof, upon the high seas, under colour of any commission from any foreign prince or State, or on pretence of authority from any person, such offender shall, notwithstanding the pretence of authority, be deemed, adjudged, and taken to be, a pirate, felon, and robber, and on being thereof convicted, shall suffer death.

And be it enacted, That every person who shall either upon the land or seas, knowingly and wittingly aid and assist, procure, command, counsel or advise, any person or persons to do or commit any murder or robbery, or other piracy aforesaid, upon the high seas, which shall affect the life of such person, and such person or persons shall thereupon do or commit any such piracy or robbery, then all and every such person, so as aforesaid aiding, assisting, procuring, commanding, counselling, or advising the same, either upon the land or the sea, shall be, and they are hereby declared, deemed, and adjudged to be, accessary to such piracies before the fact, and every such person, being thereof convicted, shall suffer death.

And be it enacted, That after any murder, felony, robbery, or other piracy whatsoever, aforesaid, is or shall be committed by any pirate or robber, every person who,

knowing that such pirate or robber has done or committed any such piracy or robbery, shall, on the land or at sea, receive, entertain, or conceal, any such pirate or robber, or receive or take into his custody any ship, vessel, goods, or chattels, which have been, by any such pirate or robber, piratically and feloniously taken, shall be, and are hereby declared, deemed and adjudged, to be accessary to such piracy or robbery, after the fact; and on conviction thereof, shall be imprisoned, not exceeding three years, and fined, not exceeding five hundred dollars.

And be it enacted, That if any seaman or other person shall commit manslaughter upon the high seas, or confederate, or attempt or endeavour to corrupt any commander, master, such person or persons so offending, and being thereof convicted, shall be imprisoned not exceeding three years, and fined not exceeding one thousand dollars.

Source: U.S. Congress, "Crimes Act," 1790. The First Federal Congress Project at George Washington University. Available online at URL: http://www2.gwu.edu/~ffcp/exhibit/p6/p6_7Large.jpg.

21. The Indian Tribes Act, 1790

And be it further enacted, That if any citizen or inhabitant of the United States, or of either of the territorial districts of the United States, shall go into any town, settlement or territory belonging to any nation or tribe of Indians, and shall there commit any crime upon, or trespass against, the person or property of any peaceable and friendly Indian or Indians, which, if committed within the jurisdiction of any state, or within the jurisdiction of either of the said districts, against a citizen or white inhabitant thereof, would be punishable by the laws of such state or district, such offender or offenders shall be subject to the same punishment, and shall be proceeded against in the same manner as if the offence had been committed within the jurisdiction of the state or district to which he or they may belong, against a citizen or white inhabitant thereof.

And be it further enacted, That for any of the crimes or offences aforesaid, the like proceedings shall be had for apprehending, imprisoning or bailing the offender, as the case may be, and for recognizing the witnesses for their appearance to testify in the case, and where the offender shall be committed, or the witnesses shall be in a district other than that in which the offence is to be tried, for the removal of the offender and the witnesses or either of them, as the case may be, to the district in which the trial is to be had, as by the act to establish the judicial courts of the United States, are directed for any crimes or offenses against the United States.

And be it further enacted, That this act shall be in force for the term of two years, and from thence to the end of the next session of Congress, and no longer.

Source: U.S. Congress, "An Act to Regulate Trade and Intercourse with the Indian Tribes." July 22, 1790. The Avalon Project at Yale Law School. Available online at URL: http://www.yale.edu/lawweb/avalon/statutes/native/na024.htm.

22. The Fugitive Slave Act of 1793

Be it enacted, &c., That whenever the Executive authority of any State in the Union, or of either of the Territories Northwest or South of the river Ohio, shall demand any person as a fugitive from justice, of the Executive authority of any such State or Territory to which such person shall have fled, and shall moreover produce a copy of an indictment fund, or an affidavit made before a magistrate of any State or Territory as aforesaid, charging the person so demanded with having committed treason, felony, or other crime, certified as authentic by the Governor or Chief Magistrate of the State or Territory from whence the person was so charged fled, it shall be the duty of the executive authority of the State or Territory to which such person shall have fled, to cause him or her arrest to be given to the Executive authority making such demand, or to the agent when he shall appear; but, if no such agent shall appear within six months from the time of the arrest, the prisoner may be discharged: and all costs or expenses incurred in the apprehending, securing, and transmitting such fugitive to the State or Territory making such demand, shall be paid by the State or Territory.

And be it further enacted, That any agent appointed as aforesaid, who shall receive the fugitive into his custody, shall be empowered to transport him or her to the State or Territory from which he or she shall have fled. And if any person or persons shall, by force, set at liberty, or rescue the fugitive from such agent while transporting, as aforesaid, the person or persons so offending shall, on conviction, be fined not exceeding five hundred dollars, and be imprisoned not exceeding one year.

And be it also enacted, That when a person held to labor in any of the United States, or in either of the Territories on the Northwest or South of the river Ohio, under the laws thereof, shall escape into any other part of the said States or Territory, the person to whom such labor or service may be due, his agent or attorney, is hereby em-

powered to seize or arrest such fugitive from labor, and to take him or her before any Judge of the Circuit or District Courts of the United States, residing or being within the State, or before any magistrate of a county, city, or town corporate, wherein such seizure or arrest shall be made, and upon proof to the satisfaction of such Judge or magistrate, either by oral testimony or affidavit taken before and certified by a magistrate of such State or Territory, that the person so seized or arrested, doth, under the laws, of the State or Territory from which he or she fled, owe service or labor to the person claiming him or her, it shall be the duty of such Judge or magistrate to give a certificate thereof to such claimant, his agent, or attorney, which shall be sufficient warrant for removing the said fugitive from labor to the State or Territory from which he or she fled.

And be it further enacted, That any person who shall knowingly and willingly obstruct or hinder such claimant, his agent, or attorney, in so seizing or arresting such fugitive from labor, or shall rescue such fugitive from such claimant, his agent or attorney, when so arrested pursuant to the authority herein given and declared; or shall harbor or conceal such persons after notice that he or she was a fugitive from labor, as aforesaid, shall, for either of the said offences, forfeit and pay the sum of five hundred dollars. Which penalty may be recovered by and for the benefit of such claimant, by action of debt, in any Court proper to try the same, saving moreover to the person claiming such labor or service his right of action for or on account of the said injuries, or either of them.

Source: U.S. Congress, An Act Respecting Fugitives from Justice, and Persons Escaping from the Service of Their Masters, February 12, 1793. The Independence Hall Association. Available online at URL: http://www.ushistory.org/presidentshouse/slaves/slaveact1793.htm.

23. The Alien Enemies Act, 1798

Be it enacted . . . That whenever there shall be a declared war between the United States and any foreign nation or government, or any invasion or predatory incursion shall be perpetrated, attempted, or threatened against the territory of the United States, by any foreign nation or government, and the President of the United States shall make public proclamation of the event, all natives, citizens, denizens, or subjects of the hostile nation or government, being males of the age of fourteen years and upwards, who shall be within the United States, and not actually naturalized, shall be liable to be apprehended, restrained, secured and removed, as alien enemies . . . Provided, that aliens resident within the United States, who shall become liable as enemies, in the manner aforesaid, and who shall not be chargeable with actual hostility, or other crime against the public safety, shall be allowed, for the recovery, disposal, and removal of their goods and effects, and for their departure, the full time which is, or shall be stipulated by any treaty [where applicable] . . . [or] according to the dictates of humanity and national hospitality.

Source: U.S. Congress, "An Act Respecting Alien Enemies," July 6, 1798. The Avalon Project at Yale Law School. Available online at URL: http://www.yale. edu/lawweb/avalon/statutes/alien.htm.

24. Excerpts from the Sedition Act of 1798

Be it enacted . . . That if any persons shall unlawfully combine or conspire together, with intent to oppose any measure or measures of the government of the United States, which are or shall be directed by proper authority, or to impede the operation of any law of the United States, or to intimidate or prevent any person holding a place or office in or under the government of the United States, from undertaking, performing or executing his trust or duty, and if any person or persons, with intent as aforesaid, shall counsel, advise or attempt to procure any insurrection, riot, unlawful assembly, or combination, whether such conspiracy, threatening, counsel, advice, or attempt shall have the proposed effect or not, he or they shall be deemed guilty of a high misdemeanor, and on conviction, before any court of the United States having jurisdiction thereof, shall be punished by a fine not exceeding five thousand dollars, and by imprisonment during a term not less than six months nor exceeding five years . . .

And be it further enacted, That if any person shall write, print, utter or publish, or shall cause or procure to be written, printed, uttered or published, or shall knowingly and willingly assist or aid in writing, printing, uttering or publishing any false, scandalous and malicious writing or writings against the government of the United States, or either house of the Congress of the United States, or the President of the United States, with intent to defame the said government, or either house of the said Congress, or the said President, or to bring them, or either of them, into contempt or disrepute; or to excite against them, or either or any of them, the hatred of the good people of the United States, or to stir up sedition within the United States, or to excite any unlawful combinations therein, for opposing or resisting any law of the United States,

or any act of the President of the United States, done in pursuance of any such law, or of the powers in him vested by the constitution of the United States, or to resist, oppose, or defeat any such law or act, or to aid, encourage or abet any hostile designs of any foreign nation against the United States, their people or government, then such person, being thereof convicted before any court of the United States having jurisdiction thereof, shall be punished by a fine not exceeding two thousand dollars, and by imprisonment not exceeding two years.

And be it further enacted, That if any person shall be prosecuted under this act, for the writing or publishing any libel aforesaid, it shall be lawful for the defendant, upon the trial of the cause, to give in evidence in his defence, the truth of the matter contained in the publication charged as a libel. And the jury who shall try the cause, shall have a right to determine the law and the fact, under the direction of the court, as in other cases.

And be it further enacted, That this act shall continue and be in force until the third day of March, one thousand eight hundred and one, and no longer: Provided, that the expiration of the act shall not prevent or defeat a prosecution and punishment of any offence against the law, during the time it shall be in force.

Source: U.S. Congress, "Addendum to An Act for the Punishment of Certain Crimes Against the United States" [generally known the Sedition Act], July 14, 1798. The Avalon Project at Yale Law School. Available online at URL: http://www.yale.edu/lawweb/avalon/ statutes/sedact.htm.

25. The Virginia Resolution of 1798

RESOLVED, That the General Assembly of Virginia, doth unequivocally express a firm resolution to maintain and defend the Constitution of the United States, and the Constitution of this State, against every aggression either foreign or domestic, and that they will support the government of the United States in all measures warranted by the former.

That this assembly most solemnly declares a warm attachment to the Union of the States, to maintain which it pledges all its powers; and that for this end, it is their duty to watch over and oppose every infraction of those principles which constitute the only basis of that Union, because a faithful observance of them, can alone secure its existence and the public happiness . . .

That the General Assembly doth also express its deep regret, that a spirit has in sundry instances, been manifested by the federal government, to enlarge its powers by forced constructions of the constitutional charter which defines them; and that implications have appeared of a design to expound certain general phrases (which having been copied from the very limited grant of power, in the former articles of confederation were the less liable to be misconstrued) so as to destroy the meaning and effect, of the particular enumeration which necessarily explains and limits the general phrases; and so as to consolidate the states by degrees, into one sovereignty, the obvious tendency and inevitable consequence of which would be, to transform the present republican system of the United States, into an absolute, or at best a mixed monarchy.

That the General Assembly doth particularly protest against the palpable and alarming infractions of the Constitution, in the two late cases of the "Alien and Sedition Acts" passed at the last session of Congress; the first of which exercises a power nowhere delegated to the federal government, and which by uniting legislative and judicial powers to those of executive, subverts the general principles of free government; as well as the particular organization, and positive provisions of the federal constitution; and the other of which acts, exercises in like manner, a power not delegated by the constitution, but on the contrary, expressly and positively forbidden by one of the amendments thererto; a power, which more than any other, ought to produce universal alarm, because it is leveled against that right of freely examining public characters and measures, and of free communication among the people thereon, which has ever been justly deemed, the only effectual guardian of every other right.

That this state having by its Convention, which ratified the federal Constitution, expressly declared, that among other essential rights, "the Liberty of Conscience and of the Press cannot be cancelled, abridged, restrained, or modified by any authority of the United States," and from its extreme anxiety to guard these rights from every possible attack of sophistry or ambition, having with other states, recommended an amendment for that purpose, which amendment was, in due time, annexed to the Constitution; it would mark a reproachable inconsistency, and criminal degeneracy, if an indifference were now shewn, to the most palpable violation of one of the Rights, thus declared and secured; and to the establishment of a precedent which may be fatal to the other.

Source: Virginia Senate, Resolution of December 24, 1798. The Avalon Project at Yale Law School. Available online at URL: http://www.yale.edu/lawweb/avalon/virres.htm.

26. The Kentucky Resolution of 1799

THE representatives of the good people of this commonwealth in general assembly convened, having maturely considered the answers of sundry states in the Union, to their resolutions passed at the last session, respecting certain unconstitutional laws of Congress, commonly called the alien and sedition laws, would be faithless indeed to themselves, and to those they represent, were they silently to acquiesce in principles and doctrines attempted to be maintained in all those answers, that of Virginia only excepted. To again enter the field of argument, and attempt more fully or forcibly to expose the unconstitutionality of those obnoxious laws, would, it is apprehended be as unnecessary as unavailing . . .

[I]n order that no pretext or arguments may be drawn from a supposed acquiescence on the part of this commonwealth in the constitutionality of those laws, and be thereby used as precedents for similar future violations of federal compact; this commonwealth does now enter against them, its SOLEMN PROTEST.

Source: Kentucky Senate, Resolution of December 3, 1799. The Avalon Project at Yale Law School. Available online at URL: http://www.yale.edu/lawweb/avalon/kenres.htm.

27. Excerpts from Instructions for the London Metropolitan Police, 1829

The following provisional instructions for the different ranks of the police force are not to be understood as containing certain rules of conduct under every variety of circumstances that may occur in the performance of their duty; something must necessarily be left to the intelligence and discretion of individuals; and according to the degree in which they show themselves possessed of those qualities, and to the zeal, activity, and judgment they display on all occasions, will be their claims to future promotion and reward.

It should be understood at the outset, that the object to be attained is "the prevention of crime."

To this great end every effort of the police is to be directed. The security of person and property, the preservation of the public tranquility, and all the other objects of a police establishment, will thus be better effected than by the detection and punishment of the offender after he has succeeded in committing the crime. This should constantly be kept in mind by every member of the police force, as the guide for his own conduct. Officers and police constables should endeavour to distinguish themselves by such vigilance and activity as may render it impossible for any one to commit a crime within that portion of the town under their charge.

When many offencers are committed, it must appear to the commissioners that the police is not properly conducted in that division; and the absence of crime will be considered the best proof of the complete efficiency of the police. In a division where this security and good order have been effected, the officers and men belonging to it may feel assured that such good conduct will be noticed by rewards and promotion.

Local Divisions.

1. The metropolitan police district will be formed into police divisions.
2. That part of the district which is taken under the charge of the police force, in the first instance, comprising a large proportion of town, is formed into five regular police divisions.
3. The number of men and officers, and the constitution of the force, are the same in each division; but in laying out the division, attention has been paid to local and other circumstances determining the number of men required, so that the superficial contents of the divisions differ greatly, and consequently that portion of each committed to the care of one man.
4. Each division is again divided into eight sections.
5. Each section into eight beats.
6. The limits of each of these is clearly defined; each is numbered, and the number entered into a book to be kept for the purpose.
7. Each division has an appropriate local name, and is also designated by a letter of the alphabet.
8. There is in every division a station or watch-house, placed as conveniently for the whole as may be ...

Police Force.

1. The Police force consists of as many companies as there are Police Local Divisions, one company being allotted to each division.
2. Each company is formed as follows:—1 Superintendent, 4 Inspectors, 16 Serjeants, and 144 Police Constables.
3. The company is divided into sixteen parties, each consisting of one serjeant and nine men.

4. The whole company is under the command of the superintendent.
5. Each man is conspicuously marked with the letter of his division, and a number, corresponding with his name in the books, so that he can at all times be known to the public.
6. The first 16 numbers in each division denote the serjeants.
7. A smaller police company is attached to the office of the commissioners, for the duty in the immediate neighbourhood, and is also applicable to general purposes.

Conditions.

The conditions upon which each man is to be admitted into the Police Force are stated here, that no complaint may be made hereafter upon their being enforced. The Commissioners of Police desire it to be understood at the same time, that they reserve their power to alter or annul any of these; and also to make such new rules as may be found expedient.

1. He shall devote his whole time to the police service.
2. He shall serve and reside wherever he is appointed.
3. He shall promptly obey all lawful orders which he may receive from the persons placed in authority over him.
4. He shall conform himself to all the regulations which may be made, from time to time, for the good of the service.
5. He shall not, upon any occasion, or under any pretence whatsoever, take money from any person without the express permission of the commissioners.
6. He shall get such articles of clothes as the commissioners shall direct, from the respective contractors, and pay for them, ready money, or by deductions made from his weekly pay, under the directions of the commissioners.
7. He shall furnish himself with new clothes whenever the commissioners may direct.
8. He shall, at all times, appear in his complete police dress.
9. He shall allow a deduction of 1s. a week to be made from his pay, if unmarried, when lodgings are found for him.
10. If married, when lodgings are found, an agreement will be made in each particular case.
11. He shall pay all such debts contracted by him, as the commissioners shall direct.
12. He shall receive his pay weekly, on such day as shall be appointed.

13. His pay as common constable is 3*s.* per day, subject to the deductions above mentioned, for clothes and lodgings.
14. He shall be supplied with an account-book, which he is to have to produce at all times, when required.
15. He shall not quit the police force, without giving a month's previous notice; in case he shall quit without such notice, all pay then due shall be forfeited.
16. He shall not use, or allow to be used, the baton, marked "Police Force," except while he belongs to the police service.

Each police constable is liable to dismissal, or such other punishment as may by law be inflicted for the breach of any of the foregoing rules. Also, the Commissioners will, if they shall think fit, dismiss him without assigning any reason.

Outline of General Duty.

1. The duty will commence each evening at an hour regulated by the setting of the sun; when any change becomes necessary, it will be specified in orders.
2. One part of the force, for duty from the commencement of the evening till midnight, the second night relief; in like manner may be a first and second day relief.
3. One half of the entire force will be on duty at night, consisting of two inspectors and eight serjeants, with their respective parties, at one time; and these will be relieved by the other half, at the hours and in the manner hereinafter specified.
4. Each serjeant's party, when on duty, will have charge of its respective section of the division, each police constable having a beat appropriated to him, within the section.
5. In case any constables should be absent from sickness or any other cause, his place will be supplied from the reserve of his section.
6. There will be nine men belonging to each serjeant's party, and only eight beats in a section; thus one man of each section will remain at the division station, forming a reserve of eight men for the whole division, to supply occasional absences, and to be ready for such duties as may be required there.
7. If from sickness of one of the men, or any other cause, the reserve men at the division station be required for duty, their place must be supplied by the men of the relief going off duty; when this becomes necessary, the reserve party, formed of the men going off duty, will be permitted to take their rest at the station, as far as circumstances will permit . . .

Police Constable.

Every police constable in the force may hope to so rise by intelligence and good conduct to the superior stations. It is therefore recommended to each man to endeavour, by studying these instructions, and by reflecting upon the nature of the duty he has to perform, to qualify himself for such promotion. But . . . he will most certainly recommend himself . . . by a diligent discharge of his sworn duties, and a strict obedience to . . . his superiors, recollecting that he who has been accustomed to . . . discipline, will be considered best qualified to enforce it hereafter . . .

He will be held responsible for the security of the lives, and safety of all property, of every person within his beat, and for the . . . peace and general good order of the whole, during the time he is on duty.

He must understand what powers he possesses to effect these objectives, either by arresting criminals, disturbers of the person, and evil-disposed persons, by searching houses when he is required, by taking bundles, and other articles carried at night by suspicious persons; and he is recommended to read carefully the instructions to him respecting the general duties of a constable . . .

As it is more important to prevent and punish the commission of great crimes than of the lesser offences, the constable has a greater power in cases of felonies than in those of mere misdemeanors.

But the first duty of a constable is always to prevent the commission of a crime . . .

As when a lunatic, or a drunken person, or a man in a violent passion, threatens the life of another, or when people are fighting furiously, or breaking into a house, or doing such things which are likely to lead to the commission of any felony, the constable should interfere and arrest the parties.

So any person having in his possession any pick-lock key, crow, jack, bit, or other implement, with intent feloniously to break into any dwelling-house, warehouse, coach-house, stable, or out-building, or being armed with any . . . offensive weapon, or having upon him any instrument with intent to commit any felonious act . . .

In each of these cases the constable must judge from the situation and behaviour of the party what his intention is. In some cases no doubt can exist, as when the party is a nefarious thief, or acting with those who are thieves, or when the party is seen to try people's pockets in a crowd, attempt to break into a house, or has endeavoured to carry off any property secretly from another! but the constable shall not act hastily, if the intentions are not this clear, but content himself with watching closely the suspected party, and he will probably soon discover what his intentions really are.

The constable must arrest any one he sees in the act of committing a felony.

Also any one whom another positively charges with having committed a felony.

So upon the suspicions of another, if the grounds of the suspicion appear to the constable to be reasonable, and the party entertaining them go with the constable.

Source: Quoted from "New Police Instructions," *The Times* (London), September 25, 1829, p. 3.

28. Excerpts from the Fugitive Slave Act of 1850

And be it further enacted, That when a person held to service or labor in any State or Territory of the United States, has heretofore or shall hereafter escape into another State or Territory of the United States, the person or persons to whom such service or labor may be due, or his, her, or their agent or attorney, duly authorized, by power of attorney, in writing, acknowledged and certified under the seal of some legal officer or court of the State or Territory in which the same may be executed, may pursue and reclaim such fugitive person, either by procuring a warrant from some one of the courts, judges, or commissioners aforesaid, of the proper circuit, district, or county, for the apprehension of such fugitive from service or labor, or by seizing and arresting such fugitive, where the same can be done without process . . .

In no trial or hearing under this act shall the testimony of such alleged fugitive be admitted in evidence; and the certificates in this and the first [fourth] section mentioned, shall be conclusive of the right of the person or persons in whose favor granted, to remove such fugitive to the State or Territory from which he escaped, and shall prevent all molestation of such person or persons by any process issued by any court, judge, magistrate, or other person whomsoever.

And be it further enacted, That any person who shall knowingly and willingly obstruct, hinder, or prevent such claimant, his agent or attorney, or any person or persons lawfully assisting him, her, or them, from arresting such a fugitive from service or labor, either with or without process as aforesaid, or shall rescue, or attempt to rescue, such fugitive from service or labor, from the custody of such claimant, his or her agent or attorney, or other person or persons lawfully assisting as aforesaid, when so arrested, pursuant to the authority herein given and declared; or shall aid, abet, or assist such person so owing service or la-

bor as aforesaid, directly or indirectly, to escape from such claimant, his agent or attorney, or other person or persons legally authorized as aforesaid; or shall harbor or conceal such fugitive, so as to prevent the discovery and arrest of such person, after notice or knowledge of the fact that such person was a fugitive from service or labor as aforesaid, shall, for either of said offences, be subject to a fine not exceeding one thousand dollars, and imprisonment not exceeding six months, by indictment and conviction before the District Court of the United States for the district in which such offence may have been committed, or before the proper court of criminal jurisdiction . . .

Source: U.S. Congress, The Fugitive Slave Act of 1850. The Avalon Project at Yale Law School. Available online at URL: http://www.yale.edu/lawweb/avalon/ fugitive.htm.

29. The Thirteenth Amendment to the U.S. Constitution, 1865

Neither slavery nor involuntary servitude, except as punishment for a crime whereof the party shall have been duly convicted, shall exist in the United States, or in any place subject to their jurisdiction . . .

Source: The Thirteenth Amendment to the U.S. Constitution, ratified December 6, 1865.

30. Excerpts from the Mississippi Black Codes, 1865

Every freedman, free negro and mulatto shall, on the second Monday of January, one thousand eight hundred and sixty six, and annually thereafter, have a lawful home or employment, and shall have written evidence thereof . . .

All contracts for labor made with freedmen, free negroes and mulattoes for a longer period than one month shall be in writing, and a duplicate, attested and read to said freedman, free negro or mulatto . . . and if the laborer shall quit the service of the employer before the expiration of his term of service, without good cause, he shall forfeit his wages for that year up to the time of quitting . . .

Every civil officer shall, and every person may, arrest and carry back to his or her legal employer any freedman, free negro, or mulatto who shall have quit the service of his or her employer before the expiration of his or her term of service without good cause; and said officer and person shall be entitled to receive for arresting and carrying back every deserting employee aforesaid the sum of five dollars, and ten cents per mile from the place of arrest to the place of delivery; and the same shall be paid by the employer, and held as a set off for so much against the wages of said deserting employee . . .

Upon affidavit made by the employer . . . or [any] other credible person, before any justice of the peace or member of the board of police, that any freedman, free negro or mulatto legally employed by said employer has illegally deserted said employment, such justice of the peace or member of the board of police issue his warrant or warrants, returnable before himself or other such officer . . . commanding him to arrest said deserter, and return him or her to said employer . . .

If any person shall persuade or attempt to persuade, entice, or cause any freedman, free negro or mulatto to desert from the legal employment of any person before the expiration of his or her term of service, or shall knowingly employ any such deserting freedman, free negro or mulatto, or shall knowingly give or sell to any such deserting freedman, free negro or mulatto, any food, raiment, or other thing, he or she shall be guilty of a misdemeanor, and, upon conviction, shall be fined not less than twenty-five dollars and not more than two hundred dollars and costs . . . Provided, if any person shall, or shall attempt to, persuade, entice, or cause any freedman, free negro or mulatto to desert from any legal employment of any person, with the view to employ said freedman, free negro or mulatto without the limits of this State, such costs; and if said fine and costs shall not be immediately paid, the court shall sentence said convict to not exceeding six months imprisonment in the county jail.

Source: The Mississippi State Legislature, "An Act to Confer Civil Rights on Freedman, and for Other Purposes" (The Mississippi Black Codes), November 25, 1865. About.com African-American History. Available online at URL: http://afroamhistory.about.com/library/blmississippi_blackcodes.htm.

31. Excerpts from the U.S. Civil Rights Act of 1866

[A]ll persons born in the United States and not subject to any foreign power, excluding Indians not taxed, are hereby declared to be citizens of the United States; and such citizens, of every race and color, without regard to any previous condition of slavery or involuntary servitude, except as punishment for crime whereof the party shall have been duly convicted, shall have the same right . . . to make and enforce contracts, to sue, be parties, and give evidence, to inherit, purchase, lease, sell, hold, and convey real and

personal property, and to full and equal benefit of all laws and proceedings for the security of person and property, as it is enjoyed by white citizens, and shall be subject to like punishment, pains, and penalties, and to none other . . .

[A]ny person who, under color of any law, statute, ordinance, regulation, or custom, shall subject, or cause to be subjected, any inhabitant of any State or Territory to the deprivation of right secured or protected by this act, or to different punishment, pains, or penalties on account of such person having at any time ever been held in a condition of slavery or involuntary servitude . . . or by reason of his color race . . . shall be deemed guilty of a misdemeanor and, on conviction, shall be punished by fine not exceeding one thousand dollars, or imprisonment not exceeding one year, or both . . .

Source: U.S. Congress, "An Act to Protect All Persons in the United States in Their Civil Rights, and Furnish the Means of Their Vindication" [The Civil Rights Act of 1866], April 9, 1866. "Reconstruction: The Second Civil War" (PBS). Available online at URL: http://www.pbs.org/wgbh/amex/reconstruction/activism/ps_1866.html.

32. The Fourteenth Amendment to the U.S. Constitution, 1868

Section. 1.
All persons born or naturalized in the United States and subject to the jurisdiction thereof, are citizens of the United States and of the State wherein they reside. No State shall make or enforce any law which shall abridge the privileges or immunities of citizens of the United States; nor shall any State deprive any person of life, liberty, or property, without due process of law; nor deny to any person within its jurisdiction the equal protection of the laws.

Section. 2.
Representatives shall be apportioned among the several States according to their respective numbers, counting the whole number of persons in each State, excluding Indians not taxed. But when the right to vote at any election for the choice of electors for President and Vice President of the United States, Representatives in Congress, the Executive and Judicial officers of a State, or the members of the Legislature thereof, is denied to any of the male inhabitants of such State, being twenty-one years of age, and citizens of the United States, or in any way abridged, except for participation in rebellion, or other crime, the basis of representation therein shall be reduced in the proportion which the number of such male citizens shall

bear to the whole number of male citizens twenty-one years of age in such State.

Section. 3.

No person shall be a Senator or Representative in Congress, or elector of President and Vice President, or hold any office, civil or military, under the United States, or under any State, who, having previously taken an oath, as a member of Congress, or as an officer of the United States, or as a member of any State legislature, or as an executive or judicial officer of any State, to support the Constitution of the United States, shall have engaged in insurrection or rebellion against the same, or given aid or comfort to the enemies thereof. But Congress may by a vote of two-thirds of each House, remove such disability.

Section. 4.

The validity of the public debt of the United States, authorized by law, including debts incurred for payment of pensions and bounties for services in suppressing insurrection or rebellion, shall not be questioned. But neither the United States nor any State shall assume or pay any debt or obligation incurred in aid of insurrection or rebellion against the United States, or any claim for the loss or emancipation of any slave; but all such debts, obligations and claims shall be held illegal and void.

Section. 5.

The Congress shall have power to enforce, by appropriate legislation, the provisions of this article.

Source: The Fourteenth Amendment to the U.S. Constitution, ratified on July 9, 1868.

33. Excerpts from the Declaration of Principles Adopted and Promulgated by National Congress on Penitentiary and Reformatory Discipline, 1870

   I. Crime is an intentional violation of duties imposed by law, which inflicts an injury upon others. Criminals are persons convicted of crime by competent courts. Punishment is suffering inflicted upon the criminal for the wrong done by him, with a special view to secure his reformation.

   II. The treatment of criminals by society is for the protection of society. But since treatment is directed to the criminal rather than to the crime, its great object should be his moral regeneration. Hence the supreme aim of prison discipline is the reformation of criminals, not the infliction of vindictive suffering.

   III. The progressive classification of prisoners, based on character and worked on some well-adjusted mark system, should be established in all prisons above the common jail.

   IV. Since hope is a more potent agent than fear, it should be make an ever-present force in the minds of prisoners, by a well-devised and skillfully-applied system of rewards for good conduct, industry, and attention to learning. Rewards, more than punishments, are essential to every good prison system.

   V. The prisoner's destiny should be placed, measurably, in his own hands; he must be put into circumstances where he will be able, though his own exertions, to continually better his own condition. A regulated self-interest must be brought into play, and made constantly operative. . . .

   VIII. Peremptory sentences ought to be replaced by those of indeterminate length. Sentences limited only by satisfactory proof of regeneration should be substituted for those measured by mere lapse of time.

   IX. Of all reformatory agencies, religion is first in importance, because most potent in its action upon human heart and life.

   X. Education is a vital force in the reformation of fallen men and women. Its tendency is to quicken the intellect, inspire self-respect, excite to higher aims, and afford a healthful substitute for low and vicious amusements. Education is, therefore, a matter of primary importance in prisons, and should be carried to the utmost extent consistent with the other purposes of such institutions.

   XI. In order to the reformation of imprisoned criminals, there must be not only a sincere desire and intention to that end, but a serious conviction, in the minds of the prison officers, that they are capable of being reformed, since no man can heartily maintain a discipline at war with his inward beliefs; no man can earnestly strive to accomplish what in his heart he despairs of accomplishing.

   XII. A system of prison discipline, to be truly reformatory, must gain the will of the convict. He is to be amended; but how is this possible with his mind in a state of hostility? No system can hope to succeed, which does not secure this harmony of wills, so that the prisoner shall choose for himself what his officer chooses for him. But, to this end, the officer must really choose the good of the prisoner, and the prisoner must remain in his choice long enough for virtue to become a habit. This consent of wills is an essential condition of reformation.

XIII. The interest of society and the interest of the convicted criminal are really identical, and they should be made practically so. At present there is a combat between crime and laws. Each sets the other at defiance, and, as a rule, there is little kindly feeling, and few friendly acts, on either side. It would be otherwise if criminals, on conviction, instead of being cast off, were rather made the objects of a generous parental care; that is, if they were trained to virtue, and not merely sentenced to suffering.

XIV. The prisoner's self-respect should be cultivated to the utmost, and every effort made to give back to him his manhood. There is no greater mistake in the whole compass of penal discipline, than its studied imposition of degradation as a part of punishment. Such imposition destroys every better impulse and aspiration. It crushes the weak, irritates the strong, and indisposes all to submission and reform. It is trampling where we ought to raise, and is therefore as unchristian in principle as it is unwise in policy.

XV. In prison administration, moral forces should be relied upon, with as little admixture of physical force as possible, and organized persuasion be made to take the place of coercive restraint, the object being to make upright and industrious freemen, rather than orderly and obedient prisoners. Brute force may make good prisoners; moral training alone will make good citizens. To the latter of these ends, the living soul must be won; to the former, only the inert and obedient body.

Source: Enoch Wines, ed., *Transactions of the National Congress of Penitentiary and Reformatory Discipline, Held at Cincinnati, Ohio, October 12–18, 1870.*

34. Appointment, Qualification, and Duties of U.S. Marshals, 1898

Attention is directed to the following provisions of the Revised Statutes:

Sec. 779.

Marshals shall be appointed for a term of four years.

Sec. 1876.

There shall be appointed a marshal for each Territory. He shall execute all process issuing from the Territorial court when exercising their jurisdiction as circuit and district courts of the United States. He shall have the power and perform the duties, and be subject to the regulations and penalties, imposed by law on the marshals for the several judicial districts of the United States. He shall hold his office for four years and until his successor is appointed and qualified, unless sooner removed by the President.

Sec. 787.

It shall be the duty of the marshal of each district to attend the district and circuit courts when sitting therein, and to execute, throughout the district, all lawful precepts directed to him, and issued under the authority of the United States, and he shall have power to command all necessary assistance in the execution of his duty.

Sec. 788.

The marshals and their deputies shall have, in each State, the same powers, in executing the laws of the United States, as the sheriffs and their deputies in such State may have, by law in executing the laws thereof . . .

Attention is invited to the view of this Department that an economical and satisfactory administration of the office of United States marshal depends largely upon the degree of the personal attention which the marshal gives to the duties of his office and upon the honesty and efficiency of the deputies employed by him. It is expected of the marshal that he will personally make such investigation from time to time as will enable him to ascertain whether his field deputies are in fact performing personally all the services for which they are claiming credit, whether all mileage has been actually traveled, and whether the actual expenses for which credit is claimed have been in fact incurred, as indicated by the receipts furnished. The marshal will be held responsible for dishonest or fraudulent practices of his deputies if he does not use the resources at his command to protect the Government against abuses. Examiners of this Department will report upon this matter in their investigations of the manner in which marshals and their deputies perform their official duties.

It is the duty of the marshal, whenever practicable, to aid in serving the process and orders of the courts. He should dismiss at once any deputy who is incompetent, inattentive to his duties, or whom he has reason to believe guilty of any fraud or dishonesty.

Source: U.S. Department of Justice, Attorney General's Office, *Instructions to United States Marshals, Attorneys, Clerks, and Commissioners* 1898, quoted in Vila and Morris, *The Role of Police in American Society,* pp. 68–69.

35. The Illinois Juvenile Court Law of 1907

An act relating to children who are now or may hereafter become dependent, neglected, or delinquent, to define these terms, and to provide for the treatment, control, maintenance, adoption, and guardianship of the person of such children

Section 1. (Definitions).

All persons under 21 shall, for the purposes of this act only, be considered wards of the state. "Dependent child" and "neglected child" shall mean any boy who, while under 17, or any girl who, while under 18, is homeless; or a public charge; or lacks parental care; or habitually begs; or lives with any vicious or disreputable person; or whose home, through fault of parent or other custodian, is unfit; and any child who, while under 10, is found begging or peddling, or furnishing any music for gain upon the street, or taking part in public entertainments.

"Delinquent child" shall mean any boy who, while under 17, or girl who, while under 18, violates any state law, or is incorrigible, or chooses evil associates; or is a runaway, or is growing up in idleness or crime; or frequents a house of ill repute, gaming place, or dram shop; or idly roams the streets at night; or habitually trespasses upon railroad property; or is guilty of public profanity, or of indecency. . . .

Source: "Illinois Juvenile Court Law, in Force July 1, 1907," in Hart, *Juvenile Court Laws in the United States,* pp. 26–27.

36. Excerpt from Timothy Hurley, *Origin of the Illinois Juvenile Court Law,* 1907

There is something in the half-famished cry of a neglected, ill-treated child that reaches the heart of the most unsympathetic adult, touches the chords of sympathy that have been silent, perhaps for years, and sets them to vibrating. The helpless wail of a poverty-stricken, sin-environed child is maddening to one interested in that branch of sociology which deals with the saving of the child. It forces him to go deeper and deeper into the causes which produce such pitiful and shameful conditions, in the hope of finding, if possible, some remedy for them.

Potentially, the Juvenile Court law, as adopted by the Legislature of the State of Illinois, provides the solution of the entire economic problem—the problem of ignorance, poverty, and crime. The possibilities and probabilities of the Illinois Juvenile Court law broaden and deepen as the student of economics analyzes it section by section, sentence by sentence. It appears to the enthusiast to be the very ultima thule of legislation, securing, if intelligently enforced, the greatest possible good for the greatest number of people, and bringing about in time a millennial condition, as each phase of the law is developed.

The real meaning of the Juvenile Court law, the motives underlying its adoption and the attitude taken by the court and officers in administering it must be thoroughly understood in every detail before an intelligent conclusion can be reached as to the results already accomplished by the workings of the law, and the possible results may be brought about in the future.

The fundamental idea of the Juvenile Court is so simple it seems anyone ought to understand it. It is, to be perfectly plain, a return to paternalism. It is the acknowledgment by the State of its relationship as the parent to every child within its borders. Civilization for years lost sight of this relationship and as a consequence the utter demoralization of society was threatened. The child, suffering for the sins of its natural parents, the outcast, illegitimate child, so to speak, of the state, committed some petty depredation, was arrested and at the first arrest became a criminal with his hand raised against every man and every man's hand raised against him.

The state recognized its duty towards the child only to the extent of providing prisons in which to lock him up when, driven by the forces of evil on all sides, he became a criminal, a menace to his fellow beings and a direct charge upon the state for the period of his natural life.

What chance was there for these poor little waifs of fortune, these human derelicts, drifting, rudderless, upon the turbid stream of life? If they walked the streets, as they usually did, they became steeped in the very dregs of degradation. If the arm of the law exerted itself to the extent of forcing them to remain at home the conditions surrounding them were often infinitely worse than they would have been had the children been allowed to remain on the streets. What could one expect from such conditions except the result that was inevitable—the ultimate outlawry of the child? The little ones did not eat three times a day—nay, an entire day frequently passed without a morsel of food passing their mouths. Sometimes the child had shoes to cover its feet. More often, however, the little feet were unprotected even in the cold of frosty winter. Often he had no covering for his head and no protecting woolens underneath the single tattered garment that served to cover his nakedness, but offered little shelter from the elements. This pallid child of fortune—ill fortune—swore like a fiend, haunted saloons and places of general ill repute, mixed in the society of thieves and people with the most vicious tendencies, bawled along the streets, shouted and fought, stole when opportunity offered, and was frightened at nothing except the form of a blue-coated policeman looming in the distance. Weather-beaten, feverish from lack of nourishment or because of the liquor which they had imbibed, these children of the street presented a problem which the child saving societies were unable to cope with because there was no law under which they could work in attempting to save the little ones from their awful surroundings. If they were arrested and taken to jail their doom was sealed forever. The stigma remained on their forehead as long as they lived. From the date of their first arrest and incarceration in jail with older criminals they became outlaws in every sense which that word implies.

Those interested in saving the little ones from the fearful future which seemed to be yawning for them realized that the fountainhead of the evil, vice and crime as well as of virtue and honor, was to be found in the home surroundings of the child. The wisest efforts to reform abuses were thwarted by homes that were depraved. It was realized that the real criminal was not the individual himself, but the entire social body that permitted conditions to exist which could produce only criminals. It was realized also that a great good would be accomplished if some way could be devised by which the home surroundings of the child could be corrected and by which, if possible, the parents could be educated to be more serious and to be cleaner both physically and mentally. Failing in this, it was felt if means could be found by which the child could be removed from the home and placed where proper influences would surround it, three-fourths of the depravity and sin which had been cursing both the individual in particular and society in general might be removed. Then, in time, as the children grew up into self-respecting, law-abiding men and women instead of legal outcasts, the corrective influence would be more far-reaching in its results and the final outcome would be that all the refuse of humanity would be cast aside into a heap and society would rest on a secure, wholesome basis.

Such a condition of affairs was dreamed of by those interested in humanity. Remembering that the state has after all, the right, in the absence of proper care from the natural parents, to step in and take upon itself the work which the natural parents had proved themselves unable to do, they evolved from their necessity the Juvenile Court law of the State of Illinois . . .

It is not the object of the Juvenile Court to punish the children brought before it. In fact, the entire thought of those who framed the law was to banish all idea of crime and punishment and to overcome entirely the positive evil of a jail commitment and a former trial. Far from appearing to punish the child, it is the one thought of the Juvenile Court to inquire into his home surroundings, and if they are found to be such as to cause the growing citizen to be not only his own worst enemy, but a menace to the public at large as well, the Juvenile Court pursues one of two courses. Either it removes him entirely from the surroundings that make for vice and place him in some institution or in a private home where his evil tendencies may be corrected, or, if it seems possible that through the agencies which the court may bring to bear, the home life of the child may be improved, the court permits the parents to retain control of the little one until it is proved conclusively that they are unable or unfit to care for him. It was intended by the framers of the Juvenile Court law that the court, in administering the law, should go much deeper into the study of child-life than a mere attempt at punishment for any small, specific depredation would permit. It was intended that the court should search out and remove the primary cause of the deflection from the paths of rectitude . . .

The probation system is the cord upon which all the pearls of the Juvenile Court are strung. It is the keynote of a beautiful symphony. Without it the Juvenile Court could not exist. Upon the intelligence and application of the probation officer depends the successful operation of the court. The state of Illinois could not furnish institutions enough to care for all the children brought before the court. All children are not in circumstances which would warrant the court in taking them from their parents, and yet they must be followed up and their future conduct and the conduct of their parents must be enquired into. The probation system enables the court to leave the child in his own home, and at the same time provides some one who shall act at once as guardian to the child and as teacher to the parents, educating them to a point where they are capable of themselves assuming the powers of guardianship towards their own child. With the great right arm of the law of the State of Illinois to back him, the probation officer can go into the home and demand to know the cause of the dependency and to build upon its ruins the foundations of a higher, better citizenship. He becomes practically a member of the family and teaches that family lessons of cleanliness and decency, of truth and integrity. Threats may be necessary in some instances to enforce the lessons he teaches, but whether by threats or cajolery, by appealing to their fear of the law or by rousing the ambition that lies latent in each human soul, he teaches the lesson and transforms the entire family into individuals whom the state need never again hesitate to own as citizens . . .

To sum up, then, the foundation idea of the Juvenile Court law in providing for the care of the dependent or delinquent child is not an idea of punishment for crime or for mendicancy, for the law does away entirely with all idea of crime or beggary as applied to a child. The work of the court is to inquire into the causes of the dependency or delinquency, to find why the child went wrong in the first place, to remove the cause of the fall from grace, and to start the little one on the right road.

Source: Timothy Hurley, *Origin of the Illinois Juvenile Court Law,* 1907, pp. 55–63.

37. The U.S. Espionage Act of 1917, Including the Sedition Act Revisions of 1918

Section 2

Whoever, with intent or reason to believe that it is to be used to the injury or the United States or to the advantage of a foreign nation, communicates, delivers, or transmits, or attempts to, or aids, or induces another to, communicate, deliver or transmit, to any foreign government, or to any faction or party or military or naval force within a foreign country, whether recognized or unrecognized by the United States, or to any representative, officer, agent, employee, subject, or citizen thereof, either directly or indirectly, any document, writing, code book, signal book, sketch, photograph, photographic negative, blue print, plan, map, model, note, instrument, appliance, or information relating to the national defence, shall be punished by imprisonment for not more than twenty years: *Provided,* That whoever shall violate the provisions of subsection:

(a) of this section in time of war shall be punished by death or by imprisonment for not more than thirty years; and

(b) whoever, in time of war, with intent that the same shall be communicated to the enemy, shall collect, record, publish or communicate, or attempt to elicit any information with respect to the movement, numbers, description, condition, or disposition of any of the armed forces, ships, aircraft, or war materials of the United States, or with respect to the plans or conduct, or supposed plans or conduct of any naval or military operations, or with respect to any works or measures undertaken for or connected with, or intended for the fortification of any place, or any other information relating to the public defence, which might be useful to the enemy, shall be punished by death or by imprisonment for not more than thirty years.

Section 3

Whoever, when the United States is at war, shall wilfully make or convey false reports or false statements with intent to interfere with the operation or success of the military or naval forces of the United States or to promote the success of its enemies and whoever when the United States is at war, shall wilfully cause or attempt to cause insubordination, disloyalty, mutiny, refusal of duty, in the military or naval forces of the United States, or shall wilfully obstruct the recruiting or enlistment service of the United States, to the injury of the service or of the United States, shall be punished by a fine of not more than $10,000 or imprisonment for not more than twenty years, or both.

Section 4

If two or more persons conspire to violate the provisions of section two or three of this title, and one or more of such persons does any act to effect the object of the conspiracy, each of the parties to such conspiracy shall be punished as in said sections provided in the case of the doing of the act the accomplishment of which is the object of such conspiracy . . .

Section 5

Whoever harbours or conceals any person who he knows, or has reasonable grounds to believe or suspect, has committed, or is about to commit, an offence under this title shall be punished by a fine of not more than $10,000 or by imprisonment for not more than two years, or both.

Source: U.S. Congress, from the "Espionage Act of 1917." Sections 3 and 4 are collectively referred to as the Sedition Act. Quoted in U.S. History Documents and Speeches. Available online at URL: http://www.historicaldocuments.com/EspionageAct.htm.

38. The Eighteenth Amendment to the U.S. Constitution, 1919

Section 1.

After one year from the ratification of this article the manufacture, sale, or transportation of intoxicating liquors within, the importation thereof into, or the exportation thereof from the United States and all territory subject to the jurisdiction thereof for beverage purposes is hereby prohibited.

Section 2.

The Congress and the several States shall have concurrent power to enforce this article by appropriate legislation.

Section 3.

This article shall be inoperative unless it shall have been ratified as an amendment to the Constitution by the legislatures of the several States, as provided in the Constitution, within seven years from the date of the submission hereof to the States by the Congress.

Source: The Eighteenth Amendment to the U.S. Constitution, ratified January 16, 1919. Repealed in 1933.

39. Excerpts from the Wickersham Commission's Report on Lawlessness in Law Enforcement, 1931

The widest inquiry into the shortcomings of the administration of justice, which the President enjoined upon this commission, necessarily involves the duty of investigating the justice of complaints, often made, that in their zeal to accomplish results Government officials themselves frequently lose sight of the fact that they are servants of the law, subject to its mandates and peculiarly charged with the duty to observe its spirit and its letter. They should always remember that there is no more sinister sophism than that the end justifies the employment of illegal means to bring offenders to justice . . .

The phrase "third degree," as employed in this report, is used to mean "the employment of methods which inflict suffering, physical or mental, upon a person, in order to obtain from that person information about a crime." As the report avers, "The third degree is a secret and illegal practice." Hence the difficulty of discovering the facts as to the extent and manner it is practiced . . .

The practice of the third degree involves the violation of such fundamental rights as those of (1) personal liberty; (2) bail; (3) protection from personal assault and battery; (4) the presumption of innocence until conviction of guilt by due process of law; and (5) the right to employ counsel, who shall have access to him at reasonable hours. Holding prisoners *incommunicado* in order to persuade or extort confession is all too frequently resorted to by the police. As the report shows, courts give no approval to any of these practices, and convictions of crime based upon confessions of guilt secured by such methods are very generally set aside.

After reviewing the evidence obtainable the authors of the report reach the conclusion that the third degree— that is, the use of physical brutality, or other forms of cruelty, to obtain involuntary confessions or admissions—is widespread. Protracted questioning of prisoners is commonly employed. Threats and methods of intimidation, adjusted to the age or mentality of the victim, are frequently used, either by themselves or in combination with some of the other practices mentioned. Physical brutality,

illegal detention, and refusal to allow access of counsel to the prisoner is common . . .

Source: The National Commission on Law Observance and Enforcement (the Wickersham Commission), from the introduction to its *Report on Lawlessness in Law Enforcement* (1931), pp. 1, 3–4.

40. The Twenty-first Amendment to the U.S. Constitution, 1933

Section 1.

The eighteenth article of amendment to the Constitution of the United States is hereby repealed.

Section 2.

The transportation or importation into any State, Territory, or possession of the United States for delivery or use therein of intoxicating liquors, in violation of the laws thereof, is hereby prohibited.

Section 3.

This article shall be inoperative unless it shall have been ratified as an amendment to the Constitution by conventions in the several States, as provided in the Constitution, within seven years from the date of the submission hereof to the States by the Congress.

Source: The Twenty-First Amendment to the U.S. Constitution, ratified December 5, 1933.

41. Excerpts from the Marijuana Tax Act, 1937

SEC. 2. (a)

Every person who imports, manufactures, produces, compounds, sells, deals in, dispenses, prescribes, administers, or gives away marijuana shall (1) within fifteen days after the effective date of this Act, or (2) before engaging after the expiration of such fifteen-day period in any of the above mentioned activities, and (3) thereafter, on or before July 1 of each year, pay the following special taxes respectively . . .

SEC. 4. (a)

It shall be unlawful for any person required to register and pay the special tax under the provisions of section 2 to import, manufacture, produce, compound, sell, deal in, dispense, distribute, prescribe, administer, or give away marihuana without having so registered and paid such tax . . .

SEC. 9. (a)

Any marihuana which has been imported, manufactured, compounded, transferred, or produced in violation of any of the provisions of this Act shall be subject to seizure and forfeiture and, except as inconsistent with the provisions of this Act, all the provisions of internal-revenue laws relating to searches, seizures, and forfeitures are extended to include marihuana . . .

SEC. 12.
Any person who is convicted of a violation of any provision of this Act shall be fined not more than $2,000 or imprisoned not more than five years, or both, in the discretion of the court . . .

Source: U.S. Congress, the Marihuana Tax Act of 1937, quoted in the Schaffer Library of Drug Policy. Available online at URL: http://www.druglibrary.org/schaffer/ hemp/taxact/mjtaxact.htm.

42. Excerpt from the Narcotic Control Act, 1956

Sec. 107
SALE OF HEROIN TO JUVENILES—PENALTIES
. . . Not withstanding any other provision of law, whoever, having attained the age of eighteen years, knowingly sells, gives away, furnishes, or dispenses, facilitates the sale, giving, furnishing, or dispensing, or conspires to sell, give away, furnish, or dispense, any heroin unlawfully imported or otherwise brought into the United States, to any person who has not attained the age of eighteen years, may be fined not more than $20,000, shall be imprisoned for life, or for not less than ten years, except that the offender shall suffer death if the jury in its discretion shall so direct.

Source: U.S. Congress, from the Narcotic Control Act of 1956; quoted in Belenko, *Drugs and Drug Policy in America*, p. 205.

43. Preface to the Omnibus Crime Control Act of 1968

Congress finds that the high incidence of crime in the United States threatens the peace, security, and general welfare of the Nation and its citizens. To prevent crime and to insure the greater safety of the people, law enforcement efforts must be better coordinated, intensified, and made more effective at all levels of government.

Congress finds further that crime is essentially a local problem that must be dealt with by State and local governments if it is to be controlled effectively.

It is therefore the declared policy of the Congress to assist State and local governments in strengthening and improving law enforcement at every level by national

assistance. It is the purpose of this title to (1) encourage States and units of general local government to prepare and adopt comprehensive plans based upon their evaluation of State and local problems of law enforcement; (2) authorize grants to States and units of local government in order to improve and strengthen law enforcement; and (3) encourage research and development directed toward the improvement of law enforcement and the development of new methods for the prevention and reduction of crime and the detection and apprehension of criminals.

Source: Preface to the U.S. Congress's "Omnibus Crime Control and Safe Streets Act of 1968," quoted in Vila and Morris, *The Role of Police in American Society*, pp. 193–194.

44. The Racketeer Influenced and Corrupt Organizations (RICO) Laws of 1970

(a) It shall be unlawful for any person who has received any income derived, directly or indirectly, from a pattern of racketeering activity or through collection of an unlawful debt in which such person has participated as a principal within the meaning of section 2, title 18, United States Code, to use or invest, directly or indirectly, any part of such income, or the proceeds of such income, in acquisition of any interest in, or the establishment or operation of, any enterprise which is engaged in, or the activities of which affect, interstate or foreign commerce. A purchase of securities on the open market for purposes of investment, and without the intention of controlling or participating in the control of the issuer, or of assisting another to do so, shall not be unlawful under this subsection if the securities of the issuer held by the purchaser, the members of his immediate family, and his or their accomplices in any pattern or racketeering activity or the collection of an unlawful debt after such purchase do not amount in the aggregate to one percent of the outstanding securities of any one class, and do not confer, either in law or in fact, the power to elect one or more directors of the issuer.

(b) It shall be unlawful for any person through a pattern of racketeering activity or through collection of an unlawful debt to acquire or maintain, directly or indirectly, any interest in or control of any enterprise which is engaged in, or the activities of which affect, interstate or foreign commerce.

(c) It shall be unlawful for any person employed by or associated with any enterprise engaged in, or the activities of which affect, interstate or foreign commerce, to conduct or participate, directly or indirectly, in the conduct of such enterprise's affairs through a pattern of racketeering activity or collection of unlawful debt.

(d) It shall be unlawful for any person to conspire to violate any of the provisions of subsection (a), (b), or (c) of this section.

Source: Section 1962 of the U.S. Code, Title 18, Part I, Chapter 96, as amended by the "Racketeer Influenced and Corrupt Organizations (RICO) Act of 1970," quoted by the Cornell University Legal Information Institute. Available online at URL: http://www.law.cornell.edu/uscode/html/uscode18/usc_sup_01_18_10_I_20_96.html.

45. Excerpt from the Report of the President's Task Force on Victims of Crime, 1982

You are a 50-year-old woman living alone. You are asleep one night when suddenly you awaken to find a man standing over you with a knife at your throat. As you start to scream, he beats and cuts you. He then rapes you. While you watch helplessly, he searches the house, taking your jewelry, other valuables, and money. He smashes furniture and windows in a display of senseless violence. His rampage ended, he rips out the telephone line, threatens you again, and disappears into the night.

At least, you have survived. Terrified, you rush to the first lighted house on the block. While you wait for the police, you pray that your attacker was bluffing when he said he'd return if you called them. Finally, what you expect to be help arrives.

The police ask questions, take notes, dust for fingerprints, make photographs. When you tell them you were raped, they take you to the hospital. Bleeding from cuts, your front teeth knocked out, bruised and in pain, you are told that your wounds are superficial, that rape itself is not considered an injury. Awaiting treatment, you sit alone for hours, suffering the stares of curious passersby. You feel dirty, bruised, disheveled, and abandoned. When your turn comes for examination, the intern seems irritated because he has been called out to treat you. While he treats you, he says that he hates to get involved in rape cases because he doesn't like going to court. He asks if you "knew the man you had sex with."

The nurse says she wouldn't be out alone at this time of night. It seems pointless to explain that the attacker broke into your house and had a knife. An officer says you must go through this process, then the hospital sends you a bill for the examination that the investigators insisted upon. They give you a box filled with test tubes and swabs and envelopes and tell you to hold on to it. They'll run some tests if they ever catch your rapist.

Finally, you get home somehow, in a cab you paid for and wearing a hospital gown because they took your clothes as evidence. Everything that the attacker touched seems soiled. You're afraid to be in your house alone. The one place where you were always safe, at home, is sanctuary no longer. You are afraid to remain, yet terrified to leave your home unprotected.

You didn't realize when you gave the police your name and address that it would be given to the press and to the defendant through the police reports. Your friends call to say they saw this information in the paper, your picture on television. You haven't yet absorbed what's happened to you when you get calls from insurance companies and firms that sell security devices. But these calls pale in comparison to the threats that come from the defendant and his friends.

You're astonished to discover that your attacker has been arrested, yet while in custody he has free and unmonitored access to a phone. He can threaten you from jail. The judge orders him not to annoy you, but when the phone calls are brought to his attention, the judge does nothing.

At least you can be assured that the man who attacked you is in custody, or so you think. No one tells you when he is released on his promise to come to court. No one ever asks you if you've been threatened. The judge is never told that the defendant said he'd kill you if you told or that he'd get even if he went to jail. Horrified, you ask how he got out after what he did. You're told the judge can't consider whether he'll be dangerous, only whether he'll come back to court. He's been accused and convicted before, but he always came to court; so he must be released.

You learn only by accident that he's at large; this discovery comes when you turn a corner and confront him. He knows where you live. He's been there. Besides, your name and address were in the paper and in the reports he's seen. Now nowhere is safe. He watches you from across the street; he follows you on the bus. Will he come back in the night? What do you do? Give up your home? Lose your job? Assume a different name? Get your mail at the post office? Carry a weapon? Even if you wanted to, could you afford to do these things?

You try to return to normal. You don't want to talk about what happened, so you decide not to tell your coworkers about the attack. A few days go by and the police unexpectedly come to your place of work. They show their badges to the receptionist and ask to see you. They want you to look at some photographs, but they don't explain that to your co-workers. You try to explain later that you're the victim, not the accused.

The phone rings and the police want you to come to a line-up. It may be 1:00 a.m. or in the middle of your work day, but you have to go; the suspect and his lawyer are waiting. It will not be the last time you are forced to conform your life to their convenience. You appear at the police station and the line-up begins. The suspect's lawyer sits next to you, but he does not watch the stage he stares at you. It will not be the last time you must endure his scrutiny.

Source: President's Task Force on Victims of Crime, Final Report,
December 1982, pp. 3–5.

46. Excerpt from the Illinois Domestic Violence Act of 1986

This Act shall be liberally construed and applied to promote its underlying purposes, which are to:

(1) Recognize domestic violence as a serious crime against the individual and society which produces family disharmony in thousands of Illinois families, promotes a pattern of escalating violence which frequently culminates in intra-family homicide, and creates an emotional atmosphere that is not conducive to healthy childhood development;

(2) Recognize domestic violence against high risk adults with disabilities, who are particularly vulnerable due to impairments in ability to seek or obtain protection, as a serious problem which takes on many forms, including physical abuse, sexual abuse, neglect, and exploitation, and facilitate accessibility of remedies under the Act in order to provide immediate and effective assistance and protection;

(3) Recognize that the legal system has ineffectively dealt with family violence in the past, allowing abusers to escape effective prosecution or financial liability, and has not adequately acknowledged the criminal nature of domestic violence; that, although many laws have changed, in practice there is still widespread failure to appropriately protect and assist victims;

(4) Support the efforts of victims of domestic violence to avoid further abuse by promptly entering and diligently enforcing court orders which prohibit abuse and, when necessary, reduce the abuser's access to the victim and address any related issues of child custody and economic support, so that victims are not trapped in abusive situations by fear of retaliation, loss of a child, financial dependence, or loss of accessible housing or services ;

(5) Clarify the responsibilities and support the efforts of law enforcement officers to provide immediate, effective assistance and protection for victims of domestic violence, recognizing that law enforcement officers often become the secondary victims of domestic violence, as evidenced by the high rates of police injuries and deaths that occur in response to domestic violence calls; and

(6) Expand the civil and criminal remedies for victims of domestic violence; including, when necessary, the remedies which effect physical separation of the parties to prevent further abuse.

Source: From the "Illinois Domestic Violence Act of 1986." Transcribed and made available online by the Illinois Coalition Against Domestic Violence. Available online at URL: http://www.ilcadv.org.

47. Florida law allowing minors to be charged as adults, 1994

1. If the child was 14 years of age or older, and if the child has been previously adjudicated delinquent for an act classified as a felony, which adjudication was for the commission of, attempt to commit, or conspiracy to commit murder, sexual battery, armed or strong-armed robbery, carjacking, home-invasion robbery, aggravated battery, aggravated assault, or burglary with an assault or battery, and the child is currently charged with a second or subsequent violent crime against a person; or

2. If the child was 14 years of age or older at the time of commission of a fourth or subsequent alleged felony offense and the child was previously adjudicated delinquent or had adjudication withheld for or was found to have committed, or to have attempted or conspired to commit, three offenses that are felony offenses if committed by an adult, and one or more of such felony offenses involved the use or possession of a firearm or violence against a person;

The state attorney shall request the court to transfer and certify the child for prosecution as an adult or shall provide written reasons to the court for not making such request, or proceed pursuant to s. 985.227(1). Upon the state attorney's request, the court shall either enter an order transferring the case and certifying the case for trial as if the child were an adult or provide written reasons for not issuing such an order.

Source: State of Florida, Statute 985.226(2)(b), taking into account amendments made in 1994 to allow the prosecution of juveniles as adults.

48. Excerpts from the USA PATRIOT Act of 2001

SEC. 215. Access to Records and Other Items under the Foreign Intelligence Surveillance Act.

Title V of the Foreign Intelligence Surveillance Act of 1978 (50 U.S.C. 1861 et seq.) is amended by striking sections 501 through 503 and inserting the following:

SEC. 501. Access to Certain Business Records for Foreign Intelligence and International Terrorism Investigations.

(a)(1) The Director of the Federal Bureau of Investigation or a designee of the Director (whose rank shall be no lower than Assistant Special Agent in Charge) may make an application for an order requiring the production of any tangible things (including books, records, papers, documents, and other items) for an investigation to protect against international terrorism or clandestine intelligence activities, provided that such investigation of a United States person is not conducted solely upon the basis of activities protected by the first amendment to the Constitution . . .

SEC. 502. Congressional Oversight.

(a) On a semiannual basis, the Attorney General shall fully inform the Permanent Select Committee on Intelligence of the House of Representatives and the Select Committee on Intelligence of the Senate concerning all requests for the production of tangible things under section 402.

(b) On a semiannual basis, the Attorney General shall provide to the Committees on the Judiciary of the House of Representatives and the Senate a report setting forth with respect to the preceding 6-month period—

(1) the total number of applications made for orders approving requests for the production of tangible things under section 402; and

(2) the total number of such orders either granted, modified, or denied.

SEC. 216. Modification of Authorities Relating to Use of Pen Registers and Trap and Trace Devices.

(A) GENERAL LIMITATIONS- SECTION 3121(C) OF TITLE 18, UNITED STATES CODE, IS AMENDED—

(1) by inserting "or trap and trace device" after "pen register";

(2) by inserting ", routing, addressing," after "dialing"; and

(3) by striking "call processing" and inserting "the processing and transmitting of wire or electronic communications so as not to include the contents of any wire or electronic communications."

(B) ISSUANCE OF ORDERS-

(1) IN GENERAL- SECTION 3123(A) OF TITLE 18, UNITED STATES CODE, IS AMENDED TO READ AS FOLLOWS:

(A) IN GENERAL-

(1) ATTORNEY FOR THE GOVERNMENT

Upon an application made under section 3122(a)(1), the court shall enter an ex parte order authorizing the installation and use of a pen register or trap and trace device anywhere within the United States, if the court finds that the attorney for the Government has certified to the court that the information likely to be obtained by such installation and use is relevant to an ongoing criminal investigation. The order, upon service of that order, shall apply to any person or entity providing wire or electronic communication service in the United States whose assistance may facilitate the execution of the order. Whenever such an order is served on any person or entity not specifically named in the order, upon request of such person or entity, the attorney for the Government or law enforcement or investigative officer that is serving the order shall provide written or electronic certification that the order applies to the person or entity being served . . .

Sources: Sections 215 and 216 of the "USA PATRIOT Act of 2001" (H.R. 3162), passed by the U.S. House of Representatives on October 24, 2001. The Library of Congress, THOMAS. Available online at URL: http://thomas.loc.gov.

Appendix B
Biographies of Major Personalities

Adams, John (1735–1826) *second president of the United States*

A Massachusetts lawyer and politician, Adams assumed a major role in the American movement for independence from Britain; he served in the Continental Congress, wrote the state constitution of Massachusetts of 1780, acted as American envoy to both France and Britain, served as vice president under George Washington, and finally served as president between 1797 and 1801. His long career intersected with the history of crime and justice in two notable instances. First, as an attorney in Boston prior to the Revolutionary War, he successfully defended both the American patriot John Hancock against smuggling charges in 1768 and Captain John Preston, the British officer in charge of troops that fired on an American crowd in the so-called Boston Massacre of 1770. Second, as president he signed the Alien and Sedition Acts in 1798, giving the federal government extensive but short-lived powers to prosecute its political opponents.

Addams, Jane (1860–1935) *social reformer*

Addams was the leading figure in U.S. social reform in the late 19th and early 20th centuries. Born in Cedarville, Illinois, the daughter of a successful miller and banker, she enjoyed an education unusual for women of her time, eventually graduating from Rockford Female Seminary in 1881, one of the first generation of U.S. women to earn a college degree. Like other educated women of the day, she spent some years searching for an application for her skills. On a trip to Europe, she discovered the famous social settlement Toynbee Hall in London. Inspired, she decided to establish a similar institution in the United States. In 1889, together with college friend Ellen Gates Starr, she rented a dilapidated mansion on the near west side of Chicago and opened it as the Hull-House Social Settlement. This institution provided a home for social activists who wished to work with the city's immigrant poor and a community center for the neighborhood. It offered clubs, meeting space, vocational and domestic education, and English-language classes, among other services. Hull-House also provided short-term housing for a generation of Chicago social activists and reformers. Using Hull-House as a base of operation, Addams challenged Chicago's corrupt political system, mediated in labor disputes, and advocated the creation of a juvenile court. Her memoir, *Twenty Years at Hull-House* (1910), chronicles her experiences; *The Spirit of Youth and the City Streets* (1909) analyzes the sources of juvenile delinquency. Addams later became active in the Progressive Party's 1912 electoral campaign and cofounded the Women's Peace Party in 1915. In the 1920s, her defense of dissenters made her a target of much public criticism, but she remained active in the international peace movement. In 1931, Addams won the Nobel Peace Prize for her efforts.

Agron, Salvador (Capeman) (1943–1986) *murderer*

Known as the "Capeman," Agron became prominent after the August 29, 1959, murders of two youths in a New York City playground. A 15-year-old loosely affiliated with a gang called the Vampires, Agron went to the playground that night with his peers looking for other boys who had offended them, argued with the boys they found there, and in the ensuing melee apparently stabbed them. Upon his arrest, Agron (who wore a black cape with a red lining) contributed to a demonic public image by acting the part of a hostile tough. In fact, he was a thin boy whose family had emigrated from Puerto Rico when he was nine years old. In New York, he had trouble in school, was institutionalized briefly in the Wyltwick School for Boys, and participated in the gang because it offered some measure of acceptance. Agron's arrest prompted a major public controversy about juvenile gangs in U.S. cities. He was convicted for the killings and sentenced to death, although his penalty was later commuted. Agron served more than 20 years in prison before he was released in 1979. In 1998, musician Paul Simon produced a Broadway musical based on his life called *The Capeman.*

Altgeld, John Peter (1847–1902) *governor of Illinois*

Altgeld earned a reputation as one of the most progressive political figures of the late 19th century largely due to his interventions into criminal justice issues and labor disputes. Born in Germany, he grew up in Mansfield, Ohio, served briefly in the Civil War, then studied law in Missouri and joined the bar in 1871. Altgeld relocated to Chicago in 1874, and he began a career in both real estate and politics; his construction business generated connections that served his political career in the Democratic Party. Altgeld also became interested in social problems. In 1884, he published an exposé, *Our Penal Machinery and Its Victims,* examining discrimination in the criminal justice system. Elected a superior court judge in 1886 and governor of Illinois in 1892, he also became involved in the major conflicts of the day. In 1893, he pardoned the three surviving anarchists convicted of participating in the 1886 bomb-throwing incident in Haymarket Square; not only did he release them, he argued against the legal basis of their conviction. In 1894, Altgeld sought unsuccessfully to resolve the strike against the Pullman railroad car company. He intended to use state troops to maintain order, but President Grover Cleveland overruled him and used federal troops to end the strike. In 1896, Altgeld led a movement within the Democratic Party to prevent Cleveland's renomination for president but lost his own governorship, a victim of his unpopular decisions in office.

Anslinger, Harry Jacob (1892–1975) *law enforcement officer*

As the first U.S. Commissioner of Narcotics, serving between 1930 and 1962, Anslinger shaped American drug policy for much of the 20th century. Anslinger was born in Altoona, Pennsylvania, and attended Pennsylvania State College. After working for the U.S. War Department during World War I, he held a series of diplomatic positions abroad. During the 1920s, his work focused on the problem of illegal smuggling of foreign liquor into the United States during Prohibition. In 1930, he was appointed head of the U.S. Narcotics Bureau, where he applied the same law enforcement and interdiction approach to the U.S. drug problem. In particular, Anslinger's Narcotics Bureau targeted organized crime, prosecuting figures including New York mobster Charles (Lucky) Luciano for their roles in the narcotics trade. Anslinger rejected medical approaches to drug treatment and demand reduction in favor of a law enforcement model of cutting off the supply of drugs. Anslinger also orchestrated a national concern over the hazards of marijuana in the 1930s, and he contributed to congressional passage of the Marihuana Tax Act of 1937. Having shaped U.S. drug policy, Anslinger retired in 1962 and died at home in Pennsylvania in 1975.

Ashcroft, John D. (1942–) *U.S. attorney general*

As U.S. attorney general between 2001 and 2004, Ashcroft was one of the chief architects of the "war on terrorism." Ashcroft was born in Chicago but raised in Springfield, Missouri, as a member of the evangelical Assembly of God church. He graduated from Yale University in 1964, earned a law degree at the University of Chicago, and returned to Missouri to practice law. There, he became active in the Republican Party and began a career in politics, serving as state auditor, attorney general, and two terms as governor. As a state politician, Ashcroft became known for his conservative, faith-based agenda; for example, he sought to tighten Missouri's laws regulating abortions. In 1994, he won an open seat in the U.S. Senate; in his six years there, his voting record earned 100 percent approval ratings from the American Conservative Union and the Christian Coalition. In 2000, after he lost his bid for reelection, newly elected President George W. Bush nominated Ashcroft to be attorney general. Ashcroft's term as the head of the Justice Department was shaped by the terrorist attacks of September 11, 2001. Ashcroft became one of the public faces of the Bush administration's response to terrorism: He coordinated the ensuing investigations, approved the detention of more than 1,000 suspects, and helped design new legislation substantially expanding federal surveillance and law enforcement powers.

Barker, Kate (Ma Barker) (1871–1935) *alleged criminal*

Barker was a contradictory figure. Portrayed by the FBI as the mastermind of a bandit gang including Alvin "Creepy" Karpis and her four sons, other evidence indicates that she merely aided them with a string of hideouts and protection.

Born Arizona Donnie Clark near Springfield, Missouri, she grew up in poverty, married a farm worker named George Barker in 1892, and bore four sons between 1894 and 1902. As the boys grew up, they frequently ran into trouble with the law; most served prison time by the late 1920s. Two widely publicized kidnappings of millionaires in 1932, both of which netted them large ransoms, made her sons prominent bandits. According to publicity issued at the time by the FBI and to J. Edgar Hoover's later recollections, Ma Barker was their ringleader. According to later testimony by Karpis, however, Ma Barker simply looked after her boys and had no role in planning their offenses. Nonetheless, law enforcement officials saw her as a threat. After the 1935 arrest of one son, Doc, the FBI tracked Ma Barker and another son, Fred, to a house in Florida. When a gun battle ended, police entered the house and found Ma and Fred dead.

Bartelme, Mary (1866–1954) lawyer, judge

The first female judge of the Cook County Juvenile Court, Bartelme was a key figure in the treatment of female juvenile delinquency. She graduated from Northwestern University Law School in 1894 (the only woman in her class) and was admitted to the Illinois bar that same year. In 1897, the governor of Illinois appointed her a public guardian for Cook County, giving her responsibility for placing orphans. She served in this position until 1913, working closely with other Chicago child welfare activists and the juvenile court. In 1913, Judge Merritt Pinckney appointed Bartelme to a semiofficial position within the Cook County Juvenile Court hearing cases involving female delinquency; because so many girls' cases involved sexuality, court officials believed that a female judge was needed. In 1923, Bartelme was elected to her own term as a circuit court judge, a position she held until she retired in 1933. As a judge, Bartelme continued to hear girls' cases and to try to protect them from the moral hazards that Progressive era reformers believed to pervade urban life.

Bass, Sam (1851–1878) outlaw

A Texas outlaw whose career evolved from swindles involving horse racing and cattle herding to robbing stagecoaches and trains, Bass became known for a surprisingly successful 1877 train robbery in Big Springs, Nebraska, in which he and his gang escaped with more than $60,000 in $20 gold pieces. Bass never repeated this success, returning to a career of small-time stagecoach and train hold-ups, but his earlier heist attracted the attention of the Texas Rangers.

They convinced a member of his gang, Jim Murphy, to divulge Bass's location, and as a result Bass was killed in a gunfight with sheriff's deputies in 1878.

Bean, Roy (ca. 1825–1903) judge

One of the larger-than-life personalities of the American West, Bean was unofficially appointed justice of the peace for Langtry, Texas, in 1882, when the Texas Rangers staged a trial at his saloon. For the next 20 years, Bean acted as judge for Pecos County based out of his own saloon, declaring himself the "Law West of the Pecos." Lacking legal training, he gained a reputation for making idiosyncratic decisions based on his own informal sense of justice; he also used his court as a source of personal profit, fining defendants for arbitrary offenses.

Beccaria, Cesare Bonesano (1738–1794) Italian philosopher

A philosopher of law and economics, Beccaria's thinking substantially influenced American attitudes and practice regarding crime and punishment. Drawing on the Enlightenment's emphasis on rationality, Beccaria's major work, *Essays on Crimes and Punishment* (1764), argued that punishments should be predictable and proportionate to crimes. Beccaria critiqued earlier practices such as torture as both cruel and inconsistent: Instead, he favored punishments that would be sufficiently severe to deter crime but that could also be used with certainty. Beccaria's work, published in the United States in 1777, influenced American thinkers such as Thomas Jefferson and Benjamin Rush.

Berkowitz, David (Son of Sam) (1953–) murderer

A notorious serial killer of the 1970s, Berkowitz claimed that voices in his head, including that of a neighbor's dog, instructed him to kill. He shot 13 people in New York City in 1976 and 1977, killing six. Arrested and pronounced sufficiently sane to stand trial, Berkowitz was convicted in 1978 and sentenced to serve 365 years in prison.

Bertillon, Alphonse (1853–1914) French criminologist

As chief of the department of identification in the Paris prefecture of police, Bertillon devised the first system of identifying criminals. Published in 1890, his system classified offenders by 11 bodily measurements plus the color of hair, skin, and eyes. It served to distinguish first-time offenders from recidivists. *Bertillonage*, as the system was known, was adopted by police throughout the United States and

Europe, and it became the standard method for organizing data about offenders at the turn of the 20th century.

Billington, John (ca. 1580–1630) *murderer*
A migrant who arrived on the *Mayflower*, Billington was convicted of killing John Newcomen in Massachusetts. He was the first English colonist executed in the New World.

Billy the Kid (William H. Bonney, Henry McCarty) (1859–1881) *outlaw*
Billy the Kid was one of the most prominent gunslingers of the Old West. Little is known about his early life (even his real name—possibly William H. Bonney or Henry McCarty—is uncertain), but he reportedly killed his first man at age 16. In the late 1870s, he became a key participant in the Lincoln County, New Mexico, "wars" over cattle ranching land. His actions in the war earned him a price on his head, and he was ultimately shot dead by Pat Garrett.

bin Laden, Osama (1957–) *terrorist*
The leader of the al-Qaeda terrorist network, Osama bin Laden is considered the person most responsible for the September 11, 2001, attacks on the United States. He was born in Saudi Arabia as the 17th son of a billionaire with close links to the Saudi royal family; after graduating from college, he assumed control of millions of dollars of his family's assets. When the Soviet Union invaded Afghanistan in 1979, bin Laden used his fortune to support the resistance; he also became a zealous advocate of the Islamic faith. In the late 1980s, he came to believe that the United States exercised too much power in the Islamic world. These concerns were exacerbated when the United States stationed troops in Saudi Arabia during the Persian Gulf War. Operating from Afghanistan, bin Laden apparently formed his own terrorist group, al-Qaeda, which was responsible for the bombing of two U.S. embassies in Africa in 1998 and the bombing of the USS *Cole*, an American naval destroyer, in Yemen in 2000. On September 11, 2001, 19 al-Qaeda terrorists hijacked four U.S. airliners. They flew two into the World Trade Center in New York City, flew another into the Pentagon in Washington, D.C., and crashed the fourth into a field in Pennsylvania; in total, they killed approximately 3,000 victims. In the wake of the attacks, the U.S. government substantially disrupted al-Qaeda's operations and pursued bin Laden.

Booth, John Wilkes (1838–1865) *actor, assassin*
A prominent U.S. actor, Booth murdered President Abraham Lincoln in April 1865. Born in Bel Air, Maryland, Booth pursued a career as an actor beginning in Richmond, Virginia, in 1855. He found little initial success, but by 1860 he used his charisma to win acclaim in Shakespearian roles. During the U.S. Civil War, he became a fierce partisan for the Confederacy and as early as 1863 plotted a conspiracy to kidnap Lincoln. On April 14, 1865, just days after the end of the war, Booth learned that Lincoln would attend a performance at Ford's Theater that night. During the show, Booth snuck into Lincoln's box and shot him in the head, fatally wounding him. Booth escaped by jumping to the stage, breaking his leg in the process. Authorities caught up with Booth on April 26 and surrounded him in a barn; when he refused to surrender, they set the barn on fire, and he died in the conflagration. Booth's accomplices were subsequently tried and convicted; four were sentenced to death, and the doctor who set his broken leg was sentenced to life in prison.

Borden, Lizzie Andrew (1860–1927) *alleged murderer*
Although Borden was born, lived, and died in relative obscurity in Fall River, Massachusetts, she is remembered for her role in one of the most famous trials in U.S. history. When on August 4, 1892, her father and stepmother were found brutally murdered in the home that they shared with 32-year-old Lizzie, she became the only suspect in the killings. Lacking witnesses, a confession, or a murder weapon, local authorities indicted her on the basis of circumstantial evidence. The ensuing trial became a sensation, attracting nationwide press coverage. Popularly believed to have been guilty, Borden was nonetheless acquitted in 1893.

Bowen, Louise de Koven (1859–1953) *philanthropist*
The daughter of a wealthy Chicago businessman and the wife of a Providence banker, Bowen used her considerable financial resources to support social work during the late 19th and early 20th century in Chicago. From her first contact with Jane Addams's Hull-House Social Settlement in 1893, Bowen became its most generous donor, eventually giving almost $1 million. She was also actively involved in its work, particularly issues involving juvenile delinquency. Bowen lobbied for the creation of Cook County's juvenile court in 1899, served as president of the Juvenile Protective Association, and wrote numerous pamphlets and articles examining the problem of delinquency.

Brace, Charles Loring (1826–1890) *activist, philanthropist*

Born in Litchfield, Connecticut, to an old New England family, Brace became a leading innovator in treating orphans and juvenile offenders. After graduating from Yale in 1846 and studying at the Yale Divinity School, Brace decided to lead a life of activism rather than pursue the ministry. In 1853, he helped found and became the leader of the New York Children's Aid Society (CAS), an organization that relocated urban children at risk for delinquency from cities to the countryside, where it found them homes and jobs with rural families. In more than 50 years of operation, the CAS reportedly moved more than 90,000 young people west on its so-called orphan trains. Brace's most famous book, *The Dangerous Classes of New York* (1872), explained his philosophy: Urban settings had an irredeemably degrading effect on young people, but these same youths might be saved through exposure to rural life and hard work and by being given opportunities to help themselves.

Breckinridge, Sophonisba (1866–1948) *social activist*

Breckinridge was one of the first generation of professionally trained women to engage with issues of social reform. Born in Kentucky, she graduated from Wellesley College in 1888 in one of the first classes of American women to earn a college degree. After teaching briefly in Washington, D.C., she studied law in Kentucky (joining the Kentucky bar in 1895), earned a Ph.D. in political science at the University of Chicago in 1901, and earned a J.D. at the University of Chicago Law School in 1904. She taught political economy at the University of Chicago between 1904 and 1942 and helped establish its School of Social Service Administration in 1920. Breckinridge also became a prominent activist in Chicago, working closely with Jane Addams and Hull-House and using her scholarly training to investigate social problems. Together with Edith Abbott she wrote prominent studies such as *The Delinquent Child and the Home* (1912). Her scholarship in the 1920s and the 1930s focused on the role of federal and state governments in promoting social and family welfare.

Brockway, Zebulon Reed (1827–1920) *penologist, prison administrator*

After dabbling in business as a young man, Zebulon Brockway, the son of an old Connecticut family, pursued prison administration as a career and became the most prominent penologist of his day. As head of the Detroit House of Correction between 1861 and 1872 and as superintendent of the Elmira, New York, State Reformatory for Men between 1876 and 1900, Brockway implemented new ideas such as indeterminate sentences. Having a variable term of incarceration would either provide inmates with an incentive to reform themselves or a mechanism to maintain custody over those who remained incorrigible. Brockway's address to the 1870 National Congress on Penitentiary and Reformatory Discipline in Cincinnati became the basis for a school of thought focused on inmate reform called the "new penology."

Brown, John (1800–1859) *abolitionist*

John Brown was a prominent opponent of slavery in the United States. Born in Connecticut, he engaged in a number of marginally successful business ventures, mainly in Ohio and upstate New York. Driven by his Protestant faith, Brown's main interest was in ending slavery. He believed in taking action to further his cause; he was active in the Underground Railroad, helping escaped slaves flee to the North and to Canada, and after 1849 he relocated his family to New Elba, New York, to operate a farm that trained free blacks in agriculture. Following the 1854 Kansas-Nebraska Act, five of Brown's sons moved to Kansas to join the free-state forces battling pro-slavery forces for control of the state. Brown later joined them, bringing rifles to arm his side. In reprisal for the burning of the free-state capital of Lawrence, Brown led a raid on a proslavery settlement at Pottawatomie Creek in 1856, killing five unarmed men. Brown escaped punishment and became known nationally as a promoter and fund-raiser for the abolitionist cause. In 1859, Brown assembled a group of 18 men to attack the federal armory at Harpers Ferry, Virginia; he intended to seize the weapons stored there and to initiate a slave rebellion. Although the raid was initially successful, Virginia militia recaptured the armory and killed most of his men. Brown was arrested, tried, and executed. Brown's daring raid and unrepentant condemnation of slavery during his trial, however, made him a hero for opponents of slavery on the eve of the Civil War.

Bundy, Ted (1946–1989) *serial killer*

Bundy was responsible for the deaths of at least 28 women in the 1970s. A law student at the University of Utah, he apparently kidnapped and killed a number of women in Utah, Oregon, and Washington in the early 1970s. He was arrested in 1975, but prosecutors could generate only circumstantial evidence to link him to the crimes, so they tried and convicted him only for a failed kidnapping a year earlier. In 1977, Bundy escaped from prison, traveled to Florida, snuck into a sorority house at Florida State University, and attacked four women, killing two as well as another woman later that night. Arrested again, this time he was tried and convicted for all three murders and sentenced to death. Shortly before his 1989 execution, Bundy confessed to 28 murders.

Burr, Aaron (1756–1836) *politician, vice president of the United States*

A New York lawyer who fought in the Revolutionary War, Aaron Burr became vice president of the United States under Thomas Jefferson. Throughout his career, he engaged in a political rivalry with fellow New Yorker Alexander Hamilton, the U.S. Treasury secretary under George Washington. In 1804, their rivalry culminated in a duel with pistols near Weehawken, New Jersey, in which Hamilton was killed. Burr left office soon after the duel and began plotting a military expedition in the American Southwest, with the apparent intention of separating this territory from the United States. Arrested in 1807 and tried for treason, Burr was acquitted, but his political career was finished.

Capone, Alphonse (Al Capone, Scarface) (1899–1947) *gangster*

Al Capone dominated organized crime in Chicago during Prohibition. Born to Italian immigrant parents in Brooklyn, New York, Capone became a leader among New York street gangs while still a teenager. During that time, an opponent cut his cheek with a razor, giving him his nickname "Scarface." In 1919, he relocated from New York to Chicago to avoid a murder charge and went to work for a former associate, Johnny Torrio. Capone quickly moved up in Torrio's organization and eventually succeeded him. When Prohibition made alcohol illegal in 1920, a strong demand persisted, which Capone and his organization filled through bootlegging and smuggling. In 1927, alone Capone's group reportedly enjoyed revenues of more than $60 million from illegal alcohol. Unlike many other gangsters, Capone was very much a public figure. In Chicago, he presented himself to the press as a genial host and as a friend of the poor by bankrolling food kitchens. At the same time, he used brutal means to defend his business interests. In 1929, his men gunned down seven members of a rival gang in the famous "St. Valentine's Day Massacre." Federal agents finally arrested and tried Capone in 1931, when the U.S. Treasury

Department charged him with income tax evasion. He was sentenced first to a federal penitentiary in Georgia and then later to Alcatraz Island, where he became that prison's most famous inmate. He was released due to failing health in 1939 and lived a quiet life until his death in 1947.

Capote, Truman (1924–1984) *writer*

Born in New Orleans, Louisiana, Capote was one of the most wide-ranging and controversial literary figures of the middle of the 20th century. He contributed to the literature on crime and justice with *In Cold Blood* (1965). In this work, Capote established a new literary form that he called the "nonfiction novel." The book examines the murders of Kansas farmer Herbert W. Clutter and his family, who were attacked and killed in their home by two ex-convicts in November 1959. Telling the stories both of the victims and of the killers, the book combined the accuracy of journalism with the emotion of fiction and raised questions about the U.S. legal system and capital punishment.

Cloward, Richard A. (1926–2001) *sociologist*

A sociologist who taught at Columbia University between 1954 and his death in 2001, Cloward was a leading advocate of expanding social welfare services for inner-city youths, arguing that economic circumstances could be linked to crime and delinquency. In his 1960 *Delinquency and Opportunity: A Theory of Delinquent Gangs*, Cloward and coauthor Lloyd Ohlin argued that juvenile crime was a rational response to the lack of economic and social opportunities available to urban youths. Using this theory as a guide, Cloward created the Mobilization for Youth program in New York City to work with potential delinquents and to determine what services communities wanted. Cloward's ideas and efforts became a model adopted by Lyndon Johnson's Great Society programs later in the 1960s. Cloward's later work, particularly his 1971 *Regulating the Poor: The Functions of Public Welfare* (written with frequent collaborator Frances Fox Piven), examined the role that social welfare services played in American society.

Comstock, Anthony (1844–1915) *purity reformer*

A New York dry goods salesman and Civil War veteran raised in the Congregational Church, Comstock found his calling as a crusader against vice. In 1871, as a member of the Young Men's Christian Association (YMCA), he convinced his fellow activists to form a Society for the

Suppression of Vice to enforce state obscenity laws and to support new laws governing the mailing of obscene materials through the U.S. Post Office. In 1873, the U.S. Congress passed the Comstock Law banning the mailing of not only sexually explicit material but also any information about birth control or abortion. The post office subsequently appointed Comstock a special agent in charge of enforcing this law, a position that he held for the rest of his life and from which he used criminal sanctions to vigorously oppose the dissemination of information about sexuality.

Couzens, James Joseph (1872–1936) *businessman, police administrator, politician*

An immigrant from Canada as a young man, Couzens parlayed a successful career in business into an equally successful career in politics and public service. Moving from Toronto, Ontario, to Detroit, Michigan, in 1890, Couzens initially worked for a railroad company in which he moved up rapidly. In 1903, he became one of the original 12 investors in the Ford Motor Company. While Henry Ford provided the ideas, Couzens implemented them, eventually becoming general manager of the company and realizing concepts such as a moving assembly line and a $5-per-day wage. Couzens became immensely wealthy as a result of his initial investment and resigned from Ford in 1915. Rather than retire, he pursued a career in public service first as the head of the Detroit Street Railway Commission and between 1916 and 1918 as commissioner of Detroit's police. As head of the police department, Couzens attempted to implement the same types of efficiency-maximizing reforms that he had used at Ford. At the same time, he also became an advocate of a social service–oriented, "child-friendly" style of policing. In the process he became one of the more influential police reformers of the early 20th century. Couzens later served as Detroit's mayor during the troubled 1920s, became a philanthropist (endowing the Children's Fund of Michigan), and ultimately served as a U.S. senator from Michigan between 1924 and his death in 1936. Although a Republican, he supported the New Deal.

Cox, Archibald (1912–2004) *lawyer*

A high-profile lawyer and legal educator, Cox is best known for serving as the special prosecutor during the Watergate investigation. Cox graduated from Harvard Law School in 1937, and after working in government during World War II, he returned to the university to teach. Between 1961 and 1965, Cox served as solicitor

general of the United States. In this position, he argued the Kennedy and Johnson administrations' cases before the Supreme Court in a number of civil rights cases. In 1973, during the political scandal resulting from the burglary of the Democratic Party's national headquarters at the Watergate Hotel, the Nixon administration appointed Cox to head up the special investigation. Upon discovering that President Nixon had recorded all of his White House conversations on audiotapes, Cox requested that the administration give them to the investigators. Rather than comply, Nixon ordered that Cox be fired. In a series of events known as the "Saturday Night Massacre," Nixon's attorney general and assistant attorney general resigned in protest, before the current solicitor general finally fired Cox. Cox returned to teaching and writing about the law, and he served as chair of Common Cause, a citizens' advocacy group, between 1980 and 1992. His example provided a model for later special prosecutors.

Cummings, Homer Stillé (1870–1956) *U.S. attorney general*

As the U.S. attorney general for President Franklin D. Roosevelt between 1933 and 1939, Cummings helped initiate a new and more expansive federal role in crime control. Born in Chicago, Cummings earned his bachelor's degree from Yale University in 1891 and his law degree there in 1893. He established a private practice in Stamford, Connecticut, also became involved in Democratic Party politics, and served as mayor of Stamford, corporation counsel, and state's attorney. As U.S. attorney general he helped implement Roosevelt's "war on crime." He supervised the Federal Bureau of Investigation (FBI) under J. Edgar Hoover and reformed the federal prison system. In particular, Cummings was responsible for establishing a new federal high-security prison, which opened on Alcatraz Island in San Francisco Bay in 1934.

Czolgosz, Leon (1873–1901) *assassin*

Born in Poland, Leon Czolgosz immigrated to the United States as a boy, growing up in a lumber town in northern Michigan and the industrial city of Cleveland, Ohio. As a young man he became disenchanted with the economic ramifications of industrializing the United States and gravitated toward radical ideologies. Proclaiming himself an anarchist, he blamed U.S. political leaders for the problems of working men. As President William McKinley shook hands with members of the crowd at the Pan-American Exposition in Buffalo, New York, on September 6, 1901, Czolgosz walked up to him and shot him in the stomach. As guards arrested Czolgosz, he proclaimed "I done my duty." McKinley lingered for eight days but died on September 14. Czolgosz was promptly put on trial on September 23, convicted, and executed at Auburn Penitentiary on October 29.

Dahmer, Jeffrey (1960–1994) *serial killer*

A confessed serial killer, Jeffrey Dahmer committed crimes that became a bizarre fascination for the U.S. public. Dahmer was born in Milwaukee, Wisconsin, grew up in Bath, Ohio, and lived his adult life in Wisconsin. Following his 1991 arrest, he admitted to killing 17 boys and young men beginning in 1978. Most of his victims were African-American youths whom Dahmer engaged in consensual sex with and photographed nude before killing. He admitted to eating the flesh of at least two. When his defense that he was not guilty by reason of insanity was rejected, Dahmer was convicted of 15 counts of murder. He was killed in prison in 1994.

Darrow, Clarence Seward (1857–1938) *lawyer*

Perhaps the most famous defense attorney in U.S. history, Darrow participated in almost every high-profile case of the early 20th century. Darrow grew up in Farmdale, Ohio, spent one year at Allegheny College, studied law for another year at the University of Michigan, and then gained most of his training "reading law" with a firm in Youngstown, Ohio; he joined the bar in 1878 and practiced in small towns throughout Ohio. In 1887, Darrow relocated to Chicago, where he initially worked as the city's corporation council and as a general lawyer for the Chicago and North Western Railway. In 1894, he reversed course from practicing corporate law to work instead on the side of labor. In that year, he defended Eugene V. Debs, the head of the American Railway Union against the Pullman Palace Car Company. In 1906 and 1907, he defended William "Big Bill" Haywood, the leader of the Industrial Workers of the World (IWW), and in 1911 he defended James and J. J. McNamara, union men who would confess to blowing up the headquarters of the antilabor *Los Angeles Times*. This case led to a break between Darrow and the labor movement; when Darrow convinced the brothers to plead guilty to avoid the death penalty, unionists regarded this move as a betrayal. In later years, Darrow took on high-profile criminal cases that also allowed him a platform to advance dissenting social views. In 1924, he successfully defended two Chicago teenagers, Richard Loeb and Nathan Leopold, accused of murdering a 14-year-old boy. In 1925, in the so-called Monkey Trial, he defended

John Thomas Scopes, a Dayton, Tennessee, schoolteacher accused of teaching the theory of evolution. In 1926, he defended Dr. Ossian Sweet, an African-American physician who had moved into an all-white neighborhood in Detroit accused of shooting into a mob that attacked his home. In his later years Darrow wrote a number of books advocating freethinking.

Davis, Katherine Bement (1860–1935) *penal administrator*

Katherine Davis was the superintendent of New York's female reformatory, Bedford Hill, between 1901 and 1914. Davis was born in Buffalo, New York, and educated at Vassar College; she earned a Ph.D. in political economics at the University of Chicago. After teaching at Vassar, she was appointed to head Bedford Hills in 1901. There she introduced the latest in criminological thinking and cottage-style architecture to house inmates in small groups. Contemporary medical models of crime and delinquency that saw offenders—particularly female offenders—as mentally inferior influenced Davis. She gained funding from John D. Rockefeller, Jr., to establish a Laboratory of Social Hygiene adjacent to the reformatory to study female delinquency. She also introduced democratic reforms in the institution, including an "honors cottage" to reward the most cooperative prisoners. After Davis left Bedford in 1914, her tenure received much subsequent criticism. Inmates described physical brutality if they violated rules, but public attention centered on reports of race mixing and lesbianism at Bedford.

Debs, Eugene V. (1855–1926) *labor leader*

As the turn-of-the-20th-century leader of the American Railway Union and the Socialist Party, Debs frequently ran afoul of the law. He was born in Terre Haute, Indiana, and worked briefly as a firefighter before becoming the head of a firefighter's union. In 1893, he became the first president of the American Railway Union. In 1894, when workers struck the Pullman Palace Car Company in Chicago, Debs acceded to a sympathy strike by railway unions across the country; it shut down rail transport throughout the western United States. A legal injunction, however, ended the strike and led Debs to serve six months in prison for contempt of court. In prison, Debs became an advocate of socialism. The Socialist Party of America nominated Debs for president five times, in 1900, 1904, 1908, 1912, and 1920. As a candidate, Debs made a democratic version of socialism politically appealing. He earned as much as 6 percent of the popular vote in the 1912 election. His opposition to World War I led to further conflicts with the law. Debs was arrested and convicted for violating the wartime Espionage Act for a series of speeches condemning the war and the repression of dissent. He was sentenced to 10 years in prison and served more than two between April 1919 and his pardon in 1921; during this time, he ran for president from his jail cell, winning more than 900,000 votes.

DeSalvo, Albert (The Boston Strangler) (1931–1973) *accused serial killer*

Between 1962 and 1964, a dozen women were sexually assaulted and murdered in the Boston, Massachussetts, area. The killings became known as the "silk stockings murders," the perpetrator known as "The Phantom Strangler" or, more famously, "The Boston Strangler." Albert DeSalvo was convicted of the murders and sent to prison, where he was murdered in 1973. Evidence suggests that there may have been more than one perpetrator, and the real identity of the Boston Strangler remains a subject of debate.

Dillinger, John (1903–1934) *criminal*

John Dillinger's brief but spectacular career as an armed robber made him a national icon. Born in Indianapolis, Indiana, Dillinger joined the navy as a young man to avoid trouble with the law, but he deserted soon after. After being arrested for robbing a grocery store in 1925, he spent eight years in prison only to become a full-time criminal following his release in 1933. His career was highlighted by frequent bank robberies, shootouts with police, arrests, and escapes from jail. Following one escape, Dillinger teamed up with four escaped convicts to form a gang; following another escape, Dillinger stole a police car and drove it across state lines, thereby violating federal law and inviting the attention of the FBI. In 1934, the FBI made Dillinger its highest priority. Only a tip that Dillinger would be at Chicago's Biograph movie theater on the night of July 22, 1934, allowed federal agents to surprise him there and gun him down.

Dix, Dorothea Lynde (1802–1887) *reformer*

An educator and activist, Dorothea Dix's efforts to improve conditions for mental patients and the insane led to substantial reforms in U.S. jails and asylums. Born in Maine, she ran away to Massachusetts at the age of 12. When she was 14, she opened a school in Worchester, Massachusetts; only at 17 did she go to Boston to live with her grandmother and to complete her education. In 1821, still only 19 years old, she opened a school for young ladies in her grandmother's home and taught there until ill health forced her to stop in 1835. She found new direction in 1841, when she visited the East Cambridge Jail in Massachusetts as a volunteer Sunday school teacher and discovered both appalling physical conditions and indiscriminate mixing of criminals, paupers, and the insane. She then spent two years touring correctional institutions, taking note of conditions and lobbying for reform. In 1843, she appeared before the Massachusetts legislature to argue that the mentally ill should be housed in facilities separate from criminals and the poor. Dix continued to inspect jails, hospitals, and almshouses throughout the Northeast, publishing her findings in 1845 as *Remarks on Prisons and Prison Discipline*. Frustrated in her efforts to secure federal funding for a new system of asylums in 1848, she traveled to Europe, inspecting jail and asylum conditions there as well. During the U.S. Civil War, she volunteered as a nurse and helped organize health care for the Union army. Both her activism and her wartime efforts drew attention to jail and asylum conditions in the United States, and they ultimately fostered the creation of new institutions for the mentally ill.

Dugdale, Richard Louis (1841–1883) *sociologist*

A sociologist interested in heredity, Richard Dugdale conducted research that helped to foster a connection between crime and biology in U.S. thinking of the late 19th century. As a researcher investigating conditions in 13 county jails for the Prison Committee of New York, he noted the relationships between offenders in jail and, using his own funds, decided to examine further. The resulting study, *The Jukes: A Study in Crime, Pauperism, Disease, and Heredity*, published in 1877, traced the connections between more than 700 persons associated with the pseudonymous "Juke" family in upstate New York, the vast majority of whom had received public relief, had been prosecuted for crimes, or had been treated for venereal disease. By demonstrating these familial links, Dugdale made a case that crime and poverty could be linked to a form of biological "degeneracy." Dugdale's research became the foremost evidence of its day that biological and inherited factors shaped criminal behavior.

Dummer, Ethel Sturges (1866–1954) *philanthropist*

Ethel Dummer helped to underwrite the expansion of the mental hygiene movement and treatment for delinquent girls in the early 20th century. Born into a wealthy family and married to successful banker William Francis

Dummer, Ethel Dummer was taught from an early age that the wealthy had special social service obligations. Involved with Chicago's universe of social reform, in 1909 she provided the funds to create the Juvenile Psychopathic Institute affiliated with the Cook County Juvenile Court and chose Dr. William Healy to be its first director. In later years, she also provided financial support for Miriam Van Waters to establish the El Retiro School for delinquent girls in Los Angeles, California.

Dwight, Theodore William (1822–1892) *lawyer*

As a professor of law, first at Hamilton College and later at Columbia College, Theodore William Dwight aimed to teach his students the principles of U.S. law through lectures and textbooks; he used only cases to illustrate these principles. In addition to his work as a law professor, Dwight also participated in issues related to criminal justice. Beginning with an investigation of prisons in New York, he and Enoch C. Wines undertook a much larger investigation of prison conditions published as *Report on the Prisons and Reformatories of the United States and Canada* in 1867. Their criticism of the prison system as emphasizing retribution over rehabilitation led prison reformers to gather at the 1870 National Congress on Penitentiary and Reformatory Discipline and to formulate a more balanced approach to corrections called the "new penology."

Dyer, Mary (unknown–1660) *Quaker martyr*

The wife of William Dyer, Mary Dyer migrated from England to the Massachusetts Bay Colony sometime in 1635. During the Antinomian Controversy, she and her husband openly supported Anne Hutchinson. When Hutchinson was expelled from the Puritan church, the Dyers accompanied her and helped found Rhode Island in 1638. Returning to England in the 1650s, Mary Dyer soon converted to Quakerism. Returning to the American colonies in 1657, Dyer was arrested in Boston for preaching Quakerism. Persistent in advocating her faith, she was arrested and jailed in Boston a total of four times and finally hanged in 1660.

Earp, Wyatt Barry Stapp (1848–1929) *lawman*

A vigorous self-promoter, Earp was one of the most famous lawmen in the American West in the latter half of the 19th century. Born in Illinois, Earp moved west, becoming a deputy marshal and deputy sheriff in Dodge City, Kansas. In 1879, Earp and his brothers moved to Tombstone, Arizona, where they sought to establish order in a region filled with cattle rustlers and stagecoach rob-

bers. On October 26, 1881, Earp, two of his brothers, and John "Doc" Holliday engaged in the famous shoot-out at the O.K. Corral in Tombstone. Killing three of their opponents cemented Earp's reputation as one of the leading lawmen in the West. After two of his brothers were later killed in retribution, Earp, along with Holliday, engaged in a vigilante campaign to gain revenge, which ultimately forced him to leave Arizona. Earp lived his final years in California.

Elias, Norbert (1897–1990) *German sociologist*

A noted sociologist, Norbert Elias's analysis of "the civilizing process" exerted considerable influence over European and U.S. scholars of crime and homicide. Born in Breslau, Germany (now part of Poland), Elias was educated throughout Europe and taught in Britain, France, and the Netherlands. The translation of his 1939 work, *Über den Prozess der Zivilisation*, into English as *The Civilizing Process* in 1978 and 1982 generated his enduring influence. In this work, he demonstrated that, over centuries, Western peoples gradually developed rules to help them restrain their emotions and learn to interact with one another. Historians of crime have adapted Elias's ideas to explain the long-term decline in homicide and violence in European and Westernized societies from the late Middle Ages until the 20th century.

Faurot, Joseph A. (1872–1942) *police officer*

As a member of the New York Police Department (NYPD), Faurot helped pioneer the use of fingerprinting to investigate crime in the United States. Having seen fingerprinting demonstrated at the St. Louis World's Fair in 1904, Faurot went to London to learn more about the technique at Scotland Yard. Upon his return, he used fingerprints to solve a number of homicide cases. The NYPD adopted fingerprinting as its official method of identifying criminals in 1911, and Faurot remained its leading advocate until he retired in 1930.

Fish, Albert (1870–1936) *murderer*

Albert Fish killed and mutilated as many as 16 children in and around New York City in the 1920s and 1930s. He was detected and arrested only in 1934, after he sent an anonymous letter to the family of one his victims bragging of his murder of their 10-year-old daughter in 1928. Fish was convicted in 1935 and executed in the electric chair at Sing Sing prison in 1936.

Floyd, Charles Arthur (Pretty Boy Floyd) (1901–1934) *criminal*

A famous outlaw of the 1930s, Pretty Boy Floyd gained a reputation as a social bandit, a Robin Hood figure who robbed banks to help the poor people of his home. Born and raised in Akins, Oklahoma, in the Cookson Hills, Floyd grew up as a farmer. When dust bowl conditions became pervasive in Oklahoma in the 1920s, however, he turned to crime. Floyd was convicted of robbing a payroll service in 1925, and he spent four years at the Missouri State Penitentiary in Jefferson City. He emerged in 1929 as a hardened criminal, conducting a series of bank robberies in Ohio, Kentucky, and Missouri. Floyd avoided the law with the support of both Kansas City organized crime figures, whom he paid, and Oklahoma farmers, who regarded him as a folk hero. In 1933, Floyd was identified as one of a group of machine-gunners who attacked and killed an FBI agent and three local police officers in Kansas City. Although Floyd publicly denied this crime, the Kansas City Massacre transformed him into a primary target for the FBI. Agents led by Melvin Purvis caught up with Floyd near East Liverpool, Ohio, on October 22, 1934, and shot him dead as he sought to escape.

Forrest, Nathan Bedford (1821–1877) *general*

A Confederate general during the U.S. Civil War, Nathan Forrest subsequently helped found the Ku Klux Klan. Forrest was born in Tennessee and became wealthy as a trader in real estate and slaves, eventually purchasing cotton plantations in Mississippi and Arkansas. When the Civil War began, he enlisted as a private in the Confederate army, but after he raised and equipped a battalion, he was promptly promoted, first to lieutenant colonel and by July 1862 to brigadier general. He became the most effective and feared cavalry commander in the Confederate army, leading daring raids against Union forces throughout the western theater. He became known to the northern press and U.S. Congress after a raid on Fort Pillow, Tennessee, in which his men killed more than 200 Union defenders of the fort, mostly African Americans, many as they were fleeing. His actions at Fort Pillow subsequently became a rallying cry for Union soldiers. After the war, Forrest returned to his plantation in Tennessee and became involved in railroad construction. He also helped lead the opposition to Reconstruction in Tennessee, helping to organize the Ku Klux Klan among Confederate veterans with the goal of terrorizing blacks into submis-

sion. Forrest was active in reactionary politics in his later years but when called to testify before Congress about the Ku Klux Klan denied knowledge of its activities.

Fosdick, Raymond B. (1883–1972) *lawyer*

In his varied career, Fosdick wrote two seminal investigations of police procedure, *European Police Systems* (1915) and *American Police Systems* (1920). Born in Buffalo, New York, Raymond Fosdick earned a bachelor's degree from Princeton University in 1905 and a master's in 1906; while there he began a lasting friendship with university president Woodrow Wilson. Upon graduation, he studied law in New York, worked for a social settlement house, and became assistant corporation counsel for the city, investigating municipal corruption and becoming acquainted with John D. Rockefeller. Later in his career, his political connections helped him earn positions as the chairman of the World War I Commission on Training Camp Activities and president of the Rockefeller Foundation. His investigations of police paralleled his other activities in that they examined a wide range of agencies and promoted the most efficient practices for others to emulate.

Foucault, Michel Paul (1926–1984) *French philosopher*

Michel Foucault was a late 20th-century French philosopher whose work challenged the empirical foundations of Western thought. Born in Poitiers, France, he studied with the Marxist philosopher Louis Althusser at the École Normale Supérieure in Paris and then taught at the University of Clermont-Ferrand, the University of Paris at Vincennes, and in the Department of History of Human Thought at the Collège de France. His writings—widely translated and read throughout the world beginning in the 1970s—suggested that history was built not on events and individuals but on systems of knowledge, which themselves became mechanisms of power. These knowledges and powers were, in turn, contained within discourses or means of presenting ideas. Foucault helped shift scholarly thinking away from empirical data and toward a more relativistic analysis of discourse. His 1975 book *Surveiller et punir: Naissance de la prison* (translated in 1977 as *Discipline and Punish: The Birth of the Prison*) used incarceration as an example of the process; he argued that the emergence of penitentiaries in the early 19th century represented a shift in forms of social control from physical coercion to a more subtle and diffuse form of surveillance; punishments of the body were replaced by more insidious punishments of the mind and of the spirit. Foucault's theoretical work inspired much subsequent, more concrete, research on the history of crime and justice.

Frank, Leo (1884–1915) *engineer*

Leo Frank was lynched on August 16, 1915, outside Marietta, Georgia, after that state's governor commuted his death sentence for the 1913 murder of 13-year-old Mary Phagan. Raised in New York City, Frank was trained in mechanical engineering at Columbia University and obtained his degree in 1906. He soon moved to Atlanta to work as the superintendent of the National Pencil Factory. In 1913, the body of a 13-year-old white employee, Phagan, was found in the factory. After Frank was arrested for the crime, the local press was filled with inflammatory coverage; in particular, Atlanta newspapers emphasized that being a Jew and an outsider made Frank seem a more likely killer. In a sensationalized trial, Frank was convicted and sentenced to death. The case also generated national publicity in Frank's favor; as his lawyers appealed, groups in northern cities came to his aid. Outsiders flooded the Georgia governor with petitions containing more than a million signatures demanding Frank's release. On June 21, 1915, Governor John M. Slaton commuted his sentence to life in prison, expecting a new trial. Two months later, however, a vigilante group removed Frank from the Georgia prison farm where he was being held and hanged him.

Fuld, Leonhard Felix (1883–1965) *writer, scholar*

Considered one of the first police reformers, Leonhard Fuld never worked as a police officer or administrator. Instead, he was a highly trained scholar who wrote his doctoral dissertation on policing in the United States and Europe. His research, published as *Police Administration* (1909), became a handbook for police professionalization. In particular, he advocated higher standards of education and training for officers. Fuld helped plan the New York Police Academy but did not further pursue a career in law enforcement; instead, he became successful in real estate and the stock market.

Gacy, John Wayne (The Killer Clown) (1942–1994) *serial killer*

Between 1972 and 1978, John Wayne Gacy kidnapped, raped, and murdered at least 33 young men and boys, hiding many of their bodies under a staircase in his house. He was convicted in 1980 and executed by lethal injection in 1994.

Garrett, Pat (1850–1908) *lawman*

The sheriff of Lincoln County, New Mexico, Garrett is best known for pursuing Billy the Kid. Garrett arrested Billy the Kid in December 1880, but he escaped from jail in April 1881. Garrett tracked him to the home of a mutual acquaintance and killed him in July 1881.

Garrison, William Lloyd (1805–1879) *abolitionist*

William Lloyd Garrison was one of the leading opponents of slavery between the 1830s and 1860s. Born in Newburyport, Massachusetts, he initially became a printer's apprentice and later a journalist employed by a number of newspapers concerned with temperance and abolition. He founded his own newspaper, *The Liberator,* in 1831 to espouse his increasingly radical views on slavery; it called for the immediate emancipation of slaves without compensation to owners. Although the paper's circulation never exceeded 3,000, it became a central forum for abolitionism and made Garrison a leading figure in the movement. He helped found both the Massachusetts Anti-Slavery Society and the American Anti-Slavery Society. His views also attracted such antipathy that a Boston mob attacked him in 1835. In the 1850s, as the issue of slavery became increasingly contentious, Garrison remained a pacifist and avoided political disputes. Nonetheless, he remained a symbolic leader of the abolition movement.

Gates, Daryl F. (1926–   ) *police officer*

Daryl Gates served as chief of the Los Angeles Police Department (LAPD) between 1978 and 1992, one of its most difficult eras. He was born in Glendale, California, in 1926, graduated from the University of Southern California, and joined the LAPD in 1949. He became chauffeur and protégé for Chief William Parker and adopted Parker's proactive approach to policing. When Gates took over the LAPD in 1978, he dealt with budget cuts and reduced numbers of officers by implementing an aggressive style of policing akin to Parker's. Gates is credited with policing the 1984 Olympics, which ended without trouble, and with initiating D.A.R.E., a program to bring police officers into schools to teach children how to resist pressure to use drugs. His tenure was also marked by controversy, most notably the videotaped beating of Rodney King in 1991 and the 1992 riots that followed the acquittal of the four officers involved in that incident. Gates retired in June 1992, less than two months after the riots.

Glueck, Sheldon (1896–1980) **and Glueck, Eleanor Touroff** (1898–1972) *criminologists*

The two Gluecks, professors at Harvard Law School, were known for their innovative studies of juvenile delinquency. Sheldon Glueck was born in 1896 in Warsaw, Poland, but grew up in Milwaukee, Wisconsin; he graduated from National University Law School in New York in 1920. Through his brother, Dr. Bernard Glueck, Sheldon Glueck met a social settlement worker, Eleanor Touroff. They were married in 1922. Both continued their educations at Harvard University, from where they received their doctorates in 1924 and 1925, respectively. Each went on to serve on the faculty at Harvard where they engaged in innovative longitudinal studies of young offenders. The Gluecks were the first scholars to systematically examine the outcomes of correctional treatment by tracking juvenile delinquents not only in correctional institutions but also for years after they were released. Their first research project followed 500 male offenders who had been incarcerated at the Massachusetts Reformatory over a span of 15 years. Their second research project similarly followed women who had been incarcerated at the Women's Reformatory in Framingham, Massachusetts. A third major research effort examined juveniles who had been referred by the Boston Juvenile Court to its psychiatric clinic; this resulted in the influential book *One Thousand Juvenile Delinquents* (1934). Their most famous work, *Unraveling Juvenile Delinquency* (1950), followed the careers of 500 boys who became offenders and 500 boys from similar disadvantaged Boston neighborhoods who did not. The Gluecks' work set a new scientific standard for research in both the causes and the treatment of delinquency.

Guiteau, Charles Julius (1841–1882) *assassin*

Charles Guiteau was a self-taught lawyer and low-level operative in the Republican Party. He campaigned on behalf of James A. Garfield in 1880 and in return expected to be appointed ambassador to France. His services declined, Guiteau grew incensed and stalked the president, seeking revenge. On July 1, 1881, Guiteau approached President Garfield at a Washington, D.C., train station and shot him in the back; Garfield died two months later. Guiteau was arrested immediately and placed on trial. Probably insane, Guiteau conducted his own defense and claimed that God had ordered him to kill Garfield. In spite of his mental instability, Guiteau was convicted and hanged on June 30, 1882.

Gunness, Belle (1859–1908) *murderer*

Belle Gunness was among the first known female serial killers in the United States. A Norwegian immigrant and widow, she routinely advertised for male suitors who would visit her but rarely stayed long. When her LaPorte, Indiana, farmhouse burned to the ground in 1908, investigators found two bodies in the house and the remains of at least nine adult men on the grounds of the farm. Gunness, who was presumed to have died in the fire, had apparently lured a string of men to her home, convinced them to give her money and valuables, and killed them.

Hardin, John Wesley (1853–1895) *outlaw*

The son of a Methodist preacher, John Wesley Hardin murdered a man at age 15 in 1868 and lived much of his life acquiring a reputation as a ruthless killer and outlaw. Captured by the Texas Rangers in 1877, he served 16 years in prison. During that time, he studied law, and after his release in 1894 he set up a law practice. He died, however, just one year later in a barroom brawl. His journal, published posthumously in 1896 under the title *Gunfighter*, is the only extant autobiography of a western gunslinger.

Harris, Eric (1981–1999) **and Dylan Klebold** (1981–1999) *spree killers*

These two teenagers carried out the largest and most prominent school massacre during a wave of school killings in the late 1990s. Both were seniors at Columbine High School in Littleton, Colorado, at the time of the attack. Harris was born and raised in Wichita, Kansas, but had moved to the Littleton area in 1993. Klebold was born in Lakewood, Colorado, and lived in the area his entire life. The two became friends in high school and claimed to have been unpopular and targets of bullying during this time. They reacted by posting violent content on a Web site, experimenting with bomb making, and making plans to exact revenge on students at their high school. On the morning of April 20, 1999, Harris and Klebold went to Columbine High School and shot 37 people (killing 13) before taking their own lives.

Hauptmann, Bruno Richard (1899–1936) *carpenter, murderer*

Born in Saxony, Germany, in 1899, Bruno Hauptmann served in the German army during World War I. Following the war, he was twice arrested for burglary. In order to avoid prison after the second arrest, he stowed away on a ship sailing to the United States. Living in New York City in 1925, Hauptmann married another German immigrant and worked as a carpenter. In 1934, he was arrested for murdering the son of aviator Charles Lindbergh, the first man to fly solo across the Atlantic Ocean and perhaps the most prominent celebrity of his day. Two years earlier, the baby had been taken from Lindbergh's country home. Paying the ransom demanded in semiliterate notes did not yield the child's return, and ultimately his body was found near where he had been taken. Hauptmann was linked to the crime in 1934, when he was discovered spending the numbered bills used in the ransom. His 1935 trial in New Jersey became one of the most highly publicized cases of the 20th century. The jury convicted Hauptmann on the basis of largely circumstantial evidence and sentenced him to death. His execution was delayed, however, as prosecutors sought to convince him to name other partners in his crime and as his attorney sought to exonerate him. Hauptmann denied the offense to the end and was put to death in the electric chair at New Jersey State Prison on April 3, 1936.

Healy, William (1869–1963) *psychiatrist*
William Healy was a pioneer in applying psychological approaches to juvenile delinquency. After studying at Harvard University with William James, Healy was appointed to be the first director of Chicago's Juvenile Psychopathic Institute in 1909. This institution, which originated as an adjunct to the Cook County Juvenile Court, began as a treatment center for juvenile offenders and later evolved into providing therapy for nondelinquent youths as well. In 1915, Healy published his research based on individual case studies as *The Individual Delinquent*. This work offered a multicausal explanation of delinquency and reoriented existing debates over whether social or hereditary factors represented the primary source of adolescent misbehavior. In 1917, Healy left Chicago and took over the Judge Baker Foundation of the Boston Juvenile Court. By the 1920s, Healy led a shift in work with juvenile offenders that emphasized psychiatric treatment. Together with his research assistant and later wife, Augustana Bronner, he wrote a number of influential books, including *New Light on Delinquency and Its Treatment* (1936).

Hearst, Patricia (Patty Hearst) (1954–) *heiress*
The granddaughter of newspaper publisher William Randolph Hearst, Patricia Hearst was kidnapped and held for ransom in 1974 by an obscure Oakland, California, radical group, the Symbionese Liberation Army. Although her parents paid the ransom, she was not returned. Instead, she was apparently brainwashed and joined her captors. Security cameras showed her participating in an April 1974 San Francisco bank robbery carrying weapons and aiding her captors. Arrested a year later, she was convicted in 1976 for her part in the robbery and sent to prison; President Jimmy Carter commuted her sentence in 1979.

Hickman, William Edward (1908–1928) *kidnapper, murderer*
After committing a notorious kidnapping-murder, Edward Hickman became the subject of one of the most widely publicized manhunts of the 1920s. A college student who claimed to be seeking money, Hickman kidnapped, killed, and mutilated 12-year-old Marian Parker in Los Angeles, California, in December 1927. Then, pretending that the girl was still alive, he accepted a $7,500 ransom from her father and abandoned her body. The Los Angeles Police Department initiated a nationwide pursuit of a man who fit the killer's description. He was arrested in Oregon, returned to Los Angeles under the glare of publicity over the Christmas holidays, tried, convicted, and subsequently hanged on February 4, 1928.

Hickok, James Butler (Wild Bill Hickok) (1837–1876) *gunfighter*
Dime novelists made Wild Bill Hickok one of the most romanticized figures of the Old West. He earned his reputation when he killed a man in 1861 while working for a Nebraska freighting company. Although the facts of the case did not favor Hickok, he was nonetheless acquitted on the grounds of self-defense and became a hero in the press. After serving as a scout for the Union army during the Civil War, Hickok became deputy U.S. marshal in Fort Riley, Kansas, in 1866, sheriff of Hays, Kansas, in 1869, and city marshal in Abilene, Kansas, in 1871. At least in the first two positions, he helped establish order in lawless western towns and burnished his own reputation while also drinking and gambling heavily. Hickok subsequently drifted in Kansas, Missouri, Wyoming, and the Dakotas, dabbling in land speculation. He was killed in 1876 in Deadwood, Dakota Territory, shot in the back of the head while playing poker.

Hinckley, John W., Jr. (1955–) *attempted assassin*
John Hinckley, Jr., shot President Ronald Reagan on March 30, 1981. A loner, he was obsessed with the 1976 film *Taxi Driver*, in which a character played by Robert De Niro attempts to assassinate a U.S. senator in an effort

to impress the character of a child prostitute played by Jodie Foster. Hinckley stalked Foster and believed that killing Reagan would impress the actress. Hinckley fired six shots at Reagan's party outside a Washington, D.C., hotel, wounding the president, his press secretary James Brady, a police officer, and a secret service officer; he was arrested immediately. At his trial, Hinckley was found not guilty by reason of insanity and confined to St. Elizabeth's Hospital in Washington.

Hiss, Alger (1904–1996) accused spy

When *Time* magazine editor Whittaker Chambers accused Alger Hiss of being a communist in 1948, members of the House Un-American Activities Committee (HUAC) hit the jackpot. Hiss, president of the Carnegie Endowment for International Peace and a former U.S. State Department official, was exactly the kind of highly placed figure who would validate fears that the government had been overrun by Soviet infiltrators. After Hiss denied providing information to the Soviet Union before the committee and sued Chambers for libel, Chambers produced five rolls of classified microfilm and claimed that they had been provided to him by Hiss during the 1930s. The statute of limitations on espionage had run out by 1948, but Hiss was convicted on perjury charges for allegedly lying to the HUAC and served nearly four years in a federal prison. For the rest of his life, he continued to deny accusations that he was a Soviet spy and insisted that he had been falsely convicted of perjury.

Hobbes, Thomas (1588–1679) English philosopher

Hobbes remains the key figure who emerged from 17th-century modern classical philosophy. His political thinking, articulated most prominently in *Leviathan* (1651), suggests that society is governed by a binding social contract. Society is merely an artifact invented by humans, but without society life is "solitary, poor, nasty, brutish and short." People, he suggested, merely struggled for self-preservation; humans, however, could surrender or transfer their will to the state. This social contract binds individuals together under the absolute power of a commonwealth. Elements of Hobbes's thinking influenced the American revolution of the 18th century.

Holliday, John Henry (Doc Holliday) (1851–1887) dentist, gunman

A dentist and gambler in the 19th-century American West, Holliday became friends with Wyatt Earp and fought with him in the 1881 shootout at the O.K. Corral in Tombstone, Arizona.

Hoover, John Edgar (J. Edgar Hoover) (1895–1972) law enforcement official

Appointed director of the Bureau of Investigation in 1924, Hoover remained at the head of that agency and its successor, the Federal Bureau of Investigation (FBI), until his death in 1972. In that time, he played perhaps the largest role of any American in shaping modern law enforcement. Born and raised in Washington, D.C., Hoover developed early in life core ideas that Protestant morality was the driving force behind American values and that ideas and movements foreign to these values or to the United States were to be regulated and controlled. He earned a master of law degree at George Washington University in 1917 and found work with the Alien Enemy Bureau of the U.S. Justice Department. In 1919, in response to a wave of terrorist bombings, Attorney General A. Mitchell Palmer put Hoover in charge of a new effort to target foreign radicals; Hoover used immigration law to deport 249 Russian-born dissenters. Following this success, Palmer placed Hoover in charge of a series of raids in January 1920 that led to the arrests of more than 4,000 suspected radicals. These raids created a public outcry over the abuse of U.S. citizens and cost Palmer his public standing, but they established Hoover as a master organizer. In 1921, he was appointed assistant director of the Bureau of Investigation; in 1924, he was appointed its director. Only 29 years old, he already had enough stature that he would accept the position only with complete freedom to remake the bureau. As the director, Hoover eliminated corruption, instituted new personnel and promotion policies, and centralized administrative power to himself. He also instituted innovations such as fingerprinting, forensic investigation, and scientific management of data about crime. Congress extended the FBI's authority so that it now had jurisdiction over interstate crimes such as kidnapping and bank robbery. Hoover also created a public relations machine that built up criminals into major public enemies, then celebrated the FBI's successes in capturing or killing them. In the mid-1930s, books, radio shows, and film serials all built a virtual cult of personality around Hoover. The FBI had become a clearinghouse for information for local police and, in effect, a national police agency. As early as the 1930s, Hoover also obtained authorization to engage in covert spying against domestic radicals, especially fascists and communists, which became Hoover's primary agenda following World War II. In the 1950s, Hoover developed a counterintelligence program (COINTELPRO) for FBI agents to infiltrate the American communist movement; in the 1960s, COINTELPRO expanded so that it also targeted the Civil Rights movement, the New Left student movements, and radical white organizations such as the Ku Klux Klan. During this time, the FBI devoted little attention to organized crime, political corruption, or white-collar offenses. Only after Hoover's death in 1972 and the Watergate scandals ending in 1974 did the extent of FBI violations of civil liberties under Hoover's leadership come to light.

Howard, John (1726–1790) *prison reformer*

Howard was the leading 18th-century advocate of prison reform in Britain. Appointed the High Sheriff of Bedfordshire in 1773, part of his duties involved inspecting local prisons. Appalled by what he discovered, Howard came to believe that justice could be tempered with humanity. His work pressured Parliament to pass acts in 1774 abolishing fees that prisoners paid to their jailers and improving health conditions in jails. In 1775, Howard conducted a tour of prisons in England, Scotland, Ireland, France, Holland, Flanders, and Switzerland, comparing conditions. He published his findings in *State of the Prisons in England and Wales . . . and an Account of Some Foreign Prisons* (1777). Howard's work inspired 19th- and early 20th-century prison reform societies that took his name in Britain, Canada, and the United States.

Hutchinson, Anne Marbury (1591–1643) *religious dissenter*

Born in England the daughter of an Anglican minister, Hutchinson became a leading critic of Puritanism in the New World. After her father's death in 1611, Anne Marbury married William Hutchinson, a prominent cloth merchant, maintained their household, raised their children, and gradually adopted the Puritan faith. In the early 1630s, the Hutchinsons followed the migration of Puritans to the Massachusetts Bay Colony in America. There, Hutchinson held prayer meetings in her home. In these meetings, Hutchinson's preaching departed from Puritan orthodoxy and challenged the clergy; rather than arguing that salvation was achieved through a combination of grace and good works, she argued that salvation could be achieved through grace alone. This position divided the Puritans, sparking the Antinomian Controversy.

In 1637, the colony's government placed Hutchinson on trial for sedition; when she proclaimed that she came to her views through direct communication with God, the court banished her from Massachusetts. Hutchinson relocated to Rhode Island and later to the Dutch colony of New Netherland, where she was killed in a 1643 Indian attack as part of Kieft's War.

Jackson, George (1941–1971) *activist*

George Jackson, a California prison inmate, leading Marxist, and author of the prison memoir *Soledad Brother* (1970), was killed by guards during an attempted prison escape in August 1971. His controversial death provoked considerable outrage among militant activists and most likely contributed to the Attica prison riots.

James, Jesse Woodson (1847–1882) *outlaw*

Born into a slave-owning family in western Missouri, Jesse James and his older brother Frank supported the Confederate cause during the U.S. Civil War. Because Missouri was officially under Union control, they joined an informal band of pro-Confederate guerrillas led by Frank Quantrill and fought their own brutal, small-scale war against Union forces and supporters in their state. Following the end of the war, Jesse and Frank James continued to support the Confederate cause; they joined forces with other guerrilla veterans as a band of outlaws, robbing trains, banks, and other symbols of an encroaching industrial economy associated with the North. Jesse James was also an inveterate self-promoter. Through an alliance with journalists, he presented himself to the public as both falsely accused and as a bandit who upheld the rural, southern values of Missouri farmers. James reached the peak of his fame when he and his band tried to rob the First National Bank of Northfield, Minnesota, in 1876. Not only was he wounded and many of his band captured or killed, this daring and violent incursion cost James public support. James continued to operate sporadically as a bandit, but the governor of Missouri offered a reward for his capture or death. In 1882, a new recruit betrayed James by shooting him in the back to claim the money. Frank James turned himself in to authorities soon after.

Jefferson, Thomas (1743–1826) *third president of the United States*

Broadly influential beyond his career in national politics, Thomas Jefferson's thinking also helped shape the practice of criminal justice. Drawing on the work of Italian philosopher Cesare Beccaria, Jefferson's *Notes on the State of Virginia* (1785) argued that punishments should bear a rational and proportional relationship to crimes committed and made a principled case against the death penalty. Jefferson's philosophy suggested that punishments such as incarceration, applied consistently and predictably, would serve as a better deterrent than more severe penalties applied erratically. His thinking helped pave the way for the expansion of prisons in the 19th century.

Jewett, Helen (Dorcas Doyen) (1813–1836)
prostitute, murder victim

Born with the name Dorcas Doyen near Augusta, Maine, Helen Jewett became a well-known prostitute in New York City in the 1830s. Her death made her even more famous. She was found murdered in her brothel with the bed set on fire to conceal the crime. Her killing became a tabloid sensation; penny newspapers competed to learn and to tell the story of how a young woman raised as a servant in the home of a prominent Maine judge grew up to be a courtesan. The press also followed closely the arrest of her paramour, 19-year-old Richard Robinson, his subsequent trial, and his eventual acquittal.

Jones, Jim (1931–1978) *cult leader*

During the mid-1970s, Jim Jones attracted a large following as leader of the Peoples Temple, a church that taught racial integration and social justice. Over time, his church became a bizarre personality cult in which Jones demanded absolute obedience, claiming to be the incarnation of Jesus, Buddha, and Lenin. When the group was investigated on tax evasion charges, he fled with approximately 1,000 followers to Guyana and established the new, self-sufficient village of Jonestown. A member of Congress flew to Jonestown on a fact-finding mission in November 1978 and was shot to death, along with five members of his entourage, by Jones's guards. When investigators returned to the scene, they found 913 Jonestown residents, including Jones, dead—most as the result of suicide, some as the result of murder.

Kaczynski, Theodore ("Unabomber")
(1942–) *terrorist*

Theodore Kaczynski carried out a series of mail bombings between 1975 and his arrest in 1996 that killed three people and seriously injured 23 others. He was the subject of one of the longest and most expensive FBI investigations ever. Kaczynski was born and raised in Illinois. He graduated from high school at age 16, earned his bachelor's degree from Harvard University in 1962, earned

a Ph.D. in mathematics from the University of Michigan in 1967, and served as an assistant professor at the University of California at Berkeley before resigning in 1969. At that point he became a recluse, spending much of the next two and a half decades at a Montana cabin. He also became increasingly angry at modern industrial society and lashed out by sending small difficult-to-trace bombs through the mail to university researchers, airlines, and computer firms. In 1995, he sent a manifesto, *Industrial Society and Its Future*, to several national newspapers, offering to cease his bombings if they published it. Reading the manifesto in the *New York Times*, however, helped Kaczynski's brother David to identify him as the Unabomber. With this information, the FBI apprehended him. In 1997, Kaczynski pleaded guilty to all charges against him in exchange for a sentence of life in prison without the possibility of parole.

Kanka, Megan (1986–1994) *murder victim*

In July 1994, seven-year-old Megan Kanka was playing outside her family's home in a New Jersey suburb. A neighbor lured her inside his home, where he raped and murdered her. Upon learning that the neighbor had been previously incarcerated for assaulting another child, Megan's parents successfully organized a petition campaign to create the New Jersey Sex Offender Registry, known as Megan's Law. This initiative, later adopted by most states and the federal government, required convicted sex offenders to register their addresses with local law enforcement agencies so that the public could be informed of their presence.

Kefauver, Estes (1903–1963) *politician*

U.S. senator Estes Kefauver, a Democrat from Tennessee, distinguished himself by leading legislative hearings into organized crime and juvenile delinquency in the 1950s. Kefauver graduated from the University of Tennessee in 1924, earned a law degree from Yale University in 1927, and returned home to practice corporate law in Chattanooga. He gained a seat in the U.S. House of Representatives in 1939, won election to the Senate in 1948, and ran unsuccessfully for the presidency in 1952. His career in the Senate was highlighted by televised hearings into organized crime conducted in a dozen cities in 1950 and 1951. In 1954, Kefauver's Senate Subcommittee to Investigate Juvenile Delinquency conducted hearings on that problem; they focused on the influence that crime and horror comic books had on children and provided a forum for Dr. Frederic Wertham to air his ideas. Kefauver remained a senator until his death in 1963.

Kemmler, William (ca. 1860–1890) *murderer, first person executed in electric chair*
Convicted of killing his common-law wife in 1889, Kemmler was sentenced to be the first person to die in the electric chair in New York's Auburn Penitentiary in 1890. His lawyer's appeal—arguing that death by electricity constituted cruel and unusual punishment—was rejected by the state supreme court on the grounds that the electric chair was actually a humanitarian form of execution. Kemmler's execution on August 6, 1890, required two applications of electricity, one lasting 17 seconds and the other more than minute.

Kennedy, Robert F. (1925–1968) *politician, U.S. attorney general*
Much of Robert F. Kennedy's political career revolved around criminal justice. Born to a prominent political family in Brookline, Massachusetts, Kennedy earned a bachelor's degree from Harvard University in 1946 and a law degree from the University of Virginia in 1951. He worked as counsel for various congressional committees in the 1950s, becoming chief counsel for the Senate Select Committee on Improper Activities in the Labor or Management Field under Senator George McClellan in 1957. In this position, he led an investigation of corruption within the International Brotherhood of Teamsters, particularly targeting the union's leader, Jimmy Hoffa. In 1960, Kennedy successfully managed the presidential campaign of his brother John F. Kennedy; he was in turn appointed attorney general in his brother's administration. As attorney general Robert Kennedy was in charge of implementing his brother's somewhat ambivalent policies on African-American civil rights. On the one hand, the Kennedy Justice Department pushed federal law enforcement agencies such as the FBI to protect civil rights workers. On the other hand, it urged civil rights advocates themselves to exercise restraint. Following his brother's 1963 assassination, Robert Kennedy resigned from the Justice Department and in 1964 won election to the U.S. Senate from New York. In 1968 Robert Kennedy joined the race for the presidency, but on June 4 he was assassinated by Sirhan Sirhan in Los Angeles, California.

Kieft, Willem (1597–1647) *governor of the Dutch colony New Netherland*
Appointed governor of the Dutch colony New Netherland (present-day New York) in 1637, Kieft arrived in 1638 to find his capital, New Amsterdam (today New York City), in disarray. He assumed authority over colonial administration, replaced the existing judicial system with his own control, and demanded tribute from surrounding Indian tribes. In 1643, Kieft ordered an attack on a nearby Indian village that resulted in at least 80 deaths. In retribution, Indians attacked Dutch settlers throughout the colony, forcing the survivors to flee to New Amsterdam for protection. Blamed for the ensuing war, Kieft was removed from office in 1646. He died in a 1647 shipwreck while returning to Europe.

Klaas, Polly (1981–1993) *victim*
Polly Klaas was a 12-year-old girl kidnapped at knifepoint from her bedroom in her Petaluma, California, home on October 1, 1993. In spite of a communitywide effort to rescue her, her body was discovered two months later. Klaas's kidnapping and death generated nationwide concern about the problem of missing children. It sparked both private efforts to address the issue and law enforcement campaigns to respond to it more effectively.

Kohler, Frederick J. (1864–1934) *police chief*
Frederick Kohler was a leading police reformer of the early 20th century. The son of a stoneworker, he joined the Cleveland police force in 1889, became a captain in 1900, and was appointed chief in 1903. Beginning in 1907, Kohler initiated a new effort to apply the "golden rule" to minor offenses, asking his officers to warn and release men, women, and children whom they might otherwise have arrested for drunkenness, disorderly conduct, vagrancy, or delinquency. He also initiated a "sunrise court" to quickly hear cases involving people held overnight first thing in the morning and to send them on their way. These innovations reduced arrests sharply but helped make him a target for criticism. Removed from office, Kohler later was elected county commissioner in 1918, mayor between 1922 and 1924, and sheriff between 1924 and 1926.

Las Casas, Bartolomé de (1474–1566) *Spanish priest*
Bartolomé de Las Casas was the leading organizer of a 16-century movement in Spain to protect Indians in Spanish America. As a young man, he sailed to the West Indies with a Spanish expedition, fought in wars against indigenous peoples, and acquired land and slaves for himself. As he matured, he became more aware of the plight of the Native Americans and urged the Spanish Crown to establish model colonies where Spanish and Indians worked together. Throughout the 1530s and 1540s he campaigned for laws that would guarantee equitable treatment of Native Americans. Las Casas is known best for his many pamphlets and tracts condemning Spanish

cruelty toward Indians, including *Brief Account of the Destruction of the Indies* (1552).

Lathrop, Julia (1858–1932) *social worker*

A Chicago reformer at the turn of the 20th century, Lathrop helped create and nurture the Cook County Juvenile Court. She was born in Rockford, Illinois, attended the Rockford Female Seminary, and then transferred to Vassar College, from which she graduated in 1880. In 1890, Lathrop went to Chicago to live and work at Jane Addams's Hull-House. From there, she participated in numerous investigations of social conditions. Illinois governor John P. Altgeld appointed her to the Illinois Board of Public Charities in 1892, where she served until 1901, until she resigned in protest over political patronage. In this position, she led studies of the state's institutions for juvenile delinquents and the mentally ill. In 1899, she helped frame the Illinois Juvenile Court Act, the world's first, and in subsequent decades remained a major supporter of the court, helping to organize its Juvenile Psychopathic Institute in 1911. President William Howard Taft appointed her head of the new federal Children's Bureau in 1912, where she served until 1921.

Leopold, Nathan F., Jr. (1904–1971) Loeb, and Richard A. (1905–1936) *murderers*

In 1924, 19-year-old Nathan Leopold and 18-year-old Richard Loeb clubbed to death 14-year-old Bobby Franks. Both Leopold and Loeb came from extremely wealthy families in the Chicago suburb of Kenwood, Illinois. Each was also spectacularly successful in academia: Leopold reportedly spoke nine languages and graduated from the University of Chicago at age 18, and Loeb graduated from the University of Michigan at 17. On May 21, 1924, the two friends convinced the Franks boy to join them in a rented car as he walked home from school, killed him, dumped the body near a railroad embankment 20 miles outside Chicago, and devised an elaborate plan to make the crime seem like a kidnapping for ransom. When they were arrested, the families hired attorney Clarence Darrow to defend them. Darrow convinced the youths to plead guilty and then saved them from execution by arguing against capital punishment itself and by maintaining that Leopold and Loeb were too young to pay the ultimate penalty. They were instead sentenced to prison for life plus 99 years. Loeb was stabbed to death in a shower-room brawl in 1936. Leopold was paroled in 1958 after serving more than 33 years in prison and moved to Puerto Rico, where he died in 1971.

Lexow, Clarence (1852–1910) *lawyer, politician*

As a Republican member of the New York State Senate, Lexow chaired and lent his name to the famous 1895 committee investigating corruption in the New York City Police Department. Lexow himself had been elected to the state senate only two years earlier, in 1893, and apparently saw the committee as a tactical means of undermining the Democratic Party's control of New York City politics and policing. Vigorous investigators, however, transformed the committee into a forum for a much larger critique of police practices. Lexow himself assumed a neutral role in the hearings, proposing only modest reforms in the final report.

Lincoln, Abraham (1809–1865) *16th president of the United States*

As president, Abraham Lincoln led the United States through its Civil War, helped restore the Union, and contributed to the final abolition of slavery. In order to accomplish his wartime goals, he extended his executive powers, including his powers over criminal justice. In particular, he suspended the right of habeas corpus (a protection against being imprisoned without charges), first in 1861 along the borders of Maryland and the District of Columbia, then in 1862 for the entire nation, in order to contain protests and dissent against the war effort. Under this provision, Lincoln ordered the arrest of secessionist legislators in border states. Criminal violence also cut short Lincoln's life: Assassin John Wilkes Booth shot him on the night of April 14, 1865, and he died the next morning.

Lindsey, Benjamin Barr (1869–1943) *judge*

A judge and social reformer, Benjamin Lindsey became the foremost proponent of juvenile courts in the United States. Born in Jackson, Tennessee, Lindsey moved to Denver, Colorado, as a young man, studied law there, and joined the bar in 1894 at the age of 29. In 1899, he was appointed public guardian and administrator in the Denver courts, and in 1901 he was appointed to an unexpired term as a county judge. From this position, he became an advocate of children in courts, trying to treat them humanely and to address the sources of their problems rather than merely to punish them. Lindsey remained on the bench until 1924. During this time, his court evolved into the Juvenile and Family Court of Denver. A prolific writer and engaging speaker, Lindsey promoted juvenile courts widely and contributed to their spread across urban America. In the 1920s, he became increasingly concerned with changing values regarding sexuality, family, and marriage and wrote two important books: *The Revolt of Modern Youth* (1925) and *The Companionate Marriage* (1927). Relocating to Los Angeles, California, he was elected to a county judgeship in 1934, where he continued to advocate new legislation to aid children and families before the law.

Locke, John (1632–1704) *English political philosopher*

John Locke is often credited with initiating the empiricist tradition in English philosophy. Rejecting theories of knowledge not based on experience, Locke argued that human knowledge began with sensation, reflection, and evidence. His political thinking also reflected this iconoclastic orientation. In his *Second Treatise on Government* (1690) he rejected theories of government based on monarchical power and instead argued that people willingly enter into civil society, giving up a certain degree of freedom in exchange for a government that reflects their shared interests and protects their rights to freedom and to property.

Lombroso, Cesare (1835–1909) *Italian criminologist*

Lombroso exerted enormous influence over late 19th-century criminology in Europe and the United States with his argument that many criminals were throwbacks to an earlier stage of human evolution. His ideas became the centerpiece for theories of crime based on heredity rather than environment. Born in Verona, Italy, in 1835, he studied psychiatry and forensic medicine throughout Europe and spent much of his professional life at the Universities of Pavia and Turin. Lombroso's 1876 book, *L'uomo delinquente,* maintained that through systematic measurements and comparison of prison inmates certain physical characteristics distinguished "born criminals" from noncriminals. In particular, mental impairments and physical defects such as sloping foreheads, asymmetrical faces, and unusually long arms characterized criminals. These problems, he suggested, resulted from atavism, or evolutionary reversions to lower forms. While American thinkers such as Richard Dugdale worked on tracks parallel to Lombroso, Lombroso's work was not published in the United States until the 20th century. Only then did he have his greatest influence.

Lovejoy, Elijah Parish (1802–1837) *abolitionist*

Elijah Lovejoy was born in 1802 in Albion, Maine, graduated from Waterville College, worked as a schoolteacher and journalist, and studied for the ministry before relocating to St. Louis, Missouri, to edit a Presbyterian newspaper, *The Observer.* From this platform, he issued outspoken editorials denouncing slavery. Threats of violence forced him to relocate from St. Louis to Alton, Illinois. Even so, between 1835 and 1837 mobs destroyed three different printing presses used by *The Observer.* Attempted intimidation made Lovejoy more strident in his abolitionist views. Finally, in November 1837, a mob surrounded the warehouse where Lovejoy had located his newest press, and Lovejoy was killed in an exchange of gunfire. In death, he became a symbol of freedom of the press and a martyr to the abolitionist cause.

Lynds, Elam (1784–1855) *prison administrator*

A state prison official in New York, Elam Lynds is credited with creating the "Auburn" system of prisons, which used silent labor among prisoners in common workshops to inculcate discipline and penitence. Lynds was appointed principal keeper of the state penitentiary at Auburn when it opened in 1817, only to be forced out in 1825. He was then placed in charge of building and managing a new prison that became Sing Sing, completing the institution in four years. At all of his prison posts, he was known for using convict labor and encouraging his staff to use physical punishments to enforce discipline.

McCarthy, Joseph (1908–1957) *politician*

A U.S. senator from Wisconsin, Joseph McCarthy lent his name to a larger anticommunist movement in the 1950s. McCarthy became the leading figure in the movement when he declared in a February 1950 speech in Wheeling, West Virginia, that he could identify large numbers of current and former communists working in the U.S. State Department. From that point on, McCarthy used his position on a special Senate investigating committee to levy accusations at opponents within and outside the federal government intended to destroy their political standing. McCarthy's style of baseless accusation eventually undermined the larger anticommunist movement, as in 1954, when his televised hearings charging subversion in the U.S. Army leadership backfired. Following this embarrassing display, McCarthy's colleagues in the Senate voted to censure him. He died in relative obscurity in 1957.

MacCormick, Austin Harbutt (1893–1979) *penal reformer*

Austin MacCormick was a pioneer in prison administration and in using prisons to rehabilitate inmates. After graduating from Bowdoin College in 1915 with a senior essay on penal reform heavily influenced by Thomas Mott Osborne, MacCormick found himself working as

Osborne's assistant at the Portsmouth, New Hampshire, Naval Prison between 1917 and 1921. There, MacCormick became Osborne's protégé, developed progressive theories of penology, and earned a reputation for rehabilitating offenders. In the 1920s, MacCormick conducted several investigations of prison conditions, published as *Handbook of American Prisons* (1926) and *The Education of Adult Prisoners* (1931). In 1934, MacCormick became head of New York City's penitentiary, Welfare Island. He quickly transformed it from an institution dominated by criminals and gangsters into a well-run penal facility. In 1937, MacCormick used the opportunity of New York replacing Welfare Island with the modern Riker's Island facility to improve classification and control of inmates. After he retired in 1940, MacCormick became executive director of the Osborne Association, a research agency aimed at studying crime and improving prison life. In 1951, he joined the faculty of the University of California at Berkeley's School of Criminology.

Mack, Julian William (1866–1943) *lawyer, judge*

From his position as an attorney and judge, Julian Mack became a leader in social welfare causes. He grew up in the German Jewish community in Cincinnati, Ohio, and attended Harvard Law School, where he earned an LL.B. in 1887. Practicing law in Chicago, Illinois, after 1890, he became involved in the city's social welfare causes. When he was elected to the judiciary in 1903, he chose to serve on Chicago's pioneering juvenile court, established just four years earlier. From his position, he developed a deeper interest in social reform and became a national advocate of juvenile courts. In 1911, President William Howard Taft appointed Mack to the federal judiciary, where he served in various posts until his retirement in 1941.

Manson, Charles (1934–) *murderer*

Charles Manson was the head of a California cult responsible for a string of gruesome murders in 1969. Charles Manson was born to a 16-year-old single mother in Cincinnati, Ohio, in 1934 and spent much of his childhood and youth drifting in and out of foster care and juvenile correctional facilities. As a young adult, he found his way to California, making his living as a petty thief. In the later 1960s, Manson attracted followers—mainly young middle-class women—to form a cult mingling countercultural values, drug use, and apocalyptic religion. On August 10, 1969, five brutally mutilated bodies were found at a Beverly Hills mansion rented to film director Roman Polanski; among the dead was Polanski's eight-

months-pregnant wife, actress Sharon Tate. The next day, two more bodies were found at a nearby estate. Three months later, police linked Manson and his followers to the crime. Over the course of almost two years between the crimes and his conviction in 1971, Manson held a fascination for the American public, presenting himself as a Christ-like figure who reflected the dark side of American society. Sentenced to death in 1971, his sentence was commuted to life in prison in 1972; he has been incarcerated at Corcoran State Prison since.

Marshall, John (1755–1835) *chief justice of the U.S. Supreme Court*

As the fourth chief justice of the U. S. Supreme Court, Marshall helped define the role of the judiciary in the American government and established the beginnings of constitutional law. Born in Virginia, he fought for the patriots in the American Revolutionary War between 1775 and 1781. He also studied law during his service, and following the war he joined the Virginia bar and became involved in politics. He subsequently participated in the Constitutional Convention in 1787, served in a number of positions in the federal government in the 1790s, and was appointed chief justice of the Supreme Court in 1800. During his long tenure on the court—he served until his death in 1835—the Marshall Court helped define the operations of American constitutional law. Most famously, his opinion in *Marbury v. Madison* (1803) established the principle of judicial review by the courts on the constitutionality of legislative actions.

Mason, George (1725–1792) *politician*

A Revolutionary-era Virginia statesman, Mason was an indefatigable defender of individual rights. During the American Revolution, he served in the Continental Congress and drafted the Virginia Declaration of Rights in 1776, which became a model for the other colonies as they became independent states. In 1787, he participated in the Constitutional Convention, insisting that the founding document include a bill of rights guaranteeing individual freedoms and refusing to endorse the Constitution without one. He actively opposed the Constitution's ratification in Virginia, only endorsing it after the first 10 amendments were added.

Matsell, George Washington (1811–1877) *police chief*

Born in New York City in 1811, Matsell became the first chief of the New York Municipal Police. Active in Democratic Party politics, he served in the New York militia and beginning in 1843 as a magistrate in New York City's jail, the Tombs. With the formation of New York's Municipal Police in 1845, he was appointed its chief. In 1849, he focused most of his semiannual reports on the problems of delinquent and vagrant children who crowded New York's streets. While his main concern was that these street urchins would grow up to join a dangerous class, his analysis did illuminate the conditions in which they lived and inspired a wave of reform efforts in subsequent years, including the work of Charles Loring Brace and the Children's Aid Society. In 1857, when the state legislature created a separate, state-managed New York Metropolitan Police Department in an effort to usurp control of policing from Mayor Fernando Wood, Matsell sided with Wood. Matsell and the municipal police barricaded themselves in city hall and fought off an attack by the Metropolitan Police. An appeals court, however, sided with the state agency, abolishing Matsell's force. When New York City regained control of its police in 1873, Matsell was again appointed superintendent.

McVeigh, Timothy (1968–2001) *terrorist*

McVeigh bombed the Alfred P. Murrah Federal Building in Oklahoma City on April 19, 1995, killing 168 people, including 19 children. McVeigh was born and raised near Buffalo, New York. After graduating from high school, he joined the U.S. Army and served in Kuwait in the 1991 Persian Gulf conflict. McVeigh became obsessed with guns and distrustful of the federal government; after leaving the service, he became involved with antigovernment paramilitary groups. In April 1995, McVeigh rented a truck, loaded it with 4,800 pounds of homemade explosives, and detonated it outside the federal building. He was arrested two hours after the bombing for a traffic violation, was carrying illegal weapons, and was quickly linked to the attack. On June 2, 1997, McVeigh was convicted in federal court on 11 charges, including eight murders of federal agents. On June 11, 2001, he was executed by lethal injection.

M'Naghten, Daniel (Daniel McNaghten)
(1816–1865) *murderer*

Born in Glasgow, Scotland, Daniel M'Naghten was a skilled lathe operator and businessman who gradually became convinced that Tory politicians were persecuting him. On January 20, 1843, he followed Edward Drummond, the private secretary to Prime Minister Robert Peel, as he left Peel's residence and shot Drummond twice

in the stomach. At M'Naghten's trial, his defense attorneys argued that although he had not displayed classic signs of mental illness, the courts should consider new breakthroughs in psychiatry; prominent medical experts argued that he was clearly insane. The jury acquitted, and in spite of a public outcry the case set the standard for deciding insanity cases that would last for the next century.

Mudgett, Herman (Dr. H. H. Holmes)
(1861–1896) *murderer*

America's first known serial killer was born in New Hampshire, studied medicine at the University of Michigan, and moved to Chicago, Illinois, where he made his living operating a pharmacy and a hotel. Both businesses, however, were fronts for insurance fraud and murder, and Mudgett used them to lure mainly young women who would become his victims during the 1893 Chicago World's Fair. Mudgett was caught in 1896 as a result of an insurance scam that went wrong. When police raided his hotel, they found elaborate mechanisms to dispose of bodies. Convicted and sentenced to hang, Mudgett confessed to 27 murders. His crimes become well-known to 21st-century readers through Erik Larson's book *The Devil in the White City* (2003).

Muhammad, John Allen (John Allen Williams)
(1960–   ) *murderer*

Muhammad was one of two men convicted of being the Washington, D.C., "Beltway Sniper" who carried out a three-week shooting spree, killing 10 people, in 2002. Muhammad, born John Allen Williams, served in the Louisiana National Guard and between 1985 and 1994 in the U.S. Army. Although described as an "unremarkable" soldier, he did attain a rating as an "expert" marksman. In October 2002, Muhammad and a teenage companion, John Lee Malvo, apparently began a spree of sniper shootings of motorists along the "Capital Beltway," the highway that runs through Virginia and Maryland and loops around Washington, D.C. The shootings prompted public panic and an intense manhunt. Police ultimately arrested Muhammad and Malvo on October 24, 2002. In 2003, Muhammad was convicted on multiple charges and sentenced to death.

Ness, Eliot (1903–1957) *law enforcement officer*

Ness gained fame as the Justice Department officer whose work led to the 1931 arrest and conviction of Al Capone. After graduating from the University of Chicago in 1925, Ness worked first as an investigator for a credit agency, then

344 Crime and Punishment in America

joined the U.S. Treasury Department's Prohibition Bureau, and finally headed the task force targeting Capone. His men were called "the untouchables" due to their reported incorruptibility. Between 1935 and 1941, Ness served as the Public Safety Director for Cleveland, Ohio. His term there was marred by the notorious "Torso Murders," which were never solved. Ness's work with the Justice Department became famous due to the 1960s television series *The Untouchables* and the 1987 film of the same name in which he was portrayed by Kevin Costner.

Olson, Harry (1867–1935) *lawyer, judge*

As chief justice of the Municipal Court of Chicago between 1906 and 1930, Olson presided over a pioneering institution that attempted to impose order over a chaotic legal system and to implement the principle of sociological jurisprudence. Born in Chicago, Olson earned his law degree from that city's Union College in 1891. After serving eight years as the assistant state's attorney for Cook County, he was chosen to be the first chief justice of the Municipal Court in 1906. The Municipal Court promised to systematize the jurisdictions and powers of each of the variety of courts operating in Chicago and Cook County. Olson's main duty was to assign cases to appropriate forums, and in doing that he was a tremendous success, winning praise from leaders in the legal profession. The Municipal Court also became the home for a number of specialized courts dealing with particular problems, such as a Court of Domestic Relations begun in 1911 to hear bastardy, child support, and abandonment cases, a Morals Court started in 1913 for prostitution cases, and a Boys' Court established in 1915 for youths between ages 17 and 21. Olson's main interest was in applying new ideas of eugenics to cases involving domesticity, youth, and sexuality. In 1914, he obtained funding to establish a Psychopathic Institute operating along eugenic principles to work alongside the Municipal Court; under his leadership, the court sent thousands of offenders to the Psychopathic Institute for examination. Olson remained a leader in the American eugenics movement throughout the 1920s.

Osborne, Thomas Mott (1859–1926) *prison reformer*

A New York State businessman and manufacturer of agricultural implements, Osborne advocated prison reform in the early 20th century, believing that inmates needed as much freedom as possible within the institution in preparation for life outside. Appointed to a state prison com-

mission in 1913, he tested his theory by serving a week as an inmate at the Auburn penitentiary. His account of his experiences behind bars, *Within Prison Walls* (1914), drew public attention to the ways in which incarceration affected inmates. Serving as warden of Sing Sing prison between 1914 and 1916, and as commanding officer of the Portsmouth Naval Prison between 1917 and 1920, Osborne sought to implement a new model of prison administration called the Mutual Welfare League in which inmates exercised some democratic control over their own living conditions.

Oswald, Lee Harvey (1939–1963) *assassin*

Oswald shot and killed President John F. Kennedy in Dallas, Texas, in 1963. Born in New Orleans, Louisiana, in 1939, Oswald joined the U.S. Marine Corps in 1956 at age 17. As a young man, he became interested in communism and after his military discharge moved to the Soviet Union. Upon returning to the United States in 1962, he became politically active in pro-Cuban, pro-Communist activities. On November 22, 1963, Oswald took a sniper's rifle to the sixth floor of the Texas School Book Depository in Dallas, Texas. As the president's motorcade passed the building, three shots were fired, killing Kennedy. When a Dallas police officer questioned Oswald near his home an hour later, Oswald killed the policeman. He was soon arrested and linked to the assassination, which he denied. Two days later, on November 24, Oswald was shot to death by Jack Ruby, a nightclub owner, as he was being transferred from a police station to the county jail. Although a federal commission headed by Earl Warren, the chief justice of the U.S. Supreme Court, found in 1964 that Oswald was the sole gunman, many Americans continued to believe that a more elaborate conspiracy was responsible for the president's murder.

Parker, Bonnie (1910–1934) and Clyde Barrow (1909–1934) ("Bonnie and Clyde") *interstate bandits*

The most visible members of the Barrow Gang, Bonnie Parker and Clyde Barrow were responsible for a string of armed bank robberies and murders in the central United States during the early 1930s. The couple first met near Dallas, Texas, in 1930. Barrow was a small-time burglar, in and out of jail, and Parker reportedly fell in love with him. In August 1932, they ran away together and began a spree of thefts and occasional bank robberies, frequently resorting to gunfire to escape. By the time they were killed, they were suspected of 13 murders, including those of at least three law enforcement officers. On May 23, 1934, a group of police officers and a prominent former member of the Texas Rangers, Frank Hamer, ambushed Parker and Barrow on a highway near Sailes, Louisiana, shooting them to death. Parker's poems "The Story of Bonnie and Clyde" and "Suicide Sal" helped to enhance the reputation of the two in life, and the 1967 film *Bonnie and Clyde* transformed them into icons in death.

Parker, William H. (1902–1966) *police chief*

As chief of the Los Angeles Police Department (LAPD) between 1950 and 1966, Parker established the model for modern law enforcement leadership. Parker, who grew up in Deadwood, South Dakota, joined the LAPD in 1927 at age 25. As a patrolman in a department known at the time for corruption, he had a reputation for upright honesty and a rigorous belief in enforcing the law. Becoming chief in 1950, Parker combined a much more centralized administration with the goal of tough crime fighting. These reforms produced a new model of authoritative, interventionist law enforcement suited to managing a sprawling city with the smallest per capita urban police force in America. Parker called this model "proactive policing," and the LAPD earned a reputation as the best police force in America. Parker was also a master publicist. He established a close working relationship with Jack Webb, the producer and star of the television series *Dragnet*, which aired between 1951 and 1959. Webb received access to the LAPD in exchange for giving Parker and his staff script approval and an opportunity to use the show to promote their own values. Parker also wrote widely about his policing techniques for scholarly, police, and public audiences and was featured frequently in magazine articles. Parker's model, however, did not lack its problems or its critics. Parker reduced corruption in the LAPD but tolerated police violence and brutality as necessary to fighting crime. Proactive policing encouraged intensive surveillance and harassment of minority communities. When the Watts riots erupted in Los Angeles's African-American community in 1965, the interventionist stance of the LAPD took much of the blame. Nonetheless, Parker retained enormous influence within policing even after his death in 1966. His protégés headed the LAPD until 1992, and many police departments across the country emulated his example.

Parris, Samuel (1653–1720) *clergyman*

A Puritan minister, his 1689 appointment to lead a congregation in Salem, Massachusetts, contributed to the ensuing witchcraft trials. In February 1692, his daughter and two other girls were afflicted with mysterious agitations. The community became convinced that the devil was attacking parishioners through witches, and a number of the accused were arrested. During the ensuing trials Parris accepted "spectral evidence," testimony of demonic activity that only the afflicted could perceive. In the course of the summer, 19 people were executed as a result of the trials, which ended when a new session of the superior court rejected "spectral evidence" and acquitted the remaining defendants. An inquiry in 1694 forced Parris to apologize to the congregation but vindicated him of any wrongdoing. In 1697, he left the clergy in a dispute over parsonage land and went into business in Boston.

Peel, Sir Robert (1788–1850) *British statesman*

A British career politician, Peel is best remembered for helping to establish the world's first official police force in London in 1829; members are often called "bobbies" or "peelers" to acknowledge him. Peel was the son of a British manufacturer and member of Parliament; he, too, was groomed for government. After he graduated from Oxford University, his father helped him procure a seat in the House of Commons at age 21. Throughout his career Peel concerned himself with reforming Britain's criminal justice system by replacing its heavy reliance on the threat of capital punishment with a more systematic and predictable bureaucracy of prisons and police. In particular, he overcame objections to a full-time police force and sponsored the Metropolitan Police Act of 1829. This law created the basis for modern systems of policing that operated as a cross between military and civilian forces. Peel later served as prime minister during 1834–35 and 1841–46.

Pinkerton, Allan (1819–1884) *private detective*

A Scottish immigrant, Pinkerton became the head of the United States' most famous detective agency. He migrated from Glasgow to the United States in 1842 and worked as a cooper and later became a sheriff in Illinois. In 1850, he became the first detective for Chicago's new police force and quickly organized his own private detective agency as well. When American policing was in its infancy, private agencies did the actual work of investigating crimes and recovering stolen property; Pinkerton's agency gained a reputation as one of the most effective and honest. After the Civil War, Pinkerton's agency expanded into a national operation under the direction of his two sons. They protected rail transport, sought to capture bandits such as Jesse and Frank James, and provided armed guards to industry in order to battle labor agitation. By the time of Pinkerton's death, his name had become synonymous with both private security and strikebreaking.

Poe, Edgar Allan (1809–1849) *writer, poet*
Poe is credited with helping to invent the American mystery and horror genres. During his lifetime, he was best known as a literary critic and magazine editor. Excessive drinking, however, made it difficult for him to hold a job and to support a family. In spite of this, he produced a prolific array of short stories and poems of enduring importance, including "The Fall of the House of Usher," "The Murders in the Rue Morgue," and "The Raven."

Prosser, Gabriel (ca. 1776–1800) *slave insurrectionist*
An African-American slave born in Henrico County, Virginia, Prosser attempted a large-scale revolt in Richmond. Prosser was an unusually talented leader and detailed planner; he assembled hundreds of slaves to take part in a three-pronged coordinated attack on Virginia's capital in 1800. The plan was undermined, however, by betrayals of slaves who warned their masters, allowing Governor James Monroe to assemble a militia, and by torrential rainstorms that delayed the attack. Prosser was captured two weeks after the intended attack, but he refused to divulge the identities of his co-conspirators. He was executed on October 7, 1800, one of 35 slaves hanged for participating in the conspiracy.

Purvis, Melvin (1903–1960) *FBI agent*
Purvis was the FBI agent credited with killing John Dillinger and Pretty Boy Floyd in 1934. A graduate of the University of South Carolina, Purvis practiced law briefly before joining the U.S. Department of Justice in 1927. As the agent in charge of the FBI's field office in Chicago, Illinois, he was responsible for investigating a wave of bank robberies and kidnappings in the Midwest in the early 1930s. At the behest of FBI director J. Edgar Hoover, Purvis concentrated on the most notorious bandit, John Dillinger. In July 1934, Purvis set up Dillinger as he emerged from the Biograph Theater in Chicago and had him killed. Later that same year, Purvis was also the agent in charge when the FBI shot down another prominent bandit, Charles Arthur "Pretty Boy" Floyd, in East Liverpool, Ohio. Purvis became a national hero as a result of his exploits and published a self-aggrandizing autobiography, *American Agent,* in 1936. This publicity, however, also contributed to a division between him and

Hoover, who pressured him to resign from the FBI. Moreover, when Purvis sought jobs as either a spokesman or a security expert for various corporations, Hoover exerted pressure to prevent him from being hired. This split lasted until Purvis's death in 1960.

Quantrill, William Clarke (1837–1865) *brigand*
An outlaw as a young man, Quantrill became the widely feared leader of a band of Confederate guerrillas during the Civil War. He was briefly a member of the Confederate army, but by 1862 Quantrill operated on his own at the head of a band of outlaws fighting an unofficial and unmerciful war in Missouri and Kansas in support of the Southern cause. His band would eventually include Frank and Jesse James. On August 21, 1863, Quantrill led a large band of men into Lawrence, Kansas, burned the town, and massacred more than 150 men, women, and children. Later that year, Quantrill's raiders defeated a small body of Union army cavalry, capturing and executing 17 noncombatants. In 1865, Quantrill was fatally wounded by a band of Union irregulars in Kentucky. He died in June 1865 near Louisville.

Rader, Dennis (BTK) (1945–   ) *serial killer*
An anonymous serial killer known only as "BTK" terrorized Wichita, Kansas, for decades until the killer's need for attention revealed his identity. The killer, whose nickname came from a letter he wrote to the media following a murder (which included the phrase "Bind Them, Torture Them, Kill Them"), claimed at least 10 victims between 1974 and 1991. In 2004, media coverage of the 30th anniversary of the first BTK murder brought Rader out of the shadows. A floppy diskette containing one of his letters was traced to a local Lutheran church, where Rader served as board president. Confronted with physical evidence linking him to the murders, Rader confessed in disturbingly graphic detail. He was sentenced to life imprisonment.

Ray, James Earl (1928–1998) *assassin*
Ray confessed to the 1968 murder of civil rights leader Martin Luther King, Jr., and then spent the remaining 30 years of his life denying that he was the sole assassin. Born in Alton, Missouri, he grew up in a troubled home and drifted from job to job as a young man. He apparently hated the African-American Civil Rights movement, especially King. A con-man and small-time thief, Ray served three terms in prison for burglary, robbery, and forgery, ultimately escaping from a low-security prison farm in 1967. On April 4, 1968, King was shot while standing on the balcony of a Memphis

hotel. All evidence pointed to Ray, and he fled to London and Portugal. Apprehended in June 1968, Ray confessed to the killing in order to avoid a possible death penalty. Ray, however, consistently maintained that he had been set up as the "patsy" for a larger conspiracy against King and three days after being sentenced to a 99-year prison term asked to recant his confession. By the 1990s, Ray convinced the King family that he was not the sole killer, and they urged the U.S. Justice Department to reopen their investigation. His death in 1998, however, made a new examination of the case unlikely.

Reagan, Nancy (1923–   ) *first lady of the United States*

As the wife of President Ronald Reagan, Reagan led a publicity campaign encouraging children and youths to "just say no" to drugs. Her efforts provided a moral exhortation that paralleled the "war on drugs" waged by her husband's administration.

Rockefeller, Nelson (1908–1979) *53rd governor of New York*

Although widely regarded as a moderate Republican whose centrist 1964 presidential primary campaign was ultimately outmaneuvered by that of archconservative Barry Goldwater, Rockefeller implemented conservative policies with respect to criminal justice. He authorized the recapture of Attica prison during the 1971 riot and spearheaded the passage of the "Rockefeller laws" of 1973, which imposed exceptionally harsh penalties for drug-related offenses.

Roosevelt, Theodore (1858–1919) *26th president of the United States*

Theodore Roosevelt experienced an astonishing rise through U.S. politics and became the model of a modern president. Born in a prominent New York family, he graduated from Harvard University in 1880 and was elected to the first of three terms as a New York state assemblyman in 1882, rapidly becoming both a celebrity and the leader of a reform wing of the Republican Party. After both his mother and his wife died within hours of each other in 1884, Roosevelt temporarily relocated to his ranch in the Dakota Territory, becoming an outdoorsman and a historical writer. Roosevelt remarried and returned to politics, becoming head of the federal Civil Service Commission in 1889 and in 1895 president of New York City's police commissioners. As the head of the police department, he became a vigorous reformer, trying to modernize the force, eliminate graft, and improve morale in the wake of the

revelations of the 1894 Lexow Committee. After serving two years on the NYPD's board, Roosevelt went on to his career in national politics. He became William McKinley's assistant secretary for the navy in 1897, resigned in 1898 to organize a volunteer cavalry regiment to fight in the Spanish-American War, was elected New York's governor in November 1898, and became McKinley's vice president early in 1901; with McKinley's death in September 1901, he assumed the presidency. In 1908, he established the Bureau of Investigation over the objections of many in Congress; this agency would evolve into the FBI.

Rosenberg, Julius (1918–1953) **and** Ethel Rosenberg (1915–1953) *alleged spies*

Julius and Ethel Rosenberg were both executed in 1953 for espionage for their roles in transferring atomic secrets to the Soviet Union. Both were leftists, Jews, and active in trade union activities from the Lower East Side of New York City. They came to public attention in 1950 with the arrest of Klaus Fuchs, a British scientist who had apparently sold nuclear secrets to the Soviet Union, helping that country develop an atomic weapon in 1949. Fuchs identified his go-between with the Soviets as a Philadelphia chemist named Harry Gold, who in turn identified David Greenglass, a former technician at the Los Alamos nuclear laboratory, as another conspirator. Greenglass identified his brother-in-law and partner in an unsuccessful machine shop, Julius Rosenberg, as the mastermind. Julius and Ethel, both prosecuted for selling atomic secrets, claimed innocence, maintaining that Greenglass was simply lying. Their 1951 trial created a national sensation both because of the heinous allegations and because of the apparent lack of evidence against them. Decrypted messages used by the FBI in their investigation but made public only in the late 1990s reveal that Julius did, in fact, coordinate a group of engineers working in defense facilities to supply technical data to the Soviets. These messages also reveal that his offenses were not so extensive as alleged at the trial and that Ethel had little role. Their plight generated tremendous sympathy among American Jews and leftists, especially after both were sentenced to death, but that could not save them from being executed each in an electric chair in 1953.

Rousseau, Jean-Jacques (1712–1778) *French philosopher*

The leading thinker of the French Enlightenment, Rousseau influenced American thinking about rights, about government, and indirectly, about criminal justice. In *Discourse on the Origin and Basis of Inequality Among Men* (1754), he argued that humans are equal in nature and become unequal only when society makes them so; in his *The Social Contract* (1762), he argued that the ideal government is a direct democracy controlled by the will of its citizens. His writings contributed to American consciousness about rights and apprehensions about a strong state. At the same time, they also contributed to an emerging 18th-century discourse that punishments should be proportionate to crimes.

Rudolph, Eric (1966–) *domestic terrorist*

Between 1996 and 1998, right-wing terrorist Eric Rudolph bombed Atlanta Georgia's Centennial Park during the 1996 Summer Olympics, two abortion clinics, and a lesbian and gay bar. He claimed that his attacks, which killed three people and injured more than 150 others, were motivated by his opposition to "abortion on demand" and what he described as "the homosexual agenda." Rudolph has also been connected to white supremacist paramilitary groups. He was arrested in 2003 and sentenced to five consecutive life terms in 2005.

Rush, Benjamin (1745–1813) *physician*

A Philadelphia physician, Rush also became a political and social activist, campaigning for penal reform and against the death penalty. A native of the Philadelphia area, Rush earned his doctorate at the University of Edinburgh in Scotland in 1768, then returned home to practice medicine. He became an activist for the abolition of slavery (helping to organize an antislavery society in 1774) and for the rights of American colonists (joining the Continental Congress in 1775 and signing the Declaration of Independence in 1776). After practicing medicine in Philadelphia during the Revolutionary War, Rush was appointed professor at the University of Pennsylvania in 1789. From there, he became a widely influential teacher and thinker. Rush also became an outspoken critic of Pennsylvania's penal practices, especially the "wheelbarrow law" of 1786, and he condemned the use of the death penalty in his 1787 pamphlet "An Enquiry into the Effects of Public Punishments Upon Criminal and Upon Society."

Sacco, Nicola (1891–1927) and
Vanzetti, Bartolomeo (1888–1927) *political activists, alleged killers*

Italian-born anarchists Sacco and Vanzetti were the subjects of one of the most controversial trials of the 1920s. Both immigrated to the United States as young men, met in the Boston area, and drifted into political radicalism.

Vanzetti, the more intellectual of the two, held a variety of jobs. Sacco was married and worked for a shoe factory. They were arrested together in May 1920 for the April 15 robbery of a shoe factory in South Braintree, Massachusetts, in which the paymaster and a guard were murdered. Their six-week trial used ballistic evidence to link them to the crime and raised suspicions that their political belief in anarchism made them criminals. Although both maintained their innocence, Sacco and Vanzetti were convicted and sentenced to death. Appeals transformed the case into a national cause célèbre, as intellectuals came to regard their conviction as a microcosm of repression of dissent and immigrants in the 1920s. Their attorneys mobilized public sentiment about the case, raised doubts about the reliability of the evidence, and suggested that the whole trial had been conducted in a biased and hostile atmosphere. All appeals were rejected, however, and the two men were executed on August 22, 1927.

Scott, Dred (1795–1858) *slave*

An African-American slave, Scott's unsuccessful lawsuit to secure his freedom established a precedent in defining slavery in the United States and became a step on the path to the Civil War. Scott was born in Virginia, but he was moved by various owners to Missouri (a slave state), Illinois (a free state), and Wisconsin (a free territory at that time). When in the 1840s Scott's efforts to purchase his freedom were rejected, he sued his owner on the basis of false imprisonment, arguing that having been transported to areas that banned slavery, he should be free. Scott's case ultimately reached the U.S. Supreme Court; in 1857, it ruled against him. Chief Justice Roger Taney's decision maintained that since Scott was a slave, he was not a citizen and therefore had no right to bring a suit. Taney ruled further that federal restrictions on slavery were unconstitutional, so slave owners could bring slaves with them into free states. In the heightened tensions of the 1850s, this ruling further divided advocates and opponents of slavery. Following the ruling, Scott's owners freed him, and he worked as a hotel porter in St. Louis, Missouri, until his death of tuberculosis less than two years later.

Shaw, Clifford R. (1896–1957) *sociologist*

As a sociologist and activist in Chicago, Illinois, Shaw helped develop new approaches to preventing juvenile delinquency. Shaw was born in a small town in rural Indiana and applied the lessons he learned there to dealing with delinquency in larger cities as well. He earned a bachelor's degree from Adrian College in Michigan and pursued graduate studies at the University of Chicago between 1919 and 1924. He never finished his Ph.D., but while in school he worked as both a parole officer and a probation officer. Appointed director of the newly created Illinois Institute for Juvenile Research in 1927, Shaw and fellow sociologist Henry McKay analyzed data on children appearing in juvenile court and found them to be concentrated in commercial and industrial areas. From these findings, Shaw and McKay developed a theory that "social disorganization"—characteristic of communities with little institutional guidance for youths—was a key factor contributing to delinquency. This research led to their seminal works *Delinquency Areas* (1929) and *Juvenile Delinquency in Urban Areas* (1942). During this time, Shaw also began collecting individual "life histories" of young offenders in order to determine what experiences led some youths and not others to engage in delinquent offenses. This research led to Shaw's best-known book, *The Jack-Roller* (1930), as well as *The Natural History of a Delinquent Career* (1931) and *Brothers in Crime* (1938). In 1932, Shaw established the Chicago Area Project (CAP) in three high-crime neighborhoods. This agency sought to address community needs, improve social organization, and place social workers on the streets with potential delinquents. The CAP expanded to other Chicago neighborhoods in the 1940s and 1950s, and Shaw remained its executive director until his death in 1957. The CAP remains the model for modern community-based social work agencies, and Shaw and McKay's thinking continues to influence discussion of the sources of crime and delinquency.

Shays, Daniel (1747–1825) *farmer, insurrectionist*
An American Revolutionary War officer, Shays led a rebellion of Massachusetts farmers against the early United States in 1786 and 1787. A farm laborer, he returned from the Revolutionary War to become a political leader in western Massachusetts. He served in a number of local offices in the 1780s, a decade in which monetary policy and taxation created difficult economic circumstances; when farmers failed to pay their debts, courts foreclosed on their lands and sent them to jail. In 1786, he and other western Massachusetts farmers took up arms and forced the courts to close. In 1787, Shays led 1,200 men in an effort to capture the federal armory at Springfield, Massachusetts. Defeated, Shays fled the state. Although he was eventually pardoned, Shays lived the rest of his life in western New York.

Siegel, Benjamin (Bugsy Siegel) (1906–1947)
gangster
A leading organizer of gambling, Siegel played a key role in making Las Vegas, Nevada, the nation's capital for casinos. Siegel was born in Brooklyn, New York, in 1906 and became involved in organized crime from an early age. Climbing through the criminal ranks in the 1920s and 1930s, Siegel relocated to California and through that state's gangsters met leading players in Hollywood. There, he established a number of illegal gambling operations and a well-known floating casino. Siegel achieved his greatest prominence in 1945, when he opened the Flamingo, a hotel in Las Vegas, bankrolled by money from organized crime. As the first legalized gambling casino in the United States, the Flamingo became famous, helped transform Las Vegas from a sleepy desert town into a major metropolis, and brought substantial profits for Siegel. Siegel was shot to death in 1947, apparently by organized crime figures as a result of a dispute over repaying the original hotel investment.

Simpson, Orenthal James (O. J. Simpson) (1947–   ) *football player, alleged murderer*
An American football player, O. J. Simpson achieved notoriety when he was arrested and tried for the murders of his ex-wife, Nicole Brown Simpson, and her friend Ron Goldman. Simpson was born in San Francisco, California, and achieved fame playing football first at the University of Southern California (where he won the Heisman Trophy as the nation's best college football player in 1968), then as a professional, mainly with the Buffalo Bills. After his playing days ended he enjoyed a second career as a moderately successful actor in movies and television commercials. Simpson (who is African American) married his second wife, Nicole Brown (who was white), in 1985; their marriage was marked by domestic violence, and they divorced in 1992. In June 1994, Nicole Brown Simpson and Goldman were found slashed to death outside her Los Angeles condominium; O. J. Simpson was the only suspect. After initially fleeing police during a nationally televised low-speed chase in his white Ford Bronco, Simpson eventually turned himself in. The ensuing trial lasted more than a year. Simpson's team of prominent defense lawyers, led by Johnnie Cochran, demonstrated that the Los Angeles Police Department (LAPD) had made numerous errors in their initial investigation; they strongly implied that white police officers had sought to "frame" an African-American celebrity accused of killing a white woman. The trial divided American public opinion along

racial lines, especially when in October 1995 the jury found Simpson not guilty. In 1997, a subsequent civil suit brought by the Brown family found Simpson liable in the slayings and ordered him to pay $8.5 million in compensatory damages to the families of the deceased. Simpson has persistently maintained his innocence. In 2007, Simpson was arrested in Las Vegas, Nevada, for robbery; in 2008, he was convicted and sentenced to at least nine years in prison.

Sirhan, Sirhan Bishara (1944–   ) *assassin*
Sirhan murdered senator and presidential candidate Robert F. Kennedy. As Kennedy was leaving the Ambassador Hotel in Los Angeles, California, on June 5, 1968, after winning the California primary, Sirhan shot him eight times at close range with a .22 caliber pistol. Kennedy died the next day. Sirhan was born in Palestine in 1944, but his family immigrated to California when he was 12. He attended public and private schools and studied for two years at Pomona City College. Sirhan claimed to be motivated by his opposition to Senator Kennedy's support for Israel. In his trials, his attorneys argued that he was not guilty by reason of insanity, but he was nonetheless convicted in 1969. Originally sentenced to death, his sentence was later commuted to life in prison.

Speck, Richard (1941–1991) *spree killer*
In June 1966, a 24-year-old drifter named Richard Speck broke into a women's dormitory and brutally murdered eight student nurses. Originally sentenced to the electric chair, he was resentenced to life imprisonment after a moratorium on capital punishment was declared in 1972.

Starkweather, Charles (1938–1959) *murderer*
At age 18, high school dropout Charles Starkweather and his 14-year-old girlfriend, Caril Ann Fugate, went on a cross-country killing spree that has retained a curious fascination in American culture. Beginning with a gas station hold-up on December 1, 1957, they killed 11 people in Nebraska and Wyoming before being captured in early 1958. Denying his lawyers' plea of insanity, Starkweather was convicted of murder; he was executed on June 25, 1959. His and Fugate's story was adapted into Terrence Malick's 1973 film *Badlands* and partly inspired Oliver Stone's 1994 *Natural Born Killers*.

Sylvester, Richard (1859–1930) *police chief*
Chief of the Washington, D.C., Metropolitan Police Department from 1898 to 1915, Sylvester was a lead-ing police reformer. He began his career as a journalist, and after he took a desk job with the Washington, D.C., police in 1894, he wrote a history of the department that propelled him into the chief's office by 1898. Sylvester's real influence came as the president of the International Association of Chiefs of Police between 1901 and 1915. There, he led a movement for police professionalization, guiding his fellow police administrators to become more efficient and more technologically adept yet still fulfill a wide variety of social welfare functions in the community. After he left the Washington police Sylvester served another 15 years as director of security for the DuPont Corporation in Wilmington, Delaware.

Thaw, Harry Kendall (1871–1947) *socialite, alleged murderer*
The playboy son of a wealthy Pittsburgh family, Thaw gained notoriety in 1906 by shooting to death the architect Stanford White. His family, which earned its money in the railroad and canal businesses, sent Thaw first to the Western University of Pennsylvania (now called the University of Pittsburgh) and later to Harvard University, but he never graduated and attracted more attention as the host of lavish New York parties. In 1905, he married Evelyn Nesbit, a chorus girl and model originally from Pittsburgh who had previously been romantically involved with White. On June 25, 1906, Thaw shot White dead, claiming that he had "ruined" his wife. Thaw's two trials generated enormous publicity and discussion of his mental state. In the end, he was found not guilty by reason of insanity and spent five years in a state mental hospital. Thaw moved in and out of the glare of publicity in his later years, tried to restore his reputation, engaged in a number of other high-profile legal disputes, and spent another seven years in a mental hospital.

Tieri, Frank ("The Old Man") (1904–1981) *head of the Genovese crime family*
In 1981, Frank Tieri earned the distinction of becoming the first organized crime boss to be convicted under the federal Racketeer Influenced Corrupt Organizations (RICO) Act. He died in prison of natural causes two months later.

Till, Emmett (1941–1955) *murder victim*
On August 28, 1955, an African-American teenager named Emmett Till was brutally murdered in rural Mississippi. An all-white jury acquitted his murderers, white supremacists Roy Bryant and J. W. Milam, who bragged

about the murder in a *Look* magazine interview a year later. No federal charges were ever filed, and Bryant and Milam eventually died of natural causes. The unpunished murder of Till galvanized the early Civil Rights movement.

Tirrell, Albert (1824–1880) *murderer*

Tirrell, a married, middle-class Bostonian, murdered prostitute Maria Bickford on October 27, 1845. In the spectacular trial that ensued, his defense attorney, Rufus Choate, argued that Tirrell was a victim of somnambulism, and that he had killed Bickford while sleepwalking and was neither conscious of nor responsible for his actions. He was found not guilty, and he experienced notoriety in his later years as pamphleteers published fantastic accounts of his crime.

Tocqueville, Alexis de (1805–1859) *French statesman, writer*

Tocqueville was the author of two major commentaries on the United States, *On the Penitentiary System in the United States and Its Application in France* (1831, with Gustave de Beaumont) and *Democracy in America* (1835). Born in an aristocratic family, he studied law as a young man and was appointed assistant magistrate at Versailles in 1827. Tocqueville lost his position, however, following the 1830 revolution, and he decided to travel to the United States to study prison reform. His resulting work publicized the new ideas and innovations behind the Pennsylvania and Auburn systems of penitentiaries, both new in the 1830s. His later book, *Democracy in America*, became an enduring analysis of the Jacksonian United States. Tocqueville returned to France and served in a number of government posts until he retired in 1851.

Torrio, Johnny (1882–1957) *gangster*

Torrio was a Chicago gangster who helped organize the business of prostitution in the late 1910s. In the 1920s, he saw a golden opportunity in Prohibition and established a bootlegging operation that paralleled the corporations so influential in that decade; Torrio purchased idle breweries, established distribution, and ensured political protection. In 1925, Torrio retired from organized crime and allowed his protégé, Al Capone, to succeed him.

Turner, Nat (1800–1831) *slave, insurrectionist*

An African-American slave in Southampton County, Virginia, Turner led a major uprising in 1831. Turner was born in Virginia and grew up as the property of a number of small farmers. As a young man, he experienced a series of religious revelations and became a preacher within the surrounding African-American communities. In the early 1830s, he concluded that the "Spirit" intended for him to lead a slave rebellion. On August 22, 1831, he gathered friends and followers, assembling as many as 50 insurgents, to attack whites on surrounding farms. Beginning with Turner's own master, they killed 57 whites in one night. The county and state militias quickly mobilized as many as 3,000 men to confront the insurgents and end the rebellion. They killed more than 100 slaves, captured more, and drove Turner into hiding. He was captured on October 30, tried and convicted on November 5, and executed on November 11. While in jail awaiting trial, Turner dictated his version of events to lawyer Thomas R. Gray, who published his account as a pamphlet, *The Confessions of Nat Turner.*

Tuthill, Richard (1841–1920) *judge*

A distinguished career jurist, Tuthill was chosen in 1899 to be the first judge of the Cook County (Chicago) Juvenile Court, the world's first. Born in Jackson County, Illinois, Tuthill graduated from Middlebury College in Vermont in 1863, then served as a scout in the Union army during the Civil War. Resigning from the army at the end of the war, he was admitted to the Tennessee bar in 1868 and practiced law in Nashville between 1868 and 1873, when he returned to Illinois. A member of the Republican Party, he served as Chicago's city attorney and U.S. district attorney before being elected judge of the Circuit Court of Cook County, a position he held for the rest of his life. In this post, he became very active in boys' cases and a leader in the movement to establish a juvenile court for Chicago. With the creation of this institution in 1899, his fellow jurists chose him to be its first judge. Leading the juvenile court between 1899 and 1905, Tuthill established practical precedents for future juvenile court judges.

Van Waters, Miriam (1887–1974) *penal administrator*

Van Waters was an innovative leader in female corrections between the 1920s and the 1940s. Born in Pennsylvania, she grew up in Oregon and graduated from the University of Oregon in 1908; she earned her Ph.D. from Clark University in Worchester, Massachusetts, in 1913. Van Waters decided to pursue a career in social reform rather than academia, working with girls in juvenile detention centers in Boston and in Portland,

Oregon. Relocating to Los Angeles in 1917, she was appointed superintendent of the county juvenile home. In 1919, she was also placed in charge of El Retiro, an experimental, county-operated facility for wayward girls. There, Van Waters allowed inmate self-government and a wide range of educational options and encouraged a sense of belonging among her girls. In contrast to other reformers of her day, she also sought to guide young women's sexuality rather than to repress it. In 1932, Van Waters became the superintendent of the Massachusetts Women's Reformatory at Framingham, a position that she held until 1957. There, Van Waters became the standard bearer for more liberal penal practices, especially for female inmates.

Vardaman, James Kimble (1861–1930) *politician*
Born during the Civil War, Vardaman became a leading Mississippi politician of the early 20th century by appealing to discontented small farmers. He made his initial career in journalism, editing the *Greenwood* (Mississippi) *Enterprise* between 1890 and 1896 and the *Greenwood Commonwealth* between 1896 and 1903. During this time, he also served as state senator and twice ran unsuccessfully for governor. Finally elected governor in 1903 after traveling the state appealing to poor white male voters, he assumed office in 1904. There, he dealt with problems in the criminal justice system, opening the new Parchman State Penitentiary in 1904. This institution, modeled on a cotton plantation, incarcerated its overwhelmingly African-American population in conditions that paralleled those of slavery. Vardaman left the governor's office in 1908, and he later served in the U.S. Senate between 1913 and 1919.

Vollmer, August (1876–1955) *police administrator*
Vollmer was the leading voice for police reform and professionalization in the early 20th century. He was appointed town marshal for Berkeley, California, in 1905, became that city's police chief in 1909, and served in that position until 1932, an exceptionally long administration for the time. As police chief, Vollmer modernized his department. He instituted one of the nation's first police training programs, improved the educational qualifications of new officers by hiring college graduates, implemented new communications systems, adopted new crime investigations technologies such as fingerprinting, and put his officers first on bicycles and then in automobiles. Vollmer also became increasingly interested in preventing crime. To fight juvenile delinquency, he established a juvenile bureau headed by a psychiatric social worker, Elizabeth Lossing, and he worked closely with parents and community groups. In 1919, he created the Berkeley Coordinating Committee, a loose group of representatives from most of the city's educational and social service agencies that monitored at-risk youths and proposed interventions, which became a model for similar groups nationwide in the 1930s. Elected president of the California Police Chiefs Association in 1907 and of the International Association of Chiefs of Police in 1922, Vollmer used his positions to promote police professionalization. He also learned the limits of reform. On a sabbatical from Berkeley, he served as chief of the Los Angeles Police Department (LAPD) for one year in 1923 and 1924 and reorganized the department, but he found it impossible to overcome the LAPD's entrenched corruption and inefficiency. Vollmer nonetheless became the leading figure in police administration in the 1920s and 1930s, teaching courses at the University of California, Berkeley, helping other colleges establish programs in criminal justice, consulting with outside police departments, and writing numerous books advocating more efficient policing. Vollmer took his own life in 1955.

Walsh, John (1945–) **and Reve Walsh** (1951–) *victims' rights advocates*
After their six-year-old son, Adam, was abducted and murdered in 1981, the Walshes lobbied Congress full-time on behalf of the parents of missing children. The National Center for Missing and Exploited Children, established in 1984, was created largely as a result of their activism. In 1988, John Walsh was hired as host of Fox's *America's Most Wanted*.

Warren, Earl (1891–1974) *Supreme Court justice*
As chief justice of the U.S. Supreme Court between 1953 and 1969, Warren led a judicial revolution that particularly impacted issues of racial segregation and criminal justice. Warren was born in Los Angeles in 1891, earned his bachelor's and law degrees at the University of California, Berkeley, and joined the California bar in 1914. Active in Republican Party politics, he was elected California's attorney general in 1938. After the Japanese attack on Pearl Harbor on December 7, 1941, Warren advocated removing Japanese Americans from California. Elected governor in 1942, he helped implement a federal policy of Japanese-American internment; later in life, he admitted that this was a major mistake. Warren was elected governor twice more, ran unsuccessfully for vice president in 1948 alongside Thomas Dewey, and helped Dwight D. Eisenhower become president in 1952.

Eisenhower in turn appointed Warren to be chief justice of the Supreme Court in 1953. Experienced in politics rather than the judiciary, Warren proved adept at forging consensus among his fellow justices and using the judicial bench as an instrument of change. In 1954, Warren led the Court to issue a unanimous decision in *Brown v. Board of Education of Topeka, Kansas,* which found racially segregated schools to be unconstitutional. In the 1960s, a series of decisions by the Warren Court substantially expanded the rights of defendants in criminal trials. Cases such as *Mapp v. Ohio* (1961) and *Miranda v. Arizona* (1966) defined defendants' protections against unwarranted searches and coerced confessions. More fundamentally, these cases also solidified the legal doctrine that the federal protections explicit in the Fourth, Fifth, Sixth, and Eighth Amendments to the U.S. Constitution were implicitly incorporated in the Fourteenth and, therefore, applied to state and local as well as federal courts. While serving as chief justice, Warren also chaired the federal commission investigating the assassination of President John F. Kennedy; the 1964 Warren Commission Report concluded that Lee Harvey Oswald was the sole assassin.

Wells, Alice Stebbins (1873–1957) *police officer*
Wells was one of the first and most prominent female police officers in the United States. Born in Manhattan, Kansas, she was educated at Oberlin College and at the Hartford Theological Seminary before moving to Los Angeles, where she worked as an assistant pastor and social worker. In 1910, at age 37, she petitioned the Los Angeles City Council for a position on the Los Angeles Police Department (LAPD). Wells believed that women could perform some police duties better than men, such as comforting and questioning abused children and preventing women and children from becoming involved in crime and vice. The Good Government League, which had supported candidates elected to council in 1909, supported her cause, and she was appointed to the LAPD in 1910. Wells served in the LAPD's Juvenile Bureau and its successor agencies between 1910 and her retirement in 1940. She worked mainly with young and female offenders, setting a model for policewomen in other departments for much of the 20th century. Wells also became a leading advocate in the movement to encourage other police departments to hire female officers, speaking and publishing widely. She believed that putting police power in the hands of educated women interested in the good of society would contribute to a larger effort to reform urban life.

Wells-Barnett, Ida B. (1862–1931) *journalist*
Through her journalism, Ida B. Wells led a campaign against lynching and racial segregation. Born a slave in Holly Springs, Mississippi, in 1862, she was educated in freedpeople's schools and later at Fisk University. She eventually became a public school teacher in Memphis, Tennessee. Through an affiliation with a Memphis literary society, she became a reporter for and part owner of the *Memphis Free Press* in 1887. Her outspoken editorials against racial segregation, however, cost her her teaching position in 1891. In 1892, her newspaper condemned the lynching of three African-American businessmen, suggesting that the white community was jealous of their success. In response, a mob destroyed her newspaper's presses. Wells, who had already left Memphis at the time of the attack, could not return, and she became a journalist working out of New York, condemning racial violence and segregation in the South. She published a number of pamphlets, including *On Lynchings, Southern Horrors, A Red Record,* and *Mob Rule in New Orleans.* In 1895, she relocated to Chicago and married Frederick Barnett. While raising their children, she remained active in the cause of civil rights, helping to found the National Association for the Advancement of Colored People (NAACP) in 1909.

Wertham, Frederic (1895–1981) *psychiatrist*
A forensic psychiatrist best known for his work on the connection between comic books and juvenile delinquency, Wertham had a long career examining the relationship of culture and violence. Born in Nuremberg, Germany, Wertham was educated in Europe, earning his medical degree in 1921. In 1922, he moved to the United States to work at a psychiatric clinic at Johns Hopkins University and later at Bellevue Hospital in New York City. In the 1930s, he became a prominent forensic psychiatrist, working with accused criminals and testifying in court. He also worked on behalf of indigent African Americans; his testimony on the psychological impact of segregation contributed to one of the cases that would become *Brown v. Board of Education of Topeka, Kansas* (1954). In 1950, Senator Estes Kefauver appointed Wertham a psychiatric consultant for the Senate Subcommittee for the Study of Organized Crime. His work in this capacity focused on how the emerging mass media impacted juvenile delinquency. His resulting book, *The Seduction of the Innocent* (1954), explicitly linked juvenile violence to comic books featuring crime and horror. Read widely, this book helped prompt the comic book industry to adopt a code governing the content of each publication. In later years,

Wertham continued his scholarly work analyzing the connections between mass culture and violence.

Whitin, Frederick H. (1872–1926) *purity reformer*

As the executive secretary of New York City's Committee of Fourteen between 1906 and 1926, Whitin led a movement to eliminate vice and prostitution. Born and educated in New York, Whitin worked as the full-time administrator for the city's most influential group of volunteer reformers. Under his leadership in the early 1910s, they successfully minimized the influence of "Raines Law Hotels," saloons used for prostitution, by sending investigators into them pretending to be customers and then reporting the results to the police. In the 1920s, Whitin led a broad but unsuccessful campaign to prosecute men for purchasing prostitutes' services.

Whitman, Charles ("The Texas Tower Sniper") (1941–1966) *spree killer*

In August 1966, Charles Whitman, a former marine, huddled in the top of the 307-foot tower on the campus of the University of Texas and fired at students for more than an hour and a half, shooting 45 people (and killing 14) before he was finally shot dead by law enforcement officials.

Williams, Alexander S. (Clubber Williams) (1839–1917) *police officer*

A New York City police officer, "Clubber" Williams earned his nickname for his skill with a nightstick. Born in Nova Scotia, Canada, in 1839, he moved to New York as a child and worked as a ship's carpenter before being appointed to the police force in 1866. Assigned to some of the city's toughest precincts, Williams used his size, strength, and fighting ability to manage street gangs. He is noted for claiming, "There is more law at the end of the policeman's nightstick than in all the decisions of the Supreme Court." In 1876, he was assigned to the Twenty-Ninth Precinct, encompassing New York's entertainment district, which he dubbed the Tenderloin when he remarked, "I have had chuck for a long time and now I am going to eat tenderloin." Williams profited financially from graft gained protecting prostitution and gambling, and he profited politically from his ability to minimize crime and disorder via strong-arm tactics. His methods, however, led to a number of assault cases against him and more than 350 formal complaints. In 1894, the Lexow Committee's investigation of corruption and brutality within the New York Police Department focused on Williams as a major target. When Theodore Roosevelt became police commissioner in 1895, he helped engineer Williams's retirement. Nonetheless, Williams left policing with a substantial personal fortune and an estate in Connecticut.

Wilson, James Q. (1931–) *criminologist*

Wilson was one of the most influential thinkers on criminal justice in the late 20th century. Born in Long Beach, California, in 1931, he graduated from the University of Redlands in 1952, served three years in the U.S. Navy, and then earned his Ph.D. at the University of Chicago in 1959. He taught political science at Harvard University between 1961 and 1987, served on the faculty of UCLA between 1985 and 1997, and then became the Ronald Reagan Professor of Public Policy at Pepperdine University. His early work, including *Varieties of Police Behavior* (1968), established him as an important scholar, but *Thinking about Crime* (1975) elevated Wilson to the status of a leading public intellectual. In this book, he articulated a conservative argument for crime control. Rejecting a view that crime was a function of social forces such as poverty that could be impacted by government programs, Wilson instead argued that deterrence is the best model for reducing crime. He maintained that, on the one hand, people who committed crimes lacked inhibitions and were more willing than most to take chances while, on the other hand, they could also rationally weigh the costs and benefits of their actions and would refrain from committing offenses if the costs were sufficiently great. This viewpoint helped justify policy decisions in the late 1970s and 1980s to increase criminal sanctions. Wilson's later work focused increasingly on the relationship between morality and public policy. He earned many distinctions over his career; in 2003, President George W. Bush presented him with the Presidential Medal of Freedom, the nation's highest civilian award.

Wilson, Orlando Winfield (1900–1972) *police administrator*

Wilson was the leading innovator in policing of his day. Born in South Dakota, his family moved to California when he was a child. Attending the University of California, Berkeley, Wilson both studied under August Vollmer and worked for him as a patrolman in the Berkeley Police Department. After his graduation, he became police chief in Fullerton, California, and between 1928 and 1939 in Wichita, Kansas. Wilson earned his national reputation in Wichita, initiating innovations such as marked police vehicles, two-way radio dispatch, and the use of lie detector machines. He also became a leader in police management, writing widely on the most efficient means to implement these new technologies and on how to apply professional ethics to policing. His textbook, *Police Administration* (first published in 1950), influenced a generation of law enforcement officials. Wilson also taught police administration at Berkeley between 1939 and 1960, and he served as dean there between 1950 and 1960. In 1960, Mayor Richard J. Daley lured Wilson to Chicago to apply his ideas on police administration to one of the nation's biggest and most troubled forces. As Chicago's police chief between 1960 and 1967, Wilson separated policing from politics, tightened discipline, updated communications and record-keeping, replaced foot patrols with automotive ones, and improved police response time and morale. Wilson also sought to improve the Chicago Police Department's relations with the African-American community by recruiting more black officers and insisting on police restraint in racially charged confrontations. However, Wilson's model of leadership did not persist past his retirement in 1967.

Wines, Enoch Cobb (1806–1879) *minister, educator*
Although Wines had experienced only middling success as the head of classical academies for boys and as a Congregational minister, he had a lasting impact as a prison reformer. As the secretary of the Prison Association of New York, together with law professor Theodore Dwight, he visited prisons throughout the Northeast to investigate operations and conditions. Published as *Report on the Prisons and Reformatories of the United States and Canada* in 1867, their work drew national attention to problems of overcrowding and inefficient administration. This work led prison reformers to gather at the 1870 National Congress on Penitentiary and Reformatory Discipline and helped launch a more balanced approach to corrections called the "new penology."

Winthrop, John (1588–1649) *Puritan leader*
A lawyer and landowner in England, Winthrop became a leader in the Puritan migration to the New World. A zealous Puritan, in 1629 he agreed to go to America with the Massachusetts Bay Company and was soon elected governor of the colony. As the Puritan migrants sailed in 1630, Winthrop justified the move in a sermon called "A Model of Christian Charity" in which he argued that the Massachusetts colony would be a "city upon a hill," a model to the rest of world of the life that could be achieved by their religious community. Upon arrival Winthrop helped establish the colony and served intermit-

tently as its governor between 1630 and 1648. During this time, he was also a key figure enforcing Puritan orthodoxy in religious controversies involving Roger Williams and Anne Hutchinson.

Wirz, Henry (1823–1865) *military officer*
The commandant of the Andersonville prison camp in Georgia during the Civil War, Wirz was the only Confederate officer who was hanged for war crimes. Wirz was born and grew up in Zurich, Switzerland, but immigrated to the United States in 1849, finally settling in Louisiana. When the Civil War broke out in 1861, he joined the Confederate army as an infantryman and rapidly worked his way up the ranks, commanding stockades in Richmond, Virginia, and Tuscaloosa, Alabama. He also served as a diplomat for President Jefferson Davis. In March 1864, he was appointed commandant of the Andersonville prison camp. Without supplies or competent management, the camp became a death trap for Union prisoners of war; of the 45,000 men housed there in its less than one year of operation, more than 12,000 died. When Union forces captured Andersonville, they discovered the horrific conditions and arrested Wirz. In 1865, Wirz was tried for conspiracy and murder, convicted, and executed.

Wuornos, Aileen (1956–) *murderer*
A former prostitute and drifter, Wuornos was arrested in 1991 in Florida in connection with a series of murders. She eventually confessed to killing six men in the late 1980s and early 1990s, and she was sentenced to death for each murder. She has been the subject of two documentaries directed by Nick Broomfield, *Aileen Wuornos: The Selling of a Serial Killer* (1992) and *Aileen: The Life and Death of a Serial Killer* (2003). The actress Charlize Theron won an Academy Award for portraying Wuornos in a 2003 feature film based on her life, *Monster.*

Zenger, John Peter (1697–1746) *printer, publisher*
A New York publisher, Zenger was arrested and tried in 1734 for printing "seditious and libelous" material critical of the colony's government in his *New-York Weekly Journal.* Zenger's lawyers—advocates of free speech and opponents of the current governor—argued successfully that the truth of the charges made the printed material lawful; Zenger was freed after serving 10 months in jail. Zenger's case had little immediate effect on legal culture, but it did foreshadow the later 18th century concept that free speech and political criticism should be protected under the law.

Appendix C
Maps

1. Reported Lynchings by State, 1882–1968
2. Number of Reported Violent Crimes per 100,000 Residents, by State, 2006
3. Capital Punishment in the United States, 1976–2008
4. Number of Incarcerations per 100,000 Residents, by State, 2006

Reported Lynchings by State, 1882–1968

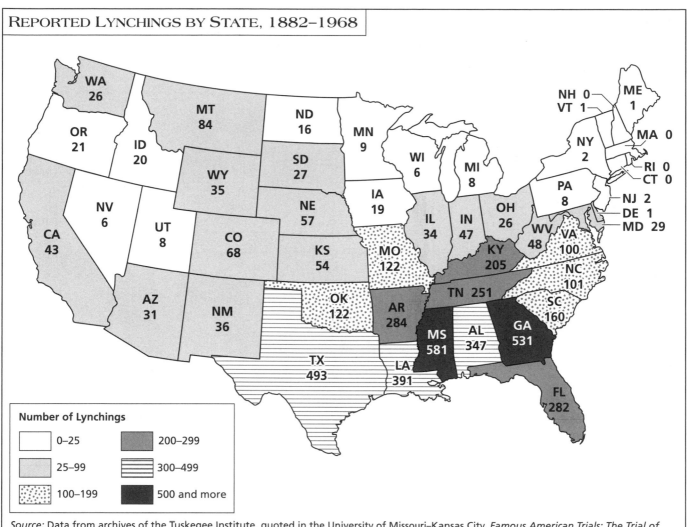

WA 26
OR 21
MT 84
ND 16
MN 9
ID 20
SD 27
WY 35
NE 57
IA 19
NV 6
UT 8
CO 68
KS 54
MO 122
CA 43
AZ 31
NM 36
OK 122
IL 34
IN 47
MI 8
WI 6
OH 26
KY 205
TN 251
AR 284
TX 493
LA 391
MS 581
AL 347
GA 531
FL 282
WV 48
VA 100
NC 101
SC 160
PA 8
NH 0
VT 1
ME 1
MA 0
NY 2
RI 0
CT 0
NJ 2
DE 1
MD 29

Number of Lynchings

0–25	200–299
25–99	300–499
100–199	500 and more

Source: Data from archives of the Tuskegee Institute, quoted in the University of Missouri–Kansas City. *Famous American Trials: The Trial of Sheriff Joseph Shipp, et al.* Available online. URL: http://www.law.umkc.edu/faculty/projects/ftrials/shipp/lynchingsstate.html. Accessed November 17, 2005.

© Infobase Publishing

NUMBER OF REPORTED VIOLENT CRIMES PER 100,000 RESIDENTS, BY STATE, 2006

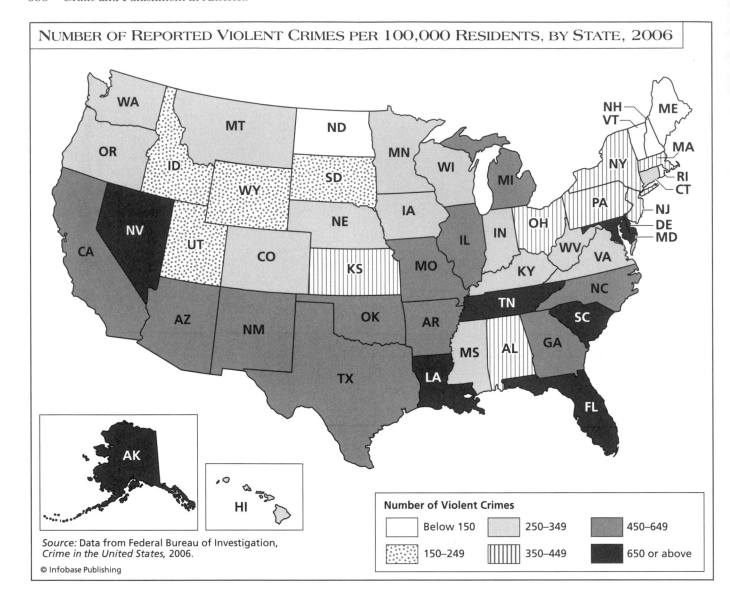

Source: Data from Federal Bureau of Investigation, *Crime in the United States,* 2006.

© Infobase Publishing

Number of Violent Crimes

Below 150

150–249

250–349

350–449

450–649

650 or above

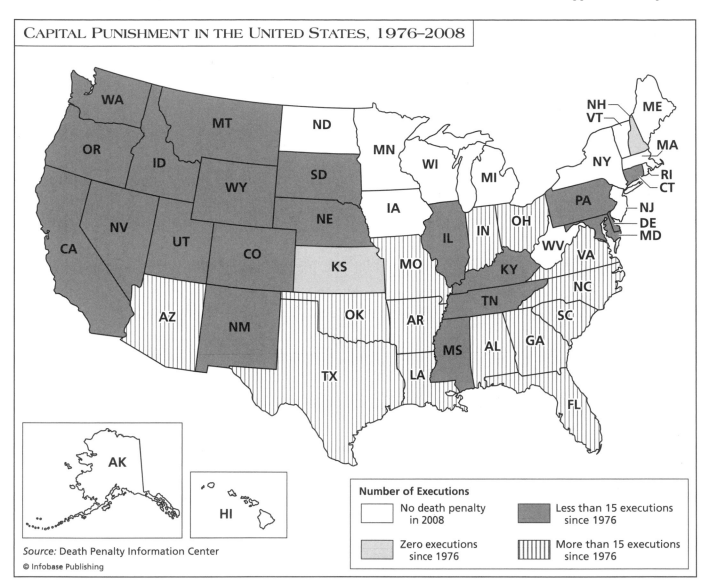

CAPITAL PUNISHMENT IN THE UNITED STATES, 1976–2008

Number of Executions

No death penalty in 2008

Zero executions since 1976

Less than 15 executions since 1976

More than 15 executions since 1976

Source: Death Penalty Information Center

© Infobase Publishing

INCARCERATION RATE PER 100,000 RESIDENTS, BY STATE, 2006

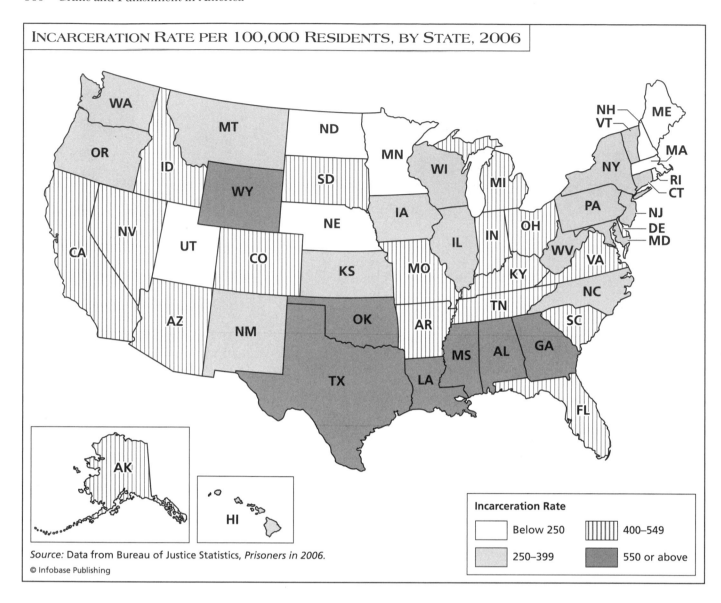

Incarceration Rate

Below 250	400–549
250–399	550 or above

Source: Data from Bureau of Justice Statistics, *Prisoners in 2006.*

© Infobase Publishing

Appendix D
Graphs and Tables

1. Deaths by Homicide in the United States, 1900–2002
2. Index Crimes Known to Police, 1960–2003
3. Prisoners in the United States, 1925–2003
4. Executions under Civil Authority in the United States, 1930–2004
5. Persons under Death Sentences in the United States, 1953–2003
6. Terrorism in the United States, 1980–2001
7. Direct Expenditure on Criminal Justice by Level of Government, 1982–2001
8. Bias-Motivated (Hate) Crimes Known to Police, 1992–2003

DEATHS BY HOMICIDE IN THE UNITED STATES, 1900–2002

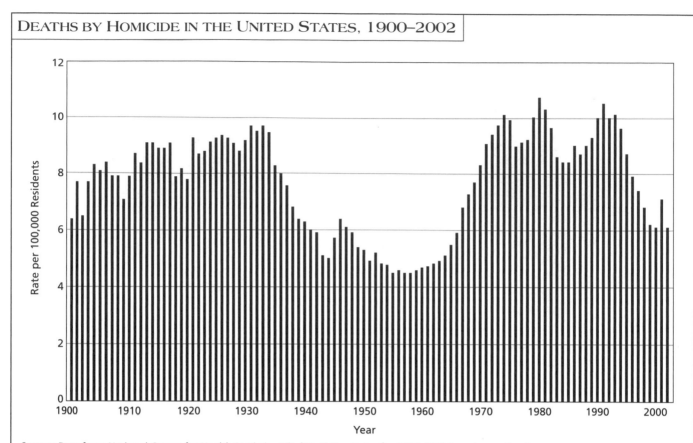

Source: Data from National Center for Health Statistics, Vital Statistics. Rates for 1900–1932 based on estimates compensating for undercount in homicide reporting. See Douglas Lee Eckberg, "Estimates of Early Twentieth-Century U.S. Homicide Rates: An Econometric Forecasting Approach," *Demography* 32 (February 1995): pp. 1–16.

© Infobase Publishing

INDEX CRIMES KNOWN TO POLICE, 1960–2003

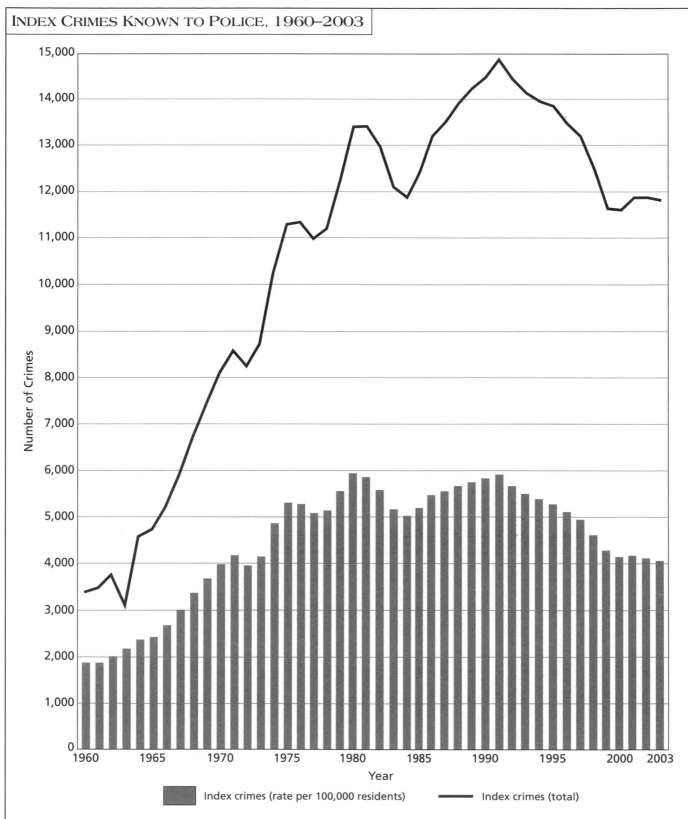

Note: "Index crimes" constitute murder and nonnegligent manslaughter, forcible rape, robbery, aggravated assault, burglary, larceny/theft, and motor vehicle theft.

Source: Data from the Bureau of Justice Statistics, *Sourcebook of Criminal Justice Statistics, 2002.* Available online. URL: http://www.albany.edu/sourcebook/. Accessed June 23, 2005, and the Federal Bureau of Investigation, *Crime in the United States 2004.* Available online. URL: http://www.fbi.gov/ucr/ucr.htm. Accessed October 27, 2005.

PRISONERS IN THE UNITED STATES, 1925–2003

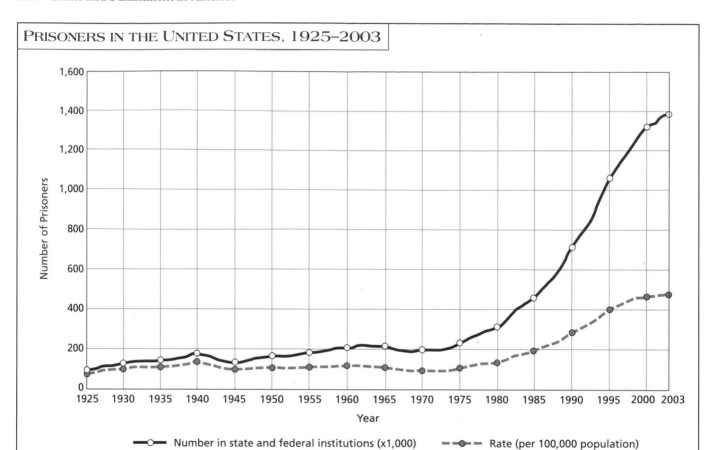

Number in state and federal institutions (x1,000)   Rate (per 100,000 population)

Note: Prison population data are compiled by a year-end census of prisoners in state and federal institutions on December 31.

Source: Bureau of Justice Statistics. *Sourcebook of Criminal Justice Statistics, 2002* (2004), p. 495. Available online. URL: http://www.albany.edu/sourcebook/. Accessed June 27, 2005.

© Infobase Publishing

EXECUTIONS UNDER CIVIL AUTHORITY IN THE UNITED STATES, 1930–2004

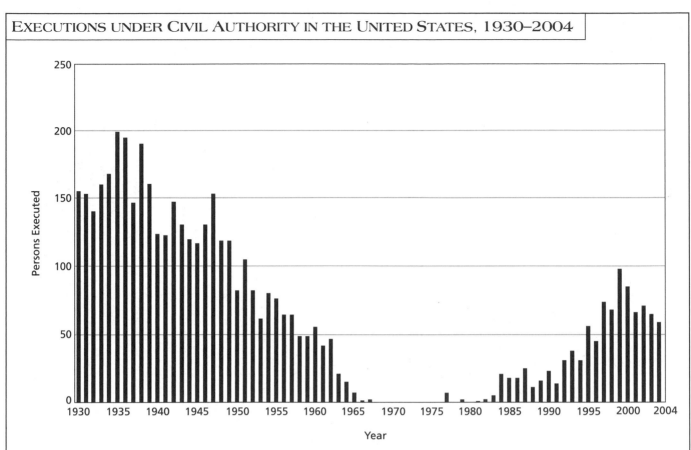

Source: Bureau of Justice Statistics. *Sourcebook of Criminal Justice Statistics, 2002* (Government Printing Office, 2004), p. 534.
Available online. URL: http://www.albany.edu/sourcebook. Accessed June 27, 2005.
© Infobase Publishing

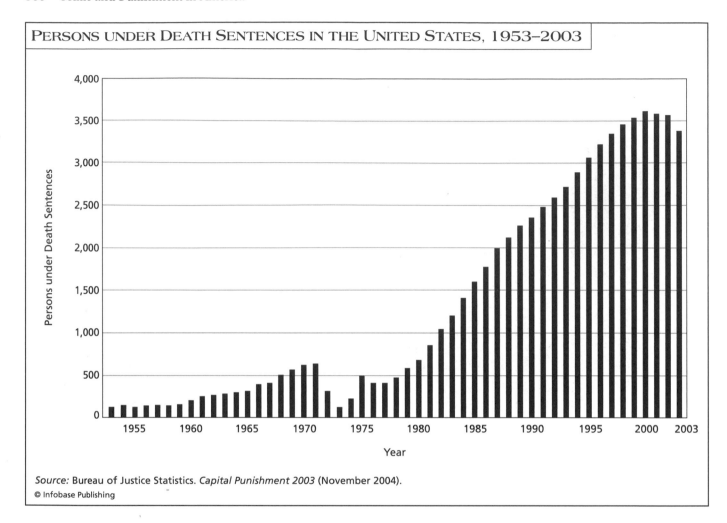

PERSONS UNDER DEATH SENTENCES IN THE UNITED STATES, 1953–2003

Source: Bureau of Justice Statistics. *Capital Punishment 2003* (November 2004).

© Infobase Publishing

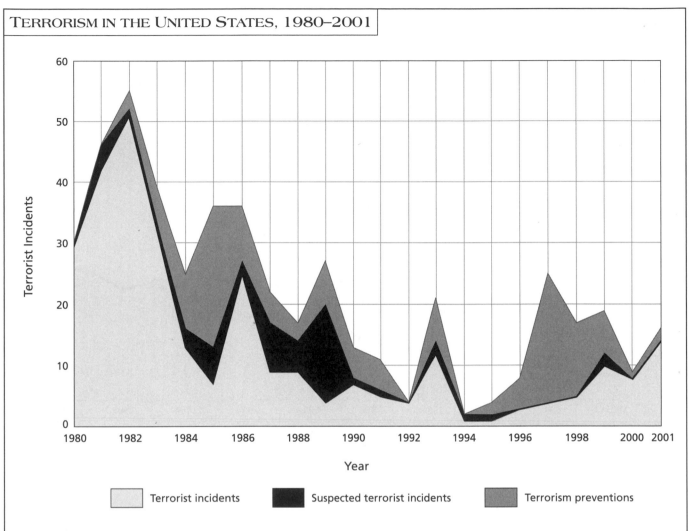

TERRORISM IN THE UNITED STATES, 1980–2001

Terrorist incidents   Suspected terrorist incidents   Terrorism preventions

Note: A terrorist incident is a violent act or an act dangerous to human life, in violation of the criminal laws
of the United States or any state, to intimidate or coerce a government, the civilian population, or any segment thereof
in furtherance of political or social objectives.

Sources: Data from Bureau of Justice Statistics. *Sourcebook of Criminal Justice Statistics, 2002* (Government Printing Office, 2004),
p. 339. Available online. URL: http://www.albany.edu/sourcebook/. Accessed June 27, 2005. Data from FBI. *Terrorism in the United States,
2000/2001.* Available online. URL: http://www.fbi.gov/publications/terror/terror2000_2001.htm. Accessed June 29, 2005.

DIRECT EXPENDITURE ON CRIMINAL JUSTICE BY LEVEL OF GOVERNMENT, 1982–2001

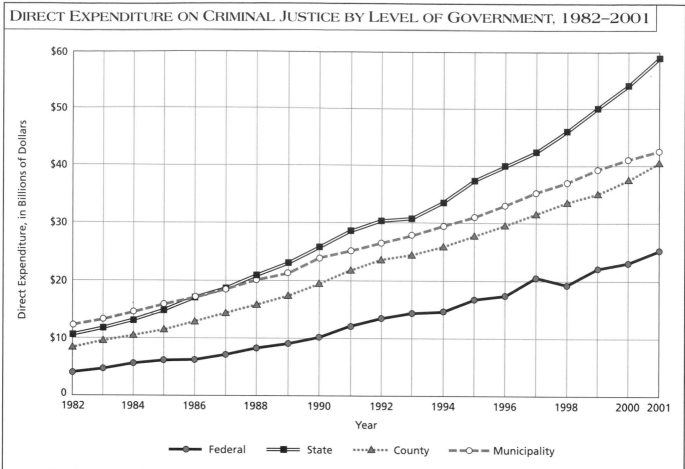

Source: Data from Bureau of Justice Statistics. *Justice Employment and Expenditure Extracts, 1982–2001,* Tables 1 and 3.

© Infobase Publishing

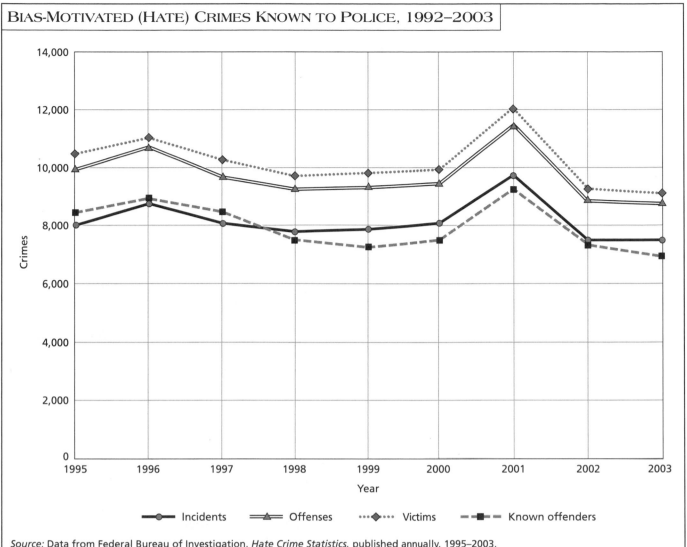

BIAS-MOTIVATED (HATE) CRIMES KNOWN TO POLICE, 1992–2003

Incidents   Offenses   Victims   Known offenders

Source: Data from Federal Bureau of Investigation. *Hate Crime Statistics,* published annually, 1995–2003.

© Infobase Publishing

Glossary

Alcatraz A rocky island in San Francisco Bay that served as a U.S. federal penitentiary between 1934 and 1963. It housed some of the most famous convicts in federal custody, including Al Capone, George "Machine Gun" Kelly, and Alvin Karpis. In 1969, American Indian activists occupied the island, demanding that the federal government recognize treaty obligations, and maintained control until forced to leave in 1971.

Alien and Sedition Acts Legislation signed by President John Adams in 1798, which gave the federal government the power to detain and deport resident aliens and to fine and/or imprison anyone who criticized government officials. The law was targeted at the French and supporters of presidential candidate Thomas Jefferson, respectively. Adams lost to Jefferson in 1800, and the acts expired shortly thereafter.

Andersonville Prison An infamous military prison operated by the Confederacy during the U.S. Civil War in which approximately 13,000 Union soldiers died from starvation, malnutrition, disease, and abuse.

anthrax An infection caused by direct exposure to the bacteria *Bacillus anthracis*. Anthrax is difficult to spread from human to human, but it can be easily contracted through contact with spores or infected livestock or can be weaponized and used for biological warfare. In September 2001, an unknown figure sent live anthrax spores to unwitting recipients through the mail, infecting 22 and killing five.

Antinomian Controversy A theological controversy that took place between 1636 and 1638 in colonial Massachusetts that led to the expulsion of the charismatic preacher Anne Hutchinson.

Auburn system An approach to prison management that emphasized hard labor in absolute silence. Pioneered by future Sing Sing prison warden Elam Lynds at Auburn Prison in New York in the 1820s, it represented a major rival to the **Pennsylvania system.**

audiencias Courts established by the government of New Spain during the 16th and 17th centuries that were created to oversee disputes involving Spanish colonists in the New World.

Bertillon system A means of identifying suspects based on precise body measurements. Invented by Alphonse Bertillon in 1882, it was the primary means of suspect identification until the end of the century.

bill of attainder A bill passed by a legislature finding a person guilty of treason—and seizing any relevant land and other assets and imposing whatever punishment the legislature deems appropriate—without benefit of trial. Used by British authorities during the colonial era, then used by the colonists themselves during the Revolutionary War as a means of claiming land held by loyalists. Outlawed by Article I, Section 9 of the U.S. Constitution.

Black Codes Laws passed by southern states in the immediate aftermath of the U.S. Civil War as a means of imposing slavery-like restrictions on newly freed African Americans. Although theoretically outlawed by the Fourteenth and Fifteenth Amendments, many of the same regulations that formed the basis of the Black Codes persisted until the civil rights reforms of the 1960s.

blasphemy Statements offensive to popular religious sensibilities. While initially regarded as a capital offense in the colonial era, it was later protected by the First Amendment.

Bureau of Narcotics and Dangerous Drugs (BNDD) A federal drug control agency located within the U.S. Department of Justice. Formed in 1968 through the merger of the Federal Bureau of Narcotics and the Food and Drug Administration's Bureau of Drug Abuse Control, it was folded into the newly created **Drug Enforcement Administration** in 1973.

Children's Aid Society Founded by Charles Loring Brace in 1853, the Children's Aid Society attempted to prevent urban juvenile delinquency by relocating troubled youths to rural areas.

COINTELPRO (Counter Intelligence Program)   A program by the Federal Bureau of Investigation (FBI) to investigate and disrupt radical groups within the United States. Operating between 1956 and 1971, it targeted communist and socialist groups, student anti–Vietnam War activists, black nationalists, and white supremacists.

Columbine massacre   A shooting that took place on April 20, 1999, at Littleton High School in Jefferson County, Colorado, in which two students killed 12 other students and a teacher before committing suicide.

Crimes Act of 1790   A law that classified treason and certain interstate crimes as federal offenses, establishing a system of federal law enforcement. Punishment for some offenses (most notably treason) included both death and mutilation of the corpse.

criminal anthropology   An intellectual discipline popular during the late 19th century but largely rejected later, that criminal behavior could be predicted based on genetics or visible physical characteristics.

Drug Enforcement Administration (DEA)   The U.S. federal government's main law enforcement agency focused on policing illegal drugs. It was created in 1973 through the merger of all federal agents (including Customs agents and Central Intelligence Agency officers) previously working on drug-related issues.

electric chair   A method of execution, first used in New York in 1890, in which the condemned sit in a wired chair, electrodes are connected to them, and an electrical current is passed through their bodies. It was the preferred method of execution in the United States for much of the 20th century.

Elmira Reformatory   Established in New York State in 1877 under the leadership of prison reformer Zebulon Brockway, Elmira abandoned the old approaches of punitive labor and enforced solitary contemplation in favor of a parole-based system that rewarded good behavior.

encomienda   The primary social institution of colonial Spain, in which American Indians were used as serfs and forced to work under the authority of a Spanish master.

English Bill of Rights   Promulgated in 1689, the Act Declaring the Rights and Liberties of the Subjects and Settling the Succession of the Crown, popularly known as the English Bill of Rights, granted free speech to members of Parliament, prohibited cruel and unusual punishment, and established jury trials, among other things. Although imperfect (with many punitive clauses directed against Roman Catholics, for instance), it served as a model for many of the criminal justice provisions found a century later in the U.S. Bill of Rights.

Enlightenment, the   A philosophical movement of 18th-century Europe that emphasized free thought, natural rights, and individualism.

Federal Bureau of Investigation (FBI)   The principal investigative and law enforcement agency of the U.S. federal government. Part of the Justice Department, it operates under the supervision of the U.S. attorney general. From its founding in 1908 through spring of 1934, it was called the Bureau of Investigation; between 1934 and fall of 1935 it was called the Division of Investigation; and since 1935 it has had its current title. Although federal law limits its jurisdiction to offenses that cross state lines, the actual range of crimes that the FBI investigates has expanded over time. Moreover, it has come to serve as a coordinating agency and central information clearinghouse for local police.

Federal Bureau of Narcotics (FBN)   The major federal agency dealing with illegal drugs between its founding as an independent organization in 1930 and its merger with other agencies in 1968.

Fugitive Slave Act of 1793   A federal law establishing that northern states must transfer any known escaped slaves in custody to their masters.

Fugitive Slave Act of 1850   An expansion of the **Fugitive Slave Act of 1793,** holding northern states accountable for actually capturing fugitive slaves, mandating stiff penalties against those who refused to participate, and establishing that slaves have no right to trial by jury.

Guantánamo Bay naval base   A U.S. military base located on the southeastern coast of Cuba, most famous for housing alleged Taliban combatants and al-Qaeda associates in the wake of the 9/11 attacks and the Afghanistan War.

habeas corpus   Latin for "you shall have the body." The right of all citizens, following arrest, to appear before a judge and be released if criminal justice authorities cannot produce evidence to warrant their continued detention. Protected by Article I, Section 9, of the U.S. Constitution.

hate crime A crime motivated by prejudice, constituting an attack both against the victim and against the larger community to which the victim belongs. The FBI recognizes hate crimes that are perpetrated on the basis of disability, ethnicity, national origin, race, religion, and sexual orientation.

incorporation doctrine The gradual application of the U.S. Bill of Rights to cover state law as well as federal law by way of the Fourteenth Amendment. Until the 20th century the Bill of Rights was not regarded as binding on state law.

International Association of Chiefs of Police (IACP) The major professional organization for police administrators, mainly in the United States. It was founded in 1893 as the National Police Chiefs Union and assumed its current name in 1900. The annual meetings of the IACP have provided a forum for police leaders to exchange and disseminate new ideas.

judicial revolution Term describing the major changes in U.S. constitutional law enacted by the U.S. Supreme Court under the leadership of Chief Justice Earl Warren between 1953 and 1969. During the judicial revolution a series of decisions—most notably *Mapp v. Ohio* (1961) and *Miranda v. Arizona* (1966)—substantially expanded and clarified the rights of criminal defendants and applied federal standards to state and local judicial procedures.

juvenile courts Courts designed to hear cases involving juvenile delinquency, dependency, and neglect separately from cases involving adults. Juvenile court jurisdictions vary by state, but they generally include young offenders up to age 17. They segregate juveniles from adults throughout the judicial process and try to offer rehabilitative treatments. Because their avowed purpose is to help young offenders rather than to punish them, juvenile courts can consider a wider range of misbehaviors than simple violations of the law and can operate without fully providing due process protections that exist in criminal courts for adults. The first juvenile court was established in Cook County (Chicago), Illinois, in 1899.

Kerner Commission (National Advisory Commission on Civil Disorders) A federal investigation of the urban riots of the 1960s sponsored by President Lyndon Johnson and chaired by former Illinois governor Otto Kerner. Its 1968 report targeted racial and economic disparities as major sources of unrest.

Ku Klux Klan (KKK) A white supremacist group founded in the U.S. South in the aftermath of the Civil War aimed at restoring white political and social power through violence against African Americans. It was revived in the 1910s and 1920s with a membership estimated at more than 3 million, concentrated in the South but also prevalent in midwestern states such as Indiana, Ohio, and Michigan. The KKK contracted sharply in the 1930s, but its members actively engaged in violent resistance to the Civil Rights movement in the South in the 1950s and 1960s.

Law Enforcement Assistance Administration (LEAA) Agency created by the 1968 Omnibus Crime Control and Safe Streets Act to provide federal block grant funding to state and local police agencies. It was eliminated in 1982.

Lexow Committee An 1894 and 1895 investigation into police corruption in New York City. It was named for its chairman, state senator Clarence Lexow.

lynching An illegal execution generally conducted in response to an alleged crime or violation of social norms.

Mafia Italian for "bravado." A general term referring to loosely organized Sicilian crime families and their offshoots in the United States. Sometimes used in a general sense to refer to all organized crime.

Magna Carta Latin for "great charter." A British document, agreed upon in the year 1215, that limited the power of the monarch.

Mann Act A federal law passed in 1910 that made it a crime to transport members of the opposite sex across state lines for "immoral purposes." Originally passed to combat interstate prostitution and arbitrarily enforced as an antifornication statute, it was later used almost exclusively in cases where one of the parties was a minor.

masterless men A term referring to a class of low-income men living in Britain during the pre–Revolutionary War era. Perceived as the nation's "criminal element," they were frequently forced into captivity as indentured servants.

Megan's Law A term referring to a federal law passed in 1996 and state laws passed as early as 1994 that allow local law enforcement agencies to maintain publicly accessible databases of sex offenders. Inspired by the case of Megan Kanka, a seven-year-old New Jersey girl who was raped and murdered by a convicted sex offender who lived near her home.

Miranda rule A law enforcement officer's obligation under the Supreme Court's ruling in *Miranda v. Arizona* (1966) to inform suspects of their right to remain silent and to have an attorney present before commencing interrogation.

National Crime Victimization Survey (NCVS) The main source of information about crime victimization in the United States. Compiled annually since 1973 through representative surveys of the nation's households, the National Crime Victimization Survey is generally considered a more accurate measure of the actual prevalence of crime than are other gauges such as the Uniform Crime Reports.

New Penology A movement influential during the late 19th century that emphasized a reward-based prison system that allowed for parole and took other measures to encourage positive changes in prisoners' behavior.

oidores Judges who served in New Spain's *audiencia* court system.

Omnibus Crime Control and Safe Streets Act A 1968 law that substantially expanded the federal role in law enforcement. It established the Law Enforcement Assistance Administration (LEAA) to make grants to state and local governments to support policing and clarified federal rules involving surveillance, investigations, and wire-tapping.

parens patrie Latin for "parent of the country." A legal doctrine used to justify special treatment of juveniles in courts and corrections. The notion emerged in English common law in the 1500s that in cases where a parent died and left an estate to a minor child, courts could intervene and manage the estate until the beneficiary reached adulthood. As applied to juvenile justice in the United States, *parens patrie* allowed courts to act in what they saw as the best interests of dependent and delinquent children. In the 19th century, it justified correctional agencies holding juveniles; in the 20th century, it justified informal juvenile court proceedings (which often ignored due process procedures) because they intended to rehabilitate young offenders. The concept of *parens patrie* was substantially undermined in the 1960s by a series of decisions by the U.S. Supreme Court, particularly *In re Gault* (1966).

Pennsylvania system The prison system initiated at Walnut Street Jail after its 1790 restructuring at the hands of Quaker reformers, who transformed it into the first American *penitentiary*—literally, a place where prisoners would learn to become penitent, or repent, through solitary confinement and religious instruction. It gained its most widespread application at Pennsylvania's Eastern State Penitentiary in the 1820s and competed with the Auburn system, which emphasized hard labor and silence.

penology The study of prisons.

President's Commission on Law Enforcement and Administration of Justice A major investigation of crime in the United States initiated by President Lyndon Johnson in 1965. It published its findings in 1967 under the title *The Challenge of Crime in a Free Society.*

Progressive Era The period in American history lasting from approximately 1890 to 1913 marked by optimism, faith in human progress, and considerable humanitarian reforms. In particular, the Progressive Era saw the establishment of juvenile courts and reforms of policing and corrections.

Prohibition A national policy that lasted from 1920 to 1933 forbidding the manufacture, distribution, and sale of alcohol. Prohibition was authorized by the Eighteenth Amendment and repealed by the Twenty-First Amendment.

prosecutor/prosecuting attorney A lawyer, usually employed by a county or state government, whose job is to construct cases against alleged criminals and to try to achieve their conviction.

public defender A lawyer, usually employed by a county or state government, whose job is to defend accused criminals unable to pay for their own representation.

al-Qaeda Arabic for "the base." A loosely organized international terrorist organization that first became active in the 1990s. It is based on a violent and extreme version of Wahhabism, a small Islamic tradition that opposes secular innovations and focuses on the sanctity of Saudi Arabian holy sites.

racial profiling The unofficial law enforcement practice of targeting members of specific racial or ethnic groups.

ratelwacht Dutch for "rattle guard." The first organized police force in North America, established in 1658 in Dutch-ruled New Amsterdam (now New York City). These night watchmen were so named because of the loud rattles they carried, which they used to call attention to criminal activity.

recidivism   The tendency of known or convicted criminals to commit further criminal offenses.

Red Scare   Periods in U.S. history marked by fear and aggression toward perceived foreign threats and foreign ideologies (especially communism), in which immigrants and ideological nonconformists were targeted. The first Red Scare, lasting from about 1919 until about 1921, was sparked by World War I and a series of high-profile terrorist attacks. The second Red Scare, sparked by World War II and lasting until the collapse of Joseph McCarthy's investigations in 1954, centered on fear of the Soviet Union—the only nation that could have been regarded as equal in power to the United States at that point in history.

retributive justice   A theory of justice focusing on punishing criminals harshly in hopes of creating a deterrent effect.

Salem witch trials   A series of trials that took place in Salem, Massachusetts, in 1692, in which the Puritan government executed 20 people for witchcraft based on witnesses' purported mystical revelations.

Scottsboro trials   A series of Alabama rape trials that began in 1931 against nine black youths who were accused, based on weak evidence, of raping two white women.

sedition   Unlawful criticism of the government or government officials. Sedition was criminalized under the Alien and Sedition Acts of 1798 and the Sedition Act of 1918, but such laws have since been declared unconstitutional for civilian purposes (although a seldom-enforced sedition clause still technically applies to active military personnel).

serial killer   A murderer who kills three or more victims separately, with periods between murders during which he or she passes for a normal member of society.

Shays' Rebellion   A 1786–1787 revolt by Massachusetts farmers, led by Captain Daniel Shays, against what they perceived to be unfair tax and foreclosure policies in the wake of the Revolutionary War. Actions by Shays and his supporters generated concerns about the weakness of the federal government under the Articles of Confederation and prompted calls for revision that led to the writing of the U.S. Constitution.

slave patrols   Public employees who operated in slave states during parts of the 18th and 19th centuries with the explicit purpose of capturing slaves who had escaped or were traveling without proper authorization. In the 19th century, slave patrols evolved into some of the first police forces in the United States in cities such as New Orleans, Louisiana, and Charleston, South Carolina.

stocks   A humiliation device commonly used during the colonial era in which the head and hands of prisoners were restrained inside a hinge-loaded wooden contraption—forcing them to stand in a ridiculous and uncomfortable position.

superpredators   A term coined in the early 1990s by political scientist John DiIulio to refer to an entire generation of urban juvenile delinquents, who, he argued, would soon overrun the country. His theory fell into disuse as violent crime rates decreased in the late 1990s and early 2000s.

Texas Rangers   Members of Texas's state police force, founded in 1823, who initially focused on small-scale conflict with American Indians but later dealt successfully with a wider array of crimes.

Underground Railroad   An illegal secret abolitionist network established decades prior to the U.S. Civil War through which southern slaves were able to escape to Canada.

Uniform Crime Reports (UCR)   The oldest standard system of measuring crime used in the United States. Uniform Crime Reports were first assembled and published in 1930 by the Federal Bureau of Investigation (FBI). They established a common format to collect data on crimes known to the police. Organized and printed annually, the Uniform Crime Reports provide a quantitative basis for assessing crime.

USA PATRIOT Act   The Uniting and Strengthening America by Providing Appropriate Tools Required to Intercept and Obstruct Terrorism Act, passed by Congress on October 12, 2001, in response to the 9/11 attacks. The act, which included controversial provisions expanding federal surveillance powers, was renewed in March 2006.

Violence Against Women Act   Federal legislation passed in 1994 that expanded prosecution of violence against women, toughened pretrial incarceration standards in cases where retaliatory violence would be likely, and allowed victims of violence to file civil cases.

Walnut Street Jail Constructed in 1776 in Philadelphia, Pennsylvania, as a conventional jail, Walnut Street Jail was reformed in 1790 and became the first American penitentiary. The term *penitentiary* had a very literal meaning at the time; the purpose of Walnut Street Jail was to encourage prisoners to repent of their past deeds, an approach that became known as the **Pennsylvania system.**

war on drugs A phrase most strongly associated with the presidencies of Ronald Reagan and George H. W. Bush in the mid-1980s through the early 1990s (although a number of presidents had used it previously). It refers to aggressive federal prosecution of drug-related offenses intended to shut down the illegal drug trade.

war on terror A phrase coined by President George W. Bush in 2001, it refers generally to a vast array of international military and law enforcement efforts intended to dismantle terrorist networks.

Whiskey Rebellion A revolt that took place during the summer of 1794 near Pittsburgh, Pennsylvania, in which several thousand grain farmers marched on Pittsburgh in opposition to the excise tax on whiskey. In response, President George Washington assembled and led an army of 13,000 men in western Pennsylvania (the only time that a sitting president ever personally commanded military forces), which prompted the rebels to disperse.

White League A violent white supremacist group similar to the **Ku Klux Klan,** the White League was extremely powerful in Louisiana in the years following the Civil War. Although they quietly infiltrated Louisiana's economy and native political infrastructure, they were also frequently willing to use violent methods to get their way, slaughtering more than 100 African-American militia members in the Colfax Massacre of April 1873 and capturing New Orleans for three days in September 1874.

Wickersham Commission (National Commission on Law Observance and Law Enforcement) Federal commission appointed by President Herbert Hoover in 1929 to examine the operations of criminal justice in the United States and, in particular, to investigate the effectiveness of Prohibition. Its 14-volume report, issued in 1931, represented the first national effort to understand criminal justice as a system. Volume 11, on *Lawlessness in Law Enforcement*, focused public attention on the problem of police brutality.

writ of assistance A general search warrant issued by royal charter to officials during the colonial era, allowing them to search any residence or building they chose to prevent smuggling. Writs of assistance were specifically outlawed by the Fourth Amendment.

Notes

Introduction

1. Ann L. Pastore and Kathleen Maguire, eds., *Sourcebook of Criminal Justice Statistics 2003*. U.S. Department of Justice, Bureau of Justice Statistics. (Washington, D.C.: U.S. Government Printing Office, 2005), pp. 478, 14, 42, 68, 80.
2. Internet Movie Database. Available online at URL: http://www.imbd.com.
3. Federal Bureau of Investigation, *Crime in the United States* (Washington, D.C.: U.S. Government Printing Office, 2003). Available online at URL: http://www.fbi.gov/ucr/03cius.htm.
4. Lawrence M. Friedman and Robert V. Percival, *The Roots of Justice: Crime and Punishment in Alameda County, California, 1870–1910* (Chapel Hill: University of North Carolina Press, 1981), pp. 80–81.
5. Death Penalty Information Center, State-by-State Information for California. Available online at URL: http://www.deathpenaltyinfo.org/state.

Chapter 1

1. Quoted from Thomas Jefferson, letter to Edward Carrington, January 16, 1787, in Julian P. Boyd, ed., *The Papers of Thomas Jefferson, Volume 11: January 1787 to August 1787* (Princeton, N.J.: Princeton University Press, 1955), pp. 48–49.
2. Lawrence Friedman, *Crime and Punishment in American History.* (New York: Basic Books, 1994), p. 103.
3. See V. A. C. Gatrell, *The Hanging Tree: Execution and the English People, 1770–1868* (New York: Oxford University Press, 1994); Peter Linebaugh, *The London Hanged: Crime and Civil Society in the Eighteenth Century* (Cambridge: Cambridge University Press, 1992).
4. Samuel Walker, *Popular Justice: A History of American Criminal Justice,* 2nd ed. (New York: Oxford University Press, 1998), pp. 17–18.
5. William Waller Hening, *Statutes at Large: Being a Collection of All the Laws of Virginia from the First Session of the Legislature in the Year 1619,* vol. 2 (New York, 1823), pp. 269–271.

6. John Winthrop, "A Modell of Christian Charity" (1630). Available online at URL: http://history.hanover.edu/texts/winthmod.html.
7. Isaac Jogues, "Novum Belgium, 1646," reprinted in J. Franklin Jameson, ed., *Narratives of New Netherland, 1609–1664* (New York: Charles Scribner's Sons, 1909). Available online at URL: http://www.gutenberg.org/etext/3161.

Chapter 2

1. Colin Bonwick, *The American Revolution* (Charlottesville: University of Virginia Press, 1991), p. 17.
2. U.S. Department of Commerce, Bureau of the Census, *Historical Statistics of the United States,* vol. 1 (Washington, D.C.: U.S. Government Printing Office, 1975).
3. Charles Francis Adams, *The Works of John Adams with Life,* vol. 10 (Boston: Little Brown, 1850–1856), p. 345.
4. The U.S. Constitution, Amendment IV.
5. The U.S. Constitution, Article I, Section 9.
6. Quoted in David J. Brewer, ed., *The World's Best Orations: From the Earliest Period to the Present Time,* vol. 8 (St. Louis: Kaiser, 1899), pp. 3128–3129.
7. Quoted in John W. Johnson, ed., *Historic U.S. Court Cases: An Encyclopedia,* vol. 1 (London: Routledge, 2001), p. 24.
8. John Locke, *Two Treatises of Government: An Essay Concerning the True Original, Extent and End of Civil Government,* ed. Richard Cox (1690; Arlington Heights, Ill.: Harlan Davidson, 1982).
9. Declaration of Independence.
10. Jackson Turner Main, *The Antifederalists: Critics of the Constitution, 1781–1788* (1961; Chapel Hill: University of North Carolina Press, 2004), p. 226.
11. John Smilie, from a speech given before the Pennsylvania Ratifying Convention, November 28, 1787. Quoted in the "Founders' Constitution" (University of Chicago Press). Available online at URL: http://presspubs.uchicago.edu/founders/documents/v1ch14s28.html.

12. From "Leonidas," a London resident writing an editorial for the July 30, 1788, edition of the *London Times,* p. 2.

13. John Winthrop, "A Modell of Christian Charity" (1630). Available online at URL: http://history. hanover.edu/texts/winthmod.html.

Chapter 3

1. U.S. Department of Commerce, Bureau of the Census, *Historical Statistics of the United States,* vol. 1 (Washington, D.C.: U.S. Government Printing Office, 1975).

2. U.S. Congress, "An Act for the Punishment of Certain Crimes Against the United States" (Sedition Act), July 14, 1798. Available online from the Constitution Society at URL: http://www.constitution.org/rf/sedition_1798.htm.

3. Donald Henderson Stewart, *The Opposition Press of the Federalist Period* (Albany: State University of New York Press, 1969), p. 538.

4. Ron Chernow, *Alexander Hamilton* (New York: Penguin Books, 2004), p. 634.

5. Quoted in Eliza Steelwater, *The Hangman's Knot: Lynching, Legal Execution, and America's Struggle with the Death Penalty* (Boulder, Colo.: Westview Press, 1999), p. 55.

6. Quoted in Carl Sifakis, *The Encyclopedia of American Crime,* 2nd ed., vol. 2 (New York: Facts On File, 2001), p. 558.

Chapter 4

1. U.S. Department of Commerce, Bureau of the Census, *Historical Statistics of the United States,* vol. 1 (Washington, D.C.: U.S. Government Printing Office, 1975).

2. Kenneth S. Greenberg, ed., *The Confessions of Nat Turner and Related Documents* (1831; Boston: Bedford/St. Martin's, 1996), p. 46.

3. Ibid., pp. 18–20.

4. George W. Matsell, "Report of the Chief of Police Concerning Destitution and Crime among Children of the City (1849)," in *Juvenile Offenders for a Thousand Years: Selected Readings from Anglo-Saxon Times to 1900,* ed. Wiley B. Sanders (Chapel Hill: University of North Carolina Press, 1970), p. 379.

5. Clay Gish, "Rescuing the 'Waifs and Strays' of the City: The Western Emigration Program of the Children's Aid Society," *Journal of Social History* 33, no. 1 (Fall 1999): pp. 121–142; see also Marilyn Irvin Holt, *The Orphan Trains: Placing Out in America* (Lincoln: University of Nebraska Press, 1994).

6. "American Psychiatric Association Honors Dorothea Dix with First Posthumous Fellowship," *Psychiatric Services* 56 (April 2005), pp. 502–503.

7. Quoted in Carl Sifakis, *The Encyclopedia of American Crime,* 2nd ed. (New York: Facts On File, 2001), p. 463: see also Patricia Cline Cohen, *The Murder of Helen Jewett: The Life and Death of a Prostitute in Nineteenth-Century New York* (New York: Vintage Books, 1998).

8. Sifakis, *Encyclopedia of American Crime,* p. 86.

Chapter 5

1. Charles Wilson, *Baptized in Blood: The Religion of the Lost Cause, 1865–1920* (Athens: University of Georgia Press, 1980), p. 112.

2. Joseph J. Ellis, *Founding Brothers: The Revolutionary Generation* (New York: Vintage, 2000), p. 102

3. John Mack Faragher, et al., *Out of Many: A History of the American People,* 4th ed. (Upper Saddle River, N.J.: Prentice Hall, 2003).

4. See William Waller Hening, *Statutes at Large: Being a Collection of All the Laws of Virginia from the First Session of the Legislature, in the Year 1619,* vol. 3 (1823), p. 459.

5. Most Southern states exacted penalties against both slaves learning to read and others (slave or free) who attempted to teach them; in Louisiana, the penalty for the latter offense was death. For more on antiliteracy codes, see Janet Duitsman Cornelius, *When I Can Read My Title Clear: Literacy, Slavery, and Religion in the Antebellum South* (Columbia: University of South Carolina Press, 1991).

6. For more on northern laws responding to the Fugitive Slave Act of 1850, see Thomas D. Morris, *Free Men All: The Personal Liberty Laws of the North, 1780–1861* (Baltimore: Johns Hopkins University Press, 1974).

7. The U.S. Supreme Court had already ruled in favor of southern states in *Prigg v. Pennsylvania,* 41 U.S. 539 (1842), but the North remained largely defiant.

8. See Kwame Anthony Appiah and Henry Louis Gates Jr., eds., *Africana: The Encyclopedia of the African and African American Experience* (New York: Basic Civitas, 1999), p. 793.

9. The U.S. Constitution, Article I, Section 9.

10. Abraham Lincoln, letter to General Winfield Scott, April 27, 1861. TeachingAmericanHistory.org. Available online at URL: http://teachingamericanhistory. org/library/index.asp?document=414.

11. Paul A. Cimbala and Randall Miller, *Union Soldiers and the Northern Home Front: Wartime Experiences, Postwar Adjustments* (New York: Fordham University Press, 2002).

12. See "New York Draft Riots," Home of the American Civil War. Available online at URL: http://www.civilwarhome.com/draftriots.htm.

13. Elliott J. Gorn, "'Good-Bye Boys, I die a True American': Homicide, Native and Working-Class Culture in Antebellum New York City." *Journal of American History* 74, no. 2 (September 1987), pp. 388–410.

14. Faragher, et al., *Out of Many.*

15. See Charles P. Roland, *American Iliad: The Story of the Civil War* (Lexington: University Press of Kentucky, 2004), p. 94.

16. Jefferson Davis, Second Inaugural Address, February 22, 1862. Jefferson Davis Documents, Rice University. Available online at URL: http://jeffersondavis.rice.edu/docs.cfm.

17. See Christine Quigley, *Skulls and Skeletons: Human Bone Collections and Accumulations* (Jefferson, N.C.: McFarland, 2001), p. 43.

18. Andersonville was the subject of several issues of *Harper's Weekly* in June 1865.

19. Quoted in Carolyn Kleiner, "The Demon of Andersonville," *Legal Affairs* (September/October 2002). Available online at URL: http://www.legalaffairs.org/printerfriendly.msp?id=247.

20. Robert E. Lee's surrender terms to Ulysses S. Grant, April 9, 1865. Quoted in Jay Winik, *April 1865: The Month That Saved America* (New York: HarperCollins, 2002), p. 187.

21. See Jessica McElrath, "The Black Codes of 1865," About.com: African-American History. Available online at URL: http://afroamhistory.about.com/od/blackcodes/a/blackcodes1865.htm

22. Ibid.

Chapter 6

1. U.S. Department of Commerce, Bureau of the Census, *Historical Statistics of the United States*, vol. 1 (Washington, D.C.: U.S. Government Printing Office, 1975).

2. Eric Foner, *Reconstruction: America's Unfinished Revolution, 1863–1877* (New York: HarperCollins, 1988), p. 558; Nicholas Lemann, *Redemption; The Lost Rattle and the Civil War* (New York: Farrar, Straus, and Giroux, 2006), p. 86.

3. Lemann, *Redemption*, pp. 15–26.

4. Frederick E. Hoxie, ed., *Encyclopedia of North American Indians* (New York: Houghton Mifflin, 1996), pp. 695–697.

5. Discussed in detail in Colin Beavan, *Fingerprints: The Origins of Crime Detection and the Murder Case That Launched Forensic Science* (New York: Hyperion, 2001).

6. Quoted in Carl Sifakis, *The Encyclopedia of American Crime*, 2nd ed. (New York: Facts On File, 2001), p. 73.

7. Ibid., p. 72.

8. Ibid., pp. 683–684.

9. For a good analysis of the Hickock mythos, see Steven Lubet, "Slap Leather! Legal Culture, Wild Bill Hickock, and the Gunslinger Myth," *UCLA Law Review* 48, no. 6 (2001), pp. 1545–1556.

10. Sifakis, *Encyclopedia of American Crime*, p. 289.

11. This discussion is derived mainly from T. J. Stiles, *Jesse James: Last Rebel of the Civil War*. New York: Alfred A. Knopf, 2002.

12. Stewart L. Udall, *The Forgotten Founders: Rethinking the History of the Old West* (Washington, D.C.: Island Press, 2004), p. 172.

13. Sifakis, *Encyclopedia of American Crime*, p. 91.

14. "Texas Rangers," Handbook of Texas Online. Available online at URL: http://www.tsha.utexas.edu/handbook/online/articles/TT/met4.html.

15. Quoted in Rick Miller, *Sam Bass & Gang* (Austin, Tex.: State House Press, 1999), p. 1.

16. Leon Claire Metz, *John Wesley Hardin: Dark Angel of Texas* (Norman: University of Oklahoma Press, 1998).

17. "Texas Rangers," Handbook of Texas Online. Available online at URL: http://www.tsha.utexas.edu/handbook/online/articles/TT/met4.html.

18. See Edgardo Rothman, "The Failure of Reform: United States, 1865–1965," in *The Oxford History of the Prison*, ed. Norval Morris and David J. Rothman (New York: Oxford University Press, 1997), pp. 154.

19. Reprinted in Alexander W. Pisciotta, *Benevolent Repression: Social Control and the American Reformatory-Prison Movement* (New York: New York University Press, 1994), p. 157.

20. Quoted in Lawrence M. Friedman, *Crime and Punishment in American History* (New York: Basic Books, 1993), p. 142.

21. Ibid., p. 142.

Chapter 7

1. John Whiteclay Chambers II, *The Tyranny of Change: America in the Progressive Era, 1890–1920*, 2nd ed. (New Brunswick, N.J.: Rutgers University Press, 2000), p. xi.

2. Thomas Lee Philpott, *The Slum and the Ghetto: Immigrants, Blacks, and Reformers in Chicago, 1880–1930* (Belmont, Calif.: Wadsworth, 1991), pp. 5–41.

3. Chambers, *Tyranny of Change*, p. 11.

4. Erik Larson, *The Devil in the White City: Murder, Magic, and Madness at the Fair That Changed Americ* (New York: Crown Publishers, 2003), pp. 394–395.

5. Douglas Lee Eckberg, "Estimates of Early 20th-Century U.S. Homicide Rates: An Econometric Forecasting Approach," *Demography* 32, no. 1 (February 1995), pp. 1–16. See also Roger Lane, *Murder in America: A History* (Columbus: Ohio State University Press, 1997), p. 181.

6. Lane, *Murder in America*, pp. 185–188. See also Lane, *Violent Death in the City: Suicide, Accident, and Murder in 19th-Century Pennsylvania*, 2nd ed. (1979; Columbus: Ohio State University Press, 1999), pp. 53–76.

7. Lane, *Violent Death in the City*, pp. 119–141.

8. Eric H. Monkonnen, *Murder in New York City* (Berkeley: University of California Press, 2001), pp. 20–25.

9. Jeffrey S. Adler, "'Halting the Slaughter of the Innocents': The Civilizing Process and the Surge in Violence in Turn-of-the-Century Chicago." *Social Science History* 25 (Spring 2001), pp. 29–52. See also Leigh B. Bienen and Brandon Rottinghaus, "Learning from the Past, Living in the Present: Understanding Homicide in Chicago, 1870–1930," *Journal of Criminal Law and Criminology* 92, no. 3 (Spring/Summer 2002), pp. 441 and 516–533.

10. Jeffrey S. Adler, *First in Violence, Deepest in Dirt: Homicide in Chicago, 1875–1920* (Cambridge, Mass.: Harvard University Press, 2006), pp. 120–158.

11. Samuel Walker, *Popular Justice: A History of American Criminal Justice*, 2nd ed. (New York: Oxford University Press, 1998), p. 62.

12. Marilynn S. Johnson, *Street Justice: A History of Police Violence in New York City* (Boston: Beacon Press, 2003), p. 41.

13. Walker, *A Critical History of Police Reform* (Lexington, Mass.: D.C. Heath, 1977), pp. 56–61.

14. Lawrence M. Friedman and Robert V. Percival, *The Roots of Justice: Crime and Punishment in Alameda County, California, 1870–1910* (Chapel Hill: University of North Carolina Press, 1981), pp. 173–181.

15. Ben B. Lindsey. "The Reformation of Juvenile Delinquents through the Juvenile Court," in *Children's Courts in the United States: Their Origin, Development, and Results*, ed. Samuel J. Barrow (Washington, D.C.: U.S. Government Printing Office, 1904).

16. Adam Fairclough, *Better Day Coming: Blacks and Equality, 1890–2000* (New York: Penguin, 2001), p. 14.

17. Lane, *Murder in America*, p. 151.

18. Ibid., pp. 151–156.

19. Ibid.

20. David M. Oshinsky, *"Worse Than Slavery": Parchman Farm and the Ordeal of Jim Crow Justice* (New York: Free Press, 1996), p. 137.

Chapter 8

1. Nathan Miller, *New World Coming: The 1920s and the Making of Modern America* (New York: Simon & Schuster, 2003), p. 16.

2. Robert M. Saunders, *In Search of Woodrow Wilson: Beliefs and Behavior* (Westport, Conn.: Greenwood Press, 1998), p. 229.

3. John Whiteclay Chambers II, *The Tyranny of Change: America in the Progressive Era, 1890–1920*, 2nd edition (New Brunswick, N.J.: Rutgers University Press, 2000), p. 245.

4. Ibid., p. 246.

5. Geoffrey R. Stone, *Perilous Times: Free Speech in Wartime from the Sedition Act of 1798 to the War on Terrorism* (New York: W.W. Norton, 2004), p. 12.

6. Nick Salvatore, *Eugene V. Debs: Citizen and Socialist* (Urbana: University of Illinois Press, 1982), pp. 291–302.

7. Thomas Watt Gregory, "The Annual Report of the Attorney General of the United States to the Senate and House of Representatives," December 4, 1917.

8. Michael McGerr, *A Fierce Discontent: The Rise and Fall of the Progressive Movement in America, 1870–1920* (New York: Free Press, 2003), p. 290.

9. Chambers, *Tyranny of Change*, pp. 268–269; Eric Arneson, *Black Protest and the Great Migration: A Brief History with Documents* (Boston: Bedford/St. Martin's, 2003), pp. 7–15.

10. Chambers, *Tyranny of Change*, p. 269.

11. Ibid., pp. 269–270.

12. Ibid., pp. 270–271; Richard Gid Powers, *Secrecy and Power: The Life of J. Edgar Hoover* (New York: Free Press, 1987), pp. 56–129.

13. In *Schenck v. United States*, 249 U.S. 47 (1919) and *Abrams v. United States*, 250 U.S. 616 (1919).

14. Chambers, *Tyranny of Change*, p. 272.

15. U.S. Constitution, Amendment 18.

16. Richard C. Lindberg, *To Serve and Collect: Chicago Politics and Police Corruption from the Lager Beer Riot to the Summerdale Scandal, 1855–1960* (1991; Carbondale: Southern Illinois University Press, 1998), pp. 156–159.

17. "Virtue for Tiny Tots," *Chicago Tribune* (February 4, 1930), p. 14.

18. Anthony Bianco, *Ghosts of 42nd Street: A History of America's Most Infamous Block* (New York: HarperCollins, 2004), p. 80.

19. Paula Fass, "Finding History in Woodside, California," *American Places: Encounters with History*, William E. Leuchtenburg, ed. (Oxford and New York: Oxford University Press, 2000), p. 118.

20. Gilbert Geis and Leigh B. Bienen, *Crimes of the Century: From Leopold and Loeb to O. J. Simpson* (Boston: Northeastern University Press, 1998), pp. 13–47.

21. Michael Newton, *The Encyclopedia of Kidnappings* (New York: Facts on File, 2002), p. 220.

22. Ibid., p. 169.

23. Stuart Banner, *The Death Penalty: An American History* (Cambridge, Mass.: Harvard University Press, 2003), pp. 226–227.

24. Ronald Kessler, *The Bureau: The Secret History of the FBI* (New York: St. Martin's Press, 2003), p. 30.

25. In *United States v. Jackson*, 390 U.S. 570 (1968).

26. Carl Sifakis, *The Encyclopedia of American Crime*, 2nd ed. (New York: Facts On File, 2001), vol. 1, pp. 263–267.

27. Federal Bureau of Investigation, "Famous Cases: Bonnie and Clyde." Available online at URL: http://www.fbi.gov/libref/historic/famcases/clyde/clyde.htm.

Chapter 9

1. Unemployment data from U.S. Department of Commerce, Bureau of the Census, *Historical Statistics of the United States, Colonial Times to 1970*, Bicentennial Edition, Part 1 (Washington, D.C.: U.S. Government Printing Office, 1975), p. 135. On the Great Depression and New Deal more generally, one recent scholarly overview is David M. Kennedy, *Freedom from Fear: The American People in Depression and War, 1929–1945* (New York: Oxford University Press, 1999).

2. The discussion of the Scottsboro cases is distilled from a number of sources including Douglas Linder, ed., *Famous American Trials: The "Scottsboro Boys" Trial.* Available online at URL: http://www.law.umkc.edu/faculty/projects/FTrials/scottsboro/scottsb.htm; Gilbert Geis and Leigh B. Bienen, *Crimes of the Century: From Leopold and Loeb to O.J. Simpson* (Boston: Northeastern University Press, 1998), pp. 49–88; Adam Fairclough, *Better Day Coming: Blacks and Equality, 1890–2000* (New York: Penguin, 2001), pp. 133–140.

3. Quoted in Geis and Bienen, *Crimes of the Century*, p. 61.

4. Jill Jonnes, *Hep-Cats, Narcs, and Pipe Dreams: A History of America's Romance with Illegal Drugs* (New York: Scribner, 1996), pp. 121–128.

5. Ibid., (New York: Scribner, 1996), pp. 128–129.

6. Ibid., p. 129. Fines translated to 2007 dollars using "The Inflation Calculator," an on-line conversion tool utilizing data from the Consumer Price Index. Available online at URL: http://www.westegg.com/inflation.

7. Jonnes, *Hep-Cats, Narcs, and Pipe Dreams*, pp. 119–140, 161–162.

8. Ibid., pp. 162–163.

9. Angelo N. Ancheta, *Race, Rights, and the Asian American Experience* (New Brunswick, N.J.: Rutgers University Press, 1998), p. 31.

10. Rose D. Scherini, "When Italian Americans Were 'Enemy Aliens,'" in *Una Storia Segreta: The World War II Evacuation and Internment of Italian Americans*, ed. Lawrence Distasi (Berkeley, Calif.: Heyday Books, 2001), p. 31.

11. Winston S. Churchill, "The Sinews of Peace," March 5, 1946.

12. John Mack Faragher et al., *Out of Many*, 4th ed. (Upper Saddle River, N.J.: Pearson Prentice Hall, 2003), pp. 812, 814.

13. Ellen Schrecker, *The Age of McCarthyism: A Brief History With Documents*, 2nd ed. (Boston: Bedford/St. Martin's, 2002), pp. 43–45.

14. Ibid., pp. 66–67, 229–236.

15. Gilbert Geis and Leigh B. Bienen, *Crimes of the Century: From Leopold and Loeb to O. J. Simpson* (Boston: Northeastern University Press, 1998), pp. 127–157.

16. Reprinted in Schrecker, *Age of McCarthyism*, p. 237. This is the version of the speech entered into the Congressional Record on February 20. Before his Wheeling audience on February 9, McCarthy reportedly claimed to have 205 names on the list.

17. National Center for Health Statistics, *Vital Statistics*. See also Figure A1.

18. Ann L. Pastore and Kathleen Maguire, eds., *Sourcebook of Criminal Justice Statistics 2003*. U.S. Department of Justice, Bureau of Justice Statistics (Washington, D.C.: U.S. Government Printing Office, 2005), p. 500.

19. James Gilbert, *A Cycle of Outrage: America's Reaction to the Juvenile Delinquent in the 1950s* (New York: Oxford University Press, 1986), pp. 28–29.

20. Edward J. Escobar, *Race, Police, and the Making of a Political Identity: Mexican Americans and the Los Angeles*

Police Department, 1900–1945 (Berkeley: University of California Press, 1999), p. 194.

21. Gilbert, *Cycle of Outrage*, pp. 66–67.

22. Ibid., p. 64.

23. Ibid., pp. 143–161; Bradford M. Wright, *Comic Book Nation: The Transformation of Youth Culture in America* (Baltimore: Johns Hopkins University Press, 2001), pp. 154–179.

24. Eric C. Schneider, *Vampires, Dragons, and Egyptian Kings: Youth Gangs in Postwar New York* (Princeton, N.J.: Princeton University Press, 1999), pp. 3–26, 78–105.

25. Thomas Hine, *The Rise and Fall of the American Teenager* (New York: Perennial, 1999), p. 8.

26. William Graebner, *Coming of Age in Buffalo: Youth and Authority in the Postwar Era* (Philadelphia: Temple University Press, 1990), pp. 99–106.

27. Steven Schlossman, "The California Experience in Juvenile Justice: Some Historical Perspectives" (Sacramento: California Bureau of Criminal Statistics, 1989), pp. 6–10.

28. Schneider, *Vampires, Gangs, and Egyptian Kings*, pp. 188–197.

29. Joe Domanick, *To Protect and to Serve: The LAPD's Century of War in the City of Dreams* (New York: Pocket Books, 1994), pp. 104–129.

30. Ibid., p. 110.

31. William Bradford Hule, "The Shocking Story of Appeared Killing in Mississippi," *Look* (January 1956); republished *The American Experience: The Murder of Emmett Till.* Available online at URL: http://www.pbs.org/wgbh/amex/till/sfeatures/sf_look_confession.html.

Chapter 10

1. Roger Lane, *Murder in America: A History* (Columbus: Ohio State University Press, 1997), pp. 269–271.

2. Lane, *Murder in America*, pp. 277–278.

3. David Goldfield et al., *The American Journey*, 4th ed. (Upper Saddle River, N.J.: Pearson Prentice Hall, 2007), pp. 913.

4. John Mack Faragher et al., *Out of Many*, 5th ed. (Upper Saddle River, N.J.: Pearson Prentice Hall, 2006), p. 929.

5. Tom Hayden et al., "Port Huron Statement," mimeographed (n.p., Students for a Democratic Society, 1962); in *A History of Our Time: Readings on Postwar America*, ed. William H. Chafe and Harvard Sitkoff (New York: Oxford University Press, 1999), p. 291.

6. Todd Gitlin, *The Sixties: Years of Hope, Days of Rage* (New York: Bantam Books, 1987), pp. 248–254.

7. William H. Chafe, *The Unfinished Journey: America since World War II*, 5th ed. (New York: Oxford University Press, 2003), pp. 405–406.

8. Chafe, *Unfinished Journey*, pp. 374–375; Douglas Linder, "Famous Trials: The 'Chicago Seven' Trial." Available online at URL: http://www.law.umkc.edu/faculty/projects/ftrials/Chicago7/chicago7.html.

9. David Cunningham, "Understanding State Responses to Left- versus Right-Wing Threats: The FBI's Repression of the New Left and the Ku Klux Klan," *Social Science History* 27, no. 3 (Fall 2003): 327–371.

10. Harvard Sitkoff, *The Struggle for Black Equality, 1954–1992*, revised ed. (New York: Hill & Wang, 1993), pp. 161–164; quotation from 163.

11. Ibid., pp. 161–164.

12. David M. Oshinsky, *"Worse Than Slavery": Parchman Farm and the Ordeal of Jim Crow Justice* (New York: Free Press, 1996), pp. 233–236.

13. Sitkoff, *The Struggle for Black Equality*, pp. 120–135.

14. Marilynn S. Johnson, *Street Justice: A History of Police Violence in New York City* (Boston: Beacon Press, 2003), pp. 234–236.

15. Adam Fairclough, *Better Day Coming: Blacks and Equality, 1890–2000* (New York: Penguin Books, 2001), pp. 295–296.

16. Sitkoff, *The Struggle for Black Equality*, pp. 187–190.

17. National Advisory Commission on Civil Disorders, *Report* (Washington, D.C.: U.S. Government Printing Office, 1968), p. 1.

18. Quoted in Sitkoff, *The Struggle for Black Equality*, p. 199.

19. Hoover is quoted proudly by the Black Panthers in "What Was the Black Panther Party?" Available online at URL: http://www.blackpanther.org/legacynew.htm. See also Sitkoff, *Struggle for Black Equality*, p. 204.

20. *Mapp v. Ohio*, 367 U.S. 643 (1961); *Gideon v. Wainwright*, 372 U.S. 335 (1963); *Miranda v. Arizona*, 384 U.S. 436 (1966); Samuel Walker, *Popular Justice: A History of American Criminal Justice*, 2nd ed. (New York: Oxford University Press, 1998), pp. 181–184.

21. *In re Gault*, 387 U.S. 1 (1967); Thomas J. Bernard, *The Cycle of Juvenile Justice* (New York: Oxford University Press, 1992), pp. 114–120.

22. President's Commission on Law Enforcement and Administration of Justice, *The Challenge of Crime in a Free Society* (Washington, D.C.: U.S. Government Print-

ing Office, 1967), pp. v–xi; Walker, *Popular Justice*, pp. 202–205.

23. JoAnne O'Bryant, "Crime Control: The Federal Response" (Congressional Research Service, March 5, 2003), pp. 2–3; Walker, *Popular Justice*, pp. 204–205.

24. W. Marvin Dulaney, *Black Police in America* (Bloomington: Indiana University Press, 1996), pp. 72–77, 112–113; Walker, *Popular Justice*, p. 198.

25. National Center for Health Statistics, *Vital Statistics of the United States.*

26. Ann L. Pastore and Kathleen Maguire, eds., *Sourcebook of Criminal Justice Statistics 2003*. U.S. Department of Justice, Bureau of Justice Statistics. (Washington, D.C.: U.S. Government Printing Office, 2005), p. 278.

27. Eric H. Monkkonen, *Murder in New York City* (Berkeley: University of California Press, 2001), pp. 8–10.

28. Lane, *Murder in America*, pp. 295–303.

29. Ibid., pp. 294–295.

30. Douglas Linder, "Famous Trials: The Trial of Charles Manson," (2002). Available online at URL: http://www.law.umkc.edu/faculty/projects/ftrials/manson/manson.html; Lane, *Murder in America*, pp. 282–283.

31. Walker, *Popular Justice*, pp. 191–193, 199–200; Michael F. Flamm, *Law and Order: Street Crime, Civil Disorder, and the Crisis of Liberalism* (New York: Columbia University Press, 2005).

Chapter 11

1. National Center for Health Statistics, *Vital Statistics*; James Alan Fox and Marianne W. Zawitz, "Homicide Trends in the United States," Bureau of Justice Statistics, September 2004. Available online at URL: http://www.ojp.usdoj.gov/bjs/homicide/homtrnd.htm.

2. Ann L. Pastore and Kathleen Maguire, eds., *Sourcebook of Criminal Justice Statistics 2003*. U.S. Department of Justice, Bureau of Justice Statistics (Washington, D.C.: U.S. Government Printing Office, 2005), p. 278.

3. Michael R. Rand, James P. Lynch, and David Cantor, "National Crime Victimization, 1973–95" (U.S. Department of Justice, Office of Justice Programs, April 1997, NCJ-163069), p, 2.

4. Jimmy Carter, "Energy and National Goals," 15 July 1979, reprinted in Daniel Horowitz, ed., *Jimmy Carter and the Energy Crisis of the 1970s: A Brief History with Documents* (Boston: Bedford/St. Martin's, 2005), p. 111.

5. Richard Gid Powers, *Secrecy and Power: The Life of J. Edgar Hoover* (New York: Free Press, 1987), pp. 486–487.

6. Walker, *Popular Justice*, p. 205.

7. Samuel Walker, *Sense and Nonsense about Crime and Drugs: A Policy Guide*, 3rd ed. (Belmont, Calif.: Wadsworth Publishing, 1994), pp. 208–209.

8. Walker, *Sense and Nonsense about Crime and Drugs*, p. 77.

9. Samuel Walker, *Popular Justice: A History of American Criminal Justice*, 2nd ed. (New York: Oxford University Press, 1998), pp. 199–201.

10. Scott Christianson, *With Liberty for Some: 500 Years of Imprisonment in America* (Boston: Northeastern University Press, 1998), pp. 268–269.

11. Christianson, *With Liberty for Some*, pp. 269–270.

12. Francis X. Clines, "Attica Endures," *New York Times*, September 17, 2006, section 4, p. 13.

13. David W. Chen, "Judge Approves $8 Million Deal for Victims of Attica Torture," *New York Times*, February 16, 2000, section B, p. 6.

14. Senate Government Operations Committee, *Federal Drug Enforcement: Hearings Before the Permanent Subcommittee on Investigations of the Committee on Government Operations* (Washington, D.C.: U.S. Government Printing Office, 1975), p. 880.

15. Edward M. Brecher, "Drug Laws and Drug Enforcement: A Review and Evaluation Based on 111 Years of Experience," in *Perspectives on Drug Use in the United States*, ed. Bernard Segal (Binghamton, N.Y.: Haworth Press, 1986), p. 17.

16. Peter Andreas, *Border Games: Policing the U.S.-Mexico Divide* (Ithaca, N.Y.: Cornell University Press, 2001), p. 41.

17. President's Commission on Organized Crime, *America's Habit: Drug Abuse, Drug Trafficking, and Organized Crime* (Washington, D.C.: U.S. Government Printing Office, 1986), p. 106.

18. Ernest Drucker, "Population Impact of Mass Incarceration under New York's Rockefeller Drug Laws," *Journal of Urban Health: Bulletin of the New York Academy of Medicine* 79, no. 3 (September 2002), p. 1.

19. Ibid., p. 3.

20. Eric Schlosser, "The Prison Industrial Complex," *Atlantic Monthly* (December 1998), pp. 56–57.

21. "Poll Finds Support for Drug Law Reform," *Albany Times Union*, May 22, 1999.

22. See, for example, Ronald F. Becker, *Criminal Investigation, Second Edition: A Contemporary Perspective* (Boston: Jones and Bartlett, 2005), p. 168.

23. Hans Zeisel and Alec M. Gallup, "Death Penalty Sentiment in the United States," *Journal of Quantitative Criminology* 5, no. 3 (September 1989), pp. 285–296.

24. Justice Potter Stewart, from his majority ruling in *Furman v. Georgia*, 408 U.S. 238 (1972).

Chapter 12

1. Ann L. Pastore and Kathleen Maguire, eds., *Sourcebook of Criminal Justice Statistics 2003*. U.S. Department of Justice, Bureau of Justice Statistics (Washington, D.C.: U.S. Government Printing Office, 2005), p. 278.

2. Ibid., p. 129.

3. Deborah Vagins and Jesselyn McCurdy, *Cracks in the System* (Washington, D.C.: American Civil Liberties Union, 2006), p. ii.

4. Pastore and Maguire, *Sourcebook*, p. 478.

5. Eve S. Buzawa and Carl G. Buzawa, *Domestic Violence: The Changing Criminal Justice Response* (Westport, Conn.: Auburn House, 1992), p. 176.

6. Quoted in Regina G. Lawrence, *The Politics of Force: Media and the Construction of Police Brutality* (Berkeley: University of California Press, 2001), p. 210.

7. Ibid., p. 150.

8. Ibid., p. 210.

9. Quoted in Warren Christopher, ed., *Report of the Independent Commission on the Los Angeles Police Department* (Los Angeles: The Commission, 1991), p. xii.

10. Ibid., p. 73.

11. Ibid., p. xi.

12. Quoted in Lou Cannon, *Official Negligence: How Rodney King and the Riots Changed Los Angeles and the LAPD* (Boulder, Colo.: Westview Press, 1997), p. 21.

13. Douglas Linder, "A Chronology of Events Surrounding the Trial of Los Angeles Police Officers for the Beating of Rodney King," *Famous American Trials: The Rodney King Trial*. Available online at URL: http://www.law.umkc.edu/faculty/projects/ftrials/lapd/kingchronology.html.

Chapter 13

1. National Center for Health Statistics, *Vital Statistics*; James Alan Fox and Marianne W. Zawitz, "Homicide Trends in the United States" (Bureau of Justice Statistics, September 2004). Available online at URL: http://www.ojp.usdoj.gov/bjs/homicide/homtrnd.htm.

2. Federal Bureau of Investigation, *Crime in the United States, 2003* (Washington, D.C.: Federal Bureau of Investigation, 2004). Available online at URL: http://www.fbi.gov/ucr/03cius.htm.

3. Ann L. Pastore and Kathleen Maguire, eds., *Sourcebook of Criminal Justice Statistics 2003*. U.S. Department of Justice, Bureau of Justice Statistics (Washington, D.C.: U.S. Government Printing Office, 2005), p. 106.

4. Linda Williams, *Playing the Race Card: Melodramas of Black and White from Uncle Tom to O. J. Simpson* (Princeton, N.J.: Princeton University Press, 2001), p. 281.

5. Cited in William Raspberry, "O. J. and Race," *New Orleans Times-Picayune* (July 9, 1994), p. B7.

6. Cited in Eric Sundquist, "For Many, Trial Was a Black-and-White Issue," *Virginian-Pilot* (October 4, 1995), p. A7.

7. Mark England and Darlene McCormick, "The Sinful Messiah, Part One," *Waco Tribune-Herald* (February 27, 1993), p. 7A; this was the first article of a seven-part series published in the *Waco Tribune-Herald*.

8. "Murrah Building Bombing—a Look at Numbers," from the Web site of the Oklahoma City National Memorial. Available online at URL: http://www.oklahomacitynationalmemorial.org.

9. Quoted in Lois Romano and Tom Kenworthy, "McVeigh Guilty on All 11 Counts," *Washington Post* (June 3, 1997), p. A-01.

10. The nature of the experiments is documented in Alston Chase, *Harvard and the Unabomber: The Education of an American Terrorist* (New York: W.W. Norton, 2003).

11. Steven R. Donziger, ed., *The Real War on Crime: The Report of the National Criminal Justice Commission* (New York: HarperPerennial, 1996), pp. 25–26.

12. Michael P. Roth, *Crime and Punishment: A History of the Criminal Justice System* (Belmont, Calif.: Thomson Wadsworth, 2005), p. 311.

13. Willard M. Oliver and James F. Hilgenberg, Jr., *A History of Crime and Criminal Justice in America* (Boston: Pearson, 2006), pp. 321–322.

14. Pastore and Maguire, *Sourcebook of Criminal Justice Statistics 2003,* p. 500.

15. Ibid., p. 488.

16. Ibid., p. 478.

17. Ibid., p. 505.

18. Ibid., p, 519.
19. Eric Schlosser, "The Prison-Industrial Complex," *The Atlantic Monthly* 282 (December 1998), pp. 51–78.
20. Roth, *Crime and Punishment*, p. 316.
21. Ibid., pp. 315–317.
22. Ibid., pp. 320–321.
23. Thomas P. Bonczar and Tracy L. Snell, "Capital Punishment 2004," Bureau of Justice Statistics Bulletin (November 2005), pp. 3, 10.
24. Fox and Zawitz, "Homicide Trends in the United States."
25. Ibid.
26. John J. DiIulio, Jr. "The Coming of the Super-Predators," *The Weekly Standard* 1 (November 27, 1995): p. 23. See also William J. Bennett, John J. DiIulio, Jr., and John P. Walters, *Body Count: Moral Poverty—And How to Win America's War against Crime and Drugs* (New York: Simon & Schuster, 1996).
27. Alfred Blumstein, "Youth Violence, Guns, and the Illicit-Drug Industry," *Journal of Criminal Law and Criminology* 86, no. 1 (Fall 1995): p. 29.
28. Blumstein, "Youth Violence," pp. 10–36; Alfred Blumstein and Richard Rosenfeld, "Explaining Recent Trends in U.S. Homicide Rates," *Journal of Criminal Law and Criminology* 88 (1998): pp. 1175–1216.
29. Fox and Zawitz, "Homicide Trends in the United States."
30. George L. Kelling and Catherine M. Coles, *Fixing Broken Windows: Restoring Order and Reducing Crime in Our Communities* (New York: Free Press, 1996).
31. Oliver and Hilgenberg, *History of Crime and Criminal Justice*, pp. 325–326; Roth, *Crime and Punishment*, pp. 338–339.
32. Quoted in David S. Tanenhaus and Steven A. Drizin, "'Owing to the Extreme Youth of the Accused': The Changing Legal Response to Juvenile Homicide," *Journal of Criminal Law and Criminology* 92, no. 3 (Spring/Summer 2002): p. 641.
33. Ibid., p. 664.
34. Ibid., p. 643.
35. Hon. John B. Leete, "Treatment and Rehabilitation or Hard Time: Is the Focus of Juvenile Justice Changing?" *Akron Law Review* 29 (Spring 1996): pp. 491–508.
36. Tanenhaus and Drizen, "'Owing to the Extreme Youth of the Accused,'" pp. 664–671, 678–689. See also David S. Tanenhaus, *Juvenile Justice in the Making* (New York: Oxford University Press, 2004), pp. xxi–xxvii, 159–163.
37. Mark Denbeaux and Joshua Denbeaux, *Report on Guantanamo Detainees: A Profile of 517 Detainees Through Analysis of Department of Defense Data* (South Orange, N.J.: Seton Hall University Press, 2006).
38. Richard Gissel, *Digital Underworld: Computer Crime and Resulting Issues* (MacroTech Press, 2005), p. 185.
39. Jennifer LeClaire, "Symantec Report: Cybercrime on the Rise," *E-Commerce Times* (March 7, 2006). Available online at URL: http://www.ecommercetimes.com/story/49225.html.
40. Ibid.

Bibliography

Cases

Ableman v. Booth, 62 U.S. 506 (1858).

Abrams v. United States, 250 U.S. 616 (1919).

Cabey v. Goetz, Supreme Court of the State of New York, Index No. 6747–1985 (January 30, 1985).

Dred Scott v. Sandford. 60 U.S. 393 (1856).

Ex parte Merryman, 7 Fed. Cas. 144 (1861).

Ex parte Milligan, 71 U.S. 2 (1866).

Frank v. Maryland. 359 U.S. 360 (1959).

Furman v. Georgia. 408 U.S. 238 (1972).

Gideon v. Wainwright, 372 U.S. 335 (1963).

Hamdi v. Rumsfeld, 542 U.S. 507 (2004).

In re Gault, 387 U.S. 1 (1967).

Mapp v. Ohio, 367 U.S. 643 (1961).

Marbury v. Madison, 5 U.S. 137 (1803).

Miranda v. Arizona, 384 U.S. 436 (1966).

Powell v. Alabama, 287 U.S. 45 (1932).

Prigg v. Pennsylvania, 41 U.S. 539 (1842).

Schenck v. United States, 249 U.S. 47 (1919).

United States v. Jackson, 390 U.S. 570 (1968).

Weeks v. United States, 232 U.S. 383 (1914).

Newspapers and News Outlets

Adirondack Record-Elizabethtown Post

Albany Times Union

BBC News. Available online. URL: http://news.bbc.co.uk/.

Burlington Hawk Eyecommunist

CBS News. Available online. URL: http://www.cbsnews.com/.

Chicago Daily Tribune / Tribune

Cincinnati Post

CNN.com. Available online. URL: http://www.cnn.com/.

Daily Advertiser

Daily Nevada State Journal

Dallas Morning News

Findley (OH) Courier

Fort Wayne Daily Gazette

Huron Reflector

Lawrence Journal World

The Liberator

Los Angeles Times
New Orleans Times-Picayune
New York Daily Times
New York Herald
New York Times
New York Transcript
New York Tribune
New York Weekly Journal
Ohio Statesman
Pennsylvania Gazette
The Times (London)
Times News (Lehighton, PA)
Virginian-Pilot
Waco Tribune-Herald
Washington Post

Primary and Secondary Sources

Adams, Charles Francis. *The Works of John Adams with Life.* Vol. 10. Boston: Little, Brown, 1850–1856.

Adler, Jeffrey S. "'My Mother-in-Law Is to Blame, But I'll Walk on Her Neck Yet': Homicide in Late Nineteenth-Century Chicago." *Journal of Social History* 31 (Winter 1997): 253–276.

———. "'The Negro Would Be More Than an Angel to Withstand Such Treatment': African-American Homicide in Chicago, 1875–1910." In *Lethal Imagination: Violence and Brutality in American History,* ed. Michael A. Bellesiles. New York: New York University Press, 1999.

———. "'Halting the Slaughter of the Innocents': The Civilizing Process and the Surge in Violence in Turn-of-the-Century Chicago." *Social Science History* 25 (Spring 2001): 29–52.

———. "'I Loved Joe, but I Had to Shoot Him': Homicide by Women in Turn-of-the Century Chicago." *Journal of Criminal Law and Criminology* 92 (Spring / Summer 2002): 867–897.

———. "'On the Borders of Snakeland': Evolutionary Psychology and Plebian Violence in Industrial Chicago, 1875–1920." *Journal of Social History* 36 (Spring 2003): 541–560.

———. *First in Violence, Deepest in Dirt: Homicide in Chicago, 1875–1920.* Cambridge, Mass.: Harvard University Press, 2006.

———. "'It was his first offense. We might as well let him go.': Homicide and Criminal Justice in Chicago, 1875–1920." *Journal of Social History* 40 (Fall 2006): 5–24.

Alexander, Ruth. *The "Girl Problem": Female Sexual Delinquency in New York, 1900–1930.* Ithaca, N.Y.: Cornell University Press, 1995.

American Civil Liberties Union. *Sanctioned Bias: Racial Profiling since 9/11.* February 2004. Available online. URL: http://www.aclu.org/safefree/resources/17017pub20040226.html. Accessed on October 6, 2009.

"American Psychiatric Association Honors Dorothea Dix with First Posthumous Fellowship." *Psychiatric Services* 56 (April 2005): 502–503.

The American Experience: The Murder of Emmett Till. Available online. URL: http://www.pbs.org/wgbh/amex/till/sfeature/sf_look_confession.html. Accessed on July 4, 2008.

Anccheta, Angelo N. *Race, Rights, and the Asian American Experience.* New Brunswick, N.J.: Rutgers University Press, 1998.

Andreas, Peter. *Border Games: Policing the U.S.-Mexico Divide.* Ithaca, N.Y.: Cornell University Press, 2001.

Appiah, Kwame Anthony, and Henry Louis Gates Jr., eds. *Africana: The Encyclopedia of the African and African American Experience.* New York: Basic Civitas, 1999.

Appier, Janis. *Policing Women: The Sexual Politics of Law Enforcement and the LAPD.* Philadelphia: Temple University Press, 1998.

Aptheker, Herbert, ed. *A Documentary History of the Negro People in the United States.* New York: Citadel Press, 1951.

Arneson, Eric. *Black Protest and the Great Migration: A Brief History with Documents.* Boston: Bedford/St. Martin's, 2003.

The Avalon Project at Yale Law School. *Documents in Law, History, and Diplomacy.* Available online. URL: http://www.yale.edu/lawweb/avalon/avalon.htm. Accessed on May 11, 2007.

Ayers, Edward. *Vengeance and Justice: Crime and Punishment in the Nineteenth-Century American South.* New York: Oxford University Press, 1984.

Ayers, William. *A Kind and Just Parent: The Children of Juvenile Court.* Boston: Beacon Press, 1997.

Bacon, Thomas. *Laws of Maryland.* Archives of Maryland. Available online. URL: http://archivesofmaryland.net/html/index.html. Accessed on July 8, 2008.

Banner, Stuart. *The Death Penalty: An American History.* Cambridge, Mass.: Harvard University Press, 2002.

Bartley, Diane. "John Walsh: Fighting Back." *Saturday Evening Post* (April 1990), p. 1.

Beavan, Colin. *Fingerprints: The Origins of Crime Detection and the Murder Case That Launched Forensic Science.* New York: Hyperion, 2001.

Beaumont, Gustave de, and Alexis de Tocqueville. *On the Penitentiary System in the United States and Its Application in France.* 1833. Carbondale: Southern Illinois University Press, 1979.

Beccaria, Cesare. *An Essay on Crimes and Punishments.* Translated by Edward D. Ingraham. 1764. Philadelphia: Philip H. Nicklin, 1810. The Constitution Society. Available online. URL: http://www.constitution.org/cb/crim_pun.htm. Accessed on May 18, 2007.

Beckett, Katherine, and Theodore Sasson. *The Politics of Injustice.* Thousand Oaks, Calif.: Pine Forge Press, 2000.

Becker, Ronald F. *Criminal Investigation, Second Edition: A Contemporary Perspective.* Boston: Jones and Bartlett, 2005.

Belenko, Steven R., ed. *Drugs and Drug Policy in America: A Documentary History.* Westport, Conn.: Greenwood Press, 2000.

Bellesiles, Michael A. *Arming America: The Origins of a National Gun Culture.* New York: Alfred A. Knopf, 2000.

Bennett, William J., John J. DiIulio, Jr., and John P. Walters. *Body Count: Moral Poverty and How to Win America's War against Crime and Drugs.* New York: Simon & Schuster, 1996.

Bernard, Thomas J. *The Cycle of Juvenile Justice.* New York: Oxford University Press, 1992.

Bernstein, Richard. *Out of the Blue: The Story of September 11, 2001, from Jihad to Ground Zero.* New York: Times Books, 2002.

Besharov, Douglas J. *Recognizing Child Abuse: A Guide for the Concerned.* New York: Free Press, 1990.

Bianco, Anthony. *Ghosts of 42nd Street: A History of America's Most Infamous Block.* New York: HarperCollins, 2004.

Bienen, Leigh B., and Brandon Rottinghaus. "Learning from the Past, Living in the Present: Understanding Homicide in Chicago, 1870–1930." *Journal of Criminal Law and Criminology* 92, no. 3 (Spring/Summer 2002): 437–554.

Blumstein, Alfred. "Youth Violence, Guns, and the Illicit Drug Industry." *Journal of Criminal Law and Criminology* 86, no. 1 (Fall 1995): 10–36.

Blumstein, Alfred, and Richard Rosenfeld. "Explaining Recent Trends in U.S. Homicide Rates." *Journal of Criminal Law and Criminology* 88 (1998): 1175–1216.

Blumstein, Alfred, and Joel Wallman, eds. *The Crime Drop in America.* New York: Cambridge University Press, 2000.

Bonczar, Thomas P., and Tracy L. Snell. "Capital Punishment 2004." Bureau of Justice Statistics Bulletin, U.S. Department of Justice, November 2005.

Bonwick, Colin. *The American Revolution.* Charlottesville: University of Virginia Press, 1991.

Borden, Morton, ed. *The Anti-Federalist Papers.* East Lansing: Michigan State University Press, 1965.

Boyle, Kevin. *Arc of Justice: A Saga of Race, Civil Rights, and Murder in the Jazz Age.* New York: Henry Holt, 2004.

Brace, Charles Loring. *The Dangerous Classes of New York, and Twenty Years' Work among Them.* New York: Wynkoop & Hallenbeck, 1872.

Braithwaite, John. *Crime, Shame, and Reintegration.* New York: Cambridge University Press, 1989.

Brearley, H. C. *Homicide in the United States.* Chapel Hill: University of North Carolina Press, 1932.

Brecher, Edward M. "Drug Laws and Drug Enforcement: A Review and Evaluation Based on 111 Years of Experience." In *Perspectives on Drug Use in the United States,* edited by Bernard Segal. Binghamton, N.Y.: Haworth Press, 1986.

Brewer, David J., ed. *The World's Best Orations: From the Earliest Period to the Present Time.* Vol. 8. St. Louis: Kaiser, 1899.

Brown, Richard Maxwell. *Strain of Violence: Historical Studies of American Violence and Vigilantism.* New York: Oxford University Press, 1975.

———. *No Duty to Retreat: Violence and Values in American History and Society.* New York: Oxford University Press, 1991.

Brumberg, Joan Jacobs. *Kansas Charley: The Story of a Nineteenth-Century Boy Murderer.* New York: Viking, 2003.

Bugliosi, Vincent, with Curt Gentry. *Helter Skelter: The True Story of the Manson Murders.* New York: Norton, 1974.

Burrough, Bryan. *Public Enemies: America's Greatest Crime Wave and the Birth of the FBI, 1933–34.* New York: Penguin, 2004.

Bush, George W. Radio Address. September 15, 2001. Available online. URL: http://www.whitehouse.gov/news/releases/2001/09/20010915.html. Accessed on July 6, 2006

Butler, Lindley S., and Alan D. Watson, eds. *The North Carolina Experience: An Interpretive and Documentary History.* Chapel Hill: University of North Carolina Press, 1984.

Butterfield, Fox. *All God's Children: The Bosket Family and the American Tradition of Violence.* New York: William Morrow, 1995.

Buzawa, Eve S., and Carl G. Buzawa. *Domestic Violence: The Changing Criminal Justice Response.* Westport, Conn.: Auburn House, 1992.

Cannon, Lou. *Official Negligence: How Rodney King and the Riots Changed Los Angeles and the LAPD.* Boulder, Colo.: Westview Press, 1997.

Carte, Gene E., and Elaine H. Carte. *Police Reform in the United States: The Era of August Vollmer, 1905–1932.* Berkeley: University of California Press, 1975.

Chafe, William H. *The Unfinished Journey: America since World War II.* 5th ed. New York: Oxford University Press, 2003.

Chafe, William H., and Harvard Sitkoff, eds. *A History of Our Time: Readings on Postwar America.* 5th ed. New York: Oxford University Press, 1999.

Chambers, John Whiteclay, II. *The Tyranny of Change: American in the Progressive Era, 1890–1920.* 2d ed. New Brunswick, N.J.: Rutgers University Press, 2000.

Champlain, Samuel de. *The Voyages and Explorations of Samuel de Champlain, 1604–1616.* Translated by Annie Nettleton Bourne. Vol. 1. 1632. New York: Allerton, 1922.

Chase, Alston. *Harvard and the Unabomber: The Education of an American Terrorist.* New York: W.W. Norton, 2003.

Chernow, Ron. *Alexander Hamilton.* New York: Penguin Books, 2004.

Chudacoff, Howard P., and Judith E. Smith. *The Evolution of American Urban Society.* 5th ed. Upper Saddle River, N.J.: Prentice Hall, 2000.

Christianson, Scott. *With Liberty for Some: 500 Years of Imprisonment in America.* Boston: Northeastern University Press, 1998.

Christopher, Warren, ed. *Report of the Independent Commission on the Los Angeles Police Department.* Los Angeles: The Commission, 1991.

Churchill, Winston S. *Never Give In! The Best of Winston Churchill s Speeches.* New York: Hyperion. 2003.

Cimbala, Paul A., and Randall Miller. *Union Soldiers and the Northern Home Front: Wartime Experiences, Postwar Adjustments.* New York: Fordham University Press, 2002.

CNN. O. J. Simpson Trial Transcripts. January 31, 1995. TRNO 6-5.

———. "Transcript: Bin Laden Determined to Strike in U.S." Available online. URL: http://www.cnn.com/2004/ALLPOLITIC/04/10/august6.memo. Accessed on July 6, 2006.

Cohen, Andrew Wender. *The Racketeer's Progress: Chicago and the Struggle for the Modern American Economy, 1900–1940.* Cambridge: Cambridge University Press, 2004.

Cohen, Patricia Cline. *The Murder of Helen Jewett: The Life and Death of a Prostitute in Nineteenth-Century New York.* New York: Vintage Books, 1998.

Colvin, Mark. *Penitentiaries, Reformatories, and Chain Gangs: Social Theory and the History of Punishment in Nineteenth-Century America.* New York: St. Martin's Press, 1997.

"The Comics Code." *Lambiek's Comiclopedia.* Available online. URL: http://www.lambiek.net/comics/code_text.htm. Accessed on May 18, 2007.

Cook, Philip J., and John H. Laub. "The Unprecedented Epidemic in Youth Violence." In *Crime and Justice: An Annual Review of Research,* vol. 24, *Youth Violence,* edited by Michael Tonry and Mark H. Moore. Chicago: University of Chicago Press, 1998.

Cornelius, Janet Duitsman. *When I Can Read My Title Clear: Literacy, Slavery, and Religion in the Antebellum South.* Columbia: University of South Carolina Press, 1991.

Courtwright, David T. *Violent Land: Single Men and Social Disorder from the Frontier to the Inner City.* Cambridge, Mass.: Harvard University Press, 1996.

Cunningham, David. "Understanding State Responses to Left- versus Right-Wing Threats: The FBI's Repression of the New Left and the Ku Klux Klan." *Social Science History* 27, no. 3 (Fall 2003): 327–371.

Custer, George. "My Life on the Plains." *Galaxy,* April 1872, 473–474.

Darrow, Clarence S. *Resist Not Evil.* 1902. Reprint, Montclair, N.J.: Patterson Smith, 1972.

Davis, Angela Y. *Are Prisons Obsolete?* New York: Seven Stories Press, 2003.

Davis, Mike. *City of Quartz: Excavating the Future in Los Angeles.* 1990. Reprint. New York: Vintage Books, 1992.

Davis, Jefferson. "Second Inaugural Address," February 22, 1862. Jefferson Davis Documents, Rice University. Available online. URL: http://jeffersondavis.rice. edu/docs.cfm. Accessed on May 31, 2007.

Death Penalty Information Center, State-by-State Information for California. Available online. URL: "http://www.deathpenaltyinfo.org/state" www.deathpenalty-info.org/state. Accessed on May 29, 2007.

Denbeaux, Mark, and Joshua Denbeaux. *Report on Guantanamo Detainees: A Profile of 517 Detainees through Analysis of Department of Defense Data.* South Orange, N.J.: Seton Hall University Press, 2006.

Deparle, Jason. "Executions Aren't News." *Washington Monthly* (March 1986).

Dickens, Charles. *Bleak House.* 1853. Reprint, New York: Charles Scribner's Sons, 1911.

———. *The Letters of Charles Dickens.* 12 vols. Edited by Madeline House, Graham Story, and Kathleen Tillotson. Oxford: Clarendon Press, 1974.

DiIulio, John J., Jr. "The Coming of the Super-Predators." *The Weekly Standard* 1 (November 27, 1995).

Dix, Dorothea. "Memorial to the Massachusetts Legislature." 1843. USINFO at the U.S. Department of State. Available online. URL: http://usinfo.state.gov/usa/infousa/facts/democrac/15.htm. Accessed on May 17, 2007.

Dodge, L. Mara. "'Our Juvenile Court Has Become More Like a Criminal Court': A Century of Reform at the Cook County (Chicago) Juvenile Court." *Michigan Historical Review* 26 (Fall 2000): 51–89.

———. *Whores and Thieves of the Worst Kind: A Study of Women, Crime, and Prisons, 1835– 2000.* DeKalb: Northern Illinois University Press, 2002.

Domanick, Joe. *To Protect and to Serve: The LAPD's Century of War in the City of Dreams.* New York: Pocket Books, 1994.

Donaldson, Greg. *The Ville: Cops and Kids in Urban America.* New York: Anchor Books, 1994.

Donziger, Steven R., ed. *The Real War on Crime: The Report of the National Criminal Justice Commission.* New York: Harper Perrenial, 1996.

Douglass, Frederick. *Narrative of the Life of Frederick Douglass, An American Slave, Written by Himself.* 1845. Reprint, Boston: Bedford/St. Martin's, 1993.

Drucker, Ernest. "Population Impact of Mass Incarceration under New York's Rockefeller Drug Laws," *Journal of Urban Health: Bulletin of the New York Academy of Medicine* (September 2002).

Dugdale, Richard L. *The Jukes: A Study in Crime, Pauperism, Disease, and Heredity.* 4th ed. New York: G. P. Putnam's Sons, 1877. Reprint, New York: Arno Press, 1970.

Dulaney, W. Marvin. *Black Police in America.* Bloomington: Indiana University Press, 1996.

Dyer, Joel. *Harvest of Rage: Why Oklahoma City Is Only the Beginning.* Boulder, Colo.: Westview Press, 1997.

Eartherly, Billy J. "Drug-Law Enforcement: Should We Arrest Pushers or Users?" *Journal of Political Economy* 82, no. 1 (January–February 1974): 210–214.

Eckberg, Douglas Lee. "Estimates of Early Twentieth-Century U.S. Homicide Rates: An Econometric Forecasting Approach." *Demography* 32, no. 1 (February 1995): 1–16.

———. "Stalking the Elusive Homicide: A Capture-Recapture Approach to the Estimation of Post-Reconstruction South Carolina Killings." *Social Science History* 25 (Spring 2001): 67–92.

Ellis, Joseph J. *Founding Brothers: The Revolutionary Generation.* New York: Vintage, 2000.

Erlen, Jonathon, and Joseph F. Spillane, eds. *Federal Drug Control: The Evolution of Policy and Practice.* Binghamton, N.Y.: Pharmaceutical Products Press, 2004.

Escobar, Edward J. *Race, Police, and the Making of a Political Identity: Mexican Americans and the Los Angeles Police Department, 1900–1945.* Berkeley: University of California Press, 1999.

Fairclough, Adam. *Better Day Coming: Blacks and Equality, 1890–2000.* New York: Penguin Books, 2001.

Faragher, John Mack, Mari Jo Buhle, Daniel Czitrom, and Susan H. Armitage. *Out of Many: A History of the American People.* 4th ed. Upper Saddle River, N.J.: Pearson Prentice Hall, 2003.

———. *Out of Many: A History of the American People.* 5th ed. Upper Saddle River, N.J.: Pearson Prentice Hall, 2006.

Fass, Paula. "Finding History in Woodside, California." In *American Places: Encounters with History,* ed. William E. Leuchtenberg. Oxford: Oxford University Press, 2000.

Faulds, Henry. *Guide to Finger-Print Identification.* Hanley, U.K.: Wood, Mitchell, and Co., 1905.

Federal Bureau of Investigation. *Crime in the United States.* Published annually. Washington, D.C.: Federal Bureau of Investigation, U.S. Department of Justice, 1998–2003.

———. "Famous Cases: Bonnie and Clyde," Available online. URL: http://www.fbi.gov/libref/historic/famcases/clyde/clyde.htm. Accessed on May 18, 2007.

———. *Hate Crime Statistics.* Published annually. Washington, D.C.: Federal Bureau of Investigation, U.S. Department of Justice, 1992–2003.

———. *Terrorism in the United States.* Washington, D.C.: Federal Bureau of Investigation, U.S. Department of Justice, 2000/2001.

———. *Uniform Crime Reports.* Published annually. Washington, D.C.: Federal Bureau of Investigation, U.S. Department of Justice, 1930–1997.

The Federalist Papers. New York: New American Library, 1961.

Feld, Barry C. *Bad Kids: Race and the Transformation of the Juvenile Court.* New York: Oxford University Press, 1999.

Flamm, Michael F. *Law and Order: Street Crime, Civil Disorder, and the Crisis of Liberalism.* New York: Columbia University Press, 2005.

Fogelson, Robert M. *Big-City Police.* Cambridge, Mass.: Harvard University Press, 1977.

Foner, Eric. *Reconstruction: America's Unfinished Revolution, 1863–1877.* New York: Harper & Row, 1988.

Foucault, Michel. *Discipline and Punish: The Birth of the Prison.* Translated by Alan Sheridan. New York: Vintage, 1979.

The Founders Constitution. University of Chicago Press. Available online. URL: http://press-pubs.uchicago.edu/founders. Accessed on October 6, 2009.

Fox, James Alan, and Marianne W. Zawitz, "Homicide Trends in the United States." Bureau of Justice Statistics, September 2004. Available online. URL: http://www.ojp.usdoj.gov/bjs/homicide/homtrnd.htm. Updated on June 29, 2006.

Franklin, Benjamin. *The Works of Benjamin Franklin.* Edited by John Bigelow. New York: G.P. Putnam's Sons/The Knickerbocker Press, 1904.

Freedman, Estelle B. *Their Sisters' Keepers: Women's Prison Reform in America, 1830–1930.* Ann Arbor: University of Michigan Press, 1981.

———. *Maternal Justice: Miriam Van Waters and the Female Reform Tradition.* Chicago: University of Chicago Press, 1996.

Fried, Albert, ed. *McCarthyism: The Great American Red Scare: A Documentary History.* New York: Oxford University Press, 1997.

Friedman, Lawrence M. *Crime and Punishment in American History.* New York: Basic Books, 1993.

Friedman, Lawrence M., and Robert V. Percival. *The Roots of Justice: Crime and Punishment in Alameda County, California, 1870–1910.* Chapel Hill: University of North Carolina Press, 1981.

Fuld, Leonhard Felix. *Police Administration.* New York: G.P. Putnam's Sons, 1909.

Garland, David. *Punishment in Modern Society: A Study in Social Theory.* Chicago: University of Chicago Press, 1990.

———. *The Culture of Control: Crime and Social Order in Contemporary Society.* Chicago: University of Chicago Press, 2001.

Garraty, John A., and Mark C. Carnes, eds. *American National Biography.* 24 vols. New York: Oxford University Press, 1999.

Gatrell, V. A. C. *The Hanging Tree: Execution and the English People, 1770–1868.* New York: Oxford University Press, 1994.

Geis, Gilbert, and Leigh B. Bienen. *Crimes of the Century: From Leopold and Loeb to O. J. Simpson.* Boston: Northeastern University Press, 1998.

Getis, Victoria. *The Juvenile Court and the Progressives.* Urbana and Chicago: University of Illinois Press, 2000.

Gilbert, James. *A Cycle of Outrage: America's Reaction to the Juvenile Delinquent in the 1950s.* New York: Oxford University Press, 1986.

Gilfoyle, Timothy J. *City of Eros: New York City, Prostitution, and the Commercialization of Sex, 1790–1920.* New York: W.W. Norton, 1992.

———. "Street-Rats and Gutter-Snipes: Child Pickpockets and Street Culture in New York City, 1850–1900." *Journal of Social History* 37 (Summer 2004): 853–882.

Gish, Clay. "Rescuing the 'Waifs and Strays' of the City: The Western Emigration Programs of the Children's Aid Society." *Journal of Social History* 33, no. 1 (Fall 1999): 121–142.

Gissel, Richard. *Digital Underworld: Computer Crime and Resulting Issues.* Scottsdale, Ariz. MacroTech Press, 2005.

Gitlin, Todd. *The Sixties: Years of Hope, Days of Rage.* New York: Bantam Books, 1987.

Goldfield, David, Carl Abbott, Virginia DeJohn Anderson, Jo Ann E. Argersinger, Peter H. Argersinger, William L. Barney, and Robert M. Weir. *The American Journey: A History of American People.* 4th ed. Upper Saddle River, N.J.: Pearson Prentice Hall, 2007.

Gordon, Linda. *Heroes of Their Own Lives: The Politics and History of Family Violence: Boston, 1880–1960.* New York: Viking, 1988.

Gorn, Elliott J. "'Good-Bye Boys, I Die a True American': Homicide, Nativism, and Working-Class Culture in Antebellum New York City." *Journal of American History* 74, no. 2 (September 1987): 388–410.

Gourley, G. Douglas. "Police Public Relations." *Annals of the American Academy of Political and Social Science* 291 (January 1954): 135–142.

Graebner, William. *Coming of Age in Buffalo: Youth and Authority in the Postwar Era.* Philadelphia: Temple University Press, 1990.

Greenberg, Kenneth S., ed. *The Confessions of Nat Turner and Related Documents.* Boston: Bedford/St. Martin's, 1996.

Gregory, Thomas Watt. "The Annual Report of the Attorney General of the United States to the Senate and House of Representatives." December 4, 1917.

Hall, David D. *The Antinomian Controversy, 1636–1638: A Documentary History.* Durham, N.C.: Duke University Press, 1990.

Haller, Mark H. "Urban Crime and Criminal Justice: The Chicago Case." *Journal of American History* 57, no. 3 (December 1970): 619–635.

———. "Civic Reformers and Police Leadership: Chicago, 1905–1935." In *Police in Urban Society,* ed. Harlan Hahn, 39–56. Beverly Hills, Calif.: Sage Publications, 1971.

———. "Organized Crime in Urban Society: Chicago in the Twentieth Century." *Journal of Social History* 5, no. 2 (Winter 1971–72): 210–234.

———. "Urban Vice and Civic Reform: Chicago in the Early Twentieth Century." In *Cities in American History,* ed. Kenneth T. Jackson and Stanley K Schultz, 290–305. New York: Alfred K. Knopf, 1972.

———. "Historical Roots of Police Behavior: Chicago, 1890–1925." *Law and Society Review* 10, no. 2 (1976): 303–323.

Hamilton, Jeanne. "The Nunnery as Menace." Eternal Word Television Network Libraries. 1996. Available online. URL: http://www.ewtn.com/library/HUMAN ITY/BURNING.TXT. Accessed on May 18, 2007.

Hart, Hastings H., ed. *Juvenile Court Laws in the United States.* New York: Charities Publication Committee, 1910.

Hawes, Joseph M. *Children in Urban Society: Juvenile Delinquency in Nineteenth-Century America.* New York: Oxford University Press, 1971.

Hening, William Waller. *Statutes at Large: Being a Collection of All the Laws of Virginia from the First Session of the Legislature in the Year 1619.* Vol. 3 Philadelphia 1823.

Herivel, Tara, and Paul Wright. *Prison Nation: The Warehousing of America's Poor.* New York: Routledge, 2003.

Hindus, Michael S. *Prison and Plantation: Crime, Justice, and Authority in Massachusetts and South Carolina, 1767–1878.* Chapel Hill: University of North Carolina Press, 1980.

Hine, Thomas. *The Rise and Fall of the American Teenager.* New York: Perennial, 1999.

Hinton, Paula K. "'The Unspeakable Mrs. Gunness': The Deviant Woman in Early-Twentieth-Century America." In *Lethal Imagination: Violence and Brutality in American History,* ed. Michael A. Bellesiles. New York: New York University Press, 1999.

Hobbes, Thomas. *Leviathan.* Edited with an introduction by J. C. A. Gaskin. 1660. New York: Oxford University Press, 1996.

Hoffman, Frederick L. *Race Traits of the American Negro.* New York: The Macmillan Company, 1896.

Hofstadter, Richard, and Michael Wallace, eds. *American Violence: A Documentary History.* New York: Vintage Books, 1970.

Holt, Marilyn Irvin. *The Orphan Trains: Placing Out in America.* Lincoln: University of Nebraska Press, 1994.

Hoover, J. Edgar. "Wild Children." *American Magazine* 136 (July 1943), 40–41, 103–105.

House Committee on Un-American Activities. *Hearings on H.R. 1884 and H.R. 2122.* 80th Congress, 1st Session. March 26, 1947.

Horowitz, Daniel, ed. *Jimmy Carter and the Energy Crisis of the 1970s: A Brief History with Documents.* Boston: Bedford/St. Martin's, 2005.

Hoxie, Frederick E. ed. *Encyclopedia of North American Indians.* New York: Houghton Mifflin, 1996.

Hurley, Dan. "Cycles of Craving: Society's Drugs of Choice Appear to Come in Waves: LSD and Marijuana, Cocaine, Now Crack." *Psychology Today* (July/August 1989).

Hurley, Timothy D. *Origin of the Illinois Juvenile Court Law: Juvenile Courts and What They Have Accomplished.* 3rd ed. Chicago: Visitation and Aid Society, 1907.

Illinois Association for Criminal Justice. *The Illinois Crime Survey.* 1929. Reprint. Montclair, N.J.: Patterson-Smith, 1968.

Illinois Coalition against Domestic Violence. "Illinois Domestic Violence Act of 1986." Available online. URL: http://www.ilcadv.org. Accessed on May 18, 2007.

"The Inflation Calculator." Available online. URL: http://www.westegg.com/inflation. Accessed on May 2, 2007.

Internet Movie Database. Available online. URL: http://www.imbd.com. Updated on May 29, 2007.

Jackson, Bruce. "Attica: An Anniversary of Death." *Artvoice* (September 9, 1999). Available online. URL: http://www.acsu.buffalo.edu/~bjackson/attica.htm. Accessed on May 18, 2007.

Jameson, J. Franklin, ed. *Narratives of New Netherland, 1609–1664.* New York: Charles Scribner's Sons, 1909. Project Gutenberg. Available online. URL: http://www.gutenberg.org/etext/3161. Accesssed on June 30, 2008.

Jefferson, Thomas. *Notes on the State of Virginia,* 1785. The Electronic Text Center at the University of Virginia Library. Available online. URL: http://etext.lib.virginia.edu/toc/modeng/public/JefVirg.html. Accessed on May 18, 2007.

———. *The Papers of Thomas Jefferson, Volume 11: January 1787 to August 1787.* Edited by Julian P. Boyd. Princeton, N.J.: Princeton University Press, 1955.

Jennings, Dean. "Portrait of a Police Chief." *Saturday Evening Post* (May 7, 1960), 44–45, 86–89.

Johnson, David R. *Policing the Urban Underworld: The Impact of Crime on the Development of the American Police, 1800–1887.* Philadelphia: Temple University Press, 1979.

———. *American Law Enforcement: A History.* St. Louis, Mo.: Forum Press, 1981.

———. *Illegal Tender: Counterfeiting and the Secret Service in Nineteenth Century America.* Washington, D.C.: Smithsonian Institution Press, 1995.

Johnson, John W., ed. *Historic U.S. Court Cases: An Encyclopedia.* Vol. 1. London: Routledge, 2001.

Johnson, Marilynn S. *Street Justice: A History of Police Violence in New York City.* Boston: Beacon Press, 2003.

Jonnes, Jill. *Hep-Cats, Narcs, and Pipe Dreams: A History of America's Romance with Illegal Drugs.* New York: Scribner, 1996.

Kelling, George L., and Catherine M. Coles. *Fixing Broken Windows: Restoring Order and Reducing Crime in Our Communities.* New York: Free Press, 1996.

Kennedy, David M. *Freedom from Fear: The American People in Depression and War, 1929–1945.* New York: Oxford University Press, 1999.

Kennedy, Randall. *Race, Crime, and the Law.* New York: Vintage, 1998.

Kessler, Ronald. *The Bureau: The Secret History of the FBI.* New York: St. Martin's Press, 2003.

Kleiner, Carolyn. "The Demon of Andersonville." *Legal Affairs* (September/October 2002). Available online. URL: http://www.legalaffairs.org/printerfriendly.msp?id=247. Accessed on May 31, 2007.

Kohler, Fred J. "Arrests of First Offenders," *International Association of Chiefs of Police, 15th Annual Session,* Detroit, Michigan, June 2–5, 1908; reprinted in *Proceedings of the Annual Conventions of the International Association of Chiefs of Police,* 1906–1912, Vol. 2 (New York: Arno Press, 1971), 30–32.

Lane, Roger. *Policing the City: Boston, 1822–1885.* Cambridge, Mass.: Harvard University Press, 1967.

———. *Violent Death in the City: Suicide, Accident, and Murder in Nineteenth-Century Philadelphia.* 2nd ed. 1979; Columbus: Ohio State University Press, 1999.

————. *Roots of Violence in Black Philadelphia. 1860–1900.* Cambridge, Mass.: Harvard University Press, 1986.

————. *Murder in America: A History.* Columbus: Ohio State University Press, 1997.

Larson, Erik. *The Devil in the White City: Murder, Magic, and Madness at the Fair That Changed America.* New York: Crown Publishers, 2003.

Lawrence, Regina G. *The Politics of Force: Media and the Construction of Police Brutality.* Berkeley: University of California Press, 2001.

LeClaire, Jennifer. "Symantec Report: Cybercrime on the Rise." *E-Commerce Times* (March 7, 2006). Available online. URL: http://www.ecommercetimes.com/story/49225.html. Accessed on May 12, 2007.

Leete, Hon. John B. "Treatment and Rehabilitation or Hard Time: Is the Focus of Juvenile Justice Changing?" *Akron Law Review* 29, no. 3 (Spring 1996): 491–508.

Lemann, Nicholas. *Redemption: The Last Battle of the Civil War.* New York: Farrar, Straus and Giroux, 2006.

Leyden, John. "Blaster Worm Spreading Rapidly." *The Register* (August 12, 2003).

Leyton, Elliott. *Hunting Humans: The Rise of the Modern Multiple Murderer.* New York: Carroll & Graf, 2003.

Lincoln, Abraham. Letter to General Winfield Scott, April 27, 1861. TeachingAmericanHistory.org. Available online. URL: http://teachingamericanhistory.org/library/index.asp?document=414. Accessed on May 31, 2007.

Linder, Douglas, ed. *Famous Trials: Illinois v. Nathan Leopold and Richard Loeb.* Available online. URL: http://www.law.umkc.edu/faculty/projects/ftrials/leoploeb/leopold.htm. Accessed on May 19, 2007.

————. *Famous American Trials: Los Angeles Police Officers' (Rodney King Beating) Trials, 1992 and 1993.* Available online. URL: http://www.law.umkc.edu/faculty/projects/ftrials/lapd/lapd.html. Accessed on May 16, 2007.

————. *Famous American Trials: The O. J. Simpson Trial.* Available online. URL: http://www.law.umkc.edu/faculty/projects/ftrials/Simpson/simpson.htm. Accessed on May 19, 2007.

————. *Famous Trials: The 'Chicago Seven' Trial.* Available online. URL: http://www.law.umkc.edu/faculty/projects/ftrials/Chicago7/chicago7.html. Accessed on March 14, 2006.

————. *Famous Trials: The Rosenberg Trial.* Available online. URL: http://www.law.umkc.edu/faculty/projects/ftrials/rosenb/ROSENB.HTM. Accessed on July 6, 2008.

————. *Famous American Trials: The "Scottsboro Boys" Trial.* Available online. URL: http://www.law.umkc.edu/faculty/projects/FTrials/scottsboro/scottsb.htm. Accessed on May 19, 2007.

————. *Famous Trials: The Trial of Lizzie Borden.* Available online. URL: http://www.law.umkc.edu/faculty/projects/ftrials/Lizzie Borden/bordenhome.html. Accessed on July 6, 2008.

————. *Famous Trials: The Trial of Sacco and Vanzetti.* Available online. URL: http://www.law.umkc.edu/faculty/projects/ftrials/SaccoV/SaccoV.htm. Accessed on May 18, 2007.

Lindsey, Ben B. "The Reformation of Juvenile Delinquents through the Juvenile Court." In *Children's Courts in the United States: Their Origin, Development, and Results,* ed. Samuel J. Barrow. Washington, D.C.: U.S. Government Printing Office, 1904.

Lindberg, Richard C. *To Serve and Collect: Chicago Politics and Police Corruption from the Lager Beer Riot to the Summerdale Scandal, 1855–1960.* 1991. Reprint, Carbondale: Southern Illinois University Press, 1998.

Linebaugh, Peter. *The London Hanged: Crime and Civil Society in the Eighteenth Century.* Cambridge: Cambridge University Press, 1992.

Liss, Julia, and Steven Schlossman. "The Contours of Crime Prevention in August Vollmer's Berkeley." *Research in Law, Deviance, and Social Control* 6 (1984): 79–107.

Littleton Police Department. Littleton, Colorado. Columbine Files.

Locke, John. *Second Treatise of Government: An Essay Concerning the True Original, Extent and End of Civil Government,* edited by Richard Cox. 1690. Reprint, Arlington Heights, Ill.: Harlan Davidson, 1982.

Lorence, James J., ed. *Enduring Voices.* Volume 2: From 1865. Boston: Houghton Mifflin, 2000.

Lubet, Steven. "Slap Leather! Legal Culture, Wild Bill Hickock, and the Gunslinger Myth." *UCLA Law Review* 48, no. 6 (2001): 1545–1556.

Mack, Julian W. "The Juvenile Court." *Harvard Law Review* 23 (December 1909–10): 104–122.

Maguire, Mark, Rod Morgan, and Robert Reiner, eds. *The Oxford Handbook of Criminology.* New York: Oxford University Press, 2002.

Main, Jackson Turner. *The Antifederalists: Critics of the Constitution, 1781–1788.* 1961; Chapel Hill: University of North Carolina Press, 2004.

Mano, D. Keith. "The Goetz Confession." *National Review* (May 13, 1988).

Martinez, Ramiro. *Latino Homicide: Immigration, Violence, and Community.* New York: Routledge, 2002.

Massachusetts, Colony of. "Massachusetts Body of Liberties," 1641. Hanover Historical Texts Project. Available online. URL: http://history.hanover.edu/texts/masslib.html. Accessed on May 19, 2007.

Massaquoi, Hans J. "How to Stop Police Brutality." *Ebony* (July 1991), p. 58.

Masur, Louis P. *Rites of Execution: Capital Punishment and the Transformation of American Culture, 1776–1865.* New York: Oxford University Press, 1991.

Mauer, Marc. *Race to Incarcerate.* New York: New Press, 2001.

Mauer, Marc, and Meda Chesney-Lind, eds. *Invisible Punishment: The Collateral Consequences of Mass Imprisonment.* New York: New Press, 2003.

"McCarthy-Welch Exchange," 1954. *American Rhetoric.* Available online. URL: http://www.americanrhetoric.com/speeches/welch-mccarthy.html. Accessed on July 6, 2008.

McElrath, Jessica. "The Black Codes of 1865." About.com: African-American History. Available online. URL: http://afroamhistory.about.com/od/blackcodes/a/blackcodes1865.htm. Accessed on May 31, 2007.

McGerr, Michael. *A Fierce Discontent: The Rise and Fall of the Progressive Movement in America, 1870–1920.* New York: Free Press, 2003.

McGrath, Roger D. *Gunfighters, Highwaymen, and Vigilantes: Violence on the Frontier.* Berkeley: University of California Press, 1984.

McKelvey, Blake. *American Prisons: A History of Good Intentions.* Montclair, N.J.: Patterson Smith, 1977.

McLennan, Rebecca. "Punishment's 'Square Deal': Prisoners and Their Keepers in 1920s New York." *Journal of Urban History* 29, no. 5 (July 2003): 597–619.

McShane, Marilyn D., and Frank P. Williams III, eds. *Encyclopedia of American Prisons.* New York: Garland Publishing, 1996.

McWilliams, Peter. *Ain't Nobody's Business If You Do: The Absurdity of Consensual Crimes in Our Free Country.* Los Angeles: Prelude Press, 1996.

McNamee, Gwen Hoerr, ed. *A Noble Social Experiment? The First 100 Years of Cook County Juvenile Court, 1899–1999.* Chicago: Chicago Bar Association, 1999.

Mennel, Robert M. *Thorns and Thistles: Juvenile Delinquents in the United States, 1825–1940.* Hanover, N.H.: University Press of New England, 1973.

Meranze, Michael. *Laboratories of Virtue: Punishment, Revolution, and Authority in Pennsylvania, 1760–1835.* Chapel Hill: University of North Carolina Press, 1996.

Metz, Leon Claire. *John Wesley Hardin: Dark Angel of Texas.* Norman: University of Oklahoma Press, 1998.

Miethe, Terance D., and Wendy C. Regoeczi. *Rethinking Homicide: Exploring the Structure and Process Underlying Deadly Situations.* New York: Cambridge University Press, 2004.

Miller, Jerome G. *Search and Destroy: African-American Males in the Criminal Justice System.* New York: Cambridge University Press, 1996.

Miller, Kent S., and Betty Davis Miller. *To Kill and Be Killed: Case Studies from Florida's Death Row.* St. Louis, Mo.: Hope Publishing, 1989.

Miller, Nathan. *New World Coming: The 1920s and the Making of Modern America.* New York: Simon & Schuster, 2003.

Miller, Rick. *Sam Bass & Gang.* Austin, Tex.: State House Press, 1999.

Miller, Wilbur R. *Cops and Bobbies: Police Authority in New York and London, 1830–1870.* 2nd ed. Columbus: Ohio State University Press, 1999.

Minton, Robert J., ed. *Inside: Prison American Style.* New York: Random House, 1971.

Mississippi, State of. "An Act to Confer Civil Rights on Freedman, and for Other Purposes" (The Mississippi Black Codes). November 25, 1865. About.com African-American History. Available online. URL: http://afroamhistory.about.com/library/blmississippi_blackcodes.htm. Accessed on May 18, 2007.

Monkkonen, Eric H. *Police in Urban America, 1850–1920.* Cambridge: Cambridge University Press, 1981.

———. *America Becomes Urban: The Development of U.S. Cities and Towns, 1780–1980.* Berkeley: University of California Press, 1988.

———. *Crime, Justice, History.* Columbus: Ohio State University Press, 2002.

———. *Murder in New York City.* Berkeley: University of California Press, 2001.

Montesquieu, Charles de. *The Spirit of the Laws.* 1748. Translated by Thomas Nugent. 1748. Reprint, London: G. Bell and Sons, 1914.

Morris, Norval, and David J. Rothman, eds. *The Oxford History of the Prison: The Practice of Punishment in Western Society.* New York: Oxford University Press, 1998.

Morris, Thomas D. *Free Men All: The Personal Liberty Laws of the North, 1780–1861.* Baltimore: Johns Hopkins University Press, 1974.

Musto, David F. *The American Disease: Origins of Narcotic Control.* Expanded ed. New York: Oxford University Press, 1987.

Nabokov, Peter, ed. *Native American Testimony: A Chronicle of Indian-White Relations from Prophecy to the Present, 1492–1992.* New York: Penguin, 1992.

Nash, Jay Robert. *Encyclopedia of World Crime: Criminal Justice, Criminology, and Law Enforcement.* 6 vols. Wilmette, Ill.: CrimeBooks, Inc., 1990.

———. *Bloodletters and Badmen: A Narrative Encyclopedia of American Criminals from the Pilgrims to the Present.* New York: M. Evans and Company, 1995.

The National Archives Experience. "Declaration of Independence" (1776). Available online. URL: http://www.archives.gov/national_archives_experience/charters/declaration.html. Accessed on June 30, 2008.

National Center for Health Statistics. *Vital Statistics of the United States.* Published annually. Washington, D.C., 1890–2003.

National Commission on Law Observance and Enforcement [Wickersham Commission]. *Report No. 11: Report on Lawlessness in Law Enforcement.* Washington, D.C.: U.S. Government Printing Office, 1931; Reprint, Montclair, N.J.: Patterson Smith, 1968.

————. *Report No. 14: Report on Police.* Washington, D.C.: U.S. Government Printing Office, 1931; Reprint, Montclair, N.J.: Patterson Smith, 1968.

National Commission on Terrorist Attacks Upon the United States. *The 9/11 Commission Report.* New York: Norton, 2004.

National Research Council and Institute of Medicine. *Juvenile Crime, Juvenile Justice.* Joan McCord, Cathy Spatz Widon, Nancy A. Crowell, eds. Committee on Law and Justice and Board on Children, Youth, and Families. Washington, D.C.: National Academy Press, 2001.

Neely, Mark E., Jr. *The Fate of Liberty: Abraham Lincoln and Civil Liberties.* New York: Oxford University Press, 1991.

Newton, Michael. *The Encyclopedia of Kidnappings.* New York: Facts On File, 2002.

"New York Draft Riots." Home of the American Civil War. Available online. URL: http://www.civilwarhome.com/draftriots.htm. Accessed on May 31, 2007.

Nickerson, Catherine Ross. "'The Deftness of Her Sex': Innocence, Guilt, and Gender in the Trial of Lizzie Borden." In *Lethal Imagination: Violence and Brutality in American History,* ed. Michael A. Bellesiles. New York: New York University Press, 1999.

Norris, Joel. *Serial Killers.* New York: Anchor, 1989.

Nussbaum, Martha. *Hiding from Humanity: Disgust, Shame, and the Law.* Princeton, N.J.: Princeton University Press, 2004.

O'Bryant, JoAnne. "Crime Control: The Federal Response." Congressional Research Service, March 5, 2003.

Odem, Mary E. *Delinquent Daughters: Protecting and Policing Adolescent Female Sexuality in the United States, 1885–1920.* Chapel Hill: University of North Carolina Press, 1995.

Oklahoma City National Memorial Website. Available online. URL: http://www.oklahomacitynationalmemorial.org. Accessed on May 12, 2007.

Oliver, Willard M., and James F. Hilgenberg, Jr. *A History of Crime and Criminal Justice in America.* Boston: Pearson, 2006.

Osborne, Thomas Mott. *Within Prison Walls: Being a Narrative of Personal Experience during a Week of Voluntary Confinement in the State Prison at Auburn, New York.* 1914. Reprint, New York: D. Appleton and Company, 1921.

Oshinsky, David M. *"Worse Than Slavery": Parchman Farm and the Ordeal of Jim Crow Justice.* New York: Free Press, 1996.

Otis, James. "Against the Writs of Assistance," February 24, 1761. Constitution Society Home Page Address. Available online. URL: http://www.constitution.org/bor/otis_against_writs.htm. Accessed on October 6, 2009.

Pagán, Eduardo Obregón. *Murder at the Sleepy Lagoon: Zoot Suits, Race, and Riot in Wartime L.A.* Chapel Hill: University of North Carolina Press, 2003.

Paine, Thomas. *Common Sense.* 1776. New York: Penguin Books, 1986.

Parry, J. H. *The Audiencia of New Galicia in the Sixteenth Century: A Study in Spanish Colonial Government.* Cambridge: Cambridge University Press, 1948.

Pastore, Ann L., and Kathleen Maguire, eds. *Sourcebook of Criminal Justice Statistics, 2003.* U.S. Department of Justice, Bureau of Justice Statistics. Washington, D.C.: U.S. Government Printing Office, 2005. Also available online. URL: http://www.albany.edu/sourcebook/. Accessed on May 2, 2007.

Peabody, Selim H., ed. *American Patriotism: Speeches, Letters, and Other Papers Which Illustrate the Foundation, the Development, the Preservation of the United States of America.* New York: American Book Exchange, 1880.

Philadelphia in 1830–1: Or, a Brief Account of the Various Institutions and Public Objects in this Metropolis, forming a Complete Guide for Strangers and a Useful Compendium for the Inhabitants. Philadelphia: Carey and Hart, 1830.

Philpott, Thomas Lee. *The Slum and the Ghetto: Immigrants, Blacks, and Reformers in Chicago, 1880–1930.* 1978; Belmont, Calif.: Wadsworth, 1991.

Pisciotta, Alexander W. *Benevolent Repression: Social Control and the American Reformatory-Prison Movement.* New York: New York University Press, 1994.

Platt, Anthony M. *The Child Savers: The Invention of Delinquency.* 2nd ed. 1969; Chicago: University of Chicago, 1977.

Poe, Edgar Allan. "The Murders in the Rue Morgue." In *Tales.* New York: Wiley and Putnam, 1845.

Potter, Clair Bond. *War on Crime: Bandits, G-men, and the Politics of Mass Culture.* New Brunswick, N.J.: Rutgers University Press, 1998.

Powers, Edwin. *Crime and Punishment in Early Massachusetts, 1620–1692: A Documentary History.* Boston: Beacon Press, 1966.

Powers, Richard Gid. *Secrecy and Power: The Life of J. Edgar Hoover.* New York: Free Press, 1987.

President's Commission on Law Enforcement and Administration of Justice. *The Challenge of Crime in a Free Society.* Washington, D.C.: U.S. Government Printing Office, 1967.

President's Commission on Organized Crime. *America's Habit: Drug Abuse, Drug Trafficking, and Organized Crime.* Washington, D.C.: U.S. Government Printing Office, 1986.

President's Task Force on Victims of Crime. *Final Report, December 1982.* Washington, D.C.: U.S. Government Printing Office, 1982.

Prison Discipline Society (Boston, Massachusetts). *First Annual Report of the Board of Managers of the Prison Discipline Society.* Boston, 1826.

Quigley, Christine. *Skulls and Skeletons: Human Bone Collections and Accumulations.* Jefferson, N.C.: McFarland, 2001.

Rafter, Nicole Hahn. *Partial Justice: Women in State Prisons, 1800–1935.* Boston: Northeastern University Press, 1985.

———. *Creating Born Criminals.* Urbana: University of Illinois Press, 1997.

———. *Shots in the Mirror: Crime Films and Society.* New York: Oxford University Press, 2000.

Rauchway, Eric. *Murdering McKinley: The Making of Theodore Roosevelt's America.* New York: Hill & Wang, 2003.

Rand, Michael R., James P. Lynch, and David Cantor. "National Crime Victimization, 1973–95." U.S. Department of Justice, Office of Justice Programs, April 1997, NCJ-163069.

Reagan, Ronald. "Address to the Nation on the Campaign against Drug Abuse." September 14, 1986. Ronald Reagan Presidential Library. Available online. URL: http://www.reagan.utexas.edu/archives/speeches/1986/091486a.htm. Accessed on May 18, 2007.

Redfield, H. V. *Homicide, North and South: Being a Comparative View of Crime against the Person in Several Parts of the United States.* Introduction by Douglas Eckberg. 1880. Reprint. Columbus: Ohio State University Press, 2000.

Reiman, Jeffrey. *The Rich Get Richer and the Poor Get Prison: Ideology, Class, and Criminal Justice.* 7th ed. Boston: Allyn & Bacon, 2003.

Richardson, James F. *The New York Police: Colonial Times to 1901.* New York: Oxford University Press, 1970.

Rivera, Luis N. *A Violent Evangelism: The Political and Religious Conquest of the Americas.* Louisville, Ky.: Westminster John Knox Press, 1992.

Robertson, Stephen. *Crimes against Children: Sexual Violence and Legal Culture in New York City, 1880–1960.* Chapel Hill: University of North Carolina Press, 2005.

Roland, Charles P. *American Iliad: The Story of the Civil War.* Lexington: University Press of Kentucky, 2004.

Rosenheim, Margaret K., Franklin E. Zimring, David S. Tanenhaus, and Bernadine Dohrn, eds. *A Century of Juvenile Justice.* Chicago: University of Chicago Press, 2002.

Roth, Michael P. *Crime and Punishment: A History of the Criminal Justice System.* Belmont, Calif.: Thomson Wadsworth, 2005.

Rothman, David J. *The Discovery of the Asylum: Social Order and Disorder in the New Republic.* Boston: Little, Brown, 1971.

———. *Conscience and Convenience: The Asylum and Its Alternatives in Progressive America.* Boston: Little, Brown, 1980.

Rothman, Edgardo. "The Failure of Reform: United States, 1865–1965." In *The Oxford History of the Prison,* ed. Norval Morris and David J. Rothman, 151–177. New York: Oxford University Press, 1997.

Rousseau, Jean-Jacques. *A Discourse on Political Economy.* Translated by G. D. H. Cole. 1755. The Constitution Society. Available online. URL: http://www.constitution.org/jjr/polecon.htm. Accessed on May 18, 2007.

Rubenking, Janet. "IDentity Theft: What, Me Worry?" *PC Magazine* (March 2004).

Rush, Benjamin. "An Enquiry Into the Effects of Public Punishments Upon Criminals and Upon Society." In *Essays, Literary, Moral, and Philosophical.* Philadelphia: Thomas & Samuel F. Bradford, 1798.

Ruth, David E. *Inventing the Public Enemy: The Gangster in American Culture, 1918–1934.* Chicago: University of Chicago Press, 1996.

Salvatore, Nick. *Eugene V. Debs: Citizen and Socialist.* Urbana: University of Illinois Press, 1982.

Sampson, Robert J., and John H. Laub. *Crime in the Making: Pathways and Turning Points Through Life.* Cambridge, Mass.: Harvard University Press, 1993.

Sanders, Wiley Britton, ed. *Juvenile Offenders for a Thousand Years: Selected Readings from Anglo-Saxon Times to 1900.* Chapel Hill: University of North Carolina Press, 1970.

Sarat, Austin, ed. *The Killing State: Capital Punishment in Law, Politics, and Culture.* New York: Oxford University Press, 2001.

Saunders, Robert M. *In Search of Woodrow Wilson: Beliefs and Behavior.* Westport, Conn.: Greenwood Press, 1998.

Schaffer Library of Drug Policy. Available online. URL: http://www.druglibrary.org/schaffer/. Accessed on May 18, 2007.

Schechter, Susan. *Women and Male Violence: The Visions and Struggles of the Battered Women's Movement.* Boston: South End Press, 1982.

Scherini, Rose D. "When Italian Americans Were 'Enemy Aliens.'" In *Una Storia Segreta: The Secret History of Italian American Evacuation and Internment during World War II,* ed. Lawrence Distasi. Berkeley, Calif.: Heyday Books, 2001.

Schlosser, Eric. "The Prison-Industrial Complex." *The Atlantic Monthly* 282 (December 1998): 51–78.

Schlossman, Steven L. *Love and the American Delinquent: The Theory and Practice of "Progressive" Juvenile Justice, 1825–1920.* Chicago: University of Chicago Press, 1977. Republished as *Transforming Juvenile Justice: Reform Ideals and Institutional Realities, 1825–1920.* DeKalb: Northern Illinois University Press, 2005.

———. "The California Experience in Juvenile Justice: Some Historical Perspectives." Sacramento: California Bureau of Criminal Statistics, 1989.

Schlossman, Steven L., and Michael Sedlak. "The Chicago Area Project Revisited." *Crime and Delinquency* 26 (July 1983): 398–462.

Schlossman, Steven L., and Stephanie Wallach. "The Crime of Precocious Sexuality: Female Juvenile Delinquency in the Progressive Era." *Harvard Education Review* 48, no. 1 (February 1978): 65–94.

Schneider, Eric C. *In the Web of Class: Delinquents and Reformers in Boston, 1810s–1930s.* New York: New York University Press, 1992.

———. *Vampires, Dragons, and Egyptian Kings: Youth Gangs in Postwar New York.* Princeton, N.J.: Princeton University Press, 1999.

Schneider, John C. *Detroit and the Problem of Order, 1830–1880: A Geography of Crime, Riot, and Policing.* Lincoln: University of Nebraska Press, 1980.

Shrecker, Ellen. *The Age of McCarthyism: A Brief History with Documents.* 2nd ed. Boston: Bedford/St. Martin's, 2002.

Schultz, Nancy Lusignan. "Burning Down the House," *Sextant* 4, no. 2 (1993). Available online. URL: http://www.salemstate.edu/sextant/v4n2/schultz.html. Accessed on May 19, 2007.

Schulz, Dorothy Moses. *From Social Worker to Crimefighter: Women in United States Municipal Policing.* Westport, Conn.: Praeger, 1995.

Shi, David, and Holly A. Mayer, eds. *For the Record: A Documentary History of America.* 2nd ed. 2 vols. New York: W.W. Norton and Company, 2004.

Shoemaker, Donald J. *Theories of Delinquency: An Examination of Explanations of Delinquent Behavior.* 2nd ed. New York: Oxford University Press, 1990.

Sicherman, Barbara, and Carol Hurd Green, eds. *Notable American Women: The Modern Period.* Cambridge, Mass.: Belknap Press of Harvard University Press, 1980.

Sifakis, Carl. *The Encyclopedia of American Crime.* 2nd ed. Vols. 1–2. New York: Facts On File, 2001.

Silliman, Jael, and Anannya Bhattacharjee, eds. *Policing the National Body: Sex, Race, and Criminalization.* Cambridge, Mass.: South End Press, 2002.

Simpson, Sally S. *Corporate Crime, Law, and Social Control.* New York: Cambridge University Press, 2002.

Sitkoff, Harvard. *The Struggle for Black Equality, 1954–1992.* Revised ed. New York: Hill & Wang, 1993.

Skolnick, Jerome H. *Justice without Trial: Law Enforcement in Democratic Society.* New York: John Wiley & Sons, 1966.

Skolnick, Jerome H., and James J. Fyfe. *Above the Law: Police and the Excessive Use of Force.* New York: Free Press, 1993.

Snell, Tracy L. "Capital Punishment, 2005." Bureau of Justice Statistics Bulletin. Washington, D.C.: U.S. Department of Justice, December 2006.

Snow, Robert L. *Terrorists among Us: The Militia Threat.* Cambridge, Mass.: Da Capo Press, 2001.

Spillane, Joseph F. *Cocaine: From Medical Marvel to Modern Menace in the United States, 1884–1920.* Baltimore, Md.: Johns Hopkins University Press, 2000.

Steelwater, Eliza. *The Hangman's Knot: Lynching, Legal Execution, and America's Struggle with the Death Penalty.* Boulder, Colo.: Westview Press, 2003.

Steinberg, Allen. *The Transformation of Criminal Justice: Philadelphia, 1800–1880.* Chapel Hill: University of North Carolina Press, 1989.

Stewart, Donald Henderson. *The Opposition Press of the Federalist Period.* Albany: State University of New York Press, 1969.

Stiles, T. J. *Jesse James: Last Rebel of the Civil War.* New York: Alfred A. Knopf, 2002.

Stone, Geoffrey R. *Perilous Times: Free Speech in Wartime from the Sedition Act of 1798 to the War on Terrorism.* New York: W.W. Norton, 2004.

Sublett, Jesse. "Lone on the Range: Texas Lawmen of Lore." *Texas Monthly.* Available online. URL: http://www.texasmonthly.com/1000-01-01/webextra49-5.php. Accessed on October 8, 2009.

Sullivan, Mercer L. *"Getting Paid": Youth Crime and Work in the Inner City.* Ithaca, N.Y.: Cornell University Press, 1989.

Sylvester, Richard. "Principles of Police Administration." *Journal of Criminal Law and Criminology* 1 (September 1910): 411–416.

Tanenhaus, David S. *Juvenile Justice in the Making.* New York: Oxford University Press, 2004.

Tanenhaus, David S., and Steven A. Drizin. "'Owing to the Extreme Youth of the Accused': The Changing Legal Response to Juvenile Homicide." *Journal of Criminal Law and Criminology* 92, no. 3 (Spring/Summer 2002): 641–705.

"Texas Rangers." Handbook of Texas Online. Available online. URL: http://www.tsha.utexas.edu/handbook/online/articles/TT/met4.html. Accessed on May 31, 2007.

Tonry, Michael, ed. *The Future of Imprisonment.* New York: Oxford University Press, 2004.

Tregaskis, Richard. "The Cops' Favorite Make-Believe Cop." *Saturday Evening Post* (September 26, 1953), 24–25, 107–109.

Trost, Jennifer. *Gateway to Justice: The Juvenile Court and Progressive Child Welfare in a Southern City.* Athens: University of Georgia Press, 2005.

Tyler, Moses Coit. *The Literary History of the American Revolution, 1763–1783.* New York: G.P. Putnam s Sons, 1897. 2 vols.

Udall, Stewart L. *The Forgotten Founders: Rethinking the History of the Old West.* Washington, D.C.: Island Press, 2004.

Ullman, Joan. "'I Carried It Too Far, That's for Sure.'" *Psychology Today* (May/June 1992).

United States. "An Act for the Punishment of Certain Crimes Against the United States" (Sedition Act), July 14, 1798. The Constitution Society. Available online. URL: http://www.constitution.org/rf/sedition_1798.htm. Accessed on May 30, 2007.

———. "An Act Respecting Fugitives from Justice, and Persons Escaping from the Service of Their Masters." 1793. The Independence Hall Association. Available online. URL: http://www.ushistory.org/presidentshouse/history/slaveact1793.htm. Accessed on June 30, 2008.

———. "Treaty with the Delawares [Lenape tribe]." September 17, 1778. Oklahoma State University Library Electronic Publishing Center. Available online. URL: http://digital.library.okstate.edu/kappler/Vol2/treaties/del0003.htm. Accessed on May 18, 2007.

———. "An Act to Protect All Persons in the United States in Their Civil Rights, and Furnish the Means of Their Vindication" [The Civil Rights Act of 1866], April 9, 1866. *Reconstruction: The Second Civil War* (PBS). Available online. URL: http://www.pbs.org/wgbh/amex/reconstruction/activism/ps_1866.html. Accessed on May 19, 2007.

———. "Espionage Act of May 16, 1918." U.S. History Documents and Speeches. Available online. URL: http://www.historicaldocuments.com/EspionageAct.htm. Accessed on May 18, 2007.

———. "Punishment of Crimes Act." 1790. The First Federal Congress Project at George Washington University. Available online. URL: http://www2.gwu.edu/~ffcp/exhibit/p6/p6_7.html. Accessed on June 30, 2008.

———. "Racketeer Influenced and Corrupt Organizations (RICO) Act of 1970." Cornell University Legal Information Institute. Available online. URL: http://www.law.cornell.edu/uscode/html/uscode18/usc_sup_01_18_10_I_20_96.html. Accessed on November 2, 2005.

———. "Treaty with the Cherokee Nation." November 28, 1785. "The New Nation, 1783–1815," at the Library of Congress. Available online. URL: http://lcweb2.loc.gov/learn/features/timeline/newnatn/nativeam/cherokee.html Accessed on May 18, 2007.

United States. Department of Commerce. Bureau of the Census. *Historical Statistics of the United States, Colonial Times to 1970,* Bicentennial Edition. Washington, D.C.: U.S. Government Printing Office, 1975.

United States. Library of Congress. THOMAS, Legislative Information on the Internet. Available online. URL: http://thomas.loc.gov. Accessed on May 18, 2007.

United States. National Advisory Commission on Civil Disorders. *Report.* Washington, D.C.: U.S. Government Printing Office, 1968.

United States. National Archives and Records Administration. *The National Archives Experience: The Charters of Freedom.* Available online. URL: http://www.archives.gov/national-archives-experience/charters/charters.html. Accessed on May 11, 2007.

United States. National Archives and Records Administration. *Weekly Compilation of Presidential Documents.*

United States Senate. Government Operations Committee. *Federal Drug Enforcement: Hearings Before the Permanent Subcommittee on Investigations of the Committee on Government Operations.* Washington, D.C.: U.S. Government Printing Office, 1975.

Vagins, Deborah, Deborah, and Jesselyn McCurdy. *Cracks in the System.* Washington, D.C.: American Civil Liberties Union, 2006.

Vandal, Gilles. *Rethinking Southern Violence: Homicides in Post-Civil War Louisiana, 1866–1884.* Columbus: Ohio State University Press, 2000.

Vila, Bryan, and Cynthia Morris. *Capital Punishment in the United States: A Documentary History.* Westport, Conn.: Greenwood Press, 1997.

———. *The Role of Police in American Society: A Documentary History.* Westport, Conn.: Greenwood Press, 1999.

Virginia. "An Act Concerning Servants and Slaves." 1705. Virginia Statutes on Slaves and Servants. Available online. URL: http://www.law.du.edu/russell/lh/alh/docs/virginiaslaverystatutes.html. Accessed on March 24, 2006.

Vollmer, August. "Predelinquency." *Journal of Criminal Law and Criminology* 14 (August 1923): 279–283.

von Hoffman, Alexander. "An Officer of the Neighborhood: A Boston Patrolman on the Beat in 1895." *Journal of Social History* 26, no. 2 (Winter 1992): 309–330.

Walker, David. *Appeal.* 1829. Documenting the American South. Available online. URL: http://docsouth.unc.edu/nc/walker/walker.html. Accessed on May 18, 2007.

Walker, Samuel. *A Critical History of Police Reform.* Lexington, Mass.: D.C. Heath, 1977.

———. *Popular Justice: A History of American Criminal Justice.* 2nd ed. New York: Oxford University Press, 1998.

———. *Sense and Nonsense about Crime and Drugs: A Policy Guide.* 3rd ed. Belmont, Calif.: Wadsworth Publishing Company, 1994.

Warr, Mark. *Companions in Crime: The Social Aspects of Criminal Conduct.* New York: Cambridge University Press, 2002.

Warren Commission. *Report of the President's Commission on the Assassination of President John F. Kennedy.* Washington D.C.: U.S. Government Printing Office, 1964.

Watts, Eugene J. "Police Priorities in Twentieth Century St. Louis." *Journal of Social History* 14, no. 4 (Summer 1981): 649–673.

——. "Police Response to Crime and Disorder in Twentieth-Century St. Louis." *Journal of American History* 70 (June 1983): 340–348.

Wells, Alice Stebbins. "Women on the Police Force." *The American City* 8 (April 1913): 401.

"What Was the Black Panther Party?" Available online. URL: http://www.black panther.org/legacynew.htm. Accessed on March 9, 2006.

Who Was Who in America. Chicago: Marquis Publishing, 1966.

Williams, Linda. *Playing the Race Card: Melodramas of Black and White from Uncle Tom to O. J. Simpson.* Princeton, N.J.: Princeton University Press, 2001.

Willrich, Michael. *City of Courts: Socializing Justice in Progressive Era Chicago.* Cambridge: Cambridge University Press, 2003.

Wilson, Charles. *Baptized in Blood: The Religion of the Lost Cause, 1865–1920.* Athens: University of Georgia Press, 1980.

Wilson, James Q. *Varieties of Police Behavior: The Management of Law and Order in Eight Communities.* Cambridge, Mass.: Harvard University Press, 1968.

——. *Thinking about Crime.* New York: Basic Books, 1975.

Wines, Enoch, ed. *Transactions of the National Congress of Penitentiary and Reformatory Discipline.* 1871. Reprint, American Correctional Association, 1970.

Winik, Jay. *April 1865: The Month That Saved America.* New York: HarperCollins, 2002.

Winthrop, John. "A Modell of Christian Charity." 1630. Available online. URL: http://history.hanover.edu/texts/winthmod.html. Accessed on May 29, 2007.

Wolcott, David B. *Cops and Kids: Policing Juvenile Delinquency in Urban America, 1890–1940.* Columbus: Ohio State University Press, 2005.

Wolcott, David, and Steven Schlossman. "Punishing Serious Juvenile Offenders: Crime, Racial Disparity, and the Incarceration of Adolescents in Adult Prison in Late 19th- and Early 20th-Century Pennsylvania." In *Beyond Empiricism: Institutions and Intentions in the Study of Crime,* ed. Joan McCord, 39–68. New Brunswick, N.J.: Transaction Publishers, 2004.

Wolfgang, Marvin E. *Patterns in Criminal Homicide.* Philadelphia: University of Pennsylvania Press, 1958.

Woods, Gerald. *The Police in Los Angeles: Reform and Professionalization.* New York: Garland Publishing, 1993.

Wright, Bradford M. *Comic Book Nation: The Transformation of Youth Culture in America.* Baltimore: Johns Hopkins University Press, 2001.

Zeisel, Hans, and Alec M. Gallup. "Death Penalty Sentiment in the United States." *Journal of Quantitative Criminology* 5, no. 3 (September 1989): 285–296.

Zimring, Franklin E. *American Youth Violence.* New York: Oxford University Press, 1998.

——. *The Contradictions of American Capital Punishment.* New York: Oxford University Press, 2003.

Zimring, Franklin E., and Gordon Hawkins. *Incapacitation: Penal Confinement and the Restraint of Crime.* New York: Oxford University Press, 1995.

——. *Crime Is Not the Problem: Lethal Violence in America.* New York: Oxford University Press, 1997.

Zinn, Howard, and Anthony Arnove, eds. *Voices of a People's History of the United States.* New York: Seven Stories Press, 2004.

Index

Locators in *italic* indicate illustrations. Locators in **boldface** indicate main entries/topics and biographies. Locators followed by *m* indicate maps. Locators followed by *t* indicate graphs and tables. Locators followed by *g* indicate glossary entries. Locators followed by *c* indicate chronology entries.

A

Abanes, Richard 285
Aberdeen Saturday Pioneer 116
Abernathy, Ralph *215*
Ableman v. Booth 62, 84, 92*c*
abortion clinic bombing 269, 283*c*
Abraham, Nathaniel 275, 283*c*
Abu Ghraib Prison 279, 283*c*
ACLU. *See* American Civil Liberties Union (ACLU)
An Act for the Punishment of Certain Crimes. *See* Crimes Act of 1790
An act legalizing the killing of slaves, Virginia, 1669 297
Act 33 274, 282*c*
Adams, Ansel *177*
Adams, John 22, 24, 36, 42–45, *51*, 51–52*c*, **322**
Addams, Jane **322**
"Address to the Nation on the Campaign against Drug Abuse" (Reagan) 253–254
Adirondack Record-Elizabethtown Post 167
Adriaenzen, Maryn 19–20
African Americans. *See also* slavery
    drugs and 174–175, 240
    juvenile offenders 274–275
    migration of 125, 148, 181, 205
    militias 101, 112*c*
    in police departments 222
    segregation 122, 131–133, 171–174, 199
    treatment of in criminal justice system ix, 226, 272
    violence against 101–102, 111*c*, 112*c*, 113*c*, 114–115, 125, 148, 273
    voting rights 100–101
Agca, Mehmet Ali 251*c*
Agron, Salvador 181, 191, 208*c*, **322–323**
Alabama Supreme Court 162*c*, 172
Alcatraz 370*g*
Alcatraz Federal Penitentiary 158, 185*c*, 202, 208*c*, 210*c*
Alexander VI (pope) 5, 7
Alfred P. Murrah Federal Building *266*, 267, 282*c*, 283*c*, 285
Alien and Sedition Acts **42–45**, 51*c*, 370*g*
Alien Enemies Act 305–306
Alien Friends Act 43
Allen, Barry 254
Almeida, Paulo de 283*c*
Altgeld, John Peter **323**
Alton Observer 60

American Civil Liberties Union (ACLU) 278, 291–292
American Communist Party 179, 197, 208*c*
American Economic Review 235–236
American Indian Territory of Arkansas 103
The American Magazine 174, 185*c*, 190–191
American Militias (Abanes) 285
American Protective League (APL) 148
American Revolution 23–24, 33*c*, 42
American Socialist Party 148
America's Most Wanted 241, 251*c*, 255–256
Amistad slave ship 70*c*
anarchists 150
Anderson, Jack 237
Andersonville Prison 81, 89, 93*c*, *98*, 99, 370*g*
Anglin, Clarence 208*c*
Anglin, John 208*c*
Annals of the American Academy of Political and Social Science 191–192
Anslinger, Harry Jacob 162*c*, 170, 174–175, 185*c*, **323**
Answer to the Representation of New Netherland 20
anthrax 370*g*
anti-abolitionist riots 60, 69*c*
anti-Catholic sentiment 63, 69*c*, 74, 87
Anti-Drug Abuse Act of 1986 239, 251*c*
antidrug education 238–240, 253–254
The Antifederalist Papers 37–38
anti-immigrant sentiments 147, 149–150
anti-Irish sentiments 87, 88
Anti-Literacy Act 31*c*
Anti-Lynching Crusaders 161*c*
antilynching legislation 161*c*
Antinomian Controversy 10, 18–19, 370*g*
Anti-Riot Act of 1968 210*c*
Anti-Slavery Convention of American Women 70*c*
antislavery newspapers 60
anti-stalking legislation 242, 251*c*
antiwar movement 147–148, 159*c*, 195–198, *197*, 209*c*, 220
Appeal (Walker) 47, 52*c*, 56
Appointment, Qualification, and Duties of U.S. Marshals 313
Army-McCarthy hearings 186*c*, 189–190
Army of God 269
"Arrests of First Offenders" (Kohler) 138
Articles of Confederation 28, 33*c*
Ashcroft, John D. **323**
assassinations
    attempts 238, *239*, 251*c*
    of civil rights workers 198–199, 208*c*, 209*c*, 210*c*, 214–216
    political 146–147, **193–195**, 208*c*, 209*c*, 211–212
Astor Place Opera House 63, *64*, 70*c*
asylum movement 66
ATF. *See* Bureau of Alcohol, Tobacco and Firearms (ATF)
Atlanta Federal Prison 148
Attica Correctional Facility 223, 232*c*, 234

"Attica Uprising Not Preplanned, Blue-Ribbon Inquiry Concludes" (Goldman) 234
Auburn Penitentiary 50, 52*c*, 130, 134*c*, 135*c*, 142–143, 223
Auburn system 50, 57, 370*g*
audiencia (judicial court) 13*c*, 370*g*
Aurora 44
Austin, Stephen F. 107
Austria 146–147
The Autobiography of Malcolm X (Malcolm X) 200
"The Automobile as a Police Department Adjunct" 139
automobiles, use of in policing 126, 139
Aztec kingdom 1–2, *2*, 6, 13*c*

B

Bache, Benjamin Franklin 44
Bailey, F. Lee 261
Baker, Lewis 87, 92*c*
Baldwin, Lola 127
"The Ballad of Sam Bass" 118
Bank of Maryland 63, 69*c*
bank robberies 106, 156–158, 167
Barber, Lois 99
"Bare Tale of Negro Beatings" (Moore) 213–214
Barker, Fred 158, 185*c*
Barker, Kate 158, 185*c*, **323–324**
Barker-Karpis Gang 158
Barrow, Clyde 156–157, 162*c*, 167, 185*c*, **344–345**
"Barrow and Woman Are Slain by Police" 167
Bartelme, Mary **324**
Bartley, Diane 255–256
Bass, Sam 107–108, 112*c*, 118, **324**
Bates, Karen Grigsby 258–259
Bates, Ruby 172, 173
Baum, L. Frank 116
BBC News 290–291
Bean, Roy 103, *104*, 112*c*, 113*c*, **324**
Beattie, Taylor 114
Beatty, Warren 156
Beauford, Clay 114
Beazley, Anne 17
Beccaria, Cesare Bonesano 25–26, 31*c*, *37*, 37, 48, **324**
"Beckwith's 2d Trial Ends in Hung Jury" (Herbers) 213
Beecher, Edward 72
Behan, John 105
Belstone, A. L. 136
Bennett, William J. 239, 251*c*
Berkeley, William 17
Berkowitz, David 228, 233*c*, 236, **324**
Bernstein, Richard B. 290
Bertillon, Alphonse 113*c*, 126, **324–325**
Bertillon system 370*g*
Besharov, Douglas J. 256
Bias, Len 239, 251*c*

Bias-Motivated (Hate) Crimes Known to Police, 1992–2003 369*t*
bias-motivated crimes 271, 281*c*, 282*c*, 369*t*, 372*g*
Bickford, Maria 67, 68, 70*c*
"Big Overhaul of Juvenile Justice Planned" (Peterson) 288
Billington, John **325**
bill of attainder **24–25**, 28, 370*g*
Bill of Rights, U.S. 28, 29, 33*c*, 37–40, 51*c*, 303. *See also specific amendments*
Billy the Kid 106–107, 112*c*, 116–117, **325**
Bingham, Stephen 223
bin Laden, Osama 277, 289, *291*, 291, **325**
"Bin Laden Determined to Strike in US" 289
"Bin Laden's Warning" (BBC News) 290–291
Birney, James *69*, 69*c*
Blackboard Jungle 181
Black Codes 90–91, 131–132, 370*g*
Black Hand 146–147
Black Hills War 102
black nationalism 200
blackout 220, 233*c*
Black Panther Party 201–202, 209*c*
Black Power 200–201, 222
Blackwell's Island penitentiary 57
Blaise, Madelaine 236–237
blasphemy 10, 14*c*, 370*g*
Blaster/LOVESAN e-mail virus 279
Blaster worm 293
"Blaster Worm Spreading Rapidly" (Leyden) 293
Bleak House (Dickens) 68, 80
Blumstein, Alfred 273
Boggs Act 175–176, 186*c*
Bolshevik Revolution 147, 177
bombings. *See also* terrorism
    in 1990s **267–269**
    abortion clinics 269, 283*c*
    during Civil Rights movement 199, 208*c*, 213
    at J.P. Morgan Building 150, 160*c*
    in mail 159*c*
    Oklahoma City bombing **265–267**, *266*, 282*c*, 283*c*, 285
    al-Qaeda 267, 277, 281*c*
"Bomb Negro Church: Birmingham Children Victims; 21 Injured" 213
Bonanno crime family 233*c*, 236
Bondly, Beal 72
Bonney, William H. 106, **325**
Bonnie and Clyde 156
Booth, John Wilkes **325**
Booth, Sherman M. 83–84
bootlegging 152
Borden, Abby 122–123, 134*c*
Borden, Andrew 122–123, 134*c*
Borden, Lizzie Andrew 122–123, 134*c*, 136, *136*, **325**
Boston xi, 63–64, 65, 70*c*, 71*c*, *130*
Boston House of Reformation 52*c*
Boston Massacre 24, *32*, 32*c*
Boston Police Department 71*c*
Boston Port Act 24, 32*c*
"Boston Strangler" 205, **330**
Boston Tea Party 23, *23*, 32*c*
Boumediene v. Bush 283*c*
Bowen, Louise de Koven **325**
Bowery Boys 87
Boyd, Joshua 88
Brace, Charles Loring 66, 71*c*, **326**
Bracker, Milton 191
Bradford, David 47
Bradley, Tom 247, 248
Brady, James 270
Brady, William 107

Brady Handgun Violence Prevention Act 270, 281*c*
Branch, Ben 216
Branch Davidian cult 264–265, *265*, 281*c*
Brasco, Donnie 233*c*
Bratton, William J. 273–274
bread riots 89, 93*c*
Breckinridge, Sophonisba **326**
Brennan, William J. 230
Brockway, Zebulon Reed 109, 110, 112*c*, **326**
"broken windows" model of policing 274
Bronson, Charles 241
Brooks, Charles, Jr. 251*c*
Brooks, Preston 92*c*
Brown, John 84, 85, 92*c*, 95–96, **326**
Brown, Rap 235
Brown v. Board of Education of Topeka, Kansas 184, 186*c*
Bryant, Roy and Carolyn 183–184, 186*c*
"BTK killer" 243, 251*c*, **346**
Buckner, Thomas 97–98
Buford (ship) 160*c*
Bundy, Ted 228, 233*c*, 236–237, 242–243, 251*c*, **326–327**
Bureau of Alcohol, Tobacco and Firearms (ATF) 264–265, 281*c*
Bureau of Investigation xi, 127, 156, 157, 161*c*, 162*c*. *See also* Federal Bureau of Investigation (FBI)
Bureau of Narcotics and Dangerous Drugs (BNDD) 162*c*, 174, 176, 224, 370*g*
Burns, Anthony 71*c*
Burr, Aaron x, *44*, 45, 52*c*, 55, **327**
Bush, George H. W. 239, 242, *247*, 248, 251*c*
Bush, George W. 278–279, 283*c*, 289, 291
"Butcher Bill" 87, 92*c*
Butler, Andrew 92*c*
"By Authority by the President of the United States of America, a Proclamation" (Washington) 53–55

C

Cabey, Darrell 241, 254–255
Cabey v. Goetz 254–255
Cagney, James 162*c*
Cahill, Frank 106
California 62, 242, 251*c*, 271, 282*c*. *See also* Los Angeles
California, University of 126, 182, 195, 196, 268
California Forestry Association 268
California Governor's Commission on the Los Angeles Riot 214
California Highway Patrol *201*, 248
California v. Stewart 217
California Youth Authority (CYA) 182
Callahan, William 173
Calley, William 220, 232*c*, 233*c*
Cannon, Jack 102
Canty, Troy 255
Capital punishment. *See* death penalty
Capital Punishment in the United States, 1976–2008 359*m*
Capone, Alphonse viii, 152–153, *160*, 160*c*, 161*c*, 162*c*, **327**
Capote, Truman **327**
"Capture of Nat Turner" 73
Carmichael, Stokely 200
Carneal, Michael 275, 282*c*
Carnegie Endowment for International Peace 178
Caroline, Fort, Florida 6
Carter, Jimmy 221, 233*c*

Cartier, Jacques 13*c*
Casscles, J. Leland 234
Catholic charities 129
Catholic Church 7, 12, 13*c*, 33*c*, 63, 69*c*, 74, 87
Cenci, Beatrice *37*
Census Bureau 121, 203
Centennial Olympic Park 268–269, 282*c*
Center on Child Abuse and Neglect 256
Central Intelligence Agency (CIA) 279, 283*c*
"Central Park Jogger" 238, 251*c*
The Challenge of Crime in a Free Society 203, 209*c*, 218–219
Chambers, Whittaker 178–179, 185*c*
Champlain, Samuel de 17
Chaney, James 198, 208*c*
Channing, Henry 65
Chapin, Charles 159*c*
Chapman, Jay 245
Charles I (king of Spain) 13*c*
Charter of West New Jersey 298
Cherokee nation 2, 4, 59–60, 69*c*, 301
Chicago
    Democratic National Convention 196–198, *197*, 209*c*, 210*c*, 212–213
    juvenile courts 129, 134*c*, 142
    Ku Klux Klan in *171*
    murder rate 124–125
    organized crime in 152–153, 160*c*, 161*c*, 164–165
    race riots 148, 159–160*c*, 163, 200
    serial killers 123–124
    soup kitchen *160*
    South Water Street *122*
Chicago Area Project 182
Chicago Bar Association 129
Chicago Daily Tribune 164
Chicago Police Department 196–198. *See also* Democratic National Convention
"Chicago Seven" 196–197, 210*c*
Chicago Tribune 153, 187, 213–214, 216, 217–218, 236
Chicago Women's Club 129
child abduction. *See* kidnapping
child abuse. *See* domestic violence
child pornography 280
children, attacks on 271, 281*c*. *See also* kidnapping
Children's Aid Society (CAS) 66, 71*c*, 78, 370–371*g*
Children's Bureau, U.S. 180
Choate, Rufus 70*c*
Christian fundamentalism 263, 269
Christian Identity movement 269
Christopher, Warren 247
Christopher Commission 247, 248, 251*c*
CIA. *See* Central Intelligence Agency (CIA)
Cincinnati, Ohio 71*c*. *See also* National Congress on Penitentiary and Reformatory Discipline; riots
Cincinnati Post 288
cities. *See* urban crime
citizen participation, in criminal justice **240–242**
civilian review boards 204
civil liberties **202–203**, 216–217
Civil Rights Acts 199, 204, 311
Civil Rights movement
    assassinations 198–199, 208*c*, 209*c*, 210*c*, 214–216
    bombings 199, 208*c*, 213
    demonstrations 195, 208*c*
    effects of 222
    law enforcement and 198–199
    racially motivated killings and 171, 184
    violent reaction to x, **198–199**, 213–216
Claiborne, Billy 105

Clanton gang 105–106, 112*c*
Clark, Marcia 261, 284
Clark, Tom 216–217
Clay County Savings Bank 106
Cleveland Survey of Criminal Justice 161*c*
Clinton, Bill
    criminal justice reform 242, 270, 271, 281*c*,
      282*c*, 286–287
    in general 264, 267, *281*
Clinton, Hillary *281*
Cloward, Richard A. **327**
Clum, John P. 114
CNN.com 289
cocaine 238–240, 251*c*, 253–254, 273
Cochran, Johnnie 261, 284–285
Coercion Acts. *See* Intolerable Acts
COINTELPRO (Counter Intelligence Program)
    197–199, 202, 208*c*, 209*c*, 212, 221, 371*g*
Coker v. Georgia 230, 233*c*
cold war **176–180**
Collins, Wilkie 68
Collis, Addie Mae 213
colonies, crime in 17–19
Colorado Fuel and Mine Company 159*c*
Colosimo, Big Jim 152, 160*c*
Columbia University 196, 209*c*
Columbine High School massacre 275–276, 283*c*,
    288–289, 371*g*
Columbus, Christopher 5, 13*c*
comic books 181, 186*c*
"The Comics Code" 191
Comics Magazine Association of America 186*c*
Common Sense (Paine) 34
communism 178
Communist Party–USA 179, 197, 208*c*
community-based corrections 221
community values, reflected by criminal law viii
Comprehensive Drug Abuse Prevention and Con-
    trol Act (CDAPCA) 224, 232*c*
Compromise of 1850 62
computer hackers 279
Comstock, Anthony **327–328**
Confederate State of America 86, 89, 92*c*, 93*c*
The Confessions of Nat Turner 72–73
Congress, U.S. 29, 195, 208*c*
congressional hearings 178–180, 181
Congress of Racial Equality (CORE) 199, 200
Connor, Eugene T. "Bull" 199, 208*c*
Consejo de Indias 6, 13*c*
Constitution, U.S. 28, 30, 33*c*, 301–302. *See also*
    Bill of Rights, U.S.
Constitutional Convention 33*c*
consumer culture 205
contract labor system 50
Controlled Substances Act 224, 232*c*
convict leasing 132
Cooper v. Pate 208*c*
Copeland, John A. 96
Coppola, Francis Ford 232*c*
Cops viii
"The Cops' Favorite Make-Believe Cop" (Tregas-
    kis) 191
CORE 199, 200
Cornell University 196
Corven, Phillip 17
Cotton, John 10
cotton gin 41, *42*
Council of the Indies 6, 13*c*
counsel, right to 28
counterfeiting of federal records 46
counterintelligence programs. *See* COINTELPRO
    (Counter Intelligence Program)
county system of law enforcement 10
The Courier 286

"Courting Passion in the Camera's Eye" (Blaise
    and Ketzenbach) 236–237
courts xi–xii, **128–131**. *See also* juvenile courts;
    prisons and jails; punishment; Supreme Court
Court TV 260, 262
Couzens, James Joseph **328**
Cowlings, Al 261
Cox, Archibald **328**
Cox, Brian 243
Crazy Horse 102
crime 35, **204–205**, 217–219. *See also* specific issues
crime commissions **153–154**, 167–169
Crimes Act of 1790 46–47, 51*c*, 303–304, 371*g*
crime statistics
    incarceration vii
    index crimes ix, 205, 260, 363*t*
    lynchings by state 357*m*
    murder rate 124–125, 180, 204–205, 220,
      238, 260, 272–273, 276, 362*t*
    violent crimes by state 358*m*
criminal anthropology 109–110, 371*g*
criminal identification 126, 137
criminal investigation 126
criminal justice
    during Civil War period **86–89**, 97–99
    direct expenditures on 368*t*
    philosophies of 36–37
    reform of
      in antebellum period **65–66**
      Clinton and 242, 270, 271, 281*c*, 282*c*,
        286–287
      eyewitness testimony 76–78, 118–120
      legislative **203–204**
      after September 11, 2001 **277–279**
    after World War II **180**
Criminal Justice in Cleveland 161*c*
The Criminal Man (Lombroso) 109, 112*c*
criminal responsibility, age of 128
criminal scientists 126
"crisis of confidence" 221, 233*c*
Crosby, Peter 101
Cross, J. H. 213
Crouse, Ex parte 65, 70*c*
Crouse, Mary Ann 65
cruel and unusual punishment 28, 230
Crum, Allen 218
Cuauhtémoc (Aztec ruler) 6, 13*c*
Cummings, Homer Stillé 157, 162*c*, **328**
Custer, George 116
"Cycles of Craving" (Hurley) 254
Czolgosz, Leon **328–329**

D

Dahmer, Jeffrey 243, *244*, 252*c*, 257, **329**
Daily Gazette 74–75
Daily Nevada State Journal 117
Daingerfield, John E. 95–96
Daley, Richard J. 196, *197*
Dallas Morning News 218, 234
Darden, Christopher 261, 284, 285
D.A.R.E. program 239, 251*c*
Darrow, Clarence Seward 131, 134*c*, 141, 155,
    161*c*, 165–167, **329**
Darwin, Charles 109
Davis, Dolores 251*c*
Davis, Jefferson 81, 86, 89, *92*, 92*c*, 93*c*
Davis, Katherine Bement 131, 134*c*, **329**
Davis, Rennie 196
Day, William R. 167–168
DEA. *See* Drug Enforcement Administration (DEA)
death penalty
    ban on **229–231**, 232*c*, 237

in Crimes Act of 1790 46
electric chair 131, 134*c*, 140–141, 245, 251*c*,
    371*g*
in English law 8–9
expanded use of 272
federal offenses and 270
gas chamber 161*c*, 245, 251*c*, 252*c*
hanging *105*
history of xii
lethal injection **245**, 251*c*
Massachusetts Body of Liberties 14*c*
means of 140, *250*, 257
poverty-related crime *8*, 8–9
race and 229–230
for rape 230, 233*c*
rates of per state 359*m*
reform of 131, 140–141
reinstatement of 233*c*, 237
Sacco and Vanzetti 161*c*
statistics 365*t*, 366*t*
views of 25–26, 48
*Deaths by Homicide in the United States,
    1900–2002* 362*t*
Death Wish 241
Debs, Eugene V. 148, 151, 159*c*, 161*c*, 163,
    329–330
Debs v. United States 159*c*
Declaration of Independence 25–27, 29, 33*c*,
    300
Declaration of Principles Adopted and Promul-
    gated by National Congress on Penitentiary and
    Reformatory Discipline 312–313
A Declaration on the Execution of Two Quaker
    Women, Massachusetts, 1659 297
Declaratory Act 23, 31*c*
Deddeh, Peter 274
Dee, Henry 213
Defense Advanced Research Project Area 278
defense attorneys 128
Defense Department 278
De la Beckwith, Byron 198, 213
Delaware Declaration of Rights 28, 33*c*
Dellinger, David 196
Democratic National Convention 196–198, *197*,
    209*c*, 210*c*, 212–213
Democratic Party 44, 64, 107
Democratic-Republican Party 42, 44
demographic changes in U.S. 58, 100, 121
Denbeaux, Mark 279
Deparle, Jason 257
Department of Correctional Services 223
Dershowitz, Alan 261
DeSalvo, Albert 205, **330**
desegregation 199
"detached workers" 182
detective stories viii, 58, 68, 70*c*, 80
deterrence 221
Detroit 87–88, 93*c*, 97–98, 161*c*, 176, 185*c*, 200,
    209*c*
Detroit House of Correction 109
Diallo, Amadou 282*c*, 283*c*
Dickens, Charles 57, 68, 80
DiIulio, John J., Jr. 273, 287–288
Dillinger, John 156–158, 162*c*, 185*c*, **330**
direct democracy 25
Direct Expenditure on Criminal Justice by Level of
    Government, 1982-2001 368*t*
Dirty Harry 240
A Discourse on Political Economy (Rousseau) 37
*Discourse on the Origin and Basis of Inequality Among
    Men* (Rousseau) 25, 31*c*
district attorneys 128
Dix, Dorothea Lynde x, 66, 70*c*, 76–77, **330**
Domestic Abuse Intervention Project (DAIP) 242

domestic terrorism
  eyewitness testimony 285–286
  in 1990s **267–269**
  Oklahoma City bombing **265–267**, *266*,
    282*c*, 283*c*, 285
  Olympic bombing, Atlanta 268–269, 282*c*,
    283*c*
  rise of **262–265**
domestic violence **242**, 251*c*, 256, 374*g*
Douglas, William O. 237
Douglass, Frederick 70*c*, 72
Doyen, Dorcas. *See* Jewett, Helen
Doyle, Sir Arthur Conan viii, 68
draft 86–88, 93*c*
draft riots 86, 87–88, 93*c*, *97*, 98
Dragnet vii, 183, 191–192
Dred Scott v. Sandford 84, 92*c*, 94–95
Drug Abuse Resistance Education (D.A.R.E.) 239,
  251*c*
drug culture 175
"drug czar" 239, 251*c*
drug enforcement, modern **224–225**, 234–236
Drug Enforcement Administration (DEA) 224,
  233*c*, 370*g*, 371*g*
Drug Free Federal Workplace 239, 251*c*
"Drug-Law Enforcement" (Eartherly) 235–236
drugs, illegal
  addiction 224
  African Americans and 174–175, 240
  anti–drug education 238–240, 253–254
  cocaine 238–240, 251*c*, 253–254, 273
  Harrison Narcotics Tax Act of 1914 127,
    159*c*, 161*c*, 174
  heroin 225
  marijuana 174–175, 185*c*, 225, *225*, *235*,
    239, 271
  modern drug enforcement **224–225**,
    234–236
  murders and 272
  Rockefeller drug laws **226**, 233*c*, 235
  trafficking 170, 174, 224, 270
  war on viii, xi, 176, 186*c*, 188, 239, 271, 375*g*
duels *44*, 45, 52*c*, 55
due process clause 172, 209*c*, 216–217, 240
Dugdale, Richard Louis viii, 110, 112*c*, 120, **330**
Dummer, Ethel Sturges **330–331**
Dunaway, Faye 156
Dutch West India Company 11
Duties on Distilled Spirits Act 51*c*
Dwight, Theodore William 93*c*, 109, **331**
Dyer, Joel 285
Dyer, Leonidas 161*c*
Dyer, Mary 15*c*, **331**

E

Eappan, Matthew 282*c*
Earp, Morgan 105–106
Earp, Virgil 105–106
Earp, Wyatt Barry Stapp 105–106, 112*c*, **331**
Eartherly, Billy J. 235–236
East Cambridge Jail 66, 70*c*
Eastern State Penitentiary 50, 52*c*
East India Company 23–24, 32*c*
Ebony 257–258
EC Comics 181
economic opportunity, crime and 203, 205
economy, structural changes to 221
editorial cartoons *61*
Edwards, Charles 213
Edwards, John 284
Edwards, Tracy 243
Edwards, Willie 208*c*

The Effectiveness of Correctional Treatment (Lipton et
  al) 233*c*
Eighteenth Amendment 151, 159*c*, 316–317
Eighth Amendment 230, 232*c*, 237, 303
Eisenhower, Dwight D. 176, 179–180, 186*c*, 188
electoral tie 52*c*
electric chair 131, 134*c*, 140–141, 245, 251*c*, 371*g*
Elias, Norbert **331**
Elkins v. United States 216
Elmira Reformatory 109, 112*c*, 371*g*
e-mail virus 279
Emancipation Proclamation 87, 90, 93*c*
embassy bombings 277, 289
Emerson family 84
encomienda system 5–6, 13*c*, 16, 371*g*
enemy combatants 278–279, 283*c*
energy crisis 221
enforced silence 50
English Bill of Rights 11, 15*c*, 28, 299, 371*g*
English law, in New World **7–11**
English Toleration Act 15*c*
Enlightenment 25–27, 35, 50, 371*g*
"An Enquiry Into the Effects of Public Punish-
  ments Upon Criminals and Upon Society"
  (Rush) 33*c*, 40
Enrollment Act 86, 93*c*
Epstein, Charles 268
Espionage Act of 1917 148, 159*c*, 316
eugenics movement 110, 118–120
Eunick, Tiffany 275
Evans, John Louis 245, 251*c*
Evarts, William M. 120
Evers, Medgar 184, 198, 208*c*, 213
evolution, theory of 109
Excise Act of 1791 47, 51*c*
exclusionary rule 202
"Executions Aren't News" (Deparle) 257
Executions under Civil Authority in the United
  States, 1930–2004 365*t*
Executive Orders 176, 178, 185*c*, 239, 251*c*
expenditures on criminal justice 368*t*
"The Expense of the New Government" 38
ex post facto laws 28
extradition 5, 28

F

Family Violence Prevention and Services Act of
  1984 242, 251*c*
Farrell, William E. 235
Faulds, Henry 112*c*, 126, 137
Faulkner, Thomas 88
Faurot, Joseph A. **331**
FBI. *See* Federal Bureau of Investigation (FBI)
fear of crime **205–207**, 209*c*, 210*c*, 217–219
Federal Bureau of Investigation (FBI). *See also*
  COINTELPRO (Counter Intelligence Pro-
  gram); organized crime
    assassination investigations 198–199
    background 371*g*
    and Black Panther Party 201–202, 209*c*
    establishment of 157–158
    expansion of 170
    juvenile delinquency statistics 180
    Ku Klux Klan 208*c*
    as part of national criminal justice system
      146
    predecessor to xi, 127, 156
    Waco incident 264–265
Federal Bureau of Narcotics (FBN) 170, 371*g*
Federal Bureau of Prisons 272
federal crime control **156–158**, 167–169,
  174–176

federal crime policy in 1990s **270–271**
federal government, role of in criminal justice
  x–xiii, 46, 368*t*
The Federalist Papers 39
Federalists 42
Federal Kidnapping Act 155–156
federal law, development of 28, 45–46
Ferdinand II (king of Spain) 5
Fifteenth Amendment 100, 111*c*
Fifth Amendment 209*c*, 271, 303
Fillmore, Millard 62
films vii–ix, 161*c*, 162*c*, 181, 208*c*, 240, 243. *See
  also specific films*
Finch, Abraham 14*c*
"Find Kidnapped Chicago Boy's Body in River"
  187
fingerprints 112*c*, 126, *127*, 137
First Amendment 161*c*, 303
*First Annual Report of the Board of Managers of the
  Prison Discipline Society* 56
First Balkan War of 1912 146
First Continental Congress 33*c*
FISA. See Foreign Intelligence Surveillance Act
  (FISA)
Fish, Albert **331**
Five Points Gang 152
Florida law allowing minors to be charged as
  adults, 1994 320–321
Floyd, Charles Arthur viii, 157, 158, 162*c*, 185*c*,
  332
Focault, Michel Paul **332–333**
FOIA 221
Fonda, Henry 156
Force Act 101, 111*c*
forced labor prisons 48
Ford, Bob 106, 112*c*
foreign affairs 42–45, 51*c*
Foreign Intelligence Surveillance Act (FISA) 278
Forrest, Edwin 70*c*
Forrest, Nathan Bedford **332**
Fort Caroline, Florida 6
Fort Sumter 86, 92*c*
Fort Wayne Daily Gazette 116–117
Fosdick, Raymond B. **332**
Foster, Stephen 34
Foucault, Michel Paul **332**
Fourteenth Amendment
  Black Codes 90
  due process clause 172, 209*c*, 216–217, 240
  incorporation doctrine 161*c*, 203, 372*g*
  passage of 93*c*
  proposal of 81
  text of 311–312
Fourth Amendment 24, 202, 216
Fox Television 241, 251*c*, 255–256
France, U.S. relations with 42–43, 44, 51*c*
Frank, Leo 159*c*, **333**
Frank Leslie's Illustrated Weekly 136
Franklin, Benjamin 30, 34
Franks, Bobby 155, 161*c*
Franz Ferdinand (archduke of Austria) 146–147,
  159*c*
Free Democrat 83
Freedom of Information Act (FOIA) 221
Freedom Rides 199
Free Speech 134*c*
free speech movement 195
French and Indian War 22
"French Connection" 225, 232*c*
French trade **6**, *7*
Frethorne, Richard 17–18
Froines, John 196
Fugitive Slave Act of 1793 51*c*, *61*, 61, 72, 83,
  305, 371*g*

Fugitive Slave Act of 1850 58, *61*, 62, 70*c*, 71*c*, 83–84, 92*c*, 310, 371*g*
Fuhrman, Mark 262
Fuld, Leonhard Felix 135*c*, 138–139, **333**
Fuller, C. J. 140
Furman v. Georgia 230–231, 232*c*, 237

G

Gacy, John Wayne 228, 233*c*, 236, 243, **333**
Gaines, William M. 181
Gallup Organization 230, 238, 260
gambling 152
gang-related murders 272
Gangs of New York 87
Garrett, Pat 107, 112*c*, 117, **333**
Garrison, William Lloyd 60, 69*c*, **333**
garrote device *250*
gas chamber 161*c*, 245, 251*c*, 252*c*
Gasnier, Louis 174–175
Gates, Daryl F. 248, **333**
Gates, J. G. 114
Gault, Gerald 202–203
Gault, In re 202–203, 209*c*
Gein, Ed 208*c*
Gelernter, David 268
gender. *See also* women
    Antinomian Controversy 10, 18–19, 370*g*
    under colonial law 9
    in Comanche society 2
    diversity of in police departments 204
    history of crime and x
    Puritan gender roles 10–11
    serial killers 124
Geneva Conventions 278, 283*c*
Genovese crime family 227
George II (king of Great Britain) 24
George III (king of Great Britain) 33*c*
German Americans, hostility toward 147
Gettysburg, Battle of *90*
G. I. Bill of Rights 180
Gideon v. Wainwright 202, 208*c*
Gilchrist, James 234
Gilmore, Gary 231, 233*c*, 237
"Gilmore's Death Row Behavior" (Anderson and Whitten) 237
Gitlow v. New York 161*c*
Glueck, Eleanor Touroff **334**
Glueck, Sheldon **334**
The Godfather 226, 232*c*
Goetz, Bernhard 241, 251*c*, 254–255
"The Goetz Confession" (Mano) 255
Golden, Drew 275, 282*c*
"golden rule" policing 126, 135*c*, 138
Goldman, Emma 150
Goldman, John J. 234
Goldman, Ronald viii, 261–262, 281*c*, 282*c*, *285*
Goldwater, Barry 206
Goodman, Andrew 198, 208*c*
Gore, Al and Tipper *281*
Gorillas in the Mist 247
Gorman, John 236
Gourley, G. Douglas 191–192
government, role of in criminal justice **x–xiii**
Graham's Magazine 80
Grant, Ulysses S. 89, 93*c*
grants 204
Gray, Jimmy Lee 245, 251*c*
Gray, L. Patrick 221, 233*c*
Gray, Thomas R. 73
Great Britain 6, **7–11**, 15*c*, 42–43, 51*c*, 69*c*
Great Depression 162*c*, 170
Great Society xi, 193, 202, 203

Greenberg, Margaret Whitehead 73
Greene, Ronnie Jr. 275
Greenglass, David 179
Greer, William R. 211
Gregg v. Georgia 231, 233*c*
Gregory, Thomas Watt 148
"The Grievances of the American Colonies" (Foster) 34
Gross, Jane 253
Guantánamo Bay naval base 278, 283*c*, 371*g*
guerrilla warfare 84
Guide to Finger-Print Identification (Faulds) 137
Guiliani, Rudolph W. 236, 273
"Guiliani Says Trials Weaken the Mob" (Oreskes) 236
Guiteau, Charles Julius **334**
Gulf of Tonkin Resolution 195, 208*c*
gun control 270, 281*c*
Gunness, Belle 124, 135*c*, **334**

H

habeas corpus
    definition of 371*g*
    enemy combatants 278–279, 283*c*
    suspension of 81, 86, 88–89, 92–93*c*, 97, 101, 111*c*
Habeas Corpus Act 86
Hager, J. H. 139
Hamdan v. Rumsfeld 278–279
Hamdi, Yasser 279
Hamdi v. Rumsfeld 292–293
Hamilton, Alexander x, 39, *44*, 45, 52*c*, 55
Hamilton Township, NJ 271
hanging *105*
hanging judge 103
Hanson, Lee 290
Hanson, Peter 290
Hardin, John Wesley 104, 107–108, 112*c*, **334**
Harding, Donald Eugene 245, 252*c*
Harding, Warren G. 150–151, 161*c*
hard labor 48–50
harmony ethic 2, 4
Harpers Ferry, raid on 85, 92*c*, 95–96
Harper's Weekly 89, *115*
Harris, Eric 275, 283*c*, 288–289, **334**
Harris, Thomas 251*c*
Harrison, Francis 35
Harrison Narcotics Tax Act of 1914 127, 159*c*, 161*c*, 174
Harvard University 196
Harvest of Rage (Dyer) 285
hate crimes 271, 281*c*, 282*c*, 369*t*, 372*g*
Hate Crimes Statistics Act of 1990 271, 281*c*
Hauptmann, Bruno Richard 155, 167, 185*c*, **334–335**
Hayden, Michael V. 283*c*
Hayden, Tom 196
Headley, Joel Tyler 98
Healy, William **335**
Hearst, Patricia **335**
HEAS alert system 278
Heith, John *105*
Hennessy, David C. 152
Herbers, John 213
Hernandez, Antonio 191
heroin 225
Hess, Paul 216
Hickman, Edward 161*c*
Hickman, William Edward 155, **335**
Hickok, James Butler 103–105, 112*c*, 116, **335**
Hicks, Giles 72
Higgins, Lois Lundell 217

Hill, Clinton J. 212
Hill Street Blues vii–viii
Hinckley, John W., Jr. *239*, 250*c*, **335–336**
Hirabayashi v. United States 176
Hispanics 102, 108–109, 174–176, 185*c*, 226, 272
Hiss, Alger 178–179, 185*c*, 186*c*, **336**
Hitchcock, Alfred 208*c*
Hobbes, Thomas 17, **336**
Hoffman, Abbie 196
Hoffman, Frederick L. 143–144
Holliday, George 248
Holliday, John Henry 105, 112*c*, **336**
Holmes, Abraham 38–39
Holmes, H. H. 123, 134*c*, **343**
Homeland Security, Department of (DHS) 278
Homeland Security Advisory System (HEAS) alert system 278
homicide. *See* murder; murder rate
homosexuality 9, 14*c*, 271, 282*c*
Hoover, Herbert 154, 155
Hoover, John Edgar
    background **336–337**
    on the Black Panther Party 201–202
    death of 221, 232*c*
    FBI and *157*, 157–158, 161*c*, 162*c*, 170, 185*c*, 190–191, 199
    at Justice Department 150
Hopkins, Anthony 243, 251*c*
Horrocks, Michael 289
Horton, James 173
House Committee on Un-American Activities. *See* House Un-American Activities Committee (HUAC)
House Judiciary Committee 233*c*
House of Representatives 178
houses of refuge 52*c*, 65
House Un-American Activities Committee (HUAC) 185*c*
housing, racism in 161*c*
Howard, John **337**
Howell, Vernon 264
"How to Stop Police Brutality" (Massaquoi) 257–258
"How We Can Stop Narcotic Sales" (Whitman) 188
HUAC. *See* House Un-American Activities Committee (HUAC)
Hule, William Bradford 188
humiliation in stocks 9
Humphrey, Hubert H. 196, 207
Hurley, Dan 254
Hurley, Timothy 314–316
Huron Reflector 79
Hutchinson, Anne Marbury 10, 13*c*, *18*, 18–19, **337**

I

"I Carried It Too Far, That's for Sure" (Ullman) 257
identity theft **279–280**, 293
"Identity Theft: What, Me Worry?" (Rubenking) 293
"I Knew It Wouldn't Be Right" (Popyk) 288
Illinois Association for Criminal Justice 164–165
Illinois Crime Survey 161*c*
Illinois Domestic Violence Act of 1986 320
Illinois Juvenile Court Law of 1907 313–314
Illinois v. Leopold and Loeb 165–167
immigration ix, 58, 63, 87, 100, 121, 181
"Immune Criminals and the Why of It" 164
Impartial Administration of Justice Act 24, 32*c*
importation, in English colonies 21

imprisonment 9, 48–50. *See also* prisons and jails; punishment
"Improvements in Police Work" (McKelvey) 137
incarceration statistics vii, 180, 271, 360*m*, 364*t*
incorporation doctrine 161*c*, 203, 372*g*
indentured servants 9, 13*c*, 14*c*, 17–18
Independent Commission on the Los Angeles Police Department 247, 251*c*
indeterminate sentences 129–130
index crimes ix, 205, 260, 363*t*. *See also* routine crime
Index Crimes Known to Police, 1960–2003 363*t*
Indian Appropriations Act 102, 111*c*
Indiana Women's Prison 112*c*
Indian Tribes Act 304–305
indictments, establishment of 28
Industrial Society and Its Future (Kaczynski) 268, 282*c*, 286
Industrial Workers of the World (IWW) 150, 159*c*
"Inmate Killed in Prison Riot" 234
insanity defense 65
Instructions for the London Metropolitan Police 307–310
Inter Caetera 5
International Association of Chiefs of Police (IACP) 125, 134*c*, 372*g*
International Labor Day 149
International Labor Defense (ILD) 172
international terrorism **276–277**, 289–291
Internet crime **279–280**, 293
internment camps 176, *177*, 185*c*
interrogation methods 279, 283*c*
interstate crime 170
Intolerable Acts 24, 32*c*
Iraq War 261, 279
Irish Dead Rabbits 87
Isabella I (queen of Spain) 5
Italian Black Hand 152
Ito, Lance 261, 284

J

Jackson, Andrew *59*, 59–60, 69*c*
Jackson, George 222–223, 232*c*, **337**
Jackson, Jesse *215*, 216
Jaffe, Jerome 224
James, Frank 106, 112*c*, 113*c*
James, Jesse Woodson viii, 106, 112*c*, 117, *117*, **337**
James II (king of England) 28
Jamestown, Virginia 8, 13*c*
James-Younger gang 112*c*
Japanese Americans, internment of 176, *177*, 185*c*
Jay Treaty of 1795 42
Jefferson, Thomas
    Bill of Rights and 29, 33*c*
    in general 1, 31*c*, 48, 300, **337–338**
    Notes on the State of Virginia 25–26, 302–303
    as president *26*, 42–45, 47, 51–52*c*
Jennings, A. J. 136
Jennings, Dean 192
Jet (magazine) 184
Jewell, Richard 268–269
Jewett, Helen 66–67, 68, 69*c*, **338**
Jim Crow 99, 101, 131–133
Jogues, Isaac 12
John Paul II (pope) 251*c*
Johnson, Andrew 88
Johnson, Lyndon B. xi, 194–195, 198, 200, 203–204, 206, 208*c*
Johnson, Mitchell 275, 282*c*
"John Walsh: Fighting Back" (Bartley) 255–256

Joint Select Committee to Inquire into the Conditions of Affairs in the Late Insurrectionary States 101, 111*c*
Jon, Gee 161*c*
Jones, Jim 229, *229*, 233*c*, **338**
Jones, Margaret 19
Jourdain, J. B. 99
The Journal of New Netherland 19–20
J.P. Morgan Building 150, 160*c*
judicial revolution 372*g*
Judiciary Act of 1789 45–46
The Jukes (Dugdale) 110, 112*c*, 120
jurisdictional limitations 156
jury trial, right to 27, 28
Justice Department 150, 156, 160*c*, 241, 264
"just say no" antidrug campaign 239
"The Juvenile Court" (Mack) 142
Juvenile Court Act 129
juvenile courts xiii, *128*, 128–129, 134*c*, 141–142, 202–203, 209*c*, 372*g*
juvenile delinquency **180–182**
    adult criminal courts and 274–275, 288–289
    causes of 65–66, 186*c*
    eyewitness testimony 76–78, 141–142, 190–191
    gangs 180–181
    institutions for 49, 71*c*
    as new class of offenders 58
    in newspapers 180–181
    photograph *130*
    view of in early 20th century 126
juvenile institutions 52*c*, 65, 76
juvenile justice, toughening of 241–242, **274–276**, 288–289

K

Kaczynski, David 268
Kaczynski, Theodore 260, 267–268, 272, 282*c*, 286, **338**
Kanka, Megan 271, 281*c*, **338**
Kansas City Massacre 162*c*
Kansas-Nebraska Act 84
Kardashian, Robert 261
Karpis, Alvin 185*c*
Kaufman, Irving 186*c*, 188–189
Kefauver, Estes 175, 181, 186*c*, **338**
Kefauver Committee 175
Kellerman, Roy H. 211–212
Kelling, George 273
Kelly, George "Machine Gun" 157
Kemmler, In Re 140
Kemmler, William 131, 134*c*, 140–141, 245, **339**
Kennan, George 177–178
Kennedy, David 99
Kennedy, Jacqueline 211–212
Kennedy, John F. 193–194, *194*, 208*c*, 211–212
Kennedy, Robert F. 194, 209*c*, **339**
Kentucky Resolution of 1799 43–44, 51*c*, 307
Kenya, U.S. embassy in 277, 289
Kerner, Otto 200
Kerner Commission 200, 205, 206, 209*c*, 372*g*
Ketzenbach, John 236–237
kidnapping **154–156**
    eyewitness testimony 165–167
    Kanka 271, 281*c*, **338**
    Leopold and Loeb 155, 161*c*, 165–167, **340**
    Lindbergh baby 155–156, 162*c*, 167, 185*c*
    media coverage of 155–156
    petition against 40
    Walsh 240–241, 250*c*
Kieft, Willem 11–12, 14*c*, **339**
Kieft's War 12

Kilpatrick, Carroll 234
King, Martin Luther, Jr. 195, *209*, 209*c*, 210*c*, 214–216, *215*
King, Rodney **245–248**, *246*, 251*c*, 252*c*, 258–259
Kinkel, Kip 275, 276, 282*c*
KKK. *See* Ku Klux Klan (KKK)
Klaas, Polly **339**
Klebold, Dylan 275, 283*c*, **334**
Knights of the White Camellia 100
Kohler, Frederick J. 126–127, 135*c*, 138, **339**
Koon, Stacey 245
Korean War 178
Korematsu v. United States 176
Koresh, David 264–265
Ku Klux Klan (KKK)
    background 372*g*, 375*g*
    COINTELPRO (Counter Intelligence Program) 208*c*
    denial of African American right to vote 100–101
    emergence of 81, 90–91, 93*c*
    habeas corpus and 101, 111*c*
    image of *91*
    in northern states 148
    photograph of *111*, *171*
Ku Klux Klan Act 111*c*

L

LaBianca murders 206
labor movement, harassment of 148
labor strikes 113*c*, 148, 149, 159*c*
L.A. Confidential 208*c*
Lamoreaux, Annette 291
Lanape Nation 301
Lang, Fritz 156
Lanman, Thomas 72
LAPD. *See* Los Angeles Police Department (LAPD)
Las Casas, Bartolomé de 6, 13*c*, 16–17, **339–340**
Lathrop, Julia **340**
Latinos. *See* Hispanics
Law and Order viii
"law and order" as a political issue 206–207
Law Enforcement Assistance Administration (LEAA) xi, 204, 372*g*
Lawlessness in Law Enforcement 154
lawmen in Old West 103–106
Lawrence, W. H. 188
Leach, Kimberly 233*c*
Leasing Act 132
Lecter, Hannibal 243, 251*c*
Lee, Robert E. 85, 89, 93*c*
legislative assent 45
Lenox, David 53
Leonidas (English journalist) 39
Leopold, Nathan F., Jr. 155, 161*c*, 165–167, **340**
lethal injection **245**, 251*c*
Leviathan (Hobbes) 17
Lexow, Clarence **340**
Lexow Committee 125, 134*c*, 137, 372*g*
Leyden, John 293
Liberator, The 69*c*, 73
Liberty Place, Battle of 101, 112*c*
Liddy, G. Gordon 233*c*
Liebowitz, Samuel 172–173
The Lights of New York 161*c*
Lincoln, Abraham 69*c*, 81, 85, *87*, 93*c*, **340**. *See also habeas corpus*
Lindbergh, Charles 155–156, 162*c*
Lindbergh, Charles, Jr. 155, 162*c*, 167, 185*c*
Lindbergh Law **154–156**, 162*c*
Linder v. United States 161*c*

Lindsey, Ben Barr 129, 134*c*, 141–142, **340–341**
Lipton, Douglas 233*c*
Little Caesar 162*c*
local government, and criminal justice x–xiii, 368*t*
Locke, John 15*c*, 25, 35, *35*, **341**
Loeb, Richard A. 155, 161*c*, 165–167, **340**
Lomax, John A. 118
Lombroso, Cesare viii, 109–110, 112*c*, **341**
London Metropolitan Police 63–64, 75–76, 307–310
London Times 29, 39, 75–76
Long, Huey "Kingfish" *145*
Longstreet, James 101, 112*c*
Look (magazine) 184, 186*c*, 188
Lorraine Motel 195, *215*
Los Angeles
    assassinations 194
    kidnapping 155
    race riots 200, 214
    riots in 1990s **248–249**, 252*c*, *258*, 258–259
    Watts neighborhood riots 200, *201*, 208*c*, 214
Los Angeles Police Department (LAPD). *See also* King, Rodney; race riots
    Independent Commission on the Los Angeles Police Department 247, 251*c*
    juvenile delinquency statistics 180
    Los Angeles riots **248–249**, 252*c*, *258*, 258–259
    professionalization of 182–183
    racism 247
    reform and 191–192
    Simpson murder trial. *See* Simpson, O. J.
    women in 127, 135*c*
Los Angeles Times 213, 234
Louima, Abner 282*c*
Lovejoy, Elijah Parish 60–61, 70*c*, 72, **341**
loyalty oaths 178, 185*c*
Loyalty-Security program 178, 185*c*
Lucas, Charles 17
Ludlow Massacre 159*c*
L'Uomo Delinquente (Lombroso) 109, 112*c*
Lux, Henry 216
lynching
    background 372*g*
    campaign against 134*c*, 143–144
    in general 102, 112*c*, 132, 171
    number of by state 357*m*
    photograph of *132*
    rape 159*c*, 160–161*c*
    by state 357*m*
    of Till. *See* Till, Emmett
    during World War I 148, 159*c*
"Lynch Law in America" (Wells) 144
Lynds, Elam 50, 52*c*, 57, 70*c*, **341**

M

MacCormick, Austin Harbutt **341–342**
Mack, Julian William 142, **342**
Macready, William 70*c*
Madison, James 1, 29, *29*, 33*c*, 43, 45
Mafia. *See also* St. Valentine's Day Massacre
    background 372*g*
    in Chicago 152–153, 160*c*, 161*c*, 164–165
    drugs and 174–175
    federal response to 233*c*, 236
    in popular culture 161*c*, **226–227**
    Prohibition and 164–165
    prostitution 152
    rise of **151–153**
Magna Carta 28, 372*g*
Maguire, Micha 234
mail bombs 159*c*

Malcolm X 199–200, 208*c*
mandatory arrest policies 242
mandatory prison sentences 221, 226, 239, **269–270**
Manhattan Project 179
Manhunter 243
Mann Act 127, 135*c*, 372*g*
Mano, D. Keith 255
Manson, Charles 206, 210*c*, **342**
Manzanar Relocation Camp *177*
Mapp v. Ohio 202, 206, 208*c*, 216–217
Marbury v. Madison 45–46, 52*c*, 55
Margolick, David 284
Marihuana Tax Act of 1937 175, 185*c*, 317–318
marijuana 174–175, 185*c*, 225, *225*, *235*, 239, 271, 282*c*
"Marijuana: Assassin of Youth!" (Anslinger) 174, 185*c*
Marshall, John 46, 55, **342**
Marshall, Thurgood 230
Marshal Service xi, 313
Marten, Ambros 19
Martin, David Dene 257
Martinez, Ramiro 218
"Martin Luther King Slain" 216
Martinson, Robert 221, 233*c*
Maryland 9, 13*c*, 14*c*, 21, 41, 86
Maryland Declaration of Rights 28, 33*c*, 301
Maryland Public Morality Codes 296
"The Mary Rogers' Mystery Explained" 79
Mason, A. H. 114
Mason, George 27, 28, 33*c*, 300, **342**
Massachusetts Anti-Slavery Society 69*c*
Massachusetts Bay Colony *18*
Massachusetts Body of Liberties 14*c*, 296
Massachusetts Declaration of Rights 28, 33*c*
Massachusetts General Court 14*c*, 15*c*
Massachusetts Government Act 24, 33*c*
Massaquoi, Hans J. 257–258
mass consumer culture 205
masterless men 372*g*
Massino, Joe 233*c*
Masterson, William "Bat" 105
Mather, Richard 19
Matsell, George Washington 65, 77, **342–343**
Matteawan Asylum for the Criminally Insane 123
Maxwell, Pete 117
McCall, Jack 105
McCanles, Dave 103–104
McCarthy, Henry 106, **325**
McCarthy, Joseph 151, 179–180, 186*c*, 189–190, **341**
McCone, John 214
McCord, James 233*c*
McKay, Robert B. 224, 232*c*
McKay Commission 224, 232*c*
McKelvey, W. J. 137
McKinley, William xi
McKissick, Floyd 200
McLaury, Frank 105
McLaury, Tom 105
McLennan County Jail 162*c*
McNaghten, Daniel **343**
McNair, Denise 213
McNeely, Wylie 161*c*
McPherson, Harry 235
McVeigh, Timothy
    antigovernment sentiments 260, 285
    background **343**
    execution of 270, 283*c*
    Oklahoma City bombing **265–267**, *266*, 282*c*, 283*c*, 285
media. *See also* newspapers
    24-hour news cycle 260

coverage of high-profile trials viii, **122–125**, 136, 261–262
    murder coverage **66–68**, 78–80, **122–125**, 136, 205–207
    police, depictions of 183
    sensationalism 229
medical marijuana 271, 282*c*. *See also* marijuana
Megan's Law 271, 282*c*, 372–373*g*
Meili, Trisha 238
"Memorial to the Massachusetts Legislature" (Dix) 76–77
Memphis, Tennessee 134*c*, 195, 209*c*, *215*
Menendez, Erik and Lyle 262, 282*c*
mentally handicapped facilities 66, 70*c*
Merryman, Ex Parte 88, 92–93*c*
Merryman, John 88, 92–93*c*
Metropolitan Police for the City of New York 64–65. *See also* New York Police Department (NYPD)
Mexico 6, 13*c*, 224–225
migration of African Americans 125, 148, 181, 205
Milam, J. W. 183–184, 186*c*, 188
Miles, Robert A. 218
Military Tribunals Act of 2006 279
militias, African American 101, 112*c*
Miller, Betty Davis 257
Miller, Horace 101
Miller, Kent S. 257
Milligan, Ex Parte 88–89
Milligan, Lambden 88
Miranda rule 373*g*
Miranda v. Arizona 202, 206, 209*c*, 217
Missing Children Act 250*c*
Mississippi Black Codes 310–311
Missouri Compromise 92*c*
Mitchell, John 233*c*
M'Naghten, Daniel **343**
molasses **21–24**
Molasses Act of 1733 22, 31*c*
Montesquieu, Charles de 31*c*, 36–37
Montgomery bus boycott 184
The Moonstone (Collins) 68
Moore, Charles 213
Moore, Eugene A. 275
Moore, William 213–214
Moore v. Dempsey 161*c*
moral corruption 127
Moran, George "Bugs" 153
Morris, Frank 208*c*
Morrow, Anne 155
Morton, William 107
Mosser, Thomas 268
"Most Horrible Murder and Arson" 79
movies. *See* films
Moyamensing Prison 134*c*
MSBlast worm 293
Mt. Benedict School for Girls 63, 69*c*, 74
Mudgett, Herman 123–124, 134*c*, **343**
Muhammad, John Allen **343**
murder. *See also* specific victims and killers
    under colonial law 10
    drugs and 272
    media coverage of 66–68, 78–80, 122–125, 136, 205–207
    prostitution and 66–67
    racially motivated 159*c*, 171, 184, 208*c*
murder rate
    20th-century 180, 204–205, 220, 238, 260, 272–273, 276, 362*t*
    African Americans and 125, 273
    in cities 124–125, 205
"Murders in the Rue Morgue, The" (Poe) 68, 70*c*, 80

"Murder Suspect's '2 Faces' Revealed" (Gorman and Zyda) 236
Murphy, Jim 108
Murray, Gilbert 268
Mussolini, Benito 177
My Lai massacre 220, 232c
"My Life on the Plains" (Custer) 116
"The Mystery of Marie Roget" (Poe) 68

N

NAACP. *See* National Association for the Advancement of Colored People (NAACP)
Napolitano, Dominick "Sonny Black" 236
Narcotics Control Act of 1956 176, 318
Narcots 186c
Narrative of the Life of Frederick Douglass (Douglass) 72
Narrative of the Riots at Alton (Beecher) 72
Nash, Frank 162c
National Advisory Commission on Civil Disorders 200, 209c, 214–216, 372g
National Association for the Advancement of Colored People (NAACP) 161c, 172, 184, 198, 208c
National Center for Missing and Exploited Children 241, 251c
National Commission on Law Observance and Enforcement 153, 162c, 169, 375g
National Commission on Terrorist Attacks Upon the United States 289–290
National Commission on the Causes and Prevention of Violence 212–213
National Congress on Penitentiary and Reformatory Discipline 109, 110, 111c, 118–119
National Crime Victimization Survey (NCVS) 203, 220, 373g
National Crime Victims' Rights Week 241
National Institute of Law Enforcement and Criminal Justice 204
National Institute on Drug Abuse (NIDA) 224, 233c
National Institutes of Health (NIH) 224
National Police Chiefs Union 125, 134c
National Review 255
National Rifle Association (NRA) 270
Nation of Islam 199–200, 208c
Native Americans
    under colonial law 9
    conversion to Catholicism 13c
    deaths of due to European diseases 5–6
    encomienda system 5–6, 13c, 16, 371g
    forced movement of 59, *115*
    French trade **6**
    Jefferson on 1
    police units *4*, 114
    protestors 202, 210c
    racism 102, 108, 114–116
    relationship with Dutch 12
    relationship with United States 29–30
    retribution 4
    Spanish conquest **5–6**
    Trade and Intercourse Act 51c
    treaties 102, 301
    treatment of in criminal justice system ix
Native American societies **1–5**
Nat Turner Rebellion 60, 69c, 73, 83
Naturalization Act 43
natural rights argument 24–25
Navy, U.S. 176, 185c
NBC (television network) 183, 241, 251c
Nelson, George "Baby Face" 157, 158, 185c
Nepaupuck (member of Quillipieck tribe) 13–14c

Nesbit, Evelyn 123, 136
Neshoba County, Mississippi 198
Ness, Eliot 153, **343–344**
Neville, John 53
New Amsterdam 12, 15c, 62
New Deal xi, 170
New France 6, 16–17
Newgate Prison 48
"New Government of America" (Leonidas) 39
New Left 195, 209c, 212
New Mexico State Penitentiary 233c
New Netherland **11–12**, 15c, 19–20
New Orleans, Louisiana 6, 62, 71c, 101, 112c
New Orleans Massacre 99
New Penology 111c, 118–120, 129–130, 373g
"The New Police Force Is on the Eve of Being Brought Into Action" 75–76
"A New Purified Form of Cocaine Causes Alarm as Abuse Increases" (Gross) 253
New Spain 6, 13c, 16–17
newspapers. *See also* media
    antislavery 60
    coverage of kidnappings 155–156
    coverage of murders 66–68, 78–80, 122–125, 136
    on juvenile delinquency 180–181
    on marijuana 174
Newton, Huey 201, 209c
New Women All Woman Clinic 269
New York City. *See also* Metropolitan Police for the City of New York; New York Police Department (NYPD); urban crime
    blackout 220, 233c
    bombings 150, 160c
    crime in 220, 273–274
    draft riots 86–88, 93c, *97*, 98
    houses of refuge 52c, 65
    murder rate 124, 205
    organized crime in 152
    police reform 125, 204
    riots 63, 69c, 200, 208c
    slave rebellions 27, 31c
New York City Youth Board 182
New York Daily Times 76
New York Division of Substance Abuse Services 251c
New York Evening World 159c
New York Herald 118–119
New York House of Refuge 52c
New York Municipal Police 64, 70c, 71c
New York Police Department (NYPD)
    "broken windows" model of policing 274
    police brutality 125, 200, 247, 282c, 283c
    reform of 137
    Roosevelt and 134c
New York Post 229
New York Prison Association 109, 110, 119–120
New York Society for the Prevention of Poverty 52c
New York State Reformatory *108*
New York State Special Commission on Attica 224, 232c
New York Times
    on crack cocaine 251c, 253
    crime 287–288
    juvenile delinquency 180
    Kemmler execution 140–141
    Lexow Committee 137
    1914–1933 167
    1934–1957 188, 191
    1958–1970 213
    1971–1981 234, 235, 236
    Simpson murder trial 284
    Terrorist Surveillance Program (TSP) 278

Unabomber and 268, 282c, 286
    White murder 136
New York Transcript 79
New York Tribune 79
New York Weekly Journal 36
Nicholls, Francis T. 101
Nichols, Terry *266*, 267
night watchmen 62
The 9/11 Commission Report 289–290
Nixon, Richard M.
    drug policy 224, 234
    "law and order" as a political issue 206–207
    photograph of *232*
    reelection of 233c
    resignation of 233c
    Vietnam War 220, 232c
    Watergate scandal 220–221, 232–233c
"Nixon Seeks National War on Drug Use" (Kilpatrick) 234
Nolen, W. L. 223
nonviolent methods of activism 196
Norris, Clarence 173, 185c
Norris, Joel 256–257
Norris v. Alabama 173, 174, 185c
North Carolina Declaration of Rights 28, 33c, 301
Northside Family Planning Clinic 269
North Side Gang 152–153, 161c
Northup, Solomon 70c
Notes on the State of Virginia (Jefferson) 25, 302–303
NRA. *See* National Rifle Association (NRA)
nuclear bomb 178, 185c
nullification doctrine 43
Number of Incarcerations per 100,000 Residents, by State, 2006 360m
Number of Reported Violent Crimes per 100,000 Residents, by State, 2006 358m
Nye, Bill 117
NYPD. *See* New York Police Department (NYPD)

O

Obama, Barack 283c
O'Banion, Dion 152–153, 161c
O'Brien, Margaret *127*
"Observations on the Letters of 'A Farmer' Addressed, Number III" 53
O'Connor, Sandra Day 292–293
Ocuish, Hannah 65
O'Donnell, Kenneth 211
Office for Victims of Crime 241
"Office Left His Steak; Later Shot Tower Sniper" (Recer) 218
Ohio Stateman 79
oidores 373g
oil embargo 221
O.K. Corral 105, 112c
Oklahoma City bombing **265–267**, *266*, 282c, 283c, 285
Old Bailey Experience: Criminal Jurisprudence and the Actual Working of Our Penal Code of Laws 76
"The Old Man." *See* Tieri, Frank
Old West. *See* West, U.S.
Olson, Harry **344**
Olympic bombing, Atlanta 268–269, 282c, 283c
omertà 226–227
Omnibus Crime Control Act of 1968 318
Omnibus Crime Control and Safe Streets Act 203–204, 209c, 373g
On Crimes and Punishments (Beccaria) 25, 31c, 37
"On Smuggling and Its Various Species" (Franklin) 34
"On the Skin-Furrows of the Hand" (Faulds) 112c

Operation Condor 224–225
Operation Intercept 224
opium 225, 232c
Oreskes, Michael 236
organized crime
    in Chicago 152–153, 160c, 161c, 164–165
    drugs and 174–175
    federal response to 233c, 236
    in New York City 152
    in popular culture 161c, **226–227**
    Prohibition 164–165
    prostitution 152
    rise of **151–153**
    St. Valentine's Day Massacre 153, 161c, 164,
        165
Organized Crime and Control Act 227, 232c
Origin of the Illinois Juvenile Court Law (Hurley)
    314–316
orphan trains 66
Osborne, Thomas Mott 130, 135c, 142–143,
    344
Oswald, Lee Harvey 194, 208c, **344**
Oswald, Russell G. 223
Otis, James 24, 31c, 36
"Our Criminal Classes" 118–119
outlaws, in Old West **106–107**, 116–118

P

Padilla, José 279
Paine, Thomas 34
Palmer, A. Mitchell 149–150, 159–160c
"Palmer Raids" 150
Pankhurst, Emmeline 147
paramilitary groups 101, 263, 285–286. See also
    domestic terrorism
Parchman State Penitentiary 133, 135c, 199
parens patriae 65, 70c, 202–203, 209c, 373g
Paris, Treaty of 22
Parker, Bonnie 156–157, 162c, 167, 185c, **344**
Parker, Isaac C. 103
Parker, Marion 155, 161c
Parker, Quanah 3
Parker, William H. 182–183, 186c, 192, **345**
parole 109, 129–130
Parris, Samuel 10–11, 15c, **345**
patriot movement 262–263
Patterson, Haywood 171, 172, 173–174, 185c
paupers 110
PC Magazine 293
Pearl Harbor 176, 185c
Peel, Sir Robert 63, **345**
Pendleton, Nathaniel 55
penitentiaries **48–50**, 56–57. See also prisons and
    jails
Penn, William 15c, 31c, 299
Pennsylvania Charter of Privileges 31c, 299
Pennsylvania Declaration of Rights 28, 33c, 300
The Pennsylvania Gazette 53
Pennsylvania system 49–50, 52c, 370g, 373g, 375g
penny papers 67
penology 373g
Pentagon, U.S. 277, 283c
People's Temple 229
permanent settlements 13c
Persons under Death Sentences in the United
    States, 1953–2003 366t
Petersburg Intelligencer 73
Peterson, Iver 288
Phagan, Mary 159c
Philadelphia 65, 69c, 70c, 71c, 124, 204
Philadelphia House of Refuge 52c, 65
Philadelphia riots of 1834 60

Philadelphia Society for Alleviating the Miseries of
    Public Prisons 48
Philadelphia Society for Assisting Distressed
    Prisoners 48
Philanthropist, The 69c
Phips, William 15c
phishing 279–280, 283c, 293
physical measurements of criminals 126
physical punishment 50
Pierce, William 266
Pinkerton, Allan **345–346**
Pinkerton National Detective Agency 106, 112c
piracy 46
Pistone, Joseph 233c, 236
Pitezel, Benjamin 123, 134c
plea bargaining 128
Plessy v. Ferguson 131
Plymouth Colony 13c
Poe, Edgar Allan viii, 68, 70c, 80, **346**
Polanski, Roman 206
Policastro, Marc 290
police. See also police riots; race riots; riots; specific
    departments
    African Americans in 222
    automobiles used by 126, 139
    "broken windows" model of policing 274
    brutality 125, 200, 247, 282c, 283c
    civilian review boards 204
    Civil Rights movement. See Civil Rights
        movement
    corruption in 153–154
    creation of xi, 63–64, 70c
    crime commissions **153–154**, 167–169
    development of 62–65, 70–71c, 75–76
    diversity in hiring 204, 217, 222
    gender 204
    "golden rule" policing 126, 135c, 138
    media and 183
    mismanagement of cases 240–241
    Native American unit 4, 114
    police unions and 222
    professionalization of **62–65**, **182–183**,
        191–192
    racism 257–258
    radio calls 126
    reform of **125–127**, 137–140, 204
    relationship to public 126–127, 204
    social reform and 127
    training program 126
    uniforms 76
    urban politics and 64, 125–126
    women in 127, 139–140, 204, 217, 222, 222
Police Administration (Fuld) 135c, 138–139
"Police Public Relations" (Gourley) 191–192
police riots 196–198, 209–210c, 212–213
Policewoman's Manual (Higgins) 217
political assassinations **193–195**, 208c, 209c,
    211–212. See also assassinations
Poole, William "Butcher Bill" 87, 92c
popular culture **vii–ix**, 226–227. See also films;
    media
popular fear of crime **205–207**, 209c, 210c,
    217–219
Popular Justice (Walker) 9
Popular Science 182
population growth 58, 100
Popyk, Lisa 288
Port Huron statement 195
"Portrait of a Police Chief" (Jennings) 192
Pottawatomie massacre 84, 92c
Poussaint, Alvin F. 257–258
poverty 63, 65–66
poverty-related crime 8, 8–9
Powell, James 200

Powell, Laurence 246–247
Powell v. Alabama 162c, 172, 174, 187
Powhatan confederacy 16
Prager, Robert 147, 159c
presidential election of 1800 43–44, 51–52c
Presidential Task Force on Victims of Crime 241,
    251c
"President Launches Drive on Narcotics"
    (Lawrence) 188
President's Commission on Law Enforcement and
    Administration of Justice 203, 205, 206, 209c,
    218–219, 373g
President's Task Force on Victims of Crime, Final
    Report 319–320
press, freedom of 28
Price, Victoria 172, 173
Prigg v. Pennsylvania 61, 70c, 72
Princip, Gavrilo 146–147, 159c
"Principles of Police Administration" (Sylvester)
    139
prisoners
    under death sentences 366t
    number of 364t
    racism and 222–223, 234
    rehabilitation of 50, **109–110**, 130, 203, 221
    torture of 82, 224, 279, 283c
Prisoners in the United States, 1925–2003 364t
prisons and jails. See also prisoners; punishment;
    specific prisons
    African Americans in 226, 272
    expansion of xii, **271–272**
    first modern penitentiaries **48–50**, 56–57
    mandatory sentences 226, **269–270**
    maximum security 272
    population 240, **271–272**
    private sector and 272
    racially disparate effect of crack cocaine laws
        240
    reform of 65, 93c, **109–110**
    riots in **222–224**, 232c, 233c, 234
    Rush on 48
    secret prisons 279
    social reform and **128–131**, 140–143
    in South 132–133
    supermax 272
    for women 131
"Prisons Are a Bargain, by Any Measure" (DiIulio)
    287–288
"Prisons Feel a Mood of Protest" 234
proactive policing 183
probation officers 129
Proclamation of Amnesty and Reconstruction 93c
Prohibition 151, 151–153, 160c, 162c, 164–165,
    373g
Proposition 215 271, 282c
prosecutor/prosecuting attorney 373g
prosecutors 128
Prosser, Gabriel 47, 51–52c, **346**
prostitution 66–67, 127, 135c, 152, 372g
Psycho 208c
Psychology Today 254, 257
public defender systems 202, 208c, 373g
The Public Enemy vii, 162c
public opinion polls 230, 238, 260, 272
public order offenses 126–127
public penance 10
public transportation, desegregation of 199
Puerto Rican immigration 181
Punch, John 14c
punishment. See also Rockefeller drug laws
    cruel and unusual punishment 28, 230
    hard labor and 48–50
    humiliation 9, 65
    increased penalties 286–287

mandatory sentences 221, 226, 239, **269–270**
new sentencing practices 129–130
physical 50
public penance 128
purpose of 25
rehabilitation 50, **109–110**, 130, 203, 221
Rush on 40
solitary confinement 50
whipping 9, 48
Puritans viii, 9, 10–11, 12, *14. See also* Salem witch trials
Purvis, Melvin **346**
Purvis, Robert 95
Puzo, Mario 226

Q

al-Qaeda 277, 278, 283c, 289, *291*, 373g
Quakers 15c, 48–49, 62, 297
Quantrill, William Clarke 93c, 106, **346**
Quartering Act 24, 33c
Quebec 13c
Quebec Act 24, 33c
Quillipieck tribe 13–14c
Quinn, William 223

R

race. *See also* African Americans; Hispanics; racism
associated with urban crime 205
death penalty and 229–230
discrimination 143–144, 170, 174
juvenile offenders in adult criminal courts 274–275
murder and 125, 171, 184, 273
power and ix–x
profiling 278, 291–292, 373g
southern prisons and 132–133
race riots. *See also* riots
during 1960s 199–202, 208c, 209c, 214–216
in Chicago 148, 159–160c, 163, 200
Detroit 97–98, 176, 185c, 200, 209c
effect on popularity of Civil Rights movement 222
in New York City 200, 208c
as violent resistance **199–202**
Watts neighborhood 200, *201*, 208c, 214
during World War I 148, 159–160c, 163
during World War II 176
Race Traits of the American Negro (Hoffman) 143–144
racism
in criminal justice system **100–102**
in housing 161c
Los Angeles Police Department and 247
against Native Americans 102, 108, 114–116
police and 257–258
prisoners and 222–223, 234
racially motivated killings 171, 184
Simpson murder trial. *See* Simpson, O. J.
in South **100–102, 131–133**
Texas Rangers 108–109
"Racism II" (Maguire) 234
Racketeer Influenced and Corrupt Organizations (RICO) statute of 1970 227, 232c, 233c, 318–319
Rader, Dennis 243, 244, 251c, **346**
radio 183. *See also* media
radio calls, use of in policing 126
Rahman, Omar Abdel 289
Rainey, Lawrence 198
Ramseur, James 254
Ransdall, Hollace 187

rape 159c, 160–161c, 172–173, 230, 233c
Raritans 12
ratelwacht 373–374g
rationalism 25
Ray, James Earl 195, 209c, 210c, **346–347**
Reader's Guide to Periodical Literature 181
Reagan, Nancy 239, 251c, **347**
Reagan, Ronald
antidrug education 239, 251c, 253–254
assassination attempts 239
crime victims 241, 250c, 251c
as governor 196
photograph of *239*
Rebel Without a Cause 181
Recer, Paul 218
recidivism 374g
Recognizing Child Abuse (Besharov) 256
Red Scare **149–151**, 163–164, 177, **178**, 188–190, 374g
Red Squads 198
Red Summer of 1919 149
Reefer Madness 174–175, 185c
reformation of criminals 40, 48, 109–110
"The Reformation of Juvenile Delinquents through the Juvenile Court" (Lindsey) 141–142
reform of criminal justice. *See also* juvenile courts
in antebellum period **65–66**
Clinton and 242, 270, 271, 281c, 282c, 286–287
eyewitness testimony 76–78, 118–120
legislative **203–204**
after September 11 **277–279**
reform schools 66
refuge, houses of 52c, 65
The Register 293
Regulators 107
rehabilitation 50, **109–110**, 130, 203, 221
relative deprivation 205
religion, freedom of 28
religious cults 229, 233c
religious profiling 278
Religious Toleration Act 11
Remarks on Prisons and Prison Discipline (Dix) 66, 70c
Remote Procedure Call (RPC) 293
Reno, Janet 264–265
Reported Lynchings by State, 1882-1968 357m
"Report of the Chief of Police Concerning Destitution and Crime among Children in the City" (Matsell) 77
Report of the President's Commission on the Assassination of President Kennedy 212
"The Report of the Select Committee on the Metropolitan Police" 75
Report on Lawlessness in Law Enforcement (Wickersham Commission) 317
The Representation of New Netherland 20
Republican Party 85
Republican Women's Club 179
Requerimiento 13c
Resist Not Evil (Darrow) 131, 134c, 141
Ressam, Ahmed 289
Ressler, Robert 227
retribution 4, 10, 374g
revenge 25
Richmond Bread Riot 89, 93c
RICO. *See* Racketeer Influenced and Corrupt Organizations (RICO) Statute of 1970
Ridge, Tom 274
Rights in Conflict (Walker) 212–213
riots. *See also* police riots; race riots
in antebellum period 58, 63, 69c, 70c, 72–75
antiabolitionist 60, 69c
in border states 92c
bread riots 89, 93c

in Cincinnati 63, 69c, 70c, 74–75
Democratic National Convention 196–198, *197*, 209c, 210c, 212–213
draft 86, 87–88, 93c, *97*, 98
Los Angeles riots **248–249**, 252c, *258*, 258–259
in New York City 63, 69c
in prisons **222–224**, 232c, 233c, 234
"zoot suit" 176, 185c
Rio Verde Indians 114
robberies 106, 112c, 156–158, 167
Robertson, Carol 213
Robertson, Daniel 94
Robertson, Harriet 94
Robinson, Edward G. 162c
Robinson, Francis P. 78
Robinson, Richard P. 67, 69c
Roche, Pat 164
Rockefeller, Nelson 223, 226, 233c, 235, **347**
Rockefeller drug laws **226**, 233c, 235
Rogers, Don 239, 251c
Rogers, Mary 67–68, 70c, 79
Roosevelt, Franklin D. 157, 162c, 170, 176
Roosevelt, Theodore xi, 125, 127, *134*, 134c, **347**
"The Rose Man of Sing Sing" 159c
Rosenberg, Ethel 179, *186*, 188–189, **347**
Rosenberg, Julius 179, 186c, 188–189, **347**
Ross, Charley 112c, 155
Rousseau, Jean-Jacques 1, 25, 31c, 37, **347–348**
routine crime **ix–x**, 124–125, 180. *See also* index crimes
roving wiretaps 278
Rubenking, Janet 293
Rubin, Jerry 196
Ruby, Jack 194, 208c
Ruby Ridge incident **263–264**
Rudolph, Eric 268–269, 283c, **348**
rule of law **45–48**, 53–56
Rush, Benjamin 33c, 40, 48, *49*, **348**
Russel, Majors, and Waddell 103
Ryan, Leo J. 229

S

Sacco, Nicola *149*, 150, 160c, 161c, **348**
Saldana, Theresa 242, 250c
Salem witch trials viii, 10–11, *11*, 15c, 19, 374g
San Carlos Police Force 114
San Martín, Matías de 17
San Francisco State University 196
San Quentin Prison 232c
Saracini, Victor 289
Saturday Evening Post 180, 191, 192, 255–256
Scarface. *See* Capone, Alphonse "Scarface"
Scarface (film) vii, 162c
Schaeffer, Rebecca 242, 251c
Schechter, Susan 256
school shootings **274–276**, 283c, 288–289, 371g
Schwermer, Michael 198, 208c
scientific crime investigation 182
Scott, Dred 84, 92c, 94–95, **348**
Scott, Henry 160c
Scott, Winfield 86, 92c, 97
Scottsboro Boys 162c, 171–174, 185c, 187
Scottsboro trials 374g
SDS. *See* Students for a Democratic Society (SDS)
Seale, Bobby 196, 201, 209c, 223
"Search for Mass Slayer" 217–218
search warrants. *See* writ of assistance
Second Continental Congress 27, 33c
The Second Treatise of Government (Locke) 25, 35
secret prisons 279

Secret Service xi, 211
sedition 374*g*
Sedition Act of 1798 43, 44, 45, 306
Sedition Act of 1918 148, 150, 151
Sedition Act Revisions of 1918 316
The Seduction of the Innocent (Wertham) 181, 186*c*
segregation 122, 131–133, 171–174, 199
Select Committee to Study Governmental Operations with Respect to Intelligence Activities 212
selective incapacitation 221
self-incrimination 202
"Senate Passes Assembly's Version of Antidrug Bill" (Farrell) 235
Senate Subcommittee to Investigate the Causes of Delinquency 181, 186*c*
sentences, indeterminate 129–130
separate but equal 131
September 11, 2001, terrorist attacks 261, *276*, **276–277**, 283*c*, 289–291
Serbia 146–147
serial killers
    background 374*g*
    definition of **227–229**, 233*c*
    eyewitness testimony 236–237
    gender 124
    popular fear of crime and **205–207**, 209*c*, 210*c*, 217–219
    as public figures **242–244**, 251*c*, 252*c*, 256–257
    at turn of 20th century 123–124, 134*c*
Serial Killers (Norris) 256–257
serial murder, definition of **227–229**, 233*c*
Seven Years' War 22
sex offender registries 271
shaken baby syndrome 282*c*
Shanks, A. R. 164
Shapiro, Robert 261
sharecropping 133
Shaw, Clifford R. **348–349**
Shays, Daniel 47, **349**
Shays' Rebellion 47, 374*g*
Shepard, Matthew 271, 282*c*
"The Shocking Story of Approved Killing in Mississippi" (Hule) 188
Short Account of the Destruction of the West Indies (De Las Casas) 6, 13*c*
Siddiqui, Muhammad 291–292
Sidney, Sylvia 156
Siegel, Benjamin *175*, **349**
Signal Corps, U.S. 179
The Silence of the Lambs vii, 243, 251*c*
Simi Valley 248
Simpson, Nicole Brown viii, 261–262, 281*c*, 282*c*, 284, *285*
Simpson, Orenthal James viii, 260, **261–262**, 281*c*, 282*c*, 284–285, *285*, **349–350**
"Simpson Team Reads of Officer's Slurs" (Margolick) 284
Sing-Sing Prison 50, 52*c*, 57, 70*c*, 130, 159*c*, 234
Sirhan, Sirhan Bishara 194, 209*c*, **350**
Sitting Bull *102*, 102
Sixteenth Street Baptist Church 199, 208*c*, 213
Sixth Amendment 202, 208*c*, 303
60 Minutes II 283*c*
Slater and Morrill Shoe Factory 150
slave codes 31*c*, 41, 83
slave patrols 62, 374*g*
slave rebellions. *See also* slavery
    abolitionist sketch *73*
    in antebellum period 60, 70*c*, 72–75
    as avenue of resistance ix
    in Early Republic 30
    fear of 47–48, 83
    in New York City 27, 31*c*

Prosser and 51–52*c*
    in Virginia 15*c*
slavery
    abolition of 27, 69*c*, 87, 90, 93*c*
    ban on importation of 52*c*
    as challenge to early American system 41
    under colonial law 9, 15*c*
    eyewitness testimony 72
    final years of 94–97
    fraud 17
    fugitive slave laws. *See* Fugitive Slave Act of 1793; Fugitive Slave Act of 1850
    guerrilla warfare 84
    introduction of 6, 13*c*
    overview of ix–x
    paradox of highlighted by Enlightenment 27
    punishments 48
    regional differences on 59, **82–86**
    torture *82*
    trade 13*c*, 30, 40, 41
    treatment of slaves 82–83
slave ship *30*
Smilie, John 28–29
Smith, John 16
smuggling 11–12, 19–20, 21–22, 24, 34
SNCC. *See* Student Nonviolent Coordinating Committee (SNCC)
Snow, Robert L. 285–286
social conditioning 109
The Social Contract (Rousseau) 25, 31*c*
social contracts 26–27
social harmony ideal 29
social history, routine crime and **ix–x**
Socialist Party 150, 159*c*
Socialist Workers Party 208*c*
social reform 127, **128–131**, 140–143
Society for the Prevention of Pauperism 65
Soledad Brother 223
Soledad Prison 223, 234
solitary confinement 50. *See also* punishment
"Son of Sam" 228, 233*c*, 236, 242–243, **324**
Sons of Liberty 22
soup kitchen *160*
South, U.S.. *See also* Civil Rights movement; slavery
    Civil Rights movement, reaction to **198–199**, 213–216
    criminal justice during Progressive Era **131–133**
    criminal justice in 1930s **171–174**
    prisons in 132–133
    racism in criminal justice system **100–102**
    segregation 122, 131–133, 171–174, 199
South Carolina 27, 31*c*, 62, 69*c*, 85–86, 92*c*
South Chicago Community Hospital 206, 209*c*
Southern Christian Leadership Conference (SCLC) 199, 208*c*
South Water Street *122*
"Soviet Ark" 160*c*
Soviet Union 177, 178, 185*c*
Spanish Armada 13*c*
Spanish conquest **5–6**
speakeasies 152
Special Action Office for Drug Abuse Prevention (SAODAP) 224
Special Committee to Investigate Organized Crime in Interstate Commerce 175, 186*c*
Speck, Richard 205–206, 209*c*, 217–218, **350**
speech, freedom of 28
spinning wheel *14*
The Spirit of the Laws (Montesquieu) 31*c*, 36–37
spree killers 228
spy software 280
spyware 280
Stack, Robert 241, 251*c*

Stafford, Humphrey 17
stagflation 221
stalking 242, 250*c*, 251*c*
Stamp Act 22–23, 31*c*
Stamp Act Congress 22
Standards of the Comics Code Authority 191
Starkweather, Charles **350**
state, role of in criminal justice **x–xiii**
State Department 178, 186*c*
state government, expenditures on criminal justice 368*t*
statistics. *See* crime statistics
Stephens, Alpha Otis 245
Stewart, Potter 230
still, underground *151*
Still, William 94, 96–97
stock market crash 162*c*
stocks 374*g*
Stompanato, Joey 208*c*
Stone, I. F. 189
Stono Rebellion 27, 31*c*
Stop the Draft Week 196, 209*c*
Story, Joseph 72
street workers 182
strict labor discipline 50
student activism 195–198
Student Nonviolent Coordinating Committee (SNCC) 200
student occupation of universities 196, 209*c*
Students for a Democratic Society (SDS) 195, 212. *See also* New Left
Stuyvesant, Peter 12
St. Valentine's Day Massacre 153, 161*c*, 164, *165*
sugar **21–24**
Sugar Act of 1764 22, 31*c*
Sumner, Charles 92*c*
Sumter, Fort 86, 92*c*
supermax prisons 272. *See also* prisons and jails
superpredators 273, 274, 374*g*
Supreme Court. *See also specific cases*
    Alien and Sedition Acts 45
    civil liberties and **202–203**, 216–217
    on the death penalty xii, 230
    desegregation 199
    on Federal Kidnapping Act 156
    juvenile courts 202–203
    power of 29, 41
    role of 45
    on Sedition Act of 1918 150
Supreme Court building *46*
Supreme Court of Wisconsin 83
surveillance 277–278
The Survey 163
Sutherland, George 187
Sweeney, Brian David 290
Sweeney, Julie 290
Sweeney, Louise 290
Sweet, Ossian 161*c*
Sylvester, Richard 125–126, 139, **350**
Symantec Internet Security Threat Report 279
systemic unfairness in criminal justice system 203

T

Tafero, Jose 245
Taliban 278
Taney, Roger 92*c*, 94–95
Tanzania, U.S. embassy in 277, 289
tariffs 22
Tate, Lionel 275
Tate, Sharon 206
taxation, colonial objection to 21–24
taxation without representation 22

Taylor, Graham 163
tea, taxes on **21–24**, 32c
Tea Act of 1773 23, 32c
Teenage Crime Wave 181
television vii–ix, 183. *See also* media
Tell Your Children 174–175, 185c
temporary insanity 123
tenant farming 133
terrorism
    death penalty 270
    domestic
        in 1990s **267–269**
        eyewitness testimony 285–286
        Oklahoma City bombing **265–267**, *266*, 282c, 283c, 285
        Olympic bombing, Atlanta 268–269, 282c, 283c
        rise of **262–265**
    international **276–277**, 289–291
    September 11, 2001, terrorist attacks 261, *276*, **276–277**, 283c, 289–291
    statistics 367t
    war on xi, 291–293, 375g
Terrorism in the United States, 1980–2001 367t
Terrorists among Us (Snow) 285–286
Terrorist Surveillance Program (TSP) 278
Tet offensive 195, 209c
Texas, University of, at Austin 206, 209c, 218
Texas Book Depository 193, 211
Texas Highway Patrol 156
Texas Rangers 69c, **107–109**, 112c, 374g
Texas Tower Sniper 206, 209c, 218
Thaw, Harry Kendall 123, *135*, 135c, 136, **350**
theocratic system 10–11
The Times News 99
Thibodaux massacre 113c, 114
Thinking About Crime (Wilson) 221, 233c
Third Amendment 303
"third degree" 154
Thirteenth Amendment 90, 93c, 310
three strikes laws 270
Tieri, Frank 227, 233c, **350**
Till, Emmett 171, **183–184**, 186c, 187–188, **350–351**
Time magazine 261
time off for good behavior 109
Tirrell, Albert 67, 70c, **351**
Tocqueville, Alexis de **351**
To Kill and Be Killed (Miller and Miller) 257
Toleration Act 14c
Toole, Otis 240–241
"Topics of Conversation" 167
Torrio, Johnny 152, 160c, **351**
torture 224, 279, 283c
torture instruments 82
Total Information Awareness (TIA) program 278
tower sniper 206, 209c, 218
town meeting system of law enforcement 10
Townsend, Rosina 67, 78
Townshend Revenue Act 23, 31c, 32c
trade, in English colonies 21
Trade and Intercourse Act 51c
Trail of Tears 59–60
train robberies 106, 112c
treason 46–47, **178–180**, 188–189
Treasury Department xi, 153
Treaty of Montefontaine 45
Treaty of New Echota 59, 69c
Treaty with the Cherokee Nation 301
Treaty with the Lenape Nation 301
Tregaskis, Richard 191
trials
    celebrity 58, 123
    "Chicago Seven" 196–197, 210c

during cold war 178–180
in colonial Massachusetts 19
Manson family 206, 210c
media coverage of viii, 122–125, 136, 261–262
Rosenbergs 179, *186*, 186c, 188–189, **374**
Scottsboro Boys 162c, 172–174, 185c, 187, 374g
of Simpson viii, 260, **261–262**, 281c, 284–285
Till murder 171, **183–184**, 186c, 187–188, **350–351**
tribal elders 5
trojan horses 280
Truman, Harry 178, 185c
truth-in-sentencing laws 269–270
Tubman, Harriet 63, 70c
Tudor, William 36
Tuntall, John 106
Turner, Lana 208c
Turner, Nat ix, 60, 69c, 72–73, 83, **351**
The Turner Diaries 266
Turner Rebellion 60, 69c, 73, 83
Tuthill, Richard 129, 142, **351**
Twenty-first Amendment 153, 162c, 317
"2 Gang Suspects Are Denied Bail" (Bracker) 191
Two Treatises on Government (Locke) 15c
Tylenol tampering case 238, 250c

U

Ullman, Joan 257
Unabomber 268, 282c, 286, **338**
"Undercover Agent Tells of N.Y. Mafia Killings" 236
Underground Railroad 61–62, 84, *85*, 94, 96–97, 374g
unemployment 170
Uniform Crime Reports (UCR) 180, 271, 374g
Union of Russian Workers 150
United and Strengthening American by Providing Appropriate Tools Required to Intercept and Obstruct Terrorism (USA PATRIOT Act). *See* USA PATRIOT Act of 2001
United Nations 178
United States of America, establishment of 27–29
United States v. Behrman 161c
United States v. Doremus 159c
United States v. Jin Fuey Moy 159c
Unsolved Mysteries 241, 251c
urban crime **58–80**, **238–259**. *See also* juvenile delinquency; riots
    in 1990s **272–274**
    antebellum period **59–65**
    chronology of events 69–71c, 250–252c
    criminal justice reform **65–66**
    domestic violence **242**, 251c, 256
    eyewitness testimony 72–80, 253–259
    increased penalties 286–287
    increase in **204–205**
    lethal injection **245**
    media coverage of crime **66–68**
    as political issue 206–207
    population growth 58, 63, 121, 205
    professional police departments **62–65**
    serial killers as public figures **242–244**
    victims' rights and citizen participation **240–242**
urban culture 58, 65–66
urban politics, police and 64, 125–126
urban population, divisions in 63, 87
USA PATRIOT Act of 2001 277–278, 283c, 291–293, 321, 374g

U.S. Crimes Act. *See* Crimes Act of 1790
USS *Cole* 277

V

Van der Donk, Adrian 20
Van Ness, William P. 55
Van Tienhoven, Cornelius 20
Van Waters, Miriam **351–352**
Vanzetti, Bartolomeo *149*, 150, 160c, 161c, 163–164, **348**
Vardaman, James Kimble 133, **352**
Velasco, Luis de
VENOMA documents 179
Veren, Philip 19
Vermont Declaration of Rights 33c
"A Veterans Day Remembrance" (Barber) 99
Victim and Witness Protection Act 250c
victims' rights **240–242**
Vietnam War 195–198, *197*, 208c, 209c, 220, 232c
"Viewing the Charges of Police Brutality" (Wilkins) 213
vigilante justice 240–241, 251c, 254–255
Vignera v. New York 217
violence. *See also* murder
    against African Americans 101–102, 111c, 112c, 113c, 114–115, 148
    against children 271, 281c. *See also* kidnapping
    against women **242**, 251c, 256
Violence Against Women Act 374g
violent crime, number of by state 358m
Violent Crime Control and Law Enforcement Act 270, 271, 282c, 286–287
Virginia
    in general 21, 28, 86, 89
    slave codes 9, 31c, 41, 83, 299–300
    slave rebellions 60
Virginia Assembly 15c
Virginia Declaration of Rights 27, 28, 33c, 300
Virginia Resolution of 1798 43–44, 51c, 306–307
Virginia Slave Codes 299–300
Vollmer, August 126, 135c, 182, **352**
Volstead Act 160c
vote, right to 100–101

W

Waco, Texas *132*, 162c
Waco incident 264–265, *265*, 281c
Wahunsonacock (King Powhatan) 16
Walker, David 47, 52c, 56, 212–213
Walker, Samuel 9
Walker Report 212–213
Waller, William L. 213
Walling, George W. 120
Walnut Street Jail 49–50, 51c, *56*, 56–57, 375g
Walsh, Adam 240–241, 250c
Walsh, John 240–241, 251c, 255–256, **352**
Walsh, Reve 240–241, **352**
Ware, Richard Clayton 112c
Warner Brothers 161c, 162c
war on crime xi
war on drugs viii, xi, 176, 186c, 188, 239, 271, 375g
war on terror xi, 291–293, 375g
warrantless searches 278
Warren, Earl 194, 202, 206, 217, **352–353**
Warren Commission 194, 212
Washington, George 47, 51c, 53–55, *54*, 61
Washington, Jesse *132*

Washington Monthly 257
Washington Post 232–233*c*, 234, 236–237, 268, 282*c*, 286
Washington Times 87
Watergate scandal 220–221, 232–233*c*
Watts neighborhood riots 200, *201*, 208*c*, 214
Weaver, Randy 263–264
Webb, Jack 183, 191
Webb v. United States 159*c*
The Weekly Pelican 114–115
Weeks v. United States 167–168, 216
Weinshank, Albert 164
Weinter, Lee 196
Weiss, Hymie 161*c*
Welch, Joseph 189–190
Wells, Alice Stebbins x, 127, 135*c*, 139–140, **353**
Wells-Barnett, Ida B. 132, 134*c*, *144*, 144, **353**
Wertham, Frederic 181, 186*c*, 191, **353–354**
Wesley, Cynthia 213
West, U.S. **100–120**
    eyewitness testimony 114–120
    forced movement of Native Americans to 59
    lawmen in 103–106
    myths of Wild West **102–106**
    outlaws **106–107**, 116–118
    racism in criminal justice system **100–102**
    Texas Rangers **107–109**
    Wild West **102–106**
western genre 102
Westminster, Treaty of 15*c*
Westover v. United States 217
West Side Story 181, 186*c*
Whig Party 44
whipping 9, 48
Whiskey Rebellion 47, 51*c*, 53–55, *54*, 375*g*
whiskey taxes 47, 51*c*
White, Stanford 123, 135*c*, 136
White Citizens' Council 198
white flight 205, 238
Whitehead, Richard 72–73

White League 100, 101, 112*c*, 375*g*
White Man's Party 100
White Mountain Indians 114
White-Slave Traffic Act 135*c*
white supremacist groups 199. *See also specific groups*
Whitin, Frederick H. **354**
Whitman, Charles 206, 209*c*, 218, **354**
Whitman, Christine Todd 288
Whitman, Howard 188
Whitten, Les 237
Wicker, Tom 223
Wickersham, George W. 154, *154*, 162*c*
Wickersham Commission 154, 161*c*, 162*c*, 169, 317, 375*g*
"Wild Children" 190–191
The Wild One 181
Wild West. *See* West, U.S.
Wilkins, Roy 213
Wilks, Judith 233*c*
Williams, Alexander S. 125, **354**
Williams, Eugene 162*c*, 172
Williams, Hosea *215*
Williams, John Allen **343**
Wilson, James Q. 221, 233*c*, **354**
Wilson, Mallie 159*c*
Wilson, Orlando Winfield 182, **354–355**
Wilson, Woodrow 147
Wines, Enoch Cobb 93*c*, 109, **355**
Winter Garden Theater 186*c*
Winthrop, John 10, 18–19, 29, **355**
Wirz, Henry 89, 93*c*, **355**
witchcraft 10, 14*c*, 19
witch trials viii, 10–11, *11*, 15*c*, 19, 374*g*
Within Prison Walls (Osborne) 130, 142–143
Woman's Christian Temperance Union 127
Woman's Home Companion 188
women. *See also* gender
    under colonial law 9
    as police officers 127, 139–140, 204, 217, 222, *222*

    prisons for 131
    violence against **242**, 251*c*, 256
Women and Male Violence (Schechter) 256
"Women on the Police Force" (Wells) 139–140
Women's Reformatory 131, 134*c*
Woodham, Luke 275, 282*c*, 288
Woods, Fernando 64
Woodward, Louise 262, 282*c*
World's Fair, Chicago 124
World's Fair, Portland 127
World Trade Center 267, *276*, 276–277, 281*c*, 283*c*
World War I **146–148**, 159–160*c*, 163–164
World War II **176–178**, 180, 185*c*
Worthington, Ohio 70*c*
Wounded Knee massacre 102
Wright, Roy 172
writ of assistance **24–25**, 27, 28, 31*c*, 36, 375*g*
writ of *mandamus* 45–46
Wuornos, Aileen **355**

Y

Yale University 268
Yarborough, Ralph W. 211
Youngblood, Rufus W. 211–212
Young Men's Lyceum 69*c*
You Only Life Once (Lang) 156
Yousef, Ramzi 272, 289
youth activism **195–198**
youth culture, emergence of 180, 182

Z

Zenger, John Peter 36, **355**
Zobel, Hiller 282*c*
"zoot suit" riots 176, 185*c*
Zyda, Joan 236